Meal Management

Meal Management

Sixth Edition

Faye Kinder
Associate Professor Emeritus, Michigan State University

Nancy R. Green
Associate Professor, Florida State University

Natholyn Harris
Associate Professor, Florida State University

Macmillan Publishing Company
New York

Collier Macmillan Publishers
London

Macmillan Publishing Company
866 Third Avenue, New York, New York 10022

Collier Macmillan Canada, Inc.

Library of Congress Cataloging in Publication Data

Kinder, Faye.
  Meal management.

  Includes index.
  1. Food. 2. Marketing (Home economics)
3. Table. I. Green, Nancy R. II. Harris, Natholyn.
III. Title.
TX353.K45 1984   641.3   83-7944
ISBN 0-02-364150-9

Printing: 2 3 4 5 6 7 8   Year: 4 5 6 7 8 9 0 1 2

ISBN   0-02-364150-9

Preface

This is the sixth edition of *Meal Management*. Since the first edition was printed, cultural, economic, and social forces have modified such practices as where meals are eaten, when meals are eaten, what foods are consumed, and how much is eaten. New and more information is needed for meal management in the 1980's and 1990's. In an attempt to meet new needs, there has been some reorganization of the subject matter of the text as well as the updating of information. The text retains, however, information that has been found tried and true. The problems introduced at the ends of chapters in the fifth edition have been retained or modified; a few new ones have been introduced.

The authors would like to acknowledge all who have supplied illustrations for the book. Special thanks are due Alice Simpson for designing the table settings used for new photographs and to Joe Boris for expertly handling the photography. The comments, criticisms, and suggestions of Professors Patricia T. Berglund of North Dakota State University, Barbara J. Zeches of the University of Arizona, Pearl C. Baker of Framingham State College, and Eve J. McCreary of Longwood College have been incorporated where possible. The authors are grateful to all persons who have contributed in any way to the production of this work.

F.K., N.G., N.H.

Contents

TABLES   ix

FIGURES   xiii

PHOTOGRAPHS   xvii

CHAPTER 1. *Meal Management—Some Concepts and Definitions*   1

CHAPTER 2. *Technology and Food in the 1980's*   9

CHAPTER 3. *Federal Laws, Regulations, and Federal Agencies
             that Regulate the Food Supply*   25

CHAPTER 4. *Food and Energy Conservation*   66

CHAPTER 5. *Meal Management Goal 1: Good Nutrition*   80

CHAPTER 6. *Meal Management Goal 2: Meals to Match a
             Budget*   94

CHAPTER 7. *Meal Management Goal 3: Controlled Use of Time*   110

CHAPTER 8. *Meal Management Goal 4: Pleasurable Eating*   125

CHAPTER 9. *Shopping for Food: Some General Information and
             Principles*   141

CHAPTER 10. *Shopping for Meat, Poultry, and Seafood*   168

CHAPTER 11. *Shopping for Dairy Products, Nondairy Products,
             Eggs*   221

CHAPTER 12. *Shopping for Food: Cheeses*   245

CHAPTER 13. *Shopping for Food: Fruits*   276

CHAPTER 14. *Shopping for Food: Vegetables*   305

CHAPTER 15. *Shopping for Food: Grain Food Products, Legumes,
             and Nuts*   327

CHAPTER 16. *Shopping for Food: Miscellaneous*   344

CHAPTER 17. *Meal Service Styles*   361

CHAPTER 18. *Setting the Table*   371

CHAPTER 19.   *Table Appointments*   398
CHAPTER 20.   *Waiting on the Table*   420
CHAPTER 21.   *Etiquette of the Table*   433
CHAPTER 22.   *Meals for Guests*   450
CHAPTER 23.   *Teas, Receptions, and Other Occasions*   479

APPENDIX A.   *Format for Menus*   503
APPENDIX B.   *Purchasing Guides*   505
APPENDIX C.   *Temperature of Food and Control*
               of Bacteria   511
APPENDIX D.   *Frozen Food Storage*   513
APPENDIX E.   *Metric Conversions*   517
APPENDIX F.   *Suggested Menus*   519

INDEX   525

Tables

5–1. Food and Nutrition Board. National Academy of Sciences—National Research Council Recommended Daily Dietary Allowances. Revised 1979. 83
5–2. U.S. Recommended Daily Allowances (U.S. RDAs) 85
5–3. Nutritional Label 87
5–4. The Basic Seven Food Groups 89
5–5. Amino Acid Content of Plant Protein 91

6–1. Meat Selections to Match a Budget 100
6–2. The Food Plan for the Family 103

7–1. Time Used by Urban Housewives for Household Work and Food-Related Activities 111
7–2. Steps 1 and 2 in Timing Meal Preparation 119
7–3. Step 3 in Timing Meal Preparation—Tasks Listed in Descending Order of Total Time Required 119
7–4. The Time Schedule for Preparing the Meal 120
7–5. Steps 1 and 2 in Timing Meal Preparation 121
7–6. Step 3 in Timing Meal Preparation—Tasks Listed in Descending Order of Total Time Required 122
7–7. The Time Schedule for Preparing Dinner for Four 122

9–1. Cost of Selected Items as Purchased in Different Food Markets 145
9–2. Cost of National versus Store versus Generic Brands of Selected Products 147
9–3. The Costs of Two Plans for Buying Meat for Five Meals for Four Persons 157

9–4.   The Costs of Two Plans for Buying Vegetables for
Five Meals for Four Persons   158
9–5.   The Estimated Per-Serving Cost of Corn as
Established by the Product Purchased   159
9–6.   Unit Cost as Determined by Package Size   161

10–1.   Estimated Per-Serving Costs of Selected Kinds and
Cuts of Meat, Poultry, and Fish   170
10–2.   Minimum Quantities of Meat Required in Various
Food Products   213

11–1.   The Cost of One Quart of Selected Fluid Milk
Products as Purchased in Containers of Different Sizes
from Different Market Sources   223
11–2.   Cost per Quart of Nonfat Dry Milk as It Varies with
Purchase of Different Brands and Different Packages   229
11–3.   Summary of United States Standards for Quality of
Individual Shell Eggs   237

12–1.   Cheese-Making Techniques and the Resulting
Characteristics of the Cheeses   248
12–2.   Per-Pound Cost of Some Cheddar Cheeses   253
12–3.   Per-Pound Cost of Some Cheese Varieties   258
12–4.   Per-Pound Cost of Some Diet-Modified Cheeses and
Cheese Products   260
12–5.   Per-Pound Cost of Selected Cheese Products   265

13–1.   Per-Serving Cost of Selected Fresh Fruits—June, 1982   278
13–2.   Cost per Pound of Canned Peaches as Cost Differs
with Brand, Kind, and Size of Can Purchased   292
13–3.   Cost per Pound of Selected Canned Fruits   293
13–4.   Cost per Pound of Selected Frozen Fruits   294
13–5.   Cost per Pound of Selected Dried Fruits, June, 1982   296
13–6.   Per-Serving Cost and Vitamin C Value of Selected
Orange Juice Products and Citrus Flavored Products   298

14–1.   Estimated Per-Serving Cost of Selected Fresh
Vegetables   307
14–2.   Per-Serving Cost of Selected Canned Vegetables   308
14–3.   Per-Serving Cost of Selected Frozen Vegetables   309
14–4.   Cost per Ten-Ounce Carton of Frozen Vegetable
Dishes   309
14–5.   Estimated Cost of Four Servings of Potatoes as
Purchased in Different Forms   316

15–1. Per-Pound Cost of Selected Breads, Rolls, and Other
       Similar Products   330
15–2. Estimated Per-Serving Cost of Selected Sweet Goods   335
15–3. Per-Pound Cost of Selected Breakfast Cereals   337
15–4. Unit Cost of Some Ready-to-Eat Breakfast Products   338

16–1. The Total Cost of Selected Miscellaneous Purchases   359

B–1.   Guide to the Use of Foods in Cooking and Meal
       Preparation   507
B–2.   The Measure of One Pound   509
B–3.   The Measure of Cans   510

D–1.   Suggested Maximum Home-Storage Periods to
       Maintain Good Quality in Purchased Frozen Foods
       Held at 0° F   513
D–2.   Suggested Storage Periods to Maintain High Quality in
       Home-Frozen Food Products Held at 0° F   515

E–1.   Volume Conversions   517
E–2.   Weight Conversions   517

Figures

3–1. Meat inspection marks   59
3–2. Poultry inspection mark   60

4–1. Recent changes in energy prices   74

6–1. Family's weekly food cost   96
6–2. Income versus money spent for food at home and
      away   97
6–3. Regions of the U.S. versus money spent for food at
      home and away   98
6–4. Urbanization versus money spent for food at home
      and away   98

9–1. Universal Product Code   155

10–1. Per capita consumption of animal products   169
10–2. Per capita consumption of poultry   169
10–3. Beef chart—wholesale cuts of beef and their bone
      structure   172
10–4. Veal chart—wholesale cuts of veal and their bone
      structure   173
10–5. Pork chart—wholesale cuts of pork and their bone
      structure   173
10–6. Lamb chart—wholesale cuts of lamb and their bone
      structure   173
10–7. The seven basic retail cuts of meat   174
10–8. Bones identify seven groups of retail cuts   175
10–9. Retail cuts of beef—where they come from and how
      to cook them   176

10–10. Unboned steaks   177
10–11. Unboned cuts from the chuck and the round   178
10–12. Retail cuts of pork—where they come from and how
        to cook them   180
10–13. Retail cuts of veal—where they come from and how
        to cook them   181
10–14. Retail cuts of lamb—where they come from and how
        to cook them   182
10–15. Meat inspection marks   186
10–16. Poultry inspection mark   186
10–17. Combination grade and inspection symbol for poultry
        showing class of bird   186
10–18. USDA yield grade and quality grade symbols   189
10–19. U.S. Grade A and U.S. Grade B turkeys   194
10–20. Ready-to-cook chickens of U.S. Grade A, U.S. Grade
        B, and U.S. Grade C qualities   194

11–1.   Ten-year change in per capita dairy products sales   222
11–2.   Grademark for instant nonfat dry milk   229
11–3.   Grade symbols for graded butter   232
11–4.   Per capita consumption of eggs   235
11–5.   Grademark for graded eggs   236
11–6.   Grade symbol for Fresh Fancy Quality eggs   238
11–7.   Appearance of broken-out eggs   239
11–8.   Weight classes for eggs   240

13–1.   Noncitrus fruit consumption   290
13–2.   Citrus fruit consumption   290

14–1.   Per capita consumption of vegetables   306
14–2.   Per capita consumption of potatoes   306
14–3.   Canned food label showing net weight and solid
        content weight of product; also nutrition information   319

16–1.   U.S. cocoa imports and prices   352
16–2.   Per capita consumption of fats and oils   354

18–1.   Formal service—individual cover   375
18–2.   Alignment of napkin, flatware, and plate within a
        cover   376
18–3.   Possible positions of the dinner fork when no dinner
        knife is laid   378
18–4.   Possible positions of the butter spreader on the
        bread-and-butter plate   379

18–5.   Position for the butter spreader when no bread-and-butter plate is placed   380
18–6.   Serving pieces laid beside serving dishes   380
18–7.   Serving pieces laid at the server's cover   383
18–8.   Possible positions of the water glass   384
18–9.   Position of the bread-and-butter plate   386
18–10. Position of the salad plate when there is no bread-and-butter plate in the cover   386
18–11. Possible positions of the salad when a bread-and-butter plate appears in the cover   387
18–12. Possible positions of the salad service at the server's cover   389
18–13. Possible arrangements of a beverage service at the hostess's cover—beverage served during the meal and no tray used   391
18–14. A tray arranged for beverage service   392
18–15. Dining table set for service of food at the table   394
18–16. A serving table arranged for convenient use   395

19–1.   The individual pieces included in three-piece, four-piece, five-piece, and six-piece place settings   400
19–2.   Serving pieces   405

20–1.   Dessert placed for serving at the table   425
20–2.   Possible arrangements of the beverage service at the server's cover   427

21–1.   Order of serving persons at the table   436

22–1.   Tray arranged for offering a beverage in glasses   454
22–2.   Tray arranged for offering accompaniments to a beverage   455
22–3.   Tray arranged for serving coffee in demitasse   457
22–4.   Small chest set for buffet service—table service at dining table   459
22–5.   Small chest or table set with trays, appointments, and beverages   461
22–6.   Buffet arranged so that guests proceed around it—table service   466
22–7.   Buffet arranged so that guests proceed from end to end—plate service   467
22–8.   Arrangement for self-service of a hot beverage   470
22–9.   A dessert buffet   471

23–1.   A tray arranged for afternoon tea or coffee   486

23–2a. A small table arranged for tea or coffee-finger food   488

23–2b. A small table arranged for afternoon tea or dessert—
        food requires the use of a fork   489

23–2c. A small table arranged for afternoon tea or morning
        coffee—food requires the use of a butter spreader   490

23–3.   Table arrangement for a large tea—a single service
        on one side of table and cups and saucers used   491

23–4.   Table arrangement for a large tea—duplicate services
        on one side of table, cups and saucers used   492

23–5.   Table arrangement for a large tea—duplicate services
        on the two sides of the table, cups and plates used   495

23–6.   Table arrangement for a large tea—guest takes food,
        then receives beverage. Tea plates stacked with
        napkins in between   497

23–7.   Table arrangement for serving punch   498

C–1.   Temperature of food for the control of bacteria   512

Photographs

1. Table set for self-service of food American style   362
2. Table set for formal service   364
3. One cover of a formally set table   365
4. Table set for the serving of food at the table   366
5. Outdoor buffet—dining from plate in hand   368
6. Dessert flatware placed in the center of the cover above the dinner plate   381
7. Possible position of glassware when three glasses appear in the cover. Cocktail fork placed for first course   384
8. Possible position of the salad plate when a bread and butter plate appears in the cover   387
9. Well-coordinated table appointments   410
10. Table set for a small luncheon   451
11. After dinner coffee served in the living room   456
12. Buffet service arranged for guest to dine at table   460
13. Buffet supper—dining from plate in hand   462
14. Table arranged for a dessert buffet   473
15. Table arranged for afternoon tea   482
16. A tray arranged for afternoon tea or coffee   485

Meal Management

Chapter I

Meal Management— Some Concepts and Definitions

This sixth edition of *Meal Management* is written for the 1980's. The 1980's are a time when more meals are eaten outside of the home than ever before, when more meals are eaten alone—both within and outside of the home—than heretofore, when meals are eaten on the run, when many non-meals (snacks) are consumed, when shopping for food and meal preparation may be a responsibility of either spouse or a joint venture including the input of children, and when food industries prepare much of our food. It is also a time when lean cuisine is chic, when cooking schools flourish, when the annual output of new cookbooks is incredible, when becoming a gourmet or gourmand confers status, when at least three major magazines are solely devoted to gourmet cookery, and many more feature menus and recipes, when kitchens are created by designers, when cookery is considered an art form, when dining is understood to be a social grace, and when there is concern for good nutrition. Because so much has changed in recent times, there must be a rationale for the sixth edition. It is simply this: decisions and action are prerequisite to the consumption of meals and even of snacks, whether eaten in the home or not and whether they are simple, old-fashioned meals or lavish productions. Meal management is about those decisions and that action.

Meals are not instant. They require inputs of money, time, and human and mechanical energy. Furthermore, personal skills and abilities are essential to the planning, shopping, cooking, and service of meals.

The term *meal management* is used in this book to include all of the decision making and all of the hand-and-foot work that meals entail. We call the person who bears the responsibility for meals the *meal manager*. In general, that person is a homemaker; however, we know full

1

well that the meal manager may be a person of either sex or several persons who share meal management responsibilities. While this book places emphasis on managing meals for the individual or family, the goals and principles are the same for the dietition or food supervisor. We speak of the person, or persons, as the meal manager; and when a pronoun must be used, we use *she* and *her,* though we could use *he* and *his, they,* and *you.*

Meal managers make many decisions. Here are some of them: how much to spend, what to serve, where to shop, how much to buy, whether to buy prepared foods or to prepare from scratch, how to store purchased foods in order to avoid waste, how much time to spend in the kitchen, how to cook purchased foods, how to conserve energy (both human and commercial), how to serve meals, and when to serve them. Meal managers make decisions in the marketplace and in the kitchen. They make decisions that affect others, and they make personal decisions. Their decisions differ from time to time. Some of their decisions are thoughtfully made; others are routinely made as the result of experience. The meal manager engages in a variety of tasks: she is hostess, dietitian, purchasing agent, organizer of goods and tasks, kitchen supervisor, chef, waitress, scullery maid, janitor, and so on.

DECISION MAKING

The availability of a variety of goods and services compels choices— a kind and cut of meat, a way of preparing potatoes, a kind of vegetable, a brand of canned pears, a kind of breakfast cereal, a kind and brand of cake mix, and so on. When more than one course of action is open, we are forced to decide where to shop, supermarket A or supermarket B; when to shop, Tuesday or Friday; early morning or late evening; whether to serve a family meal at an established hour or to have a meal ready prepared and permit family members to dine according to personal schedules; to serve some family meals each week and require all family members to be present, or to eat meals away from home and spend accordingly, or to cope with all of the variables of having family meals at home.

It is possible to map the sequential steps of decision making. First is the recognition that there is a condition of choice. Next is the discovery of alternative choices. Then would come the weighing of the relative merits of alternative choices. Finally, the choice would come from among alternatives. This sequence of steps can be illustrated by a decision such as which potato product to buy. A trip through the supermarket will show that potatoes may be purchased other than in bags of fresh potatoes. Potatoes are available canned in various styles, frozen in various styles ready for cooking at home and frozen precooked, and dehydrated for mashing and in mixes for preparing various kinds of potato dishes. From available information and in the light of experience, it is possible to estimate the cost of comparable numbers of servings of potatoes as purchased in different ways and to estimate the time required for the preparation of a particular potato dish. A choice can be made solely on the basis of cost, or it may take into account time required for preparation, or it might be made on the basis of palatability. All choices are made from some frame of reference or are based on some set of criteria. They are made for gain, goals to be achieved, or satisfactions wanted. The meal manager's goal may be to maximize food dollars; in this situation, she would choose to buy bags of fresh potatoes many months of the year. Her goal could be to save her time—an extremely important one in the 1980's. In this situation, she might buy a canned, frozen ready-prepared, or "instant" potato product. Or her goal could be the maximum enjoyment of the potato as a food; in this situation, she might purchase fresh potatoes of a given variety and grade.

Many decisions of all meal managers are rational ones made objectively to achieve a recognized end, such as maximizing the dollars allocated for food. For example, beef is bought when it is cheaper than pork, pork when it is cheaper than beef, nonfat dry milk instead of bottled fluid milk, frozen peas instead of frozen asparagus, bananas instead of fresh strawberries, and tuna instead of shrimp. Or, the meal manager chooses corn, not beets, beef, not lamb, hamburger, not beef liver, cornflakes, not oatmeal because of food preferences. Decisions made on the basis of food likes are rational decisions. The decision to buy a ready-made cherry pie instead of baking one from basic ingredients would be a rational decision if it was directed by a limited supply of time for meal preparation. Rational decisions are thought-out decisions; they make use of information. The meal manager makes nonrational decisions too. These are decisions affected by feelings, beliefs, self-images, sentiments, and so on. These decisions effect emotional satisfactions. Meals planned and prepared for special occasions and for guests are often fashioned by nonrational decision making. These meals often require greater expenditures of time, energy, and money than is normally spent; however, these expenditures are amply rewarded in such personal satisfactions as being recognized as a great cook, as a gracious hostess, or as having great sophistication regarding food.

People have many wants; they are seekers after satisfaction. Few people can satisfy all wants; we must decide which ones to strive for—these are our goals. We contrive within the limits of our means or resources to achieve them. Our wants and resources provide the frame of reference for making decisions. To paraphrase, one can say that decision making forces us to manipulate what we have to get what we want. We discuss next what we have; thereafter, we discuss what we want.

Resources of the Meal Manager

The meal manager's resources are both human and nonhuman; the latter are of great importance because they regulate the use of the former in many households. The nonhuman resources include money and, when available, home-produced food. The money resource is used for the purchase of a range, refrigerator, freezer, dishwasher or microwave oven; small equipment such as a toaster, food processor, blender, coffee maker, or slow cooker; pots and pans for cookery; tools for cookery such as good knives for cutting and spoons for stirring; and such items as linens, potholders, paper goods, films and aluminum foil, and cleansers. The money resource is also used to furnish a place for dining and for linens, paper goods, dinnerware, beverageware, and flatware. The money resource can also buy services such as convenience foods or meals eaten away from home. Finally, money is essential for the purchase of commercial energy that is used in a variety of ways in the management of meals, such as transportation for the purchase of food, the storage of food, the cooking of food, and heating the water for dishwashing. Different families allocate nonhuman resources in different ways—they spend different sums for food and for the kitchen and dining area because families differ in their value systems and goals.

Human resources include time, energy, knowledge, skills, and abilities. To provide meals for a family, time must be invested in planning meals, in shopping for food, in the storage of food, in preparing and serving meals, in clean-up after meals, in the care of the kitchen and its equipment, and in the care of the dining area and its furnishings. The time available and the decisions on how to use it partly determine the character of family meals.

In addition to time, one or more persons must expend energy—that is, do the hand-and-foot work of preparing and serving meals. Energy is expended in shopping, storing food, cooking, table setting, waiting on the table, cleaning up after meals, and caring for the kitchen and its equipment and for the dining area and its furnishings. Here, too, the available supply of energy and the willingness to use it partly determine the character of meals. Time and energy may be equally available to many families, yet they may eat dissimilar meals, served quite differently, because willingness to devote time and energy to meals depends on the values placed on them. If the goal of eating a meal is merely refueling the body, then any food is satisfactory and any quick manner of eating suffices. Food may go from range to plate to dining counter—and as soon as it is empty, the plate may be taken to the sink and deposited. If, on the other hand, the goal is that mealtime provide a period of relaxed interaction and opportunity for congenial conversation for the family, whether guests are present or not, each dish may be meticulously prepared, the table painstakingly set the food served from the dining table, the table cleared between courses, and the meal prolonged over a last cup of coffee.

Very important among the meal manager's resources are knowledge, skills, and abilities. They determine, to no small extent, how much money, time, and energy are expended on the meal responsibility because the uses of resources are interrelated. The more knowledge, abilities, and skills one has, the less money, time, and energy need be spent to achieve a given end. The better one knows how to shop in today's markets, the better one can control food expenditures. The less money one has to spend, the more time and energy may have to be spent. The more money one has, the more ready-prepared and quick-cooking foods can be purchased, thereby reducing expenditures of time and energy. Finally, the better one knows how to organize the tasks involved and the more skill one has in food preparation and meal serving, the more control there is over the expenditures of money, time, and energy.

GOALS AND VALUES IN MEAL MANAGEMENT

It is easier to discuss goals than values. Goals are wants; they are close and meaningful. The values that prompt selected goals are less evident. In fact, most people are generally not aware of the values that motivate them. Keeping in mind that values determine goals, we first consider goals for family meals.

At least four goals for meals may be cited. The first is that of good nutrition. In the 1980's, good nutrition is more than simply providing enough food of the right kinds; it is also the avoidance of excess consumption of sugar, saturated fats, and salt (sodium). Above all, it means avoidance of overconsumption that leads to overweight.

A second goal in meal management is that meals not cost too much; that is, the goal of planned spending for food. This goal is real for almost all meal managers whether they are responsible for the meals of a small nuclear family, a commune, an army, a retirement home, a prison, a hospital, a school lunchroom, a fast-food restaurant, or a gourmet restaurant. How much money for meals is "too much" depends on the extent of the money resource. There is a minimum essential cost for the nutritionally good diet; however, nutritionally adequate meals can be purchased at widely different levels of spending. The number of dollars essential for feeding a family depends on the size of the family, the age composition of the family, and the region of residence. The estimated cost per week—United States average—of a moderate-costing plan for a family of four with school-age children was approximately $90 in March, 1982; of an economical plan, $75; and of a generous-spending plan, $120 (1). According to Department of Commerce data, the personal consumption expenditure for food in 1981 was 16.2 percent of disposable personal income. According to a survey conducted in February, 1982, high food prices, recession, and unemployment had caused many shoppers, in recent months, to modify food-buying practices so as to reduce spending (3). Control of spending for food has always been and probably will always be a goal of some meal managers.

A third goal for meals is that they please the family. This goal offers explanations as to why we spend more for meals than is required to purchase a nutritionally good diet, why some persons overeat, why some persons do not consume a nutritionally good diet, and why some families spend more time and energy on meals than others do. All persons have some food preferences; these are learned. The kinds of meals people prefer are established by such influences as ethnic background, family customs, region of residence, socioeconomic background, education, religion, and experiences.

Meals provide satisfactions such as the enjoyment of food per se. We eat what we like and we like what we eat. Fortunately, food preferences do change; for example, millions have learned to like instant coffee and store-bought bread. In the late 1980's, it is probable that the foods and dishes of which meals are now composed will undergo change whether we like it or not. It has been suggested that, with the exception of the beliefs and practices associated with a religious concept, resistance to new and different foods is not strong if economic and labor-saving advantages are to be gained (2). Perhaps the goal that meals satisfy will, before the end of the century, like so much else, just fade away.

The meal manager's last goal is to fit the responsibility for meals into the planned uses of time and human energy. Time is required for planning meals and organizing the hand-and-foot work of meals; time and energy are required for shopping, meal preparation, and clean-up after meals. The ready acceptance of convenience foods, mixes and prepared foods, and the microwave oven is evidence that a high value is placed on time; it also reflects the wish to bypass the tedious tasks of cooking. In essence, today's meal manager tailors meals to available time: fifteen minute dinners when time is short; the better part of a day for meal preparation when time permits. Time and energy are budgeted as is money. As different families budget money differently, so do they budget time and energy differently. But, out of necessity or design, all families place limits on the use of time and energy.

Man is a valuing animal. He does not find all things equally good or equally desirable, nor do all men value things in the same way. And, what people value changes with time. They organize their values into a structure according to relative importance—a hierarchy of values. Values and their relative importance establish wants and goals and thereby pattern behavior. Through history, people have valued many different things: success as measured in a given culture, equality, peace, religious freedom, the high regard of peers, self-esteem, prestige, status as determined in a given culture, beauty, plumpness, piety, health, being of service to mankind, thrift, work, leisure time, safety of person, sensuous pleasures, freedom to be oneself and do one's own thing, and so on *ad infinitum*. We have symbols for our values: long hair, love beads, the cars we drive, the kinds of books we read, the TV programs we watch, the kinds of food we eat, the kinds of meals we eat and serve, the objects we own, and, again, so on *ad infinitum*. Our wants are symbols of our values.

We do not always know what we value. The more we seek to know and understand what we value, the better we understand our wants and our behavior. Not infrequently our values are in conflict. For example, the desire to maintain a desirable body weight and the desire to eat apple pie à la mode for dessert are not always compatible. We are torn between the values of health and pleasure. Similarly, our goals are often in conflict. For example, the goal of controlled spending is in conflict with the goal of maximizing the uses of time and energy when meals are eaten outside of the home.

It is not difficult to postulate ways in which family meals reflect the values of the family and of the meal manager. The allocation of resources to meals is a clue; goals are another. The value we place on health explains the goal of good nutrition for meals. When material wants are many, money may be conservatively allocated for the purchase of meals, and the kinds of food eaten reflect this value. When the enjoyment of food, especially expensive food, takes first place, dollars, time, and energy may be allocated inordinately to meals that will surely display this enjoyment. When little time is allocated to the preparing or the eating of meals, it may be because meals per se are little valued; on the other hand, it may reflect the lack of time available for meal preparation.

SUMMARY

Meal management is decision making and action. Decisions are made in accordance with desired satifactions; but they must realistically recognize resources: the available supply of money, time and energy, and the knowledge, skills, and abilities of one or more persons. General goals for meals are that they provide good nutrition; that they not exceed in cost an established plan for spending; that they be satisfying; and that they not exceed established limits on the uses of time and energy. Meals are sources of satisfactions that are not alike for all persons or families. Neither the decisions nor the actions of meal management will be universally the same, even of very similar family groups. And, finally, the answer to, "What's for dinner?" is not as simple as the homemaker's family has always thought.

REFERENCES CITED

1. "Cost of Food at Home," *Family Economics Review,* Family Economics Research Group, Agricultural Research Service, United States Department of Agriculture, Washington, D.C. (June 1982), pp. 38–42.
2. Niehoff, Arthur, "Food Habits and Cultural Patterns," in *Food, Science, and Society,* Nutrition Foundation, Inc., New York (1969), p. 68.
3. "Poll Finds Shift in Shopping Habits," *CNI* (Community Nutrition Institute) *Weekly Report,* Vol. 12, No. 20(May 20, 1982).

Chapter 2

Technology and Food in the 1980's

The consumer in the 1980's finds a vast array of foods from which to choose. These include foods which have been frozen, canned, refrigerated, dried, and prepared to various stages as well as fresh products of high quality which are available most of the year. These products are the result of scientific research related to agriculture and technology.

RECENT DEVELOPMENTS IN AGRICULTURE

Agricultural developments can be credited to scientists who have developed crossbreeds of meat animals and improved varieties of fruits, vegetables, and grains; to scientists who developed disease-resistant plants and animals; to scientists who helped prevent and control diseases; and to scientists who helped control pests in the environment. All of this has resulted in the production of more food of better quality. Some specific recent developments are worthy of note.

There have been several recent advances in crop production which will continue to have a significant effect on agriculture in the United States. One of the most important of these is *conservation tillage,* a technique which involves leaving previous crop material on the soil surface and thus controlling soil erosion. The no-tillage system reduces the time required for preparation for planting by eliminating plowing. This system makes the production of two or more crops in one growing season more feasible and thus increases total production per unit of land.

The season for many fruits and vegetables has been extended naturally through the development of early- and late-maturing varieties and of varieties that store well, and through the adaptation of varieties to different environments. For example, peach varieties that are better adapted to warmer climates have been developed. Such advances in addition to environmental control during storage have all but eliminated season, and most fruits and vegetables are available fresh throughout the year. Varietal changes have resulted in such improvements as better color, shape, fleshiness, size, juiciness, and so on. However, the flavor and aroma of some fruits and vegetables have not always been improved; for example, there are those who are critical of the flavor of the newer varieties of tomatoes and corn-on-the-cob. Improvements of recent decades are to be seen in peaches, apricots, plums, strawberries, potatoes, sweet corn, carrots, celery, and cucumbers. Varietal improvements coupled with increased knowledge of the cultural requirements of plants both in the field and in the greenhouse have increased production.

Due to modern production practices, poultry is one of the most economical sources of animal protein. Advances have been made in breeding, feeding, processing, and packaging. These advances have given us eggs and broilers at bargain prices. Another economical source of animal protein has been made possible by the development of aquaculture or fish farming, a technique in which fish are produced under managed conditions. The channel catfish is experiencing the most commercial success, but other fish such as trout, salmon, shrimp, and oysters also offer potential for commercial culture. Fish are more efficient than beef or pork and about equal to chickens in converting food protein into their body protein.

The advent of recombinant DNA technology and the current surge of interest in biotechnology have resulted in amazing advances in knowledge and exciting possibilities for new or more efficient processes. For example, resistance genes may be introduced into plants to prevent attack by pathogenic fungi. This resistance could be accomplished in a shorter time than with routine breeding.

Science and know-how continue to be exceedingly important when production is complete; fruits and vegetables must be harvested at the optimum time, and animals must be slaughtered when they are of the best size and quality. Mechanical harvesting of fruits and vegetables has replaced hand harvesting extensively. At-harvest treatments such as vacuum cooling and hydrocooling maintain garden freshness for days in such vegetables as carrots, celery, corn-on-the-cob, and lettuce, and in fruits such as peaches and nectarines. These processes provide wide distribution of fresh fruits and vegetables. In vacuum cooling, produce is cooled in a partial vacuum from the field temperature to 35° F in minutes due to evaporation. Dipping in ice water is a technique of hydrocooling. It is used for vegetables such as potatoes which have a large mass but little surface area. This sudden drop in temperature is significant in the maintenance of the quality of freshness. Some items are packaged and go to market at this point; others, such as apples and pears, are stored for future distribution. Some freshly harvested fruits and vegetables are immediately frozen; others are processed by other methods, such as canning and dehydration.

The storage and prevention of spoilage of fruits has become so effective that apples harvested in November may remain in good condition until the following June. To deter spoilage, fruits such as lemons and peaches may receive very mild heat treatments in water or steam. Other fruits are treated with solutions containing chemicals that are effective for the specific organisms to which a fruit is susceptible: apples are dipped to prevent storage scald, a skin disorder; citrus fruits are dipped to prevent mold damage. Storage facilities in which the temperature, humidity, and atmosphere—that is, the carbon dioxide-oxygen ratio—are controlled extend the storage life of fruits and vegetables such as apples, grapes, and pears.

SCIENCE, TECHNOLOGY, AND FOOD PROCESSING

Thus far, discussion has been of science and technology in the production, the harvest, and the storage of food consumed fresh; it is, however, in the science and technology of food preservation and processing that food products derive their stability and convenience. The storage and preservation of food, modern packaging, and the use of food additives have led to today's convenience foods.

Canning Preservation

Canning is a relatively modern method of preservation; it began in the United States in the early 1800's. Foods are canned in hermetically sealed containers which are heat processed at temperatures high enough to destroy pathogenic and spoilage organisms which might be present in the raw food.

Foods are canned in metal cans and glass containers. Recently, flexible packages made from laminated films and films laminated with aluminum foil have been developed. It is predicted that the flexible package will come into greater use; it will provide canned products of better flavor because of possible shorter processing time. Further, it will be less expensive and shipping costs will be reduced because of lighter weight. Currently, cans of aluminum or tin exceed other containers in use. Tin cans are steel with a thin coating of tin on both the external and the internal surfaces. Cans for some products are further coated with enamels formulated from oleoresins to protect brightly colored fruits such as cherries from undesirable color changes; to prevent sulfur-bearing vegetables such as corn from becoming black as a result of interactions with elements in the metals; and to prevent detinning action by such foods as tomato juice. High-temperature, short-time canning has improved the quality of some canned products. Aseptic canning, wherein the food and the container are separately sterilized, has been used for canning whole milk, cream, and ready-to-eat puddings. The dairy products are packaged in foil-lined cartons. Dehydrocanning is the canning of foods that have had their water content reduced by 50 percent before processing. Canning unfavorably modifies the flavor, the color, and the texture of foods for some persons; they prefer many food products frozen instead. Although canning does give storage stability, canning does not preserve food indefinitely because there are changes in color and flavor during storage. A law that will require the mandatory open dating with the date of processing for all canned foods will probably be enacted.

Dehydration

More and more foods processed by dehydration can now be found in the supermarket. They are most noticable as the many instant products to which one adds water; they are also present but less noticed in assorted foods and mixes. There are naturally dehydrated foods, such as nuts, grains, beans, peas, and sun-dried fruits. Because of the unpredictability of the weather, these foods are often finished commercially with artificial drying. An advantage of dehydration is weight reduction by water loss. Water removal occurs at high temperatures or at low temperatures in a vacuum; quality is better in the latter instance. The treatment of certain fruits and vegetables with sulfur will help to retain color and vitamin C during drying. However, sulfur treatment is not recommended for products which are high in thiamin since sulfites are destructive of that vitamin. There are several techniques for the dehydration of food, more than those available for preservation by canning or freezing.

In tunnel drying, food passes through chambers into which heated air is blown. In spray drying, liquid foods are sprayed into cone-shaped chambers into which hot air is blown. The food is instantly dried. Milk, coffee, juices, and coffee creamers are dried in this way. In roller or drum drying, food slurries or purees are heated in a thin layer on the surface of a heated revolving drum. The dry film is removed and is then flaked or pulverized. Instant potato flakes, instant cereals, and instant sweet potatoes, applesauce, and pumpkin are some foods processed in this way. In foam-mat drying, the puree is released under pressure from a nozzle into a heated chamber for drying—as in spray drying. This process is used for milk, instant flour, coffee, tea, fruit and vegetable juices, and fruit purees.

Freeze drying is a first-class method of food preservation. It is superior to most other methods in the retention of color, flavor, texture and nutrients. It would be used more if it were not such an expansive process. Freeze drying is a two-step process that includes the initial quick freezing of the prepared product, followed by drying in a vacuum chamber. The final product retains its original cell structure, is light in weight, is shelf storable, and is of good color and flavor. The freeze-dried product is fragile and requires special packaging to protect it from shattering. Research has demonstrated that freeze-dried foods can be compressed for purposes of bulk reduction and that on hydration they are restored to normal appearance and texture. Freeze-dried foods take up water rapidly and some are subject to deterioration in oxygen; they must be packaged in an inert atmosphere in moistureproof and vaporproof wraps. Products dehydrated by freeze drying include coffee; raw and precooked meats, fish, poultry, and shellfish; such precooked vegetables as peas, spinach, corn, and carrots; cottage cheese; such fruits as peaches, strawberries, cherries, and pears; such fruit juices as orange, grapefruit, and pineapple; shrimp, chicken, and tuna salads; casserole dishes such as beef Stroganoff; and so on.

The reverse of freeze drying is dehydrofreezing, which combines the economy of dehydration with the flavor-holding advantages of freezing. The water content of fruits and vegetables is reduced by 50 percent; the product is then frozen. The process is used for processing fruits and vegetables for food manufacturing, and is used for such foods as apple slices for pies, and potatoes and vegetables for soups and stews. Explosion puffing, first used to puff cereals, has been applied to vegetables and fruits. Products are first partially dried and then placed in a pressure chamber. Release of pressure in the chamber causes the pieces to explode, much in the way that corn pops. The finished pieces are about the same size as they were before processing. The flavor is good, and the products reconstitute readily. Reverse osmosis is a process whereby water is removed from fruits placed in a concentrated sugar solution; when the water content is reduced to the desirable level, the fruit is further dried to low water content by vacuum drying. Properly packaged dehydrated foods will retain their quality when stored at room temperatures for extended periods of time. Handling and storage costs are reduced for dehydrated foods due to lighter weight and reduced product volume.

Freezing Preservation

Many diverse products are frozen—some to thaw and eat, others to heat and eat, and still others to cook and eat. Many varieties of plants are grown especially for preservation by freezing, notably peas and strawberries. New frozen food products are introduced all of the time; old ones fade away.

Depending on the refrigerant used, foods preserved by freezing are either quick frozen at temperatures from minus 10° F to minus 40° F or instant (or cryogenic) frozen at minus 100° F to minus 320° F. Prepared foods frozen in consumersized packages are quick frozen between metal plates or in cold air blasts. Products that are packaged after freezing are spread on a wire mesh belt and either pass through a freezing tunnel or are subjected to a current of icy cold air that passes up through the mesh belt and causes the food to tumble and freeze in the air. Freezing is rapid and the individual pieces do not stick together but are individually quick frozen (IQF). The IQF fruits, vegetables, and other products so frozen are readily pourable from the package and handy to use in the kitchen.

The main advantage of a quick freezing process is that it produces numerous small crystals as opposed to the larger ones which form during slow freezing. Large crystals damage cells and thus texture. However, the advantage of a quick-freezing process is lost if food is not maintained at low temperatures. Fluctuating temperatures promote the growth of larger crystals. Also, numerous undesirable changes take place in frozen food which is stored at temperatures warmer that 0° F or minus 18°C. Much care and expense is required to maintain a package of frozen food at the optimum low temperature from the time the product is frozen at the factory until the time it is selected from the home freezer for final preparation.

Microwave Processing

In March of 1968, the Food and Drug Administration approved radio frequency radiation (including microwave frequencies) for the heating of food. Microwaves are a form of electromagnetic energy that are between radio waves and infrared waves in frequency and wavelength. Microwaves are absorbed by food and cause the agitation of molecules and friction; hence, rapid heating. Dipolar molecules, such as water selectively absorb the energy. Commercially, microwave heating is being used in processing potato chips and in frying chicken. Its use permits the control of browning. The microwave oven is used extensively for cooking and heating food in restaurants, institutions, and the home.

Radiation Preservation of Food

The regulation of the use of radiation preservation or treatment of food is under the Food and Drug Administration by authority of the

Food Additives Amendment of The Food, Drug, and Cosmetic Act of 1938. The preservation of food by radiation has been extensively researched worldwide since World War II. High radiation dosage effects complete and total sterilization of food; "cold sterilization" at a lesser dosage level effects sterility comparable to canning. Low-radiation doses pasteurize, disinfect, and inhibit sprouting. Pasteurization reduces spoilage and extends the shelf life of such perishable foods as fresh fruits and vegetables, fish and shellfish. Unfortunately, radiation treatment of food reduces acceptability by affecting color and flavor and aroma. Even pasteurization causes flavor change described as "radiation flavor." It has been discovered that cooking or freezing food before radiation results in fewer undesirable changes.

In February, 1963, the Food and Drug Administration authorized the radiation sterilization of canned bacon. This product did not reach the consumer market, but it was consumed by the armed forces. In August, 1968, approval was withdrawn on the basis of adverse effects produced in animals fed irradiated foods. There is as yet no consensus on the safety of radiation-treated food. There is some loss of nutrient content, but this is comparable to the losses caused by heat treatment. Food does not contain induced radioactivity. However, there is the possibility of the production of toxic agents in the food by radiation. Radiation preservation is expensive and it will probably not be introduced in food processing unless it can offer some unique advantage over established methods. It remains in use for deinfestation of wheat and wheat flour and for the inhibition of sprouts on potatoes. The use of ultraviolet radiation for the processing and treatment of food is permitted by the Food and Drug Administration for surface microorganism control, as in the fast ripening of beef and the sterilization of water for food processing. The U.S. Department of Agriculture is conducting experiments to obtain data in support of regulatory clearance for widespread use of irradiation in food preservation.

Modern food processing techniques produce food of high quality, and in many cases the nutritive value is superior to that of its fresh counterpart. Although few methods of food preservation have been developed recently, new and better ways to preserve food are being researched.

Food Packaging

Advances in food technology have required advances in food-packaging technology; and at the same time, developments in food-packaging materials and technology have made possible advances in food technology. The consumer asks that the package be convenient, informative, and protective; the food processor asks that it sell his product and that it be protective; and the supermarket manager also asks that it be stackable and pilfer proof.

Consumers want the package to have labels that tell what the product is and how to use it. Consumers also want labels to reveal the nature of the contents (as in window-boxed products) when feasible. Consumers also require that packaging protect the contents from contamination and deterioration. Consumers have complained about the numerous different sizes of the same product and the resulting difficulty they have in determining the best buy. Customers also complain that the artwork on some packages is deceptive; showing, for example, a perfect, rich-colored, firm fruit or vegetable whereas the product in the package is really irregularly shaped and soft. There has also been much discussion about bulk versus prepackaged fresh produce. The majority of consumers prefer to purchase fresh produce from bulk display rather than prepackaged produce; this allows them to check for blemishes and bruises and to select the exact quantity needed.

The prime purpose of packaging is protection: protection from physical damage during transport and handling, protection from contamination, and protection from deteriorative changes caused by environmental factors. Protection during shipping and handling is easily obtained by the use of strong cartons, which also aid in the unitization of items. Protection from contamination means prevention of the entry of debris and microorganisms after processing the food. Only food that has been properly processed and packaged in hermetically sealed containers is free from the danger of microbial contamination.

Factors in the environment that cause the deterioration and spoilage of food are heat, oxygen, moisture and light. The effects of enzymes and the growth of microorganisms combined with some or all of these environmental factors cause rancidity, drying, moldiness, putrefaction and the loss of crispness, color, and flavor. Packaging that removes one or more of the environmental factors delays these undesirable changes.

Proper sealing of the package, packaging in a vacuum, packaging in an inert gas, and using additives (such as antioxidants, desiccants, mold inhibitors, and preservatives) in the packaging material aid in removing the environmental factors. All foods must be packaged according to kind and must be properly stored. At best, packaging and storage conditions simply delay the reactions that lead to food deterioration and ultimately to spoilage.

Some examples of good packaging are perforated film bags that control respiration and moisture loss in fresh fruits and vegetables, shrink-film packaging for lettuce, poultry, and cheese; opaque, oxygen-impermeable films for fresh and cured meats; vacuum- and nitrogen-backfilled packages for luncheon meats; and moisture- and vapor-proof packaging that prevents drying in frozen foods.

The disposal of the waste that packaging creates is an increasingly serious problem. Alhough some of the materials used in packaging food products can be recycled, not all can be. No-return bottles pose a special problem because they are difficult to destroy. It is quite likely that a method for their destruction will be discovered or that a method of producing containers that are more easily destroyed will be developed. The new, stay-on tab for aluminum beverage cans eliminates litter of the pull tabs and makes these cans 100 percent recyclable.

Increased use of the microwave oven has created the need for packaging which can move directly from the freezer to the microwave oven. Since metals cannot be used in the microwave oven, a paperboard tray coated with heat-resistant polyester has been developed. It is economically practical and certain to see increased use. Another package which will undoubtedly see wider use is the *form-fill flexible package*. This package, used for refrigerated products such as fresh pineapple and sauerkraut, is transparent and resistant to bursting, pinholing, and leaking. Printing on the package is between laminations and does not come in contact with the food.

The *retort pouch*, a flexible laminated pouch that can withstand thermal processing temperature and combines the advantages of the metal can and the plastic boil-in-bag, is finally reaching the marketing stage in the United States. It has been successfully marketed in Europe and Japan for several years. Its development is considered to be one of the most important steps in food processing technology since the development of canning. The pouch consists of three layers held together by an adhesive: an outer layer of polyester for strength; a middle layer of aluminum foil as a moisture, light, and gas barrier; and an inner layer of polyolefin as the heat-seal and food-contact material. The pouched product does not require refrigeration or freezing, is shelf stable for as long as is canned food, can be prepared by heating the pouch in boiling water, and requires less disposal space than cans. Another advantage is that pouches are lighter in weight than cans and can be packaged in uniform cardboard cartons which are stackable. The pouch does have some disadvantages: initially, it will require some form of overwrapping, such as a carton; it is limited in size; and its popularity is as yet unproved in the United States. However, most of the disadvantages of the pouch will probably be overcome in time, and it may eventually replace the tin can and the glass jar for most products.

Substitutes and Synthetic Foods

No discussion of science and technology and food can omit mention of substitute and synthetic foods and designed or engineered foods. *Synthetic products* have been defined as those that include at least one major ingredient derived from nonfarm sources. A *major nonfarm ingredient* is any substance that displaces natural agricultural materials in a food product's set of basic attributes, particularly flavor, texture viscosity, and color. Usually petroleum provides the bulk of material for synthetic ingredients. Some synthetics are fruit juice drinks, fruit juice powders and concentrates, and fruit punches. *Substitute food products* have been defined as those that contain one or more major ingredients derived from unconventional agricultural resources. Some foods considered to be substitutes are margarine, the meat analogs, nondairy coffee creamers, and nondairy whipped toppings. At the present time, substitutes exceed synthetics in number. The currently projected future food-population imbalance favors the continued development of both. If meat analogs were to replace meat in our diet, current agricultural capacity would feed four to five times as many persons as it now does. Producing agricultural products to feed animals in order to feed meat and other animal foods to man is less efficient and more costly than if man were to consume the primary crops. In general, only in the Western, or advanced countries, has it been possible to feed the primary crops to animals; the rest of the world's people eat diets composed of grains, yams, roots, legumes, and other vegetables, that is, the primary food products.

In the United States, substitutes have been accepted because of the frequent replacement of animal fat with vegetable fats and reduced cholesterol in such foods as margarine and nondairy coffee creamers. The meat analogs are used by religious groups that forbid the eating of certain meats, by vegetarians, and in institutional feeding. The food processors use textured vegetable proteins in such dishes as chili with beans, meat loaf, and Spanish rice, to name but a few.

Designed or engineered foods include those developed for overcoming malnutrition in the developing countries. They are fabricated from agricultural products with or without the addition of minerals and/or vitamins. Some are especially intended for the feeding of children. These foods are formulated from cereal grains, soybeans and other legumes, cottonseed meal, and fish protein concentrate. They are prepared for eating as gruels, soups, breads, and whatever other dishes are peculiar to the diet in a given place. In general, small quantities of the product provide a high proportion of nutrient needs other than calories.

The threat of starvation as a result of population-food imbalance has led to the research and developnent of unconventional sources of protein. Bacteria, yeasts, and fungi have been cultured in a variety of substrates to provide great quantities of protein and other nutrients. Fish-protein concentrate, oil-seed protein concentrate derived from the press cake that remains after the pressing of oil from oil-bearing seeds, leaf protein concentrate, and protein concentrate derived from the culture of algae are other unconventional food sources. The Food and Drug Administration has approved fish-protein concentrate for limited use by humans; the use of the remaining unconventional sources remains in the future for man, though some are now in use in animal feeding.

Food Additives

Just as an abundant agriculture is dependent on the use of a host of chemicals, so is the abundant supply of high quality food found in the supermarket today dependent on a host of chemicals. These are the food additives, the use of which has been both maligned and applauded. The proper use of food additives presupposes that they are safe, effective for an intended purpose, and not used to provide an opportunity for deception or to supplant good manufacturing practices. The legal aspects of food additives are discussed in Chapter 3; the discussion here is limited to the purposes of their use and to the kinds of compounds in use.

Basically, the use of additives is a response by the food industry to the enormous population growth and the changes in food consumption patterns that have taken place in the past one hundred years. Most consumers no longer grow or make their own food and have a low tolerance for food that spoils quickly. Much of the controversy about food additives stems from the irrelevant distinction between "artificial" and "natural" chemicals. There is no difference between the chemicals found in nature and the same chemical created in the laboratory. A blanket indictment of additives and preservatives is unwarranted. A better understanding of food additives may be gained by looking at a relevant distinction such as that between "intentional" and "indirect" additives. Indirect additives are substances that have no planned function in food but become (or have a possibility of becoming) part of it during some phase of production, processing, packaging, or storage. Intentional additives, also known as direct additives, are substances purposely and directly added to food. Vanilla is an example of an intentional food additive; cellophane, a material used in food packaging, is an indirect additive. Packaging materials become indirect additives when minute amounts of the molecules that make up such materials migrate from the package to the food.

Additives present in food are put there for intended purposes such as to color, flavor, enhance flavor, prevent foaming, prevent spoilage, produce a smooth texture, and so on.

Some classes of additives are described according to their function, and it may be noted that some additives function in more than one capacity, such as nitrates and nitrites and sulfur dioxide and sulfites.

Preservatives or antimicrobial additives extend the shelf life of foods, and are important in preventing food waste and in maximizing the food supply. Salt, sugar, acids, and wood smoke have been in use for centuries in preserving food. They remain in use as antimicrobial agents, but have largely been superseded by chemical preservatives. The use of chemical preservatives cannot, by law, result in deception, or adversely affect the nutritive value of a food, or permit the growth of food poisoning organisms while suppressing the growth of other organisms that would make spoilage evident. Label statement of the use of chemical preservatives in standardized foods is mandatory. Further, the label statement must specify the nature of the preservative action, for example, "added to retard mold growth." Benzoic acid and sodium benzoate are active against many bacteria, yeasts, and molds. Their use is permitted in carbonated and still beverages, fruit drinks and juices, margarine, prepared salads and salad dressings, mincemeat, and pickles. The parabens (para-hydroxybenzoate esters) are similar in action and are used in the same products, except margarine, and also in chemically-leavened baked goods, pastries, icings, toppings, and dried fruits and vegetables.

Sorbic acid and its sodium and potassium salts are particularly effective inhibitors of molds and yeasts; they are used in the foods already mentioned and in cheese and cheese products, dry sausages, and salted or smoked fish. In addition to being used directly on a food, the sorbates may be present on wrapping materials. Proprionic acid and its sodium and calcium salts are used primarily as mold inhibitors in bread, cheese, and cheese products. Proprionates are sprayed on brown-and-serve rolls, and butter wrappers are impregnated with them. Sulfur dioxide and the sulfites are antimicrobial for bacteria, yeasts, and molds; they also protect the color of fruits and vegetables by actions that deter browning. Sulfur is applied as fumes, in a dip, or by spray. Although nitrates are antimicrobial, their main use is in curing mixtures for meats, where they function to develop and fix the red color that is unique to cured meats. The safety of the nitrate additives is suspect. A committee appointed by the National Academy of Science–National Research Council at the request of the Food and Drug Administration and the U.S. Department of Agriculture recommended in 1981 that the exposure of cured meats to nitrites be reduced to the level that protection against botulism is not compromised. It was also recommended that the search for alternatives be continued. Acetic acid, acetates, and vinegar are effective against yeast and bacteria. They are used in catsup, mayonnaise, pickles, and pickled sausages.

Antioxidants also preserve food by preventing rancidity, browning, loss of color, and loss of flavor. A moderately long list of antioxidants has been approved for foods and for packaging materials. Some of them, the names of which appear in full or in abbreviated form on labels, are butylated hydroxyanisole (BHA), butylated hydroxytoluene (BHT), propyl gallate (PG), gum guaiac, tocopherols, and citric and ascorbic acid.

A group of compounds known as sequestrants function similarly to antioxidants in that they protect against rancidity and color and flavor losses, but they do so in a different manner. They are chelating agents that react with metals to alter the effects of metals in substances. Some sequestrants, the names of which appear on labels, are oxystearin, sorbitol, EDTA (ethylenediaminetetra acetate), and citric, tartaric, and pyrophosphoric acids. Their use extends the shelf life and stabilizes the flavor of salad dressings, french fried potatoes, fried and baked goods, roasted nuts, and margarine, that is, products containing fats and oils. They protect the vitamin content, especially vitamin C, of fruit juices; the color of canned vegetables and fruits and of frozen fruits; and the color and flavor of fish and shellfish processed by canning and freezing.

One of the prime requisites of a food is that it taste good; hence, an extremely important group of food additives is one that includes flavorings, flavor enhancers and potentiators. We have already noted that a number of food additives are used to protect flavor. Spices were introduced in Europe during the Crusades and, herbs were introduced during the Middle Ages. Their function was twofold: to mask the bad flavor of nearly spoiled food and to provide pleasing flavors. A glance at the labels of almost any prepared food on supermarket shelves reveals that flavor agents are both natural and artificial, though generally only the latter. Artificial flavor agents that closely resemble natural ones can be made more economically, more uniformly, and in greater concentration than the natural flavor agents. Man-made flavorings are of two types: the synthetic ones that have the same chemical composition as natural flavor agents, and simulated, or imitation, flavorings that taste like the natural flavor agents. Both are used in foods and would be described on labels as artificial flavorings. The development of meat analogs was contingent on the availability of flavor agents to provide the beef, chicken, and other flavors that cause the analogs to taste like the real thing. Likewise, cake mixes, imitation dairy foods, margarine, dessert mixes, and a host of other foods require the use of prodigious quantities of artificial flavorings.

In addition to the use of flavor agents per se, there is wide use of compounds known as flavor enhancers and flavor potentiators. While these compounds contribute little or no flavor themselves, they can influence the way in which other flavors in a product are perceived. A number of naturally occurring flavor enhancers have been identified; those in commercial production and use include monosodium glutamate (MSG), maltol, 5′-inosine monophosphate (IMP), and 5′-guanine monophosphate (GMP). They intensify flavor and appear to suppress some undesirable flavor notes. All are used in minute quantities, and the amount of MSG used to produce certain effects can be reduced by the use of 5′-nucleotides, which act synergistically with it. The flavoring of processed foods is both science and art; an otherwise convenient food may fail because of unacceptable flavor, for though flavor is an experience short in duration, it is lasting in memory.

Gums comprise a group of compounds in extensive use in processed foods. Gums derived from seaweeds were in use for centuries as thickening and gelling agents but it took twentieth-century food technology to give them the importance they now have. They are, excepting gelatin, complex carbohydrates composed of sugar units. Dissolved in water they produce viscous solutions or gels. They function as thickening, gelling, emulsifying, suspending, water-binding, and stabilizing agents. Gums from natural sources are, in decreasing order of use, gum arabic, guar gum, gelatin, carrageenan, locust bean gum, and agar. The natural sources of gums, excepting gelatin, are plants. Gums derived from seaweeds are agar, algin, carrageenan, and furcellan; from seeds, locust bean gum and guar gum; and from tree sources, gum arabic, gum tragacanth, and karaya gum. Semisynthetic gums are derived by treatment of starch and cellulose; several approved by the Food and Drug Administration for use include methyl cellulose, carboxymethyl cellulose, and propylene glycol alginate. Pectins are derived from fruits, especially citrus fruits. The names of gums appear abundantly on food labels; however, carob bean gum, gum karaya, gum tragacanth, guar gum, and oat gum may be designated as "vegetable gum." Almost all gums are used in the production of the following dairy products: ice cream and ice milk, sherbets, chocolate milk drink, cottage cheese, cream cheese, cheese spreads, whipped cream, and yogurt. Some or all of the named gums are used in bread doughs and mixes, cake mixes, cake fillings and toppings, pie fillings, puddings, cookies, and others. Gums are also used in salad dressings and French dressing; in white sauces and gravies; in syrups and toppings; in spaghetti sauces; in canned meat, fish, and poultry; in sausages and in low-calorie foods. The color additives are both artificial and natural. The natural ones include annatto, an extract from the seeds of a tropical tree; beta carotene; caramel; paprika; saffron; turmeric; and grapeskin extract. All artificial colors must be certified as safe by the Food and Drug Administration. A group of compounds called polyglycerol esters is interesting because it is comprised of defoaming agents and antispattering, antisticking, antiweeping, antilumping, and anticlouding agents. They also make peanut butter and margarines more spreadable; further, they are emulsifiers, thickeners, and stabilizers. Surfactants are extremely important in food processing: they are emulsifying agents and wetting agents. They retard the staling process in yeast-raised baked goods, among other functions. Important surfactants are the mono- and di-glycerides, propylene glycol monostearate, and polysorbate 60. These surface-active agents give shortenings and oils their easy-to-use properties. The addition of food nutrients—as in the enrichment of flour, bread, cereals, fruit beverages, milk, and salt—is important nutritionally. It is quite probable that as more foods are designed, the addition of nutrients will become increasingly important.

Although the list of intentional food additives is relatively long it is not headed by exotic substances but by such familiar substances as sucrose (table sugar), salt, and corn syrup (a mixture of fructose and dextrose). These three compounds account for 93 percent by weight of all food additives used in the United States. Thirty more additives account for the next 5.5 percent. These include such familiar substances as yeast, citric acid (occurs naturally in lemons and oranges), baking soda, vegetable colors (such as red from beets), mustard, pepper, and the carbonated gas for soda pop. The 1,900 or so remaining additives account for the balance, 1.5 percent. According to the study by the President's Science Advisory Committee, the amount of various food additives normally ingested in a year ranges from 102 pounds per person of table sugar, 15 pounds of salt, and 13 pounds of dextrose to 9.3 pounds of the remaining additives. The average use per person of each of the remaining 1,900 intentional additives per year is 0.08 ounces. This figure overstates the use of most additives, for if we look at a list of all 1,900, half of them would have an average use of less than 0.000016 pounds per person per year.

In summary, it may be stated that in the 1980's food technology makes extensive use of food additives for various purposes: to fabricate foods of acceptable quality, that is, good flavor, color, and texture; to maintain quality, that is, prevent deterioration and spoilage; to enhance nutrient content; and, of course, to provide the consumer with built-in maid and built-in chef services.

SUMMARY

During this century, our food supply has been vastly increased by developments in agriculture and animal husbandry, by improved storage techniques, and by improved methods of processing. The world population-food imbalance demands the maximum use of our food supply that science and technology can effect. These advances have not been without hazards to man, the pollution of the environment with many different kinds of chemicals, and the addition to food of substances that may or may not be totally safe. These developments have contributed to the greater need for laws to regulate the safety of the food supply.

SUGGESTED PROBLEMS

1. Read the ingredient list on three convenience food products. Identify the food additives. What are their functions?
2. Notice the packaging of six food products. From a consumer's point of view is the packaging adequate or exceptional? How would you change it?
3. Compare the cost of some food products available in several forms—canned, frozen, dehydrated, or freeze dried.
4. Find as many examples as possible of foods packaged in different types of flexible pouches.

Chapter 3

Federal Laws, Regulations, and Federal Agencies that Regulate the Food Supply

The story of adulterated food is an old one; the history of legislation to regulate adulteration and provide people with wholesome food is equally old. Two well-known examples from biblical history are the restrictions on eating pork and on eating meat from animals killed other than by prescribed slaughter. Bread and wine were adulterated in ancient Greece and Rome. A Sanskrit law of 300 B.C. imposed fines on any persons who sold adulterated grains or oils. Chinese classics of the second century B.C. relate that there were government officials responsible for preventing the manufacture of adulterated food. During the Middle Ages, as commerce expanded and the manufacture of some food was transferred from home to shop, the fraudulent practice of including cheaper materials in foods increased. Spices were in great demand; they were often highly diluted. The first English food law, the Assize of Bread proclaimed by King John in 1202, prohibited the adulteration of bread with such ingredients as ground peas or beans. In 1266, legislation was passed in England to protect the purchaser against short weight in bread and against the sale of unsound meat. In general, these early attempts at control were ineffectual. Cheating became more sophisticated and more common during the sixteenth, seventeenth, and eighteenth centuries. In the nineteenth century, the enormity of the problem came to light as the science of analytical chemistry and the microscope provided tools for detecting and measuring adulteration.

It was in England that the problem was first publicized and action taken. In 1820, a German chemist and pharmacist living in London, Frederick C. Accum, published *A Treatise on Adulteration of Food, and Culinary Poisons*. This work was published in the United States in the same year by a pirate publisher. At midcentury, Dr. Arthur H. Hassell conducted investigations for the *Lancet,* a British medical journal, revealing that scarcely any common foodstuff was free from adulteration. Aroused public opinion forced the passage of legislation to control food adulteration. The first efforts were weak, but in 1875, Parliament passed a law that, with subsequent amendments, remained the basic British food law for many years. By the end of the century, most European countries had general food statutes.

LEGISLATION IN THE UNITED STATES

In the United States, the first law on record to control the adulteration of food was passed in 1784 by Massachusetts; it penalized the seller of diseased, corrupted, or unwholesome provisions. In 1850, a pure food and drink law was passed in California. General interest in food and drug laws did not develop until after the Civil War; however, during the relatively short time since, a voluminous history of food legislation in the United States has been accumulated. Only federal legislation is discussed here. At first, the federal food laws were enacted to provide revenue, to prevent the importation of unwholesome and adulterated food, and to protect domestic agriculture. Later, the main purposes of federal legislation became the protection of the consumer from fraud and the protection of the public health. A brief history of the various enactments of the federal government follows.

History of Legislation

The first federal food law was the Tea Act of 1883; it prohibited the importation of spurious and adulterated teas. This tea act was repealed by a Tea Act of 1897, which also prohibited the importation of adulterated and spurious teas; but it also provided for the establishment of a body of tea experts who would each year—on or before February 15—establish minimum standards of quality for imported teas and for the inspection of all teas entering United States ports.

In 1886, the original Oleomargarine Act was passed. It imposed taxes on, regulated the manufacture and sale of, and controlled the importation of oleomargarine. The tax was not repealed until 1950, at which time the Food, Drug, and Cosmetic Act was amended to regulate the sale of colored margarine and the serving of colored margarine in public eating places "whether the margarine originates from an interstate source or from the state in which sold."

In 1890, an act to prohibit the importation of adulterated food and drink was enacted.

The Meat Inspection Act of 1890 provided for the inspection of salted pork and bacon and live animals intended for export. It was legislation in response to embargoes and complaints on the quality of the meat imported from the United States by European countries. The act authorized the inspection and quarantine of imported animals.

The Cattle Inspection Act of 1891 authorized the inspection of all cattle intended for export; voluntary inspection of animals before and after slaughter if they were to be shipped in interstate commerce; the tagging of inspected meats to inform consumers of the inspection; and the nonmandatory inspection of carcasses to be sent to canning and processing plants.

In 1896, the Filled Cheese Act was passed. The legislation defined cheese and imposed a tax upon and regulated the manufacture, sale, importation, and export of "filled cheese." This product is manufactured from milk or skim milk with added butter, animal fats, vegetable oils, or a combination of these ingredients in imitation of cheese.

In 1902, the Renovated or Process Butter Act defined renovated or process butter and adulterated butter. Further, it imposed a tax upon them and decreed that they could not be prepared from filthy or decomposed materials. Legislation enacted the same year prohibited the false branding of food and dairy products as to place of origin. Appropriations were also made for establishing pure food standards and to characterize adulterants.

In 1906, the first Food and Drugs Act was passed; it is discussed briefly later in this chapter. In the same year, the Meat Inspection Act was passed for the purpose of "preventing the use in interstate or foreign commerce of meat and meat food products which are unsound, unhealthful, unwholesome, or otherwise unfit for human food." This act made mandatory the inspection, examination, and certification as "Inspected and Passed" of all carcasses or parts thereof, of meat, and of meat products destined for interstate or foreign commerce. The law provided for the establishment of an inspection service for the examination and certification of the wholesomeness of animals, carcasses, or parts thereof, and of meats and meat products; and for the development of a sanitary code for slaughterhouses and meat-packing and processing plants. Further, the law decreed that no meat product could contain dyes, chemicals, preservatives, or ingredients that might render it injurious to health. Cattle, sheep, swine, and goats were covered in the law. The Imported-Meat Act of 1913 extended the provisions of the law to imported meat and meat products. The Horse-Meat Act of 1919 requires the conspicuous labeling of meat and meat products from horses as "horse-meat" and "horse-meat products."

The Wholesome Meat Act of December, 1967, applied the provisions of the Meat Inspection Act of meat and meat food products in intrastate commerce. It placed under inspection the 25 percent of all meat sold and the 15 percent of all slaughter that had previously been un-inspected. States were given two years, with an extension of one year possible, to establish inspection programs "at least equal" to federal in-spection. The law made federal inspection mandatory in the absence of satisfactory state inspection.

An act of 1910 was concerned with the adulteration and misbranding of insecticides and fungicides. The 1954 amendment to the Federal Food, Drug, and Cosmetic Act required regulation of the residues of chemical pesticides on raw agricultural products.

In 1923, the Filled Milk Act, which prohibited the shipment in inter-state commerce of filled milk, was passed. It defined filled milk as milk, skim milk, or cream in any form to which any fat or oil other than milk fat was introduced. The law exempted certain proprietary foods de-signed for feeding infants and children.

In 1923, by an act of Congress, butter was defined.

The Import Milk Act of 1927 contained provisions to ensure that all milk and cream imported into the United States came from healthy cows, was handled in sanitary establishments, and was handled under sanitary conditions; it restricted the importation of milk by requiring that the shipper hold a valid permit from the secretary of Agriculture.

The McNary-Mapes Amendment of the Food and Drug Law of 1906 was enacted in 1930. It authorized the secretary of Agriculture to pro-mulgate for canned foods—except meats—definitions and standards of identity and reasonable standards of quality, condition, and/or fill of container, when in his best judgment they would promote honesty and fair dealing in the interest of the consumer. It required that substan-dard foods be conspicuously labeled substandard in quality. The first food standards issued in July, 1939, were for canned whole tomatoes, tomato puree, and tomato paste.

In 1934, an amendment to the Food and Drug Law of 1906 provided for the inspection of seafoods at the request of packers. This amend-ment remained in force when the Food, Drug, and Cosmetic Act of 1938 replaced the 1906 law. In 1958, this responsibility for the inspec-tion of seafoods was transferred to the Bureau of Commercial Fisheries of the United States Department of the Interior. In 1968, the shellfish sanitation program came under the aegis of the Food and Drug Ad-ministration. In October, 1970, the Bureau of Commercial Fisheries was abolished. Inspection of fishery products and the promulgation of grade standards passed to the National Marine Fisheries Service of the National Oceanic and Atmospheric Administration of the United States Department of Commerce. Both the inspection and grading services of seafoods are voluntary; when they have been utilized, this fact will be noted on the label of the container in which the seafoods are packed.

In 1938, the new Federal Food, Drug, and Cosmetic Act discussed subsequently in this chapter, was passed. Four amendments to this act are the Miller Pesticide Chemicals Act of 1954, the Food Additives Amendment of 1958, the Color Additive Amendment of 1960, and the amendment included in the National Heart and Lung Authorization Bill of 1976. All of these amendments are also discussed subsequently.

The Poultry Products Inspection Act passed in 1957 established mandatory inspection of poultry and poultry products in foreign and interstate commerce. The act became effective January 1, 1959. The Wholesome Poultry Products Act of 1968 requires state inspection "at least equal" to federal inspection of poultry and poultry products in intrastate commerce.

The Fair Packaging and Labeling Act became law on November 3, 1966. It did not repeal, invalidate, or supersede the Food, Drug, and Cosmetic Act of 1938. It superseded any and all state and local laws that were less stringent or had different information requirements for the labeling of the net contents of the package of any consumer commodity. It became effective on July 1, 1967. To administer the law, numerous regulations have been promulgated. Some that are of particular interest to consumers are discussed subsequently.

In December, 1970, the Egg Products Inspection Law was enacted. It requires that plants processing eggs for interstate, intrastate, and foreign commerce operate under mandatory, continuous inspection of the United States Department of Agriculture. The law further regulates the disposition of such "restricted eggs" as checks, dirties, and incubator rejects. The law became effective for eggs broken for egg products in July, 1971, and for packaged shell eggs in July, 1972.

Legislation is an ongoing process, and it can be expected that new laws and amendments to old laws will be forthcoming.

The enactment of each piece of legislation in the interest of the consumer came as a result of the dedicated efforts of one or more persons and was often helped by the occurrence of some fortuitous, though perhaps tragic, circumstance—the publication of Upton Sinclair's *The Jungle,* the sulfanilamide tragedy of the 1930's, and the thalidomide tragedy of the 1960's. Because these laws ran counter to the interests of the industries and because of the power of industry lobbies, they were often years in the making and were not infrequently weak and watered-down versions of the laws proposed by those who spoke out for the public interst and public health. Ralph Nader characterized the Fair Packaging and Labeling Act "the most deceptive package of all." Even so, the laws have often been better than the administration of them.

In October, 1970, by executive order, the General Services Administration was instructed to establish a Consumer Product Information Coordinating Center for the purpose of collecting and disseminating such product information gathered by governmental agencies through research, development, and procurement as would be useful to consumers.

In February, 1971, an Office of Consumer Affairs in the Executive Office of the President was established by executive order. The agency's functions are to receive consumer complaints, to channel complaints to the agency that has the power to take corrective action, to represent the consumer in an advisory capacity with federal agencies, to determine the nature of consumer problems, to participate in consumer education programs, to participate in programs for improving consumer goods and services, and to assist in the dissemination of consumer product information.

The Wiley Food and Drugs Act of 1906

During the post-Civil War period, chemists of the Department of Agriculture became interested in the problem of adulterated and misbranded fertilizers, feedstuffs, and foods. In 1869, Dr. Thomas Antisell pointed out the extensive adulteration of fertilizers and feedstuffs. In 1879, Dr. Peter Collier presented evidence of adulteration in butter, oleomargarine, alcoholic beverages, and coffee. In 1879, Congressman Hendrick B. Wright of Pennsylvania introduced the first bill to secure comprehensive protection from adulterated and misbranded foods. Nearly two hundred measures were introduced between that date and the passage of the Wiley Act in 1906.

In 1883, Dr. Harvey W. Wiley became Chief Chemist of the Chemical Division of the Department of Agriculture. Under his direction, methods of detecting adulteration and determining the nature of adulterations progressed. *Bulletin 13, Food and Food Adulterants* appeared in eight parts between 1887 and 1893. The various parts reported findings on dairy products; spices and condiments; lard and lard adulterations; baking powders; tea, coffee, and cocoa products; canned vegetables; and alcoholic beverages. This bulletin was a technical reference for chemists engaged in food-control work. To arouse public interest in the problem of food adulteration, another bulletin entitled *A Popular Treatise on the Extent and Character of Food Adulterations* was published in 1890. This bulletin pointed out that fraud extended to almost every article of food and that, although many of the adulterations were not injurious to health but were only economic cheats, some adulterations were poisonous. The need for protection beyond what state laws could provide was indicated. The ultimate passage of a federal law was a triumph for Dr. Wiley, who had dedicated himself to that purpose. It was an act "For preventing the manufacture, sale, or transportation of adulterated or misbranded or poisonous or deleterious foods, drugs, medicines, and liquors, and for regulating traffic therein, and for other purposes."

The Wiley Food and Drugs Act of 1906, which became effective on January 1, 1907, defined food as "all articles used for food, drink, confectionery or condiments by man, or other animals, whether simple, mixed, or compound." Briefly, the provisions of the law were as follows:

1. The import, export, and interstate traffic of adulterated or misbranded foods and drugs were prohibited.

2. The Secretaries of the Treasury, of Agriculture, and of Commerce and Labor were empowered to make rules and regulations for carrying out the law.

3. Food and drug examinations were to be carried out by the Bureau of Chemistry of the Department of Agriculture.

4. Violations of the law were punishable by fine, imprisonment, or both. Suspected food could be seized.

5. A food was deemed adulterated:
   a. if any substance had been mixed or packed with it to reduce or injuriously affect its quality or strength;
   b. if any other substance had been substituted wholly or in part for the article supposedly being sold;
   c. if any valuable constituent of the article had been wholly or in part abstracted;
   d. if it had been treated in such way as to conceal damage or inferiority;
   e. if any posionous or deleterious substance had been added;
   f. if it consisted in whole or in part of filthy, decomposed, or putrid vegetable or animal substance; if it contained any portion of an animal unfit for food, whether manufactured or not, or if it was the product of a diseased animal or one that had died other than by slaughter.

6. A food was deemed misbranded:
   a. if it was an imitation or was offered for sale under the distinctive name of another article;
   b. if it was labeled or branded so as to deveive or mislead the purchaser;
   c. if a correct statement of contents in terms of weight or measure did not appear on a packaged item;
   d. if the package or label bore any statement, design, or device regarding ingredients or added substances that was false or misleading. However, mixtures sold under *their own distinctive*

names were required to bear on the label only the name of the food and the place of manufacture. Imitations, blends, and compounds were required to be identified as such on the label.

Enforcement of the 1906 law was difficult. There were no definitions or standards for foods that had the force of law; foods sold under their own distinctive brand names were free from the law; fines for violation were so small that payment was not a serious penalty; it was necessary to prove intent to deceive; and false and misleading information could be placed on circulars distributed separately. The law was amended several times, and numerous rules and regulations for the enforcement of the law were in effect by 1930. However, before the last amendment to the law was enacted in 1934, a new law had been introduced in the Senate.

A separate law-enforcement agency was established in 1927 in the United States Department of Agriculture. It was first known as the Food, Drug, and Insecticide Administration. In 1930, it became the Food and Drug Administration but continued as a division of the United States Department of Agriculture until 1940, when it was transferred to the Federal Security Agency, which became the United States Department of Health, Education, and Welfare in 1953. In 1980, it became the Department of Health and Human Services.

Federal Food, Drug, and Cosmetic Act of 1938 as Amended

The new law was prepared by officials of the Food and Drug Administration and staff members of the Solicitor's Office of the United States Department of Agriculture. It was designed to correct the shortcomings of the old law. It has been called the Tugwell Bill because it was sponsored by the then secretary of Agriculture, Rexford G. Tugwell; it is better known as the Copeland Bill because it was introduced in the Senate by Senator Royal S. Copeland on June 6, 1933. The bill was reintroduced four times before a law acceptable to Congress was signed by President Roosevelt on June 25, 1938, to become effective on January 1, 1939.

The Federal Food, Drug, and Cosmetic Act is an act "To prohibit the movement in interstate commerce of adultered and misbranded food, drugs, devices, and cosmetics, and for other purposes." The provisions of the law and the subsequent amendments are summarized briefly and somewhat arbitrarily under these headings: general provisions; definitions; adulterated food; misbranded food; label and labeling regulations; standards; and amendments.

General Provisions.   First and most important, underlying the law was the determination to protect the public health; second, there was the determination to protect the consumer from the fraudulent practices of unscrupulous enterprisers. To accomplish these ends, the law deems a food adulterated if it has been prepared, packed, or held under unsanitary conditions whereby it may become contaminated with filth or rendered injurious to health, or if the container may render the product injurious to health. The law and its subsequent amendments prohibit the presence in food of poisonous, deleterious, and unsafe substances—except for some substances, such as pesticide chemicals on raw agricultural products, for which tolerances are established by regulations. Adulteration and misbranding are specifically and precisely defined. A distinction between label and labeling is made. The law imposes stringent label requirements. Penalties for violations are greater than under the old law, and the power of injunction is given to the administering body. To facilitate the administration of the law, the law provided for the promulgation of reasonable standards and definitions of identity, reasonable standards of quality, and/or reasonable standards of fill of container that would have the force of law.

Definitions.   For purposes of administering the law and its amendments, hundreds of terms have been clearly defined—especially in the standards and definitions of identity promulgated under the law. Some important definitions are included here: some are quoted exactly; a few are simplified.

1. *"Food* means (a) articles used for food or drink for man or other animals, (b) chewing gum, and (c) articles used for components of any such article."
2. *Label* means a display of written, printed, or graphic matter upon the immediate container of any article, and also on the outside container or wrapper (if there is one), or a display that is easily legible through the outside container or wrapper. The term *immediate container* does not include package liners.
3. *"Labeling* means all labels and other written, printed, or graphic matter (a) upon any article or any of its containers or wrappers, or (b) accompanying such article."
4. "The term *raw agricultural commodity* means any food in its raw or natural state, including all fruits that are washed, colored, or otherwise treated in their unpeeled natural form prior to marketing."
5. *"Pesticide chemical* means any substance which, alone, in chemical combination, or in formulation with one or more other substances, is an 'economic poison' within the meaning of the Federal Insecticide,

Fungicide, and Rodenticide Act as now in force or as hereafter amended, and which is used in the production, storage, or transportation of raw agricultural commodities."

6. "*Food additive* means any substance the intended use of which results or may reasonably be expected to result, directly or indirectly, in its becoming a component or otherwise affecting the characteristics of any food (including any substance intended for use in producing, manufacturing, packing, processing, preparing, treating, packaging, transporting, or holding food; and including any source of radiation intended for any such use), if such substance is not generally recognized, among experts qualified by scientific training and experience to evaluate its safety, as having been adequately shown through scientific procedures (or, in the case of a substance used in food prior to January 1, 1958, through either scientific procedures or experience based on common use in food) to be safe under the conditions of its intended use"; except that such terms do not include color additives, pesticide chemicals, and some substances granted prior sanction pursuant to earlier legislation.

7. "*Safe* has reference to the health of man and aminals."

8. "Safe" means that after a comprehensive review of all available evidence, including (1) probable consumption of the substance under consideration; (2) any compound formed in or on the food because of its use; and (3) the cumulative effect in the diet, the Food and Drug administration can conclude that no significant risk of harm can result from the substance when used as intended.

9. "*Color additive* means a material which:
   a. is a dye, pigment, or other substance made by a process of synthesis or similar artifice, or extracted, isolated, or otherwise derived, with or without intermediate or final change of identity, from a vegetable, animal, mineral, or other source, and
   b. when added or applied to a food, drug, or cosmetic, or to the human body or any part thereof, is capable (alone or through reaction with other substance) of imparting color thereto; except that such term does not include any material which the Secretary of the Department of Health, Education and Welfare, by regulation, determines is used (or intended to be used) solely for a purpose or purposes other than coloring."

10. "The term *color* includes black, white, and intermediate grays."

Adulterated Food.   A food is deemed adulterated when any of the following is true.

1. It bears or contains any poisonous or deleterious substance that may render it injurious to health; if the substance is not an added one,

the food is not considered adulterated if the quantity present is not considered injurious to health.

2. It bears or contains any added poisonous or added deleterious substance that is unsafe.

3. It bears or contains a food additive or color additive that is deemed unsafe or that is used contrary to regulations.

4. It is a raw agricultural product and contains the residue of a chemical in excess of established tolerance or an unauthorized pesticide.

5. It consists in whole or in part of any filthy, putrid, or decomposed substance or is otherwise unfit for food.

6. It has been prepared, packed, or held under unsanitary conditions whereby it may have become contaminated with filth or rendered injurious to health.

7. It is, in whole or in part, the product of a diseased animal or of an animal that died otherwise than by slaughter.

8. The container is composed, in whole or in part, of any poisonous or deleterious substance that might render the contents injurious to health.

9. It has been intentionally subjected to radiation, unless the use of radiation was in conformity with regulations.

10. If any valuable constituent has been omitted in whole or in part, or abstracted, or if any substance has been substituted wholly or in part therefor.

11. If damage or inferiority has been concealed in any way.

12. If any substance has been added or mixed or packed with it to increase its bulk or weight, or to reduce its quality or strength, or to make it appear better or of greater value than it is.

In March 1972, the Food and Drug Administration made public the levels for natural contaminants or unavoidable defects in food that present no health hazard. The levels—most of which were defined in the 1930's—recognized that it is not possible to grow, harvest, and process some crops totally free of natural defects. Some classes of food for which defect levels have been established include chocolate and cocoa; coffee beans; fish, shellfish, and seafood; flours; assorted canned fruits; spices; dried prunes and raisins; nuts; some canned and frozen vegetables; and tomato products. The natural defects recognized as unavoidable include molds, the eggs and larvae of some insects, certain insects and insect parts, rodent hairs, as well as other defects peculiar to and natural to certain foods.

Misbranded Food.   A food is considered *misbranded* when any of the following is true.

1. If labeling is false or misleading in any particular.

2. If it is offered for sale under the name of another food.

3. If it is an imitation of another food, unless its label bears—in type of uniform size and prominence—the word *imitation* and, immediately thereafter, the name of the food imitated, for example, "Imitation Vanilla."

4. If its container is so made, formed, or filled as to be misleading.

5. If it appears in package form without a label carrying (a) the name and place of business of the manufacturer, packer, or distributor and (b) an accurate statement of the quantity of the contents in terms of weight, measure, or numerical count.

6. If labels and labeling do not present required information prominently and in terms that can be read and understood easily.

7. If a food for which the definition and standard of identity has been prescribed does not conform to this definition and standard, and the label does not bear the name of the food as specified and the common names of the optional ingredients as required.

8. If it is a food for which standards of quality and fill of container have been established, and it falls below such standards, and the label does not bear a statement of substandard quality or fill.

9. When the label of a food fabricated from two or more ingredients does not name the ingredients in order of predominance by weight— except that spices, flavorings, and colorings other than those sold in a pure state may be designated as spices, flavorings, and colorings without each being named.

10. If it contains any artificial flavoring, artificial coloring, or chemical preservative, unless it is so labeled. Exemptions include cheese, butter, and ice cream; these are not required to bear a statement of the use of artificial color.

11. If it purports to be or is represented to be for special dietary uses, unless its label bears information concerning the vitamin, mineral, and other dietary properties necessary to inform purchasers fully of its value for such uses.

Label and Labeling Regulations. General regulations for the enforcement of prohibitions of misbranding are numerous. Some are of special interest to consumers. Information required on all labels includes the following:

1. The common or usual name of undefined products; the legal name of defined products, which consists of the common or usual name plus any additional statement required by the standard.

2. The accurate statement of quantity in terms of weight, measure,

or count. The statement of quantity of contents is exclusive of wrappers and other material packed with food. If a product is liquid, the statement must be in terms of the largest applicable unit of the U.S. gallon, quart, pint, or fluid ounce, that is, one quart, not two pints or thirty-two ounces. When volume exceeds one unit and is less than the next, contents must be expressed in terms of the larger unit and a fraction thereof, for example, one quart, one pint; but not three pints; nor forty-eight ounces. If a product is solid, semisolid, viscous, or a mixture of solid and edible liquid, contents must be expressed by weight in terms of the avoirdupois pound and ounce. Pickles are an exception to this. Contents must be expressed in the largest applicable unit; one pound, not sixteen ounces. When weight exceeds one unit and is less than two units, weight is expressed in terms of the larger unit, that is, one and a half pounds or one pound, eight ounces.

The Fair Packaging and Labeling Act requires that net contents on commodities containing less than four pounds or one gallon be expressed in avoirdupois or fluid ounces, respectively, in order to facilitate value comparisons, in addition to expression in the largest whole units of pounds, pints, or quarts.

3. The name and place of business of the manufacturer, packer, or distributor. If the food is not manufactured by the company whose name appears on the label, the name must be qualified by a statement that discloses the connection such company has as "Manufactured for ____and Packed by ____," Distributed by ____." "Packed by ____." For example, a can of soup may carry any of these statements: Made by Supreme Soup Company," "Made for Supreme Soup Company and packed by Goode Soupe Company," "Distributed by Blue Sky Wholesale Distributors." The products of food manufacturers are often sold under different labels but the label must define the situation; however, the manufacturer's name need not be revealed.

Label information required under certain conditions includes the following:

1. Label statement of all ingredients including water in order of predominance for all underlined food products. This order of stating ingredients does not apply to water used for processing where the consumer can distinguish between the packing medium and the product, such as water present in a can of peas. Legislation was proposed early in 1972 that would require the naming of all ingredients in defined foods. Spices, flavorings, and coloring may be designated on the label as "spices," "flavorings," and "coloring" without the designation of each by name.

2. Declaration of optional ingredients present in defined foods if the standard of identity requires such declaration.

3. Statement of any dietary properites claimed for foods promoted for special dietary uses.

4. Declaration of use of artificial color and flavorings, and of chemical preservatives.

5. Statement of substandard quality or fill of container for any product that fails to meet established standards.

6. Description of a food as *imitation* if that food is a substitute for or resembles another food but is nutritionally inferior other than in caloric or fat content.

PROMINENCE OF REQUIRED STATEMENTS. Food products are considered misbranded if required information is not prominently displayed in terms that can be easily read and understood. Regulations for administering this requirement of the law were established. Prominence and conspicuousness of labeling are deemed lacking when:

1. Required information is not present on the part or panel of the label that is presented or displayed under customary conditions of purchase.

2. Required information fails to appear on two or more parts or panels of the label, each of which has sufficient space therefor, and each of which is designed so as to be the part or panel displayed under ordinary conditions of purchase.

3. There is insufficient label space for the presentation of required information.

4. Required information is presented without sufficient background contrast, is obscured by designs or vignettes, is crowded with other printed or graphic matter, or is presented in a style or size of type that makes reading difficult.

Failure of food packages to conform to requirements for prominence of labeling was a factor that favored the enactment of the Fair Packaging and Labeling Act of 1966. Further discussion of this act will be found on pages 49–55.

Standards. A law that prohibits adulteration and misbranding of food requires standards and regulations that provide the frame of reference for the judgment of adulteration and misbranding. Dr. Wiley and his supporters were not unaware of this fact. They hoped to obtain, subsequent to the enactment of the 1906 law, authority for the Secretary of Agriculture to promulage standards of purity in accordance with which judgments of adulteration could be made. However, only two acts to this end were accomplished under the old law: an act to define butter was passed in 1923, and a law to establish the standard of quality, condition, and fill of container for canned goods was enacted in

1930. During those years, many definitions and standards for food products were developed and adopted for use by officials enforcing the Food and Drug Act. They did not have the force of law, however. The 1938 act empowered the secretary to promulgate regulations "fixing and establishing for any food, under its common or usual name so far as practicable, a reasonable definition and standard of identity, a reasonable standard of quality, and/or reasonable standards of fill of container," when in his judgment such action would promote honesty and fair dealing in the interest of consumers. The latter two standards apply only to canned foods; the first, to a number of foods including alimentary pastes, bakery products, cereal flours and related products, chocolate and cocoa products, cheeses and cheese products, dressings for foods, fruit preserves and jellies, some canned fruits and friut juices and fruit-juice concentrates, some canned shellfish, canned salmon and tuna, egg products, margarine, frozen desserts, canned vegetables and vegetable products, frozen peas, and some processed meat food and poultry food products. Most of these definitions were established by the Food and Drug Administration. Butter was defined by a special act of the Congress; meat and poultry food products, by the appropriate division of the United States Department of Agriculture. Frequent reference is made to the specifics of definitions and standards of identity for some foods in the chapters concerned with food buying.

STANDARDS OF IDENTITY, QUALITY, AND FILL OF CONTAINER. Definitions and standards of identity are detailed definitions and prescriptions for foods and food products that are composed of two or more foods. They establish the standards that permit a judgment of adulteration and misbranding. They also, by the preciseness of definition, establish minimum quality standards for those foods for which they have been promulgated, although they are not standards for grading for quality. For example, a standard that establishes the minimum milk-fat content of ice cream not only permits detection of adulteration but also establishes the minimum quality in as much as the quality of ice creams is to no small extent determined by fat content.

Definitions and standards are often years in the making, and they are frequently modified as technological developments, consumer wants, and industry interests deem change desirable. For example, some modifications of older definitions permit the canning of some fruits in slightly sweetened water, the addition of butter to some canned vegetables, and the use of flavor enhancers in food products. All interested parties—consumers, industry, and law enforcement officials—may participate in the formulation of the definition and standard of identity for a food, which may explain why they are often long in the making.

In general, definitions and standards of identity are lengthy and technical. Some specific requirements of some definitions for some commonly consumed foods are given here: and although it will be gross oversimplification, a summary of the kinds of requirements that definitions and standards establish follows:

1. In raisin bread and raisin rolls or raisin buns, not less than fifty parts by weight of seeded or seedless raisins are used per hundred parts by weight of flour.

2. Baking chocolate contains not less than 50 percent and not more than 58 percent by weight of cocoa fat.

3. Fruit jellies are made from mixtures composed of forty-five parts by weight of fruit juice ingredients and fifty-five parts by weight of saccharine ingredients.

4. Tomato catsup can be prepared from one or a combination of the following: the liquid obtained from tomatoes of red or reddish varieties, the liquid obtained from the residue left after preparing such tomatoes for canning, or the liquid obtained from the residue from partial extraction of tomatoes. The juices are concentrated then processed by heat to prevent spoilage; the use of chemical preservatives is prohibited. The label must state that juices prepared from residues were used in production and the addition of artificial color is prohibited.

5. Cream cheese can contain no less than 33 percent of milk fat and no more than 55 percent of moisture.

6. Margarine contains no less than 80 percent of fat.

7. Cream must contain no less than 18 percent of milk fat.

8. Canned tuna is the food prepared from the flesh of an enumerated list of fish species. Only loins and other striated muscles of the fish may be processed. Packing media include oils and water. Only the species *Thunnus germo* (albacore) can be described as white tuna; it must not be darker than a prescribed Munsell value. Grated tuna consists of a mixture of pieces of uniform size that pass through a half-inch mesh screen, but the particles are discrete and do not form a paste.

9. If the milk used in making cheddar cheese is not pasteurized, the cheese made from it must be cured at a temperature of not less than 35° F for not less than sixty days.

10. Pasteurized process cheese spread must be spreadable at 70° F; during pasteurization, it must have been heated for not less than thirty seconds at a temperature of not less than 150° F.

11. Mayonnaise can contain not less than 65 percent by weight of vegetable oil.

12. Peanut butter can contain no more than 10 percent by weight of seasoning and stabilizing ingredients; the fat content of the finished food cannot exceed 55 percent. For products which do not meet the standard of identity for peanut butter, the term *peanut spread* may be used followed by the percentage of peanuts in the product. However,

a product that is nutritionally inferior to peanut butter must be labeled as an imitation of peanut butter.

From the examples presented, a summary statement can be made of the requirements that the definitions and standards of identity establish. Definitions and standards of identity

1. Establish the minimum content—and sometimes the maximum content—of one or more components of a food.
2. Establish the permissible ingredient content of a food.
3. Establish the minimum quantity of one or more ingredients in a food.
4. Name the ingredients that may be optionally included in the preparation of a food.
5. Require label statement of the use of some permissible and some optional ingredients.
6. Identify the species of plant or animal that may be used.
7. Define the meaning of terms descriptive of color and form, that is, *white, grated, cuts,* and many others.
8. Describe the product that can be processed as in canning.
9. Define packing media for many foods, such as water, syrups, juices, or oils.
10. Describe processing requirements, for example, "sealed in a container and so processed by heat as to prevent spoilage."
11. Prescribe essentials in production, such as that bread must be yeast leavened and baked.
12. Require a label statement of the use of some food additives with explanation for use.

Foods for which the definitions and standards of identity have been promulgated are not required to bear label statements of their ingredient content in order of predominance; however, a label statement of the inclusion of some permissible and some optional ingredients may be required. There are also exceptions; for example, the requirements for margarine are such that a full listing of ingredients is mandatory. A survey of some defined foods available in the supermarket discloses that some do carry label statements of their ingredient content. There exists strong opposition to the exemptions these foods enjoy. This opposition is in the interest of public health: some persons may be allergic to substances not listed; others are advised against consumption of such substances as monosodium glutamate because of health reasons. Opposition also occurs because industry has used food standardization as a means of avoiding the listing of substances that might affect consumption, such as caffeine in cola drinks. A food does not conform to the definition and standard of identity if it contains an ingredient for which there is no provision in the definition and standard (except for co-called incidental additives); if it fails to contain a required ingredient; or if the quantity of any ingredient or component fails to conform to the prescribed limitations.

The two examples of definitions and standards of identity presented are reprinted from Volume 2 of Title 21, Code of Federal Regulations. All regulations are printed originally in the *Federal Register*. The first example is for nonfat dry skim milk, a single food and is the definition as of December, 1974 (7).

> Nonfat dry milk is the product obtained by removal of water only from pasteurized skim milk. It contains not more than 5 percent by weight of moisture, and not more than 1½ percent by weight of milkfat unless otherwise indicated.

The second example is for canned fruit cocktail as revised March, 1974, and effective January, 1976. It illustrates well the specificity of definitions and standards of identity. It has implicit in it an explanation for product differences in the definitions of minimum and maximum contents of the fruit ingredients (7).

§27.40 Canned fruit cocktail; identity; label statement of optional ingredients.

(a) *Ingredients.* Canned fruit cocktail, canned cocktail fruits, canned fruits for cocktail, is the food prepared from the mixture of fresh, frozen, or previously canned fruit ingredients of mature fruits in the forms and proportions as provided in paragraph (b) of this section, and one of the optional packing media specified in paragraph (c) of this section. Such food may also contain one, or any combination of two or more, of the following safe and suitable optional ingredients:

(1) Natural and artificial flavors.

(2) Spice.

(3) Vinegar, lemon juice, or organic acids.

(4) Ascorbic acid in an amount no greater than necessary to preserve color. Such food is sealed in a container and before or after sealing is so processed by heat as to prevent spoilage.

(b) *Varietal types and styles.* The fruit ingredients referred to in paragraph (a) of this section, the forms of each, and the percent by weight of each in the mixture of drained fruit from the finished canned fruit cocktail are as follows:

(1) *Peaches.* Any firm yellow variety of the species *Prunus persica* L., excluding nectarine varieties, which are pitted, peeled, and diced, not less than 30 percent and not more than 50 percent.

(2) *Pears.* Any variety, of the species *Pyrus communis* L., or *Pyrus sinensis* L., which are peeled, cored, and diced, not less than 25 percent and not more than 45 percent.

(3) *Pineapples.* Any variety, of the species *Ananas comosus* L., which are

peeled, cored, and cut into sectors or into dice, not less than 6 percent and not more than 16 percent.

(4) *Grapes.* Any seedless variety, of the species *Vitis vinifera* L., or *Vitis labrusca* L., not less than 6 percent and not more than 20 percent.

(5) *Cherries.* Approximate halves or whole pitted cherries of the species *Prunus cerasus* L., not less than 2 percent and not more than 6 percent, of the following types:

(i) Cherries of any light, sweet variety;

(ii) Cherries artificially colored red; or

(iii) Cherries artificially colored red and flavored, natural or artificial. *Provided that* each 127.5 grams (4½ ounces avoirdupois) of the finished canned fruit cocktail and each fraction thereof greater than 56.7 grams (2 ounces avoirdupois) contain not less than 2 sectors or 3 dice of pineapple and not less than 1 approximate half of the optional cherry ingredient.

(c) *Packing media.* (1) The optional packing media referred to in paragraph (a) of this section, are:

(i) Water.

(ii) Fruit juice(s) and water.

(iii) Fruit juice(s).

Such packing media may be used as such or any one or any combination of two or more safe and suitable nutritive carbohydrate sweetener(s) may be added.

(2) When a sweetener is added as a part of any such liquid packing medium, the density range of the resulting packing medium expressed as percent by weight of sucrose (degrees Brix) as determined by the procedure prescribed shall be designated by the appropriate name for the respective density ranges, namely:

(i) When the density of the solution is 10 percent or more, but less than 14 percent, the medium shall be designated as "slightly sweetened water"; or "extra light sirup"; "slightly sweetened fruit juice(s) and water"; or "slightly sweetened fruit juice(s)", as the case may be.

(ii) When the density of the solution is 14 percent or more but less than 18 percent, the medium shall be designated as "light sirup"; "lightly sweetened fruit juice(s) and water"; or "lightly sweetened fruit juice(s)", as the case may be.

(iii) When the density of the solution is 18 percent or more but less than 22 percent, the medium shall be designated as "heavy sirup"; "heavily sweetened fruit juice(s) and water"; or "heavily sweetened fruit juice(s)", as the case may be.

(iv) When the density of the solution is 22 percent or more but not more than 35 percent, the medium shall be designated as "extra heavy sirup"; "extra heavily sweetened fruit juice(s) and water"; or "extra heavily sweetened fruit juice(s)", as the case may be.

STANDARD OF REASONABLE QUALITY. Standards of quality have been prescribed for a limited number of canned fruits and vegetables and two frozen products. The standards preclude the marketing of tough green beans, hard peas, and stringy peaches. Although the standards do not define foods as Fancy, Choice, or Good, they do declare in terms of flavor, color, size, and condition the quality level below which these products cannot be sold unless they are labeled as below standard in quality. For example, if tomatoes in a pack are poor in color, they must be labeled, "Below Standard in Quality." The type of inferiority is usually mentioned, for example, "Below Standard in Quality—Poor Color." Regulations require that the statement of substandard quality be placed on the can where it can be easily seen, that it be printed in two lines, and that it be enclosed within lines forming a rectangle the size of which is scaled to can size.

Standards of quality have been established for these canned fruits: apricots, cherries, fruit cocktail, grapefruit, peaches, pears, pineapple and pineapple juice, and plums; for these canned vegetables: green and wax beans, corn, peas, and tomatoes; and frozen peas and cherry pies. These standards of quality become the U.S. Standard or U.S. Grade C for those foods for which they have been established.

The quality standards for canned fruit cocktail are reprinted (2).

(1) Not more than 20 percent by weight of the units in the container of peach or pear, or of pineapple if the units thereof are diced, are more than ¾ inch in greatest edge dimension, or pass through the meshes of a sieve designated as ⁵/₁₆ inch in Table I of "Standard Specifications for Sieves" published March 1, 1940, in L. C. 584 of the National Bureau of Standards, U.S. Department of Commerce. If the units of pineapple are in the form of sectors, not more than 20 percent of such sectors in the container fail to conform to the following dimensions: The length of the outside arc is not more than ¾ inch but is more than ⅜ inch; the thickness is not more than ½ inch but is more than ⁵/₁₆ inch; the length (measured along the radius from the inside arc to the outside arc) is not more than 1¼ inches but is more than ¾ inch.

(2) Not more than 10 percent of the grapes in a container containing ten grapes or more, and not more than one grape in a container containing less then ten grapes, is cracked to the extent of being severed into two parts or is crushed to the extent that their normal shape is destroyed.

(3) Not more than 10 percent of the grapes in a container containing ten grapes or more, and not more than one grape in a container containing less than ten grapes, has the cap stem attached.

(4) There is present in the finished canned fruit cocktail not more than one square inch of pear peel per each one pound of drained weight of units of pear plus the weight of a proportion of the packing medium which is the same proportion as the drained weight of the units of pear bears to the drained weight of the entire contents of the can. . . .

(5) There is present in the finished canned fruit cocktail not more than one square inch of peach peel per each one pound of drained weight of units of peach plus the weight of a proportion of the packing medium which is the same proportion as the drained weight of units of peach bears to the drained weight of the entire contents of the can. . . .

(6) Not more than 15 percent of the units of cherry ingredient; and not more than 20 percent of the units of peach, pear, or grape, in the container is blemished with scab, hail injury, scar tissue or other abnormality.

(7) If the cherry ingredient is artificially colored, the color of not more than 15 percent of the units thereof in a container containing more than six units, and of not more than one unit in a container containing six or less, is other than evenly distributed in the unit or other than uniform with the color of the other units of the cherry ingredient.

STANDARDS OF FILL OF CONTAINER.   Standards of fill of container have been established for some canned foods. Standard of fill of container is defined as the maximum quantity that can be sealed and processed in a can without crushing or breaking any ingredient in the can, or as a percentage of the total capacity of the container as determined under specified conditions. For example, the standard of fill of container for canned tomatoes is a fill not less than 90 percent of the total capacity of the container. Cans filled to a lesser extent must be conspicuously labeled, "Below Standard in Fill," in type of specified kind and size, and the statement must be enclosed within lines forming a bold border around it. Standards of fill have been established for a limited list of canned products, which are: corn, mushrooms, peas, dry peas, tomatoes, applesauce, apricots, cherries, fruit cocktail, grapefruit, peaches, pears, crushed pineapple, pineapple juice, and plums. A provision of the Fair Packaging and Labeling Act prohibits the nonfunctional slack fill of packages of consumer commodities of all kinds.

Amendments to the Food, Drug, and Cosmetic Act.   When the second Food, Drug and Cosmetic Act was passed in 1938, it seemed adequate for the relatively simple foods available. But as more complex foods were produced and sophisticated packaging was developed, shortcomings in the Act were apparent. There have been three amendments to the Food, Drug, and Cosmetic Act of 1938: the Pesticide Chemicals Act of 1954, the Food Additives Amendment of 1958, and the Color Additive Amendments of 1960. When the 1938 law was written, it was believed that its provisions relating to the presence of poisonous and deleterious substances in food were sufficient. Although the law deemed a food adulterated if it contained any poisonous or deleterious substance that might render it injurious to health, it permitted this exception: it exempted from declaration as adulterated those foods containing added poisonous or deleterious substances when their use was unavoidable in good manufacturing practice so long as the quantities present did not exceed tolerance levels established by the Secretary of Agriculture. Subsequent developments in agricultural practices and food technology pointed to three inadequacies in the law. First, the administering body, the Food and Drug Administration, was forced to prove the poisonous and deleterious nature of substances added to food. Second, gathering proof of the poisonous and deleterious nature of substances required extensive research that was costly in time and money. The Food and Drug Administration had neither the funds, the facilities, nor the personnel to carry out the research necessitated by the ever-increasing use of pesticides in agriculture and additives by the food industries. Third, public health was endangered by the continued use of additives suspected of being poisonous or deleterious until such time as convincing proof could stay the use of a substance by condemning food as adulterated. All three amendments to the law place the burden of proof of safety on the manufacturers of pesticides and additives. The Food and Drug Administration issues regulations governing the use of these added substances after proof of safety has been submitted. The regulations are specific in regard to intended uses and to the quantities that may be employed for the respective uses permitted.

THE PESTICIDE CHEMICALS ACT OF 1954.   Specifically, the Pesticide Chemicals Act prohibits the marketing in interstate commerce of any raw agricultural product if it bears the residue of a pesticide chemical unless (1) the pesticide chemical is safe, (2) the residue is within the tolerance established as safe, or (3) the pesticide has been officially exempted from tolerance limitations. Pesticide use has received much attention as man has become concerned over his pollution of his environment. The United States Department of Agriculture in 1970 canceled many uses of a number of pesticides on food and feed crops. Research is in the direction of the development and the recommended use of biological, environmental, and other nonchemical means of control.

THE FOOD ADDITIVES AMENDMENT OF 1958.   The Food Additives Amendment of 1958 decrees that no new additive can be used in or on food (1) until proof of safety for intended use has been submitted to the Food and Drug Administration; (2) until the Food and Drug Administration has issued a regulation prescribing uses of the additive; and (3) unless it is used in conformity with that regulation. No additive is deemed safe if it is found to be carcinogenic for either man or animal. No additive can be used to promote deception of the consumer. The law became effective immediately for substances not in use as of January 1, 1958. It exempted "any substance used in accordance with a sanction or approval granted prior to the enactment" of the amendment. It further exempted substances in use prior to January 1, 1958, when these were generally recognized as safe (GRAS).

A substance would be considered GRAS if that substance was generally recognized by experts as having been "adequately shown" to be safe for its intended use in food. This "adequate" showing of safety could be based either on scientific procedures or if the substance was used in food before January 1, 1958, on "experience based on common use in food." The amendment covers both intentional and incidental additives, such as those that can arise from processing and packaging materials.

During the period, 1958–1962, lists of GRAS substances were published from time to time in the *Federal Register*. Few substances were added to the lists from 1962 to 1970. In 1968, cyclamates were implicated as the cause of bladder tumors in animals and in the following year questions arose about the safety of monosodium glutamate (MSG). In October, 1969, President Nixon in his Consumer Message to Congress directed the Secretary of the formerly titled Department of Health, Education, and Welfare to initiate a full review of GRAS substances. Accordingly, the Food and Drug Administration contracted with the Food Protection Committee of the National Academy of Sciences (NAS) to survey the food industry and determine: (1) the aggregate national production of all GRAS ingredients; (2) the amount of each used in any food; and (3) the expected consumption of these ingredients by consumers. This survey was completed for GRAS ingredients and regulated flavor ingredients in 1972. Tentative evaluations are published in the Federal Register for comment prior to final recommendations by the Food and Drug Administration.

Reevaluations of the safety of additives in use since 1958 have been undertaken from time to time because of changes in scientific methods and standards for establishing safety. In February, 1977, the Food and Drug Administration announced that a reevaluation of all flavors, colors, and regulated direct food additives—some 2100 compounds—and of about 10,000 indirect additives would be forthcoming.

Following a ten year study by an expert advisory group, the Food and Drug Administration announced in late 1980 the completion of the first scientific evaluation of the safety of 415 food ingredients on the GRAS list. The initial phase of the study covered the substances which had been "generally recognized as safe" for their intended use before enactment of the Food Additives Amendment in 1958. Of the 415 substances reviewed, 305 were given Class One status. This means the additives are considered safe for use at current levels and future anticipated levels. Substances in this category include vegetable oils, casein, tartrates, aluminum compounds, benzoates, and protein hydrolysates. For other substances (Classes Two–Four) more research or safer conditions of use were recommended. Some of these substances included zinc, alginates, iron, BHT, BHA, salt, sugar, and modified starches.

THE COLOR ADDITIVE AMENDMENT OF 1960.   This act established the same rules and regulations for coloring substances as the 1958 amendment did for food additives, even to the inclusion of the Delaney anti-cancer clause. A food is deemed adulterated if it does not conform to the stipulations of these amendments. According to the act, a color additive is deemed unsafe unless (1) there is in effect a regulation that prescribes conditions for its use; (2) it is used in conformity with the regulation; (3) it comes from a batch certified as safe; (4) the color additive and its use are exempted. Until these amendments were enacted only coal-tar colors had to be certified as "harmless and suitable for use." Under the present law, all colors must be safe as used and limits can be set on the amounts of color used. The food colorings used by the homemaker are safe, but she must use them judiciously. Industry is prohibited from adding color to a food to make it appear better than it is. It is legal, however, to add color to some varieties of oranges; but they must be stamped "Color Added" or with another similar phrase to inform the consumer. The addition of artificial color to a food must be stated on the label unless the food is exempted.

The Food and Drug Administration banned the use of violet No. 1 dye in April, 1973. It had been in use for twenty-two years and was the dye used by the United States Department of Agriculture for marking meat for wholesomeness and quality. In February, 1976, the use of the dye, Red No. 2, was banned after fifteen years in use. Although there is no conclusive evidence of hazard to health with the use of either color additive, neither is there unequivocal assurance of their safety. In September, 1976, both Red No. 4 and Carbon Black were delisted. Red No. 4 was used only for coloring Maraschino cherries. The safety of several dyes including Yellow No. 5 has been questioned. Yellow No. 5, widely used to color baked goods, dessert mixes, candies, ice creams, and other foods, causes allergic reactions in some individuals. As of July 1, 1981, any food containing Yellow No. 5 must have its presence indicated on the label.

More recent concerns are the need for sodium labeling and the indiscriminate addition of nutrients to foods. Both a Gallup Poll (5) and an FDA survey (1) found that consumers are concerned about overconsumption of sodium. In March 1981, FDA announced a five-point program which featured a cooperative voluntary sodium labeling effort with the food industry. The program includes:

1. The voluntary reduction of salt in processed foods.
2. The development of new regulations to deal with sodium labeling.
3. Expanded consumer education programs.
4. Continued monitoring of sodium consumption.
5. Consideration of legislature proposals to broaden sodium labeling.

Currently, labeling is voluntary but an increased number of labels are showing sodium content. It is expected that at least 50 percent of the processed foods sold in grocery stores will be labeled for sodium by the mid 1980's. (8)

The Food and Drug Administration has issued a policy regarding the addition of nutrients to foods. It discourages indiscriminate addition of nutrients to foods and does not consider it appropriate or reasonable to fortify fresh produce, meat, poultry, or fish products, or snack foods such as candies and carbonated beverages. The policy states that a nutrient may be added to a food (a) to correct a dietary insufficiency; (b) to restore a nutrient to a level representative of the food prior to storage, handling, and processing; (c) to balance the vitamin, mineral, and protein content in proportion to the total caloric content of the food; (d) to avoid nutritional inferiority by adding the nutrient to a food that replaces a traditional food; and (e) to comply with other regulations. The policy also suggests appropriate labeling claims.

Food safety legislation continues to receive attention from Congress and the presidential staff. Major food safety amendments were introduced by Congress in 1981 and again in 1982. These amendments attempt to lessen the zero tolerance level of the Delaney Clause. They define "safe" (as applied to food additives, color additives, and new animal drugs) as a reasonable certainty that the risks of a substance under the intended conditions of use are insignificant. When determining if a substance is safe, the FDA examines all relevant factors and is advised by an independent food safety committee composed of scientists.

The Fair Packaging and Labeling Act

The Fair Packaging and Labeling Act is also known as the Hart Act. The act is of major importance to consumers. It was passed by the House of Representatives in October, 1966; was signed by President Johnson in November, 1966; and became effective on July 1, 1967. No provisions of the law were self-executing; therefore, they could only be carried out by regulations issued in accordance with procedures established in the Food, Drug, and Cosmetic Act of 1938—a time-consuming process. A proposed regulation is published in the Federal Register; a period of time is established for interested parties to comment; opportunity is provided for adversely affected persons to file formal objections and to request administrative hearings on the issues in dispute. Finally, after a regulation has been adopted, a period of time is allowed for compliance.

The Food and Drug Administration published some proposed regulations for the administration of the law in March, 1967. Revised regulations were published in September, 1967, with the announcement that they would take effect without public hearing. These regulations became effective for all new packages, new label designs, and labels being reordered as of January 1, 1968. This date was extended one year to permit old labels to be used up. Since that time, many regulations have been proposed, revised, and become effective; some remain in process.

The Fair Packaging and Labeling Act is short; essentially the law (1) demands specific rules and regulations on the labeling of consumer commodities; (2) asks for the control of nonfunctional slack fill of packages; (3) provides for the control of cents-off and price promotions; and (4) provides for a way of reducing the number of packages in which consumer commodities are packaged (6).

To facilitate compliance with regulations adopted for the packaging and labeling of food, the Food and Drug Administration incorporated requirements under the Food, Drug, and Cosmetic Act and the Fair Packaging and Labeling Act into one set of regulations. These regulations added to the definitions and interpretations of terms appearing in the Food, Drug, and Cosmetic Act.

Regulations.   As previously stated, many regulations have been proposed, amended, and either become effective or failed in acceptance. The following are some edited versions of some regulations that are of interest and/or importance to meal managers.

1. The principal display panel of a food in package form shall bear a statement of the identity of the commodity. It must be identified in the common or usual name of the food. If there is no common name, appropriately descriptive terms or a commonly understood fanciful name may be used. If a food is marketed in various optional forms—such as whole, diced, sliced, and so on—the particular form shall be a prominent written part of the statement of identity, unless depicted by vignette or unless visible through the container, for example, "Small Whole Beets."

2. An imitation of another food must be prominently labeled "imitation" and must bear, immediately thereafter, the name of the food imitated. An *imitation food* is one that is a substitute for or resembles another food but is nutritionally inferior to that food. Nutritional inferiority means the reduction of an essential nutrient in measurable amount—10 percent or more of the U.S. RDA for protein, or any vitamin or mineral—per average serving; but does not include a reduction in either caloric or fat content provided the food is labeled in conformity with the regulations for the nutritional labeling of food. (See 16.)

3. The label of a packaged food must bear the name and place of business of the manufacturer, packer, or distributor. If the name is not that of the manufacturer, a statement must clarify the role of the company named on the label.

4. The principal display panel of a packaged food must bear an accurate statement of the net quantity of contents in terms of weight, measure, numerical count, or a combination of numerical count and weight or measure. This statement must appear without qualifying terms that may exaggerate, such as "big pound" or "jumbo quart." The statement, generally, will be located within the bottom 30 percent of the area of the principal display panel as a distinct item separated from any other label information and in lines that are usually parallel to the base of the package. The statement must appear in easily legible, bold-face type, and in type size established in relation to the area of the principal display panel of the package. Statements of weight must be in terms of avoirdupois pound and ounce. Statements of fluid measure must be in terms of the U.S. gallon of 231 cubic inches and in quart, pint, and fluid ounce divisions thereof. An additional, accurate statement of the net quantity in terms of the metric system of weight and measure may appear on the principal display or other panel.

5. A dual declaration of net contents is required for packages containing less than four pounds or less than one gallon. The declaration must be expressed both in ounces with identification by weight or liquid measure and, if applicable (one pint or one pound or more), followed in parentheses by a declaration in pounds for weight units, with any remainder expressed in terms of ounces or common or decimal fractions of the pound; for example, "Net Wt. 24 oz (1½ lb. or 1 lb. 8 oz. or 1.5 lb.)"; and for liquid measures, in the largest whole units—quarts, quarts and pints, or pints as appropriate—with the remainder expressed in terms of fluid ounces or common or decimal fractions of the pint or quart, for example, "Net contents 24 fluid ounces (1½ pints, 1.5 pints, or 1 pint 8 fl. oz.)."

6. On packages containing four pounds or one gallon or more, the declaration must be expressed in pounds for weight units with the remainder expressed in ounces or common or decimal fractions of the pound. In the case of fluid measure, contents must be expressed in the largest whole unit with the remainder expressed in terms of the next smaller unit, for example, "Net contents 2.5 gal. or 2½ gal. or 2 gal. 2 qt."

7. The net weight of a random package, as of meat or of fresh vegetables, is expressed in terms of the pound and decimal fractions thereof carried out to no more than two places.

8. Only the following abbreviations may be utilized in the expression of quantities: weight, wt; ounces, oz; pound, lb; gallon, gal; quart, qt; pint, pt; and fluid, fl. Use of the period and of plurals is optional.

9. The statement of the quantity of the contents of a multiunit retail package must include the number of units, the quantity per unit, and in parentheses the total quantity, that is, "6 6-oz. cans (36 fl. oz.)."

10. If the label of a food package represents the contents in terms of the number of servings, it must describe the size of the serving in terms of weight, numerical count, measure, or in other commonly understood terms of measurement, such as tablespoonfuls or cupfuls. The regulations distinguish between serving and portion this way. *Serving* means that reasonable quantity of food that is practical of consumption as part of a meal. *Portion* means the amount of a food customarily used only as an ingredient in the preparation of a meal component, that is, one cup of flour.

11. All information required to appear on the label of any package must appear either on the principal display panel or the information panel unless otherwise specified. All information must be conspicuous and in no case may the type size be less than $1/16$ inch in height; there are some exceptions to this ruling.

12. All required information must be given in the English language except in those instances when items are prepared for distribution in places where the native language is other than English.

13. The ingredients of a packaged food must be listed by their common names in order of decreasing predominance in adequate type size without crowding. The entire ingredient listing must appear on a single panel of the label. In cases where a single expensive ingredient is promoted as significant to the value of the food, declaration of the percentage of the expensive ingredient is required: that is, a blend of "cottonseed oil and olive oil" in which there was 80 percent of cottonseed oil would bear a statement of the 20 percent of olive oil. This regulation does not apply to standardized and defined products.

14. A statement of the use of artificial coloring, artificial flavoring, or chemical preservative must be present on the food or its container or its wrapper in such a way that the statement is likely to be read by the ordinary person under customary conditions of the purchase and use of the food. Exempted from the required statement of the use of artificial color are butter, ice cream, and cheddar cheese.

15. A food to which a chemical preservative(s) is(are) added shall bear a label declaration stating both the common or usual name of the ingredient(s) and a separate description of function, for example, "preservative," "to retard spoilage," "a mold inhibitor," "to help protect flavor," or "to promote color retention."

16. In July, 1976, regulations became effective which required that nutrition information appear on enriched and fortified foods, as well as on all other foods for which nutritional claims are made. The nutrition information panel appears on food labels to the right of the principal display panel.

The following information is required by these regulations:

1. The serving size and the number of servings per can, carton, or other container of a food.

2. The number of calories per serving.

3. The number of grams of carbohydrate, fat, and protein per serving.

4. The percentages of the U.S. RDA of protein, of five vitamins (vitamin A, vitamin C, thiamin, riboflavin, and niacin), and two minerals (calcium and iron) derived per serving.

Information on the following is optional unless a vitamin or mineral is added to a food or claims are made in the label or advertising about the cholesterol, fatty acid, or sodium content of a food.

1. Percentages of the U.S. RDA for twelve additional vitamins and minerals (vitamin D, vitamin E, folic acid, vitamin B_6, vitamin B_{12}, biotin, and pantothenic acid; also copper, iodine, magnesium, phosphorus, and zinc).

2. The amount of cholesterol and saturated and polyunsaturated fatty acids per serving.

3. The amount of sodium per serving.

The U.S. RDA are nutritional standards that were derived from the Recommended Daily Allowances of the Food and Nutrition Board of the National Research Council. Four sets of standards were established: for infants, for children under four, for pregnant and lactating women, and for children over four and adults. The standards used in the nutritional labeling of foods, with some exceptions, are those for children over four and adults. They are adjudged adequate for nearly all normal, healthy persons and are generous for most persons. A more complete discussion of the U.S. RDA is provided in Chapter 5.

In 1978 the Food and Drug Administration released the results of a study which detailed the extent to which nutrition labels were included on food packages. Of the processed foods carrying nutrition labels, 40 percent were required by FDA to do so and 60 percent carried such information voluntarily. The term product categories that have the largest number of products with nutrition labeling are: cereals, with 100 percent of the total supermarket sales carrying nutrition labeling; margarine, 100 percent; powdered soft drinks, 100 percent; flour, 99.5 percent; dry pasta, 92.3 percent; canned and powdered milk, 89.6 percent; frozen toppings, 81.6 percent; canned seafood, 80.6 percent; baby foods, 74.7 percent; and frozen juices and drinks, 71.8 percent.

The Food and Drug Administration and the Federal Trade Commission proposed regulations to govern the use of cents-off and reduced price promotions in 1970. The finalized regulations, which became effective in January, 1972, are in essence as follows:

1. A cents-off or other reduced-price promotion of a consumer commodity is prohibited unless that commodity has been sold thirty days prior to the offer within the geographic trade area at an ordinary and customary price—a price considered the regular price.

2. The exact amount of the price reduction must be clearly and conspicuously set forth. After June 15, 1972, packages must be marked, "Price Marked Is ____ Cents Off the Regular Price."

3. The frequency of promotions is limited to three per year with a lapse of at least thirty days between each promotion. The maximum total period of time for any promotion is limited to six months per year.

4. Reduced-price promotions of newly introduced consumer commodities and commodities newly introduced into a geographic area are not subject to the foregoing limitations but are subject to these "introductory offer" limitations. Labeling must identify the offering as introductory; it must suggest the postintroduction price; and the offer cannot exceed six months in duration.

5. The package of a food or commodity promoted as the "economy size," "thrifty pack," "bargain size," or by other qualifying term that implies reduced price is required to have an established ordinary and customary price for the regular- and other-size containers. The price per unit of weight, measure, or count of the economy size must be at least 5 percent less than the regular price per unit of weight, measure, or count of the least expensive retail size of the same consumer commodity. Only one package of a line can be labeled the "economy" package.

6. Such offers as "two-for-one," "one-cent sale," and other half-price promotions must be *bona fide,* that is, based on the regular price of thirty days prior to the promotion. The duration of and number of such promotions permitted per year are limited.

The Food and Drug Administration in conjunction with the U.S. Department of Agriculture and the Federal Trade Commission published in late 1979 a thirty-page report presenting the FDA's tentative position on food labeling and nutrition issues. The report was the result of an extensive two-year study of food labeling. The food labeling issues were divided into four categories.

Only a few of the proposed changes have been implemented as of mid-1982. The proposals, which were a result of a two-year study of food labeling, represent relatively minor refinements of the food labeling requirements that are already in existence. It is expected that this refinement will be a continuing process as more information is gained on nutritional and safety aspects of foods as well as on the most effective means of conveying information about food and nutrition to consumers.

Miscellanea

The following additional regulations and/or statements of policy are of interest.

1. Radiation sources can be used for the purpose of food inspection, inspection of packaged food, and to control food processing when used under defined conditions. No food can receive an absorbed dose of more than 1,000 rads. Gamma radiation and low-dose electron-beam radiation can be used under defined conditions for the defestation of wheat and flour made from nonirradiated wheat and to inhibit sprout development in potatoes. Ultraviolet irradiation can be used under defined conditions for microorganism control, as in the rapid ripening of beef, and for the sterilization of water used in food production.

2. Salt for table use is labeled as follows: "This salt supplies iodide, a necessary nutrient" when it has been enriched with iodine or "This salt does not supply iodide, a necessary nutrient" when unenriched with iodine.

3. A food is considered adulterated when it contains the residue of an antibiotic. Antibiotics are utilized in the feeding of animals for the purpose of controlling disease and to promote growth and development. The use of antibiotics is regulated, and there is controversy as to the safety of their use.

4. Frozen vegetables must bear a label statement of the presence of salt, whether the salt has been added to the vegetables directly or indirectly, as in processing during the freezing process.

5. The presence of monosodium glutamate (MSG) in processed foods is stated in the declaration of ingredients.

6. Effective January 1, 1978, the following restructured foods must be labeled as follows: "onion rings made from diced onions," "fish sticks/portions made from minced fish," "fried clams made from minced clams," "potato chips made from dried potatoes," and all shrimp products made from comminuted shrimp identified as "made from minced shrimp." All of these qualifying statements must be printed in type size not less than one-half that used for the name of the product.

7. Beginning January 1, 1978, the labels of all processed foods must reveal the kinds of fats and/or oils present by source; further the labels will have to describe them as "saturated" (hardened) or "partially saturated."

8. To be labeled "low-calorie," a food must contain no more than 40 kilocalories per serving and no more than 0.4 kilocalories per gram; to be labeled "reduced-calorie," a food must be at least one-third lower in calories than a similar food in which the calories have not been reduced. The regulations apply to all foods used for reducing weight or caloric intake and in the diet of diabetics.

DEPARTMENTS OF THE FEDERAL GOVERNMENT CONCERNED WITH FOOD STANDARDS AND FOOD LAWS AND THE ADMINISTRATION THEREOF

The Department of Health and Human Services

The Department of Health and Human Services was formerly the Department of Health, Education and Welfare. The Food and Drug Administration is a subunit of the Public Health Service, which is a unit of the Department of Health and Human Services.

The Food and Drug Administration. In 1940, the Food and Drug Administration was removed from the Department of Agriculture to the Federal Security Agency. In 1953, that agency became the Department of Health, Education, and Welfare and in 1980 it became the Department of Health and Human Services wherein the Food and Drug Administration was included in the Consumer Protection and Environmental Health Service of the Public Health Service. In 1970, the Food and Drug Administration became a separate entity reporting directly to the Assistant Secretary for Health and Scientific Affairs. Within it, the Bureau of Foods bears the responsibility for the administration of these laws: the Tea Importation Act, the Import Milk Act, the Federal Food, Drug, and Cosmetic Act of 1938 and amendments, parts of the Public Health Service Act, and the Fair Packaging and Labeling Act. The laws have a dual purpose: to protect the public health by ensuring the wholesomeness and safety of food and to protect the consumer from fraud by preventing adulteration and misbranding.

For administrative purposes, the Food and Drug Administration has ten regional offices and nineteen district offices equipped with laboratories and manned with chemists and inspectors.

In the administration of the laws, the Food and Drug Administration uses every means to inform industries of the requirements of the laws so that they may comply with them. When there is a violation of the law, three procedures are possible: seizure of food that violates the law; criminal prosecution of the person or firm responsible for the violation of the law; and finally, injunction proceedings to keep more of the offending food from getting into interstate commerce. Seized products may be destroyed or otherwise disposed of, or they may be reconditioned, that is, brought into compliance with the law. Criminal prosecution of a firm or person for violation of the law can lead to fine or imprisonment or both, the severity of the penalty being established by proof of intent to defraud or mislead. Some activities of the Food and Drug Administration that are of interest to consumers are these.

1. It promulgates definitions and standards of identity for food products.

2. For some canned foods, it has promulgated definitions and standards of identity, reasonable standards of quality, and reasonable standards of fill of container. Other definitions and standards are in process.

3. Six times yearly it tests the diet of a nineteen-year-old man for such contaminants as radio-nuclides, pesticide residues, salmonellae, and such poisonous elements as mercury to affirm the safety of the national food supply.

4. It formulates the regulations essential to the administration of laws, such as regulations for the safe use of food additives and color additives.

5. It has issued regulations for good manufacturing practice, that is, sanitation, in the manufacture, processing, packaging, and holding of food products.

6. In cooperation with the United States Department of Agriculture, it issues regulations for the safe use of chemical pesticides on raw agricultural products.

7. It establishes good manufacturing practices (GMP's) which detail provisions concerning personnel, plants and grounds, sanitary facilities, controls and operations, equipment and utensils, processes and controls, product coding, warehousing and distribution, record keeping, and natural or unavoidable defect levels.

8. It inspects factories and warehouses to determine the prevailing sanitary conditions and practices.

9. It inspects, examines, and tests foods to determine that they satisfy the requirements of the law.

10. During natural disasters, such as hurricanes and floods, it assists state and local officials in examining and supervising the distribution of food and drugs to prevent the use of polluted materials.

11. It acts to discover the causes of outbreaks of food poisoning.

12. It inspects imported foods to determine that they comply with domestic standards.

13. When the evidence is convincing, it prohibits the addition of substances no longer deemed safe to food products, such as the cyclamates and the previously named food dyes.

Legislation leaves no doubt as to the mission of the Food and Drug Administration. The report, made public in August, 1969, of a seven-member panel of Food and Drug Administration officials named to assess the organization, concluded that the Food and Drug Administration, as it was then constituted, could not protect the consumer from bad food. The 1969 Ralph Nader Summer Study of the Food and Drug Administration culminated in the scathing report entitled *The Chemical Feast.* Since that time the Food and Drug Administration has been reorganized and has been given more ample funds. However, the Food and Drug Administration remains under attack because it does not ban the use of additives suspected of being carcinogenic and because there is a strong suspicion that its decisions are more often in favor of the industries it is charged with policing than in favor of the consumers it is charged with protecting.

The United States Department of Agriculture

The United States Department of Agriculture, created by an act of Congress approved May, 1862, engages in manifold activities. It is not within the purview of this text to discuss them fully. All of the Department's activities are of consequence to the consumer.

On January 24, 1978, four USDA agencies—the Agricultural Research Service, the Cooperative State Research Service, the Extension Service and the National Agricultural Library—merged and became the Science and Education Administration (SEA). In order to carry out one of its main missions, that of communicating information, SEA has established a Food and Nutrition Information Center to serve state and federal agencies, private institutions, and individuals.

The U. S. Department of Agriculture engages directly, and indirectly through grants, in research leading to improved methods of food production; to improved breeds of animals and improved varieties of food plants; to improved control of and eradication of plant and animal diseases and pests; and to improved methods of harvesting, processing, and distributing agricultural products. It administers the meat, poultry, and egg inspection acts. The Department promulgates standards for grading food products according to quality; it promulgates definitions and standards of identity for foods that contain meat or poultry. It approves the formulas for, the labels for, and the packaging of processed meat food and poultry food products.

Inspection of Food. The Agricultural Marketing Service, a subunit of the United States Department of Agriculture, is responsible for the grading and voluntary and mandatory inspection services of the department. The Meat Inspection Act of 1906 made mandatory the inspection of meat and meat products destined for interstate and export commerce. The Wholesome Meat Act of 1967 applied provisions of the 1906 law to meat and meat food products in intrastate commerce. Federal inspection is mandatory in any state that has no satisfactory inspection system.

The inspection process begins with live animals, continues through slaughter and processing, includes the inspection of the plant and the machinery and all the ingredients used in the production of processed meat food products, and assures that products for which standards and definitions of identity exist conform to them.

The mark of inspection reading, "U.S. Inspected and Passed," or the abbreviated form thereof, appears directly on meat or meat food products or on the labels thereof. The mark on carcasses, primal cuts, and meat food products in animal casings, beef tongues, beef hearts, and smoked meats not in casings appears within a circle in abbreviated form—"U.S. INSP'D & P'S'D"—and includes the number of the establishment where processing and inspection occurred (Figure 3–1 left). The mark of inspection on cooked, cured, and processed meat food products carries a full statement of inspection and the number of the plant where the processing and inspection occurred (Figure 3–1 right). Only inks approved for marking carcasses and cuts derived therefrom are in use. Any approved color, excepting green, can be used for marking other meat products so long as there is acceptable contrast with the color of the product.

The Poultry Products Inspection Act of 1957 as amended made inspection mandatory for ready-to-cook poultry and poultry food products in interstate and foreign commerce. The Wholesome Poultry Products Act of 1968 requires inspection of poultry in intrastate commerce and makes federal inspection mandatory in any state without an inspection program at least equal to the federal program. Inspection regulations require that each bird be individually examined and that processing occur in a sanitary manner in approved, properly equipped

FIGURE 3–1.   Meat inspection marks. Left, the mark applied directly to carcass and cuts. Right, the mark appearing on labels on processed meat food products. (*United States Department of Agriculture photographs.*)

FIGURE 3–2. Poultry inspection mark appearing on ready-to-cook poultry and processed poultry food products. (*United States Department of Agriculture photograph.*)

establishments. The same inspection symbol is used on all inspected poultry and poultry food products (see Figure 3–2). The Egg Products Inspection Act of 1970 requires continuous, mandatory inspection of egg-processing plants. The Poultry Division administers the law.

STANDARDS FOR GRADING FOOD FOR QUALITY. Sorting or classifying food according to quality requires objective standards for evaluation. The Agricultural Marketing Act of 1946 enabled the United States Department of Agriculture to establish the Agricultural Marketing Service (since 1965, the Consumer and Marketing Service) to define standards for foods not already covered by laws and regulations. Proposed standards for grading for quality are developed in consultation with trade groups; they are used tentatively until such time as they are proved practicable, when they become official permissive standards for grading. The standards are frequently revised to reflect changes in production, use, and marketing practices. There are three types of grade standards: wholesale grades, grades for food for processing, and consumer grades. The wholesale grades for items in all classes of foods apply to large-scale shipments; allow certain percentages of tolerance for undergrade specimens; and apply to quality at the time of grading in general. The food grading services that are often operated with the cooperation of state departments of agriculture are voluntary and the users pay a fee to cover costs. The percentage of the supply officially graded varies with products and ranges from zero to 80 percent for beef. Officially graded food products carry the U.S. grade shield at the option of the packer or distributor. Supermarkets buy by grade: information on grade may be available to the consumer who asks, for example, about the lettuce or the green beans. The number of grades stocked by supermarkets may be only one as for beef or two as for butter and eggs.

Consumer grades that have been established for some foods are designed to apply to the small units of food we buy and permit less tolerance for undergrade specimens than wholesale grades. There are consumer grades for six kinds of meat: beef, veal, calf, lamb, yearling mutton, and mutton; for six kinds of poultry, including chicken and turkey; for butter; for eggs; for cheddar and Swiss cheese; for nonfat dry milk; for fruit jellies and jams; for peanut butter; for some canned fruits and vegetables; for some frozen fruits and vegetables; for some fresh vegetables; and for some other food products. We do not find all these products grade-labeled in the supermarket; however, more grade-labeled food products could readily be made available to the consumer. Consumer advocates are pressing for mandatory grade-labeling of the foods for which it is feasible. The food industries, the advertising agencies, and the mass media are strongly opposed to mandatory grade-labeling because it makes the brand image worthless.

There is no one system for designation of grade. In general, consumer grades, except for meats, are preceded by the letters *U.S.;* are enclosed within the outline of a shield (the precise shape of the shield differs for different products) and are designated by letters: AA, A, B, C, and D. For some foods there may be two grades only; for others, there may be several. For example, butter grades are U.S. Grade AA, U.S. Grade A, and U.S. Grade B. Consumer grades for potatoes are only U.S. Grade A and U.S. Grade B. However, potatoes are often sold at retail according to wholesale grades of which there are four: U.S. Fancy, U.S. No. 1, U.S. Commercial, and U.S. No. 2. Meat grades are designated by words; instead of *U.S., USDA* appears with the grade designation, for example, USDA Choice. Numbers and numbers modified by adjectives are used for wholesale grades in general. The top grade of one commodity may be the U.S. No. 1 grade; but the top grade of another may be designated as U.S. Fancy or Extra No. 1, in which case the U.S. No. 1 grade is second to the best. More standardization is needed for consumer grades. Grades are confusing to the food shopper who does not know the name of the top grade or how many grades exist for a particular product.

The attributes of foods that determine quality differ with different products; the standard used for grading butter could not be used for grading eggs. Attributes that consumers prize are flavor, color, and texture. Official graders consider other factors such as appearance, freedom from defects, size of units, degree of maturity, and so on. Grading systems permit the scoring of foods on a point system. For example, frozen peas are scored on color, defects, and tenderness and maturity; the maximum points that may be assigned to each factor are 20, 40, and 40, respectively. The grade of the product would be established by the total score unless limiting rules supersede. Official standards for grading are long and detailed documents. Many definitions are included in standards, as are methods for determining objectively measurable characteristics. When packers, processors, and distributors do their own grading of foods and when they use the grade designations of official standards, the products must conform to the grades designated or the products are considered misbranded. Further, no *U.S.* or *USDA* may appear as part of the grade designation and grade cannot appear within the outline of a shield. Further discussion of food quality is given in succeeding chapters.

The Food and Nutrition Service of the United States Department of Agriculture administers all food assistance programs. These include the food stamp program and the child nutrition programs. The latter include the school lunch program, the school breakfast program, special food service programs for children, and a special milk program.

The Department of Commerce

The Department of Commerce was established to foster, serve, and promote the nation's economy, development, and technological advancement.

Through its National Bureau of Standards this department defines standards of weights and measures that are official at all levels. Among its definitions are those of the approximate weights in avoirdupois ounces and metric equivalents per cup of some foods the homemaker uses, such as flour, sugar, and nonfat dry milk. Under the authority of the Fair Packaging and Labeling Act, this agency has achieved some success in the reduction of the number of packages of different size in which consumer commodities are packaged.

In October, 1970, the fish inspection and standards promulgation functions of the abolished Bureau of Commercial Fisheries of the United States Department of Interior were transferred to the National Marine Fisheries Service of the National Oceanic and Atmospheric Administration of the United States Department of Commerce.

The Federal Trade Commission

The role of the Federal Trade Commission is to maintain a freely competitive environment in commerce and to restrain monopoly. It is enabled to do so by several laws that resulted from the growth of big business during this century. It was established to prevent unfair and deceptive acts and practices in commerce, prevent false and misleading advertising, and deter unfair pricing practices. It acts through cease-and-desist orders and by the instigation of civil penalty suits against violators of its orders. Both the Nader Report issued in January, 1969, and the report of an investigation under the auspices of the American Bar Association revealed that consumer protection by the agency was ineffectual and that it tended to favor trade interests.

The Federal Trade Commission shares in the administration of the

Fair Packaging and Labeling Act. It participated in the formulation of the regulation of cents-off and price-reduction promotions.

It proposed a Trade Regulation Rule in late 1969 to regulate retail food store advertising and marketing practices because a report of food chain selling practices in Washington, D.C., and in San Francisco had revealed that not all advertised items were available at advertised prices in all stores of chains. The rule requires that advertised specials be sold at the advertised price or less and that the advertised items be available in amounts sufficient to meet reasonably anticipated demand. It permits the use of such specific disclaimers as "available only in stores with delicatessen departments"; but it bands the use of such general disclaimers as "not all items available in all stores." The rule became effective in July, 1971.

In 1969, the Federal Trade Commission issued a statement of policy for coupons to put an end to coupons of short expiration date and to put a stop to limitations or conditions written only in very fine print. The commission also, in 1969, promulgated regulations on games of chance in the food-retailing and gasoline industries.

Reorganization within the Federal Trade Commission in 1970 gave rise to the Bureau of Consumer Protection. The bureau investigates and provides guidance and counseling to business, consumers, and government officials; it endeavors to secure voluntary compliance with the law in matters involving deceptive and unfair practices; and it is empowered to litigate and secure compliance. Further, the bureau is responsible for establishing consumer education programs to alert the public to unfair trade practices.

In 1971, the Federal Trade Commission adopted a resolution that would require advertisers, on demand, to document advertising statements regarding a product's performance, safety, comparative price, quality, or effectiveness. Much information so derived would be made public, thereby assisting consumers in decision making. Failure to validate statements to the satisfaction of the commission would lead to charges of false advertising against a company. In late 1970 and in 1971, the Federal Trade Commission began to look seriously at and to question the nutritional claims made in the advertising of some food companies. Since that time, several companies have been queried for making false nutritional claims and/or for deceptive advertising. Some milk and milk products, salt, gelatin, sugar, and freezer meats have come under scrutiny by the commission. In 1972, the Federal Trade Commission charged four cereal makers with monopoly of the industry and "tacit conspiracy" to restrict competition, a charge that was subsequently denied. The Federal Trade Commission has a comprehensive set of guidelines for food advertising and for the regulation of nutritional claims made for foods.

Like the Food and Drug Administration, the Federal Trade Commission is much maligned because it appears to favor industry over the consumer and because of its long delays in resolving cases.

THE CODEX ALIMENTARIUS

The Codex Alimentarius Commission is an international group organized under the joint auspices of the Food and Agriculture Organization and the World Health Organization. Its purpose is to establish food standards. Because the various cultures represented different concepts of what a given food should be, difficulties have been encountered in establishing standards. Codex standards establish limits of bacterial contamination, list permitted food and color additives, define reasonable quality standards, and establish basic labeling requirements (3).

The adoption of Codex standards is voluntary and the Commission does not enforce regulations. In an attempt to comply with Codex standards, FDA and USDA must examine the effects of tightening or relaxing our current standards. They must consider whether consumers and producers would benefit and whether costs would change. Before making a final decision, FDA and USDA must solicit public comments through a Federal Register notice. Procedures are similar to those for adopting a standard for a food product not currently regulated by FDA or USDA (4).

REFERENCES CITED

1. Heinback, J. T. and Stokes, R., *Nutrition Labeling for Today's Needs: Opinions of Nutritionists, The Food Industry, and Consumers,* Food and Drug Administration, Washington, D.C. (December, 1981).
2. Judge, E. E., *The Almanac of the Canning, Freezing, and Preserving Industries,* Westminster, Maryland: E. E. Judge & Sons, Inc. 1981.
3. Kimbrell, E. F., "Codex Alimentarius Food Standards and their Relevance to U.S. Standards," *Food Technology,* 36:93 (1982).
4. Morrison, R. M., "Codex Alimentarius Commission," National Food Review, United States Department of Agriculture, Washington, D.C. (Winter, 1983).
5. The Gallup Organization, "The Gallup Study of Changing Food Preparation and Eating Habits," The Gallup Organization, Inc., Princeton, N.J. (June 1980).
6. Title 21, Code of Federal Regulations, Food and Drugs, Parts 1–199, Regulations for the Enforcement of the Food, Drug, and Cosmetic Act and the Fair Packaging and Labeling Act, Office of the Federal Register, National Archives and Records Service, General Services Administration, Washington, D.C. (1981).

7. Title 21, Code of Federal Regulations, Food and Drugs, Part 1300, Office of the Federal Register, National Archives and Records Service, General Services Administration, Washington, D.C. (1981).
8. U.S. Department of Health and Human Services, "Promoting Health/Preventing Disease: Objectives for the Nation." U.S. Government Printing Office, Washington, D.C. (January 1981).

HISTORICAL REFERENCES

1. Anderson, Oscar E., *The Health of a Nation, Harvey W. Wiley and the Fight for Pure Food.* Chicago: University of Chicago Press (1958).
2. Bishop, James E., Jr., and Henry W. Hubbard, *Let the Seller Beware,* Washington, D.C.: National Press, Inc. (1969).
3. Cox, Edward S., R. C. Fellmeth, and J. E. Schulz, *Nader's Raiders.* New York: Grove Press, Inc. (1970).
4. Kallet, A., and F. J. Schlink, *100,000,000 Guinea Pigs.* New York: Grosset & Dunlap, Inc. (1933).
5. Lamb, Ruth deForest, *American Chamber of Horrors—The Truth About Food and Drugs,* New York: Farrar and Rinehart, Inc. (1936).
6. Neal, Harry Edwards, *The Protectors—The Study of the Food and Drug Administration.* New York: Julian Messner, Inc. (1968).
7. Sanford, David, *Hot War on the Consumer.* New York: Pitman Publishing Company (1969).
8. Sinclair, Upton, *The Jungle.* New York: The New American Library of World Literature (1960). Originally published by Doubleday, Page, & Co. (1905).
9. Turner, James S., *The Chemical Feast.* New York: Grossman Publishers, Inc. (1970) (paperback).
10. Wiley, H. W., *Foods and Their Adulteration,* 3rd ed. Philadelphia: P. Blakiston's Son and Co. (1917).
11. ————, *The History of a Crime Against the Food Law.* Washington, D.C.: Harvey M. Wiley (1929).
12. ————, *Wiley's Autobiography.* Indianapolis, Indiana: Bobbs-Merrill Co., Inc. (1930).

Chapter 4
Food and Energy Conservation

In recent times the world has become acutely aware that both food and energy are limited resources. Conservation of these two important resources is desirable not only from a family viewpoint but from a global perspective as well.

FOOD CONSERVATION

According to some authorities, farm output will have to double in the next twenty years in order to feed the growing world population in the same way it is now being fed. Other sources place less emphasis on production and say that the most expedient way to increase food supplies is by reducing food wastage. In tropical areas post-harvest losses are thought to range between 25 and 50 percent. Losses are mostly due to the climate's high temperatures and high humidity accelerating the deterioration of crops stored in the open air.

In the United States, losses are estimated to be about 9 percent each year for food and fiber crops. Losses are due to physiological disorders, diseases, physical damage between field and retail store, and physical damage in the market and after purchase. Vegetables subject to highest losses are lettuce, tomatoes, sweet potatoes, bell peppers, and cucumbers. A list of the most perishable fruits would include strawberries, sweet cherries, peaches, and cantaloupes.

Food conservation means the maximum utilization of the food resource, and this means minimal waste of edible food. Studies of food waste in the home, in food stores, and in hospitals and other institutions where meals are provided have been published. During New York City's financial crisis, it was widely publicized that the city must dispose of 23,000 tons of garbage each day. A three-year study carried out in Tucson, Arizona revealed that the average food waste of families was about 10 percent of the food purchased. Most of the waste occurred in middle-class neighborhoods. Garbage as defined by this study did not include food wasted by the disposal, food fed to pets, or food dumped into a compost heap.

The popularity of the "doggie bag" is evidence that more food is served to patrons at restaurants than they can eat; this also shows that some patrons wish to prevent waste of edible food. The United States has long been a land of plenty; her citizens are often guilty of wasting food in garbage, in overeating, and in the over consumption of some foods, such as protein-rich foods. It is to be hoped that a growing awareness both of wasteful practices and of the increasing shortage in the world's food supply will produce change. Although measures could be taken to reduce food waste at the national and commercial levels, control of food waste can begin with the individual meal manager.

Control of Food Waste

For the meal manager, the control of food waste (and of money) begins during shopping. Do not overbuy, that is, buy only those quantities of food that you can use to avoid losses that can occur because of staling and spoilage. Shop only where sanitation standards are high; where refrigeration is at optimum temperatures; where freezing equipment for frozen food products is maintained at a temperature of 0° F; where produce is clean and fresh; where meats on display are properly protected; and where housekeeping is above reproach. Do not buy damaged merchandise such as torn packages, cut cartons, and bulged, dented, or rusty cans. Finally, do shop carefully, select food products in accordance with the principles proposed and discussed. Quickly transport food to the home kitchen; then, promptly and properly store.

Proper storage implies applying the best protective coverings to foods; then, placing them in the proper environment. For example, almost all fresh foods require cold storage; further, some cereal products, dried herbs and spices, coffee, and some bottled sauces profit from cool storage. Frozen food products remain of better quality when the temperature of storage is maintained at 0° F. The assortment of storage materials available in the 1980's makes food storage, whether of newly purchased foods or of leftovers, both easy and effective. Contemporary materials include glass and plastic containers, plastic wraps and bags, aluminum foil, freezer wrap, and waxed paper. All have been evaluated by Consumers Union (2). Probably most meal managers keep some or all of these in the kitchen. In general, their purpose is to keep moisture in and/or air out of food products. Aluminum foil and plastic wraps are effective because they are pliable; hence, exclude air and prevent moisture loss. Following are some suggestions for proper storage that avoid waste and spoilage.

Guidelines for Food Storage.

1. On return from shopping, take time to carefully store all purchases. Place frozen products in the freezer immediately.

2. Place fresh meats, fish, and poultry products in the coldest part of the refrigerator or in the meat keeper.

3. Place eggs in the plastic carton in which you purchased them in the refrigerator at once. They will remain usable for several weeks but will have best quality if used within two weeks.

4. Refrigerate at once all dairy products. Milk and creams remain fresh for about one week after which time they lose quality. Superpasteurized creams remain fresh for much longer so long as they remain unopened, but once opened they lose quality within one to two weeks. Dried skim milk and canned evaporated milk may be stored at room temperature until reconstituted when both must be refrigerated, and will have the same storage life as fresh milk products.

5. Wrap cheeses carefully and store in the refrigerator to guard against mold formation and loss of quality.

6. Tightly enclose butter and margarine to prevent the absorption of food odors and refrigerate. Both can be freezer stored up to two months. Lard and oils should be refrigerated, but shortenings can, in general, be held at room temperature.   ~~Instead rancidity~~

7. Once containers have been opened, jams and jellies, syrups and honey, and peanut butter should be refrigerated to prevent mold development; mayonnaise and dressings should be refrigerated to prevent development of rancidity.

8. Store all canned foods in a cool, dry place. Once cans have been opened, contents should be put into coverable glass or plastic containers and refrigerated to protect flavor and prevent spoilage.

9. Store breads, well wrapped, in a breadbox unless the environment favors mold development, in which instance place breads in the refrigerator or freezer. Bread loses softness but remains usable when refrigerated; it freezes without loss of quality. Do not waste bits and pieces of bread; dry and crumb them for culinary uses.

10. Store cereals, crackers, flours, spices, herbs, sugar, and other dry food products away from heat in tightly closed containers to keep out moisture. Where weather is hot and humid, store herbs and spices and whole grain flours in the refrigerator to prevent insect infestation, that is, the eggs are present within the food but will only hatch out if ambient conditions are right.

11. Fruits are perishable; serve them quickly to avoid waste and store

with care. Keep unripe fruits at room temperature only until they are ripe; then refrigerate. In general, store all ripe and ready-to-eat fruits in the refrigerator.

12. Vegetables are less perishable than fruits, but they too require cold temperature storage. To avoid moisture loss, store vegetables in covered containers, plastic bags, or the crisper drawers in your refrigerator. Keep them dry, especially greens, green peppers, green onions, and cucumbers. Potatoes, dry onions, hard squashes, and root vegetables can be stored in a cool, dry place. Perhaps because of the energy shortage, houses will again have some cool rooms.

Control of food waste continues during the preparation of food for cooking, during food service, and during the storage of food following cooking and service. We are not as frugal in the use of food as our forebears were, nor as some other cultures are. We tend to use only the tenderest parts and only the parts of good color. We discard the edible leaves and stems of some vegetables, the trimmings from meats and poultry, and the like. Find ways to use all edible parts. Proper cooking ensures maximum utilization of food because both overcooking and undercooking lead to waste because of loss of palatability. Plate waste can be controlled by the simple expedient of serving up foods and dishes according to the likes and capacities of those to whom the food is served. Waste of leftovers is not uncommon. Failure to use leftover food while it is still fit to eat and the improper storage of leftovers lead to waste. Always place leftover foods in proper containers and chill immediately after a meal is finished. A good meal manager makes plans for the immediate use of leftover meats and vegetables in soups, stews, and casserole dishes. Flavor changes quite rapidly in some foods after they have been cooked, especially meats and poultry. Check the contents of your refrigerator often so that you can utilize everything before it loses quality, or you forget what is there, or the food becomes unsafe for eating. In summary, the meal manager has opportunities to control the waste of food from market to garbage can or disposal. Unfortunately, these opportunities seem trivial and are often ignored.

Food Spoilage

Spoilage denotes unfitness for human consumption. Spoilage may be due to chemical changes in food or due to biological causes such as the action of enzymes, microorganisms, or insects. Different people have different concepts of what constitutes spoilage. Certainly, decomposed food is spoiled, but food which is not decomposed and which seems all right in appearance and taste may contain microorganisms or toxins that render it unfit for human consumption.

The improper handling of food from market to home kitchen as well as in the kitchen itself can lead to foodborne illness. In fact, home kitchens are more often the source of foodborne illness than any other place. Bacteria, one of the causative agents of illness, are present everywhere. Bacteria grow well under conditions of warmth, and most foods provide the nutrients and moisture essential for the growth and development of bacteria. This fact explains the recommendation that purchased foods be promptly transported from the market and promptly stored once in the home. Avoidance of contamination in the kitchen requires the maintenance of maximum sanitation standards and storage at temperatures below and above the range of 40° F to 140° F, which is the range within which most bacteria flourish. See Figure C–1 in the Appendix. Good sanitation in the home kitchen, means that the can opener, cutting board, cutting implements, mixing equipment, counter surfaces, and your hands must be scrupulously clean to avoid cross-contamination of foods, that is, the transfer of bacteria from one food to another. Thaw frozen foods in the refrigerator or cook from the frozen state to avoid the growth of bacteria present while the food is within the critical temperature zone, 40° F to 140° F. Chill all cooked food immediately for the same reason.

Outbreaks of foodborne illness caused by bacteria are often called "food poisoning." However, the term *food poisoning* should be restricted to incidences in which a poison or toxin causes the illness. The other kind of illness, called food infection, is due not to a toxin but to the activity of a large number of bacterial cells within the gastrointestinal system. Food poisonings or intoxications are, in general, of a more explosive nature than food infections, and the incubation period between time of consumption of the toxic agent and appearance of symptoms is shorter. Some bacteria which cause food illness are discussed: *Salmonellae,* a food infector; *Staphylococcus aureus, Clostridium perfringens,* and *Clostridium botulinum.* The last three organisms cause food intoxication as opposed to food infection.

The *Salmonellae* are commonly found in raw meats, poultry, fish, milk, and eggs and in food products prepared from them. Pets are also sources of *Salmonellae,* which explains the admonitions: wash your hands after handling pets and do not keep their feeding dishes in your kitchen. *Salmonellae* are destroyed by heat; it is usually food which has become contaminated after cooking that causes illness. Symptoms of Salmonella infection appear within twenty-four hours of eating a contaminated food and include fever, headache, diarrhea, abdominal discomfort, and sometimes, vomiting. Over 1,000 serotypes of *Salmonellae* have been identified. The principal serotype connected with human salmonellosis is *Salmonella typhimurium.*

Staphylococcal intoxication is a common type of food borne illness.

Although a food is the vehicle for the toxin, this foodborne illness is generally of human origin; that is, the food was contaminated by man. *S. aureus* is present on the skin, in nose and throat discharges, and in the pus of infected lesions. It produces a heat-stable enterotoxin that causes the illness. Poor sanitation standards in food handling result in the contamination of the food. Then, when food is improperly chilled or heated, it becomes an excellent medium for the rapid multiplication of the organisms and the consequent production of the toxin. Foods that are most commonly incriminated in outbreaks of staphylococcal intoxications include meat and meat products; eggs and egg products; salads, such as chicken, tuna, egg, and potato; cream-filled pastries and pies; and milk and milk products. Meals eaten away from home, delicatessen foods, and foods improperly handled and stored in the home can be unsafe because of the organism. The illness caused by *S. aureus* is characterized by diarrhea, abdominal cramps, and vomiting. Symptoms appear within four hours after eating contaminated food and may continue for twenty-four to forty-eight hours.

Illness from *Clostridium perfringens* is caused by toxins produced in the human digestive tract by the bacterium. The illness occurs about twelve hours after ingestion. Symptoms include diarrhea and abdominal discomfort. *Clostridium perfringens* is a spore-forming anaerobe, of which there are many types. The spores are resistant to curing and smoking, and some are heat resistant. *Clostridium perfringens* is widely distributed in soil, dust, water, feces, and food. Food is safe only when it has been handled in accordance with maximum sanitation standards and has been maintained at temperatures above or below the critical zone. Meat is the food category most often associated with *Clostridium perfringens*. Meats should be properly cooked, held hot and served hot, and cooled quickly after cooking if they are to be served cold. Leftover meats and meat dishes, gravy, and broths should be immediately cooled and the latter should be brought to a rolling boil before being served again.

The last bacterium of concern is *Clostridium botulinum,* a ubiquitous, spore-forming anaerobe. During spore development the organism produces a virulent toxin that is lethal to man. Botulism, the disease caused by the toxin, is uncommon. It is most often associated with home-canned vegetables that were not processed properly. The toxin can only be produced in the absence of oxygen and when temperature and environmental conditions are suitable for spore development. The spores will not activate in foods of high acid, high sugar, or high salt content or in the presence of certain chemicals such as the nitrites. The spores are not destroyed by freezing or boiling but must be subjected to temperatures above boiling for a prescribed period based on the size of the container and the density of the food being processed. The toxin is rarely present in commercially canned food; the danger of this contaminant is in home-canned nonacid foods such as corn, peas, and green beans. Often the gas created by the growth of spores causes cans and the lids of jars to lose the vacuum seal and to bulge. Swelling may be caused by other organisms, however, and because you cannot know what organism caused the swelling, you must discard with great care all food in such cans. It is important to know that the toxin can also be present in cans that do not bulge and in which signs of spoilage would not be detected by the average person. The toxin is heat-labile and is destroyed in food that is boiled for ten minutes.

Home gardening and the subsequent preservation of food by canning or freezing has become a popular activity. Do not attempt to can food without having in your possession and reading a recently published booklet that outlines procedures for safe food preservation. You can safely process fruits (except figs) and acid tomatoes in a water bath canner because a temperature higher than 212° F is not required; but follow the recommended processing time for each food that you can. You must process nonacid vegetables in a pressure canner at 10 pounds of pressure yielding a temperature of 240° F. Again, always process for the recommended time. Before you store jars of canned foods, check to make certain that all jars have a perfect seal. A jar with a proper vacuum seal will have a slightly concave top. To assure maximum quality and safety, some foods, such as pickles, relishes, preserves, and jams should be pasteurized. Pack these items into clean (sterile) jars and process for 10 minutes in a simmering water bath. This procedure sterilizes the headspace and expels air from the jar; it is effective because the foods are either acid or high in sugar content. Quality is maintained and mold development is deterred.

Conservation of food by freezing presents no health hazards. The problem associated with preservation by freezing is the maintenance and preservation of a high level of quality. The quality of the finished food depends on the varieties of fruits and vegetables frozen, the quality of the foods frozen, the care given during preparation for freezing, the quality of the packaging and the tightness of seal, the speed of the freezing process, and the temperature of storage. Although food may seem frozen at any temperature under 32° F (0° C), it is in fact only partially frozen. Freezers should be maintained at 0° F or −18° C or lower in order to reduce the deterioration of color, flavor, and texture and the loss of vitamin C in products. As with canning, follow directions in a recently published booklet, bulletin, or book on how to freeze. The storage life of home-frozen products may be shorter than that of commercially frozen products. See tables in Appendix D.

While bacteria are the spoilage agents of primary concern, fungi including molds and yeasts can also bring about food spoilage. Although yeasts do not present much concern from a food safety point of view, molds do. As molds grow they may produce mycotoxins, some of which have been shown to be pathogenic in animals.

Molds develop on all kinds of foods including fresh fruits, breads, jams and jellies, and cheeses. Mold is a furry or downy coating that varies in color from white to black and may be green or blue; the color of a mold is no clue to its possible danger. Mold is produced by minute fungi that are ubiquitous. Visible mold is the "bloom" of the fungus and where it appears there are roots and growing parts within the food. Do not scrape away moldy parts; destroy moldy food in *toto*. Moldy cheeses are no exception, except for blue-veined cheeses, which show mold only as part of the veining, and other mold-ripened cheeses, such as Camembert, and which show only the characteristic mold formation. To prevent food waste because of mold development, properly store all food products that are susceptible to mold development. Refrigeration slows up but does not prevent mold development; in fact, mold can grow on the surface of the refrigerator. Freezing deters mold development. Cooking destroys mold but does not necessarily destroy any mycotoxin that may be present.

In summary, to conserve food, that is, to avoid food waste, buy carefully, store so as to preserve quality and to keep food safe to eat, cook properly, serve planned and controlled servings, use leftovers, and preserve an abundant supply of food by canning or freezing.

ENERGY CONSERVATION IN THE KITCHEN

Cooking, whether by electricity, gas, wood, coal or kerosene, consumes energy. The relative costs of various fuels are shown in Figure 4–1. It has been estimated that only 1.1 percent of the total energy used in the United States is used for cooking in homes. While this may seem like a small amount, it is one of the few areas over which consumers can exert some control.

A major factor in the energy consumed in food preparation is the work habits of the cook. One study showed that energy usage varied as much as 50 percent among women carrying out identical meal preparation tasks with the same kitchen range. There are various common sense procedures which can be used to conserve energy.

Ranges and Cookware

The use of saucepans and frypans which fit the burner will help prevent energy losses. Even when utensils fit perfectly on an electric range only about 70 percent of the heat produced will go into the food, about

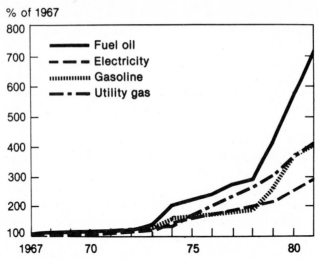

FIGURE 4–1.   Recent changes in annual average energy prices. (*Bureau of Labor Statistics.*)

ten percent goes to heat the element, and about twenty percent is lost to room air.

Keep in mind that a nonpressurized pot of water at sea level is not going to get any hotter than 212° F, regardless of how high the heat setting is. Use the lowest setting possible for maintaining the desired temperature, and don't cook food too long. Overcooking not only wastes energy but it is destructive of food quality and food nutrients. Pots and pans made of good conductors such as aluminum, cast iron, carbon steel or copper will provide good heat transfer. Good utensils with tight fitting lids are worth the investment. Less energy is required to bring about boiling if a tight fitting lid is used. Also, less water is needed and cooking time is reduced. The electric unit can be turned off before a food is completely done; it will finish cooking on the residual heat of the unit.

Ovens

The oven is an energy waster. Only about 14 percent of the heat produced during cooking in an electric range oven is actually transferred to the food. The remaining 86 percent of energy is spent as follows: 46 percent goes for heating the oven lining, 25 percent is lost through oven walls, and 15 percent is lost through the oven vent.

Gas range ovens are even less efficient than electric range ovens, for only about six percent of the heat produced is actually absorbed by the food. There is greater movement of air in gas range ovens than in electric ones and about two-thirds of the heat produced is lost through the vent.

The oven should not be used if a surface burner can be used instead. Baking for an hour in a conventional electric oven at 350° F uses 4,210 kilocalories of energy, while simmering for the same time on an eight-inch surface burner uses only 520 kilocalories of heat. Because of better insulation, a self-cleaning oven requires less energy than a conventional oven to maintain a given temperature, but the total energy used depends on the frequency of cleaning.

Emissive containers—utensils which absorb or transmit radiant energy—should be used in an oven because much of the energy in an oven is radiant energy. Emissive containers include glass that transmits radiant energy and utensils with dull, rough, dark surfaces that absorb radiant heat. It should be pointed out that products such as cookies which brown easily may burn on the bottom before completely done if baked on emissive cookie sheets. You can lower the oven temperature by twenty-five degrees when emissive cookware is used.

The oven should be used at full capacity, not solely to bake a few potatoes or a pan of biscuits. There are many foods which can be cooked in the oven. The additional food load for an oven meal causes some increases in the amount of energy used but not nearly as much as reheating the oven a time or two or heating additional surface units to cook other items.

It is not always necessary to preheat an oven. Items such as casseroles, baked vegetables or roasts do not need to be placed in a preheated oven. However, quick breads and cakes do require a preheated oven. Likewise, with the former food items, it may be possible to turn the oven off before the product is completely done. The oven door should be opened only when it is essential to do so since an oven loses about 20 percent of its heat when opened.

Pilot lights of gas ovens are wasteful of energy. It has been estimated that they consume 5 to 10 percent of all natural gas used in homes. There are new range models on the market which feature electrical ignition and eliminate the need for pilot lights.

The microwave oven may be an energy saver in cooking if used properly. The microwave oven consumes less energy than the conventional oven for comparable cooking tasks, such as cooking a roast; it might be more efficient than a range-top unit in cooking food in water, such as vegetables; but heating soups and sauces on the range uses no more energy than the microwave oven. In microwave cooking, heat is generated as food and water molecules are agitated by absorbed microwave energy. Foods are not cooked in the same way as in a conventional oven and variables affect the palatability of food prepared in microwave ovens.

For safe use of the microwave oven follow these precautions: keep the oven clean, never turn it on when it is empty, and have it inspected frequently by an authorized inspector.

Small Appliances

Some small appliances for cooking are energy conserving. The small broiler-oven is efficient for small loads of quick-cooking food, such as heating frozen ready-to-eat dishes. Because small broiler ovens are not generally well insulated, they lose heat, and are not suited for cooking long-cooking foods such as roasts. The slow-cooker and crock pot are low-wattage appliances. The crock pot, which cooks food at temperatures of 150° F to 300° F is excellent for cooking pot roasts, stews, casserole dishes, soups, and bean dishes. The electric frypan, percolator, egg cooker, griddle, and sandwich grill are appliances that use less energy than would be consumed if the same foods were prepared on a conventional range. Other appliances used in the kitchen such as the electric can opener, mixer, blender, and juicer are small energy users.

The pressure saucepan should not be overlooked, particularly for items that normally would require long, slow cooking. It shortens cooking times; a stew normally requiring several hours of cooking can be prepared in thirty minutes. In addition, as much as 16 percent less energy may be required with the pressure saucepan than with the slow cooker, and 40 percent less energy with the pressure saucepan than with the regular saucepan. The cooking time required for various products will greatly affect the amount of energy used.

Dishwashers

The need for energy associated with family meals does not end when the cooking is over; dishes and cooking utensils must be washed. In early 1980, about 43 percent of American homes wired for electricity were equipped with mechanical dishwashers. The dishwasher consumes energy in three ways: to heat water for the washing cycle, to operate a motor that circulates water during the washing cycle, and to elevate water temperature during the drying cycle. Twelve to fourteen gallons of hot water are used per load. Operate the dishwasher only when it is fully loaded. Some models have a heat/no heat drying option. Drying without heat cuts energy usage by approximately one half. Similar amounts of energy can be saved in older models by stopping the dishwasher after the last rinse and drain. The door should be left ajar to allow the dishes to dry by evaporation.

Water for mechanical dishwashers should be at least 140° F in order to adequately clean dishes. The mechanical dishwasher is considered to be the most sanitary method for washing dishes. If dishes are washed by hand, they should be scraped, rinsed and washed in hot water (120° F) containing detergent. The dishes should be rinsed by pouring boiling water over them and then be allowed to air dry.

Refrigerators and Freezers

There is less opportunity to conserve energy in the use of the refrigerator and freezer than elsewhere in the kitchen. The conventional refrigerator provides storage for fresh food but only temporary storage for frozen foods. The frozen food compartment is generally across the top of the unit and is enclosed by an inner door; it maintains a temperature of about 15° F, which is sufficient for freezing ice cubes but is suitable for only short-term storage of frozen food. The combination refrigerator-freezer has two compartments with two outer doors. The freezer compartment should maintain a temperature within the range of 0° F to 10° F with 0° F being preferred. Home freezing of food is possible and freezing storage is as good as the constancy with which the temperature of 0° F is maintained. Freezers are upright or chest models. The latter conserves energy because less cold air is lost to the environment when it is opened than from the upright model.

The significant energy cost of refrigerators and freezers is determined by whether they are of the manual defrosting, automatic defrosting, or frost-free type. Freezers are increasingly expensive to operate in that order. In a cooling device, when warm air hits a cooling surface, frost forms. In the automatic defrosting refrigerator, a timer stops the cooling unit long enough for the frost to melt, and water drains into a pan near the condenser coils and heat from them re-evaporates the water into the room. In the frost-free refrigerator and freezer, a fan blows air across the cooling plates and through the cooled area. On a timed cycle, heating elements melt the frost from the cooling plates and re-evaporate it. Because of the role of both refrigerator and freezer in the conservation of food, it is not possible to operate them at lesser energy-cost levels; however, a few simple practices can reduce energy cost somewhat. Open these appliances as infrequently as possible to reduce the loss of cold air. Test the seal of the doors frequently to assure a tight seal; close the door on a dollar bill and if it pulls out, the gasket needs replacing. Cover all liquids stored in the refrigerator, especially frost-free models, because moisture is drawn into the air from uncovered liquids making the unit work longer. Keep condenser coils clean for maximum efficiency and conservation of energy. The freezer and refrigerator both operate most efficiently when filled to the correct capacity, but do not overload as this will keep the compressor running more than it should. Space items stored in these units to permit good circulation of cold air. Use a thermometer to check storage temperatures and use the warmest setting that will maintain the proper temperatures: 36° F to 40° F in the refrigerator and 0° F in the freezer. Finally, defrost a refrigerator that requires manual defrosting often; permit no more than a one-fourth inch buildup of frost.

The Brownout and the Blackout

When you recognize that a brownout is in effect, conserve energy and protect motor-driven appliances from damage by turning off such major appliances as the air conditioner, television set, water heater, dishwasher, washer and dryer, and oven. When there is a blackout, your main concern becomes the conservation of the food contained in your freezer, refrigerator-freezer, or refrigerator. Avoid opening a freezer. Food should remain frozen in a fully loaded freezer for two days without electricity; but if the freezer is half loaded, the food will remain frozen for only about one day. The colder the temperature in the freezer, the larger it is, and the better it is insulated the longer will the food in the freezer remain frozen. To save food when a blackout continues for a longer time, or when a freezer fails to function, take the food to a freezer-locker plant if possible. You can use dry ice to extend the frozen period. Twenty-five pounds of dry ice will hold the temperature of a half full ten-cubic food freezer for three to four days. A twenty-cubic-foot freezer would require fifty pounds of dry ice. Place the ice directly on a heavy cardboard placed over the packages of frozen food. Further protect the freezer by covering it with blankets or other covering that will insulate.

Partially or wholly thawed foods require special handling. Refreezing partially thawed food products reduces quality. However, you can safely refreeze foods that retain ice crystals or if they are no warmer than 40° F. Fully thawed fruits that smell good and taste all right can be refrozen. However, they might be more tasty if made into jams or jellies. Beef, veal, and lamb that have no off-odors can also be refrozen, but never refreeze thawed ice creams, vegetables, sea foods, or ready made dishes.

The freezer compartment of the refrigerator-freezer is small, ranging from two to twelve cubic feet, with three to four cubic feet being the average. Obviously, during a power failure, food will remain frozen in this compartment for only hours, generally, not more than twenty-four. When a blackout is short, some of the food can be salvaged by cooking, although it is unlikely that any could be refrozen. During a blackout, the temperature in the refrigerator compartment will rise at a rate depending on how much it is opened, the quality of the insulation, and the closeness of the seal. Unless it is eaten, all food in this compartment will become a total loss in a relatively short period of time because of spoilage.

In summary, there can be no meaningful conservation of either food or energy, two vital resources in the United States unless individuals and families do all that they can to conserve them. To do so will require new outlooks and changes in behavior for most of us. And because the measures that we can take seem picayune in contrast to the enormity of the problems, we may lack the motivation to act.

SUGGESTED REFERENCES

1. Hunt, Fern E., "How to Save Energy Preparing Foods," *The 1980 Yearbook of Agriculture*. U.S. Department of Agriculture, Washington, D.C.
2. "Keeping Foods Fresh," *Consumer Reports,* 48:139–145 (March, 1983).
3. "Microwave Ovens," *Consumer Reports,* 46:128–141 (March 1981).
4. "Microwave Ovens," *Consumer Research Magazine* (June 1980), pp. 23–26.
5. "Money-Saving Guide to Energy in the Home." *Consumer Reports, 1978*. Garden City, N.Y.: Doubleday & Co., Inc., pp. 80–82.
6. Spies, Henry R. *et al.*, *350 Ways to Save Energy (and Money)*, New York: Crown Publishers, Inc., (1974).
7. "The Cooking Quality in New Microwave Ovens," *Consumers Research Magazine* (Sept. 1982), pp. 11–36.

Chapter 5

Meal Management Goal 1: Good Nutrition

Four goals for meals have been established. The first goal is good nutrition. The past decade has seen increasing consumer interest and concern about nutrition and its relationship to one's health. Today, some of the most pressing nutrition and diet related disease problems in the United States are associated with overconsumption. Therefore, one other concern in meal management is the avoidance of overconsumption. A good meal manager will provide meals that achieve all four goals.

NUTRITIONAL STATUS IN THE UNITED STATES

The 1977–78 Nationwide Food Consumption Survey (NFCS), conducted by the United States Department of Agriculture, collected data from approximately 3,500 households in the 48 conterminous states (6). The nutrient content of food used at home was estimated using information collected on the kinds and quantities of food used by the households during a seven day period. Six similar surveys had been conducted in 1936, 1943, 1948 (urban only), 1955, and 1965.

The NFCS found that the amounts of food used in a week by U.S. households were sufficient on the average to provide the 1974 Recommended Dietary Allowances (RDA) for food energy and 11 nutrients. Nutrients studied were protein, calcium, iron, magnesium, phosphorus, vitamin A, thiamin, riboflavin, vitamin B_6, vitamin B_{12}, and ascorbic acid.

It must be pointed out that averages conceal individual variations in nutrient levels within households. The conclusion cannot be made that all food purchased by the households was eaten nor that food was divided among household members according to nutritional need.

Only 3 percent of the households used food that failed to provide the RDA for protein. Fewer than 10 percent used food that failed to provide the RDA for phosphorus, riboflavin, and ascorbic acid. Calcium and vitamin B_6 were the nutrients most often neglected in the household food supplies. About one-third of the households used food that provided less than the RDA for these two nutrients.

Generally at each successively higher level of income, a slightly greater percentage of households used foods that met allowances. High income itself did not assure that household food met the RDA for all nutrients. The four regions of the country showed little difference in the percentage of households meeting the allowances for food energy and 11 nutrients.

One must resist the inclination to compare the results of the 1965–66 survey with the 1977–78 survey. They cannot be compared because the RDA for several nutrients have changed substantially since the earlier data were analyzed. However, comparisons of average nutritive values of food used per person in households for spring 1977 and spring 1965 indicate that food energy and fat levels were lower and levels of vitamin and minerals, except calcium, were as high or higher in 1977 than they were in 1965.

Between 1968 and 1970 the Public Health Service conducted a nutrition survey to determine the prevalence of malnutrition and related health problems in the low income segment of the United States population (2). The sample surveyed was selected from the population within ten states that had the lowest average income in each state according to the 1960 census and became known as the Ten-State Nutrition Survey. Demographic data were obtained on 24,000 families, and the nutritional status of approximately 40,000 individuals was assessed. Biochemical and dietary analyses were conducted on selected subgroups.

Evidence of malnutrition was found most frequently among blacks, followed by Spanish-Americans, and least frequently among whites. Generally, there was an increase of malnutrition as income level decreased. Among the different age groups surveyed, adolescents between the ages of ten and sixteen had the highest prevalence of unsatisfactory nutritional status. Male adolescents had more evidence of poor nutritional status than females. Elderly persons were another group with evidence of increased nutritional deficiencies. A correlation was found between the educational attainment of the homemaker and the nutritional status of the children under seventeen years of age in the home. Obesity was a significant health problem that was found to be prevalent in adult women, particularly black women. Men were less frequently obese although white males in the adolescent and the adult groups had a relatively higher prevalence of obesity than black males. Children were often either overweight or underweight.

The major findings with respect to specific nutrients are now briefly discussed. Iron status was poor in all segments of the population as demonstrated by low hemoglobin and hematocrit values. It was surprising to find the indications of poor iron status in males as they are generally considered to have adequate iron status. Low vitamin A levels were found in Mexican-Americans and in the subpopulation of young people. Although vitamin C nutriture was not a major problem among any group surveyed, lower than average serum levels were found in the elderly and in men. Nutritional status in relation to thiamin did not appear to be a problem. Riboflavin status was poor among blacks and young people. Iodine deficiency was not a problem. Protein intake was adequate or above adequate in the population surveyed; however, a relatively large segment of the pregnant and lactating women had low serum albumin levels. This may reflect inadequate standards for this group.

Schwerin et al. (9) evaluated the change in diet intake over a ten-year period by comparing the results of the First Health and Nutrition Survey (HANES I) conducted from 1971–74, the Ten-State Survey conducted 1968–70, and NFCS. They concluded that the nutrient picture had improved during the past decade. They found that more subgroups in NFCS than in HANES I met the recommended standards for iron, vitamin A, thiamin, riboflavin, and niacin. An equal number of subgroups in both samples did so for protein and ascorbic acid. Only in the cases of calcium and calories was the count in favor of HANES I.

Dietary Standards

The oldest dietary standard in this country is the *Minimum Daily Requirements of Specific Nutrients* (MDR) established by the Food and Drug Administration in 1941. The MDR provided a standard for the labeling of dietary supplements, foods for special dietary uses, and enriched and fortified foods. The amounts of certain vitamins and minerals present in those products had to be expressed on labels as percentages of the minimum daily requirements that would be supplied by a specified quantity of the product consumed during the period of one day. Since the MDR are based on requirements and individual requirements are not known, they lagged behind, and were not updated. The MDR were discontinued when FDA established the guidelines for nutritional labeling, known as the U.S. RDA.

In 1943, the first edition of the *Recommended Dietary Allowances* (RDA) was published by the Food and Nutrition Board, National Academy of Science-National Research Council. The ninth revision (1980) of the RDA is presented in Table 5–1. Allowances for calories and seventeen nutrients are given in quantitative units for seventeen population groups

TABLE 5–1. *Food and Nutrition Board, National Academy of Sciences–National Research Council Recommended Daily Dietary Allowances, Revised 1980* Designed for the maintenance of good nutrition of practically all healthy people in the U.S.A.

	Age (years)	Weight (kg)	Weight (lb)	Height (cm)	Height (in)	Protein (g)	Fat-Soluble Vitamins			Water-Soluble Vitamins							Minerals					
							Vita-min A (μg RE)[a]	Vita-min D (μg)[b]	Vita-min E (mg α-TE)[c]	Vita-min C (mg)	Thia-min (mg)	Ribo-flavin (mg)	Niacin (mg NE)[d]	Vita-min B-6 (mg)	Fola-cin (μg)	Vitamin B-12 (μg)	Cal-cium (mg)	Phos-phorus (mg)	Mag-nesium (mg)	Iron (mg)	Zinc (mg)	Iodine (μg)
Infants	0.0–0.5	6	13	60	24	kg × 2.2	420	10	3	35	0.3	0.4	6	0.3	30	0.5	360	240	50	10	3	40
	0.5–1.0	9	20	71	28	kg × 2.0	400	10	4	35	0.5	0.6	8	0.6	45	1.5	540	360	70	15	5	50
Children	1–3	13	29	90	35	23	400	10	5	45	0.7	0.8	9	0.9	100	2.0	800	800	150	15	10	70
	4–6	20	44	112	44	30	500	10	6	45	0.9	1.0	11	1.3	200	2.5	800	800	200	10	10	90
	7–10	28	62	132	52	34	700	10	7	45	1.2	1.4	16	1.6	300	3.0	800	800	250	10	10	120
Males	11–14	45	99	157	62	45	1000	10	8	50	1.4	1.6	18	1.8	400	3.0	1200	1200	350	18	15	150
	15–18	66	145	176	69	56	1000	10	10	60	1.4	1.7	18	2.0	400	3.0	1200	1200	400	18	15	150
	19–22	70	154	177	70	56	1000	7.5	10	60	1.5	1.7	19	2.2	400	3.0	800	800	350	10	15	150
	23–50	70	154	178	70	56	1000	5	10	60	1.4	1.6	18	2.2	400	3.0	800	800	350	10	15	150
	51+	70	154	178	70	56	1000	5	10	60	1.2	1.4	16	2.2	400	3.0	800	800	350	10	15	150
Females	11–14	46	101	157	62	46	800	10	8	50	1.1	1.3	15	1.8	400	3.0	1200	1200	300	18	15	150
	15–18	55	120	163	64	46	800	10	8	60	1.1	1.3	14	2.0	400	3.0	1200	1200	300	18	15	150
	19–22	55	120	163	64	44	800	7.5	8	60	1.1	1.3	14	2.0	400	3.0	800	800	300	18	15	150
	23–50	55	120	163	64	44	800	5	8	60	1.0	1.2	13	2.0	400	3.0	800	800	300	18	15	150
	51+	55	120	163	64	44	800	5	8	60	1.0	1.2	13	2.0	400	3.0	800	800	300	10	15	150
Pregnant						+30	+200	+5	+2	+20	+0.4	+0.3	+2	+0.6	+400	+1.0	+400	+400	+150	[e]	+5	+25
Lactating						+20	+400	+5	+3	+40	+0.5	+0.5	+5	+0.5	+100	+1.0	+400	+400	+150	[e]	+10	+50

Source: Reproduced with permission of the National Academy of Sciences.

[a] Retinol equivalents. 1 retinol equivalent = 1 μg retinol or 6 μg β carotene. See text for calculation of vitamin A activity of diets as retinol equivalents.

[b] As cholecalciferol. 10 μg cholecalciferol = 400 IU of vitamin D.

[c] α-tocopherol equivalents. 1 mg d-α tocopherol = 1 α-TE. See text for variation in allowances and calculation of vitamin E activity of the diet as α-tocopherol equivalents.

[d] 1 NE (niacin equivalent) is equal to 1 mg of niacin or 60 mg of dietary tryptophan.

[e] The increased requirement during pregnancy cannot be met by the iron content of habitual American diets nor by the existing iron stores of many women; therefore the use of 30–60 mg of supplemental iron is recommended. Iron needs during lactation are not substantially different from those of nonpregnant women, but continued supplementation of the mother for 2–3 months after parturition is advisable in order to replenish stores depleted by pregnancy.

according to age, sex, and condition. The allowances are established on the basis of research studies and represent the consensus of those qualified to make judgments. The allowances are designed for the maintenance of good nutrition for practically all healthy persons in the United States; they are intended to cover individual variations among most normal persons. Allowance levels are greater than minimum requirements except for calories. The RDA provide a tool for estimating the nutrient adequacy of the diets of population groups when diets are evaluated by dietary surveys. Further, the RDA provide a frame of reference for estimating the food needs of population groups and for designing models for planning meals and for food plans. The RDA were also used as a guide for establishing guidelines for nutritional labeling of foods.

The *U.S. Recommended Daily Allowances* (U.S. RDA) for food nutrients were developed in 1972 by the Food and Drug Administration to replace the MDR and to be the standard of reference for all nutritional labeling. The U.S. RDA values were derived from the highest value for each nutrient, except for calcium, phosphorus, biotin, pantothenic acid, copper, and zinc, in the 1968 RDA for males and nonpregnant, nonlactating females four or more years of age. The U.S. RDA for calcium and phosphorus are set at 1 gram each, whereas the highest value in the RDA is 1.4 grams for each. This was done because of the wide variability in the requirements (0.8–1.4 gram) depending on age; 1 gram is generally considered as meeting the human requirement in the United States, and lower values generally are supported by international groups. There had previously been no RDA for biotin, pantothenic acid, copper, and zinc although these nutrients are recognized as essential in the diet. The 1974 revision of the RDA contained a recommendation for zinc; the level that had previously been chosen for the U.S. RDA was the highest RDA value for a nonpregnant, nonlactating female over four years of age.

The Food and Drug Administration recognized that the need for nutrients varies with age and established four sets of the U.S. RDA. These sets represent the needs of infants, birth to twelve months; children under four years; adults and children four or more years of age; and pregnant and lactating women (Table 5–2). The U.S. RDA for adults are by far the most widely used. The other sets are used on appropriate items such as baby foods and special foods for pregnant and lactating females.

NUTRITIONAL LABELING

During the past decade several factors focused attention on the need for an improved system of communicating education and information

TABLE 5-2.   *U.S. Recommended Daily Allowances (U.S. RDAs)*

	Infants Birth to 12 months (Tentative)	Children under 4 Years of Age	Adults and Children 4 or More Years of Age	Pregnant or Lactating Women
Nutrients that must be declared on the label *				
Protein "low quality protein" (g)	0	0	0	0
Protein "high quality protein" (g)	20	45	45	45
Protein "proteins in general" (g)	28	65	65	65
Vitamin A (IU)	1,500	2,500	5,000	8,000
Vitamin C (ascorbic acid) (mg)	35	40	60	60
Thiamin (vitamin B_1) (mg)	0.5	0.7	1.5	1.7
Riboflavin (vitamin B_2) (mg)	0.6	0.8	1.7	2.0
Niacin (mg)	8	9	20	20
Calcium (g)	0.6	0.8	1.0	1.3
Iron (mg)	15	10	18	18
Nutrients that may be declared on the label				
Vitamin D (IU)	400	400	400	400
Vitamin E (IU)	5	10	30	30
Vitamin B_6 (mg)	0.4	0.7	2.0	2.5
Folic acid (Folacin) (mg)	0.1	0.7	0.4	0.8
Vitamin B_{12} (ug)	2	3	6	8
Phosphorus (g)	0.5	0.8	1.0	1.3
Iodine (ug)	45	70	150	150
Magnesium (mg)	70	200	400	450
Zinc (mg)	5	8	15	15
Copper (mg)	0.6	1	2	2
Biotin (mg)	0.05	0.15	0.3	0.3
Pantothenic acid (mg)	3	5	10	10

*Whenever nutrition labeling is required.

concerning nutrition. These factors included the consumerism movement, the difficulty in determining nutritional quality of an increasing number of processed and formulated foods, and the increased skepticism about the nutritional quality of the food supply in this country. Nutritional labeling has four primary objectives: to provide consumers with nutritional information about packaged foods; to assist in nutrition education of consumers; to encourage improvement of the nutritional content of food; and to safeguard the nutritional content of food (4).

The majority of products that bear nutritional labeling do so voluntarily. Nutritional labeling must be used if a product in interstate commerce is fortified or enriched, or if it makes a nutritional claim in advertising or on its label. For example, any reference to protein, fat, carbohydrate, calories, vitamins, minerals, or recommendation for use in dieting makes nutritional labeling mandatory. Products that are enriched or fortified, such as enriched bread, fortified milk, and fortified fruit juices, must bear nutritional labeling. However, a product that contains enriched flour as an ingredient need not bear nutritional labeling.

The nutritional labeling format has been standardized to contain the following items:

Serving Size.
Servings per Container.
Calorie Content per Serving.
Protein Content per Serving, in Grams.
Carbohydrate Content per Serving, in Grams.
Fat Content per Serving, in Grams.
Percentage per Serving of the U.S. RDA of Protein, Vitamin A, Vitamin C, Thiamin, Riboflavin, Niacin, Calcium, and Iron.

These items must be listed if nutritional labeling is used. Some optional nutrients may also be included. These include vitamin D, vitamin E, vitamin B_6, folic acid, vitamin B_{12}, phosphorus, iodine, magnesium, zinc, copper, biotin, and pantothenic acid. Percentages of the U.S. RDA start at 0 and are expressed in 2 percent increments up to 10 percent; in 5 percent increments from 10 to 50 percent; and in 10 percent increments above 50 percent. A food manufacturer may exercise the option of declaring a food's fatty acid and/or cholesterol content on nutritional labels. This information, if provided, must directly follow the information on fat per serving. Since FDA does not want to appear to be indicating which foods should be used for the control of heart disease, the following statement must be on the label to prevent any misinterpretation: "Information on fat (and/or cholesterol, where appropriate) content is provided for individuals who, on the advice of a physician, are modifying their total dietary intake of fat (and/or cholesterol, where appropriate)." An example of a nutritional label is shown in Table 5–3.

The nutritional labeling regulation also defines and differentiates among foods, dietary supplements, and drugs. If vitamins and/or minerals are added to a food so that a single serving provides 50 percent or more of the U.S. RDA of any one vitamin or mineral, then the food is classified as a dietary supplement and must bear this fact on the label. An example of such a food is "Total" breakfast cereal. If vitamins and/or

```
                    NUTRITION INFORMATION
                        (PER SERVING)
                    SERVING SIZE = 8 OZ.
                    SERVINGS PER CONTAINER = 1


Calories          560      Fat (Percent of
Protein           23 G       Calories 53%)        33 G
Carbohydrate      43 G       Polyunsat-
                               urated              2 G
                             Cholesterol*
                             (20 MG/100 G)        40 MG
                             Sodium (365 MG/
                               100 G)            830 MG


            PERCENTAGE OF U.S. RECOMMENDED DAILY
                  ALLOWANCES (U.S. RDA)


Protein            35      Riboflavin           15
Vitamin A          35      Niacin               25
Vitamin C                  Calcium               2
  (Ascorbic Acid)  10      Iron                 25
Thilamine (Vitamin
B₁)                15
```

*Information on fat and cholesterol content is provided for
individuals who, on the advice of a physician, are modifying
their total dietary intake of fat and cholesterol.

TABLE 5–3.   Nutritional Label. This label includes optional information on
cholesterol, fats, and sodium.

minerals are added to a food so that a single serving provides 150 percent or more of the U.S. RDA for any one vitamin or mineral, then the
food is classified as a drug and is subject to regulations for drugs.

The Food and Drug Administration's Division of Consumer Studies
conducted a national survey in 1975 to determine the consumer's use
of, and comprehension of, nutritional labeling (1). The population surveyed was representative of the United States adult who does at least
half the food shopping for the household. Sixty percent reported that
they refer to the labeling in making decisions on purchasing food. There
was a strong correlation between the amount of formal education and
the ability of a person to understand nutritional labeling. Of the people
surveyed, those with at least a high school education had a good understanding of nutritional labeling. Those who did not graduate from
high school did not understand nutritional labeling, and only one out
of three of this population had noticed nutritional labeling of food
products.

Nutritional Value of Food Eaten Away from Home

One concern of the consumer is the nutritional quality of food eaten
outside the home. Only 10 percent of all people in this country eat
lunch at home even once a week, except on weekends (3). The greatest

increase of eating outside the home is seen in the female population 25–34 years of age and in 3–5 year old children (6).

Fast-food establishments have increased in popularity in the past decade. When visiting a fast-food place, one has little choice but to buy a meal more than adequate in protein, several of the B vitamins, and iron. Fast-foods are not as high in fat as people think. Most meals are lower than 42 percent fat, the national average for the 1970's. The meals are likely to be low in calcium, vitamin A, and folacin. They are regrettably high in sodium. One can greatly vary caloric intake at a fast-food establishment. For example, a regular hamburger on bun and coffee provides 260 kcal while a high 1,085 kcal are provided by a quarter-pound cheeseburger on a bun, chocolate shake, and apple pie. If a fast food lunch has been consumed, at the next meal a good source of calcium and vitamin A is needed, such as a large raw salad and milk or a generous serving of green vegetables.

Additives to Improve Nutritional Value of Food

One of the most significant developments in food technology improves the nutritive value of refined, formulated, or processed foods. *Enrichment,* by definition, is the compensatory restoration to the original level of vitamins or minerals that routinely are lost during milling or refining. *Fortification* means the addition of nutrients that either do not occur naturally in a food or to a greater level than occurs naturally in the food. The nutrients are added to fortified food, which acts as a vehicle for the nutrients, in areas where widespread nutritional deficiencies occur and when natural routes of supplementation are not available.

The addition of iodine to salt, which began in 1924, was the first essential nutrient to be added to a staple food. The fortification of salt is optional. Fortification of margarine began in 1941 with the addition of 15,000 IU of vitamin A per pound. The enrichment of white flour, white bread, cornmeal, corn grits, and rice also began in 1941, and standards of identity for the enrichment of these products were adopted. Practically all evaporated milk canned in this country and all fresh milk is fortified with 400 IU of vitamin D. Nonfat dry milk for shipping abroad must be fortified with 5,000 IU of vitamin A and 100 IU of vitamin per 8 ounces of reconstituted fluid milk. The fortification of nonfat dry milk with vitamin D for domestic milk is not mandatory, but it is mandatory to add vitamin A. A large percentage of breakfast cereal is routinely enriched or fortified.

FOOD SELECTION FOR GOOD NUTRITION

To bridge the gap between quantitative expressions of nutrient allowances and meals planned to meet them, patterns or models for use in planning meals have been designed. In the late 1940's, the system of the "Basic Seven Food Groups" was used by people in public health and nutrition. The U.S. Department of Agriculture subsequently developed and published a food plan that was organized around "Four Basic Food Groups." Other guides include "Food for Fitness" and "Guide to Good Eating." Dr. Jean Mayer, professor of Nutrition at Harvard University, and Dr. Phillip L. White, secretary of the American Medical Association Council of Nutrition, would like to see a return to the use of the "Basic Seven Food Groups." They believe that the "Basic Seven" plans puts more emphasis on the consumption of fruits and vegetables. Table 5–4 lists the Basic Seven food groups, the number of servings recommended for each group, and the foods that belong to each group. The model shown is self-explanatory.

In general, one may encounter nutritional problems by eliminating a

TABLE 5–4. *The Basic Seven Food Groups*

Group	Number and Size of Daily Servings	Sources
1. Vegetables high in vitamin A	One serving ½ cup or more	Green, yellow, and leafy vegetables
2. Vegetables high in vitamin C	One serving ½ cup or more	Citrus fruits, tomatoes, raw cabbage, salad greens
3. Other fruits and vegetables	Two servings ½ cup or more	Noncitrus fruits, potatoes, and other vegetables not listed
4. Milk and milk products	Two servings 1 cup	
5. Meat and meat substitutes	Two servings 3 ounces 1 cup	Meat, poultry, fish, eggs, nuts, dried beans, peas, and textured vegetable protein
6. Bread and cereals	Four servings 1 slice ½ cup	Whole grain or enriched breads, cereals or paste
7. Fats	1 tablespoon	Butter, margaine, polyunsaturated oils

whole category of food. However, different members of the family have different needs depending on their sex and age. For example, a growing child needs a rich source of protein every day. Adults except for pregnant and lactating women do not need such large amounts.

The manner in which foods are combined into meals is a personal decision. Foods can be combined in any way that persons find pleasing. Some like sandwiches for breakfast and bacon and eggs for the evening meal; others want bacon and eggs for breakfast and sandwiches at noon. Perhaps our diets would improve if those who plan meals forgot traditional meal patterns. More persons might eat a good breakfast if it were other than cereal and/or toast. A grilled cheese sandwich, hamburgers, a bowl of bean soup, or even pizza might be more enticing as the first meal of the day. The availability of ready-to-eat and of heat-and-eat foods makes it easy for the meal manager to experiment and to offer different combinations within the meals of the day and on the different days of the week.

One does not have to memorize a food guide in order to provide nutritionally adequate diets. A key concept to remember is variety. By providing a variety of foods in our diet and not overconsuming food, good nutrition can generally be achieved. A variety in color and texture in a diet will mean that diet will include fruit, vegetables, grains and foods containing protein.

Nutrient Contribution of Major Food Groups

The most important contribution of meat to the human diet is protein. Practically all animal protein is of high biological value. In addition to protein, muscle meat contributes moderate amounts of thiamin, riboflavin, and iron, and generous quantities of niacin and phosphorus. The organ meats, particularly liver and kidney, furnish generous quantities of practically all the B-complex vitamins, iron, phosphorus, copper, and other trace minerals. Organ meats combine comparatively low cost with a highly desirable nutrient content. Unfortunately these meats are not very popular in the United States. With the exception of pork, which is higher in fat and thiamin, the nutritive value of most edible meats is similar. Also in the meat group are eggs and dried legumes. Egg protein is of the highest quality and is easily digested. Egg yolk is very rich in vitamin A, phosphorus, and iron. The yolk also contains liberal amounts of thiamin and vitamin D, whereas egg white is a good source of riboflavin. Since egg yolks are also a rich source of cholesterol, their consumption should be approached with moderation. Dry legumes such as beans, peas, and lentils contain incomplete protein, since they do not have all of the eight essential amino acids in the necessary quantity for humans. Legumes can become com-

TABLE 5–5. *Amino Acid Content of Plant Protein*

Plant Protein	Limiting Amino Acid	Abundant Amino Acid
Soybeans	Methionine	Tryptophan, Lysine
Wheat, rice, oats	Lysine	Methionine, Tryptophan
Legumes	Tryptophan, Methionine	Lysine
Peanuts	Lysine, Methionine, Isoleucine	Tryptophan
Sesame seeds and most nuts	Lysine, Isoleucine	Tryptophan
Corn	Tryptophan, Lysine	Methionine

plete when complemented with one another or supplemented with such high quality protein foods as cheese, milk, eggs, and meat. The limiting amino acid as well as the most abundant amino acid in some plant proteins is shown in Tabel 5–5. If one were planning a meal with no meat, milk, or eggs, it would be possible to get all of the essential amino acids by having a casserole with beans and sesame seeds; or legumes and rice; or soybeans, wheat, and sesame seeds.

Milk is distinguished by its high quality protein and its high content of calcium and phosphorus. It is also a good source of riboflavin and vitamin A. If vitamins A and D are added, skim milk is equivalent to whole milk, except that it contains fewer calories, which in many cases makes it highly desirable. Milk is a poor source of iron and vitamin C.

Vegetables vary considerably in their nutrient content. Because of the popularity of the white potato in the United States, the nutrient content of this food is of importance. The potato is high in carbohydrates and is, therefore, primarily an energy-yielding food. It contains fair amounts of vitamin C, generous amounts of potassium, and small quantities of thiamin and iron. Carrots are of value because of the large quantity of carotene that is converted to vitamin A in the body. Leafy vegetables are not important energy-yielding foods, but they provide an abundance of fiber which is an important component of a normal diet. Some vegetables are rich sources of provitamin A and are good sources of iron, calcium, folic acid, and riboflavin. The greener the leaf, the higher is the carotene content. Fresh vegetables are good sources of vitamin C.

Fruits contain more calories than vegetables. They are of value because of their vitamin, mineral, and fiber content. The citrus fruits have a high ascorbic acid content. Fruits are also good sources of potassium. Practically all dried fruits are rich in minerals and some are rich in vitamin A and riboflvin.

Cereal grains generally contain protein of low quality; however, when supplemented with simultaneously consumed protein of better quality they may aid in meeting one's total protein requirement. The vitamin and mineral constituents of grain are found mainly in the outer layers of the kernel or in the embryo. Most of this is lost in milling the grain, but phosphorus, the major mineral contribution of grains, remains. Enrichment of flour restores thiamin, riboflavin, niacin, and iron to the original level in the grain. Whole grains also provide an excellent source of fiber.

Fats and oils are primarily a source of energy and, in varying degrees, of essential fatty acids and fat soluble vitamins. In quantities normally consumed, sugar, honey, molasses, and most jams and jellies contribute calories to the diet and very few other nutrients. Alcoholic beverages contain ethyl alcohol, which yields seven calories per oxidized gram.

REFERENCES CITIED

1. Fusillo, A., "Testing Consumer's Food IQ," *FDA Consumer* 10:4 (1976).
2. "Highlights from the Ten-State Nutrition Survey," *Nutrition Today* 7:4 (1972).
3. Henderson, L. M., "Nutritional Problems Growing Out of New Patterns of Food Consumption," *American Journal of Public Health* 62:1194 (1972).
4. Institute of Food Technologists' Expert Panel on Food Safety and Nutrition, "Nutritional Labeling," *Food Technology* 28:7 (1974).
5. Marshall, William E., "Health Foods, Organic Foods, Natural Foods," *Food Technology* 28:2 (1979).
6. *Nutrient Levels in Food Used by Households in the United States, Spring 1977,* United States Department of Agriculture Science and Education Administration, (January 1981).
7. "News Notes: Washington," *Food Technology* 35:10 (1981).
8. *Recommended Dietary Allowances,* Ninth Edition, 1979, A Report of The Food and Nutrition Board, National Research Council, National Academy of Science, Washington, D.C. (1980).
9. Schwerin, H.S.; J. L. Stanton, A. M. Riley, and B. E. Brett, "How

Have the Quantity and Quality of the American Diet Changed During the Past Decade?" *Food Technology* 35:9 (1981).

SUGGESTED PROBLEMS

1. Prepare a three-day dietary for a college woman that is adequate in iron without the use of liver or iron supplements. Show values for calories and iron.
2. Plan a two-day dietary that is adequate in protein for a college woman who is a lacto-ovo vegetarian. Show values for calories and protein. Also indicate the limiting amino acids of plant protein sources.
3. Plan a two-day dietary that is adequate in protein for a college woman who is a strict vegetarian and does not consume milk and eggs. Show values for calories and protein. Also indicate the limiting amino acids for plant protein sources.
4. Compare the costs of ten items purchased in a health food store with similar items purchased in a grocery store. Read the labels and note differences in the products.
5. Using the "Basic Seven," plan nutritious meals for four days and include one meal in which you will have guests.
6. Collect information from nutritional labels on four kinds of fruit juice and record the prices of the products. Which is a better buy for vitamin C, for cost only? Are there any other nutrients that the juice supplies in generous amounts?
7. Compare the cost and nutritional label on regular bread and on diet bread. How do these products differ?
8. Compare the nutritional label and price of several breakfast cereals. What are some advantages and some undesirable qualities of each product?

SUGGESTED REFERENCES

1. Burton, Benjamin, *Human Nutrition,* 3rd ed. New York: McGraw-Hill Book Company (1976).
2. Labuza, Theodore P., *The Nutrition Crisis.* St. Paul: West Publishing Company, Inc., (1975).
3. Hamilton, E. M. and E. N. Whitney, *Nutrition Concepts and Controversies,* 2nd ed. St. Paul: West Publishing Company, Inc. (1982).
4. Whitney, E. N. and E. M. Hamilton, *Understanding Nutrition,* 2nd ed. St. Paul: West Publishing Company, Inc. (1981).

Chapter 6

Meal Management Goal 2: Meals to Match a Budget

Studies of food shopping behavior and of food consumption and food spending disclose facts that at the outset of any discussion of food budgets are both helpful and discouraging.

An attitude study (spring, 1976) of food shoppers disclosed that all but 11 percent of shoppers may be profiled into three groups (2). Eighteen percent are careful shoppers: they plan menus in advance; they make shopping lists; they take advantage of specials and sales; they compare prices; and they read labels. It may be presumed that they operate within the limits of food budgets. Thirty-two percent of food shoppers have food budgets: they use cost as a determining factor in making purchase decisions, and they follow practices that maximize the dollar and the use of time. They may be described as money/time conscious shoppers. Thirty-nine percent of food shoppers make decisions on the basis of satisfactions. For them, quality and the sensory appeal of food are more important than price. They like food shopping and food preparation and, it might be presumed, eating. It can be concluded from this study that at least one-half of meal managers are budget conscious. Furthermore, it provides some guides to budget control.

Two surveys of the late 1970's reveal information on how money is spent for food eaten at home. The United States Department of Agriculture Nationwide Food Consumption Survey (1977–78) disclosed that spending for food eaten at home per household member was approximately the same for income groups with pretax incomes of less than $20,000 per year. Spending per household member by the high income group ($20,000 and over per year) was 9 percent more than that for all other groups. However, spending for food eaten away from home increased with income; it was approximately 175 percent greater per

person in the highest income group than in the lowest. (4). A later
report (1979) disclosed that the poorest American ate food costing $622
per year while the richest American ate food costing $648 per year, a
difference of 4 percent in expenditure for food eaten at home. The
percentage of income utilized to purchase this food ranged from 25
percent for the lowest income group to 6.5 percent for the highest
income group; the average was 10.5 percent. About four percent of
pretax income was spent for food eaten away from home; however, it
ranged from 9.5 percent for the lowest income group to 3.25 percent
for the high income group. Average total food spending was 15 percent of pretax income; this ranged from 35 percent for the poor to 9.5
percent for the rich (1). Food stamps and other governmental food
assistance programs probably explain the lack of disparity in spending
for food eaten at home by different income groups.

Not only do households, on the average, spend similar sums for food
eaten at home; they also spend the at-home-food dollar similarly. According to the aforementioned United States Department of Agriculture study the at-home-food dollar, on the average, was spent as follows: 35 percent for meat, poultry, fish and shellfish, and eggs; 9 percent
for produce; 12 percent for cereals and baked goods; 13 percent for
dairy products; and 31 percent for all other foods. Some specifics on
spending are interesting. As income increased more dollars were spent
on beef, veal, and lamb; on fish and shellfish; on bakery products other
than bread, and on frozen fruits and vegetables, while less was spent
on canned vegetables, fresh potatoes, cereals, poultry, and eggs (5). According to a report by *Supermarket Business* (1980) of expenditures in
the supermarket, weekly average expenditures were as follows: 77 percent of dollars spent in the supermarket was for food, of which 32
percent was for dry groceries such as canned goods, beverages, mixes,
and so on; 29 percent was spent for meats, poultry, and fish; 13 percent, for produce; 10 percent, for dairy foods; 10 percent for cereals
and baked goods; and 6 percent for frozen foods. Twenty-three percent of the dollars spent in the supermarket was for general merchandise, paper goods, cleaning supplies, pet foods, etc. (6). From these
studies on spending for food eaten at home or carried out of the home,
guides to budget management can be derived. They are discussed subsequently.

THE FOOD BUDGET

It has already been established that good nutrition is a priority goal
of meal management. (See Chapter 5.) Fortunately, good nutrition can
be purchased within wide limits in spending, from thrift to luxury; that
is, from bean soup to caviar. The meal manager's task is to purchase

food needs with the money at hand. It was noted earlier that there are budget-conscious meal managers; there are also those who are not. This chapter addresses the former.

Budgets are established by circumstances: family composition, the general health and physical activity of family members, family income, region of residence, family food preferences, whether or not the meal manager is a wage earner, the skills and abilities of the meal manager, and, perhaps, family goals and values.

It costs more to feed some persons because their nutrient needs— that is, their food needs—are greater. For example, it costs more to feed a man than a woman of the same age unless the woman is preg-nant or lactating, in which case it costs more to feed her than him; it costs more to feed boys than girls after the age of twelve; it costs more to feed a six year old than a three year old. Family food needs are the composite of the food needs of family members. Families that are sim-ilarly composed have the same food needs, although they may spend differently for food. Dissimilar families have different total food needs and thus, different required expenditures for food (see Figure 6–1). Obviously, family size and family composition establish foods needs quantitatively. Qualitative differences in food needs also affect spend-ing for food. Families in which someone is allergic to common foods, is diabetic, or has other dietary problems require larger expenditures for food than similar families without dietary problems. Allergies to such common foods as milk, wheat, corn, or eggs necessitate the pur-chase of specially processed foods that are expensive to buy. Special foods for diabetics and for those on weight-reduction diets can also be expensive to buy. Significant determinants of the budget for food are the quantity and the kinds of food it must buy.

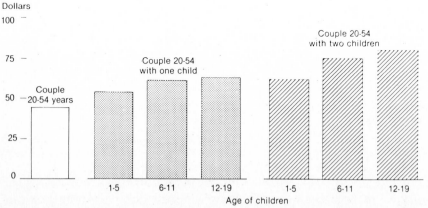

FIGURE 6–1.   Family's weekly food cost. (*USDA Low-cost Food Plan,* June 1982. *All meals at home or taken from home.*)

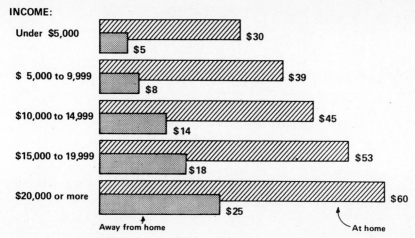

INCOME:

Under $5,000 — $30 / $5

$ 5,000 to 9,999 — $39 / $8

$10,000 to 14,999 — $45 / $14

$15,000 to 19,999 — $53 / $18

$20,000 or more — $60 / $25

Away from home — At home

FIGURE 6–2.   Income versus money spent for food at home and away—dollars per household per week. (*USDA Nationwide Food Consumption Survey,* 48 states, Spring 1977.)

Theoretically, all similar families, because they have the same needs, would spend similarly for food. Actually this does not happen. The bag of groceries that one meal manager takes home from the supermarket may contain among other items porterhouse steak and out-of-season fresh corn-on-the-cob; that of another may contain hamburger and carrots. Nutrient-wise, the two bags might be very similar; cost-wise, however, they may be quite different. It is what is purchased to fulfill food (nutrient) needs that a food budget dictates. Family income is a powerful determinant of how much the budget can be. In general, as income rises families spend more total dollars and more per capita for food, they also spend more for meals eaten away from home (see Figure 6–2). It is because the marketplace offers much variety—as noted in Chapters 10 through 16—that good nutrition can be purchased within extremes in cost. Very important to budget control is the meal manager's ability to match food choices to the money resource. This ability encompasses such skills as deciding how, where and when to shop, but especially in deciding whether a particular food product is right for the budget. We will say more about this later.

There is some difference in the cost of a market basket of foods purchased in different regions of the United States and in urban versus non-metropolitan areas (see Figures 6–3 and 6–4).

Available time and human energy resources can affect the size of the food budget. The less time and human energy are available for food shopping and meal preparation, the more dollars are used for convenience foods and for meals eaten away from home.

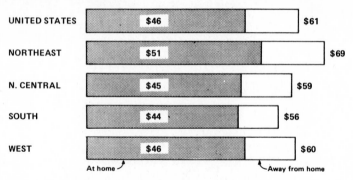

FIGURE 6–3.   Regions of the U.S. versus money spent for food at home and away—dollars per household per week. (*USDA Nationwide Food Consumption Survey*, 48 states, Spring 1977.)

Lastly, very similar families have different goals for the future and quite different value systems that influence spending patterns. Goals for the ownership of a home, a small cruiser, a home computer, or for a tour of China may so dominate family spending plans that among other economies practiced is the one of limited spending for food. Although thrift for the sake of thrift is a rare value in the late twentieth century, thrift for a purpose is not uncommon. For personal or economic reasons, some families budget spending for food; others who enjoy good food and wines may spend for food without budget in mind.

In summary, the goal of good nutrition can be accomplished within wide extremes of cost because the bags of groceries that supply food needs may contain quite different food products. What the bags con-

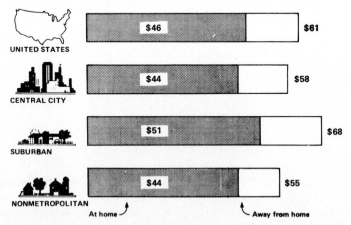

FIGURE 6–4.   Urbanization versus money spent for food at home and away—dollars per household per week. (*USDA Nationwide Food Consumption Survey*, 48 states, Spring 1977.)

tain is different even for similar families because forces interact to establish a budget for food and hence the choices of food products purchased.

How to Match Food Choices to a Budget for Food

It was noted earlier that regardless of income, households—on the average—tend to spend the at-home-food dollar similarly, although they may spend quite different total sums for food. Spending is approximately as follows: 33 percent for meat, poultry, and fish and shellfish; 15 percent for fruits and vegetables; 12 percent for cereals and baked goods; 15 percent for dairy foods including eggs; and 25 percent for dry groceries including beverages, mixes, canned foods, soups, and so on but not including paper goods and general merchandise.

Probably, the choices of what meats and what fruits and vegetables to buy are the most critical and at the same time the easiest to make. Here is how to do it.

1. Once a budget has been established, determine the daily food allowance; i.e., if the budget is on a monthly basis, divide by 30, if on a weekly basis, by seven. For example, a budget of $250 per month for a family of four—parents and two small children—allows $8.10 per day for food at home.

2. Next, determine the per-person daily allowance, that is, divide the daily allowance by the number of persons in the family. For the example set up in (1.), the per person allowance would be $2.10.

3. Next, divide the per-person allowance by three to establish how much can be spent for meat, poultry, or fish. This figure matched to the per-serving costs of meats, poultry and fish points to what matches the budget. For example, a per-person allowance of $2.10 per day permits $.70 to be used for meats. If only one serving is purchased per day, then the guide to choice making is that $.70. If lunches are carried out of the home and sometimes include luncheon meat sandwiches and if occasionally meat is served at breakfast, then that must be taken into account. Probably the simplest way to handle this is to subtract from $.70 an estimate of the cost of those items. Then, the remainder provides the guide to choice making. If chuck steak for barbecuing costs $1.98 per pound and serves out at two to three portions per pound, per-serving cost is possibly $1.00, certainly not less than $.66. Were the chuck steak served out at two portions to the pound, the per-portion cost would definitely exceed the established guide to choice making. If, on the other hand, it is served out at three servings to the pound, which it might be in the family with very small children, then that cut is a suitable choice and matches the guide well.

TABLE 6–1.   *Meat Selections to Match a Budget*

Suggested Purchases	Cost per [1] Pound	Portions per Pound	Estimated Cost per Portion
Chuck steak	$1.98	2–3	$1.00[2]
Ham shank[3]	1.18	2–3	1.18[4]
Beef liver	1.29	4	.42
Chicken, whole	.69	¾	.51
Pork chops	2.49	3	.83
Cod fillet	2.39	4	.60
Estimated cost for seven meals			$4.54

[1] June, 1982 prices.
[2] Generous serving.
[3] Served twice.
[4] Cost of two servings.

Common sense dictates that a policy for overspending the daily meat allowance be established. It can be about like this: for any choice that costs more per portion than the guide permits, make one or two choices that cost less. See Table 6–1, which suggests how choices might be made when the per-portion guide is the $.70 established in (3.) above. Estimated total spending per person for seven days would be about $4.90 (7 × $.70). The total of $4.54 leaves something for the purchase of bacon and/or luncheon meats if any lunches are carried out of the home. Obviously, the meal manager must be able to estimate the number of portions that meat cuts provide. See Chapter 10, page 170 and Appendix B for this information.

A guide for the purchase of fruits and vegetables can be established in much the same manner as was the guide for the purchase of meat. If—on the average—15 percent of the at-home-food dollar is spent for their purchase, then 15 cents of each dollar of the food budget buys whatever is to be purchased. The availability of the school lunch for children and the purchase of a noon meal away from home by many persons means that the number of portions that this 15 percent must buy differs for different families. Each meal manager accordingly estimates the number of fruit and vegetable portions the budget is to buy; perhaps, three per person, one for breakfast and at least two including potatoes for the main meal of the day.

Here is how the meal manager can establish a guide for her selection of fruits and vegetables. Determine how much 15 percent of the daily food allowance is. In the example 1. cited on page 69, the total daily food allowance was $8.10. Fifteen percent of $8.10 is $1.22. This sum, in this hypothetical situation, is to buy whatever number of portions of fruits and vegetables has been estimated. If that number is three per person and there are four persons in the family, then it is to buy twelve portions, the average cost of which would be $.10. However, the breakfast juice and the dinner potato serving do not each cost the average; in fact, $.15 can buy both when they are carefully selected, even at prices of the 1980's. Conservatively, one-half of the $.30 for the purchase of three portions per person, or $.15, would be a suggested guide to purchase of the remaining fruit or vegetable to be bought. The level of prices of the 1980's would not permit indiscriminate choice but such fresh produce as carrots, cabbage, bananas, and apples as well as some canned and frozen vegetables and some canned fruits would match the guide for selection. Again, the meal manager profits from knowing the portion yield of purchases. See Chapter 14, page 308 and Appendix B.

When the frozen prepared dinner is purchased, it is necessary to recognize that the cost of the dinner is for meat, for vegetables, and for the built-in service. When the daily meat and vegetable allowances are known, it is possible to quickly estimate the cost of the built-in service. For example, if the meat and vegetable allowance adds up to $.90, then a precooked meat loaf dinner costing $.99 has a modest cost of convenience but a serving of Chicken Kiev costing $1.69 far exceeds allowances.

There are no specific guides to spending for the other food groups. It is quite easy to spend much or little for breakfast cereals and baked goods (see Tables 15–2 and 15–3); also for products that are considered dry groceries by the trade: sauces, mixes, salad dressings, pickles, beverages, snack foods, soft drinks, and cheeses. Perhaps, each meal manager learns by trial and error what the budget for food can and cannot purchase.

Professionals of the Human Nutrition Center, United States Department of Agriculture recognize four levels of spending for food: thrifty, low-cost, moderate-cost, and liberal-cost. The different spending levels are the costs of four different plans of selecting food to meet nutritive needs. The plans differ in the quantities of food recommended for purchase in each food class but also in the choices that can be made within each food class. The cost of the thrifty plan is used in determining the amount of food stamps to be issued to households. The costs of the low-cost and the moderate-cost plans are used by the Bureau of Labor Statistics of the Department of Labor as the food component in their hypothetical annual budgets for a hypothetical urban family. The costs of the plans differ as follows: the low-cost plan costs about one third more than the thrifty plan; the moderate-cost plan, 25 percent more than the low-cost plan; and the liberal-cost plan, 20 percent more than the moderate-cost plan and fifty percent more than the low-cost plan. In general man's capacity for food consumption is limited. Spending more for food means buying different foods: tender versus less tender cuts of meat, lobster instead of cod, out-of-season fruits and vegetables instead of canned or frozen counterparts, premium priced breads and pastries instead of store brands, imported natural cheeses instead of domestic processed cheese products, ready-made dishes instead of basic ingredients, and so on ad infinitum. Spending more for food means buying more meat, more fruits and/or vegetables, more ready-made dishes, and more snack foods; it also means buying less bread and cereals. Menus for a week of three meals daily reflective of each level of spending follow. See pages 104–107.

Food budgets proposed in relation to income and family size, as suggested by professionals of the Human Nutrition Center, United States Department of Agriculture, appear in Table 6–2.

Guides to Maximizing the Food Dollar, that is, Abiding by a Budget

1. Take time to plan your shopping—what you will purchase and where you will shop. It can save time in the long run. Tentatively-made meal plans assist in the preparation of the shopping list.

2. Shop as infrequently as storage facilities permit and, of course, as the money resource permits.

3. Know the market place. Look for a warehouse store, a direct marketing outlet for fresh produce, and a supermarket that stocks generic products. Obviously, you would not shop at all of these on one shopping trip. Consumers find that once per month suffices for shopping at a warehouse store.

4. Know your guides to choice making and know how meats, fruits, and fresh vegetables serve out in portions. Know the yield in portions of canned and frozen products (see Appendix B).

5. Know the approximate, current cost of the items that you buy frequently in order to be able to recognize specials. Buy specials when they are products that you buy routinely. Use in-store coupons when they are for products that you use.

6. Buy generic products that fit your needs. Remember that canned fruits and vegetables must be labeled substandard in quality when they are less than the U.S. Grade C in quality.

7. Read labels—it is impossible to overemphasize this guide. The ingenuity of Madison Avenue and the competitive practices of management are mind-boggling.

8. Make price comparisons: the cost per unit of products available in packages of assorted sizes, the cost of national versus store brands

TABLE 6–2. *The Food Plan for the Family*

Income (before taxes)	1-Person Family	2-Person Family	3-Person Family	4-Person Family	5-Person Family	6-Person Family
$2,500–$5,000	T¹ or LC	T¹ or LC	T¹	T¹	T¹	T¹
$5,000–$10,000	MC	LC	T¹ or LC	T¹	T¹	T¹
$10,000–$15,000	L	MC	LC or MC	LC	T¹ or LC	T¹
$15,000–$20,000	L	MC	LC or MC	LC or MC	LC	T or LC
$20,000–$30,000	L	MC or L	MC or L	LC or MC	LC or MC	LC
$30,000–$40,000	L	L	L	MC or L	MC	LC or MC
$40,000 or more	L	L	L	MC or L	MC or L	MC

Source: Betty Peterkin, "Family Food Budgeting for Good Meals and Good Nutrition," Human Nutrition Information Service, United States Department of Agriculture. 1981. (5)

T Thrifty   LC Low Cost   MC Moderate Cost   L Liberal

¹Many families of this size and income are eligible for assistance through the Food Stamp Program.

	Breakfast	*Lunch or Supper*	*Dinner*
Saturday	Cereal with Sliced Bananas Coffee Cake Coffee[1] Milk[2]	Grilled Cheese Sandwiches Celery Sticks Applesauce[3] Cookies[6]	Spaghetti and Meat Casserole Cabbage Salad Rolls Cake
Sunday	Juice[5] French Toast Syrup	Peanut Butter Sandwiches Celery Sticks Cake	Liver and Bacon Mashed Potatoes Creamed Onions Bread Ice Milk Cookies[6]
Monday	Cereal Milk Toast Peanut Butter	Tomato Soup[3] Egg Sandwiches Cookies[6]	Smoked Pork Loaf[3] Scalloped Potatoes Spinach[3] Cole Slaw Bread Cake with Ice Milk
Tuesday	Juice[5] Cereal Milk Sweet Rolls	Potato Soup Bologna Sandwiches Carrot Sticks	Macaroni and Cheese Hash Brown Potatoes Cole Slaw Bread Pumpkin Pie
Wednesday	Juice[5] Cereal Milk Coffee Cake	Spaghetti with Meat and Tomato Sauce Celery Sticks Bread Plums[3]	Baked Beans[3] and Frankfurters Potatoes Carrots Cornbread Chocolate Pudding
Thursday	Juice[5] Cereal Milk Toasted Cornbread	Potato Soup Bologna Sandwiches Celery Sticks Cookies[6]	Meatballs Potatoes Corn[3] Bread Fruit Cup Cookies[6]
Friday	Tomato Juice[3] Cereal Milk Toast Jam	Cheese Rabbit on Toast Fried Potatoes Cookies[6]	Tuna-Noodle Casserole Peas[4] Celery Sticks Hot Biscuits Baked Custard

[1] Serve instant coffee at two meals daily.   [2] Serve milk to children at all meals; to adults at two meals daily.   [3] Canned.   [4] Frozen.   [5] Orange or grapefruit juice from frozen concentrate.   [6] Ready-made.

Menus for One Week of Low-Cost Meals [1]

	Breakfast	Lunch or Supper	Dinner
Saturday	Orange Juice [3] French Toast Syrup	Tuna Salad Sandwiches Lemon Pudding [4] Cookies [5]	Hamburgers on Buns French Fries [3] Mixed Relishes Bananas
Sunday	Tomato Juice [2] Bacon Eggs Toast	Grilled Cheese Sandwiches Peaches [2] Cookies [5]	Pot Roast of Beef Potatoes Onions Carrots Bread Ice Cream
Monday	Orange Juice Cereal Milk Toast Peanut Butter	Chili [2] Crackers Apples	Cold Roast Beef Hashed Brown Potatoes Green Beans [2] Bread Cake [4]
Tuesday	Orange Juice Cereal Milk Toast Peanut Butter	Creamed Eggs on Toast Celery Sticks Cookies [5]	Baked Chicken Mashed Potatoes Peas [3] Hot Biscuits Cake à la Mode
Wednesday	Orange Juice Cereal Milk Coffee Cake	Baked Beans [2] Bread Applesauce [2]	Roast Beef Hash Beets [2] Cole Slaw Bread Ice Cream
Thursday	Orange Juice Cereal Milk Toast Peanut Butter	Corn Chowder Cheese Sandwiches Jello	Liver with Bacon Potatoes Spinach [3] Bread Apple Betty
Friday	Orange Juice Cereal Milk Sweet Rolls	Egg Sandwiches Tomato Juice Plums [2] Cookies [5]	Baked Fish Baked Potatoes Buttered Cabbage Hot Rolls [3] Fruit Cup [2] Cookies [5]

[1] Consider that milk is served at all meals to children, and to adults at two meals. Coffee or tea available to adults as desired.

[2] Canned.   [3] Frozen.   [4] Mix.   [5] Ready-made.

Menus for One Week of Moderate-Cost Meals [1]

	Breakfast	Lunch or Supper	Dinner
Saturday	Bacon Eggs Toast Jam	Grilled Cheese Sandwiches Celery Sticks Pickles Apples	Swiss Steak Mashed Potatoes Corn [2] Cole Slaw Jello Cookies
Sunday	Tomato Juice French Toast Syrup	Ham Sandwiches Pears [2] Cookies [5]	Baked Ham Scalloped Potatoes Peas [3] Lettuce Salad Cake [4]
Monday	Orange Juice [3] Cereal Milk Toast Peanut Butter	Chili [2] Crackers Apples	Cold Ham Slices Lima Beans [3] Carrots Bread Cake
Tuesday	Orange Juice Cereal Milk Toast Peanut Butter Jam	Soup [2] Ham Salad Sandwiches Bananas Cookies [5]	Pork Chops Mashed Potatoes Green Beans [2] Mixed Vegetable Salad Peaches [2]
Wednesday	Orange Juice Cereal Milk English Muffins [5]	Creamed Tuna on Toast Tomato Juice Cookies [5]	Hamburgers on Buns French Fries [3] Assorted Relishes Cake à la Mode
Thursday	Orange Juice Scrambled Eggs Toast Jam	Cheese-Bologna Sandwiches Celery Sticks Pickles Jello	Fried Chicken Mashed Potatoes Spinach [3] Cole Slaw Hot Biscuits Ice Cream
Friday	Orange Juice Cereal Milk Sweet Rolls [5]	Liver Sausage Sandwiches Pickles Mixed Fruits [2]	Baked Fish Baked Potatoes Stewed Tomatoes [2] Hot Rolls Pudding [4] Cookies [5]

[1] Consider that milk is served in all meals to children and to adults at two meals. Coffee or tea is served to adults as desired.   [2] Canned.   [3] Frozen.   [4] Mix.   [5] Ready-made.

	Breakfast	Lunch or Supper	Dinner
Saturday	Grapefruit Juice[3] Poached Eggs on Toast Coffee[1] Milk[1]	Hamburgers on Buns Assorted Relishes Apples Bananas	Grilled Sirloin Steak Baked Potatoes Carrots Lettuce Salad Hot Rolls[6] Cherry Pie[6]
Sunday	Grapefruit Halves Bacon French Toast Syrup	Assorted Cold Cuts Assorted Sliced Cheeses Buttered Bread Potato Chips Pickles Radishes Apricots[2] Brownies[5]	Baked Ham Sweet Potatoes[2] Broccoli[3] Fruit Salad Hot Rolls[6] Ice Cream Cookies[6]
Monday	Orange Juice[3] Boiled Eggs Buttered Toast	Spaghetti with Meatballs[3] Celery Sticks and Relishes Bread Pears[2]	Sliced Cold Ham Potatoes Au Gratin[4] Squash[3] Cucumbers in Sour Cream Bread Butter Angel Food Cake[6]
Tuesday	Orange Juice[3] Ready-to-Eat Cereal Milk Coffee Cake[6]	Spanish Rice[5] Peas[3] Buttered Toast Brownies	Baked Chicken Potatoes Green Beans[3] Mixed Green Salad Bread Butter Angel Food Cake[6] with Ice Cream
Wednesday	Orange Juice[3] Bacon Toast Jelly	Ham and Cheese Sandwiches Assorted Relishes Angel Food Cake	Grilled Liver Potatoes Mixed Vegetables[3] Tomato Salad Grapes Apples
Thursday	Grapefruit Halves Cereal Milk English Muffins[6]	Jiffy Joes[2] on Buns Assorted Relishes Assorted Fruits Cookies[6]	Braised Pork Chops Carrots Lima Beans[3] Apple-Celery Salad Eclairs[6]
Friday	Grape Juice[2] Cereal Milk Toast Jelly	Cream of Mushroom Soup[2] Egg Sandwiches Oranges	Broiled Haddock[3] with Cucumber Sauce French Fries[3] Buttered Spinach[3] Tomato and Lettuce Salad Hot Biscuits[6] Ice Cream Cookies[6]

[1] Milk available for children at all meals; for adults at two meals; coffee, as adults wish.
[2] Canned.   [3] Frozen.   [4] Instant.   [5] Mix.   [6] Ready-prepared.

and of generic versus private-label brands, the cost of different but similar products such as breakfast cereals, crackers, breads, and so on. Possibilities are endless.

9. Note the packaging of products. Packaging is expensive and may exceed the cost of the contents of the package. Compare the cost of individually wrapped cheese slices with the cost of the same product packaged without that convenience. Bagged coffee saves the cost of a can. Compare the cost of a product packed in a glass with one packaged in plastic.

10. Study refunding and food industry coupon offers. Generally, refunding requires multiple purchases; if it does not, weigh the cost of postage against the sum of the refund. Industry coupons are frequently offered to encourage the purchase of new products which you may not find suitable. Double coupon days provide bargains if you use the couponed product.

11. Some ready-made dishes are extremely expensive when the cost of the basic ingredients is tallied against total cost. Likewise, look at the ingredient labels of seasoning mixes; they too are expensive and the seasonings they provide are easily duplicated at a lesser cost.

12. As important as any guide is the suggestion that the more food is home-prepared, the more is the dollar maximized.

13. Control your garbage losses. The garbage study made in Tuscon, Arizona suggested that one fifth of purchased food is wasted: about 16 percent as edible food, that is, plate waste and unused leftovers and the remainder as waste in food preparation (3).

SUMMARY

The goal of meals to match a budget for food is not easy of accomplishment because it requires skill in decision making. The marketplace offers such abundance and such variety that the dollar can be stretched to buy food abundantly; on the other hand, the dollar can be spent so that it buys comparatively little food. See chapters 9 through 16 for food buying information.

REFERENCES CITED

1. Gallo, Anthony, E. *et al.*, "The Rich, the Poor and the Money They Spend for Food," *National Food Review*, Economics and Statistics Service, United States Department of Agriculture, Washington, D.C. (Summer 1980), p. 16.
2. Hacklander, Effie H., "Consumer Lifestyles and Shopping Behavior," *National Food Review*, Economics and Statistics Service, United

States Department of Agriculture, Washington, D.C. (January 1978), p. 28.

3. Harrison, Gail *et al.*, "Food Waste Behavior in An Urban Population," Journal of Nutrition Education 7:13, (1975).

4. "Money Value of Food Used by Households in the United States, Spring 1977," Nationwide Food Consumption Survey 1977–78, Preliminary Report No. 1, Science and Education Administration, United States Department of Agriculture, Washington, D.C. (August 1979).

5. Smallwood, David and James Blaylock, "Impact of Household Size and Income on Food Spending Patterns," *Technical Bulletin #1650,* Economics and Statistics Service, United States Department of Agriculture, Washington, D.C. (May 1981), pp. 5–11.

6. "Thirty-fourth Annual Consumer Expenditure Study," *Supermarket Business* 36:40 (September 1981).

Chapter 7

Meal Management Goal 3: Controlled Use of Time

Four general goals for meals have been established. Two have already been discussed: good nutrition and planned spending. Perhaps the goal controlling the use of time should have been discussed first because the uses of time and human energy take first place in the plans of many meal managers. When use of these resources is limited, meals become what they are and cost what they cost because of these restrictions.

Some studies made of the use of time by homemakers for household work and food-related activities are summarized in Table 7–1. As would be anticipated, full-time homemakers spend more total time on household tasks than do employed homemakers. But what would not be anticipated is that the science and technology of the past decades have not altered the workload of the homemaker. In fact, her workload has expanded, probably because she has less paid help and less assistance from children than earlier in the century. According to these studies, she is spending a third to almost half of her time on food-related activities. This is more time than she spends on any other household task.

A survey made in 1968 by Social Research, Inc. for *Better Homes and Gardens* (11) suggests a division of time use in food-related activities. Data were derived from a survey of one thousand homemakers and are presented as median hours spent. Data are recapitulated here.

Time Spent in Average Week	Median Hours
Shopping for food	1.7
Putting away purchases	.5
Baking	1.8

Cooking	9.0
Setting table	.9
Washing dishes and tidying up	7.1
Planning meals	.9
Total	21.9

Of the total of 21.9 hours, 17.9 hours were spent in food preparation and dishwashing and tidying up. These are the major time-costs of meal management.

Until well into the twentieth century, the affluent purchased time by hiring servants. Most modern, affluent homemakers are forced to seek

TABLE 7–1.   *Time Used by Urban Housewives for Household Work and Food-Related Activities* [1]

Studies	Full-Time Homemakers [2]		Employed Homemakers [2]	
	Hours per Week All House-hold Work	Hours per Week Food Activities	Hours per Week All House-hold Work	Hours per Week Food Activities
USDA, 1920 (4) [3]	47.1	13.3	—	—
USDA, 1944 (7)	47.1	14.1	—	—
Wiegand, 1952 (10)	51.8	18.2	28.7	13.3
Anderson, 1960 (1)	49.0	20.0	31.0	15.0
Bailey, 1962 (2)	—	25.2	—	19.53
Walker, 1969 (9)	56.0	16.1	37.1	11.2
Hall, 1970 (4)	54.0	19.6	42.0	16.8
Peskin, 1976 (6)	42.6	—	20.1	—

[1] It is possible that this includes only food preparation and dishwashing in some studies, but it also includes shopping and care of food in others.

[2] Classified as *full-time* if homemaker worked 0–14 hours per week for pay and as *employed* if she worked 15 hours or more per week for pay.

[3] No distinction made on employment status; probably full-time housewives.

other ways of acquiring time. Convenience foods, fast foods, and dining out are time-savers: they are also dollar-users. Because dollars are not always available, it is necessary to explore other ways of controlling the use of time. In the discussion that follows the meal manager's energy will not be singled out for attention. Except for the elderly and the unwell, the resource of energy is a less worrisome problem than is time. We have the habit of speaking of them as one and are likely to conclude that time-saving means energy-saving and, conversely, that time-consuming tasks are energy-consuming.

The amount of time the meal responsibility requires is established by such factors as family size; standards for meals; food preferences; the efficiency of the kitchen and its equipment; the knowledge, skills, and abilities of the meal manager; and her dollar budget for food. The control of time use depends on knowledge of the diverse ways in which time is spent on meals.

HOW TIME AND ENERGY ARE USED IN MEAL MANAGEMENT

Following is a list of the ways we use time in meal management. Not all meal managers use time in all of these ways, nor does a given meal manager use time in all of these ways every week.

1. Planning menus for meals; this may include time spent looking for ideas in books and magazines. Planning may precede or follow shopping or both. It may also occur during shopping.
2. Planning shopping; this may include time spent in looking at store ads for information, for specials, for coupons, or for ideas.
3. Shopping.
4. Care and storage of food.
5. Meal preparation, that is, actual cooking and baking; may include time spent in looking for recipes.
6. Setting the table; however, this is usually done during the period of food preparation.
7. Waiting on the table.
8. Clean-up after meals.
9. Care of the kitchen and its furnishing.
10. Care of the dining area and its furnishings.

It is an impressive listing of activities and provides opportunities for inefficiencies in the use of time. It also provides opportunities for controlling time use because minutes saved from a few activities each day will add up to hours in due time.

The meal manager's problem in setting limits to the use of time for meals is complex. The best approach to the problem is to discover how much time is being used and how that time is put to use. One may discover that too much time is being spent in shopping, or too much time is spent in decision making about menus, or that too much time is spent in cooking. When excessive uses of time are recognized, it is possible to seek alternatives that save time. We discuss the former first and then discuss ways of maximizing time use.

ALTERNATIVES TO THE USE OF TIME

Alternatives to the use of time include money; knowledge, skills, and abilities; and lastly, time itself. That is, all of the meal manager's resources are alternatives to the use of time; the extent to which she can use them depends on her supply.

Money

Money buys time easily and in many ways. Unfortunately, the supply of money is often too limited for many persons to rely heavily on it as a time-saver. Here are some ways to buy time.

First, and most obvious, is the purchase of ready-made foods and dishes, such as carry-out fried chicken, ready-baked pastries, ready-to-heat dinners and breakfasts, mixes, easy-use ingredients for cooking (such as gravy mixes and instants). According to a *Better Homes and Gardens* survey, an average of 58 percent of the respondents to a questionaire said that the time-saving characteristic of convenience foods was the most important; only 24 percent said that the work-saving factor was the most important. Sixty-five percent of the working housewives in contrast to 55 percent of the nonworking housewives said time-saving was most important (3). Time-saving products come and go on the market. Those that we have found suitable stay; we spend dollars for them and buy the time we would otherwise spend in cooking and baking. All meal managers cannot use convenience foods extensively; either they do not have the dollars or there is opposition to their use in the home. The money cost of convenience and the time-saving value of convenience will be discussed (see pages 162–163). When the supplies of money and time are limited, it becomes imperative that the convenience forms bought provide maximum convenience, that is, time saved, for the dollars spent.

Second, money can buy time in the kitchen by making it a more efficient place in which to work. An expensive investment might involve the total remodeling and updating of the kitchen. However, many small investments can improve the efficiency of a kitchen. New and/or better appliances, such as a dishwasher, a garbage disposal, an electric mixer, and a pressure cooker, can save time. Not all appliances are equally valuable to all persons because each cooks and works differently in kitchens that may appear quite similar. Certainly, no appliance or gadget should be purchased until the would-be purchaser has studied it to discover what it can do for her. New and/or better cookware, such as pots and pans with tight-fitting lids and/or no-stick linings, and those that are matched to the size of range units, may save time. Good tools for preparing food, like good measuring equipment, cutting knives that hold a sharp edge, a cutting board, kitchen scissors, tongs, and effective tools for stirring food, save time. Paper goods, aluminum foil, plastic film in rolls, film bags, throwaway cookware, and special cleansers and polishes all save time. Unquestionably, all throwaway items should be conservatively used in the interest of ecology.

The improvement of storage facilities for appliances, cookware, kitchen gagets and tools, and food can make work in the kitchen easier and save time. Portable storage cabinets, portable storage shelves, on-the-door storage units, and a pegboard that permits within-arm's-reach storage of frequently used equipment are some suggestions in this category. Easy-care appointments for the dining table, such as no-iron cloths and mats, paper napkins, stainless steel flatware that requires little care, and plastic or glass-ceramic dinnerware and plastic beverageware that can be quickly handled without danger of breakage, are all ways of spending dollars and buying time. Lastly, money buys time when it hires help to come in and prepare and serve meals and clean up after them; and to clean the kitchen and the dining area. There are many ways that dollars buy and save time. The meal manager uses dollars to help her control her uses of time and energy; how extensively they can be used depends on her supply. When she decides to limit the use of dollars for meals, she cannot at the same time decide to limit the use of time. She must spend time to compensate for limited use of dollars.

Knowledge, Skills, and Abilities

The knowledge, skills, and abilities that the meal manager brings to the meal responsibility are among her most valuable resources for controlling the use of time. Among her assets are her knowledge of when to shop, where to shop, how to shop, how to choose from among the 10,000 or more items on the shelves of the supermarket, how much items cost, how to cook, what cooks quickly and what requires long cooking, how to organize the kitchen for efficient work or step-saving, how to schedule the preparation of meals, how to plan meals that satisfy, and so on. Much is gained through experience; much can be acquired through effort: the use of books, magazines, radio and television, and the help of friends, relatives, and neighbors. Knowledge, skills, and abilities are alternatives for time and also for money.

Time

Lastly, time can be invested to save time or control the use of time. A constructive use of time is to analyze one's own use of time; such a study points to leaks in time use and suggests ways of saving time. The use of time in planning ahead is rewarding. Time spent in organizing the kitchen into an efficient place in which to work is well-invested time. A kitchen may have to be arranged and rearranged several times before the most effective plan of arrangement is achieved. The maximum use of time in the kitchen to produce as much food as possible is desirable. Prepare a roast large enough for two or more meals; make up juice for tomorrow's breakfast, sandwich fillings for tomorrow's packed lunches, salad or dessert for tomorrow's dinner while preparing and cleaning up after dinner today. Make two pies and freeze one; make enough of a favorite casserole for two meals and freeze half. There is much that can be done here. Time in the kitchen is both busy time and watching time; often the latter is wasted. Use it for food production. Lastly, time spent in menu making per se can earn the meal manager time. It permits efficient shopping, the strategic placing of thirty-minute meals, and the investment of time in cooking when it is available.

Some Deterrents to Time-Saving.   Not every meal manager can reduce the use of time for meals and not all would wish to. Malloch (5) in a study of the most- and least-liked household tasks found that cooking was a most-liked task. Ronald *et al.* (7) found that 43 percent of the housewives interviewed rated cooking as their most-liked household task. Many persons like to cook; for them cooking and serving meals is what gardening or flower arrangement may be to others. Possibly the first deterrent to saving time is simply the lack of a desire to do so. Do-it-yourself cooking requires time and those who want it that way cannot save as much time as others can. Family food preferences may also be a deterrent to time-saving. Those who were born after World War II have adapted to instants and ready-mades. Those who are older remember homemade dishes and are often resistant to change.

The lack of knowledge and skills precludes time-saving by beginners; however, conscious effort to acquire knowledge and skills can result in ever-diminishing investments of time in meal management. Lastly, the most significant deterrent to reduction in the use of time is lack of money. Much can be accomplished to control the use of time without it, but having money to purchase some convenience foods and improvements in the kitchen is a boon.

TIMING MEAL PREPARATION

Meal preparation is doing many small tasks sequentially and simultaneously to the end that arrangements for dining will have been completed and all dishes of a meal will be at or near the peak of perfection and ready to serve at the desired moment in time. This is not an easy accomplishment. The question is what comes first, second, and last.

To time the preparation of meals means to order tasks systematically and to assign a time for doing each task. This ordering is decision making and precedes action. Experienced meal managers do the ordering of tasks as they proceed with meal preparation; their knowledge and skills permit it, because they have established work habits. The beginner in meal management may acquire the knowledge and skills by trial-and-error learning; however, she will acquire both more quickly by learning how to anticipate and schedule the tasks that are essential for the preparation of a given meal; that is, learn how to order and time the production of a meal.

There are at least four reasons for developing skill in timing meal preparation. The first is to have all tasks completed at the desired and designated hour. For example, the potatoes mashed at the moment the steak is done, or the table set and the salad ready so that last-minute attention can be directed to the mashing of potatoes, the broiling of steak, and the preparing of a vegetable for serving. A second reason is to have the different dishes of a meal of excellent eating quality. Some foods lose quality when held; they dry out, harden, or toughen. For many dishes there is a peak of perfection; we try for that moment. The third reason assumes that, in the long run, the total time spent in the preparation of a meal is less when tasks are carried out in a directed order than when they are done in a hit-and-miss fashion. The last reason assumes that the preparation of meals is less frustrating when one proceeds with the knowledge that all tasks have been anticipated and planned for. It is nerve-racking to discover that one forgot to start cooking the peas, to make the salad, or even to set the table.

The Characteristics of Time Schedules

First, the schedule that results from ordering tasks differs with menus. Some begin with cooking; others begin with setting the table. Some, such as that for the 30-minute dinner presented later in this chapter, concentrate the cooking in the 20 minutes just before the food goes to table. Other menus have long-cooking items; the meal manager can leave the kitchen for some time after they begin to cook, as when using the second menu presented in this Chapter. These latter menus result in broken schedules; they start, stop, and start again. In between these extremes is the menu that includes fried chicken or braised porkchops, some item that comes first in the schedule of tasks and all other tasks can be accomplished within the time allocated for the cooking of that item. What we are really saying is that there is no one schedule that works for all meals; schedules are tailored to menus. This fact makes it possible for the meal manager to tailor her menus to her established limits for the use of time.

Second, the schedules of different persons for identical menus will differ to some extent; they will reflect differences in skill in the kitchen, the efficiency and organization of kitchens, and the size of the families for which meals are being prepared. Further, schedules reflect the personality of the cook, her idiosyncrasies and habits. Third, the time schedules of different persons planning the same meal for the same number of persons will have some constants: the specific hours when different foods are put to cook on the range or in the oven; and certain tasks such as setting the table, making the salad, and placing the dinner plates to warm. Last, a schedule should be specific and detailed enough so that, as with a bus schedule, one knows where one is at a given moment. To carry the analogy further, a followed schedule should bring one to the defined destination.

Scheduling Meal Preparation

Essentials for making a schedule for meal preparation are

1. Either a cookbook or a recipe or knowledge of the time required for the cooking of the different menu items.
2. Some ability to estimate the time required to accomplish the different tasks required in preparing menu items for cooking and serving and in completing preparations for dining.
3. A pad and pencil for step-wise problem solving.
4. A clock for careful timing.

Steps in Preparing a Schedule

1. List the items of menus one under the other on the left side of a sheet of tablet paper. Add table setting. Itemize the tasks of table setting if they are not yet habit. For example, you might include under this task: lay flatware and napkins, place filled tumblers, place bread and butter, and the like.

2. Record in four vertical columns the estimated time in hours and minutes that each item will require (a) for preparation for cooking, (b) for actual cooking, (c) for preparation or serving, and (d) the totals of these estimates. Estimate realistically, especially for small tasks, such as the time you will require to make a salad, trim fresh green beans, or peel potatoes. See Table 7–2.

3. Arrange all items in decreasing order of total time required as in Table 7–3. This listing gives you two kinds of information: first, some idea of the total meal-preparation time and, second, the order in which different dishes of the menu should be prepared. Very often a meal may be prepared and the table set within the time assigned to the dish requiring the longest preparation and cooking time. Frequently, as when a stew or Swiss steak is to be prepared, time in the kitchen is much less than the cooking time of the dish requiring the longest preparation and cooking time. Again, when cooking time is short for all dishes, as it would be if steak were to be broiled and frozen vegetables used, the

time spent in the kitchen will be longer than the longest required cooking period.

4. The last and final step is the ordering of the tasks. Begin with the established hour for dining and clock cooking times backward from this; for example, if dining will be at 7:00 and one hour is required for frying chicken, put the chicken to cook at 5:50. This one hour and ten minutes allows one hour for cooking and about ten minutes for serving up the chicken and making gravy. Calculating in this fashion, establish the time to begin to cook and to remove from the range or oven all the other items that are to be cooked. Remember that food is best when it is just done and when it is served at the appropriate temperature.

Now decide when you must enter the kitchen. Next work in and around the already established tasks, the various other tasks you must accomplish. See Table 7–4.

To illustrate, we go through the four described steps for the following menu.

A Thirty-Minute Dinner

Broiled Sirloin Steak or Hamburger Patties[1]
Mashed Potatoes[2]   Buttered Peas[3]
Tossed Mixed Greens
Bread and Butter
Milk
Ice Cream   Cookies[4]
Coffee[5]

---

[1] Choice would depend on budget for food.
[2] Use potato flakes.
[3] Frozen product.
[4] Purchased ready-made.
[5] Instant.

As the name of the menu implies, the meal is quick and easy to prepare. It is the kind of meal a young homemaker who works outside the home might serve. Table 7–2 shows steps 1 and 2. The items of the menu are listed, and estimates of the time required for cooking the meat, the potatoes, and the vegetable, and for other tasks, are given. The estimates are based on the assumption that the meal manager is preparing the meal for two persons and that the prepared foods are served onto two dinner plates.

In Table 7–3, the menu items and the meal tasks are listed in descending order of the total time estimated. It is the kind of menu that

TABLE 7–2.   *Steps 1 and 2 in Time Meal Preparation*

Menu Items	Prepare for Cooking	Time in Minutes to Allow for Cooking	Prepare for Serving	Total Time in Minutes
Broiled sirloin steak or hamburger patties	5	15 [1]	5 [2]	25
Mashed potatoes	5	5	[2]	10
Peas	5	10	[2]	15
Tossed mixed greens	—	—	5 [3]	5
Bread and butter	—	—	[4]	—
Milk	—	—	[4]	—
Ice cream	—	—	[5]	—
Cookies	—	—	[4]	—
Coffee	—	5	[5]	5
Table setting	—	—	10	10

[1] thickness of one inch.
[2] Includes time for serving up potatoes and peas also.
[3] Assumes greens and dressing are ready for use.
[4] Included in table setting.
[5] Done between courses of meal; coffee is an instant product.

TABLE 7–3.   *Step 3 in Timing Meal Preparation—Tasks Listed in Descending Order of Total Time Required*

Tasks	Total Times In Minutes
Meat	25
Peas	15
Potatoes	10
Table setting	10
Tossed mixed greens	5

telescopes cooking into a short period of time. Further, it prepares foods that must go from range to table quickly for good eating. It is the kind of meal for which one does almost all the tasks but the cooking first, then cooks the food. The total time is so short that the salad, along with the water and milk can go to the table as soon as it is prepared, although one might wish to chill the salad until the last minute as the completed schedule suggests.

6:10 Place steak or patties under broiler unit and set water to heat for cooking peas and preparing potatoes.

6:15 Put peas to cook.

6:20 Or earlier, turn steak or patties. Prepare potatoes and leave on warm unit.

6:30 Approximately, serve meal, potatoes, and peas onto two warm dinner plates.

To prepare the final schedule, the time of dining has been set at 6:30. And although the dinner is called 30-minute we are allowing the meal manager 45 minutes in the kitchen. We can assume her kitchen is small; she does not take many steps between sink and range, refrigerator and sink, and range and refrigerator. We have worked out the schedule for the food preparation tasks; it is helpful to do this first, then schedule other tasks around these. Table 7–4 shows the entire plan of work—one that permits the meal manager to move leisurely.

It is best to limit timings in a schedule to critical moments in food preparation; too many timings are confusing. It would be dishonest not to admit that the best of plans can go awry. A dish may cook in less than the anticipated time; then either one holds the dish or modifies the rest of the schedule. Or a dish may not be done in the anticipated time, in which case one can hold all else and wait.

TABLE 7–4.   *The Time Schedule for Preparing the Meal*

5:45 Line small broiler pan with aluminum foil. Place steak or patties on it. Measure out peas and put into small saucepan. Prepare salad, dress, toss, serve onto plates, chill. Measure out potato flakes; set by range. Place two dinner plates on range where they will become warm and will be available at serving time. Get out bowls and underliner plates for ice cream and set on counter near refrigerator. Put cookies on plates. Place cups and saucers on counter near range. Set table, including placing bread and butter, pouring water, and pouring milk. Have milk and butter at range for peas and potatoes.

6:10 Place steak or patties under broiling unit and water on for peas and potatoes.

6:15 Put peas to cook.

6:20 Or earlier, perhaps, turn steak or patties. Prepare potatoes.

6:25 Drain and season peas.

6:30 Approximately, serve food onto dinner plates and take to table, with salads.

6:45 Or later. Put water to heat for instant coffee. Clear table. Serve ice cream into dishes and take to table. Make coffee and take to table.

A second menu, with more and different tasks to be accomplished, is suggested. Steps in arriving at the final plan and the final plan itself are given in Tables 7–5, 7–6, and 7–7. Assumptions used in timing are that dinner is to begin at 6:30 and preparation is for four persons.

Dinner for Four

Pot Roast of Beef[1]

Potatoes   Carrots

Cole Slaw

Hot Rolls

Milk

Apple Crunch[2]   Coffee

---

[1] A chuck cut weighing 4 pounds.
[2] Fresh, sliced apples with topping
of flour, sugar, butter, and spices.

This menu with suggested timing is typical of broken schedules, those that send the meal manager into the kitchen for doing some tasks, free her for a period of time, and then, return her to the kitchen for the final tasks in meal preparation. Pastries, gelatin salads and desserts, and numerous kinds of main dishes are prepared according to such broken schedules. Preparations for a guest dinner often require several sched-

TABLE 7–5.   *Steps 1 and 2 in Timing Meal Preparation*

Menu Items	Prepare for Cooking	Time in Minutes to Allow for Cooking	Prepare for Serving	Total Time in Minutes
Pot roast of beef	30	180	10[1]	220
Potatoes	5	90	—	95
Carrots	5	90	—	95
Gravy	5	—	5	10
Cole Slaw	—	—	20	20
Rolls	5	10	5	20
Milk	—	—	—[2]	—
Apple crunch	15	40	5[3]	60
Coffee	3	12	—	15
Table setting	—	—	15	15

[1] Includes time for serving up potatoes, carrots, and roast and for slicing roast.
[2] Included in table setting.
[3] For serving and adding whipped topping.

TABLE 7–6. *Step 3 in Timing Meal Preparation—Tasks Listed in Descending Order of Total Time Required*

Tasks	Total Time in Minutes
Pot roast	220 (3 hours, 40 minutes)
Potatoes	95 (1 hour, 35 minutes)
Carrots	95 (1 hour, 35 minutes)
Apple crunch	60
Cole slaw	20
Rolls	20
Coffee	15
Table setting	10
Gravy	10

TABLE 7–7. *The Time Schedule for Preparing Dinner for Four*

2:50	Brown roast in Dutch oven. Peel potatoes and carrots.
3:20	Roast into slow oven.
4:50	Potatoes and carrots put into Dutch oven with roast. Prepare apple dessert.
5:10	Dessert into oven.
5:50	Dessert out of oven. Make and chill cole slaw. Make paste for thickening gravy. Prepare rolls for heating. Set table. Place dinner plates on range. Have dessert service ready on counter. Prepare coffee maker.
6:15	Salads on table. Rolls in oven. Put roast and vegetables on platter. Slice roast. Keep warm.
6:20	Make gravy. Plug in coffee maker.
6:30	Dinner served.

ules for the preparation of the different dishes of the meal and for completion of the arrangements for dining.

No magic enables us to have everything included in a meal ready at a designated time. Timing based on estimates of required allotments of time are helpful. Each of us learns by experience, and much is learned only through experience. The period when detailed planning is essential is short for those who know how to cook. Sooner or later we reach the stage where only the final schedule is made. Even experienced hostesses and cooks who appear to do things easily make these schedules when preparing special meals.

The use of heat-and-eat dishes does not eliminate the need for timing, however much it may simplify and shorten the period of meal preparation. We repeat: it is very important to heat all frozen precooked foods at recommended temperatures and for the directed time to have them safe to eat.

How to Make the Most of Your Time

The following summary provides guidelines to the optimum use of time for meal preparation.

1. Study and observe your uses of time; know how to use time, then seek ways to curtail its use when necessity demands.
2. Set limits to the use of your time; budget it as carefully as you budget your money.
3. Become proficient in the art of timing or scheduling the preparation of meals.
4. Keep records of good menus, recipes, buffet arrangements, brand names of good products, names of satisfactory cuts of meat, and in fact, all information that you can use repeatedly. File this information systematically. Meal managers can waste a lot of time seeking information they could have at their fingertips.
5. Keep a bulletin board in the kitchen; note needs as they arise.
6. Limit the frequency of shopping trips to the minimum consistent with your storage facilities. Shopping can be wasteful of time (as well as gasoline).
7. Place items that you use routinely in your kitchen within your easy reach. Store the staples and less frequently used items on hard-to-reach, high or low shelves in your cupboard.
8. Hang all the pots and pans and gadgets that you use routinely on a pegboard. Put your knives on a magnetic or other type of holder. If there are two working areas in your kitchen, have equipment in both places.
9. Store supplies where you use them.
10. Use the oven for as much cooking as is practical—and not an extravagant use of commercial energy—because cooking foods in the oven requires little watching and active time. Cook several dishes at the same time and prepare enough for two or more meals. Have both the energy and the time pay dividends.
11. Finally, be receptive to new ideas, new products, new recipes, new methods of cooking, and new kinds of cookware and gadgets. Change old habits by adapting to the new if it will result in saving time.

REFERENCES CITED

1. Anderson, E. D., and C. Fitzsimmons, "Use of Time and Money by Employed Homemakers," *Journal of Home Economics* **52:**453 (1960).
2. Bailey, Betty W., *Food and Management Practices of Employed and Unemployed Homemaker Families,* Bulletin N.S. 98, Georgia Agricultural Experiment Stations, University of Georgia College of Agriculture, Athens, Georgia (June 1962).
3. *Better Homes and Gardens Consumer Questionnaire,* A Better Homes and Gardens Report, in *Indices,* Des Moines, Iowa (1970).
4. Hall, Florence R., and Marguerite P. Schroeder, "Time Spent on Household Tasks," *Journal of Home Economics* **62:**23 (1970).
5. Malloch, Francille, "Characteristics of Most and Least Liked Household Tasks," *Journal of Home Economics* **55:**413 (1963).
6. Peskin, Janice, "Measuring Household Production for the GNP," Family Economics Review, Agricultural Research Service, U.S. Department of Agriculture, Washington, D.C. (June, 1982).
7. "Research on Time Spent in Homemaking, An Annotated List of References," ARS 62-15, Agricultural Research Service, United States Department of Agriculture, Washington, D.C. (1967).
8. Ronald, Patricia et al., "Rating Scale for Household Tasks," *Journal of Home Economics* **63:**177 (1971).
9. Walker, Kathryn, "Homemaking Still Takes Time," *Journal of Home Economics* **61:**621 (1961).
10. Wiegand, E., *Use of Time by Full-Time and Part-Time Homemakers in Relation to Home Management,* Memoir 330, New York State College of Home Economics, Cornell University, Ithaca, New York (July 1954).
11. "Women and Food," A Better Homes and Gardens Report, in *Indices,* Des Moines, Iowa (1970).

Chapter 8

Meal Management Goal 4: Pleasurable Eating

The fourth goal for meals is that they be accepted, eaten, and enjoyed. For the meal manager—whether home manager or professional meal manager—this is the most difficult goal to achieve because the same meals are not accepted and enjoyed with the same degree of enthusiasm by all persons. In addition to satisfying hunger, the pleasures that may be derived from meals are several: visual, gustatory, aesthetic, social, emotional, and psychological. If meals only had to satisfy hunger, their planning would pose fewer problems since we have known for some time that even hungry persons reluctantly eat what is strange to them, that is, wheat or corn if their basic staple is rice, and vice versa.

This chapter discusses the food preferences of consumers in the United States, factors affecting these preferences, flavor perception, and foodways; and, last, some guidelines for making menus.

FOOD PREFERENCES OF CONSUMERS IN THE UNITED STATES

Einstein and Hornstein studied the food preferences of 50,000 students throughout the United States (4). They asked students to describe their acceptance of 207 foods as "like a lot," "like," or "dislike." The following are the foods that the largest percentage of students liked and disliked.

Liked Items	Disliked Items
Ice cream	Sautéed chicken livers
Soft rolls	Turnips

Liked Items	Disliked Items
Beef steak	Sautéed liver
Hot biscuits	French fried eggplant
Milk	Cabbage
Orange juice	Pickled beets
Roast turkey	Baked squash
Roast beef	Stewed tomatoes
Apple pie	Carrot-raisin salad
Fried chicken	Stewed prunes
Ice cream sundae	Navy bean soup
Strawberry shortcake	

Of the foods that were "liked a lot," the top 10 percent included many desserts, but only one potato item and no vegetables. Of the foods that were "disliked" the bottom 10 percent included a large number of vegetables and no desserts.

The food preferences of servicemen probably have been studied more than any other group (6, 8, 9). The servicemen's ten best-liked foods (milk, hot rolls, hot biscuits, strawberry shortcake, grilled steak, ice cream, ice cream sundae, fried chicken, French fried potatoes, and roast turkey) are also among the foods found to be most liked by college students.

In the survey of college students, it was noted that men had a greater tendency to give a "Do not know" response, and women had stronger preferences for salads and vegetables, both of which are low-calorie items. The greatest regional differences in the college survey were noted in the South, where grits, black-eyed peas, lima beans, and iced tea were among the foods preferred. Chili and lamb stew were preferred foods in the West, and clam chowder was preferred in the Northeast (4). Recently Worsley and Leitch (16) found significant differences in the way in which Australian students of different ages and from different ethnic and educational backgrounds perceived foods. For many students food selection was based on psychosocial factors.

The preference for individual foods is modified by the combination in which they appear. Combination effects have important implications in menu planning. From early studies we learned that some meat and potato combinations and some meat and vegetable combinations had higher preference than others. For example, baked ham and candied sweet potatoes and baked ham and mashed potato combinations are preferred more than baked ham and French fried potatoes; but the combination of fried fish and sweet potatoes has low acceptance, whereas the combination of fried fish and French fried potatoes has high acceptance.

The preference for individual foods is modified by the method of preparation, with food that is prepared plain scoring highest. For example, grilled steak is preferred over Swiss steak, and buttered broccoli is preferred over broccoli with cheese sauce.

Schorr *et al.* (12) studied the food preferences of 182 students in grades 7 through 12. The subjects were asked to list the food and drink they "liked most," "liked least of all," and "have never tasted." The items that appeared most frequently in the "like most" category were soda pop, followed by milk, steak, hamburger, pizza, chicken, and French fries. Liver was overwhelmingly regarded as the most unpopular item. Walker *et al.* (15) found that children preferred fruits over vegetables; the texture of raw fruits and vegetables over cooked and processed forms; and the sweet tasting over the tart or bland vegetables.

Factors Affecting Food Acceptance

Greene *et al.* (5) studied the effect of heredity on taste preference in 311 twin pairs between the ages of nine and fifteen. They found the heritability estimates uniformly low and concluded that early food intake experiences may play a role in determining enduring taste preferences.

Children's rejection of some fruits and vegetables appears to be based on prejudice, related to such factors as early negative conditioning, rejection of "baby foods," or faulty generalization from a single, unfavorable attribute such as texture, color, shape, or odor. Many vegetables were repeatedly referred to as "intensely disliked" because of a "mushy," "gooey," "icky," or "slimy" texture (beets, turnip, eggplant, okra) or the presence of seeds (tomatoes, squash) whereas the "crunchy," "crispy" texture of raw vegetables was associated with popular foods (15).

The complexity of the diet of adolescents increased with an increase in their father's and mother's occupational level and their mother's educational level. The diet of the adolescent also became more varied with his or her increased social participation and employment. The adolescent's diet complexity was not related to age, sex, family size or the number of his or her nutritional information channels (12).

Cosper and Wakefield (3) studied food choices and factors affecting food choices of women. They found that husbands exert the major influence on whether or not the wife tries a new food. Advertising had the least effect and was less influential than any other factor. With relation to food groups, the meal manager is most strongly influenced by her family's preferences in the selection of meat than in the selection of vegetables, bread, dairy products, and desserts. Personal preferences influenced many women in the selection of fruit. Other motivational factors were "it's good for you," "it tastes good," "low cost," "not fattening," and "easy to fix."

Food Flavor

Flavor has been defined as "the sensation caused by, and those properties of, any substance taken into the mouth, which stimulate one or both of the sense of taste and smell and/or also the general pain, tactile, and temperature receptors in the mouth (6)." That is, flavor is more than just what we think of as "taste." When we say "This tastes very good," we actually mean, "This has a good taste and a good aroma."

Perception of flavor is an experience short in duration but long in memory. Flavor perception varies in intensity among individuals and in the same individual from time to time. Ohloff (7) has developed the following simplified classification of flavors: fruit flavor, vegetable flavor, spice flavor, beverage flavor, meat flavor, fat flavor, cooked flavor, and stench flavor.

Aroma. Odor or aroma is perhaps the most important and least understood element of flavor. It has been estimated that we can distinguish at least 10,000 different odors and our memory for odors is precise and almost never-fading. Compared to the sense of taste, which is a dull one, our sense of smell is keen. Taste is important for the total flavor of a food, but the aroma of compounds distinguishes one food from another and causes similar food items to taste differently.

The olfactory organ is located on the roof of the nasal cavity where it occupies an area about the size of the end of the thumb on both sides of the nasal septum. The olfactory receptors in the nasal cavity can be reached only by compounds that are volatized from food. The number of volatile compounds in food is large and they represent most classes of organic chemicals. Many of these compounds are present in extremely low concentrations.

The stereochemical theory of olfaction suggests that the olfactory organ contains pores into which odorant molecules fit—a "lock and key" concept. It suggests that there are primary odors such as floral, musky, and camphorlike (11). The number of primary odors is not known, or even whether there is a discrete number, as is the case with taste. One classification system based on forty-four basic odor descriptions has been used successfully (13). Olfactory acuity is decreased by sugar, alcohol, amphetamines, and aging. Olfactory acuity diminishes after a meal and is prevented by tartaric, tannic, and acetic acids; bitter tonics; and dry red wines (1). Flavor perception is also affected by color, in that most foods have a flavor associated with their color. Flavor identification of uncolored or atypically colored candies or jellies has been shown to be difficult (2).

During eating, odor is perceived both by the smelling of food before it is eaten, while it is in the dish or cup or on the fork lifted to the mouth, and during chewing and swallowing when the motions of the palate and throat create small air movements that send odorants to the smell organ via the nasopharynx. Flavor perception is experienced briefly on breathing out. Closure of the nasal passages by swelling, as when one has a cold, causes a loss of the sense of smell. At such a time, food has only taste and mouthfeel and we are apt to comment, "It all tastes alike" or, "It is like eating cotton." The pleasure that accompanies the eating of roast beef, fresh homemade bread, spice cake, and all the other foods we like is derived primarily through the sense of smell.

The organ of smell adapts to continuous and repetitive stimulation with a consequent loss of perceptive ability called adaptation or *smell fatigue.* For example, our sensitivity to the enticing odors of the bakery and to the offensive odors of the fish market is diminished as we wait there. Adaptation to a single odor is more rapid than to the same odor accompanied by other odors. Adaptation to some odors is more rapid than to other odors. There seems to be no point of fatigue for oil of lemon and oil of cloves. The time of adaptation to an odor varies with its strength or intensity—the more intense the odor, the less rapid is its adaptation. Intense odors mask less intense odors. And, finally, the longer one is in the presence of a prevailing odor, the more intense must the stimulus for its perception be. This last observation causes one to wonder if food eaten in the kitchen, where the prevailing aroma is that of the food just prepared, is as flavorful as the same food eaten in an atmosphere free from kitchen odors.

Some culinary practices and some dining customs can be explained by reference to these observations. The fact of adaptation explains why no two bites of a single dish ever taste the same and why the last bite never tastes as good as the first. It perhaps explains the habits of eating quickly the foods we like and of eating slowly the foods we dislike. In the one instance, we unconsciously hurry so that we may enjoy the flavor of a dish before adaptation to odor is complete; in the other, we unconsciously delay until fatigue diminishes sensitivity. Because the organ of smell recovers rather quickly when the stimulus is removed or changed, enjoyment of flavors is assured when meals are composed of several dishes eaten interchangeably. Perhaps the lack of enthusiasm for one-dish meals can be explained by quick adaptation to its aroma. The suggestion that foods of similar flavor, herbs, spices, and seasonings not be repeated in meals is sound; repetition would cause rapid adaptation to a particular smell.

Fatigue to the aroma of spices is delayed longer than fatigue to other aromas—hence, the long and colorful history of their use. Used judiciously, spices undoubtedly prolong the period of enjoyment of their unique aromas. But the stronger odors of spices, herbs, and seasonings can dominate and prevent the perception of subtle odors. They should be used with a light hand, if the other ingredients of a dish or even other foods in a meal are to be tasted. For example, the delicate flavor of garden-fresh peas would pass unnoticed were they served with a lamb curry.

Aroma is modified by the temperature of food because the odorous particles that stimulate the organ of smell are more volatile at higher temperatures. Food that is too hot causes pain so that neither taste nor smell can be perceived. A degree of warmth, however, is essential for the best flavors of many foods. Very cold foods, such as ice cream, have more flavor if they are held in the mouth until somewhat warm. Fruits of delicate flavor, such as peaches, pears, and some melons, have more flavor when eaten unchilled or only slightly chilled.

Taste.   Taste is the perception of stimuli through the taste buds. Taste buds are minute depressions, located primarily on the tongue. They are also present in such areas as the soft palate, the pharynx, and the larynx. There are four basic tastes: sweet, sour, salty, and bitter. Generally each taste is perceived on a specific area of the tongue: the tip is most sensitive to sweet, the sides to sour and salty, and the back to bitter.

The salty taste is evoked by some inorganic salts. We add sodium and potassium chloride to produce the salty taste of foods. The sour taste is effected by the hydrogen ion however, pH and sourness are not always parallel. All inorganic acids taste alike when they are sampled in equal concentration; but, some organic acids such as acetic, tartaric, citric, and malic taste more sour than their hydrogen ion concentration would suggest. The sour taste of foods is present in fruits. We add vinegar, wines, and lemon juice to produce the sour taste. The sweet sensation derives from complex organic compounds, including sugar, saccharin, dulcin, and glycerin. The bitter taste is chiefly aroused by alkaloids, certain glucosides, and inorganic salts. Tannins in foods and beverages impart bitterness and astringency. In about 90 percent of tasters, saccharin has been found to have a bitter aftertaste. The bitter taste is present in fruits and vegetables, especially salad greens. Bitterness has a positive quality in coffee, tea, red wines, and other beverages. Rietz (11) says that traditional flavor combinations balance bitter-salt-sour-sweet tastes, for example, pork with apple. Man's order of sensitivity to the four tastes is bitter, sour, salt, and sweet. Taste sensitivity can be enhanced or depressed. Pharmaceuticals make use of flavors to disguise or mask tastes. For example, a salty taste is masked by syrup of orange, cinnamon, and sarsaparilla; raspberry and cocoa disguise bitterness.

Because the taste buds are stimulated by substances in solution, the texture of foods affects their taste. The taste of liquids and foods of fluid consistency is more readily perceived than that of foods that must be chewed. The taste of poorly chewed food may not be sensed. Temperature also affects the taste of food. Not all taste stimulants are similarly affected by temperature. As temperature rises from 63° F to body temperature (98.6° F), sensitivity to sweetness increases, and then decreases. Sensitivity to salt and bitter tastes decreases over the temperature range. For most persons the sensitivity to the sour taste is not modified by temperature; for some persons the response to sour taste is similar to the response to sweet taste (10). In food terms this means that apple pie eaten warm will taste sweeter than when eaten cold; that hot coffee will be less bitter than cold or iced coffee; that hot soup will taste less salty than cold soup; and that the sweetness of sugar added to tea will not be apparent until the tea has cooled in the mouth to approximately body temperature.

Taste receptors adapt or become insensitive to a stimulus that acts for some time. The degree and duration of fatigue depends on the intensity of the stimulus; the weaker the stimulus the more rapid is adaptation or fatigue to it. Persistence of taste is longest for bitterness and shortest for sweetness; sourness and saltiness fall in between, with adaptation to saltiness coming more quickly than adaptation to sourness. Adaption to one taste enhances the perception of another, as of the sourness of an apple after one eats a sweet. Some interactions of the tastes are interesting. Salt solutions reduce sensitivity to bitterness and acid; acid solutions reduce sensitivity to salt and bitter tastes; but both in small quantities enhance sweetness. Practically, in cooking and food preparation we use a pinch of salt to enhance sweetness as of a melon, a frosting, or a pudding; sugar or a sweet sauce to reduce the saltiness of ham; sugar to modify the bitterness of coffee; a bit of sugar to reduce the saltiness of the soup; and sugar to reduce the sourness of a grapefruit. The particular taste of a food is the result of the concentration of the various taste stimulants and their interactions.

All persons are not equally sensitive in perception of taste, which may explain why saltcellars, sugar bowls, and vinegar cruets have been present on dining tables through the years. Further, it may explain why some persons use two lumps of sugar, whereas others use one lump to sweeten coffee to their satisfaction. It has been reported that taste acuity diminishes with age, with the perception of sourness being least affected (1).

The Mouthfeel of Foods.   The feel of food in the mouth is the third component of flavor; it is extremely important in the acceptance of food and meals. Mechanical stimulation of sense organs present in the tongue, the gums, and the hard and soft palates results in the judgment of mouthfeel, that is, the texture of a food or beverage. Among the many adjectives we use to describe food textures are crisp, chewy, crunchy, creamy, dry, juicy, fibrous, greasy, soft, moist, tender, tough, stringy, fluffy, sticky, velvety, and gritty. For different foods we demand a different feel in the mouth. We want meat tender and juicy; bread, soft and moist; crackers, crisp and dry; pudding, smooth; and cake, velvety. Further, we like foods combined in ways to contrast texture—for example, crisp crackers with soup. Certain ingredients are introduced in the preparation of foods and in the composing of combination dishes to produce desirable textures, for example, slivered almonds with green beans.

Some texture qualities such as grittiness, fibrousness, toughness, mushiness, lumpiness, and dryness decrease food acceptability. The textures we like include smoothness, crispness, softness, lightness, and flakiness. However, we reject softness and smoothness to the exclusion of other textures, as evidenced by the dislike of soft and liquid diets. Control of food textures means control of changes that occur during the cooking and staling of foods. Undercooked foods and overcooked foods lack the sought-for textures. Staling results in dryness, hardness, toughness, and sogginess, depending on the food. Modern packaging attempts to prevent the changes in texture that decrease acceptability.

In menu planning, the meal manager purposefully introduces liked textures and an assortment of textures. The following foods are often introduced as much for their texture as for other reasons: salads of mixed greens, cole slaw, crusty rolls, mealy baked potatoes, crisp French fried potatoes, mashed potatoes, smooth and lump-free gravy, crisp fried chicken, and chocolate pudding with whipped topping.

Flavor and Visual and Auditory Senses

Color is a vital constituent of food. It is one of the first characteristics perceived by the senses and is indispensable as a means of rapid identification and ultimate acceptance of food. Almost all foods, from raw agricultural commodities to the finished product, have an associated color that is acceptable to the consumer on the basis of social, geographic, ethnic, and historical backgrounds. Foods with the same amount of flavor are judged more or less flavorful as their color is deep or pale (1).

There is an auditory aspect of flavor. Certain sounds are associated with certain foods and may have a role in flavor perception for some persons: the crunchiness of celery, the fizz of champagne and carbonated beverages, the sizzling of steak, the perking of coffee, and the like (1).

Flavor Potentiation

Cooks have always added a "pinch of this and a pinch of that" to improve food flavors. Herbs, spices, onions, chocolate, vanilla, citrus rinds, and a whole host of other items are in use to add and improve flavor. The movement of cooking out of the home kitchen and into the factory has produced a body of knowledge on how to improve food flavors through the use of flavor enhancers and flavor potentiators. They are substances that do not have flavor of their own in the quantities in which they are used; but they do affect the ways in which flavor is perceived and they are elements of the stimuli that affect this perception. The *flavor enhancer* is an intensifier of flavor. A *flavor potentiator* is defined as a compound that by itself has no sensory effect but that exaggerates the effects of other agents in a system. According to Sjöström (13), monosodium glutamate is a flavor enhancer but it also meets several of the criteria for a flavor potentiator. In the dry form, MSG tastes sweet and salty; in solution, it has all four tastes. It acts on nerve endings in the mouth to affect the impression of basic tastes and on the tactile nerve endings to produce a satisfying feeling in the oral cavity. Flavor potentiators in commercial use include the 5'-nucleotides (disodium inosinate and disodium quanylate; dioctyl sodium sulfosuccinate (DSS); and maltol). The 5'-nucleotides enhance the flavor activity of MSG and spare the MSG requirement in many foods. Alone or in combination, these compounds are important in the production of convenience foods. Here are some of their effects: they protect "freshness" in processed fruits and vegetables; they cover the sour, grainy, and starchy flavor notes of cereals; they reduce the oily mouth effects of fats and oils; they enhance flavor and protect freshness in beverages, especially fruit beverages; they suppress sulfury notes in food flavors; they enhance meaty and brothy flavors, and in soups, they give a sense of greater viscosity. Soups and stews may seem to contain more meat than they actually do.

FOODWAYS

Thus far, we have discovered that people eat what they like. They like what they know and what tastes good to them. The knowledge about foods and meals is established for each person by his culture, his family background, and his breadth of experiences, including his level of education. The culture distinguishes the edible from the inedible, for example, that chicken but not guinea pigs and peanuts but not acorns are food. Further, it establishes how food is prepared, that is, as soups, stews, or curries or boiled, fried, or roasted; it determines the number of meals as one, two, three, or more per day; and dictates how food shall be eaten, that is, with fingers, forks, or chopsticks. The food-ways of persons in the United States differ within the framework of Western culture primarily, but also of other cultures, because families are of diverse national origins or subcultures, such as Swedish, Italian, Spanish, German, Dutch, Cuban, Japanese, and Chinese. What a family considers to be food and enjoyable meals are established by such characteristics as ethnic origin, religious beliefs, region of residence, socio-economic status, standard of living, and goals and ambitions.

The foodways change. In recent years, Americans have been eating more meals away from home and more meals each day. Midmorning and midafternoon coffee breaks and the evening snacks have been added to, or eaten in place of, the traditional three meals daily. The meal manager's tasks became simpler in many ways. But the fact remains that she does plan many meals; for these she may have a higher set of standards than formerly.

GUIDELINES TO MEAL PLANNING

No set of guidelines for planning meals will assure the acceptance and enjoyment of meals by all persons. Some guidelines are based on knowledge of food preferences and flavor perception; others, on recognition that man is not entirely rational or logical about his food and meals. The primary properties of foods are judged in fixed order: appearance, odor, texture and consistency, and taste and aroma (16). Planners of meals deliberately plan meals to have eye appeal. Meals must look good to be tasted and to be enjoyed.

Food and the Eyes

To make meals visually pleasing, include some foods and dishes that are known and liked by the persons for whom the meals are planned. Introduce the new into meals in small ways and along with very well-liked foods and dishes. Second, have foods prepared in familiar ways: the pot roast with or without carrots and onions, the chicken fried with or without batter, depending on preference. Third, have the foods and dishes within a meal prepared in different ways. Do not mash everything; do not cover several dishes with a sauce; do not fry several items. Next, have the different foods and dishes appear different. Do not have small whole potatoes, small whole stewed onions, and meatballs, or macaroni and cheese, French cut green beans, and cole slaw in the same meal. Everything looks too much alike. The items seen at one time should differ in the shapes and sizes of pieces. Be sure that food looks like what it is; there is little reason to have a tomato look like a rose, a banana-pineapple salad look like a candlestick, or a cake look like a football unless at parties for children. Make certain that every constituent of a dish, other than seasonings, can be identified. Dislike of such combination dishes as stews and casserole dishes may have been born out of an inability to identify the constituents and hence to know precisely what was being eaten. For the best appearance, have the different items within a food mixture sized and shaped differently. Limit the number of mixed dishes within a meal. For people in the United States, do not serve a meal composed of lamb stew and vegetables, with Waldorf salad, and a mixed fruit cup for dessert; the meal includes too many combination dishes.

Last, use plenty of color. Man likes color in his clothing, in his surroundings, and especially in his food. The color of food assists us in identifying food of poor quality: the underripe tomato, the overripe peach, overcooked green beans, and overgrilled steak. Color assists us in identifying food flavors. Some colors stimulate the autonomic nervous system, of which the digestive system is a part; they are yellow, orange, orange-red, bright green, tan, and brown. Purple, red-purple, yellow-green, olive and mustardy tones, and gray are not pleasing (2). We like color and color variety in meals, but we do not like our foods colored artificially. We will eat blueberries but not blue bread, strawberries but not red mashed potatoes. The artificial coloring of food is best limited to such uses as heightening natural colors, like the addition of red color to a cherry pie filling. We accept colored frostings on cakes and bright red maraschino cherries because the color is part of our concept of the food. We like colored candies but not colored mayonnaise.

Some thought should always be given to the choice of the dinnerware on which food combinations are served. Modern ceramic and plastic dinnerwares are bright in color and bold in design; they look magnificent on the colorful linens on which they are so often displayed. However, their function is in the service of food and the food sometimes is overwhelmed and disadvantaged by their color. White, pink, aqua, pastel green, and yellow are the colors acclaimed as best in food service. (2).

Food and the Senses That Savor It

To maximize the enjoyment of eating, allow plenty of time for dining—flavor perception takes time. Consider the temperature of foods, the tastes, the mouthfeel or textures, and the aroma of foods. Introduce all the tastes; use them judiciously. The sweet taste is the one to be watched. We like it, but we sometimes overdo it. In general, keep it for the dessert course. Jellies, preserves, and pickled fruits are sweet, sour, and bitter. We use them along with meats. Pickles and pickle relishes are sour and sweet. Olives are salty. Oil and vinegar dressings are sour and can be made salty to enhance slightly bitter greens.

Introduce a variety of textures into a meal and use the liked ones, such as smoothness, crispness, moistness, and chewiness. Use crisp salads and crusty breads to contrast the smoothness and softness of mashed potatoes, meat loaves, macaroni and cheese, or a salmon casserole. Use a crisp cookie to contrast with the velvetiness of ice cream.

Introduce extremes in temperature; have something hot with a cold meal and something cold with a hot meal. Some persons like cold sherbet with a hot entrée. Serve hot food hot and cold food cold for optimum perception of food flavors and the tongue taste of foods. This may make it necessary to heat or chill dishes onto which food is served.

Include a variety of flavors within a meal, so that the organ for perception of aroma does not fatigue. Because the organ of smell adapts to one odor quickly, a meal composed of only one or two dishes may make dull eating. Food flavors range from the very intense to the very delicate. Foods that have intense flavors include garlic and onions; the well-ripened cheeses such as Limburger; sauerkraut; many herbs; and spices. Foods that are delicate in flavor include the staple foods: rice, potatoes, bread, and other cereals; skim milk and cottage cheese; meats such as chicken and veal; vegetables such as peas, corn, squash, and cucumber; and fruits such as the avocado, the papaya, the pear, and the banana (12). The blending of flavors in creating dishes and planning meals is an art. Unfortunately, not even experts agree on the rightness of flavor combinations. Individual differences in the ability to perceive tastes and aromas, in past experiences, and in personal preferences would explain lack of universal agreement.

A widely accepted principle of menu writing suggests that mild flavors come first in a meal, and strong ones later. Thus, a meal of several courses traditionally begins with consommé, proceeds through fish to meat or fowl, and ends with cheese and crackers. Few homemakers plan such meals, but this is a useful suggestion for first courses. Keep them mild in flavor, particularly if the main course will consist of delicately flavored foods, such as fowl with wild rice, scalloped oysters, or veal with mushrooms. Mildly flavored foods that would be suitable in the first course include, fruit juices, thin soups, and crackers spread with mild cheese spreads. Highly seasoned foods and strong cheese are more suitably served in later courses, with cocktails, or in cold suppers, unless they are eaten in small quantities.

The real art of menu planning is in the blending of flavors within a course and within a meal. Although flavor relationships are not well understood, three seem apparent. Some flavors enhance others—butter on bread and vegetables, and cream on strawberries. Some flavors mask others, and their forceful character must always be kept in mind. Peanut butter is one; nothing can compete with it. To serve a peanut butter sandwich with cream of potato soup is to lose the flavor of the soup; the sandwich should follow the soup. The blue cheeses mask the mild flavors of the lettuce, watercress, and avocado they so often dress in salads. The decision on whether or not to use a blue cheese dressing depends upon what one wants tasted: if it is the salad greens, the answer is no; if it is the cheese, yes. Mushrooms served with pork sausage can scarcely be appreciated; whereas mushrooms served with veal or chicken will be truly enjoyed. Those who eat many meals in restaurants soon learn the cover-up value of sauces and condiments.

Some flavors are pleasing when eaten together; others are less so. By and large, the traditional combinations that have stood the test of time can be depended on to please. Included in this long list are cucumbers with fish, asparagus with cheese dishes, cabbage with corned beef, onions with liver, wild rice with poultry, and carrots and onions with pot roast of beef. The planner of meals should not feel limited to the use of these; rather, she should try different combinations of flavors. Those that she finds good can be continued; those she finds poor can be abandoned. Of all the cooks in the world, French chefs have best understood the art of blending flavors; perhaps that is why French cooking is considered such a culinary art.

Few individuals are sensitive to subtle flavor relationships, just as few are sensitive to the qualities that make one painting a work of art and another just one more picture. Yet everyone enjoys some meals more than others, even when the quality of the food is the same. Could it be that careful blending of flavors makes one meal taste better than another? The homemaker who wishes to plan pleasing and satisfying meals will consider flavors, making certain that the ones she wants appreciated are not lost because stronger ones mask them.

Planning a Meal

The best menus are planned around a single food item, either a food such as roast beef or baked beans, or a combination dish such as tamale pie or chicken chop suey. This item becomes the focal point of the meal and all else either is subordinate to it or complements it. Usually meals are planned around the main dish of the main course, but they could be planned around salad, dessert, or any other dish. All other foods and dishes are then thoughtfully selected so that they enhance that important dish. Food textures, tastes, aromas, and colors are all manipulated to make the most of that dish and to give pleasure in eating. Desserts should always be planned in relation to the main course. When the latter is light, the dessert can be sweet and filling; when the main course is rich and filling, the dessert should be light and possibly tart. The first course should be planned in relation to both the main and dessert courses, but it should be light—it should whet the appetite and not satisfy it.

The sequence of decisions in planning a meal are something like this. First, decide on the main dish of the main course. Next, select the staple to serve with it; however, such a staple is sometimes omitted and two vegetables are included. Next, select the vegetable or vegetables for texture, aroma, and color. Then, decide on a salad. Lastly, plan the dessert and the first course simultaneously to avoid repetitions in foods and flavors.

Summary Guidelines to Meal Planning

1. People eat what they like. Include in meals the foods and dishes they know. Prepare them in the ways people know.
2. Include foods of different colors. Preferred colors are yellow, orange, red-orange, pink, bright green, browns, and white. Use purple, yellow-green, olive and mustardy tones, and gray sparingly. Use artificial color only to enhance natural colors.
3. Limit the number of mixtures, that is, combination dishes, in meals. Always have the ingredients of mixtures identifiable.
4. Plan so that the mass, shapes, and sizes of food items differ.
5. Introduce several food textures so that the feel in the mouth changes during eating.
6. Introduce all tastes. Use the sweet taste sparingly until toward the end of a meal; balance it with the other tastes.
7. Avoid repetitions of foods and modes of preparing foods.
8. Introduce several food flavors. Avoid repetition of similar flavors. Combine foods in accordance with preferred flavor combinations.

SUMMARY

The goal of satisfying meals is not easy to attain. It must be achieved within the limits imposed by planned uses of money and time. Not all persons like the same foods and the same meals. Foods and meals are judged before they are tasted; they must look good, but this does not imply elaborate garnishing. Flavor perception is a complex of sensations; acuity of perception differs among persons. In planning meals, use art, artifice, and science to have food both look and taste good.

REFERENCES CITED

1. Amerine, M. A., R. M. Pangborn, and E. B. Roessler, *Principles of Sensory Evaluation of Food.* New York: Acadmic Press, 1965.
2. Birren, F., "Color and Human Appetite," *Food Technology* **17**:45 (1963).
3. Cosper, Barbara A., and Lucille Wakefield, "Food Choices of Women," *Journal of American Dietetic Association* **66**:152 (1975).
4. Einstein, Margery A., and Irwin Hornstein, "Food Preferences of College Students and Nutritional Implications," *Journal of Food Science* **35**:429 (1970).
5. Greene, L. S., "Heredity and Experience: Their Relative Importance in the Development of Taste Preference in Man," *Journal of Comparative Physiology and Psychology* **89**:279 (1975).
6. "News to Note," *Food Technology* **23**:1360 (1969).
7. Ohloff, G., "Classification and Genesis of Food Flavours," *The Flavor Industry* **10**:501 (1972).
8. Peryam, David R. *et al., Food Preferences of Men in the U.S. Armed Forces,* Department of the Army, Quartermaster Research and Engineering Command, Quartermaster and Container Institute for the Armed Forces, Chicago (1960).
9. Pilgrim, F. J., "What Foods Do People Accept or Reject?" *Journal of the American Dietetic Association* **38**:439 (1961).
10. Rietz, C. A., *A Guide to the Selection, Combination, and Cooking of Foods, Vol. I: Selection and Combination.* Westport, Conn.: The Avi Publishing Company, Ind. (1961).
11. Rietz, C. A., and J. A. Wanderstock, *A Guide to the Selection, Combination, and Cooking of Foods, Vol. 2: Formulation and Cooking of Foods.* Westport, Conn.: The Avi Publishing Company, Inc. (1965).
12. Schorr, B. C. C., D. Sanjur, and E. C. Erikson, "Teen-age Food Habits," *Journal of the American Dietetic Association* **61**:415 (1972).
13. Sjöström, Loren B., "Flavor Potentiators," in *Handbook of Food Additives,* Cleveland: Chemical Rubber Company (1970) Chapter 13.
14. Von Sydon, Erik. "Flavor—Chemical or Psychophysical Concept," *Food Technology* **25**:40 (1971).
15. Walker, Mabel A., Mary M. Hill, and Frank Milliman. "Fruit and Vegetable Acceptance by Students, *Journal of the American Dietetic Association* **61**:268 (1973).
16. Worsley, A. and D. Leitch. "Students Perceptions of Favorite and Disliked Foods." *Journal of Human Nutrition* **35**:173–187 (1981).

SUGGESTED PROBLEMS

1. Choose an entrée; plan nutritious and satisfying meals for each season of the year.

2. Plan two meals that you would serve for guests who have just moved into your neighborhood. Plan the meals so that they would be accepted by most people.
3. Have each person in the class write a menu for dinner. Redistribute the menus and have each person evaluate the menu written by someone else.

Chapter 9

Shopping for Food: Some General Information and Principles

In 1981, Americans in the United States spent, on the average, 16.7 percent of disposable personal income for food; of this percentage, 12.3 percent was spent for food to be eaten within the home or carried out of the home as meals and/or snacks. Inflation, recession, and unemployment in the 1980's emphasize the significance of skills and abilities in shopping for food.

In this chapter, some general information is organized and summarized to formulate some general principles for meal managers. First, the marketplace will be examined; second, developments that currently make shopping easier than heretofore are summarized; and finally, the types of food buying decisions that meal managers make are discussed.

Not all meal managers have the same resources for shopping for food. Every meal manager can find it helpful to discover the shopping resources of the local community; to compare prices therein; and to evaluate the quality of food products offered and the kinds of services available. By so doing, the meal manager is enabled to maximize dollars, if and when that is imperative, and also to use time and energy resources effectively.

The kinds of food stores are several. They include several types of supermarkets; the combination store; warehouse stores; convenience stores; direct marketing outlets like the farmer's market; many types of specialty shops, such as the meat market, bakery, cheese shop, and delicatessen to name only a few; and the food cooperative. In one locale, there may only be a convenience store or a conventional supermarket; in another, such as in a metropolitan area, there may be multiple resources. Multi-resources are positively advantageous to the food shopper.

Progressive Grocer defines three types of supermarkets on the basis of the volume of annual sales; these are superstores, supermarkets, and supermarket-type stores. In the following discussion there will be no distinctions made; all supermarkets will be referred to by the term *supermarket* or *conventional supermarket*. Food stores are units of chain organizations or they are independents. A *chain* operates eleven or more stores whereas an *independent store* is one of a group of ten or less, it may be one of a kind. Although independents outnumber chain stores, they accounted for only 45 percent of grocery store sales in 1981.

THE SUPERMARKET

Supermarkets are the food shopper's dream come true. They are a development of the twentieth century and they developed in the United States. Many forces—technological, economic, social, agricultural, and psychological—favored the development of the supermarkets of the 1980's. We mention only a few of these forces here. The first and of greatest significance was the automobile, which made shopping possible beyond the immediate neighborhood. Second were technological advances in refrigeration, food processing, and food packaging. These made possible self-service and the sale of a diversity of products within the supermarket. Further, shopping for food could be reduced to one trip per week as soon as families had refrigerators and freezers. Third was the development of a vast body of knowledge within the industry of how to retail food efficiently at low cost. Fourth, women entered the labor market in ever-increasing numbers. They wanted self-service to minimize the time and energy investments in food shopping; they wanted one-stop shopping; and they wanted low prices and quality. Fifth, families moved to the suburbs. Lastly, incomes rose and food consumption habits changed.

History of the Supermarket

Large food markets in the United States date back to 1658 and the Faneuil Hall Market in Boston, Massachusetts. By 1918, there were 174 of these large markets in cities of over 30,000 in population. They were conglomerates of retailers of diverse kinds of foods. Each retailer occupied a booth or stall in an open-air market or an enclosed structure designated often as "the market." At these large markets, although they purchased from many different retailers, consumers could shop for all their food needs. Three evolving concepts culminated in the development of the supermarket, which was very much like the trading post or general country store that had long been a part of the American scene. These were centralization of management, self-service by the customer, and the cash-and-carry concept. Centralization of management came first. The first departmentalized food store under one ownership was established in Lowell, Massachusetts, before the Civil War; it was known as the Lowell Public Market. It was also the first market to precut meat before sale. By the turn of the century, such markets as Ralph's Grocey Company of Los Angeles and Frank Munsey's Mohican Stores had been established under central management. Clerk service and delivery service were the general rule, but self-service had been introduced. Self-service was popularized by Clarence Saunders in the Piggly Wiggly Stores that opened in 1916, in Memphis, Tennessee: Saunders also introduced the turnstile, the checkout, and cash payment for groceries in his store. The idea of self-service was successful from the beginning. Much to the surprise of many operators, it was discovered that the customer liked to browse and choose. John Hartford of the Great Atlantic and Pacific Tea Company is credited with the cash-and-carry concept. He established, in 1912, economy stores without delivery or credit. But chains were not the inventors or developers of the supermarket. The first market that could be called a supermarket was opened in Jamaica, New York, by Michael Cullen in August, 1930.

The depression of the 1930's favored the rapid growth of large self-service markets described as "cheapy" markets. These stores were departmentalized with meat, bakery, dairy, produce, and grocery departments. Established in low-rent locations on the fringes of densely populated areas, they occupied abandoned warehouses and empty department stores, garages, and factories. The interiors of these stores had crude floors, bare ceilings, glaring lights, gaudy signs, and merchandise piled everywhere. Most of the space was allocated to food merchandising although some operators leased space to dealers in hardware, paint, automobile accessories, and so on. These "cheapy" markets offered abundant parking space and one-stop shopping. They featured low food prices, a policy they could adopt because of the low cost of their facilities and because of buying practices. The warehouse store of the 1980's is reminiscent of this store. By the mid-1930's, the chains started supermarket operations; the Kroger Company in 1935 and the Great Atlantic and Pacific Tea Company in 1937. Small independent merchants who were threatened by both the supermarkets and the chains were forced to adopt the supermarket principle. This they accomplished by affiliating either with wholesaler-sponsored or retailer-sponsored groups. There was rapid increase in the number of supermarkets in the late 1930's. There was little expansion during World War II, but an important change in merchandising policy occurred. To hold and expand volume, supermarkets took on nonfood lines, products that were not previously sold in grocery stores.

Following World War II, came larger chains; more and larger stores—

superstores that gross more than $8,000,000 annually; acquisition of food processing plants such as bakeries, dairies, and meat processing plants by the chains; more services offered to customers; more emphasis on nonfood merchandise—a policy that continues to grow with the result that some supermarkets offer a stock not unlike that of a variety store; and more competition with subsequent resort to many measures to increase patronage and profit. During the 1970's and early 1980's, inflation, recession, rising energy and labor costs, and competition with the fast food industry have made food stores even more competitive.

Organization of the Supermarket

Supermarkets have six standard food departments and one or more nonfood departments. The standard food departments are the meat, the produce, the dairy, the baked goods, the frozen foods, and the dry groceries departments. In addition, supermarkets of the 1980's may have an in-store bakery, a delicatessen shop, a wine shop, a cheese shop, a coffee and tea shop, or a gourmet food shop. These latter departments are not only profitable but they also attract customers. Nonfood merchandising by supermarkets includes the selling of cosmetics, housewares, pharmaceuticals, auto supplies, flowers and plants, books, newspapers and magazines, and so on. These departments are also profitable. The locations of some of these departments is similar in supermarkets: the meat department, the dairy products, produce, the in-store bakery, and the delicatessen shop are located on the store perimeter. Other departments are located center store. Different department locations and different shelving arrangements among chains influence some shoppers to consistently patronize a particular supermarket because the search for needs in an unfamiliar setting can be time and energy consuming.

The Competitive Practices of Supermarkets

Earnings of supermarkets average about one percent of total sales. Store operating costs are fixed and rising. Profits can only be increased by increasing volume which means attracting more and more customers to buy more and more food and nonfood products. Competitive practices of supermarkets include price competition and nonprice measures.

Pricing Policies. Refer to Table 9–1 for the findings of a survey conducted by the authors in Florida (mid-1982) of the costs of 26 selected food items in six different supermarkets. All of the nonperishable items were national brand products. All of the supermarkets were units of

TABLE 9–1. *Comparing Prices in Six Supermarkets in June 1982*

	Super-Market A	Super-Market B	Super-Market C	Super-Market D	Super-Market E	Super-Market F
	Price	Price	Price	Price	Price	Price
Bananas, 1 lb.	$ .29	$ .35	$ .25	$ .25	$ .33	$ .29
Cabbage, 1 lb	..39	.49	.38	.48	.43	.43
Carrots, 1 lb.	.25	.39	.28	.22	.25	.25
Lettuce, 1 head	.68	.69	.68	.79	.78	.79
Potatoes, 5 lbs.	.88	.90	.98	1.05	1.08	1.09
Chicken, 1 lb.	.69	.75	.49	.69	.68	.69
Ground beef, 1 lb.	1.28	1.67	1.28	1.79	1.49	1.39
Ham, butt end, 1 lb.	1.18	1.17	1.08	.99	1.18	1.19
Pork loin chops, 1 lb.	2.58	2.67	2.48	2.49	2.48	2.49
Rump roast, 1 lb.	2.88	2.97	2.28	2.09	2.28	2.29
Sirloin steak, 1 lb.	3.18	2.97	3.18	3.39	3.18	3.59
Weiners, 1 lb.	1.55	1.97	1.83	1.75	1.38	1.89
Milk, whole, ½ gal.	1.25	1.27	1.25	1.27	1.27	1.27
Eggs, large, 1 doz.	.79	.75	.74	.69	.74	.75
Cheese, cheddar, 10 oz.	2.29	2.05	2.14	2.23	2.07	2.19
Margine, 1 lb.	.55	.56	.56	.55	.59	.63
Bread, 20 oz. loaf	.57	.42	.42	.42	.44	.45
Flour, 5 lb.	.98	.88	.98	.89	.98	.98
Sugar, 5 lb.	1.23	1.33	1.33	1.39	1.33	1.33
Instant coffee, 10 oz.	4.39	4.38	4.38	3.99	4.38	4.39
Rice, Uncle Ben's, 2 lb.	1.68	1.66	1.66	1.71	1.66	1.66
Mayonnaise, 1 qt.	1.33	1.33	1.33	1.35	1.33	1.37
Peanut butter, 18 oz.	1.82	1.82	1.72	1.87	1.82	1.77
Tuna, 6½ oz.	.84	.84	.82	.79	.84	.84
Cling peach halves, 29 oz.	.88	.88	.88	.83	.89	.84
Catsup, 32 oz.	1.21	1.39	1.23	1.19	1.39	1.39
Totals	35.64	36.55	34.63	35.15	35.27	36.20

chains and only two were not discount supermarkets. It will be noted that there are not great differences in the total costs of the six market baskets, the most expensive costing but 5 percent more than the least expensive. What is notable is that there are some significant differences in the cost of different items within the market basket, for example, the 10-ounce block of cheese, sirloin steak, chicken, and cabbage. These differences point to what is termed *variable price merchandising*, that is, the same or similar products, whether food or nonfood, are priced differently by different retailers who may price some products high in order to price others low. Even in units of the same chain in the same metropolitan area, pricing may be variable to permit competition with other stores within the same area. In general, low-priced products are those that the consumer is price-conscious to, for example, bread, ground beef, or milk. In contrast to variable pricing is *discount pricing*, a price policy of low prices on all products. Stores that practice discounting may be described as discount supermarkets, about which we will say more later. Another pricing policy is the offering of specials. *Specials* are items that are priced less than their regular price for a period of time, perhaps only one day. Specials may be priced less than the cost to the dealer, they are then *loss leaders*. A store coupon may be required for the purchase of a "special" product, a store may limit the number that a shopper may purchase and may also require a minimum purchase amount. Only a few of the more or less 10,000 items a supermarket stocks are specialed. Each week, sometimes twice weekly, food stores advertise their specials in the local newspapers. It should be noted, however, that not all advertised products are specials; many are products that are being promoted by the food manufacturers who in some way favor the retailer who includes the product in his advertising. For this reason, it helps the meal manager to know the current prices of the food products that she customarily buys—only then is it possible to recognize a bargain.

Another kind of price competition between supermarkets is in the extent and diversity of private label offerings, so-called store brands. Supermarkets got their start in the sale of nationally or regionally known brands of food products. The supermarket of the 1980's offers national brands, its own private label brands, products manufactured by local and/or little-known companies, and generic brands. A chain may produce its private label merchandise in its own plants or it may acquire it from manufacturers. Some large food manufacturing companies engage in dual labeling of products: that is, cornflakes, canned tuna, canned milk or frozen peas may bear the manufacturer's label but may also be variously labeled for different retailing stores. There has always been a price differential between private label products and national brands such as Del Monte or Kellogg. More recently, this cost differential has narrowed. The original intent of the private or store label was to establish store loyalty; the intent of the name or national brand is to establish brand loyalty. A company carefully protects its brand image; it is for many consumers a symbol of the quality that they seek and a guide to decision making in the marketplace. Store-brand merchandise can undersell brand name products because the latter are priced to cover the costs of advertising, promotion, and development. *Generic* label products are unbranded or no-name. They are plainly packaged and bear white or yellow labels printed in black. The label states the name of the product and provides all information required by law. Although not introduced until 1977, 80 percent of supermarkets were stocking some generic products by January, 1982. It should be noted, however, that the number of generic label products stocked is relatively small and varies from market to market. Some generic food products include peanut butter, evaporated milk, tomato products and catsup, flour, canned fruits and vegetables, coffee, canned juices and drinks, pasta products, cookies, and the list is ever-growing. Some generic nonfood products include toilet paper, facial tissue, pet foods, soaps, bleach, and health and beauty aids. Generic produce is available in some supermarkets. Generic products are primarily of USDA Grade C quality for canned foods and U.S. No. 2 and U.S. No. 3 grades for produce. Generics are priced 15 to 40 percent below private label and brand name products (11). See Table 9–2 for cost comparisons of national brands, store brands, and generic brands for some selected products.

Nonprice Competitive Practices of Food Stores. Food stores utilize several nonprice competitive practices; these are both subtle and obvious. Their purpose is to increase patronage and to expand sales volume. They can be classified into two types: in-store strategies and advertising and promotions.

Supermarkets use strategies in routing traffic through the store, they use the art and science of decor, lighting, and display, and they devise means of detaining the patron in the store. The two areas of the store,

TABLE 9–2.   *Cost of National versus Store versus Generic Brands [1] of Selected Products*

	National Brand	Store Brand	Generic Brand
Instant coffee, 10 oz.	$ 4.30	$ 3.58	$ 3.09
Bleach, 2 qt.	.71	.55	.34
Corn, No. 303 can	.53	.46	.43
Milk, evaporated, 1 can	.51	.42	.37
Peaches, No. 2½ can	.92	.69	.75
Peanut butter, 28 oz.	2.79	1.99	1.74
Pears, No. 2½ can	1.05	.93	.78
Peas, No. 303 can	.50	.42	.35
Soup, vegetable, 1 can	.36	.31	.29
Tomatoes, No. 303 can	.75	.53	.42
Tomato juice, No. 3 Cyl. can	.91	.85	.79
Totals	$13.33	$10.73	$ 9.35

[1]Prices as of June, 1982 in a chain supermarket. Prices would vary in different regions of the United Stated but price comparisons would be similar.

the perimeter area and the midstore area, are shopped differently. Positioning of the meat, produce, bakery, and dairy departments around the store perimeter assures heavy perimeter traffic. Midstore displays receive much less customer attention. To divert traffic into midstore aisles, strategies are used: good signs that identify product locations, lighted shelving, brightly lettered signs, blinking lights, positioning of the products that draw heavy traffic—coffee, bread, cookies and crackers, baking needs, paper products, canned soups, laundry supplies, cereals, and sugar—to achieve maximum coverage of midstore aisles, and placing advertised specials in light traffic areas. Techniques of display that favor increased sales include full shelf stocking with every available item visible and reachable; "sore-thumb" displays that dramatically call attention to products; end-of-aisle displays; checkout displays; multiple pricing of units; the display of go-togethers in adjacent positions, such as potato chips and pretzels beside soft drinks; and the display of candies, health and beauty aids, and nonfood goods beside such traffic-drawing items as cereals, soft drinks, and breads. Free samples, cooking demonstrations, snack bars, kiddie corners, gourmet food shops, wine cellars, and bold displays in any food or nonfood department tend to detain shoppers. Dinnerware, cookware, beverageware, flatware, cookbook series, and encyclopedias help to establish store loyalty and hence attract shoppers into a store; they also detain shoppers. Markets claim that there is an 80 percent chance that an unplanned purchase is made for each stop (4).

Although in-store strategies influence consumers, advertising and promotions take first place in the competitive world of the 1980's. Advertising may be defined as any strategy that influences consumer choice among different brands or retail stores; hence, it includes not only conventional advertising via mass media but also coupons, refunding, stamps, premiums, games, contests, and sweepstakes (2). Advertising costs are supported by local food retailers and by manufacturers of food products. It is no secret that the manufacturers of processed food products use television abundantly for advertising. Newspaper advertising is the medium most frequently utilized by local retailers of food. It would be difficult to state which influences meal managers more. However, newspaper advertising can be of great value to the shopper for food. According to surveys conducted in 1976–78 by the United States Department of Agriculture, about one-half of those surveyed always or almost always consulted newspaper advertising before going shopping (6). Store ads inform customers of price changes, of changes in food supply, and about specials. They provide in-store coupons and announce double coupon days.

Coupons are provided both by local food retailers and by food processing companies. The in-ad, i.e., retailer, coupons permit the purchase of named food or nonfood products at a discounted price in the stores of a particular chain or other food store for a limited period of time and on specified days. In-ad coupons may feature private label products and may be intended to increase store traffic. They may also feature brand name products whose price reductions are subsidized by food manufacturers. The number of couponed items that a customer may purchase may be limited. In a sense, the couponed product is a special.

Manufacturers' coupons are redeemable in any store that accepts them. Stores are paid for handling the coupons. The manufacturer's coupon is a promise of discount on the purchase of a specific product. On double coupon days, the retailer matches the discount established by the manufacturer. Billions of manufacturers' coupons are issued annually; the number issued rose from 10 billion in 1965 to 102 billion in 1981. These coupons appear in newspapers, magazines, Sunday supplements, special flyers, and in and on food packages. They cost millions of dollars annually for handling and redemption. In 1981 food shoppers redeemed five billion coupons (one in twenty issued) enough to purchase one billion dollars worth of food and merchandise. Coffee, highly processed food products, breakfast cereals, pet foods, and new product introductions were among highly couponed items (1). The average face value of coupons was 23.5 cents (1981). For the meal manager, coupon redemption requires the exercise of common sense; certainly, nothing should be purchased simply because a coupon reduces its cost by 15 cents.

The refund by manufacturers is not new; refunding has, however, become a phenomenon of the 1980's. Refunding involves sending to the manufacturer a specified number of proofs of purchase, i.e., bottle caps, can lids, box tops or bottoms, labels, or other scraps of evidence that a given product has been purchased. In return, the refunder receives money as stipulated or other privilege as promised in the offer. Refund offers are printed on forms that provide the kinds of information that the potential refunder should have, such as the expiration date of the offer, the number of proofs of purchase required, and so on. Consumers are advised of offers via newspapers, magazines, at point-of-sale displays, and by on- or in-package notices. Some newspapers report refund offers periodically and there are bulletins to which one can subscribe that report offers.

Trading stamps were in use before World War I but did not become big in food retailing until the 1950's and 1960's. Use peaked out in the late 1960's and declined until 1975 when a reversal began. In 1981, about 25 percent of supermarkets were giving trading stamps; the Southwest and the Southeast were the areas of greatest use. Sperry and Hutchinson (Green Stamps) remains the largest of the stamp companies. Stamps are redeemable for merchandise or cash. Another type of stamp is in use in the 1980's. When a specified number of these stamps have been acquired and attached to a proper form, they are negotiable for products at greatly reduced cost, for example, one dozen eggs for 29 cents or paper towels for 19 cents.

Finally, only the limits of the imaginations of Madison Avenue advertisers and marketing heads of chain organizations can define the kinds of games, contests, and other gimmicks designed to attract shoppers into this or that market to purchase this or that food or nonfood product.

The Discount Supermarket

The discount supermarket differs little from the conventional supermarket other than in pricing policy. The discount supermarket advertises low prices every day; there is less emphasis on specials. Chain supermarkets are more likely to be discounters than independent supermarkets which favor specials. Kash n' Karry Stores, a division of Lucky Stores, Inc. is a discount chain. Lucky Stores, Inc. ranked third in sales volume in 1981. Other discounting supermarkets include Pantry Pride and Family Mart Stores.

The Combination Store

The combination store, a development of the 1960's and 1970's, succeeds well. It marked a return to the general store of frontier days. As defined, 40 percent or more of floor space is devoted to nonfood merchandise; appliances, automobile accessories, clothing, footwear, gifts, hardware and paints, housewares, household linens, school supplies, and so on; the remainder of floor space, to food products. Combination stores may gross $8 million or more in sales annually. They have a margin of about 25 percent in contrast to the 20 percent margin of supermarkets and superstores. Combination stores succeed because they favor one-stop shopping, an important service to women who work outside of the home. It has been pointed out (4) that some merchandise offered in combination stores is inferior in quality to that offered in department stores for two reasons. First, buying for the combination store is by a buyer for nonfood merchandise while the buying in department stores is by specialized buyers. Secondly, manufacturers appear reluctant for their quality merchandise to be sold in low-cost operations. Be that as it may, combination stores are here to stay; they fare well because the high margin on nonfood merchandise permits the sale of food at prices favorable to consumers.

Warehouse Stores

Warehouse stores are no-frills stores that feature low prices. They provide food products at lower cost than conventional supermarkets; they minimize operating costs and customer services. They are of two types: the warehouse store and the limited assortment store. The warehouse store may be as large in size and have as many departments as the conventional supermarket. It offers 1500 to 7500 items with less variety within departments, fewer brands, and a lesser number of sizes of units. Limited assortment stores, sometimes called box stores, stock less than 1500 items; typically they sell no items requiring refrigeration. Warehouse stores are a rich shopping resource for the meal manager who must maximize food dollars.

Convenience Stores

The convenience store is a miniature supermarket, that is, it is a mini-market. Convenience stores are a food retailing development of the 1960's. They increased from about 500 in 1957 to about 13,250 in 1970. And in spite of inflation, high food prices, recession, and unemployment, convenience stores increased in number to about 40,000 in 1981; sales volume rose from $475 million in 1957 to $14 billion in 1981. Convenience stores engage in relatively little advertising and in few promotions, though they do feature some specials from time to time. Convenience store margins are higher than in supermarkets; about 30 percent in contrast to 20 percent in supermarkets. Net earnings of convenience stores before taxes are also higher; 3.8 percent in contrast to 1.3 percent in supermarkets in 1981.

The convenience store represents a return to the "corner grocery store." It is close by, it is small, its personnel are known and friendly, it is open from early morning to late evening several days per week, and it is often customized to the neighborhood. It meets the need for quick shopping between trips to the supermarket and for emergency shopping. The names of the different chains of convenience stores reflect their character: "Kwik Chek," "Stop 'n Shop," "Hop-in-Food Stores," and "Jiffy Shop." The average number of items stocked in convenience stores is about 3,000. Generally, neither fresh meat nor produce is stocked. Fast food items and fountain beverage sales are big earners. Gasoline, which is sold in about 45 percent of convenience-store operations, accounts for more than one-third of sales volume. Although consumers are aware that prices are high in these stores, they do patronize them and the stores do succeed.

Direct-to-Consumer Marketing

The direct marketing of food from producer to consumer has long been practiced world wide. In the United States, supermarkets generally usurped food sales beginning with the 1930's and until the late 1950's when direct sales staged a comeback. The Direct Marketing Act of 1976 provided funds to the states to promote direct sales which could increase income for farmers. Since then, the number of direct sales outlets has increased significantly. Various direct outlets include the traditional farmer's market, roadside stands, pick-your-own stands, and huckster vans. In addition, fruit and vegetable stands are operated by persons who buy at wholesale prices and sell to the public directly on street corners and elsewhere. Direct mail order sale of food products by food manufacturers and specialty shops has become big business. Meats, cheeses, flour, cereal products, canned soups, jellies and jams, baked goods, and fresh fruits are some foods obtainable by mail. It is quite safe to state that none are great bargains; however, some may be of superior quality, and delivery to one's door is a service.

The Food Cooperative

Food cooperatives, or co-ops, are groups that have organized to purchase food at wholesale prices and thereby eliminate intermediate services and costs. Persons within a group arrange to buy the food, transport it, sort and package it, work as cashiers, and perform all other duties that such a project entails. The recession, inflation, and high food costs caused rapid growth in the number of food co-ops. It is estimated that at least 3,000 were in existence in 1975. Some cooperatives are composed of only a few families that share responsibilities; others are larger and hire some of the services performed. The advantages of cooperative buying may be reduced food costs and fresher food; but the costs in personal time, human energy, and transportation must be reckoned. Further, supermarket specials may cost less than the same items priced at co-ops, for example, coffee, canned goods, and paper goods. The disadvantages of the food cooperative are restricted food choices and the inconveniences of a do-it-yourself operation.

THE FOOD SHOPPER'S CHOICE OF STORE

The variety in the kinds of resources for shopping for food permits the meal manager to pick and choose the one or several that offer personal advantages. Store owners and managers would like to know why some consumers shop one or more stores to the exclusion of others that are almost identical in size, layout, pricing policy, and merchandise offerings. Shoppers give these reasons for choice of store(s): cleanliness within and outside of the store; prices clearly marked on all food items and nonfood products; low prices; unit pricing signs on shelves; frequent specials; an abundant supply of fresh, good quality produce; good meat department; convenient store location; quick checkout with baggers on duty; and pleasant and helpful personnel (8). Although shopping at more than one store would not be possible or practical for some meal managers, about 25 percent of shoppers do so (6). According to *Progressive Grocer,* the average number of shopping trips per shopper was 2.5 trips per week in 1981 (8). This would suggest that a significant number of meal managers shop more than once each week.

SOME DEVELOPMENTS THAT FACILITATE FOOD SHOPPING

Unit Pricing

Unit pricing is a system that permits the customer to compare the cost of products without having to do the arithmetic. The cost per pound or ounce of products sold by weight, and by quart, pint, or fluid ounce if sold by volume is printed on a marker that is affixed to the edge of the shelf where the products are on display. This affixed marker shows the price of the displayed item plus unit cost. By using the information provided, one can select the "best buy"—the brand or the package that is least costly, such as a box of tea bags or of cocoa mix. Or, one can use the information to compare the costs of foods within a class, such as of breads, or of breakfast cereals or jams. Unit pricing is mandatory in some states; elsewhere it is voluntarily provided in food stores.

Open Date Labeling

Open date labeling is the system of date-coding packaged food products that permits the customer to read, and sometimes, interpret it. The date is shown on some items as day and month; for others, the year may be included. The date can appear at almost any place on a package, but the top and bottom of a carton or a box are the positions on which the date is most often printed. Depending on the product, the date may represent any of the following:

1. The *pull date* is the last recommended day of retail sale. Food products that are safe for consumption after this date can be sold; but they will, in general, have been separated from fresh stock and in some way the shopper will be informed of the situation. A product is not

necessarily spoiled or unusable after this date because when the product was dated, the time for its storage and use in the home was calculated even though it might have been purchased on the last day it was offered for sale. Fluid dairy products, other dairy products, ice cream, cold cuts, and refrigerated fresh dough products are some that may carry a pull date.

2. *Freshness date* establishes the period of optimum quality of a food product. After this stated time, the product may lose palatability but in no sense would it cease to be edible. Some products that bear freshness dates are cheeses, breakfast cereals, bakery products, and mayonnaise. The label of a jar of peanut butter recently viewed stated, "For full flavor, use by MR217."

3. The *expiration date* generally means "don't use after the date shown." It is a difficult date to establish and is not frequently used, although it appears on packaged dry yeast.

4. The *pack date* is the date of processing or of final packaging. It may be found on one end of a can of canned food products and on cartons of frozen foods.

Although open dating provides information to the shopper, food quality is as much dependent on methods of handling and storage care in the warehouse, supermarket, and the home kitchen as on elapsed time from moment of production.

5. *Code dating* is used by some food manufacturers on products that have a long shelf life. The code informs as to where and when a product was packaged. If a recall is required by the Food and Drug Administration for any reason, the code permits identification and subsequent withdrawal of products from store shelves.

Computerized Checkout in the Supermarket

Computerized checkout systems have been established in many supermarkets, and total computerization is expected by the mid-1980's. Since installation of a computer system is expensive, there must be advantages to the supermarket industry. Advantages of computerization to the supermarket operator include reduced labor costs, fewer pricing errors, and better inventory control. Advantages for the consumer include time saved at the checkout counter, detailed sales slips, fewer errors in pricing, fewer errors at the checkout counter, and perhaps, but only perhaps, lower prices for food as a result of supermarket savings. Where a computerized checkout system has been installed, the cost of the items in the shopping cart are tabulated by means of the Universal Product Code symbol affixed to packages as they pass over or under an electronic, optical scanner. See Figure 9–1. The scanner is

200542 205899

FIGURE 9–1.   Universal product code. (*Courtesy of Hobart Corporation.*)

connected to a computer that prints the name and price of each item on a screen at the checkout, and it also prints this information on the consumer's sales receipt. The computer must be properly and frequently pogrammed. The Universal Product Code symbol consists of a series of dark lines of varying widths with white spaces between them also of varying widths set over two sets of digits. The left half of the symbol identifies the manufacturer; the right half identifies the product. The code can be used to mark 100 billion different items by brand name.

Stores like to discontinue item marking when the electronic scanner is installed. Instead of price marking each package, shelf markings disclose the price of products. Consumer objection to this practice has resulted in legislation by six states (mid-1982) that makes item pricing mandatory with some exceptions. The six states are: Connecticut, Michigan, Minnesota, New York, Massachusetts, and California (7). Some chains have continued item pricing after installation of electronic scanners as a convenience to customers.

Nutrition Labeling of Food

Nutrition labeling of food was mentioned in the discussion of the regulations established for the administration of the Fair Packaging and Labeling Act. Nutrition labeling is also fully discussed in Chapter 4 and is thus described but briefly here.

Although nutrition labeling is mandatory only for food products to which a nutrient is added or for which some nutritional claim is made, many food products bear nutrition information. This information must be uniformly presented so that comparisons can be made. The informational content of the label includes calorie content; the quantities of protein, carbohydrate, and fat expressed in grams; and the percentage of the U.S. RDA for protein, six vitamins, and two minerals provided by a serving of a food product as that serving is defined on the label. Although the value of this information is contingent on some knowledge of nutrition, it would definitely point out, even to a beginner, the difference in nutrient content of two such canned vegetables as beets and spinach and of two ready-to-eat dishes as canned chili with beans and canned noodles with chicken. The nutrition labeling of food products is an ambitious program of the Food and Drug Administration and the United States Department of Agriculture to educate consumers in the science of nutrition.

FOOD BUYING DECISIONS

It would be difficult to underestimate the significance of the meal manager's food buying decisions. Millions of words have been written in books, in magazines and newspapers, in bulletins, in leaflets, and have been spoken on television, on radio, and in classes to inform consumers on how to spend the at-home food dollar advantageously. Much of the disseminated information can be classified so as to correlate with these three decision-making situations: where and when to shop; what to buy; and how to purchase.

Where and When to Shop

A meal manager who has researched the resources for food shopping in the area of residence is enabled to decide where and when to shop in accordance with needs. The budget for food often suggests where to shop. The discount supermarket, the warehouse store, and the farmers produce stand where available are important resources if conservative spending is indicated. Comparison shopping either in person or via advertising in the local newspaper assists the meal manager in knowing where to find specials, abundant produce, bargains in cuts of meat and groceries, and nonfood merchandise offerings at discount. When gasoline is in short supply, the location of a food market may take first place in the decision of where to shop. When time is of consequence, early in the week, early in the morning, or in the evening are generally good times to shop. Tuesdays are often double coupon days—a means of alluring customers on a slow day. Combination stores and superstores, because they offer abundant stocking can be time-saving places to shop. The meal manager's decision on where to shop may be based on budget and/or convenience; the decision on when to shop is probably a personal decision.

Decisions on What to Buy

The meal manager's decisions on what to buy are all-important. They are not easy to make because of the abundance of food products available all of the months of the year and because of the enterprise and ingenuity of the food processing industries. In some regions of the United States, fresh strawberries, melons, and garden tomatoes can be purchased when the ground is snow covered. The meal planning decision to serve baked apples or pumpkin pie instead of strawberry shortcake, or cole slaw instead of tomato salad can be critical, even difficult. To decide to buy hamburger instead of sirloin steak, or leg of lamb, or shrimp is not easy either. The decision to buy basic ingredients instead of ready-prepared dishes can be painful because it means the home cooking of meals. Again, budget is a determining factor in decision making. Families tend to eat what they can purchase and meals are what they are for that reason. See Chapter 6, pages 104 through 107 for the character of meals as the food budget shapes them. Tables 9–3 and 9–4 show how the choice of what to buy can affect spending for food. It is not easy to learn what to buy: study, trial and error learning, and experience are teachers. However, there are ways to purchase food so that dollars buy more. For this reason, the range of food choices can be wider than one often realizes.

TABLE 9–3. *The Costs of Two Plans for Buying Meat for Five Meals for Four Persons* [1]

	Cost per Market Unit	Amount to Buy for Four	Cost for Four
Plan 1. Selections			
Sirloin steak	$3.18/lb.	2 lb.	$ 6.36
Loin pork chops	2.48/lb.	1⅓ lb.	3.31
Ready-made fried chicken	3.38/2 lb.	2 lb.	3.38
Batter fried fish fillets	3.89/1½ lb.	1 lb.	2.60
Ham, canned	5.38/1½ lb.	1 lb.	3.58
Total			$19.23
Plan 2. Selections			
Hamburger	1.28/lb.	1 lb.	1.28
Blade pork chops	1.88/lb.	1½ lb.	2.82
Chicken, fryer	.68/lb.	3 lb.	2.04
Fishcakes—ready made	1.35/8	8	1.35
Frankfurters, chicken	2.15/2 lb. (20)	8	.86
Total			$ 8.35

[1] June, 1982 prices in discount supermarket.

TABLE 9–4. *The Costs of Two Plans for Buying Vegetables for Five Meals for Four Persons* [1]

	Market Unit and Cost	Amount to Buy for Four	Cost
Plan 1. Selections			
Asparagus, fresh	$1.29/lb.	1⅓ lb.	$1.72
Broccoli in Cheese Sauce	1.19/10 oz.	10 oz.[2]	1.19
Corn, fresh	.15/ear	4 ears	.60
Mixed vegetables, Italian style, frozen	1.29/10 oz.	10 oz.[2]	1.29
Peas in butter sauce, frozen	1.19/10 oz.	10 oz.[2]	1.19
Total			$5.99
Plan 2. Selections			
Beets, canned	$ .43/ #303	1 can	.43
Cabbage, fresh	.39/lb.	2 lb.[3]	.78
Carrots, fresh	.22/lb.	1 lb.[3]	.22
Corn, canned	.46/#303	1 can	.46
Peas, frozen	.50/10 oz.	10 oz.	.50
Total			$2.39

[1]June, 1982 prices in discount supermarket.
[2]Small portions.
[3]Generous portions.

Decisions on How to Buy

The significance of the how-to decisions can be simply illustrated. See Table 9–5 for how the decision to purchase corn might be accomplished. The per-serving cost of corn as estimated ranged from nine cents to thirty-two cents depending on the state of or form of corn purchased, the quality of the product purchased, and the extent to which service was added to the corn.

We use the terms *state* or *form* to indicate that a food is fresh or in its natural condition, or that it has been modified in some way by processing. Each year developments in processing modify our foods more and more. Sometimes the price advantage lies with fresh, unmodified food and sometimes with food processed in some way. Frozen orange juice concentrate, frozen peas, and frozen lima beans are nearly always less expensive than their fresh counterparts. But fresh potatoes are less expensive than many of the dehydrated and ready prepared and frozen products. Reconstituted nonfat dry milk costs less than fresh, fluid skim

TABLE 9–5. *The Estimated Per-Serving Cost of Corn as Established by the Product Purchased*

Product Purchased	Cost of Market Unit [1]	Estimated Serving Cost
Fresh corn on the cob	.15	$ .15
Frozen corn on the cob	1.29 (4 ears)	.32
Corn, frozen, 5-minute	.60/10 oz.	.15–.20 [2]
Corn, frozen, Brand A	.92/16 oz.	.15
Corn, frozen, Brand B	.84/16 oz.	.14
Corn, frozen in butter sauce	.95/10 oz.	.24–32 [2]
Corn, canned national brand	.55/No. 303	.14
Corn, canned store brand	.47/No. 303	.12
Corn, canned, generic brand	.37/No. 303	.09

[1] Prices in discount supermarket, June, 1982.
[2] Depending on serving size.

milk. Reconstituted evaporated milk costs less than fresh, fluid whole milk. Some cheese products are less expensive than natural cheeses of the same cheese varieties. Coffee brewed from ground coffee beans costs more than coffee made from an instant product. Minute rice costs more per serving than milled rice. Mixes for gravies, sauces, and seasonings are expensive in terms of their component ingredients. Some processed foods are preserved foods such as canned and frozen fish, meats, fruits, and vegetables; others are convenience products such as pre-grated cheeses, ready-made cheese and sour cream dips, prepared, rolled and panned pastry, individual portions of instant hot cereals, iced-tea mixes, and ready-to-pour pancake batter. The purchase of food plus service is discussed subsequently. But it is important to recognize that some foods are purchased in convenient forms. A little of do-it-yourself can reduce the cost of some food items. To maximize food dollars it is necessary to compare the costs of fresh with canned, frozen, and dehydrated forms and of the instants and ready-mades with do-it-yourself equivalents. For example, a graham cracker pie shell weighing six ounces can cost $.89 whereas a pound of graham cracker crumbs may cost about $1.10 and hence provide crumbs for almost three shells; and a serving of instant oatmeal to prepare in the serving bowl costs about $.15 whereas a serving of cook-before-eating oatmeal costs only five cents.

Food products are not only available in different forms, but they are also of differing quality. The grading of food for quality was discussed in Chapter 3, it will be discussed further in Chapters 10 through 16. The fact of quality differences in food products permits the meal manager to pick and choose among products and to select with budget and personal preference in mind. Certainly, the top quality whether of canned or frozen corn, fresh apples, or beef for a pot roast would provide good eating; unfortunately, the supply of top quality is limited and therefore expensive. Numerous characteristics among which are color, tenderness, degree of ripeness, size, texture, freedom from defects, flavor, taste, and aroma establish quality. Some of these attributes do and some do not greatly affect the eating satisfaction of foods. Palatability judgments of a food, whether a canned vegetable or a frozen dinner, are personal. Some consumers associate brand name with quality; others associate quality with cost. Actually, neither is a reliable guide. Because there are quality differences in the assortment of food products available to the meal manager, it is possible to control spending for food, and it is also possible to indulge in personal food wants. It is important that the meal manager recognize that small savings on this and that add up to significant sums in the course of time.

Another boon to the meal manager who wishes to maximize dollars is the availability of food products in packages of different sizes and sometimes in different packaging materials. In general, the larger is the package of a food product, the lower is the cost of a unit of the product. See Table 9–6. A quart of homogenized whole milk costs more when purchased in a quart carton than when purchased in a gallon container. An ounce of cornflakes costs less when bought in a 12-ounce box than as a single serving; a serving of frozen peas costs less when purchased in a 20-ounce bag than a 10-ounce carton; a serving of tomato juice, when purchased in a No. 3 Cylinder can, costs less than in a six-pack of individual servings; and a pound of coffee costs less when purchased in a paper bag than when bought in a metal can. Many food products can be purchased in a number of sizes of containers, whether bag, box, bottle or can. This variety in package sizes permits consumers to purchase according to personal wants but it also permits maximizing the dollar. It would be misleading not to point out that family size, storage facilities, personal food likes, and the storage qualities of a food product must be taken into account when purchasing a product. What would be economy for one consumer could be extravagance for another; for example, the purchase of an eight-ounce jar of instant coffee would be uneconomical for a single person because of the instability of instant coffee products. Many staples have good storage qualities when properly stored; hence, meal managers can buy some food products in packages that are economical.

Contemporary packaging trends are in the direction of convenient packages as exemplified by the tea bag. Packages may consist of a number of units, such as cocoa mix, nonfat dry milk, breakfast cereals, six-packs of juices, individually wrapped slices of cheese food products,

TABLE 9–6.   *Unit Cost as Determined by Package Size*

Items	Cost of Market Unit [1]	Cost of Unit
Cornflakes	$	$
12 ounces	.89	1.19/lb.
8 ounces	.64	1.28/lb.
¾ ounce	.18	3.84/lb.
Canned pears		
No. 2½ can, 29 oz.	1.05	.58/lb.
No. 303 can, 16 oz.	.75	.75/lb.
No. 82 can, 8 oz.	.54	1.08/lb.
Pasteurized process cheese spread		
2-lb. loaf	7.18	2.39/lb.
24-ounce loaf	3.74	2.49/lb.
12-ounce block	1.98	2.64/lb.
Tomato juice		
No. 3 Cylinder can, 46 oz.	.95	.12/6 oz.
12-ounce can	.30	.15/6 oz.
Six pack—6 oz./can	1.20	.20/6 oz.
Instant coffee		
10 ounces	4.30	.86/2 oz.
6 ounces	2.99	.97/2 oz.
2 ounces	1.27	1.27/2 oz.

[1] June, 1982 costs in discount supermarket.

crackers, and cookies. Packaging is expensive. In about one-fourth of all food and beverage industries, the container and packaging cost more than the value of the ingredient(s) used in product production (3). The value of the packaging is about equal to the value of the ingredients in canned fruits and vegetables. The packaging costs exceed the cost of basic ingredients in soft drinks, breakfast cereals, soups, and frozen dinners. Packaging is seen as a form of advertising by the food industries; it becomes a disposal problem for households and communities. In general, the consumer finds packages that are economical to purchase if he or she is aware that packaging can be a factor in the cost of food products.

The last of the how-to-buy decisions that the meal manager makes is the decision on how much "service" or convenience foods to purchase. They are great time savers, but they are not without cost. Some convenience foods are new—ready-to-eat chocolate pudding, ready-to-spread cake frostings, heat-and-serve rice side dishes, heat-and-eat Chicken Kiev, spoon-and-serve whipped topping, pancake batter ready for pouring, and many, many more. However, there are convenience foods that are familiar: "store bread," butter, cheese, canned soups, Jello, baking powder, and others that have been available so long that they cease to be thought of as convenience foods. Traub and Odlund (9) define convenience foods as, "any fully or partially prepared food in which a significant amount of preparation time, culinary skills, or energy inputs have been transferred from the home kitchen to the food processor and distributor." They describe products introduced before 1960 as established convenience foods and those introduced after 1960 as "new generation" convenience foods.

Convenience foods are further classified as finished foods and as semiprepared foods. Finished foods, such as canned soups and frozen ready-baked cakes and pastries, are ready for eating after heating or thawing. Semiprepared foods include mixes; they have some service yet to be performed. In general, finished foods have more service added to basic ingredients than is added to semiprepared foods. Within each category there will always be differences in the amount of service added because some dishes are more time consuming to prepare than others, for example, frozen ready-to-bake biscuits and bottled salad dressings. The more service added to basic ingredients, the less are the energy and time inputs of the cook. When dishes are made from basic ingredients, time is used in measuring, mixing, and manipulating ingredients; in trimming, slicing, or dicing; in dusting or crumbing and browning; in whipping; in washing tools and equipment; and so on. Additional time is required for cooking or chilling homemade dishes. The cooking period may require full attention, as in stirring, basting, or turning, or it may not. The total time used in food preparation consists of active time and inactive time when attention may be directed elsewhere. The use of mixes reduces active time by eliminating almost all measuring time and almost all mixing time. Ready-to-use products like canned pie fillings reduce active time. Total time is reduced as active time diminishes. The level of convenience a product offers differs for persons who differ in experience, skill, and interest in cookery. Products are evaluated personally by meal managers in terms of the convenience each offers. The level of convenience in a product may be little and the cost may be excessive, but it may be valued highly by some. Mixes for salad dressings; crumb mixtures for preparing chicken, pork chops, or fish; stuffing mix for chicken or turkey; and seasoning mixes for chili are some examples. They do not save much time, they are relatively expensive, but they do make for tasty dishes, depending on personal preferences, and they do offer the cook satisfactions.

An extensive assortment of convenience dinners, entrees, mixed vegetable dishes, and rice dishes as well as of baked goods and desserts is available in the frozen foods section of the supermarket. There are many such items at the delicatessen counter also. They can be found canned too. An in-store bakery can provide many selections among sweet goods and breads. All of these products and many more simplify meal preparation, however, cost can be such that not all budgets can accomodate their purchase.

Traub and Odlund (9) reported a study of convenience food purchases in 1979. The study, which was of all food purchases, disclosed that about one-half of at-home food dollars were spent for convenience foods. Thirty-six percent of purchases were of established convenience foods; about 13 percent of purchases were for new generation convenience foods. They selected 166 convenience foods for cost comparisons with home prepared counterparts. Fifty-eight percent of the 166 products studied cost more per serving than home-prepared counterparts; 24 percent, less; and 18 percent, the same. They reported that quality-wise, the convenience foods did not differ significantly from the home-prepared items. In 1980, the same authors (10) reported a cost up-dating of the same convenience foods. Fifty-nine percent cost more; 28 percent, less; and 13 percent, about the same as home-prepared counterparts. In 1979, Isom (5) reported comparison costs of some frozen plate dinners and frozen dinner entrees with homemade counterparts. The spread of increased cost was from 13 percent to 105 percent for the frozen dinners; and from nine to 127 percent for the frozen dinner entrees. Because the purchase of convenience food products buys time and energy inputs, some meal managers do not find it unreasonable to pay the price for them.

Judgments of the palatability, or eating qualities, of convenience foods are personal and will be influenced by past experiences with food. Persons accustomed to home-prepared food of good quality are quite uncharitable in their evaluations of precooked, frozen dinners, ready-to-bake apple pie, and instant coffee. On the other hand, persons who are long accustomed to eating precooked, frozen dinners, precooked, frozen fish sticks, bakery cakes, and instant coffee may judge them as good as homemade counterparts. The tastiness of home-cooked food depends on the skill and experience of the cook. There have always been some superior cooks and there have been poor cooks. The same is true now. The frame of reference for judgment explains the many and diverse opinions on different convenience foods.

Quality evaluations of convenience products by panels of experts have been made. These experts judge food products in accordance with defined standards of quality. Food products are scored on the basis of such attributes as tenderness, proper texture, good aroma and flavor, absence of off-flavors, proper taste, proper color, absence of defects, and absence of foreign matter. Professional evaluations that are available to the consumer are published in Consumer Reports by the Consumers Union of Mt. Vernon, New York. In these evaluations, products are sometimes described as excellent, very good, good, fair, and poor. Explanations of ratings are included and products are identified by processor and/or brand name. Some products which were evaluated in the late 1970's and early 1980's include: beef stews, frozen pot pies, cake mixes, canned soups, dehydrated soups, frozen pizza, spaghetti sauces, hot dogs, bologna, orange juice, and many more.

To conclude this discussion of convenience foods, two points can be made. First, an unbelievable variety of food products with small to great inputs of convenience can be purchased and brought into the home kitchen. Second, because the convenience inputs increase cost, the meal manager is encouraged to analyze products from these points of view: the convenience, that is, the time and energy inputs being purchased; the price paid for that convenience; and the ingredient composition of the food product purchased. A buy-and-try policy is a suitable method for rating available convenience products.

In final summary, the food shopping task of the meal manager is advantaged by these knowledges and skills: the market resources of the local area; the most favorable time to shop; where to shop in accordance with personal goals; the current costs of regularly purchased food products; the variations in the cost of food products as product costs are affected by processing, quality, and the kind of package purchased.

SOME SHOPPING GUIDES FOR MEAL MANAGERS

1. Do your own shopping, shop alone, and, to avoid overbuying, do not shop when you are hungry.

2. To conserve your time, your energy, and gasoline, shop as infrequently as your storage facilities permit.

3. Plan your shopping expedition so as to conserve your time, money, and energy.

4. Compare prices in the markets available to you. Shop at that market that provides the kinds of commodities and services that you want at the price you want to pay. Shop at more than one market if it is practical in terms of time and energy inputs.

5. Prepare a shopping list, based on menu planning. Use the advertising of your market(s) and your newspaper in preparing your list. However, do change your mind about intended purchases when you find better buys in the market(s).

6. Allow ample time for shopping and take as much time as you require to compare products, compare prices, read labels, and seek the information that you want.

7. Develop skill in estimating how many servings you will derive from cuts of meat and prepackaged fresh vegetables and fruits.

8. Know the current costs of the food items that you buy regularly. The list will not be long because you tend to purchase the same food products week after week.

9. Comparison shop and use unit price information. Compare the costs of different brands of the same food products, such as crackers, ice cream, frozen vegetables, and so on. Compare the unit costs of packages that differ in size; compare the costs of products of different quality; and compare the costs per serving of meats, fresh fruits and vegetables, frozen vegetable dishes, and so on.

10. Buy and try different brands.

11. Buy fresh foods when they are in plentiful supply, that is, in season.

12. Shop whatever day(s) of the week that your market(s) provides you with price advantages.

13. Check the weight of food products in newly designed packages, of sale items, and of multiple-priced deals; price increases may be concealed here.

14. Buy the largest package consistent with your need for food products and your ability to store them.

15. Buy by grade when you can; match quality to intended use.

16. Look for open-date coding to inform you as to the freshness life of products.

17. Take advantage of sales, specials, and coupons, but not without evaluating the products.

18. Unless your food budget is very generous, be cautious in the purchase of ready-to-eat food products. At least, try to determine if the cost of the convenience is worth what it costs you.

19. When you prepare dishes in your kitchen, ask yourself if there are not less expensive ingredients than canned soups, mayonnaise, seasoned croutons, ready-seasoned bread crumbs, soup mixes, sauce mixes, marshmallow creme, and so on. For plain cooking, look for a cookbook written before World War II.

20. Use coupons selectively. Often, the value of the coupon is a fraction of the cost of a food product that is quite costly and that you would not consider buying if you did not have the coupon.

21. Study ingredient listings, such as this one for Green Onion Dip: "water, partially hydrogenated coconut and soybean oil, dried corn syrup, sodium caseinate, modified whey, dehydrated onion, salt, food starch-modified, vinegar, lactic acid, monosodium glutamate, gelatin, sugar, mono and digylcerides, with sodium benzoate and potassium sorbate as preservatives, dehydrated green onion, hydrolyzed vegetable protein, xanthan gum, sodium phosphate, carob bean gum, guar gum, dehydrated garlic, artificial flavor and color."

REFERENCES CITED

1. Gallo, Anthony E., "Coupons: Part 1," *National Food Review*, Economics and Statistics Service, United States Department of Agriculture, Washington, D.C. (Spring 1982), p. 11.
2. Gallo, Anthony E., "Food Advertising," *National Food Review*, Economics and Statistics Service, United States Department of Agriculture, Washington, D.C. (Winter 1981), p. 7.
3. Gallo, Anthony E. and John M. Connor, "Packaging in Food Marketing," *National Food Review*, Economics and Statistics Service, United States Department of Agriculture, Washington, D.C. (Spring 1981), p. 10.
4. Horowitz, David, *Don't Get Ripped Off.* New York: Harper and Row Publishers (1979), pp. 109–110.
5. Isom, Pamela, "Frozen Prepared Plate Dinners and Entrees—Cost Versus Convenience," *Family Economics Review*, Science and Education Division, United States Department of Agriculture, Washington, D.C. (Summer 1979). p. 18.
6. Kaitz, Evelyn F., "Getting the Most for Your Food Dollar," *National Food Review*, Economics and Statistics Service, United States Department of Agriculture, Washington, D.C. (Winter 1979), p. 29.
7. Price, Charlene C. and Charles Handy, "The Electronic Scanner Checkout and Item Price Removal," *National Food Review*, Economics and Statistics Service, United States Department of Agriculture, Washington, D.C. (Winter 1982), p. 15.
8. "Shopping Habits," *Progressive Grocer* **61**:142, 146 (April 1982).
9. Traub, Larry and Dianne D. Odlund, *Convenience Foods and Home-Prepared Foods: Comparative Costs, Yield and Quality*, Economic Report 429, National Economics Division, Economics, Statistics, and Cooperative Service, United States Department of Agriculture, Washington, D.C., 1979, pp. 1–18.
10. Traub, Larry and Dianne D. Odlund, "Convenience Food Update," *National Food Review*, Economics and Statistics Division, United States Department of Agriculture, Washington, D.C. (Winter 1980), p. 17.
11. Wills, Robert L. and Rosanna L. Mentzer, "The Effect of Generics on Food Market Structure," *National Food Review*, Economics and Statistics Division, United States Department of Agriculture, Washington, D.C. (Spring 1982), p. 7.

SUGGESTED PROBLEMS

1. Some or all of the following can be found in packages of several sizes in supermarkets: breakfast cereals, canned fruits, cheese prod-

ucts, cocoa mixes, coffee creamers, cooking oils, flour, instant coffee, macaroni products, nonfat dry milk, peanut butter, sugar, tea bags, and detergents. Select six or more of these products, go to the supermarket, shop around, gather data, and then develop a table to show how unit cost differs with package size.

2. Prepare a list of six food products that are available as store brands, generic brands, and national brands. Price them and prepare a table to show comparative costs.

3. Do a study of "heat and serve" frozen dinners or entrees. To do this, go to a supermarket and choose six from among those available. Describe them in terms of their components, weight, cost, and other interesting or relevant information.

4. Prepare a list of ten items that can be purchased nearly everywhere. Price these items in two supermarkets and a convenience store. Prepare a table that shows how the items are priced similarly and how they are priced differently. How would the total costs differ?

5. Make a collection of coupons from available sources. How much are they worth?

SUGGESTED REFERENCES

1. Goldbeck, Nikki and David Goldbeck, *The Supermarket Handbook.* New York: The New American Library, Inc. (1976).

2. Hayes, Mary Anne, *Ask the Coupon Queen.* New York: Pocket Books (1979).

3. Samtur, Susan and Ted Tuleys, *Cashing In At the Checkout.* New York: Warner Books (1979).

4. Sloane, Martin, *1981 Guide to Coupons and Refunds.* New York: Bantam Books, Inc. (1981).

5. United States Department of Agriculture, *How To Buy* bulletins are available from Publications Center, Office of Governmental and Public Affairs, U.S. Department of Agriculture, Washington, D.C. 20250.

Chapter 10

Shopping for Meat, Poultry, and Seafood

Americans like to eat meat. The 1980 estimated per capita consumption of meat in the United States in retail weight was 76.5 pounds of beef, 68.3 pounds of pork, 1.5 pounds of veal, 1.3 pounds of mutton; in ready-to-cook weight, it was 500 pounds of chicken, 10.5 pounds of turkey, and in edible weight, 12.7 pounds of fish. This adds up to an amazing total of 220.8 pounds of meat, poultry, and fish for each American. In general, the consumption of animal products has decreased while the consumption of plant products increased during recent years. This is a welcome trend because it is more economical and efficient to eat plant proteins directly than to eat meat produced from plant proteins. Since 1975 the consumption of beef has decreased from 89 pounds per capita to 76.5 pounds per capita. Veal and mutton too have decreased in per capita consumption during the past five years. On the other hand, pork consumption has increased from 51 pounds per capita in 1975 to 68.3 pound per capita in 1980. This was due to an abundant supply and thus relatively low costs for pork. Poultry, including both chicken and turkey, have increased in per capita consumption while fish has remained about the same as in 1975 (See Figures 10–1 and 10–2).

Consumers tend to spend about one third of their food dollars for meat, poultry, and fish. Frequently, this occurs at the expense of good nutrition when not enough dollars are available to buy all of the foods essential for good nutrition. Meat, because it pleases, is bought instead of milk and fruits and vegetables. The meal manager's most difficult decisions and the ones that require the most knowledge and skill in planning meals and in buying food are her choices of meat. In general, *meat* means poultry and fish as well as red meat.

168

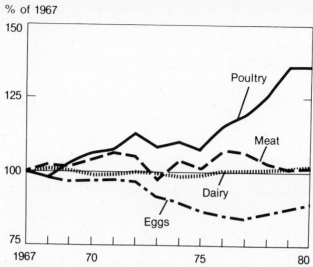

FIGURE 10–1. Per capita consumption of selected animal products. (Dairy includes butter. *USDA*.)

The meal manager requires a certain number of servings of meat for each meal. She may choose and then pay the cost or she may decide the cost and choose accordingly. The number of servings purchased for a given number of dollars is determined by the kind, the cut, and the quality of the purchased items. A dollar buys more servings of pork chops than of lamb chops, of stew than of steak, and of USDA Standard Beef than of USDA Choice beef. The costs per serving of some

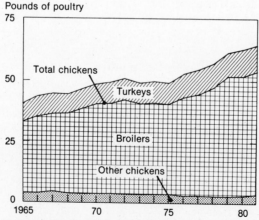

FIGURE 10–2. Per capita consumption of poultry. (*USDA 1981 preliminary*, 1982 forecast. Poultry is ready-to-cook weight.)

TABLE 10-1. *Estimated Per-Serving Costs of Selected Kinds and Cuts of Meat, Poultry, and Fish*

Kind	Cost per Pound[1]	Approximate Number of Servings per Pound[2]	Cost per Serving
Beef			
Chuck roast, bone in	$1.82	2	$0.91
Hamburger	1.52	4	0.38
Liver	1.07	4	0.27
Round Steak	3.14	4	0.785
Rib roast, bone in	3.28	2	1.64
Rump roast, boneless	2.06	3	0.69
Pork			
Chops	2.20	2½	0.88
Loin roast	1.56	2	0.78
Ham, whole	1.01	3	0.34
Lamb			
Loin chops	3.77	2	1.885
Veal			
Cutlet, boneless	6.76	4	1.69
Poultry			
Breasts, chicken	1.50	2½	0.60
Fryer, chicken	.72	1⅓	0.55
Turkey	.90	1½	0.60
Fish			
Haddock fillet, frozen	2.24	5	0.45
Ocean perch fillet, frozen	1.80	3⅓	0.545

[1] July, 1981 prices in Washington, D.C.
[2] Minimum yield per pound in general. Yields can be greater due to trimming practices and quality.

selected kinds and cuts of meat, poultry, and fish are given in Table 10-1.

To discuss the various factors that affect the cost of meat items purchased and to provide the meal manager with a frame of reference for choice making, it is necessary to define or standardize the serving. The estimated cost of a defined serving then becomes the frame of reference for decision making.

THE SIZE OF MEAT SERVING

The size of a serving of meat, poultry, or fish varies with families and for different family members. However, it is possible to think and plan in terms of standardized servings, then serve them at such ratios as four individual servings from three standardized servings or three individual servings from four standardized servings. Some meat portions are larger than the standardized serving such as steaks, small whole fish, and Rock Cornish game hens.

When the budget for food is conservative, the size of a serving may be smaller than the standardized portion. In meal planning, something less expensive may be added to compensate, perhaps dumplings or pastry, or the meat may be combined with potatoes, noodles, or vegetables.

The average, or standardized, serving is three ounces of cooked lean meat. This quantity of cooked lean meat will be derived from four to four and one-half ounces of fat-free and bone-free uncooked lean meat so long as cooking losses are no greater than 25 to 33 percent. Cooking losses of meat vary with the temperature of cooking, the length of the cooking period, the degree of doneness to which cooked, and the manner of cooking. Losses are of water and drippings. Low-temperature cooking for the shortest suitable period of time minimizes losses. The amount of meat that must be purchased to yield this four or more ounces of fat-free and bone-free lean meat is determined by the amount of fat and bone present in a cut and the size and shape of a cut. The larger the cut, the smaller is the percentage of loss, and the greater the surface area, the greater is the loss. Very young birds have a higher ratio of bone to lean than mature birds, that is, a stewing hen serves out more portions per pound than an eight-week-old fryer. Perhaps it should be noted that many persons will think that three ounces of cooked lean meat make a stingy portion.

Some items and cuts that may yield about four average portions per pound are ground beef, lamb, or ham; minute or cube steaks; liver; beef and pork tenderloins; fish fillets; center-cut ham slices; flank steak; trimmed cuts from the beef round; stew meat; and shelled frozen shrimp. Of these, liver, well-trimmed stew meat, and ground beef can be expanded to give five servings to the pound, depending, of course, on how and with what they are combined. So-called muscle boning, which simply means separating the muscles of such large cuts as the chuck and the round to fabricate steaks and roasts—which we prefer— produces lean cuts that may yield up to four servings per pound. Items that may yield three portions per pound are rib veal and pork chops; boned cuts from the shoulder of beef, pork, veal, and lamb; whole or half ham; boned beef rump roast; shrimp in the shell; and chicken breasts. Cuts that may be expected to yield two or two to three servings per pound include chicken legs (that is, the drumstick plus thigh), drumsticks, and thighs; lamb chops and lamb legs; porterhouse and sirloin steaks; bone-in rib roasts; bone-in shoulder roasts and steaks of beef; unboned lamb and pork shoulder roasts. Cuts that serve only one or one to two servings per pound include spare ribs, lamb shanks, short ribs of beef, duckling, and Rock Cornish game hen.

It is quite difficult to state precisely the number of servings a pound of meat, poultry, or fish will yield; tables often suggest yields in a range of one to two, two to three, three to four, and four to five. The range allows for variations in cuts and in the trimming practices of different supermarkets. See-through prepackaging of meats permits the buyer to assess the amount of waste, at least to some degree. The label on the package states the weight of the contents. With these bits of information, the consumer can, by examination of the packages in a display, select an approximate quantity for the desired number of servings.

CUTS OF MEAT

Animal carcasses are cut into primal or wholesale cuts, which are, in turn, cut into retail cuts. Retail cuts differ in cost per pound and preferred methods of cooking as they differ in the wholesale cut of origin. Skill in identifying the wholesale cut of origin of a retail cut is of value to the meal manager. Both bone shapes and muscle structure provide clues to identifying the part of the carcass from which a cut is derived. Beef, veal, pork, and lamb carcasses are similar in bone and muscle structure; they are cut differently into primal cuts but the retail cuts are very similar though they vary in size. Figures 10–3, 10–4, 10–5, and 10–6 show the bone structure of beef, veal, pork, and lamb carcasses and how they are cut into wholesale cuts.

Figure 10–7 shows retail cuts and carcass origin. The beef carcass is used in the illustration, but the veal, pork, or lamb carcass would have been equally satisfactory. Preferred retail cuts for all kinds of meat are rib cuts, loin cuts, sirloin cuts, and cuts from the round. This preference is explainable by meat muscle structure and inherent tenderness

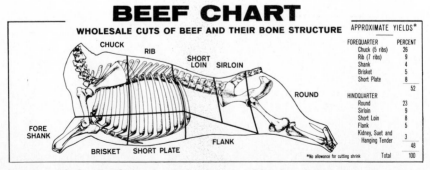

FIGURE 10–3.   Beef chart—wholesale cuts of beef and their bone structure. (*National Live Stock and Meat Board.*)

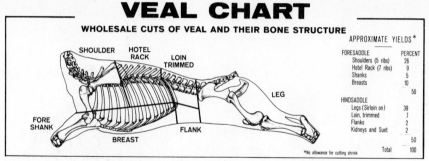

FIGURE 10–4. Veal chart—wholesale cuts of veal and their bone structure. (*National Live Stock and Meat Board.*)

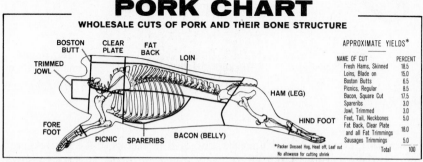

FIGURE 10–5. Pork chart—wholesale cuts of pork and their bone structure. (*National Live Stock and Meat Board.*)

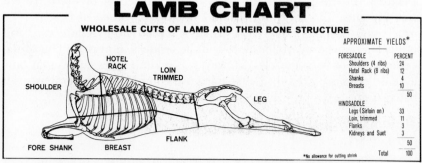

FIGURE 10–6. Lamb chart—wholesale cuts of lamb and their bone structure. (*National Live Stock and Meat Board.*)

with the possible exception of the beef round. Unless boned, these cuts are readily identified by the shapes of bone segments present in them; in the absence of bones, they are identifiable by muscle structure. Figure 10–8 shows how bone shapes reveal the carcass origin of cuts. Rib

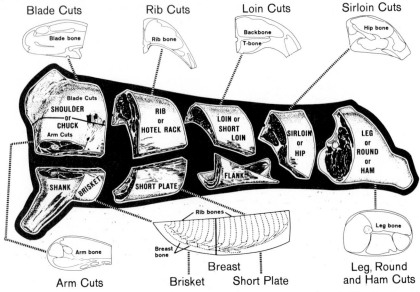

FIGURE 10–7. The seven basic retail cuts of meat. (*National Live Stock and Meat Board.*)

bones and T-bones identify roasts, chops, and steaks that are preferred and also expensive. Small circles of bone identify foreleg and round. The blade bone and the irregular shapes from the hip bone identify shoulder and sirloin cuts.

Figure 10–7 also shows the basic muscle structure of the different cuts. Rib cuts, loin cuts, and sirloin cuts are composed of two muscles principally: the *longissimus dorsi,* which is called rib eye, loin eye, and top sirloin depending on location, and the tenderloin muscle. The round is composed of four muscles. However, it is sometimes cut so that only three muscles are present. Other parts are composed of several muscles that vary in size.

Beef Cuts

Figure 10–9 shows retail cuts of beef and where they originate. Beef cuts are described as tender and less tender. An animal has muscles of locomotion and muscles that support; the latter are tender, the former are less tender. The supporting muscles lie along the animal's back; the muscles of locomotion are in the legs, shoulders, and neck. In general, tender cuts are cut from the rib, short loin, and sirloin; less tender cuts are derived from all other carcass parts (see Figure 10–3). However, all

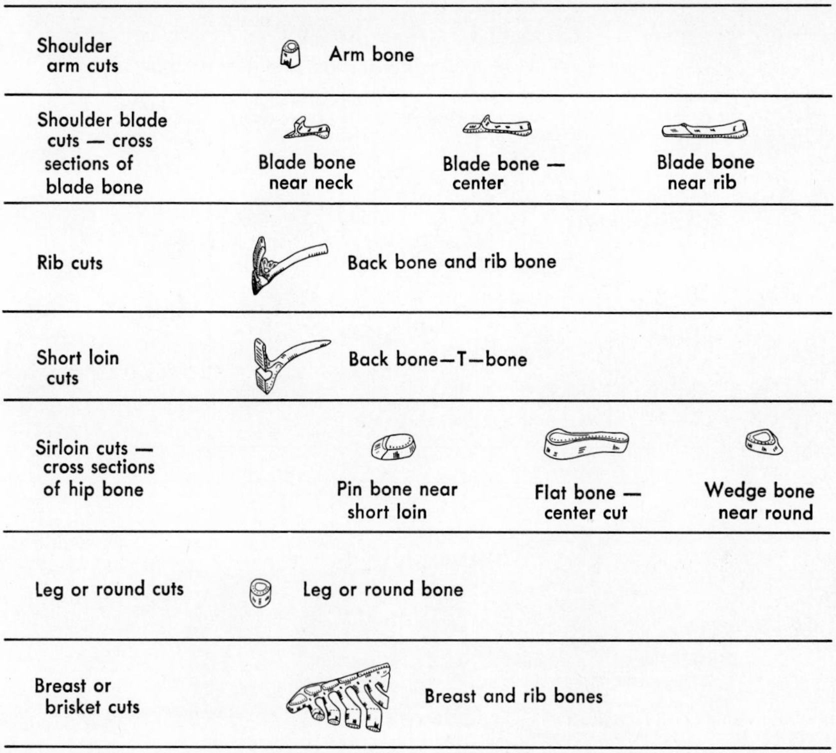

Shoulder arm cuts	Arm bone		
Shoulder blade cuts — cross sections of blade bone	Blade bone near neck	Blade bone — center	Blade bone near rib
Rib cuts	Back bone and rib bone		
Short loin cuts	Back bone—T—bone		
Sirloin cuts — cross sections of hip bone	Pin bone near short loin	Flat bone — center cut	Wedge bone near round
Leg or round cuts	Leg or round bone		
Breast or brisket cuts	Breast and rib bones		

FIGURE 10–8. Bones identify seven groups of retail cuts. (*National Live Stock and Meat Board.*)

these cuts are less tender when from low-quality carcasses. Tender cuts of meat can be cooked by dry heat methods: roasting, broiling, pan-broiling, and pan-frying. Less tender cuts of meat are made tender by moist heat methods of cooking: braising and stewing. Consumer preference is for tender cuts. The yield of a side of beef in these cuts is approximately 26 percent.

Unless they are boned, cuts from the rib section are identifiable by the curved rib bone and the presence of the large rib-eye muscle. Steaks cut from the short loin are identifiable by the T-shaped bone that derives from the backbone—although if a steak is thin, no bone may be present—and the loin eye opposed by a smaller muscle, the tenderloin, which varies in size depending on the origin of the steak (see Figure 10–8). The tenderloin muscle is a long tapering muscle that extends along the backbone through the short loin and into the sirloin with the thickest part in porterhouse steaks. The tenderloin muscle is the tenderest in the entire carcass. It is sometimes stripped from the loin and

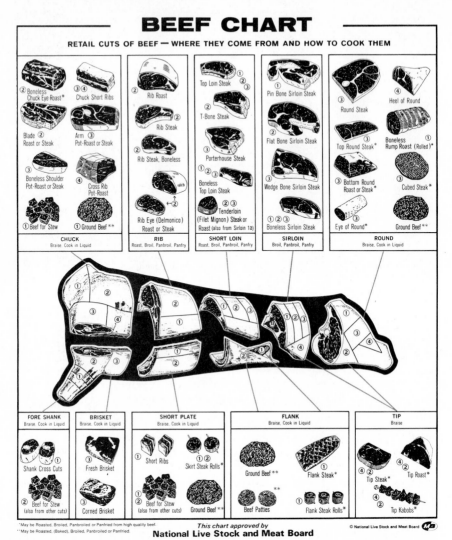

FIGURE 10–9.   Retail cuts of beef—where they come from and how to cook them. (*National Live Stock and Meat Board.*)

it may be cut into steaks called fillet mignon. It is the most expensive beef cut. Unless they are boned, sirloin steaks contain bone pieces of irregular shape that are derived from the hipbone. The shape of a hipbone varies in the different steaks. Those cut nearest the short loin contain the tip of the hipbone; they are pin-bone steaks. The next steaks contain the widest section of the hipbone; they are flat-bone or spoon-bone sirloin steaks. The next steaks contain a round or oval bone; those

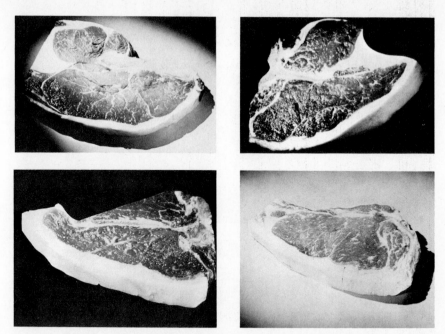

FIGURE 10–10.   Unboned steaks. Top left, flat bone sirloin steak; top right, porterhouse steak; bottom left, T-bone steak; bottom right, club steak. (*United States Department of Agriculture.*)

cut nearest the round contain a wedge-shaped bone. Refer to Figure 10–3 for concepts of the bony structure of these steaks. The best sirloin steaks are the pin-bone and flat-bone steaks because of their neat muscle structure. Figure 10–10 shows photographs of steaks from the short loin. The general appearance of the sirloin steaks cut from the part nearest the round is not as favorable as is the appearance of steaks cut nearest the short loin. Boning and muscle-boning of the sirloin gives meaty cuts with a variety of names that confuse the consumer.

Traditional cuts from the chuck that are readily identifiable are the blade and arm steaks and roasts (Figure 10–11). The seventh-rib cut, the cut adjacent to the rib section, is considered the best because it contains part of the rib eye. Boning and muscle-boning of the chuck produce roasts and steaks bearing such names as petite steak and flat-iron roast.

The beef round is sliced to give round steaks and is cut into heel-of-beef cuts and rump cuts. The round is sometimes cut into top round, bottom round, and eye-of-round sections that are sliced for steaks or cut into large pieces of pot roasts or roasting. Top round, also called inside round, is the most tender part of the round. Cuts from the round are quite free of fat. The only bone that may be present is the thigh-

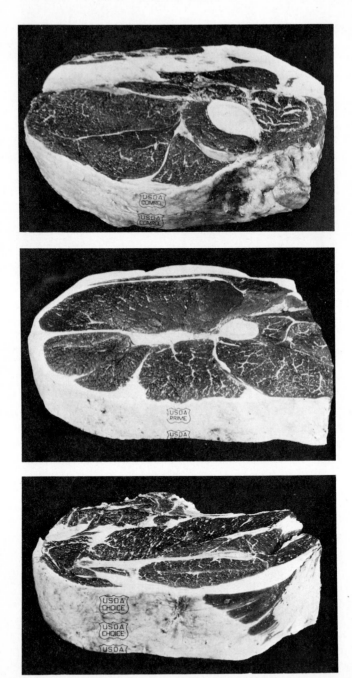

FIGURE 10–11. Unboned cuts from the chuck and the round. Top, arm cut. Center, cut from the round. Bottom, blade cut. (*United States Department of Agriculture.*)

bone, which is recognized as a small circle of bone with a center of marrow. Cuts from the round provide three to four standard portions when the bone-free cuts are bought and cooking time is not excessive. Traditional cuts from the chuck and the round are shown in Figure 10–11. Cuts from the chuck and the round are less tender cuts unless they come from high-quality carcasses. The list of tender cuts is extended by blade cuts and top round if the grade of beef is USDA Prime; by top round only if the grade is USDA Choice.

The remaining wholesale cuts provide hamburger, stew meat, short ribs, flank steak, and brisket of beef. Grinding beef to make hamburger is a means of tenderizing less tender cuts. The federal standard for hamburger requires that it contain no more than 30 percent of beef fat, no meat by-products, and no extender. Ground beef may contain as much as 30 percent beef fat, but will generally contain from 20 to 25 percent. Ground beef is priced higher than hamburger. In some markets, ground chuck, ground round, and ground sirloin are available; in general, they are priced differently, but always higher than hamburger.

Pork Cuts

Although all pork cuts are tender, only roasts are cooked by dry heat. However, thin chops can safely be pan-fried or pan-broiled. The possible presence of *trichinae,* a parasite, in pork makes it desirable that all pork cuts be cooked well done; for small cuts, this implies moist heat methods of cooking to prevent drying. There is not the variety of pork cuts that there is of beef cuts. The large loin (see Figure 10–12) is cut into chops and roasts. Roasts are center cut, blade or rib end, and sirloin loin. Chops from the loin are rib, loin, and butterfly. Rib chops are identified by the slightly curved rib bone and the presence of the rib-eye muscle outside of the curve. Loin chops are identified by the T-bone and the presence of the tenderloin and rib-eye muscles on the two sides of the T-bone. These resemble T-bone and porterhouse steaks, but they are smaller, of course. Butterfly chops are boneless; they are composed of a thick section of the rib-eye muscle partially cut through and opened out and flattened. The fore part of the carcass provides the picnic shoulder and the Boston butt. The Boston butt is cut into what may be called shoulder chops or blade steaks, or it may be boned or left unboned as Boston butt roast. The picnic shoulder is cut into arm steaks or chops, pig hocks, and roasts called arm picnic. Fresh ham cuts into pork steaks identified by a small circle of bone and boned or unboned roasts. Smoked ham is similarly cut into ham slices and butt or shank ham portions.

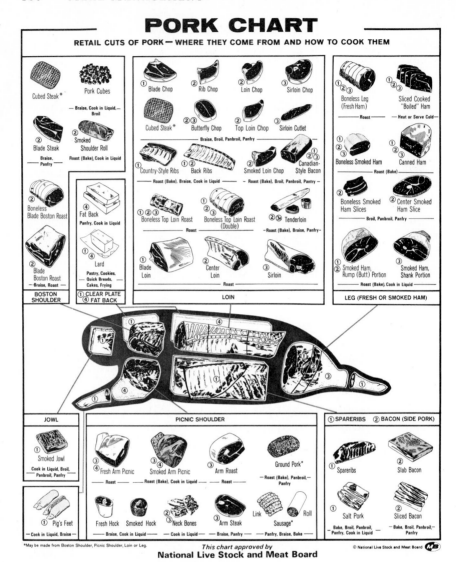

FIGURE 10–12.   Retail cuts of pork—where they come from and how to cook them. (*National Live Stock and Meat Board.*)

Veal Cuts

Veal cuts resemble beef cuts but are smaller. As with beef and pork, the shoulder cuts into blade and all roasts and steaks; the rib into rib chops or rib roast; and the loin into loin chops or sirloin steaks. The

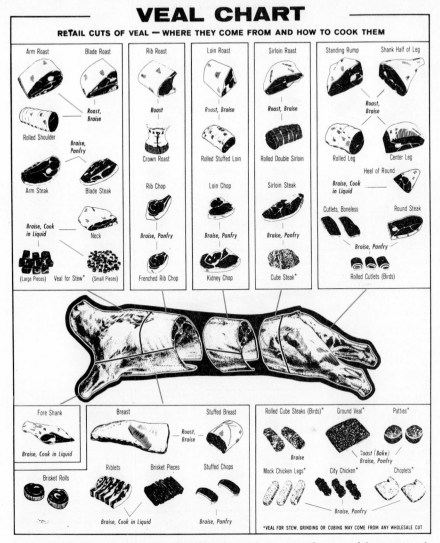

FIGURE 10–13. Retail cuts of veal—where they come from and how to cook them. (*National Live Stock and Meat Board.*)

veal round cuts into round steak, sometimes called veal cutlet and into leg or round roasts (see Figure 10–13).

Lamb Cuts

All lamb cuts are tender. The carcass is small so that cuts appear to be miniatures of beef cuts. As with beef the various wholesale cuts are

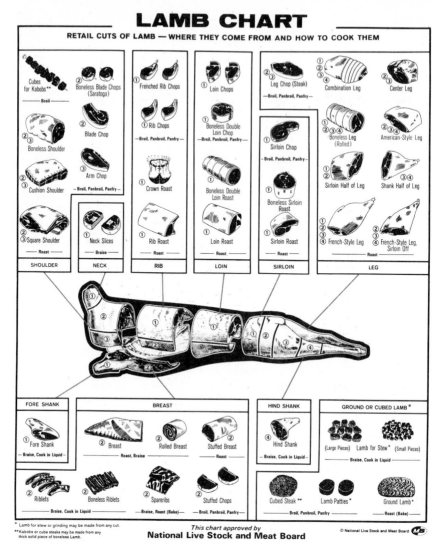

FIGURE 10–14.   Retail cuts of lamb—where they come from and how to cook them. (*National Live Stock and Meat Board.*)

cut into both roasts and chops. The shoulder cuts into blade and arm chops or boned or unboned shoulder roast (see Figure 10–14). The rib cuts into rib chops or rib roast, and the loin cuts into loin chops or roast. The leg is a roast; it may be semiboned (American-style), or unboned (French-style), Half legs are available in some markets as sirloin and shank halves. Sometimes lamb legs are cut into slices—leg chops or steaks. Lamb shanks are the forelegs.

Summary.   Different cuts of meat from the same species have similar nutrient value and comparable flavor; they may differ in tenderness and other palatability factors. For all kinds of meat, the cuts from the rib and loin sections are the most highly prized; they are also the most expensive to purchase. The lamb leg is a premium cut; it is expensive to purchase. Ham and fresh ham and the veal cutlet and the veal leg roast are excellent cuts; the pork cuts are fairly expensive; the veal cuts are very expensive. Shoulder cuts of all kinds of meat are moderately priced; when properly cooked, they make fine eating. The other parts of carcasses are the less favored parts; in general, they are cut into stew or chop-suey meat, or ground finely to coarsely for hamburger or sausage. Although not necessarily cheap, their cost per serving is less than that of other cuts.

It is possible to identify the part of the carcass from which a cut originates by the shape of the bone or bones present. In the absence of bone, most cuts are identifiable by the muscle structure. It is important to know from what part of the carcass a beef cut has been derived in order to know how to cook it.

Poultry Cuts

Chickens and turkeys are cut into parts, prepared as boneless roasts, and prepared as boneless thigh and breast fillets. All have been defined by the United States Department of Agriculture for poultry products in interstate commerce. *Poultry product* means any ready-to-cook poultry or poultry food product. *Ready-to-cook poultry* means any dressed poultry from which the protruding pinfeathers, vestigial feathers, head, shanks, oil gland, and all viscera have been removed, with or without giblets; it is ready to cook without the need of further processing. The term *giblets* means the liver from which the bile sac has been removed, the heart from which the pericardial sac has been removed, and the gizzard from which the lining and contents have been removed. *Dressed poultry* means poultry from which feathers and blood have been removed. Any packages labeled as follows will contain poultry parts as specified.

1. *Breasts, breasts with ribs, wishbones* are breast pieces separated from the carcass as the names imply. The breast may be cut into two nearly equal parts along the breastbone. No neck skin can be included in any of these.
2. *Legs* include thigh and drumstick, whether disjointed or not. Legs separated into parts that are packaged and sold separately become *thighs* and *drumsticks*. No back skin can be included on legs and thighs.

3. *Wings* must include the entire wing with skin and muscle intact, but the wing tip may be removed.

4. *Backs* include the pelvic bones and all the vertebrae posterior to the shoulder joint. The meat may not be removed from pelvic bones. But *stripped backs* will have the meat removed from the pelvic bones.

5. *Necks,* with or without neck skin, are separated from the carcass at the shoulder joint.

6. *Halves* are the nearly equal parts derived by the full-length split of the back and the breast of the carcass. *Quarters* are the halves cut crosswise at almost right angles to the backbone.

7. *Poultry roast* (or *roll,* or *bar,* or *log*) is prepared from the meat of young poultry of A Quality with respect to fleshing and fat covering. *A Quality* means the top quality designation in the United States standards for ready-to-cook poultry and parts. The meat is trimmed of tendons, cartilage, large blood vessels, blood clots, blemishes, discoloration, and other undesirable parts. Seventy-five percent or more of the outer surface must be covered with skin either attached or used as a wrap. Slices of the cooked roast should separate into no more than three parts. Label statement must reveal the combination of light and dark meat if they are present in other than natural proportions. Dark meat has long been considered fatter and less tender than white meat, but more flavorful. Young poultry is marketed at such an early age that these differences have practically ceased to exist.

8. *Boneless breast* and *boneless thigh* (also called *breast fillet* and *thigh fillet*) are deboned parts that must meet the A Quality requirements for ready-to-cook poultry parts.

Except for the poultry roast and the breast and thigh fillets, all of these cuts are abundantly available either fresh or frozen and prepackaged in the supermarket. For birds at eight to ten weeks of age, the breast is about 33 percent of its ready-to-cook weight; the two legs, about 33 percent; and the bony parts, about 34 percent (9). However, averages published by the National Broiler Council are legs with thighs, about 30 percent; breast with ribs, about 30 percent; remaining parts, 37 percent; cutting losses, 3 percent. When properly priced, the chicken parts are as good buys as the whole chicken. Proper pricing means that breasts are priced about 40 percent more; thighs, about 33 percent more; drumsticks, about 25 percent more; and legs, about 30 percent more than whole fryers. Obviously, the bony parts—wings, backs, and necks—should cost less per pound than the whole fryer (11). At all ages, males weigh more than females; this is also true for each part, or cut. When available, parts from male fryers provide more generous portions than parts from female fryers.

Fryers weigh from two and a half to four pounds of ready-to-cook weight, depending on age and sex. They are usually about nine weeks of age. The yield in cooked meat at this age is about 54 percent and the yield in skin is about 11 percent; that is a little over half of the purchased weight is edible meat (5).

THE QUALITY OF MEAT, POULTRY, AND FISH

Quality in meat, poultry, and fish has two connotations for the consumer; wholesomeness and palatability. If one of these connotations has first place, it is probably wholesomeness.

Wholesomeness as an Aspect of Quality

Wholesomeness as an aspect of quality means fit and safe for eating. It means that all meat and meat food products—animal, poultry, and fish—derive from healthy animals; and that slaughter, all processing, all transport, and all storage take place under sanitary conditions; and that all products are free from disease-producing microorganisms and filth of any kind. Federal inspection for wholesomeness is mandatory for all meat and poultry and for processed meat and poultry food products destined for interstate and foreign commerce. The Wholesome Meat Act of 1967 and the Wholesome Poultry Products Act of 1968 required that the states provide inspection equal to federal inspection for products destined for intrastate commerce. In the absence of state inspection programs equal to federal inspection, federal inspection became mandatory. See Chapter 3.

Inspection begins with live animals and continues through slaughter and processing. Animals and animal parts considered unfit for food are condemned and removed from food channels. High standards of sanitation are enforced in slaughtering and processing plants.

Processed meat and poultry food products are made according to approved formulas. The meat or poultry ingredient is reinspected to make certain that it is wholesome. All ingredients and additives used in production are inspected for wholesomeness. Inspection continues through each step in production to packaging and labeling. It is mandatory that ingredients be named in order from the one present in greatest amount to the one present in least amount. Although this labeling is informative to a degree, it does not inform as to the quantity of meat or poultry present in a product.

All federally inspected products are identified by appropriate inspection marks (see Figure 10–15). In addition to the statement of inspection, the number assigned to the processing plant is included within the inspection mark. The inspection mark for meats is stamped in a safe red or blue dye on all wholesale cuts; it may or may not be trimmed

FIGURE 10–15.   Meat inspection marks. Left, the mark on carcass and cuts. Right, the mark on processed meat food products. (*United States Department of Agriculture.*)

FIGURE 10–16.   Poultry inspection mark. (*United States Department of Agriculture.*)

FIGURE 10–17.   Combination grade and inspection symbol for poultry showing class of bird. (*United States Department of Agriculture.*)

from retail cuts. On fresh and uncooked frozen poultry and poultry parts, the inspection mark appears on the overwrap, on an insert within the package, or on the wing tip of the ready-to-cook bird. The inspection mark may stand alone or be combined with the grade (Figures 10–16 and 10–17). The inspection mark on processed meat and poultry food products, such as frozen dinners, chili con carne, and chicken pies, is printed on the box, can, or wrapper.

The wholesomeness of fish food products is assured only by the provisions of the Food, Drug, and Cosmetic Act; that is, there is no mandatory inspection of fish and fish food products during processing as there is for meat and poultry. The inspection program for fish and fish products which is being used at the present time is voluntary. A round stamp reading "U.S. Department of Commerce, Packed Under Federal Inspection" is used on fish products which have been inspected and found to be safe, wholesome and of good quality. Grading, too is voluntary. All grades are wholesome but U.S. Grade A is assigned to products which are of uniform size and free of blemishes. Currently less than one half of the processed fish products are subject to inspection and grading by the National Marine Fisheries Service.

To prevent the transmission of disease through shellfish, a shellfish sanitation program is administered jointly by the coastal shellfish producing states, the Food and Drug Administation, and the shellfish industry. Water quality is monitored and, when indicated, areas are closed to the taking of shellfish. Both oysters and clams live and breed in estuarine water that can become polluted. In 1971, oysters were found to contain cadmium in amounts greater than now considered safe. Shellfish shippers are certified and each package of shellfish should bear the certificate number of the shipper.

Palatability as an Aspect of Quality

Most consumers, except beginners perhaps, have a concept for the assessment of quality in meats, including fish and poultry. This concept includes freshness as it can be judged by color and smell; appropriate color; minimum quantities of fat and bone, except as a cut demands the presence of a distinctive bone of good size; muscle composition of a few well-shaped pieces; the potential for easy and neat carving; and a no-drip package. Consumers can be observed in the supermarket making judgments; packages of meat that fail in assessment are passed over. Of course, meat must eat well, that is, be tender, juicy, and of good flavor.

The intrinsic factors that affect the qualities of tenderness, juiciness, and flavor are known; hence, standards for the quality grading of uncooked meat, poultry, and fish can be established. They are the work of the appropriate divisions of the United States Department of Agriculture for meats and poultry and of the National Marine Fisheries Service of the United States Department of Commerce. Formerly, the Bureau of Commercial Fisheries of the United States Department of the Interior defined standards for grading fishery products. Products graded in accordance with established standards bear the appropriate grade marks. Standards have been developed for grading beef; veal and calf; lamb, yearling mutton, and mutton; chickens and turkeys; and for a variety of frozen fish fillets and steaks. Since no law requires grading of meat for quality, the packer may hire federal graders, grade his own products, or market his products without grading.

Grading for Quality

Until February, 1976, factors that were considered in grading for quality were cutability, conformation, and quality. After that date conformation per se was no longer used in the determination of quality; however, it is still considered in an indirect way since animal conformation influences other quality factors. *Cutability* refers to the amount of usable meat in a carcass. High cutability implies thick muscling and minimum fat covering. There are cutability grades for beef, pork, and lamb. *Quality* refers to the characteristics associated with tenderness, juiciness, and flavor of lean meat. These characteristics are maturity, the amount and distribution of fat, and the color, firmness, and texture of the lean. As animals and birds age, bones lose pinkness and porosity and become dense, flinty and white, lean flesh darkens and becomes coarse in texture, and fat may change in color and accumulate in excessive quantities. Meat from mature animals and birds is less tender and drier than that from younger ones. Fat is deposited as an external covering of the body, within the abdominal cavity, and between and within muscles. Fat intermingled with lean within a muscle is termed *marbling.* The presence of fat in meat protects it against drying during cooking; hence it affects juiciness. Further, good flavor is associated with the presence of fat. The color, firmness, and texture of the lean affect quality. Lean of good quality is of the proper color for its kind, firm, and fine of grain.

Grading Beef for Quality.   There are two kinds of USDA grades for beef: yield grades and palatability, or quality, grades. Yield grades were adopted in 1965. They are expressions of the percentage yields of boneless, closely trimmed retail cuts from the high-value parts of the carcass—round, loin, rib, and chuck—that is, the cutability of a carcass. Carcasses of the same quality grade can differ in yield grade. There are five yield grades from USDA Yield Grade 1 through USDA Yield Grade 5. Differences in the yields of trimmed cuts are from 82 percent to about 64 percent for carcasses of like weight from USDA Yield Grade 1 to USDA Yield Grade 5. Yield grades are based on the size of the ribeye muscle, the external and internal fat, and carcass weight. The ribeye diminishes in area and the quantity of fat increases as the grade moves from a lower to a higher number, a fact that explains the different appearance of like cuts of the same quality grade. The meat-type steer—a product of breeding and feeding management—produces a thickly muscled carcass of minimum fat content that rates high in cutability, that is, a yield grade of low number.

Palatability grades describe beef as USDA Prime, USDA Choice, and so on. The palatability grade is based on such factors as marbling, firm-

FIGURE 10–18. USDA yield grade and quality grade symbols. (*United States Department of Agriculture.*)

ness, texture, and color of the lean. Marbling and firmness are assessed in a cut surface in relation to the apparent maturity of the animal from which the carcass derived. Maturity is assessed by an evaluation of the size, shape, and ossification of the bones and cartilages and the color and texture of the lean flesh. Consumers may prefer mature beef due to its stronger, more distinctive flavor; however, mature beef often lacks tenderness if the marbling is not adequate.

The eight quality grades for beef, from the best to the poorest, are Prime, Choice, Good, Standard, Commercial, Utility, Cutter, and Canner. When federally graded, the grade name is preceded by USDA and the whole is enclosed within a shield (Figure 10–18). The grade mark is imprinted with a roller stamp the full length of the carcass and across the shoulders. Most retail cuts from graded carcasses will carry one or more or part of one of these marks. Of the top five grades, only the USDA Commercial grade is applied to mature carcasses. Very little of Prime beef reaches the supermarket; this quality is purchased by the restaurant trade. The lower three grades are seldom sold as retail cuts but are used instead in making hamburger and meat food products. USDA Choice is the grade that is most abundantly available. In 1976 several changes were incorporated into beef quality grades to reduce the variation in palatability within each grade and to more fully identify value differences in beef carcasses. Two changes in the 1976 revision of the quality grades were (1) to eliminate the increased requirement for marbling with maturity and (2) to reduce the marbling requirement for the Good grade. As a result of these changes in the grading system fewer carcasses are graded Good; more are graded Standard, Choice, and Prime (2).

As of mid-1982, further revisions in the grade designation standards were under review. In essence, the proposals would reduce marbling requirements for grades and thereby they would provide the leaner beef that consumers prefer. Further, the cost of production would be modified because the grain-feeding period could be reduced for the production of Choice Carcasses. Some new names for grades have been suggested.

Supermarkets may stock only Choice beef or they may carry one or more lower qualities. There is a wide range of quality within the Choice grade. Prices of cuts should vary with quality. In a large meat department or in a so-called meat market, it is quite possible to find identical cuts of different grades at different prices. Grade differences could demand different cooking methods. Properly cooked, both Choice and lower quality grades should be tasty; however, the cut with more marbling will probably have more flavor and be juicier.

The consumer who can buy only ungraded beef should look for lean of fine grain, creamy-white fat, and some marbling if she wants a cut of Choice quality. Good and Standard beef have lean of bright color and fine grain, bones that are red and spongy in appearance, no marbling, and a thin external fat layer. Commercial and Utility beef have lean of dark red color and coarse texture, bones that are white and dense, and a variable fat content that is yellowish instead of creamy.

Quality in Veal and Calf.   Veal and calf are two classifications of young bovine animals. Genuine *veal* comes from animals not more than three months of age that have been milk fed only. *Calf* derives from animals three to eight months of age that have been given feeds other than milk. Typical veal has lean of grayish pink color and smooth, velvety texture; the fat is soft and pliable. Calf has lean of grayish red color; the fat is harder and flaky. In the trade *veal* means all young animals up to one year of age. In some states it is permitted to describe as baby beef animals slaughtered when under fifteen months of age.

Little veal and calf are graded for retail trade. Official USDA grades include Prime, Choice, Good, Standard, and lower grades. The better quality carcasses are fatter, more juicy, and more flavorful than carcasses of the lower grades. Except for cuts from very young veal, veal and calf chops, steaks, and cutlets are traditionally cooked by moist heat methods to develop juiciness and flavor. Large cuts can be oven roasted. Veal and calf cuts are much more expensive than beef and pork cuts.

Quality in Pork.   During the 1960's, much progress was made in the production of meat-type hogs. These animals weigh about 200 pounds at five to six months of age and have larger muscles and longer sides as well as 57 percent less fat than old-type hogs. The USDA standards for grading slaughter swine, feeder pigs, and pork carcasses were revised in 1968 to reflect this. Pork carcasses are judged to be of either acceptable or unacceptable quality on the basis of firmness of fat and lean and color of lean. Pork carcasses adjudged unacceptable are graded U.S. Utility. Carcasses of acceptable quality are graded from U.S. No.

1 to U.S. No. 4 on the basis of yield in the four lean cuts: hams, loins, picnics, and Boston butts. The range in yield of these cuts is from 53 percent and over to less than 47 percent for the four grades from U.S. No. 1 to U.S. No. 4. Yield grade is based on the degree of fatness and the degree of muscling. Six degrees of muscling from very thick to very thin are recognized. Because there are no consumer grades for pork, the meal manager must grade her own. Like the expert, she should look for thick muscles and thin fat.

Fine pork has gray-pink lean that is fine in grain and firm of texture. There is some marbling of the lean. The fat is white and the bones are spongy and pinkish, a sign of immaturity. The lean of cuts from older animals is darker in color and coarse in texture. Pork should be tender, juicy, and flavorful.

Quality in Lamb, Yearling Mutton, and Mutton.   Classifications of sheep are lamb, yearling mutton, and mutton. Lamb may be baby lamb, spring lamb, and lamb. *Baby lamb* refers to animals from six to eight weeks of age. *Spring lamb* or *genuine spring lamb* comes from new-crop lambs slaughtered during the period beginning in March and terminating the week containing the first Monday in October. Older carcasses are described as lamb, yearling mutton, and mutton. As of October, 1982, new rules went into effect that permit more carcasses to be classified as lamb than formerly. The designation of *lamb* versus *yearling mutton* is based on the condition of the break between the foreleg and the feet. If one break is rough and one is smooth, the carcass can be called lamb if it possesses the other characteristics of lamb carcasses. Heretofore, both break joints had to be rough for the classification of lamb. The yearling mutton carcass has moderately wide and flat rib bones and slightly dark lean of slightly coarse texture. Mutton carcasses have spool joints at the foreleg, dark and coarse flesh. Neither lamb nor mutton is eaten widely in the United States. New Zealand and domestic lamb may be purchased, however, some consumers prefer domestic over New Zealand lamb.

USDA grades for lamb and yearling mutton are Prime, Choice, Good, Utility, and Cull; there is no Prime grade for mutton but the other grades apply. Some quality-graded lamb can be purchased in the supermarket. The five yield grades for lamb are also applicable to yearling mutton and mutton. Like the beef yield grades, the grades for lamb separate carcasses of the same quality grade according to yields of the premium cuts: chops and legs. Lamb chops and legs are high-priced; lamb shanks, lamb neck slices, and lamb breasts are less expensive. Lamb shoulder cuts are intermediate in cost. Lamb is tender and can be cooked by dry heat; yearling mutton and mutton should be cooked by moist heat.

Grading Poultry for Quality.   Modern poultry is the outcome of cross-breeding, scientific feeding, and controlled environmental conditions. Per capita consumption per year of poultry rose from 27.5 pounds in 1957–1959 to 60.0 pounds in 1980. "Chicken every Sunday" is no longer only for the affluent.

Poultry means chickens, turkeys, ducks, guineas, and geese; but only chickens, turkeys, and ducks are described here. All are marketed young—broiler and fryer chickens at eight to nine weeks of age and twenty-pound tom turkeys at five months of age—and mature. Young poultry is tender and the meat is juicy; but it may lack the flavor of mature poultry. Poultry is usually labeled to reveal age because age dictates the method of cooking.

The classes of young and mature chickens, turkeys, and ducks are described.

1. A *Rock Cornish game hen* or *Cornish game hen* is a young immature chicken bred from a Cornish chicken or the progeny of a Cornish chicken crossed with another breed of chicken. It should weigh no more than two pounds ready-to-cook weight and is usually five or six weeks of age.
2. A *broiler* or *fryer* is a young chicken, of either sex, usually nine to twelve weeks old. It has tender meat; soft, pliable, smooth-textured skin; and flexible breastbone cartilage.
3. A *roaster* is a young chicken, of either sex, usually between three and five months of age. It has tender meat, smooth-textured skin, and breastbone cartilage that may be somewhat less flexible than that of a broiler or fryer.
4. A *capon* is a surgically unsexed male chicken, usually less than eight months old. It has tender meat and soft, pliable, smooth-textured skin.
5. A *stag* is a male chicken, usually less than ten months of age. It has somewhat toughened and dark flesh, coarse skin, and a somewhat hardened breastbone cartilage.
6. A *hen* or *stewing chicken* or *fowl* is a mature female chicken, more than ten months old. The flesh is less tender than that of a roaster, and the breastbone tip is nonflexible.
7. A *cock* or *rooster* is a mature male chicken with toughened and darkened flesh, coarse skin, and a hardened breastbone tip.

In labeling practices, the first four of these classes may be described as "young chicken" and the last three, as "mature chicken" or "old chicken."

Descriptions of turkey classes follow.

1. A *fryer-roaster turkey* is a young, immature turkey of either sex, usually less than sixteen weeks old. It has tender flesh; soft, pliable, smooth-textured skin; and a flexible breastbone cartilage.

2. A *young hen turkey* is a young female turkey five to seven months old. It has tender flesh; smooth-textured, soft, and pliable skin; and a somewhat flexible breastbone cartilage.
3. A *young tom turkey* is a young male turkey with the same character- istics as a young hen turkey.
4. A *yearling hen turkey* is a fully matured female turkey, usually under fifteen months old. The flesh is reasonably tender, and the skin is reasonably smooth-textured.
5. A *yearling tom turkey* is a fully matured male turkey with the same characteristics as the yearling hen turkey.
6. A *mature turkey* or *old turkey* is a bird of either sex, older than fifteen months. It has toughened flesh and coarse skin.

For labeling purposes, the designation of sex name is optional and the first three classes may be grouped and designated as "young turkeys."

The consumption of ducks has increased in recent years, so it may be practical to define the various classes of ducks.

1. A *broiler duckling* or *fryer duckling* is a bird of either sex, less than eight weeks old, with tender flesh, a soft bill, and a soft windpipe.
2. A *roaster duckling* is a young bird of either sex, usually less than six- teen weeks old. The flesh is tender; although the bill and the wind- pipe are a little hardened, they are easily dented.
3. A *mature duck* or *old duck* is a bird of either sex over six months of age with toughened flesh and hardened bill and windpipe.

Grading of poultry for quality is voluntary and only poultry that has been federally inspected for wholesomeness can be graded. The in- spection mark and the grade mark may be combined as in Figure 10– 17. The class name is included, for example, "frying chicken." Con- sumer grades have been established for ready-to-cook birds and parts. There are three grades: U.S. Grade A, U.S. Grade B, and U.S. Grade C. The factors considered in grading are conformation, fleshing (mea- tiness), the amount of fat, and the presence or absence of such defects as bruised flesh, torn or discolored skin, and broken or disjointed bones. U.S. Grade A birds have a well-developed covering of flesh, consider- ing the kind, class, and part. The brest is rounded and the drumstick, thigh, and wing are moderately fleshed (see figures 10–19 and 10–20). U.S. Grade B birds are described as having a substantial covering of flesh on the breast and sufficient flesh on the drumstick, thigh, and wing to prevent a thin appearance. U.S. Grade C birds are those that do not meet the requirements for either U.S. Grade A or U.S. Grade B. Poultry roasts and fillets can be prepared only from top quality poul- try; they can be graded U.S. Grade A. In general, only U.S. Grade A poultry products are grade-labeled; products of lesser quality are sold unlabeled. "Breastiness" and good fleshing on the legs are marks of

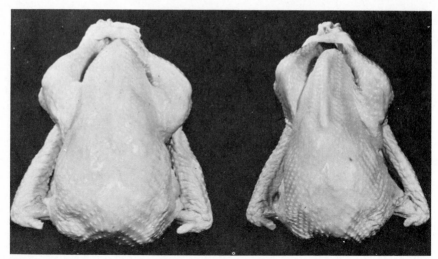

FIGURE 10–19.   U.S. Grade A and U.S. Grade B turkeys. (*United States Department of Agriculture.*)

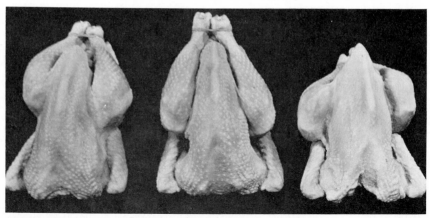

FIGURE 10–20.   Ready-to-cook chickens of U.S. Grade A, U.S. Grade B, and U.S. Grade C qualities. (*United States Department of Agriculture.*)

quality. Not much mature poultry is available in the supermarket. In general, mature poultry is cooked by moist heat, that is, stewing or braising. Older birds are preferred for some dishes, such as chicken salad, chicken pie, and creamed chicken, because of their better developed flavor. The price paid for cheap, tender chicken has been the loss of old-fashioned chicken flavor.

Fish Products.   At the present time, standards for grading have been established for the following frozen fish products by the United States

Bureau of Commercial Fisheries: fried fish sticks, raw breaded shrimp, fish blocks, haddock fillets, halibut steak, cod fillets, raw breaded fish portions, raw headless shrimp, salmon steaks, ocean perch fillets, fried scallops, fried fish portions, breaded fish steaks, and flounder and sole fillets.

The grades for fish products are U.S. Grade A and U.S. Grade B. Grades are established by evaluating such factors as flavor and odor, the appearance of the flesh, and the character of the cooked fish. U.S. Grade A fish products would be uniform in the size of the pieces, free from blemishes and defects, and of good flavor. U.S. Grade B products, although good in flavor, would not be as free of blemishes as U.S. Grade A products. The grade of fish products that is most widely distributed is U.S. Grade A. Grades define minimum fish content: raw breaded fish portions, not less than 75 percent; raw breaded fish sticks, not less than 72 percent; fried fish portions, not less than 65 percent; and fried fish sticks, not less than 60 percent by weight. Fish portions must weigh more than one and one-half ounces; fish sticks, less than one and one-half ounces, and both must be at least three-eights inches thick. Frozen fried scallops contain a minimum of 60 percent scallop meat and frozen regular breaded raw shrimp not less than 50 percent shrimp meat.

Whether fresh or frozen, fish is perishable. For this reason, frozen fish products mishandled in transit or during storage will be less than the stated grade quality. Comparisons reveal that further-processed fish products are more expensive than frozen raw fillets and steaks. They are convenience products and part of their cost is the cost of the added service.

Summary.   Quality means wholesomeness and platability. Inspection for wholesomeness of meat and poultry in interstate and intrastate commerce is mandatory; inspection of imported meat is mandatory. Inspection of fish for wholesomeness is voluntary, and inspected products will be so labeled. Standards for evaluating quality in different kinds of meat, poultry, and fish have been established. Grading for quality is voluntary and the service is paid for by the processor. The cost of the meat, poultry, or fish varies with quality, with the best being the most expensive most of the time. Proper cooking is essential for optimum palatability of all meat, poultry, and fish, even the best.

MISCELLANEOUS INFORMATION ABOUT MEATS

In this section we discuss buying meat for the freezer, cured meats, sausages, tenderizing meats, meat extenders and meat analogs, meat food products, poultry food products, and shellfish. At the end of the chapter are guides to buying meat, poultry, fish and shellfish, and a section on how to store meat.

Buying Meat for the Freezer

Although consumers purchase frozen poultry, they prefer to buy fresh red meats, especially beef, and freeze them in the home freezer or to buy them for the freezer and have them quick frozen by provisioners who provide the requisite services. A consumer must make several decisions when buying meat for the freezer. The first of these would be to consider the advantages and disadvantages of the practice, which would not be the same for all consumers. Here are some possible advantages.

1. A ready supply of meat that makes weekly shopping for meats unnecessary.
2. A supply of meat of constant quality: if the meat were excellent, this would be a boon; if only fair, it might become a disadvantage.
3. A supply of meat at, perhaps, less than the retail cost of comparable cuts. The consumer must calculate this.

These disadvantages might be listed.

1. The immediate investment of a rather large sum of money for the meat supply for several months.
2. An assortment of cuts that may or may not be those customarily eaten. No one should buy a side of beef without knowing that the percentage of tender roasts and steaks is only about 20 percent of gross weight. That would be about sixty pounds from a side of 300 pounds gross weight of medium yield grade. There would be about eighty pounds of less tender roasts and steaks and about the same weight of stew meat and hamburger plus a few pounds of brisket.
3. The need to think ahead and properly thaw meat for cooking. Although meat may be cooked from the frozen state, much of what is in the freezer will need browning and special treatment because it is less tender.
4. The determination of whether or not it will be economically feasible to make this purchase. This means comparing the cost of the freezer meat against the cost of the same assortment of cuts bought at retail. This must be done in the local market area because market conditions vary in the different regions of the United States. The ready availability of beef specials in nearly all market areas complicates these

calculations, as does the variability of the cost of meat in relation to the supply at different seasons.

Having made the decision to purchase meat for the freezer, it would next be necessary to select an honest and reliable dealer who could provide wholesome meat of the desired quality and the required services: cutting, packaging, and quick freezing; and if pork is purchased for freezing, curing service for bacon, hams, and other cuts that will not be used fresh, and service for sausage making. Third would be the choice of how much and what to buy: carcass, side, forequarter or hindquarter, wholesale cuts, or even special retail cuts. The purchase of a carcass would be the equivalent of the purchase of two sides of beef. What this entails has already been discussed. The forequarter contains the rib section for tender roasts and the chuck, which is meaty but yields less tender cuts. The hindquarter yields tender steaks, the rump, and the less tender round. The forequarter yields more meat than the hindquarter. Wholesale cuts, when these can be purchased, include the round, the chuck, the rib, and the trimmed loin. The price per pound would be the highest for the loin and the least for the forequarter. In descending order of price per pound, they would rank something like this: loin, rib, hindquarter and round, carcass, and, lastly, forequarter. Retail cuts at special prices, to be frozen in the home freezer, offer opportunities for good buys. Family preference as well as the extent of the money resource would be factors that would influence the decision on which part and how much to buy. (6)

The consumer must choose the quality to purchase. The yield grade is important for beef as well as the quality grade. Because the price per pound will vary according to the quality and yield grades, it is important to know for a certainty the grades purchased; the consumer should ask to see the USDA grade marks. The yield of beef carcasses varies according to the yield grade from about 80 percent for Yield Grade No. 1 to about 64 percent for Yield Grade No. 5. Although pork is not graded extensively, graded carcasses can be ordered. Grades are U.S. No. 1 through U.S. No. 4. Differences are in the yield of the major lean cuts: ham, loin, Boston butt, and picnic shoulder. Buy USDA Prime or USDA Choice lamb for the freezer. Both pork and lamb carcasses are from young animals, and the quality is less variable than in beef.

It is vitally important that all meat for the freezer be properly wrapped in moisture- and vapor-proof wraps to avoid freezer burn. Steaks, chops, and meat patties should be separated by waxed freezer paper to prevent their sticking together. There are time limits for satisfactory storage; therefore, all packages should be dated so that they can be used in proper sequence. See Appendix D for suggested storage times. Although thawed meat can be refrozen, it does lose quality.

Cured Meats

The curing of meat began as a means of preservation; it continues in use because curing processes effect desired color and flavor changes in products. Modern curing methods are quick. They do not always produce products that can be stored without refrigeration. The U.S. Department of Agriculture developed a voluntary program for dating processed meats and poultry that went into effect December, 1974. The regulations required that when an open calender date is shown on a processed meat or poultry product, there must be an accompanying explanatory statement indicating whether the open date is the pack date, pull date, quality assurance date, or expiration date.

A constant in the curing process is the application of curing salts. The main ingredients of the curing mixture are sodium chloride, sodium or potassium nitrate and nitrite, and sugar; in addition, the mixture may contain ascorbic or citric acid and other subtances that enhance color development and various phosphates that favor moisture retention. The curing mixture may be applied dry to the meat as in the making of salt pork and Smithfield and Italian-style hams. Curing takes place when the salts are dissolved by meat juices and then penetrate the meat. The dry curing mix may be applied to the meat, and the meat may then be covered with a solution of the mixture called the *pickle,* as in curing bacon. Or cuts may be immersed in the pickle or the pickle may be injected, as in curing hams. The pink color of cured meats is produced by the action of sodium nitrite on meat pigments. The safety of nitrite used in the curing mixture has been under question. Nitrosamines, which under certain conditions can be formed in a reaction between nitrites and amines, have been shown to be carcinogenic in laboratory animals. The most important reason for using nitrite in cured meats is its ability to inhibit the development of botulinal toxin. Nitrites are important also in the development of the organoleptic qualities (flavor, flavor stability, and color) in cured meat.

In the preparation of hams the curing solution is pumped into the ham, which is then rolled in brine, hung to drain briefly, and then smoked. *Smoked* or *cook-before-eating hams* are heated to an internal temperature of 140° F, a temperature high enough to destroy *trichinae. Fully cooked hams* are heated to an internal temperature of 150° F. Such hams can be safely eaten without further heating; however, palatability is improved if they are heated to 130° F before eating. If it has been prepared under federal inspection, a product labeled "ham" has, during the smoking process, been shrunk back in weight to its original fresh weight. Hams weighing more than original fresh weight must be labeled "ham, water added" if they contain up to 10 percent added moisture, or "imitation ham" if they contain more than 10 percent added moisture. Hams are prepared only from the hindquarter of the carcass; the products prepared from the forequarter must be designated as "smoked picnic shoulder," "smoked Boston butt," "smoked pork cuts," or other names that clearly inform that they are not ham. Forequarter cuts are priced lower than ham. Ham halves are labeled "butt half" and "shank half"; hams from which center slices are removed should be labeled "butt end" or "butt portion" and "shank end" or "shank portion" to inform the consumer that the center part of the ham has been removed. The butt part has a higher ratio of lean to bone than the shank part and is often priced higher. Boneless hams from which skin and almost all fat have been removed have been widely accepted because of their convenience and ease of serving.

Ham and other cured pork cuts are sometimes canned. Labels must inform as to whether the product within the can has been smoked or not. Although fully cooked, not all canned hams have been processed to the degree that they can be stored at room temperature. Fully processed canned hams are nonperishable and may be shelf stored. It is important to read the label to know exactly what the product is. When the meat product is put into cans, it may have an increase of up to 8 percent over curing weight; dry gelatin is put into the can to combine with the juices as they cook out during heat processing. For this reason, a product may be labeled "Fully-cooked Ham with Natural Juices, Gelatin Added." The product in the can is ham by definition but it is only part or parts of a ham, excepting in the largest cans, which may contain a whole ham. The product in the can is bone free but not fat free; it is frequently a disappointment to the consumer, who finds that it does not slice out to give pleasing looking servings. The nonperishable hams have less flavor than the perishable ones; neither has the platability qualities of uncanned ham. A Consumers Union study revealed that there was little difference in the cost per pound of edible weight between canned and uncanned hams; however, because of the greater water content of the canned hams, the cost per pound of protein was considerably less for uncanned ham than for canned hams (1).

Dry-cured and *aged hams* are produced in some regions of the United States, for example, Virginia, Kentucky, Georgia, and Tennessee. These so-called country-style hams undergo dry curing, slow smoking, and long drying. The surface of the ham is frequently rubbed with black pepper before smoking; such hams have a characteristic flavor and a firm texture, moisture loss having reduced the ham to about 85 percent of fresh weight during aging. They must be fully cooked before eating. They are priced much higher than the usual ham available in the supermarket. *Prosciutto hams* are given long, dry cures and smoked; those prepared under federal inspection can be safely eaten without cooking.

Top quality hams range in weight from eight to eighteen pounds, but much larger ones can be purchased. Lighter weight hams are priced higher than heavier hams. Center cut slices from hams are priced higher than the whole ham or the remaining parts. The product called *boiled ham* is cured and cooked, but not smoked.

Canadian style bacon is the cured boned loin; it costs more per pound than ham. It contains very little fat. It yields four to five average servings per pound; as an accompaniment to eggs it will provide about eight portions per pound.

In the preparation of *bacon,* hog bellies are trimmed into blocks; the odd-shaped pieces become bacon ends. The pieces are cured and smoked and then pressed into uniform blocks for slicing. Thin-sliced bacon averages thirty slices per pound and regular-sliced averages twenty-four slices per pound. Slab bacon that is sliced at home is the same product, though it is less perishable than the presliced bacon. Packaged, presliced bacon is perishable and quickly becomes rancid because it is fast cured; it is desirable for packaged bacon to carry the date of packaging. Bacon should be kept refrigerated and although it can be frozen, freezing is not recommended because the product loses quality. A beef cut similarly cured is called *breakfast beef;* it would be misbranding to label it "bacon."

Corned beef is prepared by the curing of brisket, plate, and rump cuts from fairly high-grade beef carcasses in pickle. All cuts contain added moisture: brisket, 20 percent more than uncured weight; others, 10 percent. When bought directly from the cure, corned beef must be fully cooked. *Pastrami* is prepared from the same beef cuts; it is dry cured, rubbed with spices and black pepper, smoked, and cooked. It may be eaten without further cooking. *Chipped* or *dried, sliced beef* is prepared by the curing and drying of cuts from the rounds of lowgrade carcasses.

Sausages

There are many varieties of sausages. Sausages are frequently named for their place of origin; for example, the frankfurter originated in Frankfurt, Germany, and bologna, in Bologna, Italy. The many sausages differ in the kind or kinds of meat used in their manufacture; in the fineness of the grind of the meat(s); in the kinds and combinations of seasonings and spices used; and in the kinds of and extent of processing. On the basis of the kind and extent of processing, sausages may be grouped into three classes: (1) fresh sausages and smoked sausages that must be cooked before eating; (2) smoked, cooked; cooked, smoked; and cooked sausages; and (3) semidry and dry sausages. Meats used in the making of sausage include pork, beef, veal, mutton, lamb, goat, chicken, and turkey; but most sausages are made from combinations of beef, pork, and veal. Meat cuts used include pork shoulders; beef chuck, brisket, and flank; and trimmings of all kinds. The use of such meat by-products as heart meat, tongue meat, and tripe is permitted unless prohibited by state law. The long list of seasonings used in sausage making includes anise, allspice, caraway, cardamom, chives, cloves, coriander, dill, garlic, ginger, mustard, nutmeg, onion, black, white and red pepper, thyme, and others. A particular seasoning may be peculiar to a particular sausage. It is permitted that some sausages contain such binders and extenders as cereal, vegetable starch, and nonfat dry milk to the extent of 3.5 percent or isolated soy protein to 2 percent of the finished product. Labels must bear a list of the ingredients in a sausage in decreasing order of predominance, excepting seasonings.

Fresh sausages that must be cooked before eating are available, in this age of convenience foods, partially cooked by parboiling. The fresh sausage most widely eaten is fresh pork sausage. It is seasoned with salt, sage, pepper, and sugar. Sausages sold in interstate commerce may contain no more than 3 percent added water and no more than 50 percent fat as derived from the meat pieces used, that is, fat may not be added in sausage making. Pork sausage labeled as "country style" or "farm style" cannot contain binder or extender. A product labeled as "sausage," "breakfast sausage," or "fresh sausage" must contain pork, but in addition it may contain beef and/or other permitted meat by-products. *Bockwurst* is a fresh sausage prepared from pork and veal and seasoned with chives, cloves, lemon, mace, sage, and white pepper. It is traditionally eaten at Easter time. *Bratwurst* as sold in the United States is made from beef, pork, and veal. It is seasoned with coriander, ginger, mustard, and lemon. Fresh *Thuringer* is similarly composed but is seasoned with caraway, celery seed, coriander, ginger, and mace. Pork sausage, breakfast sausage, and Thuringer are available smoked; they must be cooked before eating.

Smoked, cooked sausages are smoked after cooking; cooked, smoked sausages are cooked after smoking; and cooked sausages are exactly that. Smoked, cooked sausages are prepared from cured meats or the sausage mixture is cured during sausage making. In the preparation of smoked, cooked sausages, the sausage mixture is shaped by being stuffed into casings and then linked; the product is given either a light or heavy smoke; finally, the product is cooked. They may be eaten without further cooking, but their flavor is enhanced by heating. Some of the better known sausages in this group are bologna, the second of all sausage favorites; bratwurst; frankfurters, the first of all sausage favorites; knockwurst; and mettwurst. *Bologna* is made of finely cut cured beef and pork. It is usually seasoned with cloves, coriander, garlic, and ginger, though allspice, caraway, mace, nutmeg, and pepper may be included. *Bratwurst* is made of cured pork and veal or beef. It is seasoned with coriander, ginger, mustard, and lemon juice and rind. It is shaped into fat links about four inches long. *Frankfurters* are made exclusively from beef or from combinations of beef, pork, mutton, lamb, veal, goat, and poultry. Any frankfurter that contains more than 15 percent of poultry meat must be labeled "Hot Dog with Chicken Added" or some similar distinguishing name. Frankfurters can be "all meat" or they can contain 3.5 percent of nonfat dry milk and/or cereal as a binding agent. They can contain no more than 10 percent of added water; any products that exceed limits in the use of water or binder must be labeled "imitation frankfurter." They can contain no more than 30 percent fat. In the making of frankfurters, the meats are ground, curing salts and spices are added, water is added as mixing and grinding continue, and the mixture is stuffed into natural or artificial casings. The product is smoked for one to three hours, then cooked, and finally, if the product is the skinless type, the artificial casings are removed. The commonly used spices include pepper, nutmeg, mace, cinnamon, mustard, coriander, sage, and garlic. Brand differences may be differences in spicing formulas. *Knockwurst* resembles the frankfurter but contains more garlic. This sausage is served with sauerkraut and German potato salad. *Mettwurst* is prepared with cured beef and pork. It is usually spiced with allspice, coriander, ginger, and mustard. *Smokies* are made of coarsely ground beef and pork; they are similar to frankfurters but are more heavily smoked.

Liver sausage is a cooked sausage that can be made from a variety of meats and meat by-products; it must contain not less than 30 percent of liver computed on the weight of the fresh liver. It is seasoned with onions, coriander, ginger, marjoram, and mustard. *Braunschweiger* is smoked liver sausage; that is, it is a sausage that is smoked after cooking. So-called *luncheon meats* are cooked sausages. They are available in infinite variety. The meat components, seasonings, and fineness of grind differ for the different kinds.

Since 1969, cooked sausage products in interstate commerce have been limited in fat content to 30 percent in the finished product. Partially defatted pork tissue or partially defatted beef tissue may make up to 15 percent of the meat component. They may contain up to 15 percent of poultry products without a change in the name of the product; when more than 15 percent is present, poultry must appear in the product name. Labeled as "all meat," they are made only from muscle meat and contain no extenders. Labeled as "all beef," they contain only meat from beef animals.

Dry and *semidry sausages* are also known as summer sausage. The low moisture content and salt content are preservative; hence, they are less perishable than the sausages previously described. In the preparation of the dry sausages, the meats are ground and mixed with the curing ingredients and spices; the mixture is stuffed into casings; the sausages are then dried. The dry, or hard, sausages have moisture content reduced more than 20 percent; the semidry, less than 20 percent. Cervelats and salamis are the two most familiar groups of dry sausage products. Generally, the *cervelats* are semidry, though they may be dry; they are mildly seasoned and they are smoked. Generally, the salamis are dry, though they may be semidry; they are highly seasoned and may or may not be smoked. American cervelat is called *summer sausage;* it is usually made of all beef, is soft and mild in flavor, and is smoked. Swedish cervelat is made of coarsely ground beef and sometimes pork; it is seasoned with thyme, is salty, and is heavily smoked. The *salamis* originated in Europe, most of them in Italy, where the warm climate favored the abundant use of salt, spices, and drying as a means of meat preservation. Italian salamis are seasoned with garlic and hot pepper. Cooked salami is a class of salami; it includes beer salami, cotto salami, and kosher salami. These salamis are softer than the dry salamis, from which they differ mainly in that they are only briefly cured, cooked, and only briefly dried or not dried at all. *Chorizos* is a Spanish-type dry sausage made of pork and seasoned with red pepper and allspice. *Pepperoni* is an Italian dry sausage much used in making pizza. There are two types. The hot kind is made of beef and pork with chili peppers. The sweet pepperoni is usually made of all pork and is mildly seasoned. Seasonings used in both types include allspice, anise, garlic, and peppers of different kinds. *Lebanon bologna* is a semidry sausage. Its place of origin was Lebanon, Pennsylvania. It is usually an all-beef product, heavily smoked, and seasoned with cloves, coriander, garlic, and ginger.

Kosher Meats

Kosher meats and kosher further-processed meat food products are those that are clean and fit for food according to the Jewish dietary laws, which require that animals be ritually slain and that their blood be ritually drawn. All processing must be under orthodox rabbinical supervision, and only kosher ingredients and kosher equipment can be used. Equipment can be cleaned only with kosher agents—those of vegetable or synthetic origin. Three symbols mark food as kosher. The letter *K* marks food approved by the supervisory service of the Joseph Jacobs Organization of New York City. The letters *VH* are authorized by the Vaad Harabonium in Massachusetts. The U emblem is that of the Union of Orthodox Jewish Congregations of America; it is registered in the United States Patent Office. A variety of kosher products is manufactured by 400 or more companies for the million or so families that purchase kosher food. Many non-Jewish consumers purchase kosher food, perhaps for the reason that they think it superior in quality and wholesomeness.

Hamburger, Ground Beef, and Ground Beef with TVP

About one half of the beef consumed in the United States is eaten in ground forms. Some of these are defined in the regulations promulgated for the administration of the Wholesome Meat Act. *Hamburger* is chopped fresh and/or frozen beef with or without added beef fat as such and/or seasoning. Fat content cannot exceed 30 percent; and the product cannot contain added water or extenders or binders. *Ground beef* or *chopped beef* consists of chopped fresh and/or frozen beef with or without seasoning and without added beef fat, water, or extenders or binders. Fat content cannot exceed 30 percent. *Ground chuck, ground round,* and *ground sirloin* are prepared by the grinding of those cuts; they are not defined and they have fat contents of about 10 to 20 percent, 10 percent, and 20 percent, respectively. *Beef patties* consist of chopped fresh and/or frozen beef with or without added beef fat, seasonings, extenders, partially defatted beef tissue, and water. *Prefabricated steaks* may be composed of beef, veal, or combinations thereof as beef and veal or veal and beef. They cannot contain more than 30 percent fat, added water, or binder or extender. Seasonings or flavorings permitted in these products include MSG, sweetener, hydrolyzed plant protein, and selected flavor-protecting additives.

A new soy-beef product was introduced to the consumer in March, 1973, as a lower cost alternative to ground beef. The soy-beef blends were displayed in the meat counter with ground beef. Each company may choose its own name for the product and the product must bear a label indicating that textured vegetable protein (TVP) was added. The composition of the product generally was approximately 75 percent ground beef and 25 percent TVP. Since their introduction, the sales of the TVP-beef blend products have been cyclic, increasing with an increase in beef prices, and decreasing with a decrease in beef prices (3). They do not appear to pose a threat to the beef industry, but provide a means of stretching available meat when the meat supply is low. Consumer test preference for the hamburger and products containing hamburger and TVP was not significantly different if the participants did not have prior knowledge of which products contained the TVP. However, when the participant had prior knowledge of which product contained the TVP, the regular hamburger was significantly preferred over the blended product (10). Textured vegetable protein is a better medium for microbial growth than meat; therefore, necessary precautions should be taken in handling TVP products.

Tenderizing Meats

Only approximately one quarter of the cuts from a beef carcass are inherently tender. Moist heat methods of cooking tenderize less tender cuts; however, these methods are time-consuming, and they effect texture changes that many persons do not favor. Grinding or other mechanical treatment of less tender cuts makes it possible to treat the products like tender cuts; for example, hamburgers and fabricated steaks can be broiled and cube steaks can be pan-fired. In addition to these methods of tenderizing, enzymatic treatment tenderizes.

Tenderizing by enzyme action comes about in three ways. First enzymes within the tissues of the animal carcass will modify tissues chemically and physically to effect tenderizing. Considerable tenderizing occurs during the movement of fresh meat from packer to use by the consumer, a period of from six to ten days. Ribs and loins of beef of high quality and lamb and mutton are aged both to increase tenderness and to develop flavor. Two methods of aging are in use. In *dry aging,* beef is held at temperatures from 34° F to 38° F for two to six weeks. Only beef with a well-developed layer of external fat that protects against spoilage and dehydration is so aged. Humidity in the aging room is controlled to achieve the desired effect, either mold development to produce a gamey flavor or minimum dehydration. This method of aging is expensive; hence, cuts are priced accordingly. *Fastaged* beef is held at about 70° F for two days at high humidity levels; ultraviolet light is used to control spoilage. Dry-aged beef goes to the restaurant trade; fast-aged, into retail trade. Pork is not aged because rancidity develops in the fat. Veal has too little external fat to permit aging.

Proteolytic enzymes can also be applied to, or injected into, cuts commercially. In the home kitchen, a salt mixture containing the enzymes can be sprinkled over the surface of a cut. Piercing with a fork permits the enzyme to penetrate the meat. The enzyme is active between 130° F and 160° F and is inactivated as temperature rises during cooking. Enzyme treatment permits the use of dry heat methods of cooking for less tender cuts. Cuts treated commercially with enzymes must bear labels stating this fact.

A solution of a tenderizing enzyme can also be injected into animals before slaughter; hence, the enzyme will be present in all parts of the muscles. This commercial process is patented. Beef cuts so prepared may be higher priced than untreated cuts of comparable grade, but are less expensive than tender cuts from top quality carcasses.

Meat Extenders and Meat Analogs

Modern technology has produced plant protein products, sometimes called textured vegetable protein (TVP), which are used as extenders for meat in meat food products and as meat analogs. The meat analogs, described as simulated meats, synthetic meats, and imitation meats look, taste, and smell like the meats they simulate. Products that resemble beef, ham, bacon, chicken, and turkey prepared in various styles are available. The popular "Baco-Bits," which resemble crisply diced bacon, are made from soy products. Arguments in favor of the analogs are:

1. Nutritional composition can be engineered, that is, fat and cholesterol can be modified or eliminated and nutrients needed to improve the quality of the national diet can be added.
2. Quality is constant because products are made by formula.
3. They are convenient because they are ready to heat and eat.
4. Cost could be less than that of fresh meat cuts.

Meat analogs are marketed mainly to institutions, food faddists, and persons who avoid meats for religious reasons.

Soy protein products have increased in use as extenders. At moderate usage levels, the extenders do not change the flavor of a meat food product as, for example, meat loaves, sausages, or chili. The soy protein product absorbs the juices and fat that cook out of meat, thereby reducing cooking losses and resulting in juicier products. The use of extenders is limited to small percentages in products for which there are definitions and standards of identity. However, foods eaten away from home can contain higher percentages of extender because they are not regulated by the same labeling requirements as food sold at retail. In 1971 the United States Department of Agriculture permitted certain soy extenders to be used as part of the protein requirement in the school lunch program. In 1973 a ground beef-soy product was available for the consumer on the meat counter for the first time.

Slightly modified plant protein products include vegetable and cereal flours and granular products. They may not be termed protein on food labels. They are named by the plant source and a word that describes their physical form, for example soy flour, soy granules, and corn granules. The *plant protein concentrates* are prepared by a process of extraction and washing that removes fiber, carbohydrate, and minerals present in the plant source. These products may be marketed as soy protein concentrates or if more than two sources of plant protein are used it is named "vegetable," "cereal," or "plant" as in plant protein concentrate bits. The *plant protein isolates* are highest in protein content. Most of the characteristics of the plant protein source have been removed in processing so these products are not required to identify their plant source. They are identified as plant protein isolates. Mixtures of all combinations of plant protein are also on the market. When flavors are added to resemble meat, seafood, eggs and so on the flavor designation must accompany the product name such as artificially ham flavored soy protein isolate.

FISH AND SHELLFISH

Americans buy more fresh than frozen fish and shellfish, but they buy more that is canned than fresh. Per-capita consumption of fish was twelve pounds in both 1975 and 1980. The pollution of estuarine waters with sewage has decreased the take of oysters and other shellfish.

Fresh Fish

Fresh fish can be purchased in any of the following styles, depending on the kind: whole as it comes from the water; drawn—entrails removed; dressed or pan-dressed—scales, entrails and usually the head, tail, and fins removed; steaks—cross-section slices cut five-eighths to one inch thick from dressed fish; chunks—crosswise sections of large dressed fish; and fillets—the sides of fish cut lengthwise away from the backbone with or without removal of the skin. The signs of freshness in fish are readily recognizable: fresh whole fish should have bulging eyes, reddish-pink gills that are free of slime, iridescent skin, firm flesh, and a fresh, clean odor. Dressed fish, chunks, steaks, and fillets should exhibit these characteristics when relevant and, in addition, should exhibit a fresh-cut appearance without evidence of browning or drying. The pollution of lakes and rivers has reduced the supply of freshwater fish. Proper chilling of ocean catches and shipment by air favor the availability of fresh ocean fish in large urban markets.

Frozen Fish

Many species of fish are available frozen; in addition, frozen ready-to-cook breaded products and frozen precooked products can be purchased. Some products are graded and bear the proper inspection seal. People who enjoy fish and eat it for its low fat, low calorie, and high protein levels are likely to be disappointed in the frozen breaded products. According to Consumer Union, consumers will get more fish and better flavor if they buy unbreaded fresh or frozen fillets. (4) Cooking frozen fish may be a little easier but it is not faster.

Canned Fish

Approximately one half of the fish consumed in the United States is canned. Tuna, salmon, and sardines are the most frequently purchased kinds of canned fish. Canned tuna has been defined and a standard of fill of container has been established. The definition and standard of identity for canned tuna name the species of fish that may be canned and labeled as tuna; specify that only loins and other striated muscles free of skin, scales, bones, gills, blood clots, and viscera may be used; define what shall be in the can when the style of pack is labeled as "solid pack," "chunks," "flakes," or "grated tuna"; establish the color of tuna as white, light, dark, and blended, on the basis of Munsell values; name the packing media and optional ingredients; and specify that the name of a pack shall be formed by combining the designation of the form of the pack with the color of the pack, for example, "Solid-Pack White Tuna." The style of pack makes little difference in the weight of the contents of cans except that the soild-pack cans contain a little more than the other styles. Several species of tuna are canned, but of these only the Albacore is white. Cans of tuna vary widely in cost; the species and the color of the fish and the style of the pack affect cost. Solid-pack white tuna costs more than grated dark or blended tuna. The intended use would dictate the kind of pack to be purchased. Meat from fish commonly known as bonito or bonita (*Sarda chilensis*) and "yellowtail" (*Seriola dorsalis*) may not be labeled as "tuna," but must be labeled as "bonito" or "bonita" or "yellowtail." They are less expensive than tuna.

A standard of identity and fill of container for salmon has been established. Six species of salmon are canned, which differ in color, texture, and flavor. The higher priced products are deeper in color and have a higher oil content. In descending order of price, they are red or sockeye salmon, chinook or king salmon, medium red or silver-side or coho salmon, pink salmon, and chum or keta salmon. This is also a list in descending order of color from orange-red to pale pink. The king or chinook is considered the best. The less expensive salmon is a good choice for making salmon loaf and casserole dishes.

Sardines are small fish of different species of the herring family. A standard of identity for sardines has been established covering canned sardines of the species Atlantic herring (*Clupea harengus*). Sardines are imported from several countries, especially the Scandinavian ones. The European pilchard (*Sardinia pilchardus* or *Clupea pilchardus*) and brisling or sprat (*Clupea sprattus*) are commonly packed in oil and labeled as sardines. The terms *brisling sardines* and *sild sardines* are permissible in labeling small brisling and herring, respectively. All imported foods are

inspected for wholesomeness and for conformity with other requirements of United States food laws.

Anchovies have been adopted widely by an affluent society; they are
often present in Greek salad, Caesar's salad, and Green Goddess dressing. They are fish of the family *Engraulidae;* no other small fish, though
they may resemble anchovies, can be labeled as anchovies. The product
in cans is the fillets, which are packed in oil either flat or rolled around
a caper after preservation by salting or pickling. Anchovy paste contains comminuted anchovies; other ingredients present must be named
on the label.

Caviar is sturgeon roe prepared by a special process. It is imported
from Russia and Iran. It is gray to black in color, and the eggs vary in
size. Caviar prepared from other fish varieties must be identified by the
name of the fish of origin. Red caviar is prepared from salmon roe.
The best Russian caviar is very expensive.

Shellfish

Shellfish are of two types: mollusks and crustaceans. The mollusks
are bivalves; they have hard, hinged shells. Oysters, clams, and scallops
are mollusks. The crustaceans have segmented shells and include
shrimp, lobsters, and crabs. The distribution of fresh shellfish is somewhat limited, but all can be purchased frozen or canned in most markets. In general, shellfish are priced higher per portion than fish and
many cuts of meat. The best liked are shrimp, lobster, and crab.

Fresh shrimp may be purchased in a few metropolitan markets;
canned and frozen, in most supermarkets; and freeze-dried, in some
markets. Headless shrimp are block-frozen and individually quick-fro-
zen. Frozen shrimp are available in the shell, deshelled and deveined,
and cooked or uncooked. The best and most convenient of these is the
deshelled and deveined, uncooked product. In addition, breaded cooked
and ready-to-cook breaded shrimp, stuffed shrimp, cocktail shrimp with
sauce, and numerous other convenience dishes are available frozen. Although shrimp are found in all the coastal waters of the United States
from Maine to Alaska, the United States imports about half of the
quantity consumed from more than sixty countries. Shrimp from around
the world differ in color, size, and shape. The color range is from
greenish-gray to brownish-red, but regardless of color in the raw, all
cooked shrimp have the same pinkish color. They also have about the
same flavor. The term *green shrimp* refers to all or any uncooked shrimp.
Shrimp vary in size from tiny ones no larger than a dime, which may
number as many as 300 per pound, to jumbos that number ten to fifteen per pound. In the supermarket they are sold by size: small—about

sixty per pound; medium—forty to fifty per pound; large—about twenty per pound. They are priced accordingly. They are sometimes available in mixed sizes and pieces labeled "salad shrimp." Some shrimp are pencil slim and others are plump. Shrimp are sized for canning; small, medium, and large sizes can be found, although not always in the same market. Fill of container has been established for shrimp canned in nontransparent containers. Travel outside of the United States has introduced Americans to the prawn, to scampi, and to the langoustine. All are members of the same crustacean family but they are not shrimp, although they do resemble them.

The two kinds of lobsters are the true lobster and the spiny or rock lobster. The true lobster (family *Homaridae*) is taken from North Atlantic waters, has claws, and is superior in flavor to the spiny lobster. The rock or spiny lobster (family *Palinuridae*) is a sea crayfish, of which only the tail provides meat. Several kinds of spiny lobster are marketed: those from Cuba, Florida, and the Bahamas have a smooth, brownish-green shell with white spots; those from South Africa, Australia, and New Zealand, have a rough shell with color varying from maroon to brown; those from Southern California and Mexico have a smooth yellow-green shell. The meat is white, and the tails vary from small to large; frequently the small ones are more tender than the very large ones. If purchased fresh, either type of lobster should be alive and remain so until cooked by being dropped into boiling water. In many areas, lobster can be purchased only canned or frozen.

There is little fresh crab available except in coastal areas. Canned crab meat, precooked and frozen crab meat, and precooked and frozen crab dishes are widely available. Crab meat is derived from four varieties of crabs: the blue crab, the New England rock crab, the Pacific or Dungeness crab, and the king crab of Alaska. Both body and claw meat are used. The body meat of the blue crab is white, that of the claws, brownish. The meat of the New England crab is brownish. The Pacific crab has reddish claw meat and white body meat. The meat of the king crab is white with a red external surface; in general, only the claw meat is used. Soft-shelled crabs are blue crabs taken after the hard shell has been discarded and the new one is still soft. Crab meat is fairly expensive.

Oysters are bivalves. They are graded and sold by size. On the east coast, Standards are small; Selects, medium; Extra Selects, large; and Counts, extra large. Pacific oysters are similarly graded but are called by size: Small, Medium, Large, and Extra Large. However, the number of oysters per gallon is greater for Atlantic oysters than for Pacific oysters of the same size designation; that is, Selects or medium run 210 to 300 oysters per gallon, whereas Medium Pacific oysters run 64 to 96 per gallon.

Definitions and standards of identity have been promulgated for canned oysters and shucked raw oysters. Fill of container has been established for canned oysters. The standards for chucked raw oysters define conditions for controlling water content; establish size by defining the number of oysters per gallon—that is, Extra Selects are of such a size that one gallon contains more than 160 oysters but not more than 210 oysters. In the original package or can there should be no more than 10 percent liquid by weight. Oysters should be creamy white, and the liquid should be clear. There has long been a taboo on the eating of fresh oysters during the months May through August. There are two explanations for the taboo. One is that these months are the breeding season and the oysters are less succulent. The other is that oysters, and other shellfish, eaten during these months can cause food poisoning. During these months a food abundantly available to the shellfish is an organism called *Gonyaulax catanella* in Pacific coast waters or *Gymnodinium breve* in Gulf coast waters; this organism though harmless to the oyster is toxic for man.

Scallops, like oysters, are derived from bivalves. A scallop is part of the muscle used in the opening and closing of the shell. Scallops come in two sizes: the large white cubes from sea scallops and the smaller pinkish cubes from bay scallops. The smaller ones are more expensive and a greater delicacy than the larger ones. They are marketed ready-to-cook and precooked and frozen.

Several species of clams are eaten. They are not abundantly available fresh but can be purchased canned, frozen raw, and frozen fried. Pacific Coast clams are butter, littleneck, pismo, and razor clams. Atlantic Coast clams are hard, soft, and surf clams. The hard-shell clams are called *quahog* in New England.

MEAT FOOD PRODUCTS AND POULTRY FOOD PRODUCTS

Meat and poultry food products include cooked meats, sausages, ready-made dishes, and such ready-for-cooking items as breaded chops and steaks. The variety is great and is ever increasing. Turkey hot dogs and chicken wieners are examples of products that are now on the market. The poultry industry also began distributing turkey ham, turkey salami, turkey pastrami, and turkey bologna. These products are usually 100 percent turkey meat with certain spices added. They do not taste like poultry but instead taste like the meat products for which they are named. Most turkey products are less expensive than their beef and pork counterparts; all have less fat and fewer calories.

If we are to decide rationally about purchasing ready-mades, it is helpful to know the extent to which their production is regulated. For products that move in interstate commerce, the following kinds of regulations exist. First, the meat and poultry component and all other ingredients must have been inspected for wholesomeness. Second, definitions and standards of identity establish the composition of some meat and poultry food products; they establish minimum meat content and name the other ingredients that may or must be present in a product. Third, all processors are required to register complete formulas for the products they make with the Consumer and Marketing Service of the United States Department of Agriculture. These formulas and the labels for the finished products must be approved. Last, for all undefined products there must be a truthful label and a listing of ingredients in decreasing order of predominance from the one present in greatest weight to the one present in least amount. For products moving only in intrastate commerce, inspection equal to federal inspection is mandatory. However, states differ in standards for products and the labeling thereof. A large proportion of meat and poultry food products move in interstate commerce.

Defined Meat Food Products

Definitions and standards of identity or composition require that meat food products marked "all beef" or "all pork" contain no meat other than the kind named. "Meat" means only muscle tissue with natural amounts of fat. An "all," "100 percent," or "pure" meat or poultry product contains no extenders, such as cereal or nonfat dry milk. The minimum quantities of meat in some meat food products for which there are federal standards are shown in Table 10–2.

Defined Poultry Food Products

Poultry food product means any food consisting of any edible part or parts of poultry in combination with other ingredients. Some definitions and regulations have been promulgated that establish the quantities of poultry in poultry food products, the ratio of light to dark meat in them, the inclusion of skin and fat in them, and labeling requirements. These are summarized.

1. The natural proportions of skin on the whole boneless carcass are for chicken, 20 percent raw and 25 percent cooked; for turkeys, 15 percent raw and 20 percent cooked.
2. Uses of the terms light and dark meat must conform to the following specifications:

TABLE 10–2. *Minimum Quantities of Meat Required in Various Food Products*

Product	Minimum Quantity
Beans with bacon in sauce	12% bacon[1]
Beans with frankfurters in sauce	20% franks
Beans with ham in sauce	12% ham
Beef with barbecue sauce	50% beef
Beef with gravy	50% beef
Beef Stroganoff	31% beef
Chili con carne	40% beef[1]
Chili sauce with meat	6% beef[1]
Chop suey vegetables with meat	12% meat[1]
Chow mein	12% meat
Deviled ham	no more than 35% fat
Egg foo yung with meat	12% meat[1]
Egg rolls with meat	10% meat[1]
Enchiladas with meat	15% meat[1]
Frozen breakfast	15% meat
Gravy with beef	35% meat
Ham and cheese spread	12% ham
Ham chowder	10% ham
Ham spread	50% ham[1]
Hash	35% meat[1]
Lasagna with meat and sauce	12% meat[1]
Lima beans with ham or bacon	12% ham or bacon[1]
Liver paste, pudding, etc.	30% liver[1]
Macaroni and cheese with ham	12% ham[1]
Macaroni and beef in tomato sauce	12% beef
Meat casseroles	18% meat
Meat pies	18% meat
Meat salads	35% meat
Meat tacos	15% meat[1]
Meat turnovers	25% meat[1]
Omelet with bacon	12% bacon
Omelet with ham	12% ham
Pizza with meat	15% meat[1]
Pizza with sausage	12% cooked or 10% dry sausage
Pork with barbecue sauce	50% pork
Sauerkraut with wieners and juice	20% weiners[1]
Scallopine	35% meat
Spaghetti with meat and sauce	12% meat[1]
Spaghetti with meatballs	12% meat[1]
Spaghetti sauce with meat	6% meat[1]
Spanish rice with beef	20% beef
Stews	25% meat[1]
Sukiyaki	30% meat
Sweet and sour pork or beef	16% meat
Swiss steak with gravy	50% meat
Tamales	25% meat
Tamales with sauce or gravy	20% meat[1]
Veal birds	60% veal, 40% dressing
Veal Cordon Bleu	60% veal[1], 5% ham[1], plus cheese
Veal fricasse	40% meat[1]

[1] Raw meat required.

	Percent Light Meat	Percent Dark Meat
Natural proportions	50–65	50–35
Light meat	100	0
Dark meat	0	100
Light and dark meat	51–65	49–35
Dark and light meat	35–49	65–51
Mostly white meat	66 or more	34 or less
Mostly dark meat	34 or less	66 or more

3. Products containing light and dark chicken or turkey meat in other than natural proportions must clearly and conspicuously state the type(s) of meat in use in conjunction with the name of the food, for example, "Boned Turkey (Dark Meat)."

4. Cooked poultry meat used in making poultry food products must have a solids content of 34 percent; if it does not, the percentage of poultry meat required in a product must be increased in relation to the deficiency.

5. Canned, boned poultry contains light and dark meats, fats, and skin in natural proportions according to kind. Canned and boned solid-pack products must contain a minimum of 95 percent of poultry meat, including skin and fat. Canned poultry with broth must contain at least 80 percent poultry meat, skin, and fat. The percentage of poultry meat may decrease to 50 percent if statement is made of the percentage of broth.

6. Frozen poultry pies must contain not less than 14 percent of cooked, deboned poultry of the kind indicated on the label, or one and one-eighth ounces of poultry per eight-ounce pie. Note that this is less than one half of an average serving of meat.

7. Frozen poultry dinners must contain not less than two ounces or 18 percent of cooked, deboned poultry meat of the kind indicated on the label.

8. Poultry burgers must consist of 100 percent poultry meat of the kind indicated on the label. Skin and fat cannot be present in excess of natural proportions. Products containing binders or fillers must be labeled "patties" and identified as to kind, that is, "chicken patties."

9. The percentages of poultry in poultry dishes are calculated on an as-serve basis; definitions are of the minimums of cooked, deboned poultry meat of the kind named on the label. Percentages of poultry meat are as follows:

(a) Poultry soups must contain not less than 2 percent.

(b) Chop suey with poultry must contain not less than 2 percent, but poultry chop suey and poultry chow mein must contain not less than 4 percent.

(c) Poultry tamales and dumplings or noodles with poultry must contain not less than 6 percent; poultry stew, not less than 12 percent; and poultry with noodles or dumplings, not less than 15 percent.

(d) Creamed poultry, poultry cacciatore, poultry fricassee, and poultry à la king must all contain not less than 20 percent.

(e) Poultry salad, croquettes, and sliced poultry with gravy and dressing must all contain not less than 25 percent.

(f) Sliced poultry with gravy must contain not less than 35 percent.

10. Cooked poultry roasts must have been heated to an internal temperature of 160° F.

The list of defined ready-made dishes is long but incomplete. (7). The consumer must buy them and try them if she is to know their ingredient composition. However, before she buys, she can rule out some of the available products by estimating cost per portion, in accordance with the number of servings suggested on the label. For example, if shrimp Newburg will cost her $1.98 per serving and her daily meat allowance is $.70 per person, then frozen precooked shrimp Newburg is a ready-made she need not buy and try. On the other hand, if frozen prepared chicken à la king costs only $.60 per serving, she may wish to buy and try it. If she finds the quantity of chicken skimpy, she may not buy again but make her own instead, using canned chicken and a canned soup for the sauce. All ready-made meat products are convenience foods; consumers evaluate them differently because each consumer has her own particular frame of reference for judgment.

SOME GUIDES TO BUYING MEAT, POULTRY, AND FISH AND SHELLFISH

The average meal manager spends from one fourth to one third of her food dollars for meat, poultry, and fish and shellfish products, fresh, cured, canned, and frozen. Further, the average meal manager likes to maximize the dollars she spends for these products. A bad buy ends in waste and dissatisfaction. There is no other class of food purchases that requires as much knowledge or provides as much profit from experience as the purchase of meats. Supermarkets differ in the quality of the meats stocked, in trimming and boning practices, in pricing policy, in the names given retail cuts, and in packaging techniques. Further, there is evidence (8) that the weights recorded on meat packages are not always the true weights. The meal manager should research her market resources and patronize the store or stores that are honest and that provide her the quality she wants at the price she can pay.

1. Because all meat and poultry must be inspected, the consumer expects to buy only wholesome products. Never buy a torn or damaged package. If any just-purchased product, fresh or frozen, has an offensive odor or is discolored, molded, or slimy when opened in the home kitchen, return it at once to the market where it was purchased.

2. Buy graded products whenever possible. Remember that less than the best is still wholesome food; properly prepared it can be more tasty than a high-quality product poorly prepared.

3. Learn how to identify the carcass origin of retail cuts. Many fanciful names that reveal little information are in use to describe meat cuts. For example, "Sarasota Steak" might be eye-of-round steak, sirloin tip, or a steak fabricated from a special grind of beef.

4. Buy cuts according to intended use: less tender cuts for pot roasts, USDA Choice standing rib roast for roast beef, blade steak or round steak for Swiss steak, a sirloin steak for broiling, and so on. If two grades of beef are available in the market, choose from among them according to intended use.

5. From among prepackaged meats with transparent wraps, choose those with a good ratio of lean to bone and fat. Note that shoppers do just this in the supermarket.

6. Buy the quantity wanted for the intended use; too much for one meal and not enough for another may be wasteful.

7. Read the food ads in your newspaper and buy "specials." But choose selectively. They may reflect abundant supply, as of frying chickens, or they may be loss leaders to bring customers into the supermarket. To take advantage of bargains, know the current price of the items you regularly buy, for example, the price of hamburger or sirloin steak.

8. To match a purchase to your plan of spending for food, estimate the cost per serving. Know your average daily allowance for meat. Know how to overspend it to widen your choices, but do not overspend recklessly. See Chapter 6.

9. Properly priced, chicken wings and backs are good buys. You can have a pot of soup and enough chicken meat for a casserole, a salad, or sandwiches.

10. Buy the largest roast or cut of ham, or bird that your budget permits and that you can serve out satisfactorily. Dripping and moisture losses are less and the number of servings per pound average out better from large cuts than from small ones.

11. Large birds have a more favorable ratio of lean to bone than small ones.

12. In general, arm cuts have a better ratio of lean to bone than blade cuts, but the latter are more tender.

13. The butt portion of a ham has a better lean to bone ratio than the shank portion; the latter should be priced lower.

14. Compare the prices of whole and cut-up chickens, you can usually save pennies by cutting up whole birds.

15. Ready-stuffed turkeys are more expansive than the unstuffed ones.

16. Read the statement of weights on packages of luncheon meats, sausages, frankfurters, and specialty items; they are frequently smaller than the eight ounces or one pound that you think you are buying.

17. White tuna is more expensive than darker tuna; solid-pack tuna is more expensive than chunk or grated tuna; pink salmon is less expensive than red salmon. Buy according to intended use; the less expensive kinds are satisfactory for casserole dishes.

18. The best of the sirloin steaks are the pin-bone and the flat-bone cuts.

19. Properly priced, chicken parts are as good buys as whole chickens. Proper pricing means that breasts cost about 40 percent more; drumsticks, 25 percent more; and thighs, 33 percent more per pound than whole chickens.

20. Estimate and evaluate the cost of the convenience in ready-to-heat meat, poultry, and fish dishes. Consider also the time required to heat the dish to have it safe for eating. Carefully check on the quantity of meat in these dishes; it may be far less than an average meat portion. It is quite possible to broil, pan-broil, or pan-fry something for a meal in less time, at a lower cost, and with more nutrition compared to what some ready-to-heat-and-eat dishes require in resources and offer in protein.

How to Store Meat

Assuredly, you purchased wholesome meat. Keep it that way by proper handling and storage—clean to avoid contamination and cool to retard spoilage and protect quality.

1. Transport meat, poultry, and fish and shellfish from the store as rapidly as possible.

2. Wash your hands thoroughly before and after touching or handling any unwrapped products.

3. Use only clean gadgets in the handling of meats. Put them only

into clean containers. Thoroughly wash the containers and all surfaces on which raw meat or poultry have been placed.

4. The temperature in the refrigerator should be 35° F to 40° F; in the freezer 0° F or less. Place meat in the coldest part of a refrigerator that is not uniformly cold throughout.

5. Prepackaged fresh meat, poultry, fish, and shellfish may be held for one or two days in the transparent wrap, but be certain that the package is leakproof to avoid contaminating other foods. Use poultry and fish and seafood within two days. Loosely rewrap meat to be held longer than two days to permit moving air to dry the surface slightly and deter the growth of spoilage organisms. Any of these products purchased wrapped in butcher paper should be unwrapped and placed on a plate or tray and lightly covered with film or foil. Chops, steaks, and roasts may be held up to five days; but stew meat, ground meats, and variety meats are best used within two days.

6. Cured meats may be refrigerator-stored for up to one week. Cured products should be stored in the original wraps. Modern cures are non-preservative; cured meats are perishable.

7. Trim and cut into meal- or portion-sized pieces meat, poultry, fish and shellfish to be frozen for storage. Wrap tightly in moisture- and vapor-proof packaging material, foil, or film. Freeze at one time no more than two pounds per cubic foot of freezer space.

8. The storage life of frozen fresh meats is eight to twelve months for beef and lamb roasts and beef steaks; four to eight months for pork, veal, and calf roasts; three to four months for lamb, pork, and veal chops and variety meats; two to three months for ground meats and stew meats; one to two months for pork sausage; and two to three months for cooked meats. Cured meats do not freeze well because rancidity develops quickly. Freeze them only in an emergency and then use them within one month. The storage life for frozen poultry is twelve months for chicken and turkey; six months for ducks and geese; six months for cooked poultry dishes; and four months for fried chicken. The storage life for frozen fish and seafood is four to six months only; for cooked products, only two or three months. The storage life of all of these is less if the temperature within the freezer is higher than 0° F. See Appendix D.

9. Tightly wrap or store in covered containers all cooked meat, poultry, and fish and shellfish and refrigerate them promptly. Separate poultry and stuffing and store them in different containers. Use them within two days. To extend their storage life, tightly wrap and freeze them. Storage life will be two to three months. Reheat frozen casseroles, stews, and other meat-containing dishes without thawing them.

10. Frozen meat may be cooked with or without thawing but un-thawed meat requires one and one third to one and one half times

longer to cook than thawed meat. Thaw frozen meat in its wrappings in the refrigerator and cook it as soon as possible after thawing. Thawed meat is as perishable as fresh meat. Thawed meat and poultry may be refrozen if they are still icy cold and refrigerator storage was limited to one or two days. Both products will lose in palatability however.

11. Frozen poultry may be cooked with or without thawing, but commercially frozen stuffed poultry should be cooked without thawing. Frozen poultry may be thawed in any of three ways. The preferred method is to thaw it in the refrigerator in its original wrapper until it is pliable. A large bird may require up to three days for thawing. Or thaw it in cold water in its watertight wrapper for more rapid thawing. Or thaw it in a cool place; but leave it in the original wrapper and place it in a double paper bag or wrap it with newspaper or place it in a corrugated paper bag to keep its surface cool.

12. Leftover broth and gravy should be refrigerated immediately and reheated to a full rolling boil before eating.

13. The average freezer will keep food frozen for two days in the time of a blackout or a power failure. Partially thawed food can be safely refrozen.

REFERENCES CITED

1. "Canned Hams," *Consumer Reports* **35:**581 (1970).
2. Campion, D. R., and V. L. Harrison, "The New Beef Carcass Quality Grade Standards: What the Changes Mean," Livestock and Meat Situation, Economic Research Service, U.S. Department of Agriculture, Washington, D.C. (February 1976), p. 41.
3. Gallimore, William W., "Estimated Sale and Impact of Soy-Beef Blends in Grocery Stores," National Food Situation, Economic Research Service, U.S. Department of Agriculture, Washington, D.C. (February 1976), p. 37.
4. "Fish and Chips", Consumer Reports **47:**5 (1982).
5. Food Yields Summarized by Different Stages of Preparation. Agriculture Handbook No. 102 Agricultural Research Service, U.S. Department of Agriculature, Washington, D.C. (September, 1975).
6. "How to Buy Meat for Your Freezer." Home & Garden Bulletin No. 166, Food Safety and Quality Service, U.S. Department of Agriculture, Washington, D.C. (1980).
7. "Meat and Poultry Products, A Consumer Guide to Content and Labeling Requirements." Home and Garden Bulletin No. 236, Food Safety and Inspection Service. U.S. Department of Agriculture, Washington, D.C. (1981).
8. "Meats on Sale," *Consumer Reports* **35:**472 (1970).
9. Moran, E. T., Jr., and J. L. Orr, "A Characterization of the Broiler

as a Function of Sex and Age: Live Performance, Processing, Grade and Cooking Yields," *Food Technology* **23**:1077 (1970).

10. Weimer, Jon, "Taste Preference for Hamburger Containing Textured Vegetable Protein," *National Food Situation,* U.S. Department of Agriculture, Washington, D.C. (February 1976), p. 45.

11. *"Your Money's Worth in Foods,"* Home and Garden Bulletin No. 183, Science and Education Administration, U.S. Department of Agriculture, Washington, D.C. (1979).

SUGGESTED PROBLEMS

1. Select eight less expensive cuts of meat that could be grilled. What might you do to each cut before and during cooking to be sure it would be tender?

2. Prepare a table showing cost of a serving of chicken as the poultry is purchased uncut, cut-up, and in parts.

3. Shop your market area for seafood. Compare the cost of fresh (if available), frozen, and canned seafood.

4. Visit several grocery stores which sell meat. Compare cost per pound for the same cuts at different markets. Observe the extent to which fat has been trimmed from cuts.

Chapter II

Shopping for Diary Products, Nondairy Products, Eggs

The decade of the 1970's witnessed an increased consumption of low-fat milk, cheese, and fluid cream and a decreased consumption of other dairy products such as butter, fluid whole milk, and non-fat dry milk. See Figure 11–1. The consumption of eggs has declined by about 15 percent since 1967. In general, nondiary products such as whipped toppings, coffee creamers, and margarine are replacing the corresponding dairy products.

Most of the dollars spent for this group of foods are spent for milk for drinking and for use in cooking. Milk can be purchased as the fresh fluid product or as a product processed by canning or by dehydration. The fresh fluid product may be whole, low-fat, skimmed, filled, or imitation; the cost of the milk varies accordingly. Milk can be delivered to the home, or it can be bought at a supermarket or other grocery store, at a dairy store, or at some other special retail outlet, for example, from a vending machine at a gas station. Although the purchase of these products does not use a large proportion of the food dollar, the knowledge about both products and market resources assists the consumer in maximizing the food dollars. Table 11–1 shows how the cost of a quart of milk can vary, according to the product, the size of the container, and the place it is purchased. Information about, and definitions of, the different dairy and nondairy products follow. Extensive interstate commerce in dairy products makes all definitions important to consumers. Knowledge about dairy products is also needed because they are highly perishable and can easily be adulterated, contaminated, or develop undesirable characteristics. Some states have strict pull date regulations for fresh milk while others do not. Consumers Union tasters found that milk from mid-Atlantic states with tight pull date regula-

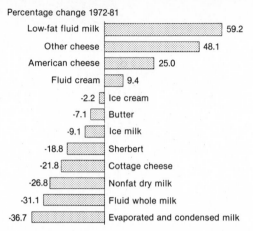

Percentage change 1972-81

Low-fat fluid milk	59.2
Other cheese	48.1
American cheese	25.0
Fluid cream	9.4
-2.2	Ice cream
-7.1	Butter
-9.1	Ice milk
-18.8	Sherbert
-21.8	Cottage cheese
-26.8	Nonfat dry milk
-31.1	Fluid whole milk
-36.7	Evaporated and condensed milk

FIGURE 11–1.   Ten-year percentage change in per capita dairy product sales, 1972–1981. (*United States Department of Agriculture.*)

tions was rated higher for flavor than milk from North Central states where dairies are allowed for the most part to set their own pull dates. (5).

DAIRY PRODUCTS

Dairy products that are discussed include whole milk, skim milk, low-fat milks, acidified and cultured milk products, flavored milk products, fortified milk products, filled milk, imitation milk, whipping cream, coffee cream, half-and-half cream, cultured cream products, frozen desserts, and butter.

Fluid Milk

The *Grade "A" Pasteurized Milk Ordinance—1965 Recommendations of the United States Public Health Service* defined milk and certain milk products and established standards for Grade A pasteurized milk and milk products (3). These standards have been adopted by many states, counties, and cities; others have established their own standards. Where the ordinance has been adopted, *milk* is defined as the lacteal secretion, practically free of colostrum, obtained by the complete milking of one or more cows; it contains not less than 3.25 percent of milk fat and not less than 8.25 percent of solids not fat. *Milk products* are defined as the different products, such as skim milk, cultured buttermilk, and evaporated milk, that result from altering milk in some way through processing. Further, where the ordinance has been adopted, only Grade A pasteurized milk and milk products may be sold to the final consumer,

TABLE 11–1. *The Cost of One Quart of Selected Fluid Milk Products as Purchased in Containers of Different Sizes from Different Market Sources* [1]

Item	Market Source	Market Unit	Cost	Cost per Quart
Homogenized	Home delivery	gallon	$2.69	$.67
Vitamin D	Home delivery	half gallon	1.49	.75
whole milk	Home delivery	quart	.89	.89
	Supermarket	gallon	2.33	.58
	Supermarket	half gallon	1.25	.63
	Supermarket	quart	.77	.77
	Convenience store	gallon	2.09	.52
	Convenience store	half gallon	1.49	.74
	Convenience store	quart	.83	.83
Skim milk	Home delivery	quart	.89	.89
	Supermarket	quart	.77	.77
	Convenience store	quart	.83	.83
Chocolate	Home delivery	quart	.89	.89
low-fat	Supermarket	quart	.99	.99
milk	Convenience store	quart	.83	.83

[1] Prices as of July 1982 in Florida.

to grocery stores, and to public eating places; but in an emergency, "ungraded" products may be sold as authorized by the local health authority. *Grade A raw milk for pasteurization* must meet the following standards: it must have been cooled immediately following milking to a temperature of 50° F or less and maintained at this temperature until processed; individual producer milk cannot exceed 100,000 bacteria per milliliter prior to commingling with other producer milk; the count of commingled milk cannot exceed 300,000 bacteria per milliliter; and there can be no detectable antibiotic residue. *Grade A pasteurized milk and milk products* must be cooled immediately after pasteurization to a temperature of 45° F or less and held at this temperature; bacterial and coliform limits are 20,000 and 10 respectively except that cultured products are exempt from bacterial limits. Milk in final packaged form for beverage use must be pasteurized or ultra-pasteurized. *Pasteurization* may be at temperatures of 191° F, 204° F, and 212° F; the holding periods thereafter are correspondingly reduced to seconds or fractions thereof. *Ultra-pasteurization* is thermal processing at or above 280° F for at least two seconds.

The composition of fluid whole milk is regulated by federal laws that set minimum standards for milk fat and solids nonfat. *Whole milk* contains not less than 3.25 percent milk fat and not less than 8.25 percent nonfat solids. *Skim milk* has the milk fat content reduced to less than

0.5 percent and it contains not less than 8.25 percent nonfat milk solids. Skim milk must be fortified with vitamin A to contain 2,000 international units per quart. Vitamin D fortification is optional, if added it must be at a level of four hundred international units per quart. *Low-fat* milk has a milk fat content between 0.5 and 2 percent and not less than 8.25 percent milk solids not fat. *Two percent* milk has a fat content of two percent and usually a solids content of ten percent. Both low-fat and two percent milk must contain added vitamin A at the same level as skim milk; the addition of vitamin D is optional. If vitamin D is added, the level is the same as for skim milk.

Whole milk that forms a cream layer has been largely replaced by homogenized milk that does not. *Homogenized milk* has been mechanically treated to break fat globules into minute particles and disperse them throughout the milk. Homogenization follows pasteurization. Homogenized milk has a softer curd, more body, and a richer flavor than unhomogenized milk.

UHT (ultra-high temperature) milk was introduced recently in the United States; it has been available on the European market for more than twenty years. The new product is shelf stable up to six months and does not require refrigeration. In UHT processing, milk is heated to 138° C. (280° F.) for a few seconds to destroy bacteria and then it is packaged in sterilized cartons made of layers of paperboard, foil, and polyethylene to keep it sterile and out of light. A packaging breakthrough came in February 1981 when the U.S. Food and Drug Administration approved the use of hydrogen peroxide for sterilizing containers separately from milk. The flavor is different from that of pasteurized milk and this may mean that time will be required for consumer acceptance. Its flavor more closely resembles that of fresh milk than that of canned milk. The use of flavors such as chocolate, vanilla, berry, and banana may expand acceptance and the flavored product may compete with the soft drink market. Researchers do not agree on whether UHT milk will have a cost advantage over pasteurized milk in the United States but everyone agrees that it offers more convenience with its longer shelf life and the elimination of the requirement for refrigeration of the unopened carton. Overall, UHT processing is comparable to pasteurization in causing little loss of nutritive value. Packaging in light-proof containers impermeable to oxygen permits UHT milk to retain almost all of its nutritional quality during storage. (7)

Acidified milk and milk products are obtained by the addition of food grade acids to pasteurized cream, half and half, milk, skim milk, and low-fat milk so that the resulting acidity is not less than 0.2 percent expressed as lactic acid. *Cultured buttermilk* is pasteurized skim milk or low-fat milk that has been soured by lactic acid producing bacteria or other similar culture. Cultured buttermilk may contain butter flakes.

Cultured milk is pasteurized whole milk that has been soured by lactic-acid-producing bacteria or other similar culture. *Yogurt* is a cultured milk product prepared from either whole or skim milk. It comes in many flavors and with added fruits. Its consumption has increased during the past decade. It is an expensive form of milk and as a dessert it is more expensive than ice cream or ice milk. It derives no special nutrient benefit from the fermentation process. Yogurt is used in cooking as a substitute for sour cream, thus reducing the calorie content and the fat content of dishes. *Frozen yogurt* was introduced in the mid 1970's and was promoted as a dessert. The only difference between regular and frozen yogurt is that the latter contains gelatin for thickening, and the fruit has been pureed. It has the appeal of ice cream, but is creamier and tarter. It is available in such flavors as strawberry, lemon and even chocolate. Frozen yogurt costs about $.10 to $.20 more than a like portion of ice cream and is more than twice as expensive as regular yogurt.

The mid-1970's saw the marketing of whole, low-fat, and skim milks with *Lactobacillus acidophilus* added. The addition of this microorganism does not change the flavor of the milk. It is a bacteria that is found in milk and is destroyed by pasteurization. It is also found in the gastrointestinal track of man.

Milk that has the flavor of chocolate is available as whole milk, low-fat milk, or skim milk; it is flavored with either chocolate or cocoa. The whole milk product flavored with chocolate is labeled "chocolate milk"; when flavored with cocoa, "chocolate-flavored milk." The low-fat products are similarly labeled as "chocolate low-fat milk" and "chocolate-flavored low-fat milk." The skim-milk products are designated as "chocolate drink" and "chocolate-flavored drink." All are sweetened, and additives that stabilize or prevent the settling of the chocolate ingredient are used. Milk products of varying fat content flavored with such flavors as maple, strawberry, coffee, and others are labeled "flavored milk," "flavored low-fat milk," and "flavored drink." *Fortified milk products* have added vitamin and mineral content. *Vitamin D milk* has the vitamin D content increased to 400 IU units per quart. Fortified skim milk contains 2,000 IU of added vitamin A and generally 400 IU units of added vitamin D. Milk for special dietary uses is available with the added vitamins thiamine, niacin, and riboflavin and the added minerals iron and/or iodine. *Reconstituted* and *recombined* milk and milk products are those that result from the recombining of milk constituents with potable water. Skim milk distributed at retail is frequently a reconstituted product prepared from nonfat dry solids and unpolluted water.

Filled milk is milk in which milk fat has been replaced by vegetable fat. It has been manufactured since 1916. In 1923 filled milk was prohibited in interstate commerce because the dairy industry to promote its interest prevailed on Congress to enact the Filled Milk Act on the grounds that filled milk was an adulterated product. In 1976 the Filled Milk Act was repealed and there are no longer any federal restrictions on the sale of filled milk. Each state is now free to establish its own regulations regarding the sale of filled milk. Filled milk has long been used by the armed forces at overseas bases because of its superior keeping qualities, and its use has been required at overseas bases since 1967. Another potential value of such products has to do with the relationship, as yet unresolved, between dietary fat and heart disease. Yet to be finalized are proposals that would require filled milk products to be labeled imitation unless they meet certain nutrient standards that would result in a product of equivalent nutrient value to the product being imitated. Filled milk is prepared from skim milk and vegetable fat or from recombined skim milk and vegetable fat plus such additives as are required to give a good product and are, of course, permitted. The vegetable fat of the first filled milks was coconut oil because it was cheap; hence, the product could be sold on the basis of price competition with whole milk. Currently, the product is prepared with vegetable fats such as soybean and corn oils, which have a more favorable ratio of unsaturated fat acids to saturated fat acids. It is usually canned. Filled milk, where it is in the marketplace, is probably a good buy; but the label ought to be read for information as to the kind of fat present, also the presence or absence of vitamins A and D. Of course, filled milk should be priced competitively.

Imitation milk is a nondairy product produced from vegetable fat, soybean protein, sodium caseinate, corn syrup solids, flavoring agents, stabilizers, emulsifiers, and water. In May, 1968, the Food and Drug Administration proposed standards of identity and standards of quality for imitation milks and creams; the proposed standards would have established nutrient contents like those of the natural products. In May, 1970, the proposals were withdrawn for imitation milks on the grounds that the quantities of these products then being produced were so negligible as not to warrant the promulgation of the proposals. Perhaps, the idea for nondairy milk, produced other than for those allergic to milk, was born too soon. If this product is purchased, the label should be carefully read for content. For instance, many contain sodium caseinate, sodium silicoaluminate, and other additives not allowed on low sodium diets.

Cream

The Food and Drug Administration sets standards of composition for different types of cream as well as milk. These standards give minimum milk fat requirements which must be met if the product is to be shipped in interstate commerce.

A number of creams have been defined; in order of increasing milk-fat content they are half-and-half, coffee cream, light whipping cream, and heavy whipping cream. The identity standards for cream products permit these safe and suitable optional ingredients: emulsifiers, stabilizers, nutritive sweeteners, and characterizing flavoring ingredients. Also these products must be homogenized, pasteurized or ultra-pasteurized. *Half-and-half*, which is a mixture of milk and cream of 10.5 percent milk-fat content has replaced coffee cream in use to such an extent that the latter is unavailable in some grocery stores. *Coffee cream*, or *light cream*, or *table cream*, contains not less than 18 percent but less than 30 percent milk fat. *Light whipping cream* has a milk-fat content of not less than 30 percent but less than 36 percent; *heavy whipping cream*, not less than 36 percent. It is not possible to whip light cream in the home kitchen without the use of a special additive. The convenience of the ready-whipped products cannot be argued; and neither can the flavor of whipped fresh cream.

Sour cream is prepared from light cream. Pasteurized and homogenized cream is inoculated with a starter of organisms that produce the body, the flavor and aroma, and the acidity characteristic of the soured cream. Filled cream is also soured, but it may lack the flavor of real cultured sour cream. When available, it is less expensive than sour cream and would be suitable for all the culinary uses made of sour cream. *Acidified sour cream* is prepared from the souring of light cream with safe and suitable acidifiers with or without the addition of lactic acid producing bacteria. *Sour half-and-half* is prepared from half-and-half cream. Sour cream and sour half-and-half can be used interchangeably for most culinary purposes except in baking, where the difference in fat content might affect the quality of the results. These products are spray-dried and are used in dry mixes for sour-cream sauce. When heated, sour cream will curdle quickly. It should be added near the end of the cooking period and used only over gentle heat. Sour cream thins when acid is added, as in salad dressing, but it rethickens on chilling. Sour cream can be whipped (it will thin momentarily and then thicken), but it will not form as stiff a foam as whipping cream. *Sour cream dressing* and *sour half-and-half dressing* have been defined and are on supermarket shelves. Both have lower fat content than the products they resemble, sour cream and sour half-and-half. (4)

Concentrated Milk Products

Fluid milk and milk products are concentrated by the removal of water; these concentrated products are evaporated milk, sweetened condensed milk, concentrated milk, nonfat dry milk, dried whole milk, and dried buttermilk. *Evaporated milk* is sterilized homogenized milk that has been reduced in volume by about 60 percent loss of water. When aseptically canned, this product undergoes less flavor change and color modification than does the canned and sterilized product. Nonfat and low fat evaporated milks are available now. They are made from the corresponding fluid milk product. When diluted with an equal volume of water, evaporated milk equals whole milk in composition. Vitamin D has been added to it in such a quantity that the vitamin D content is not less than 400 USP units per quart of diluted milk. Evaporated milk is now packaged in easy-open cans and contains an added stabilizer that retards fat separation. It costs about two thirds as much as fresh whole milk. Private-label brands are less expensive than national brands. *Sweetened condensed milk* contains added sweetener; it has been condensed by the removal of about 50 percent of the water content of whole milk. The content of milk fat is not less than 8.5 percent; of sugar, about 44 percent. The product is used mainly in cookery; it has some qualities that make it useful in the preparation of desserts and candies. *Concentrated milk* is prepared from pasteurized milk; the removal of water reduces volume to about one third. The product is not sterilized and does not contain added sugar. It must be preserved by freezing or refrigeration. The product has good flavor.

Both whole and skim milk can be dehydrated to a content of not more than 5 percent of water. Dried whole milk is used mainly in infant feeding, but it can be reconstituted and used as fresh fluid milk. To prevent the development of rancidity, dried whole milk is packed in an inert gas and is hermetically sealed in containers. Once the container is open, rancidity develops unless the milk is refrigerated. Its cost is not much different from that of fresh whole milk. Nonfat dry milk is inexpensive; when reconstituted it costs from one half to two thirds less than fluid whole milk or fluid fortified skim milk. It can be reconstituted and used like any fluid milk product. It can be used in the dry form for baking.

Because some persons do not like the flavor of reconstituted nonfat dry milk, it is often blended by the meal manager quart for quart with whole fluid milk to produce a milk with good flavor at reduced cost. Flavor varies among brands. Consumers often reject one brand but accept another for drinking. Reconstituted milk is most acceptable when served well chilled. In 1968, the definition and standard of identity for nonfat dry milk was amended to permit fortification with vitamins A and D: the consumer should buy the fortified kind. Grades for nonfat dry milk have been established; the only quality of instant nonfat dry milk is U.S. Extra Grade (Figure 11–2). There are two grades, U.S. Extra and U.S. Standard, for regular nonfat dry milk. The cost of non-

FIGURE 11–2. Grademark for instant nonfat dry milk. (*United States Department of Agriculture.*)

fat dry milk in the supermarket differs with package size, whether premeasured or not, and brand. A supermarket's own brand will cost less than the nationally advertised brands (see Table 11–2). Nonfat dry milk is used extensively by the food industries in the preparation of meat products, breads and pastries, prepared mixes, ice cream mixes, and so on. Dried buttermilk is also extensively used by the food industries. *Malted milk* is prepared from whole milk and the liquid derived from the mash of ground barley malt and wheat flour. It contains not less than 7.5 percent milk fat and not more than 3.5 percent moisture. Mixes for chocolate-malted-milk drinks contain the malted milk and chocolate, cocoa, sugar, and nonfat dry milk. Mixes for diet drinks and instant breakfasts include nonfat dry milk, flavor substances, and other

TABLE 11–2. *Cost per Quart of Nonfat Dry Milk as It Varies with Purchase of Different Brands and Different Packages* [1]

Items	Market Unit	Cost of Market Unit	Cost per Quart
Brand A			
not premeasured	20 qt.	$7.49	$.37
not premeasured	8 qt.	3.55	.44
not premeasured	3 qt.	1.43	.48
premeasured for quarts	10 qt.	4.45	.445
premeasured for quarts	5 qt.	2.45	.49
Brand B			
not premeasured	20 qt.	6.59	.33 [2]
premeasured for quarts	10 qt.	3.67	.37
Brand C			
not premeasured	20 qt.	6.27	.31
premeasured for quarts	10 qt.	3.59	.36
Brand D			
premeasured for quarts	10 qt.	4.39	.44

[1] Prices as of July, 1982 in Florida.
[2] Store brand.

ingredients. Both dried cream and dried whey are extensively used by the food industries. Even a casual reading of the labels of food products reveals their presence.

At a given time and in a given place, milk and milk products differ in cost depending on treatment, fat content, size of container, and source from which purchased (see Table 11–1). Consumers find it advantageous to comparison-shop for milk as well as for other foods. Milk costs less per unit when purchased in gallon and half-gallon containers than in quart or half-pint containers. Generally, whole milk costs more than skim milk. Fluid skim milk costs more than nonfat dry milk reconstituted by the consumer. Home-delivered milk costs more than milk purchased at the supermarket, and milk purchased from a dairy store or other special outlet costs less than milk purchased at the supermarket. The cost of fluid milk products varies in cities and regions within the United States (1).

Frozen Desserts

Frozen desserts include ice cream, frozen custard or French ice cream, ice milk, and sherbets and ices. All are made by the freezing while stirring of the ingredient mix from which each is prepared. Stirring effects the introduction of air and increases the volume of the mix 100 percent or more. Increase in volume is called *overrun;* the extent of the overrun is controlled by the regulation of the solids content and/or the weight of the finished product. All mixes must be pasteurized, and all can be homogenized. The list of milk products that can be used in the mix is very long; it includes cream, dried cream, butter, milk, concentrated milk, evaporated milk, sweetened condensed milk, and nonfat dry milk. In addition to milk ingredients, the mix may contain some or all of the following: sweetening agents; eggs; natural and/or artificial flavoring agents; characterizing ingredients, such as fruits, fruit purees, and juices; casein; artificial color; and emulsifying and stabilizing agents. The content of stabilizing agent is limited to 0.5 percent by federal definitions. Ice cream, French ice cream, ice milk, fruit sherbets, and water ices have been defined. The regulations of the states may be more stringent than federal regulations.

Ice cream has a minimum milk-fat content and total milk solids content of 10 and 20 percent, respectively, of the weight of the finished product; exemptions permit the weight of milk fat and total milk solids to be only 8 and 16 percent for ice creams in which chocolate, nuts, confections, and certain fruits are ingredients. Ice cream has not less than 1.6 pounds of total solids per gallon and weights not less than 4.5 pounds per gallon. Labels name ingredients, especially these characterizing ingredients, that is, the particular flavorings and food ingredients that characterize an ice cream. If an ice cream contains no artificial flavor, it takes the name(s) of the characterizing flavor(s), for example, "Vanilla Ice Cream." But, if an ice cream is flavored by both natural and artificial flavors and the natural one predominates, it is labeled as "flavored," that is, "Vanilla-Flavored Ice Cream." When an artificial flavor predominates or is the sole characterizing agent, the ice cream is described as "artificial" or "artificially flavored" ice cream, for example, "Artificially Flavored Vanilla Ice Cream." These labeling requirements apply to all frozen desserts. Optimum fat content imparts good body and flavor to ice cream. Available commercial ice creams differ in quality.

Frozen custard or *French ice cream* or *French custard ice cream* is ice cream in which the weight of egg-yolk solids is not less than 1.4 percent the weight of the finished product. This product is priced higher than ice cream. *Ice milk* is less rich than ice cream. Milk fat is no less than 2 percent and not more than 7 percent; total milk solids are not less than 11 percent of the finished weight. The weight of total solids can be no less than 1.3 pounds per gallon; the weight per gallon is 4.5 pounds. The natural and artificial characterizing ingredients must be named on the labels. Label statement of the use of artificial color is mandatory. Ice milk is available in hard- and soft-frozen forms.

Fruit sherbets contain not less than 1 percent and not more than 2 percent milk fat and not less than 2 percent and not more than 5 percent milk solids in the finished product. Fruit sherbets must weigh no less than 6 pounds per gallon. The characterizing ingredients of sherbet include fruits and fruit juices. The quantity of the fruit component must be 2 percent in the case of citrus fruits, 6 percent in the case of berries, and 10 percent in the case of other fruits of the finished weight of the sherbet. Label statement of characterizing ingredients and use of artificial color is mandatory. *Water ices* contain no milk products, but in other respects are like fruit sherbets.

Mellorine is a frozen dairy dessert. It may contain milk-derived nonfat solids and either vegetable or animal fat, only part of which may be milk fat, or both. Fat content is not less than 6 percent, total solids not less than 1.6 pounds per gallon and weighs not less than 4.5 pounds per gallon. Vitamin A fortification is mandatory to ensure forty international units per gram of fat in mellorine.

Frozen desserts, especially ice creams available in the supermarkets and dairy stores, differ in quality from products that just satisfy minimal requirements to products that are rich in milk fat, eggs, sugar, and other food ingredients. They differ in cost accordingly. The products of lower quality are lower priced; they are also usually lower in calories.

Frozen desserts can also differ in cost because of differences in the characterizing agents. Plain vanilla ice cream costs less to manufacture than an ice cream that contains nuts and fruits.

Butter

Butter consumption has decreased in recent years, partly because butter has remained more expensive than margarine, and also because margarine has improved in flavor and texture. Further, butter consumption has declined because of the implication of its saturated fatty acids in cardiovascular disease.

By definition, butter contains not less than 80 percent milk fat. It is churned from pasteurized specially cultured sweet or sour cream of about 33 percent milk fat content. The churned product is salted and worked to the legal moisture content. It is usually artificially colored; however, no statement of the use of artificial color is required in labeling. The quality of butter depends mainly on the quality of the cream churned. Standards for grading butter for quality have been developed. See Figure 11–3 for the grade symbols. It will be noted that the quality grade is "when graded." Milk fat is subject to the rapid development of rancidity; hence, graded butter purchased at retail is frequently less than the indicated quality, a fact that has contributed to the consumption of less butter and more margarine. Butter quality is judged mainly on flavor and aroma but also on body, texture, color, and salt. Grades are U.S. Grade AA (93 Score), U.S. Grade A (92 Score), and U.S. Grade B (90 Score). *Score* refers to the number of points a product could score out of 100. U.S. Grade AA butter is made from fresh cream; it has a delicate and pleasing flavor and aroma and smooth and creamy texture. Grade A butter is made from fresh cream; its flavor is good and it is only slightly lower in quality than U.S. Grade AA butter. U.S. Grade B butter is made from sour cream. Its flavor is like old-time country butter and it is preferred by some consumers though other consumers might describe it as having poor flavor.

FIGURE 11–3.   Grade symbols for graded butter. (*United States Department of Agriculture.*)

Reprocessed butter is prepared from low-grade butter worked with fresh milk to remove some of the objectionable flavor substances and rectify other faults. *Danish butter* is manufactured from pasteurized cream innoculated with a mixture of organisms that produce flavors resembling old-style butter churned from soured cream. *Sweet butter* is unsalted butter. Salt acts as a preservative in butter; sweet butter is more perishable than salted butter and is usually priced higher. *Whipped butter* is butter into which air or an inert gas has been introduced. Whipped butter develops rancidity more rapidly than unwhipped butter. Its appeal is its ease of spreading and lower calorie content volume for volume. Garlic butter, honey butter, and maple butter are mixtures of butter and the named ingredients. But apple or apricot butters do not contain any real butter. See page 355 for a description of fruit butters. Whipped butter and flavored butters are more expensive than butter weight for weight.

Packaging practices can modify the cost of butter of the same grade; for example, one pound blocks may cost less than one pound packaged in four four-ounce units. Ungraded butter wrapped in parchment but without further packaging is frequently specialed and may be a good buy. The best policy in buying butter is to buy and try. In supermarkets where there is a rapid turnover of products, an ungraded product may be superior in quality to a graded product that moves slowly.

NONDAIRY PRODUCTS

Nondairy products simulate—that is, are substitutes for—dairy products. The ones described here are the coffee creamers, toppings, and margarines. Imitation or nondairy milk was described earlier in this chapter. The ingredients of these products include vegetable fat, vegetable protein, sodium caseinate, sweeteners, artificial flavors, artificial color, various additives (including preservatives, gums, emulsifiers, and stabilizers), and perhaps such vitamins as vitamin A and riboflavin. Though sodium caseinate is a milk derivative, it is considered a chemical rather than a milk ingredient. Nondairy products can be designed to have special dietary properties and they have fairly good storage life, two facts that explain their ready acceptance.

Coffee Whiteners

Coffee whiteners, or coffee creamers, or coffee lighteners can simulate either coffee cream or half-and-half, or they can contain less fat than either. They can be purchased as liquid, frozen liquid, or spray-dried coffee whitener. They are bland in flavor and almost odor free. All have good storage life when compared with fresh cream, and the powdered whiteners, of which there are several brands, are shelf-stable. It should be noted, however, that they do not store indefinitely without loss of flavor. Purchase of the economy-size package may not be warranted for the small family. The list of ingredients in one such product was "water, hydrogenated palm kernel oil, sodium caseinate, sugar, di-potassium phosphate, propylene glycol monostearate, poly-sorbate 60, stearoyl-lactylate, salt, artificial flavor and color." The purposes of the additives are to give stability, dispersion, texture, and even flow. Coffee whiteners are an imitation product and do not meet the nutritional standards for the product they resemble. A merit of the product is that it lacks the fat and, therefore, the calories of cream.

Nondairy Toppings

Nondairy toppings are available as dry mixes, as liquid mix ready for whipping, in pressurized containers, and frozen ready-whipped in plastic containers. The dry mixes are the most versatile. The mix can be added to water, milk, coffee, or chocolate milk; or spices can be added to the dry mix to produce flavorful toppings. The liquid mix would be whipped in the same manner as whipping cream. The product in the aerosol container whips to good volume as it is propelled from the container. The ready-whipped topping can be spooned from the container and immediately placed on food. The products may differ in the stability of the foam. Advantages of the nondairy toppings over whipping cream are lower fat content, lower cost per serving, and greater convenience. Despite these advantages the lover of good food prefers whipping cream.

Margarine

Margarine is defined as the food in plastic form or liquid emulsion, containing not less than eighty percent fat. The regulation recognizes margarine and oleomargarine as synonymous. The product has the same fat content as butter. The fat may be of plant and/or animal origin. Oils in use in margarine manufacture include soybean oil, corn oil, safflower oil, coconut oil, natural lard, oleo oil (the fraction of beef fat fluid at room temperature), and oleo stock (beef fat rendered at low temperature). The kinds and combination of oils used vary from time to time relative to cost. The aqueous phase of margarine contains water and/or milk or milk products. Vitamin A must be added to margarine so the finished product contains not less than 15,000 IU per pound. Optional ingredients include vitamin D, salt, nutritive carbohydrate sweeteners, emulsifiers, preservatives, color additives, flavoring substances, acidulants, and alkalizers. The production of soft, easy-spread margarines with favorable polyunsaturated to saturated fatty acid ratios has improved consumer acceptance of the product. Imitation margarines with half the fat content required by the definition have half the calorie content of regular margarines. Whipped margarine, like whipped butter, has fewer calories per equal volume than regular margarine.

A relative newcomer to the market is a product composed of 60–75 percent butter. It has the advantages of having more highly unsaturated fatty acids and lower cost than butter but, at the same time, it possesses a flavor which more closely resembles butter than most margarines. The product must be labeled "margarine." Another new product in the supermarket is "spread." This product looks and tastes like margarine; however, it contains only 60 percent vegetable oil while margarine contains at least 80 percent oil. The product contains nonfat dry milk. Its main advantage is that it contains fewer calories than margarine.

Margarines are available at widely differing costs, with the most expensive ones being twice as costly as the least expensive ones. The kind of oil or oils, the treatment of the product, the packaging of the product, and the brand name account for cost differences. Store brands are less expensive than name brands. They are also frequent specials. Careful reading of information in the labeling reveals differences in composition. Freezing to extend storage life is practical.

Eggs

Per capita egg consumption has continued to decline in the past decade. In 1980 it was down to 272 eggs per person per year. (Figure 11–4.)

Until very recently, eggs were one of the few foods that the house-

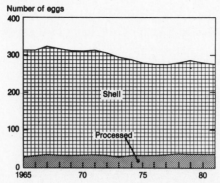

FIGURE 11–4. Per capita consumption of eggs. (*USDA 1981 preliminary,* 1982 forecast. Processed eggs converted to shell equivalent.)

wife purchased that were hardly altered by technology, about 90 percent of egg production being consumed as shell eggs. The percentage of eggs not used as shell eggs was used by the food industries as fluid, frozen, or dehydrated products. It is now possible for the consumer to purchase omelet mixtures ready for the fry pan. She can also buy seasoning mixtures for omelets; but in this instance, she must provide the eggs. Instant scrambled eggs, frozen fried eggs, canned eggnog, and many other convenient egg foods are being market tested. Pre-cooked and frozen scrambled eggs with sausage are one combination of ready-to-eat breakfasts being marketed.

In most retail markets, the consumer can purchase shell eggs by grade and size—and sometimes by shell color. Although white eggs are preferred to brown eggs in some areas and brown to white in other areas, the color of the shell per se in no way affects the quality, the flavor, or the nutrient value of the egg. The shell color is determined by the breed of chicken. In areas where white eggs are preferred to brown eggs, they command a higher price; conversely, brown eggs may cost more in areas where they are preferred.

The grading and classifying of eggs is sorting them according to quality and weight. Egg quality is determined by four primary factors: the clarity and thickness of the white, the condition of the yolk, the condition and size of the air cell, and the texture and condition of the shell. The usual method of grading eggs is by candling, that is, inspection of the interior of the unbroken egg under bright light in a darkened place. In large operations, eggs are candled en masse on conveyers that move over multiple lights. Consumer grades for shell eggs are U.S. Grade AA, U.S. Grade A, and U.S. Grade B. However, the latter grade is not often found in the supermarket as such (Figure 11–5). There is no longer a U.S. Grade C consumer grade. Since 1972 only egg processors can utilize Grade C or check quality (6). Tolerances permit small percentages of the lower grades; for example, a carton of eggs of U.S. Grade AA is permitted to contain two eggs of Grade A and two eggs of Grade B quality. In fact, each carton of Grade A and

FIGURE 11–5. Grademark for graded eggs. (*United States Department of Agriculture.*)

Grade B eggs is required to contain only eight eggs of those qualities respectively; the remaining four may be of lesser quality.

Eggs begin to lose quality immediately after laying, and deterioration is rapid unless delayed by refrigeration. Eggs that bear the USDA grade symbol must have been graded in a room wherein the temperature range was from 40° F to 70° F and held thereafter at no less than 60° F. Only eggs of "current production,"—that is, those held under refrigeration no longer than thirty days—are identified with consumer grademarks. Several changes occur in eggs as they deteriorate: the air cell enlarges, the firm white thins, and the yolk increases in water content, thereby stretching and weakening the membrane that surrounds it. Candling reveals these changes. As the firm white thins, the yolk becomes mobile and visible; the presence of blood spots in the white is detectable. Table 11–3 summarizes the grade specifications for each grade. Note that shells may not be broken and that only Grade B eggs may have stained shells. Eggs with coarse-textured shells score lower than eggs with fine-textured shells. Because eggs can deteriorate after grading, it is required that each carton be marked with either the grading date, the expiration date, or a combination of grading and expira-

TABLE 11–3. *Summary of United States Standards for Quality of Individual Shell Eggs* [1]

Quality Factor	Specifications for Each Quality Factor		
	AA Quality	A Quality	B Quality
Shell	Clean; unbroken: practically normal.	Clean; unbroken: practically normal.	Clean to very slightly stained; may be slightly abnormal.
Air cell	⅛ inch or less in depth; practically regular	³/₁₆ inch or less in depth; practically regular	⅜ inch or less in depth; may be free or bubbly.
White	Clear; firm.	Clear; may be reasonably firm.	Clear; may be slightly weak.
Yolk	Outline slightly defined; practically free from defects.	Outline may be fairly well defined; practically free from defects.	Outline may be well defined; may be slightly enlarged and flattened; may show definite but not serious defects.

[1] Source: *Regulations Governing the Grading of Shell Eggs and United States Standards, Grades, and Weight Classes for Shell Eggs;* Poultry Division, Consumer and Marketing Service, United States Department of Agriculture, Washington, D.C., July 1972.

FIGURE 11–6. Grade symbol for Fresh Fancy Quality eggs. (*United States Department of Agriculture.*)

tion dates either on the carton or on the tape used to seal the carton. The grading date may be expressed as the month and day or the number of the month and day (for example, 5-19 for May 19), or as the consecutive day of the year (for example, 129 for May 19). If the expiration date is used, it is stated as month and day or the number of the month and day preceded by the letters EXP or a statement such as, "Not to Be Sold After." The expiration date is no more than fourteen days later than the date of grading.

A second set of grade symbols may be found on graded eggs available in the supermarket. In 1959, a program for the production and marketing of quality-controlled eggs was initiated by the United States Department of Agriculture and the industry. Eggs produced under this program are Grade AA, or Fresh Fancy Quality, and Grade A, and they are further identified by the statement, "Produced and Marketed Under Federal-State Quality Control Program," which accompanies the grade symbol (Figure 11–6).

To control the quality of Fresh Fancy Quality eggs, it is required that they be gathered twice or three times daily, that they be promptly cooled to a temperature of 60° F or less, and that they be held at 60° F or less and at a relative humidity of approximately 70 percent. The quality of the eggs is determined by measurement of the height of the thick white and observation of the yolk, which must be well-rounded and quite uniform in color. The quality of the white is expressed in *Haugh units,* a numerical value derived from the weight of the egg expressed in ounces and the height of the white as measured by a micrometer. Because various factors determine the thickness of egg white, eggs from different flocks are graded separately. A flock consists of birds within sixty days of age. A flock remains on the program only so long as a biweekly sample of egg scores not less than the designated number of Haugh units and meets other stipulations. For Fresh Fancy Quality eggs, the sample must average not less than eighty-four Haugh units and not more than one egg in a sample of ten can have a Haugh value of less

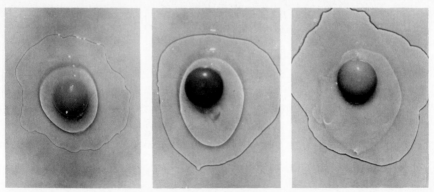

FIGURE 11–7. Appearance of broken-out eggs. From left to right, U.S. AA Grade, U.S. A Grade, and U.S. B Grade qualities. (*United States Department of Agriculture.*)

than sixty Haugh units. For U.S. Grade A quality, the sample must average not less than sixty-two Haugh units and no more than two eggs in a sample of ten can have a Haugh value of less than sixty Haugh units. Cartons of Fresh Fancy Quality eggs are required to be marked with an expiration date that is ten days from the date of packing. Packing must occur within six days of testing.

The broken-out egg quickly reveals its quality (Figure 11–7). The broken-out U.S. Grade AA egg does not spread much (it covers a small area); the white is thick and stands firmly around the yolk; the yolk appears rounded. The broken-out U.S. Grade A egg spreads some; the white does not cling as firmly around the yolk; the yolk is flattened somewhat. The broken-out U.S. Grade B egg spreads widely; the yolk is flattened. The changes are not necessarily accompanied by flavor change. Eggs with bad flavor are rarely purchased. Grade B eggs do not give a good appearance when poached or fried; but they are satisfactory for other egg dishes and for culinary uses.

Of practical concern to the consumer is information regarding the pricing of eggs in relation to size. Eggs are classified by weight per dozen as Jumbo, Extra Large, Large, Medium, Small, and Peewee. Of these classes, Extra Large, Large, and Medium are commonly available in the supermarket. Crossbreeding of chickens and scientific feeding of laying hens have increased not only egg production but the size of eggs as well. Small eggs were not uncommon a few years ago; they are rarely seen today. And eggs of Jumbo size may often be found in large supermarkets. Class and weight per dozen eggs are Jumbo, thirty ounces; Extra Large, twenty-seven ounces; Large, twenty-four ounces; Medium, twenty-one ounces; Small, eighteen ounces; and Peewee, fifteen ounces (see Figure 11–8). The weight difference between each two

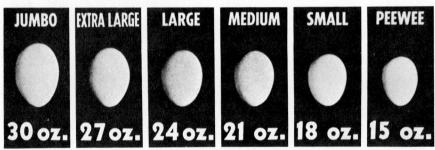

FIGURE 11–8. Weight classes for eggs. (*United States Department of Agriculture.*)

classes is three ounces. This difference provides a basis for selection among classes.

Some general guidelines for finding the best buy between one size and the next larger or smaller size are given in Table 11–4. For example, if the price of large eggs is 75 cents per dozen, extra large ones are a better buy if they are priced at less than ten cents more or 79 cents a dozen. If medium eggs are priced at 70 cents or less they are a better buy. Obviously, price comparisons must be made within the same quality grades. The consumer may decide that the smallest absolute investment is her goal; in this instance, she would purchase the smallest available size. Differences of three or six ounces divided among twelve units are not very significant. It is said that recipes assume the use of Medium or Large eggs. Some recently developed recipes express egg requirements in measure.

Purchased eggs should be refrigerated immediately in the carton in which they were purchased. Commercially, eggs may be dipped in or

TABLE 11–4. *Guidelines for Purchasing Eggs*[1]

Price per dozen of large eggs	Buy the larger size if the price difference between it and the next smaller size is less than
41–48	6
49–56	7
57–64	8
65–72	9
73–80	10
81–88	11
89–96	12

[1]*Source*: "Your Money's Worth in Foods." Home and Garden Bulletin No. 183, U.S. Department of Agriculture. Washington, D.C. (April 1979).

sprayed with colorless mineral oil as an aid to the conservation of quality. Oiling retards the losses of water and carbon dioxide and delays the chemical and physical changes that accompany sealing. Eggs are packed in cartons with the large end uppermost to prevent mechanical damage to the egg. Also, keeping the large end up prevents the air from moving from that end of the egg, a movement which could tend to dislodge the yolk.

Nearly every state has some sort of egg law. The federal standards frequently form the basis for these laws. In many states, eggs are federal-state graded. In some states only graded eggs can be sold.

In December, 1970, the Egg Products Inspection Act was passed; it became effective July 15, 1971. It requires that all eggs broken for commercial purposes be pasteurized and that the breaking process be carried out under continuous inspection.

Egg Substitutes

In the 1970's, egg substitutes that are low in cholesterol were introduced into the market. Fleischmann's marketed a synthetic egg-like fluid called *Egg Beaters. Second Nature* and *Country Cousin* are similar products that have been marketed.

Consumer Union (2) tested *Egg Beaters* and found them to be satisfactory for use in French toast, brownies, and sponge cake. Scrambled eggs and omelets from this product, however, were wet, runny, and lacked the egg aroma. *Egg Beaters* were also found to contain less protein, vitamins, and minerals than eggs. *Egg Beaters* had ten times as much carbohydrate and a greater amount of sodium, a fact that could be important to some heart patients and persons on low sodium diets. These products do, however, contain a minimal amount of cholesterol as claimed on the label. The egg substitutes cost 20 to 50 percent more than eggs. People who are allergic to eggs will probably be allergic to *Egg Beaters* since they contain egg white. Overall, Consumer Reports found *Egg Beaters* to be a passable substitute for eggs for those who must restrict their intake of cholesterol. For others, the disadvantages of poor taste and high cost do not make up for the nutritional loss when *Egg Beaters* are compared with eggs.

Summary. The variety in dairy products and in nondairy products increases with time; eggs remain simply eggs, but there has been an increase in the production of imitation eggs. Variety, quality differences, packaging styles, and different market resources make it possible for consumers to be selective. We can comparison-shop, buy and try, and then decide how to spend our dollars for the products we want and/or can buy. Dollars can buy greater or lesser quantities of dairy products, of nondairy products, and of eggs—our decisions determine whether we get the lesser or the greater quantities. The following guides suggest how to maximize the dollars for these products.

BUYING GUIDES

Milk

1. Research your market areas for a dairy store or other special markets that sell dairy products at prices lower than supermarkets.

2. Buy the largest container of fluid milk that you can use and store; the cost per unit should decrease as the container size increases.

3. Look for filled milk. If available and if priced right, it will be a good buy. Read the label to discover the kind of fat substituted for milk fat. It ought not to be coconut oil, but rather soybean or corn oil.

4. If you buy nonfat dry milk for reconstituting for drinking, comparison-shop your markets for the best product at the lowest cost. Private-label products are less expensive than national brands. All instant nonfat dry milk products are of the same grade.

5. Use as much nonfat dry milk as you can. It is your most-for-the-dollar milk. Buy it in the largest container practical for your use. You will spend more when you buy the package with measured-out units that reconstitute to one quart.

6. Use evaporated milk for an inexpensive, rich milk in cooking.

7. Use nonfat dry milk and evaporated milk for whipping whenever suitable. Many recipes have been especially developed for such intended use.

8. Use the topping mixes instead of whipping cream; they are less expensive in dollars and calories.

9. Whipping cream is sometimes specialed; buy and freeze it if you prefer it for desserts and toppings.

10. Use nondairy products in coffee; they are somewhat less expensive and may be lower in calories than dairy counterparts.

11. Make your own chocolate milk and other milk beverages, including diet drinks and "instant breakfast" mixes.

Butter

1. The pound-block of butter is often less expensive than butter packed in four-ounce sticks.

2. You can freeze butter to preserve quality.

3. Even when graded, the quality of butter is not always as good as the consumer expects. Frequently, an ungraded product of local origin will be very good. Try what the market offers.

4. Whipped butter is expensive and deteriorates rapidly. Flavored butters like garlic butter are expensive. Compare the cost ounce for ounce of the flavored and unflavored products. Make your own.

5. Unsalted butter is more expensive than salted butter and keeps less well.

6. Buy margarine instead of butter; it is much less expensive. Or use a combination of butter and margarine in cooking if you prefer the butter flavor. Butter flavoring is available for culinary uses.

Eggs

1. Buy eggs only from a refrigerated cabinet.

2. For frying or poaching, U.S. Grade A or U.S. Grade AA eggs give the best appearance. U.S. Grade B eggs are suitable for other uses.

3. Buy the size of egg that gives the best bargain.

4. Before buying omelet mixtures, calculate the cost. The convenience of the mixture is pretty expensive.

5. Color of shell is not a factor of quality.

6. Refrigerate eggs in the cartons in which they were purchased.

7. Per pound, frozen whole eggs equal ten whole Large eggs and dried whole eggs equal thirty-two eggs.

8. Two and one-half tablespoons of dried whole egg plus two and one-half tablespoons of water are equivalent to one egg.

REFERENCES CITED

1. *Estimated Retail Food Prices by Cities,* United States Department of Labor, Washington, D.C. (February 1976).
2. "Egg Beaters: Do They Beat Real Eggs?" *Consumer Reports* **39:3** (1974).
3. *Grade "A" Pasteurized Milk Ordinance—1965 Recommendations of the United States Public Health Service,* Public Health Service Publication No. 229, United States Department of Health, Education, and Welfare, Washington, D.C. (1965).
4. How to Buy Dairy Products, Home and Garden Bulletin No. 201, Food Safety and Quality Service, U.S. Department of Agriculture, Washington, D.C. (July 1979).
5. "Milk: Could it Taste Better?" *Consumer Reports* **47:6** (1982).
6. "New Laws Affecting Eggs and Egg Products Users," Poultry Division, Consumer and Marketing Service (News Release) United States Department of Agriculture, Washington, D.C. (August, 1971).
7. UHT Milk: Nutrition, Safety, and Convenience. National Food Review Economic Research Service, U.S. Department of Agriculture, Washington, D.C. (Spring 1982).

Suggested Problems

1. Compare the cost of different package sizes of whole milk, skim milk, and nonfat dry milk.
2. Compare the cost in your market area of the different sizes of eggs available. Compare with the cost of egg substitutes. Compare with the cost of eggs over a period of several months. Plot cost versus time.
3. Look at the label on an assortment of commercial products sold for preparing flavored milk drinks, milk shakes, malteds, and the like. Compare the cost. Estimate the cost of "do-it-yourself" similar products.
4. Prepare a two-day dietary adequate in calcium for a college woman who is allergic to milk. Show values for calories and calcium.
5. Prepare a two-day dietary adequate in calcium for a college woman who does not drink milk but does use it in cooking. Show values for calcium and calories.
6. Compare the cost of six brands of margarines available at the supermarket. Read the label. Suggest reasons for the differences in price.
7. Comparison shop the marketing area for butter. What are ranges in cost for different grades and different types of packaging?
8. Using one of the food composition tables available compare the nutritional make-up of sherbet, ice milk, and ice cream. Compare the cost of different brands of these products available at the supermarket.

Chapter 12

Shopping for Food: Cheeses

Although cheese is a dairy product and as such might have been discussed in the last chapter, cheeses have become of sufficient interest to consumers in the United States to warrant a separate chapter. Travel at home and abroad has introduced new varieties of cheese and different cheese dishes. Our ever-growing preoccupation with gourmet cooking and ethnic and sophisticated cookbooks has fed this interest in cheeses. Wine and cheese tastings have become popular as have such dishes as Swiss fondue and quiche Lorraine. Research and technology are producing low-fat cheeses of acceptable flavor for the calorie conscious, filled cheeses of acceptable flavor for the cholesterol conscious, and low-sodium cheese products. Few foods are as versatile as cheeses. They are suitable for any meal or snack of the day and for any part of a meal. Few foods come in such a wide variety, few are suitable in so many combinations, and few lend themselves to so many culinary purposes. This chapter suggests how to purchase cheeses, and also provides information about cheeses per se: their production; the characteristics of the different varieties, their similarities and differences; and how and with what to serve them. A dictionary of better known and widely available cheeses appears at the end of the chapter.

Historically, cheese is an ancient food. Cheese making probably developed with agriculture and animal husbandry, although legend credits the discovery of cheese to an Arab trader who filled a drinking pouch made of a sheep's stomach with milk in preparation for a desert journey. At the end of his day's journey, the pouch contained the curds and whey, both food and drink, produced as the result of the coagulation of the milk by the rennin of the sheep's stomach. In actuality, cheese making is preservation of a food by dehydration. It is believed that the art of cheese making was brought from Asia to Europe. Cheese was made in many parts of the Roman Empire, and the Romans adopted the art and took it to those countries that they conquered, including Switzerland and England. The pilgrims carried cheese with them to America, and the Dutch and English brought both the herds and the art of cheese making with them. Until the mid-nineteenth century, cheese was farm- or home-made. The first factory for the commercial production of cheese was built in 1851 near Rome, New York. Commercial cheese making began in Wisconsin in the same decade; the first Wisconsin cheese factory was built in 1864 in Sheboygan County. What was an art became a science and technology. In 1980, the per capita consumption in the United States was 18 pounds of cheese of which one-third was cottage cheese.

Because cheeses were farm made and cheese making was a folk art, there are many varieties different in size, shape, color, finish, hardness, texture, and flavor and aroma. According to Axler (1) there are 1,200 named cheeses of the world, 500 distinct varieties, and 200 very fine cheeses. New cheeses are introduced each year. The United States Department of Agriculture in its handbook on cheese varieties (8) names 800 and describes 400 varieties, but suggests that there are only 18 distinct kinds of cheeses. According to Pearl (7), more than 2,000 varieties of natural cheeses have been identified and named. Some varieties are similar; for example, the many blue-veined cheeses are similar, yet they are different in texture and piquancy of flavor, and have different names, such as the Gorgonzola of Italy, the English Stilton, and the French Roquefort; no two varieties are the same. Although the cheese-making process is simple, namely, the production and treatment of the curd of milk, there may be many steps in the process and many variables that characterize the final product. Some of these are the kind, age, composition, condition, and treatment of the milk; the mode of curd formation; the treatment of the curd—how heated, how cut, how drained, and whether stirred or not; the ripening of the curd; the kinds of ripening agents; the temperature of ripening; the length of the period of ripening; and even the kinds and quantities of microorganisms present in the air during cheese making and ripening. Some or all of these differ from place to place and account for subtle differences in cheese varieties and in the same varieties made in different places; for example, New York cheddar cheese is different from Wisconsin cheddar cheese, French Camembert differs from domestic Camembert, and Swiss cheese imported from Switzerland differs from domestic Swiss cheese.

Because it is difficult to discuss cheese making and cheese varieties without naming varieties, it is desirable to discuss their naming briefly. The names of cheeses are variously derived; many stem from place names, where the cheese originated, such as Camembert, Cheddar, Jarlsberg and Cheshire; from where the variety was first marketed, such as Limburger, Edam, and Stilton; from the monasteries and monks who made them, such as Trappist, Münster (Meunster), and Port du Salut (Port Salut). Other cheeses have been named from a special ingredient, such as sage cheese, though as presently made it no longer has fresh sage as an ingredient; pepato with added pepper; and Friesian clove; or from the shape of the cheese, such as brick, pineapple, and hand cheeses; or from a special characteristic such as the blue veining of Danish blue. A few varieties were named for saints, such as St. Claude and St. Paulin, or for persons or groups directly or indirectly connected with their development like Liederkranz, which got its name from the name of the choral society to which its originator belonged. Because most cheeses are of European origin, many variety names are European. However, many varieties made worldwide bear original names regardless of place of manufacture, for example, Swiss cheese made in Wisconsin is still called Swiss cheese, and Camembert and Fontina cheeses made in Denmark are called Danish Camembert and Danish Fontina.

The Cheese-Making Process

During the past century, the making of cheese has passed from a folk art with its attendant uncertainties and failures, as well as great successes, to a highly scientific technology with its attendant efficiency and lack of failures and, possibly, great successes. Mass-produced cheeses are frequently described as mediocre by the connoisseur, but it should be mentioned that not all homemade cheeses were great and some were truly bad.

Whether homemade or factory-made, cheeses are batch-made in vats or kettles. The steps in the process are: preparation of the milk; curd formation; treatment of the curd to compact it and remove the whey; preparation for the ripening of a cheese to be ripened or the preparation of a fresh cheese for market; ripening of all ripened cheeses; and finally, perhaps aging. The preparation of the milk includes such steps as blending milks of different milkings; blending of different kinds of milks, such as cow's milk with goat's milk; skimming; adding cream or skim milk; acidification; heating; pasteurization; and homogenization. United States law requires that all imported cheeses be made from pasteurized milk. Practically all domestic cheeses are made with pasteurized milk. The fat content of a cheese is regulated here. At the proper time, starter and/or extract of rennin or milk-clotting enzymes are added. Starters are cultures of harmless bacteria of single or multiple strains. They effect formation of lactic acid and flavor components. The acid causes coagulation of the milk proteins. Curd formation is slower when only starter is used and the curd is soft; the addition of rennin extract or of milk-clotting enzymes hastens curd formation and the curd is "meatier." The curd for cheeses to be subsequently ripened is formed with starter and a milk-clotting ingredient. When the curd has property formed, it is cut, heated, manipulated, salted, drained, and pressed, according to cheese variety. The final moisture content, the density, and, to a degree, the body and texture of the finished cheese are established in these steps. Fresh, unripened cheeses are prepared for market when the curd has been properly treated for kind; for example, creamed cottage cheese has the creaming mixture introduced. (See Table 12–1, for a correlation of cheese-making technique with the characteristics of the cheeses made.) However, for most cheese varieties a period of ripening, or curing, follows. It is the period during which the already introduced ripening agents, bacteria or molds or both, effect the changes that produce the desired flavor and aroma, the desired body and tex-

TABLE 12–1. *Cheese-Making Techniques and the Resulting Characteristics of the Cheeses*

Techniques	Cheese characteristics	Typical Varieties
Acid-coagulated curd	Tender and soft	Cottage cheese, cream cheese, Neufchâtel cheese
Curd cut and matted	Compact and firm	Cheddar and Swiss cheeses
Curd cut but not matted	Somewhat open texture	Colby, Edam, Gouda cheeses
Curd worked when hot	Plastic	Provolone, Mozzarella cheeses
Ripened throughout by bacteria with eye formation	Small to large eyes	Colby, Edam, Gouda cheeses
Ripened on surface mainly by bacteria	Soft, smooth, waxy body and mild to strong in flavor	Brick, Port du Salut, Bel Paese, Limburger, Münster, Liederkranz
Ripened throughout by molds	Blue veins, piquant flavor	Roquefort, Danablu
Ripened on surface by molds	Edible crust, soft and creamy interior, pungent flavor	Camembert, Brie, Livarot

ture, and the appropriate appearance, including the proper color. It is also during this period that rind formation occurs, for example, the thick rind of Stilton, the thin rind of Gouda, and the bloomy rinds of Brie and Camembert cheeses. Rindless cheeses are produced by wrapping cheeses in plastic. The period of ripening may be just days, as for Camembert cheese, or several months, as for cheddar cheese. The temperature and humidity for ripening, or curing, differ for different cheese varieties and for the same variety made in different places. A cheese not properly ripened is characterized as *green* or *young;* it lacks flavor and aroma and may have a texture described as *tough* or *rubbery.*

Some hard cheeses are permitted to age. This aging is a postripening period during which flavor and texture may be further improved. *Aging* means holding in storage under proper conditions and it is expensive; hence, aged cheeses are expensive and they are gourmet items purchasable generally in specialty shops and by direct mail from cheese producers. A situation confusing for the consumer exists because identity standards for some cheese varieties require that they be made from pasteurized milk or "aged for sixty days." In this instance, *aging* means only that sixty days elapsed from the time of production to the time of packaging and release for sale.

UNRIPENED CHEESES

Fresh or unripened cheeses include the several styles of cottage cheese; cream cheese; Neufchâtel cheese as made in the United States; Quesco Blanco; Greek Feta; the Italian Mozzarella alternatively called Scamorza; and ricotta cheeses. All of these are mild and delicate in flavor and aroma.

RIPENED CHEESES

The great majority of cheese varities are cured, or ripened, or permitted to mature, so that microorganisms and enzymes can effect the fermentations and changes in milk protein that result in the desired flavor and aroma, texture, and appearance peculiar to a cheese variety. The change agents, which include bacteria, molds, and possibly yeasts, may be introduced via the milk (when it is used unpasteurized), into the milk, into the curd during cheese-making, by application to the surface of the green cheese by spraying or smearing, from the environment, or a combination of these. When cheeses are made from pasteurized milk, pure cultures of organisms are introduced; because these cultures do not carry the variety of organisms or carry them in the proportions of raw milk, the domestic varieties may differ in flavor from imported varieties of the same name. The ripening process proceeds in rooms where temperature and humidity are controlled or in caves. The environment may be warm and humid or cool and dry; the time for ripening is long or short accordingly. The surface of a ripening cheese may be protected or the so-called naked cheese may rest on rush mats, hay, straw, baskets, or treated shelves. Ripening changes can occur throughout a cheese, as with cheddar cheese; from the surface to the interior, as with soft varieties like Camembert and Liederkranz; and both in the interior and from the external surface as with Bel Paese, brick, and Port du Salut. Moisture content or the softness of the cheese determines the mode of ripening. Because soft cheeses are perishable, they are kept small and/or thin; they are quickly ripened from the surface. The firmer cheeses are less perishable; they can be permitted to ripen slowly and in the interior.

The period of ripening is a most important one in the production of a fine cheese; at the same time, mishaps during this period can produce bad cheeses, such as Swiss cheese without eyes, gassy eyes or holes in a variety where none should be present, bad flavors, and a bitter taste. Unless pasteurized, a cheese continues to ripen in transit, in storage, and in the refrigerator.

CLASSIFYING CHEESE VARIETIES

No completely satisfactory method of classifying cheese varieties has yet been devised. The most commonly used system classifies by texture, that is, as soft, semisoft, hard, and very hard or cheeses for grating. The disadvantage of the system is the varying degree of hardness of different samples of the same variety and of quite similar varieties. Another system classifies cheeses by mode of ripening, as unripened, or fresh cheeses, and as cheeses ripened by bacteria, by molds, by surface organisms, or by combinations of these. Such a system groups together quite unsimilar cheeses. Another system of classification groups cheeses by country of origin, as French, Swiss, Danish, Italian, and so on. Axler contends that the cheeses of a country can be characterized—for example, the French cheeses as brilliant, the German as robust, the English as solid, and the Scandinavian as earthy (1). Marquis and Haskell (6) classify cheeses by similarities in flavor and suggest such classes as fresh country cheeses, bland and buttery cheeses, the Swisses, the Parmesans, the cheddars, flavor-relatives of cheddar, blue-veined cheeses, strong cheeses, spiced and flavored cheeses, and others. Pearl (7) suggests that natural cheeses may be classified according to their basic ingredient as whey cheeses, goat's milk, ewe's milk, or cow's milk cheeses. In the dictionary of cheeses that appears at the end of this chapter some cheeses are briefly described in alphabetical order. We endeavor here to identify some groups of cheese varieties, more especially the ones favored by consumers in the United States.

Fresh Cheeses

There are few truly fresh cheeses. They include the various cottage cheeses, cream cheeses, domestic Neufchâtel cheese, and the whey cheeses of Scandinavia. Although the assortment of cottage cheeses on supermarket shelves is large, there are only three identity standards for this food: cottage cheese dry curd or dry curd cottage cheese, low-fat cottage cheese, and cottage cheese. *Dry curd cottage cheese* contains less than 0.5 percent of milk fat and not more than 80 percent of water. It can be prepared from one or more of the following: sweet skim milk, concentrated skim milk that has been properly reconstituted, and non-fat dry milk that has been properly reconstituted. The dairy product(s) must have been pasteurized. The curd can be formed by any of these three methods: lactic-acid-forming bacteria with or without rennet and/or milk-clotting enzymes; selected food grade acids with or without rennet and/or milk-clotting enzymes, or food grade acids, D-Glucono-delta-lactone, with or without rennet and/or milk-clotting enzymes. The formed curd can be cut, warmed, stirred, and drained; then washed and drained again; and then pressed, chilled, worked, and seasoned with salt. The label on packaged dry curd cottage cheese must bear a statement of the method of curd formation as "directly set" or "curd set by direct acidification" whenever acids were added to the milk for curd formation; the common or usual names of ingredients, except that bacterial cultures may be declared as "cultured" and milk-clotting enzymes as "enzymes," followed by an explanation of use; and a statement that fat content is less than 0.5 percent.

Cottage cheese is prepared by mixing dry curd cottage cheese with a creaming mixture. It contains not less than 4 percent of milk fat and not more than 80 percent of water. The creaming mixture that must be pasteurized is prepared from "safe and suitable ingredients including, but not limited to milk or substances derived from milk. Any ingredients used that are not derived from milk shall serve a useful function . . . and shall be used in a quantity not greater than is reasonably required to accomplish the intended effect" (3). However, heat-labile ingredients may be added following pasteurization. The label must bear a statement of the fat content, of the mode of curd formation when food acids are used, and the common or usual names of all ingredients. *Low-fat cottage cheese* is prepared in the same manner as cottage cheese and must comply with all labeling requirements for cottage cheese. However, the milk fat content of low-fat cottage cheese is not less than

0.5 percent and not more than 2 percent and water content is not more than 82.5 percent. The following additives are permitted in all cottage cheeses: calcium chloride to produce a firm curd, salts of sorbic acid to retard spoilage, food grade acids, and artificial flavor substances. Low-sodium cottage cheese is available.

There are several curd styles of cottage cheese. Large-curd cottage cheese is sometimes labeled "California-style" or "popcorn cheese." Small-curd cottage cheese is also called "country-style" or "farm-style." Further, there is a whipped cream style, which is a smooth, homogeneous mixture. Some other names for cottage cheese or cheeses similar to cottage cheese are Dutch cheese, Schmierkäse, pot cheese, farmer-cheese, New York or country cheese, Pennsylvania cheese, and Amish cup cheese. Actually, these vary some in flavor, texture, and moisture content, and Amish cup cheese and Schmierkäse are briefly ripened. To improve palatability cottage cheese is often seasoned with fruits and/or vegetables.

In a study of 42 brands of cottage cheese purchased in supermarkets, Consumers Union found that less than one-third showed consistently low levels of molds, yeasts, and undesirable bacteria (4). Cartons of cottage cheese are often marked with a date which is usually a "sell-by" date.

Fresh ricotta cheese resembles cottage cheese but is smoother and sweeter. It is prepared from whey, which contains coagulable lactalbumin, derived in the making of such cheeses as cheddar and Swiss cheese, combined with either whole or skim milk. *Dry ricotta cheese* is similarly made but is cured or dried to produce a gratable cheese for culinary purposes. Other unripened whey cheese include the Scandinavian Mysöst, Gjetöst, and Primöst made by the condensation of the whey derived from the making of different cheese varieties. It is possible to include with fresh cheeses some that are briefly cured, i.e., from three or four days to one month. They include the Greek Feta, the French double and triple crêmes such as Boursin, and French Neufchâtel.

Cheddar Cheese and Related Varieties

In the United States, cheese means cheddar cheese. It is sometimes called "American," "English," "Yankee," "dairy," "store," and "rat-trap" cheese. Its name derives from the village of Cheddar in Somersetshire, England, where it was originally made. Cheddar also refers to a step in the making of the cheese, i.e., cheddaring, and to the most common style into which it was traditionally pressed, a cylinder about 14.5 inches in diameter, 12 inches thick, and weighing 70 to 78 pounds. Its flavor varies from mild to sharp, depending on the length of the ripening period and on whether or not it has been aged after ripening. Periods of ripening or curing that result in mild, medium or mellow, and sharp flavors are approximately one to three months, four to six months, and more than eight months, respectively, with five months considered the minimum to produce a cheese of good quality and one year to produce an excellent cheese. Flavor development during ripening or curing is accompanied by changes in the texture of the cheese; it becomes softer and less rubbery. Cheddar cheese ages well to produce full aroma and a waxy texture; it may be aged up to two years although one year is more common because of the cost of proper storage. The cost of this cheese can vary widely because of the cost of proper storage. It also varies because of differences in quality and aging as shown in Table 12–2.

The identity standard for cheddar cheese requires that the milk be pasteurized or that the cheese be held at a temperature of 35° F for not less than sixty days. Opinion differs on the merit of pasteurization; some believe a better cheese is made from unpasteurized milk. Most of the cheddar cheese made in the United States is made from pasteurized milk. The curd is formed by additions to the milk of lactic-acid forming bacteria and rennet or milk-clotting enzymes with or without

TABLE 12–2. *Per-Pound Cost of Some Cheddar Cheeses* [1]

Selected Items	Market Unit and Cost	Cost per Pound
Brand A, mild	$1.27/8 oz.	$2.54
medium	1.32/8 oz.	2.64
sharp	1.39/8 oz.	2.78
extra sharp	1.41/8 oz.	2.82
Brand B, mild	1.83/10 oz.	2.93
medium	1.85/10 oz.	2.96
sharp	2.07/10 oz.	3.31
extra sharp	2.10/10 oz.	3.36
Brand C, mild	1.43/8 oz.	2.86
medium	1.46/8 oz.	2.92
shredded	1.51/8 oz.	3.02
Coon Brand, sharp	2.50/10 oz.	4.00
Canadian Black Diamond, aged	9.35/lb.	9.35
New York, sharp, block	3.10/lb.	3.10
New York, extra sharp, block	4.37/lb.	4.37
Vermont	4.99/lb.	4.99
Midget Longhorn	2.17/lb.	2.17
Monterey Jack [2]	1.79/8 oz.	3.58

[1] June 1982 discount supermarket.
[2] Similar to cheddar cheese.

calcium chloride. The curd is cut, stirred, and heated with continuous stirring to separate curd and whey. The curd is then matted, or cheddared, into a cohesive mass that is cut into slabs for further drainage of whey and the development of acidity. The slabs are then cut into pieces and rinsed. The curd is salted, stirred, further drained, and pressed into forms. Enzymes that aid in the curing or development of flavor may be added during the procedures as may artificial color, the use of which need not be stated on the label. The dye in general use is yellow-orange annato which is prepared from the seed of a tree of the same name. It is also the dye used in coloring butter. The identity standard defines the cheese-making procedure as it has been described, and states further that another procedure that produces a finished cheese having the same physical and chemical properties may be utilized. The final cheese can contain no more than 39 percent of moisture and the solids must contain no less than 50 percent milk fat, that is, the cheese does not contain less than 32 percent milk fat.

Cheese varieties similar to cheddar include English Cheshire and Gloucester, Welsh Caerphilly, granular or stirred-curd cheese, Colby, Monterey, pineapple, and coon cheese. Colby is a modified cheddar cheese that originated in Vermont; it is softer, has more holes, and is milder than cheddar. Monterey, or Jack, cheese is also a modified cheddar, which originated in California. In the production of both of these cheeses, the cheddaring step is eliminated. Modifications in curd treatment result in cheeses that are different in moisture content, body and texture, and flavor and aroma.

Cheese Varieties with Eyes

Swiss cheese or Emmenthal (Emmenthaler) was originally made in the Emmenthal Valley in the Canton of Bern, Switzerland, and its name is so derived. It is one of the most difficult of all kinds to make. Proprionic-acid-forming bacteria are primarily responsible for the eye formation and the flavor of Swiss Cheese. Swiss cheese is made in many countries but none exactly duplicates the flavor and texture of Emmenthal from Switzerland. It is a creamy white, hard cheese of mild, sweet, and nutlike flavor, and it has large, shiny eyes.

Other cheeses with eyes include Gruyère, Fontina, Edam, Gouda, and Samsoe. The small eyes of these cheeses are formed mechanically during the cheese-making process and not by gas forming bacteria. Edam and Gouda cheeses are Dutch in origin. They are quite similar. Edam cheeses are small and spherical in shape. Gouda cheese is richer than Edam and the cheeses are larger although a "baby Gouda" is available. Domestic Edam cheeses are waxed or have other tightly adhering coating that may be red or another color. Domestic Gouda cheeses may or may not have a protective covering. Imported ones bear red wax coatings and the cheeses bear the Netherland's Government mark on the rind under the coating. Gruyère is Swiss in origin but much is made in France. Samsoe is the Danish and Fontina is an Italian version of this cheese type.

Blue-Veined Cheeses

In the making of blue-veined cheeses the curds are innoculated with the mold spores of *Penicillium roqueforti* prepared from bread crumbs. Then, when the cheeses are ready for curing, they are pierced or spiked to permit passage of the air essential for spore development into the interior of the cheese. The blue veins are the growing mycelia of the mold spores. They are richly productive of the enzymes that modify milk fat and protein, giving rise to the many compounds that give these cheeses their unique flavor. In addition to the mold, bacteria inside the cheese, and yeast and bacteria on the surface of the cheeses contribute to flavor development. The mold variety used in the making of blue cheeses has been in use for centuries and is apparently safe. However, when a blue-veined cheese shows development of another and different appearing mold, it should be completely discarded.

The big three of the blue-veined cheeses are Roquefort, Stilton, and Gorgonzola; others are French blue, Danish blue (Danablu), and domestic blue. The blue-veined cheeses differ in texture: the Danish blue cheeses are soft and buttery, Roquefort is firm and crumbly, and Stilton is of a pebbly consistency. Further, they differ in appearance, with the veins ranging from blue as in Roquefort to green as in Gorgonzola to blue-green as in Stilton. The body of the cheese may be white or slightly yellow. They differ in flavor from mellow to piquant. The turophile can distinguish one from the other. Roquefort cheese is made from ewe's milk set with lamb rennet, and the cheeses are cured in limestone caves in the area of the village of Roquefort in soutern France. Only cheeses made in this area may be labeled "Roquefort." Other French blue-veined cheeses are "French bleu." The United States imports more Danish blue than any other blue-veined cheese and more Gorgonzola than Roquefort. Domestic blue cheeses are considered good but not distinguished (6).

Cheeses Surface-Ripened by Molds

Cheeses surface-ripened by mold include Brie and Camembert of French origin and Crema Danica, a Danish cheese. The latter is more delicate in flavor than the other two. The ripening of these cheeses takes place from the surface inward and is by mold growth on the surface and also by bacteria and probably yeasts that grow on the surface. The cheeses are small and their thickness is only an inch or so. The interior of the cheeses may range from waxy to an almost fluid consistency, depending on how well ripened they are, and should definitely be soft and creamy yellow. The moldy crust is eaten; it is white to off-white for American Camembert, golden for French Camembert, yellow to beige for Brie, and pure white for Crema Danica.

Because the molds used in making these cheeses have been long used, it is surmised that they are safe. However, when these cheeses develop unnatural molds, they should be discarded.

Cheeses Surface-Ripened by Bacteria

The group of cheeses surface-ripened by bacteria, and probably yeasts also, is extensive; some varieties are Bel Paese, Münster, brick, Limburger, St. Paulin, Liederkranz, Port du Salut, and Livarot. All of these varieties are obtainable, either domestic or imported, in the supermarket, but the ones preferred are brick, Münster, Liederkranz, and Limburger. These varieties are characterized by a smooth, soft, waxy body. They contain more moisture than other ripened cheeses. The flavor ranges from the mild of Münster to the fullsome of Limburger. In the making of these varieties, the green cheeses are sprayed or smeared with the ripening organism *Brevibacterium linens;* they are then placed on wooden shelves impregnated with the organism. The ultimate flavor of the cheese variety is determined by the number of days the cheese remains on the shelf before being removed to the curing room.

Grana Cheeses

Grana describes a group of Italian cheeses so named because of their grainy texture when fully ripened. They are hard cheeses, as a result of ripening periods of one to two years, and are for grating; however, when young they may be used as table cheeses. Outside of Italy, and sometimes in Italy, they are known as *Parmesan.* There are two main types of grana cheeses: Grana Lombardo made north of the Po River and Grana Reggiano made south of the Po. There are subvarieties of these, all named for their place of origin. They differ mainly in the season of the year when they are made and in the details of the production process. They are large cheeses, the interior of which is yellow and the surface black from having been rubbed with a mixture of burnt umber, lamp black, and dextrin dispersed in oil. They vary in flavor from mild to sharp. The finest are Parmigiano and Reggiano. They are imported into the United States under the name "Parmesan" and "Parmesan Reggiano." They are also made domestically as well as in Argentina and in Uruguay, but none are considered as fine as the Italian varieties.

Romano cheese is another grana variety that may be eaten as a table cheese but when long-cured becomes a grating cheese. It is saltier and sharper in flavor than Parmesan.

The pregrated and prepackaged containers of the grans cheeses are compounded from different cheese varieties. The label describes what is in the container. The turophile holds them in low repute and prefers to grate Parmesan cheese immediately before use.

Pasta Filata Varieties

Pasta filata varieties include the already-mentioned Mozzarella (or Scamorza) and pizza cheeses, which are unripened, and the ripened Caciocavallo and Provolone. The former are soft and moist; the latter, firm. Pasta filata varieties are Italian cheeses characterized by the treatment of the curd following whey removal. The curd is immersed in hot water or whey and worked, stretched, and molded while plastic. The curd is truly tough and elastic.

Caciocavallo and Provolone are similarly made, and similar in flavor; however, the former contains less fat and is usually not smoked. Each variety is molded into distinctive shapes. Caciocavallo is spindle-shaped and one weighs 4 to 5 pounds. Provolone cheeses are made in different sizes and shapes and each bears a distinguishing name. The style called *Provolone* is pear-shaped and weighs between 9 and 14 pounds in the United States. Small styles are spherical. Sausage-shaped Provolone cheeses may range from small to very large—two hundred pounds or more. Most Provolone cheeses are smoked. For table use, the cheeses are cured up to four months; when cured longer, they are suitable for grating.

Spiced and Flavored Cheeses

Opinion differs on the merits of flavoring and spicing cheeses. The turophile suggests that a truly good cheese is rarely improved by such procedures and that its flavor should be savored unaltered. The probable original reasons for spicing and flavoring, pickling, and smoking cheeses were: to preserve; to mask bad flavor in a poor cheese; to introduce flavor into a poor and tasteless cheese; and finally, perhaps, to relieve the monotony of meals. Seasonings include such herbs and spices as cloves, caraway, cumin, black pepper, red pepper and paprika, sage, and clover as in sapsago cheese; port or sherry wines; brandy; onions, garlic, chives, pimentos, olives, pickles, sausage bits, and so on. Münster with caraway; cheddar with port wine; Liptauer cheese with hot red pepper, paprika, capers, anchovy paste, and other assorted seasoners; cream cheese with bacon bits; and cream cheese with olives are but a few of the great variety to be found in the supermarket. Whatever the reason for spicing or flavoring a cheese, the products are sometimes quite tasty, though they may not taste much like a good cheese. See Table 12–3 for cost comparisons of the different cheeses.

TABLE 12–3. *Per-Pound Cost of Some Cheese Varieties*

Selected Items	Cost per Unit [1]	Cost per Pound
Amish Baby Swiss	$4.25/lb.	$4.25
Blue cheese, domestic, Brand A	1.42/8 oz.	2.84
Blue cheese, domestic, Brand B	1.25/4 oz.	5.00
Blue cheese, Danish	2.29/8 oz.	4.58
Bonbel, domestic	2.29/7½ oz.	4.89
Brick cheese	1.31/8 oz.	2.62
Brie cheese, domestic	1.99/8 oz.	3.98
Brie, French	5.99/lb.	5.99
Camembert cheese, domestic	1.99/8 oz.	3.98
Colby	1.98/lb.	1.98
Cottage cheese, 4 percent milk fat, Brand A	1.10/lb.	1.10
Cottage cheese, 4 percent milk fat, Brand B	1.25/lb.	1.25
Cream cheese	.39/3 oz.	2.08
Cream cheese	.99/8 oz.	1.98
Cream cheese, soft	1.09/8 oz.	2.18
Cream cheese, whipped	.68/4 oz.	2.72
Edam cheese, domestic	2.09/7 oz.	4.78
Feta cheese	1.95/8 oz.	3.90
Fontina cheese, domestic	4.49/lb.	4.49
Gouda cheese, domestic	1.69/8 oz.	3.38
Mozzarella, part skim milk cheese	1.31/8 oz.	2.62
Neufchâtel cheese	.96/8 oz.	1.92
Muenster cheese	1.31/8 oz.	2.62
Swiss cheese, aged domestic	2.59/12 oz.	3.45
Swiss cheese, domestic	3.00/lb.	3.00
Swiss cheese, imported	4.99/lb.	4.99
Tilsit cheese, Danish	3.99/lb.	3.99
Rondelé	1.59/3½ oz.	7.26
Roquefort cheese	7.99/lb.	7.99

[1]June, 1982 costs in discount supermarket.

Cheese Products

Definitions and standards of identity have been promulgated for a long list of natural cheeses. They regulate such aspects of cheese production as the treatment of milk, the kinds of additives permitted, the minimum period of aging, the maximum moisture and mimimum fat contents of finished cheeses, and so on. Standards have likewise been promulgated for the many products in which cheeses are an ingredient, for example, cheese spreads, cheese food, and coldpack cheese.

American preference is for cheeses with mild flavors and smooth consistencies, an unnatural combination in cheese making. To achieve the desired textures and flavors, the following cheese products are manufactured: pasteurized process cheese, pasteurized blended cheese, pasteurized process cheese food, pasteurized process cheese spread, cold-pack cheese, cold-pack cheese food, cream cheese with other foods, and pasteurized Neufchâtel cheese spread with other foods. Definitions and standards of identity limit the extent to which cheese may be replaced by other ingredients and define maximum moisture content, minimum butterfat content, and minimum cheese content. Further, they define the ratio of cheeses when two or more varieties are incorporated into products, name cheese varieties that may not be cheese components, name the ingredients other than cheese that may be added, and require detailed labeling. Products that do not meet established standards are required to be labeled "imitation." Some imitation products are available on supermarket shelves. One such is made with corn oil and skim milk; another, soybean oil and sodium caseinate. Current emphasis on limited consumption of fats has contributed to good sales of these products. Some products on supermarket shelves are simply described as pasteurized process cheese product. See Table 12–4. Some of these products have fanciful names which imply that they are for the calorie conscious.

A *pasteurized process cheese* is prepared by the comminuting and mixing of one or more cheeses of the same variety or of two or more varieties, and, with the aid of an emulsifier, the heating of the mixture to form a homogeneous mass. Heating is for not less than 30 seconds at a temperature of not less than 150° F. Certain cheeses are exempted from use; they are cottage cheese, cream cheese, Neufchâtel cheese, and some others. The weight of each variety of cheese in a pasteurized process cheese made from two cheese varieties is not less than 25 percent of the total weight of both, except that the weight of the blue-veined cheeses is not less than 10 percent and the weight of Limburger is not less than 5 percent of the total weight of both. The weight of each variety in a pasteurized process cheese composed from three or more varieties is not less than 15 percent of the weight of all, except

TABLE 12–4. *Per-Pound Cost of Some Diet-Modified Cheeses and Cheese Products* [1]

Selected Items	Cost of Market Unit	Per-Pound Cost
Golden Image Imitation Colby Cheese [2]	$1.85/12 oz.	$2.47
Lite Line Pasteurized Process Cheese Product—8 percent milk fat [3]	$1.42/8 oz.	2.82
Lite 'n Lively American Flavor Pasteurized Process Cheese Product [3]	1.04/6 oz.	2.77
Semisoft Part Skim Milk Cheese	2.38/14 oz.	2.72
New Age Swiss Flavor Pasteurized Process Cheese Product [2]	1.26/8 oz.	2.52
Sandwich-Mate American Cheese Substitute [2]	1.36/12 oz.	1.81
Weight Watchers' Pasteurized Process Cheese Product [3]	1.62/10 oz.	2.59
Imitation Cream Cheese	.65/8 oz.	1.30
Low-Sodium Colby Cheese	1.47/8 oz.	2.94
Low-Cholesterol Pasteurized Process Filled Cheese Food [2,3]	1.29/8 oz.	2.58

[1] June 1982 discount supermarket price.
[2] Made with Vegetable oil.
[3] Skim milk cheese.

that the weight of blue-veined cheeses is not less than 5 percent and the weight of Limburger is not less than 3 percent of the total weight of all. Pasteurized process cheese may be smoked; or cheeses from which it is made may have been smoked before comminuting and mixing; or it may contain substances prepared by condensing or precipitating wood smoke.

The emulsifying agents permitted by the identity standards include assorted phosphate, citrate, and tartrate salts of sodium, potassium, and calcium. Optional ingredients include acidifying agents such as vinegar and acetic, lactic, and citric acids; cream; water; salt; artificial coloring; certain mold inhibitors if the pasteurized process cheese is in the form of slices or cuts in consumer-size packages; and spices and flavorings, other than any that singly or in combination with other ingredients simulate the flavor of a cheese of any age or variety. If a pasteurized process cheese has been smoked or contains an ingredient that simulates the flavor of smoking or contains added spice or flavoring or mold-inhibiting ingredients, a statement to that effect must be made on the label. Similarly, the cheese ingredients of a process cheese must be named on the label in order of predominance whenever two or more varieties are compounded, with two exceptions. First, a pasteurized process cheese made from Swiss and Gruyère cheeses in which the Gruyère variety is not less than 25 percent of the weight of both may be called "Pasteurized Process Gruyère Cheese." And second, a pasteurized process cheese compounded from cheddar cheese, Colby cheese, washed curd cheese, or granular cheese, or from a mixture of two or more of these, may be designated as "Pasteurized Process American Cheese." When these same varieties, singly or in a mixture of two or more, are combined with other varieties of cheeses, the product may be designated as "American Cheese." Although cheddar cheese may be called "American," a product called "American Cheese" is not true cheddar cheese.

Standards permit the addition of properly prepared cooked, canned, or dried fruits and vegetables, and properly prepared cooked or canned meat to pasteurized process cheese. Such additions are accompanied by slight modifications of water and fat content. Any fruit, vegetable, or meat ingredient of a process cheese must be named in the labeling. A pasteurized process cheese in the form of slices or cuts in consumer-size packages may contain a mold inhibitor. The name of the inhibitor and the reason for its use must appear on the label.

Pasteurized process cheeses in the supermarket include American, Swiss, Gruyère, brick, Limburger, and Münster. The moisture content of a pasteurized process cheese made from only one variety of cheese is no more than one percent greater than the maximum moisture content prescribed by the definition and standard of identity for the variety; but in no case is the moisture content more than 43 percent with these exceptions: it is no more than 40 percent for Colby cheese; 44 percent for Swiss cheese and Gruyère cheese; and 51 percent for Limburger cheese. Similarly, the fat content of the solids of a pasteurized process cheese made from a single variety of cheese is not less than the minimum prescribed by the definition and standard of identity for that cheese; but in no case is it less than 47 percent, with the exceptions of 43 and 45 percent for pasteurized process Swiss and Gruyère cheeses, respectively.

The moisture content of a pasteurized process cheese made from two or more varieties is not more than one percent greater than the arithmetical average of the maximum moisture contents prescribed by the definitions and standards of identity for the varieties used; but in no case is the moisture content more than 43 percent, except that a pasteurized process cheese made of a combination of cheddar, Colby, and washed curd cheese is no more than 40 percent, and a combination of Swiss and Gruyère cheeses is no more than 44 percent. Similarly, the fat content of solids is not less than the arithmetical average of the minimum fat contents prescribed by the definitions and standards of identity, for the varieties of cheese used; but in no case is it less than 47 percent, excepting that for a mixture of Swiss and Gruyère cheeses, the fat content is not less than 45 percent.

In summary, pasteurized process cheeses differ little in composition from the cheeses from which they are made, and thus have approximately the same nutrient content. Pasteurized process cheeses are often less expensive than the same natural varieties, especially the well-ripened ones. Because they have been pasteurized, the flavor of these cheeses is not subsequently changed. For some culinary purposes, they are superior to natural cheeses. When heated, pasteurized process cheeses do not curdle or form a tough, rubbery mass; they melt to a smooth and homogeneous viscous mass because of the added emulsifiers.

Pasteurized process cheese food is the food prepared by comminuting and mixing, with the aid of heat, of one or more optional cheese ingredients with certain optional dairy ingredients into a homogeneous plastic mass. The addition of dairy products to the mix reduces the quantity of cheese and, in turn, alters the moisture and fat content of the final product. Some prohibited cheese ingredients are cream cheese, Neufchâtel cheese, cottage cheese, skim-milk cheese, hard grating cheeses, and semisoft part skim-milk cheese. The weight of each variety of cheese in a cheese food made with two varieties of cheese is not less than 25 percent of the total weight of both, except that the weight of the blue-veined cheeses or Limburger cheese is not less than 10 percent. The weight of each variety of cheese in a cheese food made with three or more varieties is not less than 15 percent of the total weight of all, except that the weight of the blue-veined cheeses and Limburger cheese is not less than 5 percent. However, these limits do not apply to the quantities of cheddar, Colby, washed curd, and granular cheeses in mixtures that are designated as "American Cheese." Cheese must constitute 51 percent of the finished weight of the cheese food. Optional dairy ingredients include cream, milk, skim milk cheese whey, or condensates of these, and skim-milk cheese. Maximum water content of cheese food is 44 percent and minimum fat content is 23 percent. Other optional ingredients include emulsifying agents, acidifying agents, water, artificial color, spices or flavorings, lecithin as an anti-sticking agent, and for consumer-size packages of slices and cuts a mold inhibitor. The product may derive smoke flavor, and may contain fruits, vegetables, and meats as heretofore described. The label must bear the names of the cheese varieties in the product and the names of all optional ingredients used. Pasteurization is for not less than 30 seconds at a temperature not less than 150° F.

Pasteurized process cheese foods are snack foods and specialty cheese products. Figured in terms of the cheese component, their costs may seem excessive. These foods do, however, provide cheese products of desired texture and consistency with mild to sharp flavors.

An identity standard has been established for grated American cheese food. The optional cheese ingredients include cheddar, Colby, washed curd, and granular cheeses; optional dairy ingredients are non-fat dry milk and dried whey.

Pasteurized process cheese spread is the food prepared by the comminuting and mixing, with the aid of heat, of such cheese ingredients, such dairy ingredients, and such other ingredients as the standard permits into a homogeneous plastic mass that is spreadable at a temperature of 70° F. Permitted or optional cheese ingredients are the same as for making pasteurized process cheese food.

The moisture content of pasteurized process cheese spreads is more than 44 percent but not more than 60 percent; fat content is not less than 20 percent. Because of the higher moisture content, such water-binding agents as vegetable gums and gelatin are permitted ingredients. Other optional ingredients are the same as for pasteurized process cheese food; in addition, a sweetening agent is allowed. The weight of the cheese component must constitute not less than 51 percent of the weight of the finished product. Quantity stipulations when more than one variety of cheese is used are the same as for cheese foods. The label of a pasteurized process cheese spread must bear the common or usual names of all optional ingredients used, except that the vegetable gums need not be named but may be designated as "vegetable gum." The product must be pasteurized at a temperature of not less than 150° F for not less than 30 seconds. This product is sometimes heated—that is, melted—to make a cheese sauce; it is also suitable for use in a grilled-cheese sandwich, as is pasteurized process cheese. Pasteurized process cheese spreads are packaged for the retail trade in loaves weighing from 8 ounces to 2 pounds, in slices, pieces, and in glass jars and plastic containers. There are some differences in cost, depending on packaging and brand name.

Pasteurized cheese spread is a food that conforms to the definition and standard of identity for pasteurized process cheese spread except that no emulsifying agents are used. These products may contain fruits, vegetables, and meats.

Cream cheese with other foods is a food product prepared from cream cheese, and other ingredients, such as fruits, vegetables, meats, relishes, and pickles. Allowable water content is not more than 60 percent; fat content may not be less than 27 percent. The product may or may not be heat-processed. The label must bear a list of ingredients and a statement of the use of a color additive.

Pasteurized Neufchâtel cheese spread with other foods is a product prepared from Neufchâtel cheese. It may contain such other ingredients as fruits, vegetables, meats, and pickles; water-binding agents; dairy ingredients; artificial coloring. It must be spreadable at a temperature of 70° F. It must be heat-processed. Moisture content cannot exceed 65 percent; fat content cannot be less than 20 percent.

Both the cream cheese and the Neufchâtel cheese products are available in a wide variety of packages and flavor combinations. It is far less costly to make your own.

Cold-pack cheese, club cheese, or *crock cheese* is a product similar to pasteurized process cheese, except that it is not heat-processed. All cheeses included must have been made from pasteurized milk or held for at least sixty days at a temperature not less than 35° F before being comminuted.

Cold-pack cheese food is similar to pasteurized process cheese food except that it has not been heat-processed. Stipulations regarding milk are the same as for cold-pack cheese. This product may contain added fruits, vegetables, or meats.

In summary, the variety of products made from cheese seems infinite. Definitions and standards regulate precisely what cheese products can and cannot be. In general, the consumer will find the following information on labels of cheese products: names of cheeses; names of added dairy ingredients; names of acidifying agents; names of emulsifying and water-binding agents; names of added foods; statement of use of flavors and spices, artificial color, sweetening agents, salt and water. Frequently, statements of precentage of moisture and fat content appear on the label. Labeling regulations now require that the full name of the cheese product appear on the label in letters of uniform size, style, and color. This requirement prohibits an emphasis of "cheese" and an underemphasis of the terms that describe the true nature of the product, namely, that it is a cheese product. See Table 12–5 for the relative costs of some cheese products.

Grated Cheeses.   Identity standards for *grated cheeses* were promulgated in 1970. *Grated cheeses* are defined as the food prepared by the grinding, grating, shredding, or otherwise comminuting of cheese of one variety or a mixture of two or more varieties. Optional cheese varieties are those for which definitions and standards of identity have been promulgated, excepting cream cheese, Neufchâtel cheese, cottage cheese, cook cheese, and skim-milk cheese. Each cheese used must be present at the level of not less than 2 percent by weight of the finished food. The product is prepared by the removal of water from the cheese ingredients. The name of the food if it is made from one only variety is "grated _____ cheese," the blank being filled with the name of the cheese, such as Parmesan or Romano. When the only cheese ingredi-

TABLE 12–5. *Per-Pound Cost of Selected Cheese Products*

Items	Cost of Market Unit [1]	Costs per Pound
Pasteurized process American cheese, 8 slices	$1.04/6 oz.	$2.77
Pasteurized Process American cheese	2.52/lb.	2.52
Old English pasteurized process cheese, 8 slices	1.42/8 oz.	2.82
Pasteurized process cheese food, Brand A	1.98/12 oz.	2.64
Pasteurized process cheese food, Brand B	2.89/12 oz.	3.85
Sharp cheddar cold pack cheese food, Brand A	2.09/8 oz.	4.08
Sharp cheddar cold pack cheese food, Brand B	2.89/12 oz.	3.85
Pasteurized process cheese spread, Brand A	3.18/2 lb.	1.59
Pasteurized process cheese spread, Brand B	2.98/2 lb.	1.49
Pasteurized process cheese spread, Brand C (glass pack)	2.30/lb.	2.30
Pimiento cheese spread	1.74/lb.	1.74
Cold pack cheese food roll	2.88/10 oz.	4.61
Cheese food cheese ball with Almonds	2.15/7 oz.	4.91
Assorted pasteurized process cheese slices	1.19/5 oz.	3.81
Neufchâtel cheese spread with olives and pimiento (glass pack)	.79/5 oz.	2.53
Roka Blue cheese spread (glass pack)	.79/5 oz.	2.53

[1] June 1982 prices in discount supermarket.

ents are Romano or Parmesan cheeses, each being present at a level of not less than 25 percent by weight of the finished food, the product is labeled with these two names in the order of predominance by weight as either "Grated Parmesan and Romano Cheese" or "Grated Romano and Parmesan Cheese." The varietal designation "Reggiano" may be used for Parmesan. The label of the grated cheese made from a mixture of varieties—not including Romano and Parmesan cheeses—with each variety used being present at a level of not less than 25 percent of the weight of the finished food, bears the names of the varieties in descending order of predominance. The label of a product made with a mixture of cheese varieties in which one or more of the varieties is present at a level of not less than 25 percent—not including Parmesan or Romano cheeses—of the weight of the finished food and in which one or more other varieties are present at a level of not less than two percent, but in the aggregate not more than 10 percent, bears the names of the cheese varieties present at not less than 25 percent in order of predominance, accompanied by "with Other Grated Cheeses." This latter phrase may be in letters half as high as the names of the cheeses present in the label. For example, a label might read "Grated Swiss Cheese with Other Grated Cheeses." The varietal label "American Cheese" may be used for a mixture of two or more of these varieties: cheddar, Colby, granular, and washed curd cheeses. In summary, the labeling of a packaged grated cheese names the varieties of cheeses it contains with the exception that 10 percent of cheese components may not be named.

Other Cheese Products.   New cheese products include spray-dried American or cheddar cheese for use in pizza, dips, and by the food industries in the manufacture of mixes and easy-to-prepare dishes for consumers. Further, an assortment of dehydrated products, including the blue-veined cheeses, is in use by the food industries for food dressings, mixes, dips, and the like. Freeze-dried cottage cheese for campers and institutional feeding is also available.

QUALITY IN CHEESES

It would be encouraging to the consumer to be able to state that twentieth-century science and technology have eliminated cheeses of poor quality; unfortunately this is not true. Cheeses of mediocre, even poor, quality are to be found in the supermarket and in specialty cheese shops. Quality in cheese varieties means the aroma, flavor, texture and body, and appearance proper to a variety. For unripened cheeses, this means a fresh, clean smell like that of fresh milk or cream; a delicate flavor and a taste that ranges from sweet to slightly acid; tender, soft curds or body; and a snowy to creamy white color. For ripened cheeses, quality means freedom from noncharacteristic odors and flavors that may be described as stale, barny, moldy, yeasty, sulfury, ammoniacal, bitter, rancid, sour, flat, or weedy. Further, quality means the right body and texture—that is, softness, butteriness, or firmness—and also freedom from such defects as pastiness, crumbliness, gas holes, rubberiness, mealiness, and compactness, unless one of these is an attribute of the variety. Quality is reflected in color: white, creamy white, pale yellow, or other, depending on the variety. Finally, quality means the development of the flavor and aroma unique to a variety.

The ultimate quality of a cheese is established in a number of obvious ways: the place where it was produced; the quality of the milk used; the sanitary conditions in the place of production; the knowledge, skill, and care used in the time of production of the cheese, including the ripening period; the extent of the period of ripening; the conditions of storage after ripening; and finally, the packaging of the cheese for sale. Except for the rare exceptions of graded cheddar and Swiss cheeses, there is no guarantee of quality, whether a cheese is imported or domestic in origin. Those with expertise suggest that some varieties are superior when imported from the country of origin, such as Swiss cheese made in Switzerland; however, they agree that many domestic varieties, such as cream and Neufchâtel cheeses and Herkimer County cheddar, are excellent. Actually, true English cheddar cheese cannot be imported into the United States, though its near relatives can. Unfortunately, quality varies for a given cheese from time to time; for example, the quality of Brie, Camembert, and Liederkranz cheeses depends on how ripe they are at the time of purchase. It is probably desirable to reiterate that a cheese variety made in different places is not always the same cheese, for example, Italian versus domestic Parmesan. Lastly, it might be noted that quality judgments are personal and based on experience—as many people say they dislike a Limburger without ever tasting it.

SOME GUIDES FOR THE BUYER OF CHEESES

1. Learn to recognize quality in the cheese varieties that you buy.

2. Read the label on natural cheeses to learn as much about the cheese as labels reveal: place of production, by whom marketed, variety, degree of flavor development (as mellow or sharp), length of period of ripening, and so on, when some or all of these are given. Look for pull dates and quality assurance dates on perishable cheeses.

3. Read the labels on cheese products: the pasteurized process cheese foods, the spreads, and the cold-pack or club cheeses. Labels reveal the ingredients of these products and sometimes the moisture and fat contents.

4. Select between natural and processed cheeses with intended use in mind. You will save money by using the less expensive process cheese for sandwiches and cooking. Further, the process cheese melts to a smooth consistency, which the natural cheese rarely does.

5. Make your own spreads and dips.

6. Never buy a moldy cheese or cheese food product unless, of course, it is a blue-veined cheese or one that is surface-ripened by mold.

7. Cubes, morsels, crumbs, bits, and other so-called convenient forms of cheese or cheese products may cost more than the same product purchased in wedges or chunks.

8. Commercially prepared cheese balls and cheese logs are expensive and the quality of the cheese ingredient(s) may be poor.

9. Containers of special design, ceramic or other, may add to the cost of the cheese therein.

HOW TO STORE CHEESES

Properly packaged cheese can be satisfactorily stored for shorter or longer periods of time—depending on kind—in the refrigerator or in another cool place. The fresh unripened cheeses are perishable and should be consumed soon after purchase. The firm and ripened cheeses, such as cheddar and Swiss keep for extended periods of time, and the blue-veined varieties also store well; but the soft varieties that are sur-face-ripened by mold store only briefly without losing quality. During the storage period such changes as drying, mold development, flavor loss and/or flavor modification, and modification of body and texture can occur. To protect against changes, all cheeses should be wrapped in foil or plastic film if they cannot be kept in the original wrapper, or placed in glass or plastic containers. It is sometimes as important to prevent a cheese's contamination of other foods, like butter, as it is to protect the cheese itself. If large pieces of cheese are to be stored long, the cut surface can be scaled by dipping it in hot paraffin. Though freezing as a means of preservation is not completely satisfactory because freezing alters the body and texture of the cheese, causing it to become mealy and crumbly, some firm and semisoft varieties can be held in frozen storage for six to eight weeks. They are brick, cheddar, Edam, Gouda, mozzarella, Gruyère, Münster, Port du Salut, and provolone cheeses (7). For freezing, it is very important that the cheese be properly wrapped to prevent moisture loss and consequent texture change. Wrap in moisture-vapor-proof wrap. Pieces should be no larger than one pound. Cheeses which have been frozen should be thawed in the refrigerator and used as soon thereafter as possible. If the texture has been modified by the freezing process, the cheese may be used for culinary purposes. Process cheese products can be held for up to five months in frozen storage. Uncreamed cottage cheese may be held in freezing storage for up to one month (5).

HOW TO SERVE CHEESE

All cheeses are considered to have their best flavor and texture when served at "room temperature," which of course can range from 60° F to 80° F, Axler suggests 56° F (1). The time that the cheese is out of the refrigerator before serving will vary for different varieties and should be long enough for the flavor and aroma and body and consistency to become right. This will be longer for firm than for soft or semisoft cheeses. Following are some suggestions for serving cheeses.

1. In arranging a cheese board:
   (a) Put only cheese on it, that is, no garnishes and no breads or crackers.
   (b) Keep a reasonable distance between each variety.
   (c) Do not precut; have a knife or a server for each variety.

2. In general, serve breads and crackers on the side. Conventional choices are rye bread or pumpernickel with Swiss, German, or Dutch cheeses; French bread with French cheeses; and Italian bread with Italian cheeses. Plain and unsalted or lightly salted crackers are good with most cheeses. Melba toast, Norwegian flatbread, and sesame wafers are all good.

3. Serve sweet butter with strong and rather salty or lean and dry cheeses such as Gorgonzola or aged cheddar. English or Dijon mustard and gherkins or celery are good with cheddar-type cheeses. Thin onion slices are good with Liederkranz.

4. There are many excellent fruit and cheese combinations; apples or pears with the blue-veined cheeses; Tokay grapes with brick cheese; apples, pears, and tart plums with Camembert cheese; tart apples or melon slices with cheddar cheese; apples, orange sections, or pineapple spears with Edam or Gouda; pears with Provolone; and apples or grapes with Swiss (2). Wason suggests peaches with Gorgonzola, honeydew melon with Edam or Samsoe, and oranges with Roquefort (9).

5. Individual appointments for serving cheeses include an individual plate of dessert or salad size and individual knives; also an individual fork when fruits that require a fork for eating are served, such as melon slices or juicy peaches (that is, when the fruits are not finger foods).

6. Cheeses with or without fruits are excellent dessert courses and are becoming more and more a custom in the United States. The cheese dessert can follow almost any main course, especially a light one, but it would probably be inappropriate with Chinese or Japanese meals and Indian curries because cheese is not a food native to the diets of those countries. A cheese course may precede the sweet dessert in meals served according to European tradition.

7. Almost any beverage is suitable with cheese: coffee, tea, milk, beer, wines, and liqueurs. At the present time, cheese and wine parties are popular in the United States, as is the serving of a wine with a dessert of cheeses. For more information on the subject, consult some of the books listed at the end of this chapter. A simple rule suggests that light, dry white wines be served with cheese of delicate flavor, that full-bodied red wines be served with cheeses of stout character, and that cheeses in

the middle range be served with correspondingly middle-range wines (9).

Dictionary of Cheeses

Asiago—Italian in origin. A hard grating cheese. Yellow in color. Sharp in flavor.

American—See cheddar. Term used to identify a group of cheeses somewhat like cheddar: Colby, washed curd, stirred or granular cheeses. Also Monterey. It applies to a pasteurized process cheese compounded from two or more of the previously named near-relatives of cheddar cheese.

Appenzell (or *Appenzeller*)—Swiss in origin. More flavorful than Emmenthal and Gruyère. Wrinkled brown rind; small holes; pale yellow, deeper in color near rind.

Baker's cheese—A skim-milk cheese much like cottage cheese but softer, finer grained, more moist, and more acid. Used in making cheesecake and pastries. When creamed, it is eaten like cottage cheese.

Baronet cheese—Brand name of a cheese that is bland and buttery; has flavor not unlike Münster with an overtone of cheddar.

Beer cheese (*bierkäse*)—German in origin. Resembles brick cheese; American-made variety is milder in flavor than the German.

Bel Paese—Trade name of a fine Italian cheese. Italian import bears map of Italy and picture of a priest on the label of its chipboard box; on the Wisconsin product is the map of the Western Hemisphere. An uncooked, ripened cheese. Soft, creamy yellow interior, slightly gray surface; flavor is mild to moderately robust. Many similar cheeses are made; the group is referred to as *butter cheese.*

Bleu (*Fromage bleu*)—French name for blue-veined cheeses made in France.

Blue (*blue-veined*) *cheese*—Made in Canada, Argentina, Denmark, France, Sweden, and the United States. Semisoft, firm to crumbly texture, white interior with blue-green veining of mold; flavor peculiar to the cheese and for different varieties is from mild to sharp.

Bonbel—a French import, the brand name of a cheese that is creamy white in color and mild in flavor. It has a yellow wax coating.

Boursin—a French import. It is the name of a triple cream cheese (75 percent fat content). It is sold foil-wrapped in a small cardboard box. It is of two types: one is flavored with garlic and herbs; the other, with pepper.

Brick cheese—Domestic in origin. Not as strong as Limburger in flavor, but salty and medium to moderately sharp in flavor. Semisoft to medium firm in texture, containing many holes. Creamy yellow.

Brie—French in origin. Very perishable. Soft; interior fluid when very ripe. Interior, creamy yellow; edible crust, white flecked with brown. Mild to pungent flavor. Similar to Camembert.

Camembert—French in origin. Soft; interior fluid when fully ripe. Creamy interior with thin edible crust. Medium to pungent flavor. Continues to ripen after packaging. Similar to Brie.

Camembleu—a domestic blue-veined Camembert.

Caciocavallo—Italian in origin. Plastic-curd cheese. Resembles Provolone but less fat and usually not smoked. Firm in texture, white with tan-colored surface.

Cheddar—English in origin. Creamy white to orange in color. Semihard; firm to crumbly in texture and mild to sharp in flavor, depending on aging time.

Cheddar, English—Barred from importation into the United States.

Colby cheese—Domestic in origin. Cheddar-type cheese, but softer, more open (has more holes), milder in flavor; color ranges from creamy white to yellow-orange.

Coon—Cheddar cheese cured by special patented method. High-quality cheese cured at high temperature and high humidity. Green mold grows on surface to aid in flavor development. When fully developed, cheese is dipped in hot paraffin; heat causes green mold to turn black. Crumbly; sharp but mellow flavor.

Cream cheese—Domestic in origin. Soft, smooth cheese eaten fresh. Snow white and very mild in flavor.

Crema Danica—Danish in origin, a new variety, and imported only. Interior pale yellow; surface white; flavor delicate. Sold in a square chipboard box containing two foil-wrapped bar-shaped sticks.

Danablu—Danish blue-veined cheese. Soft, buttery texture; strong and rich in flavor, creamy white with rich blue veining.

Danbo—a Danish import. It is mild in flavor, pale yellow in color, firm in texture, and with small holes. May or may not contain caraway seeds.

Danish Havarti—a firm, creamy white, mild to full flavored cheese with small holes. *Creamy Harvarti* has a high fat content and is bland and buttery in flavor. Danish Harvarti was formerly called Danish Tilsit. Tilsit is of Dutch origin.

Danube—the brand name of a domestic Boursin.

Edam—Dutch in origin. Semisoft to hard; firmer than Gouda; cannonball shape with red wax rind; yellow; has small eyes; mild, nutty flavor. Made from partially skimmed milk. May be smoked. The surface of domestic Edam may be waxed or protected with other tightly adhering coating. Color may be red or another color.

Emmenthal (*Emmenthaler*)—Swiss cheese. No cheese similarly made has quite the same character. Semihard; firm in texture with very large, shiny eyes; ivory in color. Sweet, nutlike flavor. Swiss cheese imported from Switzerland bears "Switzerland" printed in red repeatedly on surface of cheese.

Esrom—Danish Port du Salut.

Feta—Greek in origin. Originally made from ewe's or goat's milk. Curd is heavily salted and preserved in brine. Snowy white in color; somewhat firm in texture.

Fontina—Italian in origin. Resembles Swiss Gruyère. Small eyes; semisoft to hard; yellow in color; delicate, nutty flavor.

Gjetöst—Norwegian in origin; imported only. Whey cheese made from whey from goat's milk or mixture of whey from goat's and cow's milk. Golden brown in color; firm in consistency; sweetish in taste.

Golden Image—Brand name for an imitation cheddar cheese in which corn oil replaces milk fat.

Gold-N-Rich—Brand name for a bland and buttery cheese of fine flavor. Rather like Bel Paese with a touch of cheddar.

Gorgonzola—Italian blue-veined cheese. Creamy yellow with pale green veins. Softer and milder of flavor than Roquefort cheese.

Gouda—Dutch in origin. Similar to Edam, but softer because of higher fat content. "Baby Gouda" resembles Edam. Wheels are orange or red waxed. Firm, waxy body, small eyes, mild flavor. Sometimes flavored with caraway seeds.

Grana—A group of Italian cheeses that are granular in texture, hard, sharp in flavor, and suitable for grating. See Parmesan.

Gruyère—Swiss in origin; made also in France. Similar to Swiss cheese. Small eyes; ivory to pale yellow in color with a wrinkled brown rind; mild and sweet in flavor. The pasteurized process product lacks the true flavor of the cheese.

Herkimer—Cheddar cheese made in Herkimer County, New York State. Creamy white in color; dry and crumbly in texture; and sharp in flavor. Limited in availability.

Jarlsberg—Norwegian import. It resembles Swiss cheese. It has large eyes, is soft in texture, and has a distinctive nutlike flavor.

Kuminöst—Swedish in origin. Mild, white cheese; studded with caraway seeds that give it a slightly sour taste.

Liederkranz—Domestic in origin. Made only by the Borden Company in Ohio. Similar to but milder in flavor than Limburger. Creamy white in interior; rusty orange surface; soft and smooth in texture. It is eaten in its entirety. When purchased it may not be fully ripe; it ripens in the refrigerator. Dated with date for withdrawal from sale.

Limburger—Belgian in origin. Semisoft; creamy white with reddish-yellow surface; very strong in flavor and aroma.

Liptauer—Hungarian in origin. Pickled cheese seasoned with a number of condiments: paprika, capers, chives, garlic, onions, and the like.

Mel-o-pure—Trade name of a domestic cheese. Cream-colored; firm in texture; mild in flavor, reminiscent of cheddar cheese and Bel Paese.

Monterey (or *Jack*)—Domestic in origin. A surface-ripened cheddar-type cheese first made in California. Mild in flavor.

Mozzarella—Italian in origin. Generally eaten with little or no ripening. White plastic-curd cheese; mild in flavor. Melts to a creamy smoothness and becomes somewhat elastic when heated. The Food and Drug Administration has prepared one identity standard for Mozzarella cheese and Scamorza cheese; one for part-skim Mozzarella cheese and part-skim Scamorza cheese; and one for low-moisture part-skim Mozzarella cheese and low-moisture part-skim Scamorza cheese. These three differ in moisture and fat contents, with the part-skim cheese containing not less than 30 percent milk fat calculated on the basis of the solids content.

Münster (*Muenster*)—German in origin. Resembles brick cheese but is less well ripened and milder in flavor. Semisoft; interior contains many holes; creamy white with red-orange surface that results from smearing with annatto.

Neufchâtel (*Neuchâtel*)—French in origin. Domestic Neufchâtel is unripened. White; soft and smooth in texture; very mild in flavor. Resembles cream cheese; has a lower fat content.

Parmesan—Italian in origin. Imported kind is best, bears "Parmigiano-Reggiano" stenciled on rind. A very hard cheese for grating.

Pineapple—Domestic in origin. Name derived from shape and diagonal markings on surface (which cause it to resemble a pineapple). A cheddar-type cheese.

Mysöst—Norwegian in origin. Whey cheese, brown in color, firm in consistency, sweet tasting.

Oka—Canadian Port du Salut. Made at Oka, Canada.

Pizza cheese—According to Kosikowski (5), pizza cheese is similar to low-moisture Mozzarella cheese.

Port du Salut (*Port Salut*)—French in origin, originally a monastery cheese. Flavor ranges from mild to robust, reminiscent of Limburger cheese. Semisoft and buttery; creamy yellow interior with rusty surface.

Primöst—Norwegian in origin. Whey cheese; unripened; semisoft; caramel colored; mild and sweet in flavor. Also called Mysöst.

Provolone—Italian in origin. Ripened and smoked cheese of the plastic-curd type; semihard; compact and flaky in texture. Yellow interior; golden beige surface. Made in a variety of shapes: bowl, pear, and sausage. Mellow to sharp, salty, and smoky in flavor.

Ricotta—Italian in origin. Originally a whey cheese, now made from milk and whey. Like cottage cheese when fresh; bland and semisweet in flavor. Dried to make a cheese for grating.

Romano—Italian in origin. A hard table cheese after some curing; after long curing, a very hard cheese for grating. Salty, sharp, and piquant in flavor. Yellowish interior; greenish black surface.

Rondelé—Brand name of domestic version of French Boursin.

Roquefort—Made only in France and only in the Roquefort area. Made from milk of special breed of sheep and cured in the caves of Roquefort. White with blue-green veins; semisoft to hard; sometimes crumbly. Distinctively sharp, peppery, and piquant in flavor.

Sage cheese—Domestic in origin. Cheddar-type cheese flavored with extract of sage and given a mottled green effect by the introduction of finely cut green corn. Originally seasoned with sage.

Samsoe—Danish version of Swiss cheese. Small eyes; a flavor more like Edam than Swiss cheese.

Sapsago—Swiss in origin and imported only. A very hard cheese for grating. Pale green in color because of presence of added powdered, dry clover leaves. Sharp and herblike in flavor.

Scamorza (Scamorze)—Italian in origin. Soft, mild, plastic-curd cheese to be eaten fresh. See Mozzarella cheese.

Stilton—English blue-veined cheese. (A fine cheese.) Off-white to amber at rind and much marbled with blue-green veining. Wrinkled, brown melonlike rind. Flavor combines the flavor of cheddar with the flavor of blue-veined varieties, but is milder than either Roquefort or Gorgonzola.

Swiss cheese—See Emmenthal. Characterized by large, shiny eyes; the more eyes the sharper the flavor. Ivory to yellow in color; semihard; sweet and nutlike in flavor. The most difficult of all cheeses to make, and much imitated, but no product is exactly like Emmenthal.

REFERENCES CITED

1. Axler, Bruce H., *The Cheese Handbook*. New York: Hastings House (1968).
2. *Cheese in Family Meals*, Home and Garden Bulletin No. 112, United States Department of Agriculture, Washington, D.C. (1966).
3. "Code of Federal Regulations 21, Food and Drugs," Parts 100–199, as Revised April 1, 1980, Office of the Federal Register, Washington, D.C. (1980), p. 168.
4. "Cottage Cheese," *Consumer Reports* **44:**387 (1979).
5. Kosikowski, Frank V., *Cheese and Fermented Milk Foods*. Ithaca, N.Y.: Frank V. Kosidowski (1966).
6. Marquis, Vivienne and Patricia Haskell, *The Cheese Book*. New York: Simon and Schuster, Inc. (1965).
7. Pearl, Anita May, Constance Cuttle and Barbara B. Deskins, *Completely Cheese, the Cheese Lover's Companion*. Middle Village, N.Y.: Jonathan David Publishers, Inc. (1978).

8. Sanders, G. P., *Cheese Varieties and Descriptions,* Agriculture Handbook No. 54, United States Department of Agriculture, Washington, D.C. (1953).
9. Wasson, Elizabeth, *A Salute to Cheese.* New York: Hawthorn Books, Inc. (1966).

Suggested Problems

1. Price cheddar cheeses in a supermarket. Prepare a table showing the costs of a common unit. What are the extremes? Account for the cost differences. If budget permits, have a tasting of four or five of the cheeses.
2. Price and describe the different cottage cheeses on a supermarket's shelves. Prepare a table showing the cost of a pound. Explain the differences in cost.
3. Where department budget permits, conduct a cheese tasting of generally unfamiliar cheeses.
4. Price an assortment of domestic and imported cheeses of the same kinds. Prepare a table showing the cost of a common unit.

Suggested References

1. "American Cheeses," *Consumer Reports* **48**:62, (1983).
2. Brown, Bob, *The Complete Book of Cheese.* New York: Random House, Inc. (1955).
3. Jones, Evan, *The World of Cheese.* New York: Random House, Inc. (1976).
4. McCully, Helen, *Nobody Ever Tells You These Things About Food and Drink.* New York: Holt, Rinehart, & Winston, Inc. (1967).
5. Simon, André, *Cheeses of the World,* 2nd Ed. London: Faber and Faber, Ltd. (1960).

Chapter 13
Shopping for Food: Fruits

Models and patterns for planning nutritionally adequate meals suggest a minimum of four servings of fruits and/or vegetables daily. In this century, fruit consumption trended upward into the mid-1940's but then declined into the mid-1960's. Since the 1960's, annual per capita consumption of non-citrus fruits has remained relatively constant at about 100 pounds (fresh equivalent weight) of which approximately one-half is consumed fresh. Annual per capita consumption of citrus fruits has increased to about 120 pounds (fresh equivalent basis) of which only about one-fourth is consumed fresh and about one-half as juices. See Figures 13–1 and 13–2.

Fruits in all forms—fresh, frozen, and canned—are abundantly available throughout the year. However, the fresh are often very expensive. The meal manager's decisions on which to buy are not always easy. To decide what to buy, it is desirable to compare those available on the basis of cost per serving: the fresh versus the frozen versus the canned product. For example, a serving of bananas costs less than one of strawberries even when the latter are in season; a serving of canned or frozen orange juice costs less than fresh squeezed orange juice; and canned pineapple costs less than frozen. When it is necessary to maximize the food dollar, the consumer ought to actually estimate per-serving costs and then buy accordingly, that is to say, one eats what the purse will bear.

Fruit servings are not as standardized as are some other food servings. Canned fruit servings weigh about 4 ounces including the weight of juices; frozen fruit servings may weigh only about 3 ounces because of the smaller quantity of juices. An average serving is about one-half cup of fruit. Fresh fruit servings vary with kind, so that a serving of grapes may weigh 3 ounces but one of melon may weigh much more. The size of fresh fruit servings is judged by the eye; for example, a melon may be cut into four, six, or eight servings. When of small to medium size, apples, bananas, oranges, peaches, and pears are servings. Unless whole fruits or pieces are very large, the No. 8Z can yields one to two servings of canned fruits, the No. 303 can, three to four, and the No. 2½, six to seven.

FRESH FRUITS

Because of developments in fruit production and culture, better knowledge of how to harvest, package, and store fruits, technological developments in harvesting and packaging, and rapid systems of transport, we enjoy fresh fruits throughout the year regardless of where we live—strawberries in December and plums and watermelons in March. Fresh fruits are at their best when ripe; after reaching the peak of ripeness they are highly perishable and deteriorate quickly. Quick cooling after harvesting, waxing if appropriate, proper packaging, storage at appropriate temperatures in transit and in warehouses, control of humidity, and control of the carbon dioxide-oxygen ratio in the storage atmosphere and in packaging are means of protecting quality and retarding spoilage in fresh fruits. Maintenance of the proper degree of humidity and waxing keep fruits from drying; the right carbon dioxide-oxygen ratio retards ripening and spoilage by yeasts and molds. The waxes used on foods are derived from petroleum and other natural compounds. They cannot be removed by washing a food, however, with few exceptions, they are used on products the outer surface of which is not eaten. Waxes may be a vehicle for applying insecticides, fungicides, and dyes, as well as other compounds. As of late 1982, there was no evidence that they are not safe. They are applied to a long list of fruits and vegetables including apples, cucumbers, citrus fruits, tomatoes, and melons. *Ethylene gas* is sometimes used to hasten color development of products, such as bananas and tomatoes, harvested in the unripe state. Ethylene gas effects destruction of chlorophyll and stimulates the development of red pigments. Their perishability makes fresh fruits high margin items; we often find the processed ones less expensive than the same ones fresh except at harvest time. See Table 13–1.

The perishability of fresh fruits precludes the use of consumer grades. As of July 1, 1982, commercial grades for fresh fruits were U.S. Fancy, U.S. No. 1, U.S. No. 2, and U.S. No. 3. The chief trading grade is U.S. No. 1 which represents good average quality. The U.S. Fancy grade is limited to premium products such as the especially packaged fruits shipped by gift houses at holiday time. The U.S. No. 3 grade is the lowest or poorest quality of a crop that it is practical to ship. In general,

TABLE 13–1.   *Per-Serving Cost of Selected Fresh Fruits, June, 1982* [1,2]

Selected Items	Cost and Market Unit	Estimated Servings [3]	Estimated Cost per Serving
Apples, Red Delicious, small	$ .98/5	5	$.20
Apples, Yellow Delicious, small	.98/5	5	.20
Bananas	.29/lb.	4	.075
Cantaloupe	.50 ea.	4	.125
Grapefruit	1.00/3	6	.165
Grapes	1.19/lb	5	.24
Honeyball melon	.99 ea.	4	.25
Oranges, Valencia	.88/6	6	.15
Peaches	.59/lb.	3	.20
Pears	1.80/6	6	.30
Pineapple	2.38 ea.	6	.40
Rhubarb	.99/lb.	4	.25
Strawberries	1.29/qt.	4	.32
Watermelon	.69/¼ melon	4	.17

[1] Although many of the fruits selected would be out of season in some regions of the United States, they would, in general, have been available and at comparable prices.

[2] Prices obtained in discount supermarket.

[3] Estimated number of servings was based on the size of some units.

fruits are packed and shipped by grade and are priced accordingly. A uniform grade labeling system is under review (1982) for all food products. When established, products regardless of kind will carry the same describing designations, as for example, Grade No. 1 for the best.

We do our own quality grading of fresh fruits at the supermarket. Such factors as aroma, color, condition of stem end or blossom end, appearance, and feel of skin are clues to degree of ripeness. The degree of ripeness, the size and shape of fruits, and freedom from blemishes, defects, mold, and spoilage are guides to quality. The intended use and the kind of fruit determine the quality that should be purchased. Some fruits to be eaten fresh, such as melons, strawberries, and pineapples, ought to be of the best quality; others, such as apples and plums to be stewed, can be of lesser quality.

Selecting fresh fruits requires some knowledge. Fruits mature, that is, they develop the full size and the character unique for each species and variety; then they ripen. Ripening is a relatively short period during which enzymes effect some or all of the following changes: decrease in tartness, decrease in starchiness, increase in sweetness, decrease in astringency, softening, color modification, and development of flavor and aroma. Ripening changes do not occur in fruits harvested when immature. Fruits fall into two groups with regard to the ripening period. One group includes those that are harvested when mature but not ripe and that ripen during storage, for example, apples, bananas, and pears. The second group includes those fruits that must be both mature and ripe at harvest, such as oranges, grapes, pineapples and strawberries. This latter group may develop color and some aroma if harvested unripe, but they will not become sweeter (the orange and melon, for example). In general, this is the more perishable group; once fruits in this group have reached a peak in development, they require proper treatment and storage. Even so, they deteriorate rapidly by becoming overripe because the enzymes that effected ripening continue to effect chemical changes. Overripe fruits are characterized by wateriness, extreme softness, fiberiness, and modified flavor that may range from insipid to distasteful.

Information of special interest about purchased fruits follows.

Apples

The apple is more widely grown than any other fruit. One or more apple varieties can be purchased fresh throughout the year in most supermarkets. However, the cost of fresh apples varies with the season and one's place of residence. Apple production has become an exact and complex science with the result that apples are bigger, of better shape, more colorful, and more free from defects than in the past. Although there are many named apple varieties, only about twenty varieties are commercially grown. These are grown in some thirty-four of the states, but the main apple-producing states are Washington, New York, Michigan, Virginia, California, and Pennsylvania. Low-temperature and controlled-atmosphere storage have extended the apple season from harvest to harvest. However, the longer the period of storage, the shorter will be the poststorage life of the apple; and the higher the ambient temperature, the more rapid the fruit's deterioration. Apples are better and they keep better at some times of the year than at others. Waxing protects against shriveling and improves appearance.

Apple varieties differ in shape from globular to oblate; in external color, which may be red, green, yellow, russet, or a combination of these; in flesh color, which may be creamy or snow white; in size; in flavor from sweet to sour with or without bitterness or astringency; in fullness of aroma; in flesh characteristics; in seasonal availability; and in suitability for different uses.

Summer varieties of apples come on the market in all regions of the United States. They are perishable, they are tart, and they make good apple sauce and pies. Summer varieties include the Astrachan, the Fenton, the Gravenstein, and the Yellow Transparent. Among fall and winter varieties, the apples produced and consumed in greatest quantities are the McIntosh, the Red and Golden Delicious, and the Red Rome Beauty. Apples ripen postharvest but they must be mature at harvest. The unripe apple mellows at room temperature, that is, it becomes sweeter and the texture softens. The ripe product should be refrigerated to prevent spoilage. Before native summer varieties arrive, the imported Granny Smith can be found on supermarket counters. It is bright green, crisp, and tart.

In general choices among apple varieties are limited in supermarkets. When available, good varieties for eating out of hand are Cortland, Red Delicious, Golden Delicious, Grimes Golden, Jonathan, McIntosh, Stayman, and Winesap. Good varieties for pie and apple sauce are Baldwin, Gravenstein, Rhode Island Greening, Grimes Golden, Jonathan, McIntosh, Northern Spy, Winesap, and Yellow Newton. Varieties good for baking because they retain their shape are Northern Spy, Rhode Island Greening, Rome Beauty, Winesap, and York Imperial. All-purpose varieties include Grimes Golden, Jonathan, Golden Delicious, McIntosh, Stayman, and Winesap. The flesh of two varieties, the Cortland and the Golden Delicious, does not brown when peeled and cut.

A bushel of apples weighs about 50 pounds and the number of apples per bushel ranges from 48 to 232 but nothing smaller than 175 apples per bushel is marketed fresh. Extra Large apples have a count of 48, 56, 64, and 72; Large, 80, 88, and 100; Medium, 113, 125, and 138; Small, 150, 163, and 175 per bushel. A pound of apples would have a count of from 1 to 3 to 4, depending on the size. Apples are bagged in diameter ranges, such as 2¼ to 2¾ inches; or 2½ to 3 inches. Apple sizes are usually based on these standards: small are less than 2½ inches in diameter; medium, 2½ to 3; large, over 3 inches in diameter. Cost increases with size.

Avocados

The avocado is available throughout the year. Those from California—Calavo—are in abundant supply from January to July, and those from Florida—Flavocado—from August to January. Because there are two species of avocado and many commercial varieties; those on the market differ in shape, size, color, thickness of skin, and thickness of pulp. In general, the avocado is pear-shaped though it may be almost as round as an orange. The skin may be thick or thin; smooth or pebbled; and though usually some shade of green, the skin may be purple to black. The avocado ripens after harvest. Left at room temperature the flesh softens and becomes yellow in color. It has a delicate, nutty flavor that is enhanced by salt and/or acid, such as lemon or lime juice or vinegar. An avocado is ready for eating when it feels soft under gentle pressure. When the seed rattles, the fruit is ripe. It is a tropical fruit that should be held only under mild refrigeration.

Citrus Fruits

Though much of the crop of citrus fruits is processed, the fresh fruits are available throughout the year. Supply, quality, and cost vary from time to time; the quality is best and the cost is most reasonable when the supply is the greatest. Citrus fruits are tree ripened, their storage life is limited, and their quality varies inversely with the length of the storage period.

There are six species of citrus fruits that we eat and use. The species produced in greatest quantity is the sweet orange, *Citrus simensis.* There are numerous varieties of sweet oranges, which are available almost throughout the year; and they vary in price from season to season. They differ in size, color and thickness of rind, the presence or absence of seeds, and flavor. A second species is the Mandarin orange, *Citrus reticulata.* This group includes tangerines, Satsumas, and Temple and King oranges. These are yellow to deep orange in color and are oblate in shape, that is, flattened at the poles. They are easily peeled and sectioned. The third orange species is *Citrus aurantium,* the sour and bitter oranges. This group provides the rootstock on which commercial varieties are budded. The fruits of this species are not eaten but are used in making marmalade and in the production of orange juice concentrates. Species names appear subsequently when the definitions for orange juice and orange juice concentrates are discussed. *Citrus paradisi* includes the many varieties of grapefruit; the remaining two species are lemons and limes.

Citrus-growing areas in the United States are the Gulf States—Florida, Mississippi, and Louisiana, and the western states of California, Arizona, and New Mexico; and in Texas. Oranges grown in the Gulf States are generally thin-skinned, juicy, and more often a light-orange color than the western oranges, which are thicker skinned, less juicy, and deeper in color due to environmental conditions. The oranges from Texas resemble those from both the East and the West. The Valencia is the most important commercial orange variety. It is thin-skinned, juicy, of well-colored flesh, and contains some seeds. The season of the western Valencia is from April through October; the Valencia is excellent for slicing as well as for juicing. The season for the Florida Valencia is February through May. The Valencia is slow in maturing and is present on the tree when it blooms. Fruit may "regreen" at the stem end with the flush of spring growth. This green in no way affects the quality of the orange. Oranges are required by state regulations to be well matured before being harvested and shipped out of the state. Maturity is measured by a test of sugar, acid, and solids content. The Washington Navel is the next most important orange variety. It is principally a California orange, although it is produced in the other orange-growing areas. It has a small, crinkled structure at the blossom end, which is the aborted ovary; the orange is seedless. The California Washington Navel has a thick, pebbled rind of deep orange color; the flesh is also orange in color. The Florida Navel has a thin rind of pale color, the flesh is pale in color, and the fruit is sweet. This variety peels and sections easily and is suited for slicing. California Navels are available from November through May; the Florida variety from October through January.

There are other Florida orange varieties; the season for them extends from October through May. Juice varieties include the almost seedless early Hamlin; the seedy Parson Brown; the seedy Pineapple orange; the Homosassa; and various unnamed seedling oranges. Of these the Pineapple has the best flavor. The new Murcott Honey orange, a cross between the sweet orange and tangerine, is for eating out of hand; it is sweet, is almost seedless, and has the taste of honey. These Florida oranges may have artifically colored rinds to give them a richer orange color.

There are several varieties of the species *Citrus reticulata,* or Mandarin orange. Tangerines, of which there are several varieties, are the best known of this species. They are associated with Christmas, though they are available from November to March. They are small, from two to three inches in diameter; are flattened at top and bottom; have a loose skin that is deep orange in color; have orange-colored flesh; and are sweet and juicy. The Temple orange is larger than the tangerine; it is less vivid in color than the tangerine, has a pebbled rind and a fine flavor and aroma. It is best in December. The King orange resembles the Temple orange, but it is lighter in color, has an astringent taste, and is not as flavorful as the Temple orange. The Satsuma orange is like the tangerine, though usually larger; it matures earlier than the tangerine. The Calamondin belongs to this species. It makes excellent marmalade and looks like a very small tangerine.

About half of the grapefruit crop is eaten fresh. Fresh grapefruits are marketed in all months, with the largest supplies available from January through May and the smallest quantities from June through September. The Florida season begins with September and ends in July. Florida is the biggest producer of grapefruit and Florida-derived varieties have been introduced around the world. The California season begins in October and continues through the year, with the desert valleys providing fruit from October through June and the other areas from June into September. Texas and Arizona produce grapefruit from

October through June. The main varieties of grapefruit are the seedy Duncan and its related kinds and the Marsh Seedless and its related kinds. The former is the progenitor of all other varieties. There are seedy varieties similar to the Duncan, but differences are so slight that varietal names have been dropped and they are known as Duncan or Florida Common. Characteristics of this variety and its related types are: a smooth yellow rind about one-fourth inch thick; thirty to fifty seeds per fruit; range in shape from spherical to oblate; medium to large in size, with a diameter of 3.5 to 5 inches; twelve to fourteen segments per fruit; and a truly excellent flavor. The Marsh Seedless variety originated as a seedling from the Duncan. It is similar to the Duncan in shape; has a smooth, light yellow rind; is medium to large in size; has three to eight seeds per fruit or may be seedless; is juicy and well flavored. The first pink variety, the Foster, was a bud sport discovered early in the century; it is seedy. Deriving from the Marsh Seedless as a bud sport or mutant is the Thompson, or Pink Marsh; it is pink-fleshed and seedless. The Ruby is a red-fleshed variety that originated from the Thompson as a bud sport. It has a crimson flush on the rind; its membranes as well as flesh are pigmented, but not the juice. Burgundy Red is a bud mutation of the Marsh; it has a thick rind, reddish flesh, and a few seeds. The Ruby originated in Texas, the others in Florida. The pink and pale varieties do not differ in flavor but the seedy varieties have more flavor than the seedless. The blossom half of the grapefruit is sweeter than the stem half (2).

The use of fresh lemons and limes has declined because of the availability of processed products. Virtually all lemons come from California and Arizona, whereas most limes come from Florida. Lemon picking is continuous throughout the year as the lemon tree has the unique ability of fruiting, budding, and flowering simultaneously. The lemon is picked green and cured in storage to the yellow-ripe condition. Storage life is long, up to four months, so that a supply of lemons going to market can be regulated to demand.

Limes are available most of the year but the peak season is from June to September. The commercial lime is the Persian or Tahiti lime. If permitted to mature, it becomes as large as the lemon and, like all citrus fruits, changes from green to yellow or orange if left on the tree long enough. The lime is marketed in the smaller, bright-green stage. The Key lime, also called Mexican or West Indian lime, is small and pale yellow, and of superior flavor. It has little commercial value because it is perishable after harvest.

The kumquat is a citrus fruit, a sort of elongated tiny orange. When eaten fresh or preserved, the entire fruit is eaten. It is more likely to be eaten preserved or made into marmalade.

The ugli fruit is a citrus variety, recently available in the supermarket. It is imported from Jamaica. Its flesh is delicious and has a combined flavor of orange, grapefruit, and tangerine.

Crosses within the family of citrus fruits are easily accomplished; many are of interest although of no commercial value. The only one of commercial value is the tangelo, a cross between the tangerine and the grapefruit. The four varieties of the tangelo differ principally in shape and color. The fruit looks like an orange but has the tang of grapefruit and is juicy, easy to peel, and delicious. It is available from November through February with November being the peak month.

There are U.S. grades for grapefruit, oranges, lemons, limes, and tangerines, and for tangelos from Florida. The top grade for all citrus fruits, except lemons and limes, is U.S. Fancy. U.S. No. 1 is the top grade for limes and lemons, but is the next to the best grade for the other varieties. Some citrus fruits are grade-labeled for the retail market.

In general, these citrus fruits are sized for shipping according to the number packed into the shipping carton; the larger the number the smaller the fruits within. Oranges, grapefruit, and tangerines are also packed in perforated, polyethylene bags and open-mesh bags for shipping. Hydrocooled fruit that is treated with fungicide before shipping and packaged in perforated polyethylene bags has excellent keeping quality. Labels must bear a statement of the use of fungicide and, where relevant, the use of artificial color on oranges.

After purchase, citrus fruits should be refrigerated. Lemons and limes store best in a dry closed container in the refrigerator.

Grapes

There are two types of grapes, the European and the American. The European-type grape does not slip out of its skin, but its seeds are easily removed. The American-type grape slips out of its skin and the seeds are held within the pulp. American-type grapes are grown in the East, whereas European-type grapes are grown in California. The season of the former is much shorter than that of the latter.

Most table grapes are of the European type. The different varieties mature one after the other; the season begins in June and lasts until the next spring. Table grapes are plump, firm-fleshed, sweet, and delicate in flavor. They are sprayed during production with *gibberellins,* plant-growth regulators, to produce fruit of good size. The varieties differ in color to give us white, red and purple grapes. The Perlette and the Thompson Seedless, the most popular of all the varieties, are two white varieties, that is, greenish-yellow, that are seedless. The Thompson Seedless matures a bit later and has a longer season than the Perlette. It is oval in shape, whereas the Perlette is round. Other white grapes include the Almeria and Calmaria, which are called "ladyfinger" grapes. These are elongated large grapes that grow in loose bunches. Red varieties include the Tokay, or Flame Tokay; the Emperor; the Red Malaga; and the Cardinal. The Tokay and the Red Emperor are popular varieties; the Tokay matures earlier and has a thinner skin than the Red Emperor. The latter stores extremely well and is available into the spring. The Red Malaga is a seeded, pink to reddish-purple grape of medium size and thin skin. The Cardinal is a cross between the Red Tokay and the Ribier. The Cardinal is an early red; it is large and round and of a cherry-red to reddish-purple color when ripe. The Ribier is a large, round blue-black grape. New grape varieties are introduced annually. A recent newcomer is a small seedless red grape.

Grapes must reach certain standards of maturity before they can be harvested and shipped. In buying grapes one should look for maximum color for the variety, for plumpness, and for green, pliable stems. Grapes are quite perishable; they shrink and the bunches of grapes shatter as they age.

The season for American-type grapes is short. The Concord is the best known. It is blue-black and has a silvery bloom. The Delaware is a small pink variety and the Niagara is a large white variety. These varieties are good table grapes. The Catawba is a large purplish-red grape used more for juice and wine than as a table grape.

Melons

Both the available melon varieties and the season of availability of melons have increased during the past decade. *Muskmelon* is the general name for all types of melons except the watermelon. The melon species is *Cucumis melo* and the two important botanical varieties are *reticulatis*, to which the cantaloupe belongs, and *inodorous* to which the Casaba, Crenshaw, Honeydew, Honeyball, and Persian melons belong. The watermelon is a member of the same gourd family but it is of another botanical variety, *Citrullus vulgaris*. The cantaloupe and the watermelon are grown widely in the United States but other melon varieties are grown in California, Arizona, and Texas because of favorable environmental conditions. Melons are imported from Mexico and other Latin American countries. Bright and sunny weather prior to harvest is essential if melons are to develop the sweetness that must be present at maturity. Most melons soften at the blossom end as they ripen; some pass from a firm to a softer state that may be felt under slight pressure; and some, but not all melon varieties, develop a perceptible aroma. And most will be mature but not ripe at picking. Even the best of melons are improved by a few days of storage at room temperature. During this period there is flavor development and softening of the flesh. Although they are available for many months of the year, most varieties of melons are better during the months of May through October.

Many varieties of cantaloupes have been bred for disease resistance and adaptability to different environmental conditions. Melon varieties differ in size and shape, the thickness and texture of the flesh, the external characteristics of the rind, and delicacy of flavor. Cantaloupes are round to oval in shape, and they are more or less ribbed by longitudinal furrows. Their surface is coarsely netted in gray over a ground color that is grayish or yellowish when the melon is ripe. The ripe melon has the full aroma characteristic of the cantaloupe. The flesh is salmon-orange in color. There is a sunken, calloused scar at the stem end that indicates that the melon was mature when picked. Cantaloupes are harvested at these stages of maturity: *full slip,* or hard ripe, when the stem separates from the melon under slight pressure leaving a clean stem-scar but the melon is still firm and yellow-green; *choice,* or *showing good color,* when the melons are full slip and yellowish; and *full ripe.* Melons sent to distant markets are picked full slip. Choice and ripe melons are only distributed locally. The full-slip melon is not ripe but it is mature; it will not become sweeter but flavor will develop and softening will occur when held at room temperature one or more days. Cantaloupes with the stem attached were immature at picking and will be poor in quality. Full-slip melons should not be refrigerated until they soften and become aromatic. Overripe melons are soft, watery, and poor in flavor.

The Casaba melon is nearly round but may be pointed at the stem end; the rind of the melon is furrowed lengthwise, and when ripe, the rind is yellow and the flesh is creamy white. The melon has no aroma. The flesh is juicy and sweet. The Crenshaw melon is pear-shaped, rounded at the blossom end, and pointed at the stem end. The rind is smooth and free of netting and furrows; it is gold and green in color. The flesh is salmon-colored, thick, juicy and sweet, and of excellent flavor. The melon has some aroma when ripe. The Honeyball melon is small, round, slightly netted, and green-white to pale yellow in color. The flesh is greenish-white. It is aromatic when ripe. The Honeydew melon is oval in shape; the rind is smooth; when ripe, the rind feels velvety to the touch and is creamy white to creamy yellow in color. It is only slightly aromatic. The flesh is pale green, thick, sweet, and juicy. Flavor is improved if the melon is served at room temperature and is doused with lemon or lime juice. The Persian melon resembles the cantaloupe but is much larger. It is round, the rind is netted and green or bronze-green in color. The ripe melon is aromatic. The flesh is orange in color, thick, sweet and juicy, and of fine flavor. New and different melon varieties are marketed each season.

Watermelons have been bred for different purposes and there are many varieties. They differ in size, shape, and color of rind and flesh. A 1982 seed catalogue describes a watermelon variety that has a golden rind and red flesh and a variety that has a green rind and yellow flesh. Plugging, that is, removal of a small segment of the watermelon to determine quality has been discontinued; instead, the melons are cut into halves, quarters, and smaller pieces so that quality may be visually determined. In general, the flesh should be red and the seeds black or dark brown. White seeds indicate that the fruit was immature when picked. Although it is difficult to judge the quality of an uncut melon, qualities to look for are a symmetrical shape, a bloom on the surface that gives a velvety appearance, and a yellowish rather than white underside. When the peel is scratched, it comes off of a ripe melon readily.

Pears

The main pear variety is the Bartlett; it is in season from July, when it is shipped from California, into November, when Washington and Oregon are the main suppliers. The Bartlett is picked green but mature; as it ripens, it becomes a light yellow. Fall and winter pear varieties are Anjou, Bosc, Comice, and Winter Nelis. The growing states are Washington and Oregon and the season is from November to May. The Anjou variety is not as elongated as the Bartlett; it is rounder at the blossom end. It is not as yellow as the Bartlett when ripe; it remains a pale green. It has a slight astringency. The Bosc pear is more elongated at the stem end than other varieties. When western grown, it is brownish as the result of russeting. It is a sweet pear of delicate flavor. The Comice is a plump pear, rounded at the blossom end with a short, thick neck; its full name is *Doyenne du Comice;* it is the best variety and does not ship well. It is used principally in gift packages for which each fruit can be carefully wrapped and put into special containers to permit shipment without bruising. The skin is often blushed over a pale yellowish-green. The flesh of this variety is fine in texture, juicy, and aromatic. Pears deteriorate rapidly and should be eaten soon after they reach the proper degree of ripeness.

Pineapples

The pineapple, a native of South America, is a composite fruit made up of from one hundred to two hundred berrylike fruitlets fused on a core that is a continuation of the stem that bears it. Fruits vary in height from 5 to 10 inches and in weight accordingly. Although available fresh all the year, pineapples are in best supply from March through June.

They are imported from Hawaii, Puerto Rico, Mexico, Costa Rica, Bermuda, and the Bahamas. Recently, Texas has been producing pineapples. A high proportion of the crop is processed.

The pineapple does not sweeten or ripen after picking; ideally it would be harvested when ripe. However, the fully ripe fruit is extremely perishable. Those marketed fresh are picked before full ripeness at the state called mature green. After such harvest, the shell changes color, the fruit softens, and the acid content may decrease or increase, depending on handling practices. Well-selected pineapples held at room temperature for two or three days undergo the described changes and may develop some in aroma. They are extremely perishable and should be eaten when signs point to ripeness. The fruit is sweeter at the stem end than at the crown, a reason for serving longitudinal rather than horizontal slices or for cubing and mixing the parts of the fruit. There are two important commercial varieties. The Red Spanish is small and named for its red-yellow color; its flesh is pale yellow; and the leaves of the crown are serrated. It ships well. The Smooth Cayenne has crown leaves that are smooth along the edge. It is dark green until it changes to yellow-orange; its flesh is yellow, soft, and juicy. It is a fruit of better eating qualities than the Red Spanish. Purchased fresh pineapples are often a disappointment.

Tropical and Subtropical Fruits

A significant number of tropical and subtropical fruits that were generally unknown a few years ago are now available in the supermarket. Consumers have been introduced to these fruits as they have traveled from region to region within the United States and to other countries. These fruits are commercially produced in California, Florida, and sometimes Texas; they are also imported from Mexico, other Latin American countries, and the Caribbean islands. They tend to be perishable and are in general especially packaged for shipment by air freight. Figs are highly perishable and are rarely sold fresh. They are small, seedy fruits eaten in their entirety. Color varies with variety from yellow-green to almost black. A taste for them has to be acquired. The guava is known to most persons as a kind of jelly; it is eaten as a fresh fruit where it is grown. The fruit is small and seedy like the fresh fig. One variety is yellow, another reddish. The lychee, once known only to travelers in the Orient, is now being produced in Florida. It is also called the lychee nut. The fruit is small and spherical in shape. It contains a large seed and is covered with a thin, brown coat or shell. Between seed and shell is a thin layer of yellow-green flesh that is sweet and juicy. It has no unique flavor.

The kiwi is imported from New Zealand. It is also called the Chinese gooseberry. It is about the size of a lemon and has a brown, fibery skin and green flesh with tiny black seeds. The flavor is mild and without character. The fruits keep well in the refrigerator and should be ripened at room temperature before being served alone or in combination with other fruits in salads. The mango is a tropical fruit grown in Florida, where the season is from June to mid-August. It is imported from Mexico, Puerto Rico, and the West Indies. The fruit is round to oval in shape and it has a smooth skin. The ground color is green, often blushed with red; it becomes yellow as the fruit ripens. Picked at the proper stage, the fruit ripens post-harvest. The varieties differ in size from those that are small to those that weigh as much as a pound. The flesh is yellow-orange in color, juicy, and with a flavor that is like the blended flavors of peach, pear, and pineapple. The fruit contains a large flat seed to which the flesh clings. It is a superb dessert fruit.

The nectarine is a fuzzless peach; it is not a cross but a mutation from a peach. Neither is it something new; it is a fruit that was known two hundred years ago. It is grown in California. The many varieties of nectarines mature in succession to give a season that extends from June to October, but the peak of the season is July and August. Imported fruits extend the season. The nectarine is mature but not ripe at harvest. The skin is smooth and usually of an orange-yellow ground color touched with red. The flesh may be white, yellow, or orange. The flesh is somewhat firmer and less juicy than that of a peach of the same degree of ripeness. Like the apple, it is waxed to prevent shriveling.

The papaya is not a melon, although it resembles melons, but the fruit of a herbacceous plant. It varies in size from small to very large; it has thick flesh, and contains many seeds. The flesh ranges in color from yellow to salmon-orange. It is a delicious fruit, but because it ships poorly, it is best eaten where it is grown. Those available in food stores in northern areas may be of poor quality. The persimmon available in the supermarket is an autumn fruit in season from October through December. Persimmons are grown in California. The fruit is about the size of a small to medium-sized peach and is oval-shaped; it has a smooth and glossy orange to orange-red skin. The pulp is jelly-like, sweet, and of delicate flavor. The commercial variety is seedless. It is eaten out of hand or cut into halves and eaten with a spoon.

PROCESSED FRUITS

Fruits are preserved by canning, freezing, and drying and dehydration. As shown in Figure 13–1, Americans consume more noncitrus fruit in the canned form than as frozen and dried products, but some-

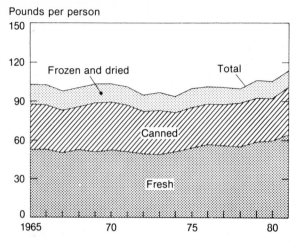

FIGURE 13–1.   Noncitrus fruit consumption, 1965–1981. Fresh-equivalent basis. Canned includes fruit and juice. (1981 preliminary statistics from *United States Department of Agriculture.*)

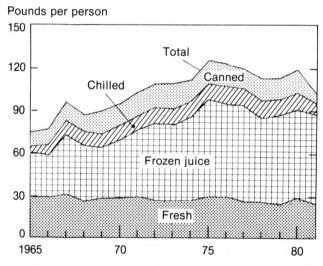

FIGURE 13–2.   Citrus fruit consumption, 1965–1981. Fresh-equivalent basis. Canned and chilled includes fruit and juice. (1981 preliminary statistics from *United States Department of Agriculture.*)

what more in the fresh than processed forms. As shown in Figure 13–2, Americans consume about as much frozen citrus juice as of the fresh fruits; however, the total of canned and chilled products and frozen juice exceeds the quantity of citrus fruits eaten fresh.

Canned Fruits

Identity standards have been established for applesauce; apricots; berries including blueberries, blackberries, red and black raspberries, strawberries, and others; both sweet and sour cherries; figs; fruit cocktail; grapefruit; seedless grapes; peaches; pears, pineapple; plums; and prunes. These standards describe the fruit ingredient that can be canned, name permitted packing media, establish the sweetness of the packing media, and name permitted optional ingredients. Permitted packing media include water, fruit juice(s) and water, fruit juice(s); any of the foregoing slightly sweetened; light syrup; heavy syrup; and extra heavy syrup. Artificial sweetening is permitted. To the metal can and glass jar used in canning, a plastic container has been added (1976). Voluntary declaration of solid content weight, the weight of food put into a can before the addition of liquids and processing, is seen on many packs. Reasonable standards of quality have been defined for apricots, cherries, fruit cocktail, grapefruit, peaches, pears, and pineapple. Standards of fill of container have been established for applesauce, apricots, fruit cocktail, grapefruit, peaches, pears, and crushed pineapple.

Canned fruits are not usually grade-labeled in the United States, although consumer groups have been lobbying for mandatory grade-labeling for some time. Permissible grade standards have been defined for canned apples, applesauce, apricots, blackberries, sour and sweet cherries, fruit cocktail, fruits for salad, grapefruit segments, free and clingstone peaches, pears, and raspberries, and for canned apple juice, grapefruit juice, grapefruit-orange juice, orange juice, and tangerine juice. Canned fruits are scored on the following factors when relevant: color, uniformity of size and symmetry of pieces or fruits, absence of defects, and character. Character refers to maturity, texture, and tenderness. The different factors are assigned a number of points for different fruits. The grade is established by the total number of points a sample scores; for example, canned pears would be U.S. Grade A, U.S. Grade B, or U.S. Grade C if the score were not less than 90, 80, or 70 points, respectively. Grade standards for canned fruits are U.S. Grade A or U.S. Fancy, U.S. Grade B or U.S. Choice, U.S. Grade C or U.S. Standard, U.S. Grade D, and Substandard. However, not all canned fruits can be graded according to all of these grades. For example, there is no U.S. Grade C for applesauce, fruit cocktail, or grapefruit, and there is no U.S. Grade D for any fruit except clingstone peaches. U.S. Grade A products are of excellent quality. They have good color, the pieces are uniform in size and shape, they are virtually free from defects, and they have ripened to the right degree and are tender. U.S. Grade B or U.S. Choice grade is of good quality, and much canned fruit is of this grade; the product may be described as having the desired characteristics to a "reasonable" extent. The color and size, and symmetry of the pieces will be less uniform; there may be a few defects, and the fruit may be slightly less tender than Grade A products. U.S. Grade C canned fruits are of fairly good quality. They are fairly uniform in color and size and symmetry of pieces, fairly free of defects, and fairly tender. All of these grades must have good flavor and aroma, possess similar varietal characteristics, and have been processed under continuous inspection. Continuous inspection assures compliance with the requirements that all ingredients be wholesome and that all steps in processing be carried out under defined sanitary conditions. Consumer interest groups are pressing for mandatory grade-labeling of canned fruits and vegetables.

Fruits are packed in different styles, such as whole, halves, slices, chunks, and peeled versus unpeeled. Price sometimes differs, with the broken slices, chunks, and unpeeled being priced lower than full slices, full halves, and peeled products. In the past, fruits were packed in syrups of different densities. The current trend is to pack fruits in water or a fruit juice. Table 13–2 shows how the cost of a unit (pound) of canned peaches can vary with the kind of purchase made, particularly

TABLE 13–2.   *Cost per Pound of Canned peaches as Cost Differs with Brand, Kind, and Size of Can Purchased*[1]

Selected Items	Market Unit and Cost	Cost per Pound
Clingstone peach halves		
Brand A, halves in heavy syrup	$1.01/No. 2½	$ .56
halves in heavy syrup	.73/No. 303	.73
Brand B, halves in heavy syrup	.95/No. 2½	.53
Brand C, halves in fruit juices	.73/No. 303	.73
Clingstone peach slices		
Brand A, slices in heavy syrup	1.01/No. 2½	.56
slices in heavy syrup	.73/No. 303	.73
slices in heavy syrup	.51/No. 8Z	1.02
Brand B, slices in heavy syrup	.95/No. 2½	.53
slices in heavy syrup	.69/No. 303	.69
slices in heavy syrup	.44/No. 8Z	.88
Brand C, slices in light syrup	.57/No. 303	.57
Freestone peaches		
Brand A, halves in heavy syrup	1.09/No. 2½	.61
Brand B, halves in heavy syrup	.95/No. 2½	.54

[1] July, 1982 prices.
[2] See Appendix B-3 for can size quantities.

TABLE 13–3.   *Cost per Pound of Selected Canned Fruits* [1]

Selected Items	Cost per Can and Market Unit	Cost per Pound [2]
Applesauce	$ .43/No. 303	$ .43
Apricots, unpeeled halves	1.23/No. 2½	.68
Apricots, unpeeled halves	.83/No. 303	.83
Apricots, whole peeled	.94/No. 303	94
Berries		
Blackberries	1.49/No. 303	1.49
Blueberries	1.49/No. 303	1.49
Gooseberries	1.25/No. 303	1.25
Red Raspberries	1.69/No. 303	1.69
Cherries, pitted black sweet	1.39/No. 303	1.39
Cherries, Royal Anne	1.39/No. 303	1.39
Cherries, red tart	1.59/No. 303	1.59
Figs	1.15/No. 303	1.15
Fruit Cocktail	1.09/No. 2½	.60
Fruit Cocktail	.73/No. 303	.73
Mandarin Oranges	.45/No. 1 Picnic	.65
Pears	.95/No. 2½	.53
Pears	.63/No. 303	.63
Pineapple Chunks	.68/no. 300	.73
Plums	.83/No. 2½	.46
Prunes	.93/No. 303	.93

[1] July, 1982, prices.
[2] In general, one pound will provide four servings. However, personal preferences may suggest three servings, or even five.

the size of the can purchased. Table 13–3 shows the cost per unit (pound) of different canned fruits. Except for the black and Royal Anne cherries and the berries, costs are fairly similar, at least of the ones commonly eaten, peaches, pears, and plums.

Canned fruit fillings for pies and other cookery are available and widely used both in the home kitchen and commercially. Their availability makes it possible to serve any kind of pie regardless of season. The fillings are also used in preparing a variety of desserts, such as brown Betty and cobblers, Ingredients of canned fruit fillings include the fruit constituent, water, sweetener, modified starch, and one or more additives for color and flavor purposes. Some available varieties include apple, blueberry, cherry, peach, and pumpkin. In general, the fillings are packed in the No. 2 can, contents weigh 20 ounces, and the measure is about two and one-half cups. No identity standards and no quality grades have been defined for these products.

Frozen Fruits

A variety of frozen fruits, fruit mixtures, and juice concentrates is available. The fruits are packed in dry sugar or sugar syrup. They are packaged in a variety of containers including paperboard or plastic cartons, cans, and bags or envelopes. Some fruits have superior palatability, that is, texture and flavor, when frozen—orange juice, raspberries, and strawberries; others, when canned—peaches, pears, and plums. The frozen fruit mixtures are available in different combinations that may include blueberries, cherries, grapes, raspberries, and pieces of melon and peach. With the exception of orange juice concentrate and strawberries, frozen fruit products tend to be more expensive than their canned counterparts. See Table 13–3 and Table 13–4. Reasons for this disparity in cost are that only foods of superior quality should be frozen whereas less than the best can be satisfactorily canned; frozen foods require special handling and equipment in transport and storage whereas canned foods do not; and frozen foods remain perishable whereas canned foods are not subject to change under normal storage conditions.

There are no definitions and standards of identity for frozen fruits and no standards of reasonable quality. However, both standards became effective December 31, 1973, for frozen cherry pies. The reasonable quality standard requires that the weight of washed and drained cherries be no less than 25 percent of the weight of the pie and that no more than 15 percent by count of the cherries be blemished. There are, however, permissive grade standards for grading almost all of the products frozen; apples; apple juice concentrate; apricots; several kinds

TABLE 13–4.   *Cost per pound of Selected Frozen Fruits* [1]

Selected Items	Cost and Market Unit	Cost per Pound
Blackberries	$1.19/12 oz.	$1.59
Blueberries	1.33/12 oz.	1.77
Cherries, Dark Sweet	1.19/12 oz.	1.59
Mixed Fruits	1.39/20 oz.	1.11
Peaches, Sliced	1.39/20 oz.	1.11
Rhubarb	.99/20 oz.	.79
Red Raspberries	1.99/12 oz.	2.66
Strawberries, Halves	1.09/10 oz.	1.74
Strawberries, Whole	1.75/20 oz.	1.40

[1] July, 1982, prices.

[2] Depending on use, generally, one pound provides five servings.

of berries including blueberries, raspberries, and strawberries; cranberries; citrus juice concentrates including lemonade and limeade; grape juice concentrate; melon balls; peaches; pineapple; and rhubarb. Quality grades include U.S. Grade A or U.S. Fancy, U.S. Grade B or U.S. Choice, and U.S. Grade C or U.S. Standard. For some frozen fruits and frozen juice concentrates, there are only two grades, U.S. Grade A and U.S. Grade C as for red tart cherries.

Chilled Fruits

Convenient chilled fruits are found in many supermarkets. They are packed in glass jars. They include grapefruit sections, orange and grapefruit sections, pineapple, peaches, and mixed fruits. They are processed by a hot-pack method in which pasteurized juice is poured over the fresh fruit. If refrigerated, the product will keep for six months. In a cold-pack method, fresh juice is poured over the fruit and a preservative is added. If refrigerated, the product will keep for fourteen days. By noting weight of contents and calculating that a serving of fruits varies between 3 and 4 ounces depending on the quantity of syrup, one can estimate the cost per serving and decide whether this particular product is more or less expensive than another form of the fruit, and if it fits the food budget. These fruits are used for salads and fruit cups especially.

Dried and Dehydrated Fruits

Preservation of fruits by sun-drying is old in time. Sun-dried fruits include raisins, figs, apricots, peaches, and pears. To deter spoilage and to prevent loss of color, fruits are subjected to the fumes of burning sulfur or are treated by being dipped in a solution of a sulfur compound. Dehydration is drying under conditions of controlled heat and humidity. Apples, blueberries, sour cherries, prunes, and bananas are some fruits that are artificially dried. Dried fruits have a somewhat different flavor than those preserved by canning or freezing and from their fresh counterparts. Standards for grading dried fruits have been developed. Quality grades are the same as for other processed fruits: U.S. Grade A or U.S. Fancy, U.S. Grade B or U.S. Choice, and U.S. Grade C or U.S. Standard. Dried fruits, especially prunes and apricots, are size-graded. Small fruits are priced lower than larger fruits.

Improved packaging of dried fruits in film bags and plastic-coated boxes has resulted in fruits of better quality and longer shelf life. Dried fruits, such as apricots, prunes, and raisins, do lose quality if held for a long time in kitchen storage and those of high moisture content, 25 percent, may develop mold unless stored in a cool place.

TABLE 13-5.   *Cost per Pound of Selected Dried Fruits,*[1] *June 1982*

Selected Items	Cost and Market Unit	Cost per Pound[2]
Apples	$1.29/6 oz.	$3.44
Apricots	2.07/6 oz.	5.52
Figs	1.15/12 oz.	1.53
Mixed fruits (apricots, peaches, pears, and prunes)	1.49/8 oz.	2.98
Peaches	1.55/8 oz.	3.10
Pineapple	1.29/6 oz.	3.44
Prunes	1.07/1 lb.	1.07

[1] Moist pack. Estimated volume gain after cooking would be 100 percent.
[2] Twelve to 14 servings per pound.

Juice concentrates have been processed by dehydration. Fruit purees are mat and foam spray-dried; juices are spray-dried. The products are powders. Spray-dried orange juice becomes instant orange juice. Freeze-dried fruit crystals for instant juices are products of the 1970's. Table 13-5 gives the cost per unit of some dried fruits.

Per-Serving Costs of Fruits.   Per-serving costs for selected fresh fruits were presented in Table 13-1. The per-pound cost of canned peaches was explored in Table 13-2. Table 13-3 showed the costs for selected canned fruits, Table 13-4 the cost for selected frozen fruits, and Table 13-5, the cost for selected dried products. The meal manager has to match her choices to her plan for spending for food. It should be noted, however, that costs are neither the same at all seasons of the year, nor are they the same in all regions of the United States at the same time. It is important for a meal manager to make comparisons, not once, but from time to time.

Fruit Juices and Beverages

The supermarket stocks a variety of products described euphemistically as "fruit beverages and punches." There is great diversity among these products in concentration, composition, and processing method. They are ready to drink, that is, single strength, like apple juice. They are concentrated and must be diluted for drinking, like orange juice concentrate. And they are available as powders. In composition, they range from "all juice," like apple juice, to "no juice," like *Kool-Aid.* In between these extremes in composition are products that contain some natural ingredients and some synthetic ingredients that provide color and flavor. Further, there are differences in fruit juices, for example, apple juice and pineapple juice are prepared without the addition of water; but cranberry juice, apricot nectar, and prune juice are prepared with added water. Fruit juices can be diluted to become ade, drink, nectar, and punch. Since July 1, 1975, it has been mandatory that all diluted orange juice beverages in interstate commerce bear statement of the percentage of orange juice therein. On January 1, 1975, it became mandatory that noncarbonated beverage products simulating any fruit in color and flavor bear statement of the absence of natural components when none were present.

Truly fresh juices are of limited availability and generally are expensive because of perishability. Some juices available in bottles and cartons in the supermarket have been pasteurized to enhance their keeping quality; they must, however, be kept refrigerated because they have not been processed long enough for sterilization. Flavor is modified by pasteurization. Canned juices have been heated long enough to destroy spoilage organisms; canning also modifies flavor. The proper dehydration of a juice and freezing the juice concentrate produce products that have good flavor when reconstituted. Table 13–6 gives the per serving costs of some selected juice and beverage products.

Citrus Fruit Beverages.   The standards of identity for orange juice and orange juice products include standards for canned, frozen, and pasteurized orange juices; canned and frozen orange juice concentrate; orange juice from concentrate; and for orange juice and concentrated orange juice with preservative, and concentrated orange juice for further processing.

Orange juice is defined as the unfermented juice of mature oranges of the species *Citrus sinensis.* In bottles or cartons, it is available in some markets where it would be called fresh orange juice. This juice, when it is available, is expensive. It is also expensive to prepare at home in many regions of the country. *Frozen orange juice* is unfermented orange juice that has been frozen. *Pasteurized orange juice* is orange juice to which may be added 10 percent by volume, but no more, of juice from mature oranges of the species *Citrus reticulata,* orange pulp and orange oil, and a sweetening agent. This juice is heat-treated to destroy viable microorganisms and to reduce enzyme activity that modifies flavor. It may be preserved by either freezing or refrigeration. This product is available in supermarkets. *Canned orange juice* may be the same combination of ingredients as pasteurized orange juice; it is sealed in containers and so processed by heat as to prevent spoilage. *Orange juice from concentrate* is prepared by the mixing of potable water with prepared orange juice concentrate. To this mixture may be added orange juice,

TABLE 13–6. *Pre-Serving Cost and Vitamin C Value of Selected Orange Juice Products and Citrus Flavored Products* [1]

Selected Items	Cost and Market Unit	Volume of Product (Fl. oz.)	Volume of Serving (Fl. oz.)	Percentage of U.S. RDA [2]	Cost per Serving (Cents)
Orange juice, fresh squeezed	$1.89/4 lb.	36	4	105	$.21
Orange juice, pasteurized	1.05/qt.	32	4	105	.13
Orange juice from concentrate	.93/qt.	32	4	100	.12
Orange juice, canned	1.03/No. 3 Cyl.	46	4	85	.09
Orange juice from frozen concentrate	.44/6 oz.	24	4	100	.07
Tang, synthetic mix	1.93/18 oz.	128	4	100	.06
Orange plus [3]	1.29/12 oz.	48	6[4]	150	.06
Orange Drink, 10 percent orange juice, Brand A	.79/No. 3 Cyl.	46	6	100	.10
Orange Nip [5]	.69/12 oz.	48	6	100	.09
Orange Punch, no orange juice	.99/No. 3 Cyl.	46	6	100	.13

[1] June, 1982 prices.
[2] U.S. RDA for vitamin C is 60 milligrams.
[3] Frozen concentrate for orange breakfast beverage, 30 percent orange juice when reconstituted.
[4] Proposed size of servings of noncarbonated breakfast beverages.
[5] Frozen concentrate for orange drink, 70 percent orange juice when reconstituted.

exclusive of canned orange juice, orange pulp and orange oil, and a sweetener. It may be heated to reduce enzyme activity and the number of viable microorganisms. This product is available in the refrigerator cabinet of the supermarket.

Both canned and frozen orange juice concentrate are defined. *Orange juice concentrates* are prepared by the removal of water from the unfermented juice of mature oranges of the species *Citrus sinensis* to which may have been added any or all of the following: 10 percent by volume before concentration of unfermented juice from *Citrus reticulata,* or hybrids, and 5 percent by volume of juice from unfermented *Citrus aurantium,* orange oil, orange pulp, orange essence, orange juice concentrate, and a sweetener. Any of the ingredients used may have been heat-treated. The diluted concentrate must have 11.8 percent of orange solids; the dilution ratio cannot be less than three plus one— that is, three volumes of water plus one of concentrate must produce orange juice. The concentrate may be frozen or sealed in containers and so processed by heat as to prevent spoilage. The wide range of possible ingredients and of the level of heat treatments of ingredients probably account for the cost and palatability differences among different brands of frozen orange juice concentrates.

There are standards for the quality grading of canned orange juice, all single strength ready-to-drink grapefruit juices, canned blended grapefruit and orange juices, canned tangerine juice, and frozen concentrated orange juice. Quality standards for canned orange juice based on scores for color, flavor, and defects are three: U.S. Grade A, U.S. Grade C, and Substandard. Quality grades for grapefruit juice apply to all single strength ready-to-drink grapefruit juices including canned grapefruit juice, "chilled" grapefruit juice, and grapefruit juice prepared from the concentrate regardless of the processing technique. There are three grades based on scores for color, flavor, and defects: U.S. Grade A, U.S. Grade B, and Substandard. Blended orange and grapefruit juices must contain no less than 25 percent of the minor ingredient.

An evaluation of processed orange juice products was presented in Consumer Reports (February, 1982). Orange juice made from frozen concentrate was judged superior in flavor. Juice which had been heat processed scored lowest. The refrigerated juices, some made from concentrate, generally were more expensive and inferior in flavor to the frozen concentrate.

Diluted orange juice products are available. In general, they are called *orange drink,* though fanciful names can be used. In general, they contain 10 percent of orange juice. They are enriched with vitamin C, and the 6-ounce serving usually provides the U.S. RDA for vitamin C. Because of the sweetening ingredients, the 6-ounce serving of the diluted drink tends to be higher in calories than the 4-ounce serving of orange juice. A concentrate for preparation of orange drink has been marketed (1975) in the No. 3 Cylinder can. After opening, it keeps fresh in the refrigerator for four weeks. It is diluted with five parts of water per part of concentrate to prepare the drink.

Imitation products from which to prepare a beverage that simulates orange juice are available and are sold under fanciful names, i.e., *Tang, Start, Bright and Early,* and *Orange Plus* as well as others. Some are frozen concentrates that must be diluted and prepared in the same manner as frozen orange juice concentrates. Others are powders that are dissolved in water. Except for Orange Plus, none contains orange juice. The imitation products are compounded from sugars, a host of food additives, including artificial color and artificial flavor plus, perhaps, orange rind, and assorted added nutrients, but especially vitamin C. See Table 13–6 for a comparison of the costs of servings of orange juice products and orange juice.

Canned and bottled lemon and lime juices are less expensive than fresh fruits in some regions of the United States during some seasons of the year. The products are more expensive when marketed in plastic squeeze containers that resemble their respective fruits than when packaged in cans or bottles. Frozen concentrates for lemonade and limeade are available. There are identity standards for lemonade and colored lemonade. The latter may be colored naturally by the addition of a colored fruit juice, such as grape juice, or it may be artificially colored.

Other Fruit Juices and Fruit Juice Beverages.   Other fruits from which juices and juice beverages are prepared include apple, apricot, cherry, cranberry, date, grape, papaya, passion fruit, pear, pineapple, guava, and prune. Standards of identity, quality, and fill of container have been established for canned pineapple juice; only the standard of identity has been established for prune juice. Quality grade standards have been defined for canned apple juice and frozen apple juice concentrate, canned grape juice and frozen grape juice concentrate, and canned pineapple juice. In general, there are two grades and the substandard quality. Canned apple juice is defined as the unfermented liquid prepared from the first-pressing juice of sound, fresh apples. It is prepared without concentration, without dilution, and without added sweetener; however, an antioxidant may be added. A development of the 1960's was the packaging of juices in six-packs of single servings. A measure of juice so purchased will, generally, cost more than if purchased in a larger container.

Dry mixes for preparing fruit-flavored beverages are generously consumed. Labels must name ingredients in decreasing order of predominance. Further, they must state the extent to which ingredients are natural and synthetic. The mixes deserve some study. Comparison of the ingredient content of the sweetened and unsweetened kinds discloses little difference except for added sugar. For example, as priced in the summer of 1982, presweetened Brand A cost 67 cents to prepare two quarts of beverage. The same brand of mix to be sweetened by the consumer cost 17 cents; to this would be added one cup of sugar to prepare two quarts of beverage. The cost of the added sugar was 15 cents (United States average cost was $1.50 for 5 pounds) for a total cost of 32 cents. The consumer paid 50 cents for the sugar in the presweetened mix, or more than triple the market cost of sugar at that time. The meal manager who buys the mixes for beverages and the canned drinks and punches ought to read labels so as to become informed about what her dollars are buying. They may be buying only sweetened, tasty water to which some vitamin C has been added. Both the water and the vitamin C can be more cheaply purchased.

SUMMARY

Fruits are available to the meal manager in great variety, both as fresh products and as processed products. There are no consumer grades for fresh fruits, although there are commercial grades for many fresh fruits. The consumer must learn to grade fresh fruits herself. There are grade standards for some processed fruits; however, not much that is available in the supermarket is graded. The fact that little that is available is graded means that the consumer can at different times buy products of quite different quality. For this reason many consumers rely on brand names as clues to quality. Fresh fruits differ in cost per serving depending on kind, region of residence, and season. The processed product is often far less expensive than the fresh counterpart, for example, frozen strawberries and orange juice prepared from frozen orange juice concentrate, canned pears, and canned applesauce. Frozen fruits are generally more expensive than canned fruits, as, for example, blueberries and red tart cherries. The cost per serving of canned fruits is determined by the quality of the product, the size of the can purchased, the style of the pack, the brand (that is, whether national brand or private label), and even where it is purchased. To some extent, the same is true of frozen fruits. Fruit juices, fruit juice beverages, and mixes for assorted beverages are so abundantly available as to confuse the consumer. It is desirable to read labels and digest the information on them before buying. Decisions on what to buy should be made on the basis of resources, preferences, experience, and information. Also fruits vary widely in their nutrient content and caloric value; this should be recognized in selection of fruit. Knowledge and skill in the marketplace are great assets.

GUIDES TO BUYING FRESH FRUITS AND FRUIT PRODUCTS

1. In general, do not buy overripe, soft, bruised, or moldy fruits.
2. Some blemishes, especially those on peels and rinds that are discarded, although they influence grade, do not necessarily affect the quality of the fruits; for example, the bronzing of citrus fruits does not affect their quality.
3. Select fruits the peels or rinds of which have the proper texture, have a proper color, and are unbroken. Any damage to peels or rinds leads to rotting and mold formation.
4. Buy citrus fruits and pineapples that feel heavy in relation to size; they will be juicy.
5. Select fruits of good color and aroma. These will be guides to ripeness; for example, strawberries should have good color and a rich aroma.
6. Some melons have no aroma that is perceivable until the fruit is cut. Although melons do not become sweeter after picking, they do soften and some develop in aroma.
7. Bananas, pears, avocados, mangoes, and apples are some fruits that ripen postharvest. They are safely purchased while unripe because they ripen at room temperature; refrigerate when ripe.
8. Both at the supermarket and at home, handle fruits gently; bruising hastens spoilage.
9. If more than one variety is available, for example, apples, buy according to the intended use.
10. When size is a factor of cost, buy according to use and remember that the biggest is not always the best.
11. Buy by weight rather than by count or measure when it is possible to do so.
12. When more than one quality of fruit is available, buy according to use, for example, top quality for freezing.
13. Buy bananas when yellow with green tips. When speckled, they are ripe and at their prime. Refrigerate them when ripe, skins will darken but the fruit remains palatable.
14. Read labels on beverage and drink containers and on mixes for punches, ades, and drinks. Except for sugar, products may be wholly synthetic or they may contain only small quantities of natural ingredients.

15. When buying canned fruits, try several different brands. The most expensive may not be the best for flavor. Packs composed of pieces irregular in shape ought to be low in cost and may be quite flavorful.

16. Frozen fruits have good flavor but may have poor texture.

17. Buy only firm, clean packs of frozen fruits. Storage without loss of quality is contingent on the holding temperature of 0° F or lower and the quality of the product at the time purchased. Storage life may be up to one year, but it may be far less if the product is not handled properly.

GUIDES TO STORAGE

1. With rare exceptions fresh fruits have a storage life limited to days; one or two days for berries except blueberries, cherries, and figs; three to five days for almost all others except bananas, mangoes, pears, and papyas picked unripe. Refrigerate them when they have ripened and use within days.

2. Stored under commercial conditions of proper temperature, humidity, and atmosphere, apples have a long storage life. Apples purchased unripe have several weeks of storage life in a cool place. Refrigerate ripe apples.

3. Store citrus fruits in a cool place. Refrigerate to extend storage life to several weeks.

4. Reconstituted juices and thawed frozen fruits have a short life even when refrigerated.

5. The palatability of canned fruits and juices will be better when the contents are removed to glass, ceramic, or plastic containers.

6. Store dried fruits in tightly closed containers at room temperature except when the weather is hot and humid. Refrigerate cooked dried fruits and use within days.

REFERENCES CITED

1. "Food Consumption, Prices, and Expenditures, 1960–1980," National Economic Division, Economic Research Service, U.S. Department of Agriculture. Statistical Bulletin No. 672. (September, 1981), pp. 20–25.
2. Miller, Erston V., and James I. Munger, *Good Fruits and How to Know Them.* Pittsburgh: Boxwood Press (1967).
3. "Orange Juice," Consumer Reports **47**:68 (1982).

SUGGESTED PROBLEMS

1. Select six readily available fresh fruits; price them in fresh and processed forms. Set up a table showing per-serving costs. What is the range in cost of each?
2. Purchase a can of cherry pie filling. Wash away the starch-thickened sweet sauce. What is the weight of the cherries? The percentage weight? Purchase a can of pie cherries. Drain and weigh the cherries. What is the cost of the cherries in the pie filling (allow ⅔ cup of sugar to sweeten the pie cherries)?
3. Survey the kinds of drinks and punches on a supermarket shelf. Set up a table showing names, principal ingredients, market unit and cost, and cost of a common unit.
4. Estimate the cost of the sugar in a presweetened drink mix.

Chapter 14

Shopping for Food: Vegetables

Models and patterns for good nutrition suggest the consumption of at least four servings of fruits and/or vegetables daily. Although vegetables are not the best-liked class of foods, they have more nutrients per kilocalorie than any other food class. Be that as it may, with varied fluctuations, annual per capita consumption of commercially produced vegetables has gradually increased during this century. Further, changes in vegetable preferences are evident. At the time of World War II, vegetable preferences of men in the armed forces were cut corn, corn-on-the-cob, green string beans, sliced tomatoes, and green peas.

During the period between 1970–1980, consumption of tomatoes, lettuce, and onions increased; they appear to be preferred fresh vegetables. Consumption of fresh beets, parsnips, and turnips declined. During 1978–80, more than one-half (54 percent) of vegetables consumed had been processed by canning or freezing. During the same period, consumption of fresh cabbage, carrots, and sweet corn decreased, consumption of frozen broccoli and carrots increased but that of frozen peas declined. Consumption data appear to reflect current vegetable preferences. Total commercial vegetable consumption (except potatoes) was in 1980 approximately 160 pounds (retail weight) per capita. Potato consumption was approximately 115 pounds (retail weight) of which more than one-half was as processed products. (See Figure 14–1 and Figure 14–2.) Home gardens would add significantly to the total of vegetables consumed.

During this century, advances in plant breeding and culture, agricultural technology inclusive of harvesting technology, and packaging technology have provided fresh vegetables in abundance and variety throughout the year, as well as varieties that process successfully during

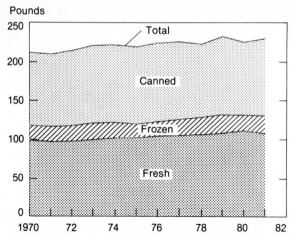

FIGURE 14–1.   Per capita consumption of vegetables. Fresh includes dehydrated onions and excludes melons. Frozen and canned on fresh-weight basis. Processed includes pickles and sauerkraut, excludes canned and frozen potatoes, and canned sweetpotatoes, baby foods, and soups. (1981 preliminary statistics from *United States Department of Agriculture*.)

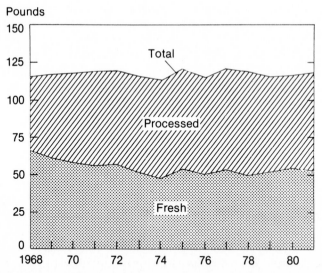

FIGURE 14–2.   Per capita consumption of potatoes. Processed on fresh-weight basis. (1981 preliminary from *United States Department of Agriculture*.)

canning and freezing. Some interesting new varieties include golden beets that do not bleed as do the red varieties; purple cauliflower and purple podded beans both of which turn green on cooking; red lettuce and red okra which turns green on cooking; several varieties of edible podded peas; and many interesting squashes. However, it is to be noted that not all new varieties that are larger or smaller, or more colorful, or hardier, or mature earlier, or are disease resistant, or produce greater yields, or that can be mechanically harvested are as tasty as old-time favorites, for example, the tomato and sweet corn.

At times, the per-serving costs of fresh vegetables exceed the per-serving costs of canned or frozen counterparts. Even in season, some fresh vegetables are more costly than others, for example, asparagus, new garden peas, fresh lima beans, and spinach. Broccoli and cauliflower cost more than cabbage. Fresh carrots and cabbage are the perennial choices of budget-conscious shoppers. Although there may always be exceptions, the wide range in the per-serving cost of fresh vegetables is narrowed by canning and freezing. See Tables 14–1, 14–2, and 14–3. Ready-prepared vegetable dishes, such as broccoli or cauliflower in cheese sauce and mixed vegetable dishes, reduce the meal

TABLE 14–1. *Estimated Per-Serving Cost of Selected Fresh Vegetables*[1]

	Cost and Market Unit	Estimated Servings per Unit	Estimated – Cost per Serving
Asparagus	$1.29/lb.	3–4[2]	$.43–32
Beans, green	.59/lb.	6	.10
Beans sprouts	.89/8 oz.	—[3]	—[3]
Beets	.59/lb.	5	.12
Bok choy	.79/lb.	—[3]	—[3]
Broccoli	.49/lb.	4	.12
Brussels sprouts	1.03/lb.	5	.21
Cabbage	.39/lb.	4–6[3]	.10–.065
Carrots	.22/lb.	5	.045
Cauliflower	.69/lb.	5	.14
Corn	.15/ear	1	.15
Eggplant	.39/lb.	3–4[3]	.13–.10
Parsnips	.99/lb.	5	.20
Snow peas	2.29/lb.	—[3]	—[3]
Spinach	1.29/10 oz.	3	.43
Tomatoes	.65/lb.	4–6[3]	.16–.11
Turnips	.49/lb.	4	.42
Yellow summer squash	.39/lb.	4	.10
Zucchini	.39/lb.	4	.10

[1] June, 1982 prices. Conventional supermarket. Some vegetables would be out of season in some regions of the United Stated but would be available perhaps at higher cost.
[2] Depending on maturity.
[3] Depending on use.

TABLE 14–2.   *Per-Serving Cost of Selected Canned Vegetables* [1]

Selected Items	Cost and Market Unit	Cost per Serving [2]
Asparagus, cuts	$ .95/No. 300 [3]	$0.24
Asparagus, spears	1.09/No. 300	.27
Beets, sliced	.47/No. 303	.12
Blue Lake green beans, cut	.55/No. 303	.14
Blue Lake green beans, whole	.58/No. 303	.145
Green beans, cut	.53/No. 303	.13
Corn, cream style	.57/No. 303	.14
Corn, whole kernel	.57/No. 303	.14
Mixed vegetables	.45/No. 303	.11
Peas	.56/No. 303	.14
Peas, tiny	.59/No. 303	.15
Peas	.39/No. 8z	.195
Spinach	.57/No. 303	.14
Tomatoes, stewed	.75/No. 303	.19
Tomatoes, whole	.65/No. 303	.16
Tomato wedges	.79/No. 303	.20
Yams	.81/No. 303	.20
Zucchini, Italian style	.69/No. 303	.17

[1] July, 1982 prices.
[2] Approximately 4 oz. per serving.
[3] See Appendix B-3 for can size quantities.

manager's work in meal preparation but increase per-serving costs. See Table 14–4. The quantities of vegetables that dollars purchase are established by choices from among the different vegetables; the state or form in which purchased, whether fresh, canned, frozen, or ready prepared; the brand purchased if processed; and, possibly, the market patronized. The farmer's market when available is a fine place for shopping for fresh produce. Store brand and generic brand canned products may provide bargains.

THE SIZE OF VEGETABLE SERVINGS

Vegetable servings are not large. When income permits, we like larger and larger meat servings and large servings of fruit; but vegetable servings rarely get larger and larger. The average serving of a vegetable—except potatoes—is, by measure, about one-half cup; by weight, about 2.5 to 3 ounces of cooked drained weight or of sauced weight. Potato servings are larger, from 3 to 4 ounces, depending on preference, and they may be much larger when baked, stuffed, or boiled whole potatoes are served, and when the food budget is conservative. Salads of mixed

TABLE 14–3. *Per-Serving Cost of Selected Frozen Vegetables*

Selected Items	Cost and Market Unit	Cost per Pound [2]	Cost per Serving [3]
Asparagus, cuts	$1.49/8 oz.	$2.98	$.50
Asparagus spears	1.89/8 oz.	3.98	.66
Beans, green, cuts	.57/9 oz.	1.01	.17
Beans, lima, baby	.73/10 oz.	1.17	.195
Beans, lima, baby	1.13/16 oz.	1.13	.19
Broccoli, chopped	.59/10 oz.	.94	.16
Broccoli, spears	.59/10 oz.	.94	.16
Brussel sprouts	.73/16 oz.	.73	.12
Cauliflower	.81/10 oz.	1.30	.22
Corn, cut	.59/10 oz.	.94	.16
Corn, cut	.89/16 oz.	.89	.15
Mixed vegetables	.89/16 oz.	.89	.15
Peas	.59/10 oz.	.94	.16
Peas	.89/16 oz.	.89	.15
Peas, tiny	1.19/16 oz.	1.19	.20
Green beans and carrots	.99/16 oz.	.99	.165
Spinach, chopped	.45/10 oz.	.80	.13
Squash, winter	.45/12 oz.	.56	.09

[1] June, 1982 prices.

[2] Per-pound cost derived for comparison purposes, also to simplify derivation of per-serving cost.

[3] Estimated per-serving cost assumes six average portions per pound, however, larger servings (five per pound) may be desired by some meal managers.

TABLE 14–4. *Cost per Ten-Ounce Carton of Frozen Vegetable Dishes* [1]

Selected Items	Cost per 10-Ounce Carton [2]
Broccoli with Cheese Sauce	$1.19
Broccoli, Carrots, and Cauliflower in Cheese Sauce	1.19
Cauliflower in Cheese Sauce	1.19
Mixed Vegetables in Butter Sauce	1.19
Chinese Style Stir-fry Vegetables	1.19
Italian Style Mixed Vegetables	1.29
Japanese Vegetables in Soy Sauce	1.15
Hawaiian Vegetables in Sweet-Sour Sauce	1.15
Lima Beans in Butter Sauce	1.09
Brussels Sprouts in Butter Sauce	1.09
Spinach in Butter Sauce	.99

[1] Cost as of June, 1982 in conventional supermarket.

[2] Four small servings, or three average servings.

greens, of mixed salad vegetables, of head lettuce, and of cabbage may weigh from 2.5 to 4 ounces per serving without dressings. Personal preferences establish the size of all of these servings for a given family.

Fresh vegetables are so prepared and packaged for distribution in the supermarket as to be almost as convenient as the canned and frozen products. Different varieties of beans and peas are shelled, corn-on-the-cob is husked, greens are trimmed and washed, root vegetables are topped, broccoli and cauliflower are trimmed, and so on. The most the cook has to do is casual trimming and rinsing. If an acceptable serving is 2.5 to 3 ounces of drained cooked weight, then many of the fresh vegetables as we buy them serve out at least four servings to the pound because the percentage of waste rarely exceeds one third of the purchased weight. Only the hard squashes, asparagus, and unpodded beans and peas have a high percentage of waste. Fresh green beans, shelled beans and peas, topped carrots, and some others may provide as many as five to six servings per pound of fresh weight. This means that what appears to be a high cost per pound for a fresh vegetable actually may be reasonable, a fact that suggests the desirability of comparing vegetable costs on a per serving basis. The No. 303 can and the No. 2 Vacuum can provide four average servings of the vegetable, and the No. 8Z can provides two servings. Ten-ounce and 9-ounce cartons of frozen vegetables provide three to four servings depending on kind and serving size. Per pound, the individually quick frozen (IQF) packs in bags easily yield six servings.

FRESH VEGETABLES

Many fresh vegetables from asparagus to zucchini can be purchased throughout the year in city supermarkets. Obviously, the statement would not hold true for small towns and villages. Costs fluctuate widely during the year because sources vary. For example, tomatoes may be locally grown, or they may be shipped from California, Florida, or Mexico when not in season locally. Fresh produce can be quality graded and often is. Different supermarkets, fruit and vegetable markets, and roadside vegetable stands may stock produce of different qualities, thus explaining price differentials. Quality is affected by weather conditions in growing areas; even the best that is available is not always of top quality. The management and care given to fresh produce within markets affect its quality—astounding quantities of produce are discarded where store policy requires that the produce offered be of the best quality. Opinion differs on prepackaging versus open selection of produce. Certainly, prepackaging avoids the situation where a shopper can pick all of the best from open stock, for example, the fattest asparagus spears, hence, leaving stock of lesser quality. It is desirable that a shopper for food be able to recognize quality in fresh produce. With few exceptions, such as the tomato, there is no concern for a proper degree of maturity or ripeness, immaturity rather than maturity being preferable in vegetables. Garden freshness is important; modern technology has effected rapid cooling and special packaging for fresh vegetables. Fresh vegetables of good quality will be crisp-appearing, of good color, and free of brown areas that point to spoilage or maturity. The use of sodium bisulfite solutions in the prevention of browning of fresh vegetables is under review by the Food and Drug Administration (1982). As with fruits, the first and the last to appear in a season may be quite expensive and may be of lesser quality than products available at the peak of the season. Some fresh vegetables will cost more per serving than others, regardless of season; for example, fresh carrots and onions are never as expensive as are fresh asparagus and spinach. Cooked fresh vegetables have a fine flavor and a firm, near-crisp texture that canned and frozen vegetables lack. Consumers do not agree on the merits of frozen over canned vegetables and vice versa.

The quality grades for fresh vegetables are under review; at present they are U.S. Fancy for top quality, U.S. No. 1, U.S. No. 2, and U.S. No. 3. The U.S. No. 1 grade is the chief trading grade and represents good, average quality. Because grading is voluntary, little grade-labeled fresh produce is found in the supermarket. Some vegetables are described.

Artichokes

The artichoke is described here because the trend toward gourmet dining and interest in vegetarian diets have made it a better known vegetable than heretofore. It is the unopened flower bud of a thistle-like perennial. More of it is inedible than is edible. The edible parts are the small, tender bit at the base of each leaflike scale that covers the bud, the young flowers within the bud, and the base on which they are borne called the artichoke heart. Buy only artichokes that are heavy, compact, plump, and of good green color. Artichoke hearts are available frozen, canned, and pickled.

Mini artichokes are available in some markets. They require some trimming of tough leaves and at top and bottom. They are cooked and eaten in their entirety either hot or cold.

Chinese Vegetables

Stir-fry and wok cooking have introduced a number of new and different vegetables, the so-called Chinese vegetables. One can find them in some supermarkets and in specialty shops in metropolitan areas where ethnic groups (from China, Japan, and Southeast Asia) reside. The vegetables have unusual names but are members of well known vegetable families. Bok or pak choy, gai lohn, and siew choy are members of the cabbage family. They are considered more delicate in flavor than common cabbage. Mao gwa, the fuzzy gourd; foo gwa, chinese bitter melon; and doan gwa, Chinese winter melon are members of the gourd family. Snow peas are the most familiar of these vegetables; these edible podded peas are favorites of home gardeners. Dow guak is the yard-long asparagus bean, so-called because the beans have a mild flavor of asparagus. These vegetables may be ingredients in stir-fry dishes; some are salad ingredients. Ginger root, a brownish knobby root is used in Oriental cookery; it was, perhaps, the first of these products to be found on supermarket counters.

Greens for Salads

Four types of lettuce and a varied assortment of greens are available for salads. The lettuce types include crisphead, butterhead, cos or romaine, and leaf lettuce. Commercially produced salad greens include curled-leaved endive, escarole, Belgian or French endive, watercress, spinach, Chinese cabbage and other Chinese greens. All greens for salads should always be young, tender, crisp, and dry. Less tender parts of heads can be cooked and served as a green vegetable. Prepared mixtures of salad greens and salad vegetables are widely available for the restaurant trade; they are also available in some supermarkets.

Lettuce. The best-known and best-liked lettuce is crisphead, or iceberg lettuce, or head lettuce, as it is more commonly known. Sizes of heads vary, with preference for those of medium size. Heads are trimmed and prepackaged for distribution; there is little, if any, waste when they are of good quality. A one-pound head will provide five or more servings and as many as sixteen lettuce cups or lettuce underliners for salads. Boston and Bibb lettuce are of the butterhead type. Heads of Boston lettuce are smaller and softer, and the leaves are smoother and greener than the leaves of iceberg lettuce. Heads of Bibb lettuce are small and loosely formed. Leaves are very tender, bright green, and delicate in flavor. A salad may be composed from a single head of Bibb lettuce, or a head may be large enough for several salads. Leaf lettuce is more delicate and perishable than iceberg lettuce; the leaves of commercial leaf lettuce are often large and branch from a stalk. Much so-called garden lettuce is leaf lettuce, of which there are many varieties. The red and partially red lettuce varieties are leaf lettuce. They are now available in supermarkets. Bibb lettuce and leaf lettuce varieties are favorites of home gardeners. Cos or romaine forms a long slender head. The leaves may be large, coarse-textured, and strong in flavor. Leaves may be dark to light in color depending on variety. Very small heads are served whole as a salad; they are considered a delicacy by some persons.

Chicory, Endive, and Escarole. Chicory, endive, and escarole are variants of the same vegetable species. Curled-leaved endive, or chicory, as it is sometimes called, is a spreading plant. The leaves are narrow, irregularly shaped, ragged and curly, deep green unless bleached, and somewhat bitter. The center leaves may be bleached to a pale greenish-yellow. Escarole has broader, less ragged-appearing leaves that are less bitter. Belgian or French endive, also called chicory and witloof, forms solid, spindle-shaped heads of yellow-tipped white leaves, which are somewhat bitter. This green is highly prized by the gourmet. It is sometimes cooked.

Onions

There are numerous varieties of onions; however, they may be classified according to three types: globe, Granex-Grano, and Spanish. Globe onions are primarily for culinary use. They are small, globular in shape, and usually have a yellow skin though it may be red or white. They are strong in flavor. Granex-Grano onions are mild in flavor. They are flattened in shape. The skin is white or yellow. Spanish onion varieties are globular in shape; they are large; and they are mild in flavor. Some onion varieties have been developed to provide slices that match the hamburger bun in size.

Green onions and scallions are any onion variety pulled before maturity; they have a white part and, continuous with it, tubular green leaves. They are used in their entirety as long as the green parts remain unspoiled. Chives are mini green onions. They are available freeze-dried. They are also pot-grown in the kitchen. Garlic is a cluster of easily separated parts called cloves. The cluster of parts is surrounded by a white onion-type skin. It is also available as a dehydrated powder and in garlic salt. The shallot, too, is a cluster of cloves of purplish-brown color. It has its own distinctive flavor that is highly prized by fine cooks. Scallions should never be substituted for the shallot. Leeks look like giant green onions. They have a short, thick white part and flat green leaves. They are always cooked as a vegetable and preferably only the white part is used, although opinion differs on this. They are more mild in flavor than onions. Leeks are widely available in the 1980's.

Potatoes

Potato consumption in the United States decreased during this century well into the 1950's when the advent of processed potato products reversed the trend. The consumption of fresh potatoes continued to decline into the mid-1970's when per capita consumption of fresh potatoes was less than 60 pounds annually. Since then, consumption has fluctuated with some years being better than others, however, consumption of the processed products still exceeds that of the fresh products. See Figure 14–2.

Fresh potato quality has improved in recent decades because of the development of disease- and pest-resistant varieties, improved cultural methods, improved technology at harvest, controlled storage conditions, and better packaging. Relatively new in potato culture is production from seeds rather than from sets, that is, potato parts that include an eye. There are many potato varieties: they can be classified in two ways: according to shape or according to cooking qualities. With regard to shape, they are either round or more or less cylindrical. According to cooking qualities, potatoes are either mealy or waxy; if they have both characteristics, they are known as all-purpose potatoes. The Irish Cobbler is such a one. Mealy potatoes are preferred for mashing and baking; waxy potatoes that remain firm and hold shape, for boiling and dishes wherein pieces are to remain discrete and unbroken. Russet varieties are mealy; red varieties and new potatoes are waxy. In general, *new* describes freshly harvested immature potatoes. So-called Idaho potatoes may be any of several varieties, the best known is the Russet Burbank. This potato may be described as Idaho regardless of place grown: Maine, Michigan, or Montana.

The Russet Burbank is cylindrical in shape, the skin russet and netted, eyes are shallow, and flesh is white. It is a splendid baker; it is also a good all-purpose potato. When of top quality and of excellent size for baking, it may be priced high. The Kahtadin is a fine potato, it is of the round type. The Kennebec is another good all-purpose potato. The White Rose is large, long, elliptical, and flattened; it is an excellent potato.

There are four commercial grades for potatoes: U.S. Fancy, U.S. No. 1, U.S. Commercial, and U.S. No. 2. Potatoes of the top three grades differ principally in requirements for size, freedom from damage caused by dirt or other foreign matter, and tolerance for defects. Some potatoes packaged for consumers are graded in accordance with commercial grades. U.S. No. 1 is the lowest grade the average consumer would wish to buy. In this grade the smallest potato allowed is one and seven-eighths inches in diameter.

Potatoes that show a green color have been sunburned during harvest or storage. They have a bitter taste that makes them unpalatable because of the presence of solanin, an alkaloid. Paring and trimming losses differ with the quality and size of potatoes; the range is from about 10 to 40 percent, with 20 percent as an overall average loss. Smaller potatoes have greater paring losses but if priced right provide more food for dollars spent than larger potatoes. Potatoes stored properly in a well-ventilated, cool place have a storage life of several months. New potatoes have a storage life of only several weeks. Potatoes store well in the refrigerator, but should be returned to room temperature for one to two days before cooking for best texture.

Processed Potato Products.   Potatoes are processed by canning, dehydration, and freezing; altogether some fifty different forms of processed potato products are available. Among canned products are small whole potatoes, sliced potatoes, German potato salad, and shoestring potatoes. Dehydration of the potato resulted in instant mashed potatoes and the cut-up forms for hash brown, au gratin, and scalloped potatoes and other dishes. In some regions of the United States and at some seasons of the year, the convenient instant product for mashed potatoes is less expensive than homemade mashed potatoes. Assorted frozen potato products and frozen potato dishes are to be found in the supermarket; of these only the French fried potato is a bargain. See table 14–5 for the estimated costs of four servings of potatoes as purchased in different forms.

Sprouted Seeds

Interest in so-called health foods; widespread adoption of stir-fry cookery; and the ever increasing popularity of sprouts as salad ingredients have made sprouted seeds available in supermarkets as well as specialty stores. Although almost any seed can be sprouted, the commonly-sprouted, available ones include soybean, mung bean, and alfalfa seed. Blends of sprouts may include radish, lentil, alfalfa, wheat, and sunflower sprouts. Sprouts differ in flavor depending on the seeds sprouted. Fenugreek, an occasional ingredient of a blend, adds spiciness to the blend. The ubiquitous presence of sprouts on the restaurant salad bar is evidence of general acceptance of sprouts as a vegetable. Occasionally sprouted cress seeds are available. The tiny leaves are harvested and used in salads and sandwiches. Home production of sprouted seeds is widely practiced.

TABLE 14–5. *Estimated Cost of Four Servings of Potatoes as Purchased in Different Forms* [1]

Selected Items	Cost and Market Unit	Quantity for Four Servings	Cost for Four Servings
Small red potatoes	$ .89/3 lb.	1 lb [2]	$ .30
Red potatoes	1.19/5 lb.	1⅓ lb.	.32
Idaho potatoes for Baking	.99/4	4	.99
Idaho Russet potatoes	1.99/10 lb.	1⅓ lb.	.25
White all-purpose potatoes	2.69/10 lb.	1⅓ lb.	.36
Canned small whole potatoes	.47/No. 303	1 can	.47
Dehydrated Au Gratin potatoes	.88/6 servg.	⅔ pack	.58
Dehydrated Hash Brown potatoes	.88/6 servg.	⅔ pack	.58
Dehydrated for mashed potatoes	.88/24 servg.	⅙ pack	.15
Dehydrated for scalloped potatoes	.78/6 servg.	⅔ pack	.52
Frozen French fries	.75/1 lb.	1 lb.	.75
Frozen French fries	2.98/5 lb.	1 lb.	.60
Frozen Hash Browns	.67/12 oz.	12 oz.	.67
Frozen Stuffed Baked Potatoes	.51/2 servg.	4 servg.	1.02
Frozen Hash Brown Potato Patties	1.12/8	4 patties	.56
Frozen Potato Planks	1.35/1½ lb.	1 lb.	.90

[1] June, 1982 prices in discount supermarket.
[2] Prepared without peeling.

Squashes

Squashes are members of the gourd family, which includes muskmelons, watermelons, cucumbers, and pumpkins. They vary in size and in internal and external color. The many varieties of squash can be grouped into two types: hard-shelled varieties and soft-shelled varieties. The hard-shelled varieties can vary in size from small Acorn types to enormous Hubbard varieties that may weigh up to 100 pounds. They are harvested when mature. They have a thick, fleshy rind and a definite seed cavity, the contents of which are not edible, though some varieties produce seeds that are edible when roasted. The soft-shelled varieties of squash are immature when harvested; there is no seed cavity and the entire fruit including its seeds is edible.

Only about 25 percent of the hard-shelled types of squash are sold fresh; most of the crop is frozen. The best known of the hard-shelled varieties are the acorn and the Hubbard; they may be either green or yellow. The Hubbard types are pear-shaped, large, and heavy. The rind is hard; the flesh is thick and golden yellow. The acorn squashes are small, furrowed, round to oval in shape, and thin fleshed. The Butternut squash is bell- or gourd-shaped with a thin, smooth rind that is beige in color. Its flesh is orange; it is smooth in texture and has a fine flavor. The Butternut is a favorite among the hard-shelled squashes. The Buttercup squash is turban-shaped, flat at the stem end and rounded at the blossom end. The flesh is bright orange, creamy in texture, and flavorsome. Hard-shelled squashes provide two to three servings per pound.

Soft-shelled squashes are very thin-skinned; in general, they are eaten in their entirety except for very small areas that are trimmed away at the stem and blossom ends. Yellow varieties are several; they differ in shape and rind texture; flesh is white. Zucchini varieties are numerous; they are green, vary in size, and are best used when immature and small. Scallop or pattypan varieties are several. They vary in color from white to pale green and in size from tiny, the size of one's palm, to several inches in diameter. All soft-shelled squashes should be eaten when young and immature; the rind should be easily pierced by the fingernail. Depending on the method of cooking, they serve out between three and four servings per pound. These soft-shelled varieties are favorites of home gardeners. Because they are mild in flavor, they require skill in cooking and some added seasonings. Both the yellow and zucchini varieties when very small and tender are used raw as salad ingredients and relishes.

Marrow varieties are few. These squashes may be small like the *Cocozelle* or very large as is the *Italian Edible Gourd.* They are cylindrical and resemble the watermelon in shape. Spaghetti squash or vegetable spaghetti is a longish oval squash. It is boiled, the fruit cut open, the seeds removed and the fibers reserved. They are seasoned and eaten in the same way as is spaghetti. Both marrow types and spaghetti squash may be purchased in some supermarkets and some vegetable markets; they are less well known than the traditional squashes.

A relatively unknown member of the squash family, the chayote also called mirlton, is now appearing on supermarket counters. It is sometimes called the vegetable pear because of its somewhat pear shape. It is small, furrowed, and ice-green in color with pale green flesh. It is prepared as are other squashes, in addition, the cooked flesh is used as a salad ingredient.

Canned Vegetables and Canned Vegetable Products

Excluding potatoes, more canned than frozen vegetables are consumed. See Figure 14–1. Improved varieties developed and grown especially for canning, improved canning technology, identity standards, and quality grade standards all contribute to good quality in canned vegetable products. Standards of identity have been promulgated for nearly all canned vegetables. Reasonable standards of quality have been defined for green and wax beans, corn, peas, and tomatoes; that is, for the preferred vegetables. Standard of fill of container has been established for corn, peas, mushrooms, and tomatoes; however, all containers must be as full as is practicable under good commercial practice. The proportion of each vegetable in a mixture of canned vegetables is not defined, but label declaration in order of predominance is mandatory, for example, "peas and carrots" or "carrots and peas." In the canning of vegetables, the use of additives is permitted to protect color, flavor, and texture; further, the use of various ingredients is permitted to make the products more tasty. Some permitted additives and ingredients are salt, sugar, and spices; seasonings such as onions and garlic; monosodium glutamate and other flavor enhancers; calcium salts to modify texture; citric acid and vinegar to modify taste; hydrolyzed vegetable protein; and vitamin C. In general, label statement of their use is mandatory. Vegetables packed whole, such as asparagus spears, beets, carrots, potatoes, and green beans, tend to be more expensive than the different cut, sliced, and diced styles. The French-cut and julienne-cut styles are lengthwise cuts; these tend to be more expensive than other cut styles.

Permissive grades have been described for many canned vegetables. The grades are U.S. Grade A or U.S. Fancy, U.S. Grade B or U.S. Extra Standard, U.S. Grade C or U.S. Standard, and Substandard (for samples that fail to meet the requirements for U.S. Grade C). The grade is determined by the number of points scored out of a possible one hundred. Products are scored for color, clarity of liquor, tenderness and maturity, uniformity of unit size, freedom from defects, and sometimes flavor. U.S. Grade A products uniformly possess desirable qualities and are practically free from defects. U.S. Grade B products are reasonably good in all respects; U.S. Grade C products are fairly good. A high proportion of canned vegetables is U.S. Grade B. Although not a factor of grade, recommended minimum drained weights are frequently suggested in the standards.

Goals of consumer groups are mandatory grade-labeling of canned vegetables and mandatory statement of drained weight. In November of 1976, the food canning industry announced that food canners will declare voluntarily the "solid content" weight of canned fruits and vegetables. *Solid content weight* is the weight of the food put into the container before adding liquid and before processing. The solid content weight declaration is placed on the principle display panel of the label to the right of or below the net weight declaration. See Figure 14–3.

Canned vegetables of top quality may cost as much as the same vegetables frozen. However, the range in cost of canned vegetables is wide; the least expensive may cost half as much as the most expensive. On

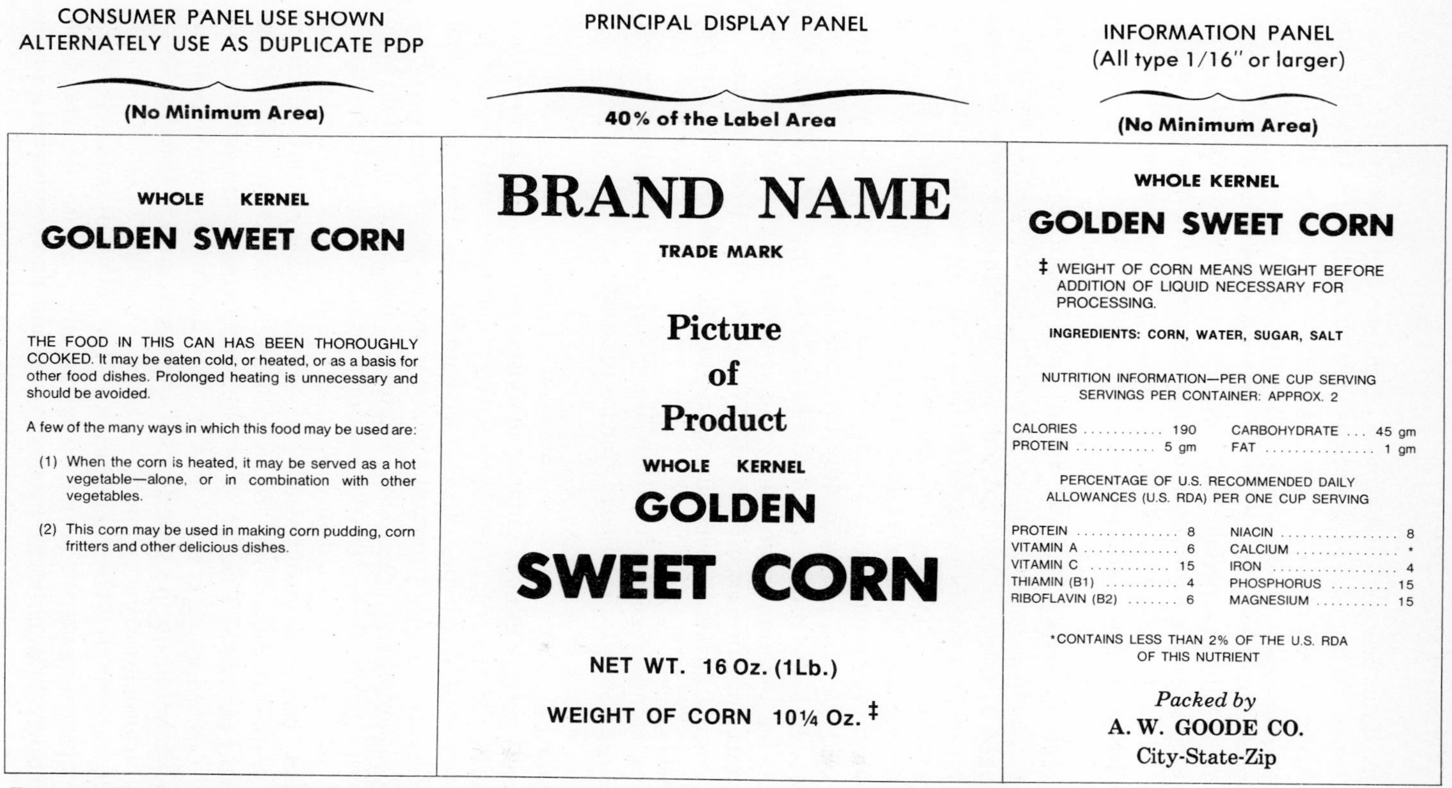
CONSUMER PANEL USE SHOWN
ALTERNATELY USE AS DUPLICATE PDP
(No Minimum Area)
WHOLE KERNEL
GOLDEN SWEET CORN
THE FOOD IN THIS CAN HAS BEEN THOROUGHLY COOKED. It may be eaten cold, or heated, or as a basis for other food dishes. Prolonged heating is unnecessary and should be avoided.
A few of the many ways in which this food may be used are:
(1) When the corn is heated, it may be served as a hot vegetable—alone, or in combination with other vegetables.
(2) This corn may be used in making corn pudding, corn fritters and other delicious dishes.
PRINCIPAL DISPLAY PANEL
40% of the Label Area
BRAND NAME
TRADE MARK
Picture
of
Product
WHOLE KERNEL
GOLDEN
SWEET CORN
NET WT. 16 Oz. (1Lb.)
WEIGHT OF CORN 10¼ Oz. ‡
INFORMATION PANEL
(All type 1/16" or larger)
(No Minimum Area)
WHOLE KERNEL
GOLDEN SWEET CORN
‡ WEIGHT OF CORN MEANS WEIGHT BEFORE ADDITION OF LIQUID NECESSARY FOR PROCESSING.
INGREDIENTS: CORN, WATER, SUGAR, SALT
NUTRITION INFORMATION—PER ONE CUP SERVING
SERVINGS PER CONTAINER: APPROX. 2
CALORIES 190
PROTEIN .... 5 gm
CARBOHYDRATE ... 45 gm
FAT .... 1 gm
PERCENTAGE OF U.S. RECOMMENDED DAILY ALLOWANCES (U.S. RDA) PER ONE CUP SERVING
PROTEIN 8
VITAMIN A 6
VITAMIN C 15
THIAMIN (B1) 4
RIBOFLAVIN (B2) 6
NIACIN 8
CALCIUM .... *
IRON 4
PHOSPHORUS 15
MAGNESIUM 15
*CONTAINS LESS THAN 2% OF THE U.S. RDA OF THIS NUTRIENT
Packed by
A. W. GOODE CO.
City-State-Zip

FIGURE 14–3. Canned food label showing net weight and solid content weight of product; also nutritioin information. (*Courtesy of the National Canners Association.*)

this basis, it can be stated that canned vegetables are less expensive than frozen ones and are often less expensive than fresh ones. Canned vegetables store conveniently and are less perishable than frozen products, however, although canned products remain safe to eat so long as their containers remain undamaged, they may lose palatability if they are held long in storage especially if the ambient temperature exceeds 75° F.

Vacuum-packed vegetables are those packed into the can without, or with a minimum quantity of packing medium. The can is exhausted and sealed, and then heat-processed in the same manner as other packs. The can used for the vacuum pack is the No. 2 Vacuum. The net weight of contents is about 12 ounces; the drained weight of the contents is about the same as the drained weight of the No. 303 can, in which the net weight of contents is about one pound. Both cans provide about four average servings of a vegetable. Other cans in use for canned vegetables include the No. 8Z Tall, the No. 1 Picnic, the No. 3 Vacuum, and the No. 2½. However, some of these are used only for specific vegetables; for example, the No. 3 Vacuum is used only for sweet potatoes and the No. 1 is used only for spinach and sauerkraut. In accordance with the provisions of the Fair Packaging and Labeling Act, not only has the number of can sizes used in canning been reduced but the number of can sizes used in processing vegetable products, such as pimientos, mushrooms, olives, juices, and tomato products, has also been reduced.

Three canned vegetable products are of sufficient interest to warrant a brief discussion: canned peas, tomato products, and olives.

Canned Peas.   Per capita consumption of canned peas exceeds that of frozen peas. A greater number of varieties of peas are canned than are frozen because of the different effects on flavor and color of the two processes. Two types of peas are canned: the Alaska or smooth-skinned early or early June pea and the wrinkled sweet-pea type. Early June peas are often canned according to size: tiny, small, medium, large, and extra large; these size designations frequently appear on labels. When sizes are combined in cans, they are described as garden run, assorted sizes, and mixed sizes. The tiny peas are considered choice and are priced accordingly. Sweet peas are not often sorted for size. Canned peas vary in brightness or dullness of color and freedom from defects according to grade. However, grade-labeled canned peas can rarely be found on the supermarket shelves. Canned vegetables of all kinds including peas are generally packed according to quality and are priced accordingly. The meal manager can only buy and try. These optional ingredients are permitted in canning peas: onions, green and red peppers, and garlic; artificial coloring; and flavor enhancers. Lastly, peas and small new potatoes are combined and canned as well as peas and carrots.

Tomato Products.   Combined annual per capita consumption of three categories of tomato products is approximately 12.5 pounds per year. These are tomato puree or pulp; tomato paste; and tomato sauce, catsup and chili sauce. There are quality grade standards for all categories and identity standards for all except tomato sauce.

The products can all be prepared from one, a combination of two, or all three of the following: the liquid obtained from mature red tomatoes; the liquid obtained from the residue from preparing tomatoes for canning, consisting of peelings and cores with or without tomato pieces; and the liquid obtained from the residue from partial extraction of juice from tomatoes. The liquid is obtained by straining so as to exclude skins, seeds, and other coarse and hard substances. It is then concentrated and seasoned as permitted. Labeling must identify the tomato ingredient(s) used in the preparation of products. *Tomato puree* or alternative *tomato pulp* contains not less than 8 percent and not more than 24 percent of tomato solids. When seasoned with salt, a label statement of the use of salt is required. When this product is prepared from the liquid obtained from red or reddish tomatoes and the tomato solids content is not less than 20 percent, it can be called *concentrated tomato juice.* When this product is diluted with three volumes of water, it is tomato juice. Tomato puree is quality graded on the basis of flavor, color, and freedom from defects. Although not a factor of quality, it may be labeled heavy, medium, or light on the basis of solids content. *Tomato paste* contains not less than 24 percent solids and may contain as much as 39 percent of natural tomato solids. It may also contain salt, spices, flavoring, and baking soda. Its concentration may be described as extra heavy, heavy, medium, or light.

Tomato sauce contains in addition to the tomato ingredient(s) salt, spices, vinegar(s), sweetener, onion, garlic, or other vegetable flavoring ingredient(s). Grades are U.S. Grade A, U.S. Grade C, and Substandard and are based on color, flavor, consistency, and freedom from defects. Brand differences among these products may be ascribable to the concentration of tomato solids and grade.

Tomato catsup may be prepared from the tomato ingredients listed for the concentrated tomato products. To the tomato ingredient(s) the following are added: salt, vinegar(s), sweetener, spices or flavorings or both, and onions or garlic or both. Grading standards provide for U.S. Grade A, U.S. Grade B, U.S. Grade C, and Substandard grades. Grading is on the basis of color, flavor, consistency, and freedom from defects. Concentration ranges according to grade from 33 percent of total solids by weight for U.S. Grade A to 25 percent for Grade C. Although there is no identity standard for chili sauce, it is defined in the U.S. standards for grades of chili sauce. *Chili sauce* is prepared from whole tomatoes to which are added salt, vinegar(s), spices, sweetener, and such chopped vegetables as green tomato, green and red peppers, celery, onion, and sweet pickle relish. Quality is established on the basis of color, flavor, consistency, character (texture of ingredients), and freedom from defects. Brand differences and cost differences among both catsup and chili sauce products may be ascribed to grade differences although grade is not declared.

Tomato juice is an unconcentrated tomato product. The identity standard requires that it be prepared from red or reddish varieties. The extracted liquid is strained of coarse material but the liquid must contain the finely divided, insoluble solids of tomato flesh. The extract may be homogenized and seasoned with salt. Tomato juice enriched with vitamin C can be marketed as an unstandardized product so long as it is properly labeled. An identity standard for yellow tomato juice requires that the product be made from yellow tomato varieties. There are standards for grading tomato juice for quality. Assigned grades are based on flavor, color, consistency, and the freedom from defects. Grades are U.S. Grade A, U.S. Grade C, and Substandard. Some difference in the cost of products on supermarket shelves can be ascribed to grade difference although they are not declared. Tomato juice of the same brand will vary in cost per unit of measure as the size of the container varies. The six-pack is probably the most expensive way to purchase the product. However, these small sizes may prove to be more economical if waste is eliminated.

Olives.   Olives, like mushrooms and artichokes, have lost status as a luxury food. Domestically, they are produced in California; they are also imported from Spain, Portugal, Italy, and Greece. The olive is a fruit rather than a vegetable. It contains a bitter principle. It is straw-colored when ripe but turns jet-black if left on the tree; oil is removed at the jet-black state. To produce the Spanish style or green olive, olives are harvested when straw-colored, treated with lye to remove the bitter principle, then allowed to undergo lactic acid fermentation. They may be bottled without pitting or may be pitted and stuffed with such items as pimientos, pickled onions, almonds, or anchovies. They are sized and bottled in brine. The ripe black olive is harvested when straw-colored and undergoes lactic acid fermentation; it is treated with lye and exposed to the air between lye treatments for the development of the black color. Ripe olives are packed according to size, which may range from Small with about 135 per pound to Super Colossal with 32 or less per pound. Green ripe olives receive no lactic acid fermentation and during the lye treatment are not exposed to the air so that they retain their natural color. So-called Italian or Greek olives, or olives given a dry, salt cure, are harvested when black. They are treated with salt for partial removal of the bitter principle. The salting removes moisture and gives the olive its wrinkled appearance. It retains some of the bitter principle, which gives it a bitterish taste. These olives are bottled without brine, in brine, or in oil, and with or without garlic.

Frozen Vegetables

More than four billion pounds of vegetables were frozen in 1980. In descending order of quantities, they were potato products—more than three billion pounds—peas, cut corn, green and wax beans, broccoli, carrots, and spinach. The development of varieties especially for freezing, quick freezing at the site of harvest, and improvements in freezing technology have resulted in an ever increasing variety of frozen vegetable products of improved quality as well as an increasing number of frozen vegetable dishes. The list of frozen vegetable dishes is long. Although they come and go, some are here to stay, such as corn souffle, creamed peas and potatoes, creamed onions, cauliflower in cheese sauce, and green beans with mushrooms or almonds. The ethnic influence is evident in such mixtures as Japanese and Chinese Style vegetables. These dishes consist of an assortment of vegetables with a sauce and, frequently, a topping of crumbs, croutons, or other ingredients. For example, San Francisco Style vegetables are composed of Frenched green beans, bean sprouts, celery, mushrooms, and red peppers in a sauce; a separate packet of topping is a part of the package. Also available are bags of plain, unseasoned mixtures of IQF, (individually quick frozen), vegetables that bear such names as California Mix, Vegetables del Sol, and Vegetables Orient. The unseasoned mixtures are somewhat similar to the frozen vegetable dishes but are less expensive.

No standards or definitions of identity and no standards of reasonable quality have been established for frozen vegetables other than peas. Standards for grading have been defined for many frozen vegetables. They are graded on the basis of color, freedom from defects, and character. The number of grades differs with different vegetables: for some, such as peas, there are three possible grades and the Substandard classification; for others, such as broccoli, there are only two grades and the Substandard classification. Grades are designated as U.S. Grade A or U.S. Fancy, U.S. Grade B or U.S. Extra Standard, and U.S. Grade C or U.S. Standard. Any product failing to meet the requirements of the lowest defined grade would be classed as Substandard and would have to be so labeled. Quality-graded frozen vegetables are available in supermarkets, although not as extensively as in the past. To remain of good quality, frozen vegetables, like all frozen food products, must be held at a constant temperature of 0° F or lower. This means that storage life in a good freezer may be from eight to twelve months; but in the freezer compartment of a refrigerator-freezer may be shorter because temperature therein is rarely constant.

The frozen vegetable may cost more per serving than the same vegetable canned. However, it may cost more or less than the fresh counterpart, depending on the vegetable. Prime examples of frozen vegetables costing less than the fresh are frozen peas and frozen lima beans. Private-label frozen vegetables generally cost less per serving than national brands. The cost per serving varies with the size of the package purchased—the 10-ounce carton versus the 2-pound bag—as well as with the style of processing, whole versus chopped or cuts. Frozen prepared dishes, of course, cost more than the same vegetables purchased without this added service. See Tables 14–3 to 14–5.

Summary. Vegetables are available in great variety both fresh and processed by canning, dehydration, or freezing. Fresh vegetables differ in cost per portion. Depending on the season and the region of residence, the fresh product may cost more than the processed one and frozen products may exceed canned ones in cost. The cost per serving of canned products is established by the quality purchased, the size of the can purchased, the style of the pack, the brand, and the market where they are purchased. The same may be said for frozen products. The addition of the gourmet touch to frozen vegetables adds to the cost. Both frozen and canned vegetables are frequent supermarket specials. Decisions on what to buy must be made by the meal manager on the bases of her resources and personal preferences.

BUYING AND STORAGE GUIDES

Fresh Vegetables

1. Except for tomatoes, winter squashes, potatoes, and a few others, immaturity is preferred in vegetables. This is true for peas, green and wax beans, corn, cucumbers, radishes, soft-shelled squashes, carrots, asparagus, broccoli, and others. Learn to recognize signs of maturity, such as dry or dull appearance in contrast to a shiny appearance, a dull or yellowish green instead of a bright green, thickening and coarsening in the texture of the skin, and browning.

2. Select vegetables that are of good color and that appear crisp. Avoid those with defects.

3. Look for signs of decay in prepackaged greens, green beans, let-

tuce, radishes, spinach, and others. Also, look for areas of spoilage on unpackaged vegetables that are kept moist on ice on vegetable counters.

4. Buy fresh produce when it is in season where you live for the maximum enjoyment of vegetables, or better still, grow your own.

5. To match choices to your food budget, compare the cost of fresh, canned, and frozen products on the cost-per-serving base.

6. Ripen unripe tomatoes tightly wrapped in a brown paper bag at room temperature but not in direct sunlight. Store ripe tomatoes uncovered in your refrigerator.

7. Fresh vegetables are perishable and should be stored in covered containers, plastic bags, or in the crisper drawer of the refrigerator. Drain well and dry thoroughly any vegetable that you wash; moisture hastens spoilage.

8. Mature onions, potatoes, sweet potatoes, winter squashes, and rutabagas can be stored for a short time at room temperature although a temperature of 50° to 60° F is more satisfactory.

Canned and Frozen Vegetables

1. Packs described as "Fancy" must conform to the quality requirements of the U.S. Fancy grade.

2. Do not buy rusty, leaking, badly dented, or bulging cans of food.

3. Buy clean, firm packages of frozen products from clean cabinets maintained at a temperature of 0° F or less. Let frozen products be the last you put into your cart. At the checkout counter insist that they be packaged to protect them from temperature change.

4. Labels must reveal the style of contents of packs as whole, cuts, chopped, pieces, quarters, dices, slabs, and so on. Buy according to intended use.

5. Any package that states the number of servings must also define the size of the serving in common measures—ounces or cups.

6. Special sauces and seasonings increase cost; buy plain unseasoned products and do your own seasoning to save pennies.

7. Read nutrition information.

8. Though price is not a true guide to quality, most canned and frozen vegetables are packaged and priced according to quality.

9. Frozen products remain of good quality only when stored in a freezer at 0° F or less. How long the products you buy will remain of good quality depends on the quality at the time of purchase—an unknown. Eight to 12 months is the suggested maximum storage period for top quality products stored in a freezer. Canned products lose quality when stored for extended periods, especially if the ambient temperature exceeds 75° F.

REFERENCES CITED

1. "Food Consumption, Prices and Expenditures, 1960–1980," Statistical Bulletin No. 672. Economic Research Service. U.S. Department of Agriculture, Washington, D.C. (September 1981).
2. *Gallup Survey—The National Poll of Patron Preferences, Prejudices, and Trends,* Vols. 1 and 2, *Food Service Magazine,* Madison, Wisconsin (1967, 1969).
3. Peryam, David R. *et al., Food Preferences of Men in the Armed Services,* Department of the Army, Quartermaster Research and Engineering Command, and Container Institute for Armed Forces, Chicago (1960).

SUGGESTED PROBLEMS

1. Update the tables in this chapter (as assigned by the instructor).
2. What is the range in cost per pound of fresh, canned, and frozen vegetables where you live. Per serving?
3. Establish a reasonable sum of money and then make three choices of vegetables that you can purchase for that sum. Reduce that figure by one third and make three choices that could be purchased for that sum.
4. Survey the assortment of either canned peas or canned corn by brand and can size in a large supermarket. Prepare a table showing brand, cost and size of market unit, and cost of a common unit of the product.

Chapter 15

Shopping for Food: Grain Products, Legumes, and Nuts

Approximately two-thirds of that at-home food dollar is spent for the food products discussed in Chapters 6 through 14. The remaining approximate one-third is spent for an assortment of food products and miscellaneous items that includes grain food products such as breads, baked goods, semiprepared baked goods, flour and flour mixes, and cereals and cereal products; dry beans and peas; nuts and nut food products; fats and oils; salad dressings; food dressings; sweeteners; jams, jellies, and syrups; beverages; baking supplies; and assorted other food products such as condiments, herbs, and spices. As with the other food products that have been discussed, the choices made and the manner of purchase determine how much of these foods the dollar buys.

In this Chapter, we discuss only grain food products, dry beans and peas, soybean products, and nuts and nut food products. Inflation, recession, unemployment, and an increased interest in natural foods, organically grown foods, food additives, so-called health foods, the world food crisis, and vegetarian diets may give these foods greater significance than they have previously had.

Because they are used in reference to breads, cereals, and flours, it is desirable to define the following terms: enriched, fortified, restored, natural, organic, and health foods. *Enriched* means that the product(s) contain added amounts of thiamine, riboflavin, niacin, and iron as these amounts are established by enrichment standards promulgated by the Food and Drug Administration. *Fortified* means that amounts of nutrients that may or may not have been present in the original grain have been added. *Restored* means that the finished product contains, after processing, the approximate amounts of nutrients present in the original grains. *Natural* as applied to a food suggests that the food has

327

undergone no or only minimal processing and that it contains no added chemical ingredients such as preservatives. *Natural* as applied to a cereal means that the product has been processed and packaged without the use of additives and that no part of the grain (seed) has been removed by milling. However, the product may contain added sugar and/or salt. As of mid-1982, there are no federal regulations governing the use of the term "natural" in advertising or labeling, that is, there is no legal definition of the term. *Organic* as applied to food means production without the use of synthetic fertilizers, synthetic pesticides (insecticides, herbicides, and fungicides) or other synthetic substance. *Health food* describes a food that has some health-promoting qualities ascribed to it by someone. The Food and Drug Administration does not permit the use of the term on food labels. A goodly assortment of these foods is to be found on supermarket shelves as well as in health-food stores. In general, foods described as organic, natural, or as health products are more expensive than counterparts not so described.

GRAIN FOOD PRODUCTS

A relatively small proportion of the at-home food dollar is spent for grain foods, approximately 13 percent. In decreasing order of consumption, the following grains are eaten by Americans in the United States: wheat, corn, rice, barley, rye, millet, wild rice, and buckwheat. Wheat is first with annual consumption approximately 120 pounds per capita. Corn and rice consumption are about eight to nine pounds of each per year. They are eaten differently in different regions of the United States with residents of the South and Southeast being large consumers of both grains. All of these cereal grains (except wild rice) are made into meals and flours of differing degrees of fineness from which diverse products are made both commercially and in the home kitchen. Rice, barley, and corn kernels are eaten as such in dishes that are often regional in origin.

Grain food products that are discussed include: flours, breakfast foods—breakfast cereals and breakfast food products; baked goods; noodles and pasta; and miscellaneous cereals.

Flours

In general, unless qualified, *flour* means wheat flour. More specifically, it means general-purpose, all-purpose, or family flour, which is produced by removal of up to 28 percent of the branny layers of the wheat kernel in the milling process. Flours are milled from hard and soft wheats that differ in protein content; hence, flours differ in the degrees to which they develop gluten. All-purpose flour is blended from soft and hard wheats so as to be suitable for making yeast breads that require gluten development and also for making cakes and pastries that do not. All-purpose flour may be bleached or unbleached. Bleaching results in a snowy-white flour, whereas unbleached flour is creamy white. Bleaching is effected by chemicals, the kinds and amounts of which are regulated by the Food and Drug Administration. Bleached flour must always be labeled as such. *Cake flour* is a low-protein flour prepared from soft wheats. Although cake flour is preferred for cake baking, all-purpose flour can be used when a proper measuring adjustment is made. *Bread flour* is milled from hard, high-protein wheats. It is used in commercial bread making; it is also available to the consumer. *Enriched flour* is flour to which thiamin, riboflavin, niacin, and iron have been added according to defined standards to replace some of the nutrients lost during milling. The addition of calcium is optional. *Self-rising* flour is all-purpose flour to which leavening agents—soda and one or more acid ingredients—are added in the proper proportion for home baking of quick breads and cakes; it is not recommended for yeast breads. *Instant flour* is flour that has been so treated that it blends readily with liquids. It is used for gravies and sauces rather than for baking. It is more expensive than all-purpose flour. *Whole wheat* or *Graham flour* is milled so as to contain all of the constituents of the wheat kernel. It has poor gluten-forming properties, and is, generally, combined with some white flour in order to produce a light loaf. *Gluten flour* is wheat flour milled so as to have a high gluten content. It is used in commercial baked goods, flours, and cereals. *Pastry flour* is milled from soft wheats and is used in the making of pastries and specialty items. Other flours used in bread making include rye flour, corn flour and cornmeal, soy flour and soy grits, buckwheat flour, and peanut flour. The addition of soy products to wheat breads retards staling and produces products that are tender and moist. *Rye flours* are light, medium, and dark in color. Rye is a poor gluten former; rye breads usually contain some wheat flour.

Baked Goods

Baked goods include breads and rolls and such similar products as waffles, pancakes, baking powder biscuits, bagels, crackers, and snack confections, as well as sweet goods, such as sweet rolls, coffee cakes, cakes, pies, cookies, doughnuts, and fruit breads. All of these products are available in an almost endless variety. Some products are fresh baked, others are prebaked and frozen, and some are premade and baked by the canning process. Further, many items are available in varying degrees of preparation from dry mix to ready-to-bake. The returns for one dollar spent depend on the selections made: a loaf of supermarket store bread at 45 cents for a 20-ounce loaf versus a one-pound loaf of California sour dough for 99 cents; Chocolate Cremes at 99 cents per pound versus Chocolate Yum Yums at $1.65 for 5½ ounces; or bakery chocolate cake at $2.99 versus German Chocolate Cake at $4.98 for the same quantity of cake. Not only must the meal manager decide what to buy but also whether or not to buy, that is, consider home production as an alternative.

Bread and Rolls. Definitions and standards of identity for white breads, rolls, and buns; enriched bread, rolls and buns; milk bread, rolls, and buns; raisin bread, rolls, and buns have been promulgated. The definitions require that all ingredients from which the bread products are fabricated be safe and suitable and that all ingredients be declared on labels. Optional ingredients for *white bread* products include these: wheat flour, nonwheat flours and grits, wheat and nonwheat starches, nutritive sweeteners, water, yeast, shortening, egg products, and various ingredients and additives peculiar to the commercial production of bread products. It is required that finished products contain not less than 62 percent of total solids. The standards for enriched bread products, milk bread products, raisin bread products, and whole wheat bread products are similar to those for white bread with certain exceptions. *Enriched bread* products must be enriched according to currently defined standards with thiamin, riboflavin, niacin, and iron; further enrichment with calcium is permitted. It has been proposed by the Food and Nutrition Board of the National Academy of Sciences/National Research Council that bread be further enriched with magnesium, zinc, vitamin A, folic acid, and B_6. As of mid-1982 very little bread was so enriched. The labels of the enriched products must bear statement of the percentages of the U.S. RDA for the added nutrients that can be obtained from a defined quantity of the product, usually one serving of the bread product. Much commercial white bread is enriched. *Milk bread* contains not less than 8.2 parts of milk solids per 100 parts of flour. Milk is the only moistening ingredient permitted in this bread. *Raisin bread* products are required to contain not less than 50 parts by weight of raisins per 100 parts of flour. Raisin bread may be iced. *Whole Wheat* bread products must be made entirely of whole wheat flour. A bread product prepared from white flour plus whole wheat flour is described as *wheaten* or *wheat*.

The following are some nonstandardized breads: rye bread, pumpernickel bread, potato bread, gluten bread, and sour dough bread. Most *rye breads* are made with a light rye flour in combination with wheat flour. *Pumpernickel rye bread* is made with a dark rye flour and the dough is made sour by special fermentation with acid-producing bacteria. Mixed grain breads were introduced and widely accepted during the 1970's.

The traditional *low calorie, "slenderizing,"* and *diet breads* differ little in calorie content from other breads. The omission of shortening and sugar from a formula alters calorie content little because the quantities of these ingredients in the formula are small. Slices of bread may vary in calorie content because of differences in thickness, weight, size, or in the texture of the bread. Weight for weight, breads are similar in calorie content.

Breads vary in nutrient content as they vary in ingredient composition. The percentage of nonfat dry milk varies in bread formulas from 4 to more than 10 percent. Milk adds calcium and protein and improves the quality of the wheat proteins. Eggs, wheat germ, sprouted grain seeds, whole grain flours, and soy flour or grits all add nutrients when they are ingredients. The levels of enrichment of enriched flours, breads and rolls, and farina give these products a nutrient content that is superior to whole grain products in the nutrients of enrichment: thiamin, riboflavin, niacin, and iron. The about 70 percent extraction of wheat in the production of white flour reduces the content of the B-vitamins pyridoxine, folic acid, and pantothenic acid, vitamin E, and the trace minerals zinc, selenium, and manganese. Whole grain products are usually superior to enriched products in these nutrients, however, fiber and phytates present in whole grain products may reduce the availability of some nutrients.

Consumers Union has reported a study of the nutritive qualities and tastiness of 39 commercial breads. (1) To measure the relative nutritional qualities of the breads, they were fed to weanling rats. There were differences in the degree to which different breads supported growth in the weanling rats. In general, the white breads were superior in nutritional quality to the whole grain and rye breads. The authors offer two explanations for this superiority of the white breads. First, because white breads often contain milk, eggs, whey, or soy flour, the quality of the wheat proteins is enhanced. Whole wheat breads contain these ingredients less often; rye breads, not at all. Secondly, the presence of fiber and phytates may reduce the availability of some nutrients in whole grain breads. The authors are careful to point out that for persons who eat a varied diet, the kinds of bread consumed may be relatively unimportant nutritionally. They further suggest that the meal manager read ingredient listings of the labels of the breads purchased so as to determine the extent to which the breads contain milk, eggs, or soy flour.

As to the tastiness of the 39 commercial breads, to no one's surprise no commercial loaf had the good flavor of home baked bread, although some breads fared well when judged for tastiness: three white breads, two whole wheat breads, a rye bread, and a branola white loaf.

Bread making is a folk art. It is sad that mom's bread like mom's apple pie has been displaced by the products of science and technology. The kinds of flour and the kinds and quantities of ingredients are important in determining both nutritional quality and tastiness in breads. Wrapping bread to keep it sanitary results in a soft crust. There is today (1982) a resurgence of interest in making bread at home—so much so that bread flour is widely available in supermarkets. Some interesting books about breads and bread making are listed at the end of this chapter.

A wide variety of dinner rolls and buns can be purchased in several stages of preparation: mix, ready-to-bake, partially baked brown and serve, ready-baked and frozen, and fresh ready-baked; the same is true for English muffins, waffles, pancakes, baking powder biscuits, and muffins. In general, cost increases with the amount of included service and perishability; a serving or like weight of these products usually costs more than a like weight of bread. National brands cost more than store brands. Table 15–1 shows the relative costs for selected breads, rolls, and similar products.

Crackers and snack confections are available in abundant variety, and a super shopper has to pick and choose from among them. For example, it is possible to purchase saltines for approximately 99 cents per pound, it is also possible to spend 99 cents for 4½ ounces of a special, unsalted cracker.

A convenience bread product that bears examination is the stuffing mix. The contents of the package of one such product was six ounces of dry bread crumbs (crusts included) and one package of seasonings. Ingredients were as follows: "bromated and enriched flour; sugar; dried onion; salt; hydrogenated cottonseed, soybean, and palm kernel oils; hydrolyzed vegetable protein (for flavor); dried celery with sulfur dioxide added as preservative; yeast; defatted soy flour; modified wheat starch; spices; caramel color; whey (from milk); dried parsley; chicken fat; calcium proprionate (preservative); onion powder; natural flavor; turmeric; dehydrated chicken meat; monosodium glutamate (flavor enhancer); artificial flavor; citric acid, BHA, TBHQ, and propyl gallate (preservatives)." To this mix one had to add one-fourth cup of butter or margarine and an amount of water to produce the desired consistency of the finished stuffing. The cost of the product, exclusive of the butter or margarine, would have purchased two 20-ounce loaves of supermarket brand bread (1982). The solids content of bread being not less than 62 percent, the two loaves of bread would provide some 25

TABLE 15–1.   *Per-Pound Cost[1] of Selected Breads, Rolls, and Other Similar Products*

Selected Items	Cost and Market Unit	Cost per Pound
Bread, white enriched, store brand	$ .42/20 oz.	$ .34
Bread, white enriched, Brand A	.85/lb.	.85
Bread, white enriched, Brand B	.89/lb.	.89
Bread, Sourdough (frozen)	1.39/16 oz.	1.39
Bread, French Style	.89/lb.	.89
Bread, Greek Style	.85/lb.	.85
Bread, Hawaiian	1.59/lb.	1.59
Bread, Italian Style	.89/lb.	.89
Bread, Pita	1.39/20 oz. (12)	1.11
Bread, whole wheat, Brand A	.99/lb.	.99
Bread, whole wheat, Brand B	.91/lb.	.91
Bread, rye, Brand A	1.19/lb.	1.19
Bread, rye, Brand B	.99/lb.	.99
Bread, rye, Pumpernickel	.99/lb.	.99
Bread, raisin	1.69/lb.	1.69
Rolls, Brown and Serve	.94/12 oz. (12)	1.25
Rolls, ready-to-eat, Brand A	1.13/6½ oz. (6)	2.88
Rolls, ready-to-eat, Brand B	.92/10 oz. (24)	1.47
Rolls, ready-to-eat, in-store bakery	1.49/20 oz. (24)	1.00
Muffins, English, Brand A	.95/12 oz. (6)	1.27
Muffins, English, Brand B	.84/12 oz. (6)	1.12
Muffins, Blueberry, heat and serve	1.49/11½ oz. (6)	2.08
Muffins, Blueberry, in-store bakery	1.47/10 oz. (6)	2.35
Muffins, Bran, in-store bakery	1.17/10 oz. (6)	1.87
Biscuits, Baking Powder	.86/9½ oz. (12)	1.47
Biscuits, Buttermilk	.83/12 oz. (12)	1.12
Bagels	.59/12 oz. (6)	.80
Hamburger, Buns, store brand	.47/11 oz. (8)	.68
Hamburger Buns, Brand A	.91/13 oz. (8)	1.12
Hamburger Buns, Brand B	.93/10 oz. (8)	1.44
Waffles, ready-made	.93/10 oz. (8)	1.49

[1]June, 1982 costs.

ounces of dry bread crumbs. Various meal managers evaluate the product differently.

Sweet Goods.   Sweet goods include sweet rolls, coffee cakes, cakes, sweet breads, muffins, doughnuts, pies, cookies, and so on. As was true for breads, all of these goods can be bought with differing levels of added service with cost varying accordingly. Mixes for cakes are available in superdeluxe, deluxe, plain, and thrifty varieties and in bewildering assortments of kinds and flavors. Some are mixes to which the cook adds water, oil or butter or margarine, eggs, or other ingredients; some include filling and glaze. Available ready-to-spread frostings add to the ease of cake production. Further, mixes can be purchased for making cookies and brownies. Ready-to-bake cookie doughs make cookie making simpler still. In the same vein, rolled and panned pie shells, canned pie fillings, pie filling mixes, and ready-to-bake pies from the supermarket freezer compartment make home pie production "as easy as pie." Needless to say, some of the quick and easy alternatives to home production give better eating than others. Obviously, the easiest and quickest route to sweet goods is the purchase of them ready for eating. Any and all can be bought at different levels of cost in almost any supermarket. There will be an infinite variety of ready-to-munch cookies made by the cracker and cookie industries, also by national and local bakers, and by in-store bakeries. Cakes, pies, sweet rolls, coffee cakes, and many other baked goods are produced by national and local bakers and in-store bakeries; some will be fresh and some will be found in the freezer compartment. There is wide variation in cost. See Table 15–2. The meal manager fits purchases to budget. Time permitting, she may decide to prepare sweet goods from a mix or even from basic ingredients. Surveys show that as income increases, more of the at-home food dollar is spent for sweet goods (2).

Alimentary Pastes or Pasta

The *alimentary pastes,* or *pasta,* are dry wheat-dough products that require cooking; familiar ones are spaghetti and macaroni. Except for noddles, which contain egg, all the various forms and shapes are made from the same basic dough, have the same texture, are similarly bland in flavor, and could be used interchangeably were it not that certain dishes traditionally require the use of certain shapes—lasagna, for example, requires the broad noodle, crinkled on the edges. There are four classes of shapes: cord-shaped like some spaghetti, vermicelli, twists, and fusilli; tube-shaped like macaroni, some spaghetti, ziti, and manicotti; ribbon-shaped like noodles; and the odd-shaped kinds like shells, bows, rote (wheel-shaped), and many others.

Definitions and standards of identity have been promulgated for a long list of products in this class including the enriched products. Macaroni products are prepared by the drying of formed units of dough made from semolina, durum flour, farina, flour, or any combination of two or more of these with water, and with or without one or more of the permitted optional ingredients. Noodle products are prepared from

TABLE 15–2. *Estimated Per-Serving Cost* [1] *of Selected Sweet Goods*

Selected Items	Cost of Market Unit	Estimated Per-Serving Cost
Breakfast sweet rolls, thaw and eat	$1.89/6 [2]	$.32
Breakfast sweet rolls, in-store bakery	1.39/6	.23
Breakfast cinnamon rolls, deli	.25/1	.25
Coffee cake, bakery	1.99/8	.25
Coffee cake, Brand A	2.39/8	.30
Coffee cake, Brand B	1.89/6	.32
Chocolate whipped cream cake	3.29/8	.41
Coconut cake, thaw and eat	1.69/8	.21
Chocolate cake, ready baked	2.29/9	.25
Black Forest cake, thaw and eat	2.99/8	.37
Pound cake, Brand A	1.69/8	.21
Pound cake, Brand B	2.49/8	.31
Cream-filled cup cakes, frozen (6)	1.89/6	.32
German chocolate cake	4.98/9	.55
Carrot cake	1.92/8	.24
Doughnuts, Brand A	1.96/12	.12
Doughnuts, Brand B	.79/6	.13
Boston cream pie, thaw and serve	1.89/8	.24
Chocolate eclair	.50/1	.50
Pie, apple, bake and serve	1.79/4	.45
Pie, blueberry, ready-baked	1.99/4	.50
Pie, cherry, bake and serve	2.39/4	.33
Pie, peach, bake and serve	1.93/6	.32
Pie, pecan, thaw and serve	2.69/8	.37
Chocolate chip cookies, in-store bakery	1.79/12 oz.	.15/oz.
Chocolate chip cookies, national brand	1.99/15 oz.	.13/oz.
Chocolate chip cookies, bakery	1.89/12 oz.	.16/oz.
Chocolate chip cookies, Danish import	4.59/1 lb.	.27/oz.

[1] June, 1982 prices in conventional supermarket.
[2] Estimated number of servings of market units.

the same flours and any of several forms of egg (that is, fresh, frozen, or dried), with or without water, and with or without certain optional ingredients. The identity standards, in addition to prescribing ingredient composition, establish the solids content and the level of enrichment for fortified products, and require label statement of the use of certain optional ingredients. The optional ingredient disodium phosphate, which is added to hasten cooking, must be named on the label. The best pasta products are made from semolina or durum flour; they hold their shape well during cooking and retain the firmness characteristic of pasta. The products are packaged in packages of assorted sizes; per unit of weight, the cost of the product should decrease with increase in package size.

Many convenience foods contain some type of pasta. There are such quick-and-easy canned dishes as spaghetti with meatballs, spaghetti or macaroni with meat sauce, and macaroni with cheese. Similar products in a great variety are available precooked and frozen. Prepackaged easy-to-make dishes contain the pasta and a sauce or other ingredients. And, finally, the "helpers" are these familiar economical convenience products that contain spaghetti, macaroni, noodles, or sometimes rice. As of the early 1980's, pasta cost about 75 cents per pound; the "helpers," about $1.00 for a package weighing 8 ounces. In addition to the pasta or rice, the packages contain some sort of seasoning or sauce mix. The tuna, or another basic ingredient must be added at additional cost to that of the "helper." One-half pound of any of the pasta provides four generous servings of the dishes in which they are ingredients.

Cereal Breakfast Foods

Breakfast cereals and breakfast food products are available in variety in the 1980's. They have replaced, more or less, the old-time bacon or ham, eggs, and fried potato breakfast. All family members are able to prepare their own breakfasts of juice and cereal in the 1980's, some or all of the days of the week. Supermarkets devote many feet of shelving to the display of breakfast foods.

Breakfast Cereals.   Breakfast cereals are not defined or standardized except for farina, enriched farina, and enriched corn grits. However, many cereals are enriched or fortified with added nutrients; some are natural. Labeling requirements make mandatory the naming of all ingredients of which a cereal is composed and the declaration of the added quantities of vitamins and minerals as percentages of the U.S. RDA supplied by a serving (generally, one ounce). Breakfast cereals may be prepared from a single grain, such as are cornflakes, or from a mixture of grains. They often bear fanciful names. Hot cereals may be regular, quick, instant, or precooked.

Generally, ready-for-eating cereals cost more than the cook-before-eating kinds. Ready-sweetened ones cost more than the unsweetened kinds. Fruited cereals cost more than plain counterparts. Pre-measured, precooked cereals cost more than the cook-before-eating counterpart such as oatmeal. Per unit of weight, the cereal in a large box costs less than the cereal in a smaller box or variety pack. The per-pound costs of selected cereals are presented in Table 15–3. In general, an ounce of cereal provides an average serving.

TABLE 15–3. *Per-Pound Cost of Selected Breakfast Cereals*[1]

Selected Items	Cost and Market Unit	Cost per Pound
Corn Products		
Corn Flakes	$ .88/10 oz.	$1.41
Sugar Frosted Corn Flakes	1.93/20 oz.	1.54
Corn Pops	1.82/15 oz.	1.94
Corn Chex	1.32/12 oz.	1.76
Corn Puffs	1.15/9oz.	2.04
Chocolate Flavored Corn Puffs	1.69/12 oz.	1.35
Corn Total	1.67/10 oz.	2.67
Oat Products		
Cheerios	1.23/10 oz.	1.97
Granola	1.69/16 oz.	1.69
Life	1.83/20 oz.	1.46
Mixed Gain Products		
Buc Wheats	1.97/17 oz.	1.85
Product 19	1.58/12 oz.	2.11
Special K	1.93/12 oz.	2.57
Team	1.24/13 oz.	1.53
Raisin Rice and Rye	1.49/13 oz.	1.83
Wheat Products		
Grape-Nut Flakes	1.19/12 oz.	1.59
Shredded Wheat	.93/10 oz.	1.49
Frosted Mini Wheats	1.59/16 oz.	1.59
Wheaties	1.19/12 oz.	1.59
Puffed Wheat	.79/4 oz.	3.16
Total Wheat	1.65/12 oz.	2.20
Cook-before-eating Cereals		
Cream of Rice	1.05/16 oz.	1.05
Cream of Wheat	.83/14 oz.	.95
Oatmeal	.97/18 oz.	.86
Mix'n'Eat Cream of Wheat (10) servings	1.25/10 oz.	2.00
Instant oatmeal (8) servings	1.25/12 oz.	1.67

[1]June, 1982 prices in conventional supermarket.

In 1981, Consumers Union reported on the relative nutritional qualities of 57 different cereals (3). Nutritional quality was determined in growth studies with rats. Among the cereals ranking high in nutritive value were the old-time favorites: *Grape-Nuts* and *Shredded Wheat*. In the studies, no milk was fed with the cereals. For this reason, nutritive quality as reported cannot be presumed to be the same for humans who would consume milk with the cereal. This study has been widely criticized. Current concern about breakfast cereals is less with their nutritional value than with their sugar and salt contents.

Granolas are mixtures of grains, seeds, dried fruits, nuts, and honey. The grains may be assorted cereal flakes, oats, wheat germ, or soy flakes. The seeds may be sesame, sunflower, squash, or pumpkin seeds. The fruits include raisins, currants, dates, dried apricots, as well as others. As would be anticipated, they are more expensive than plainer cereals. Some persons prepare their own granolas. Vegetarians favor them. Granolas are higher in fat content than other breakfast cereals. Therefore, they are also higher in calories. If coconut is used in their preparation, they are high in saturated fat in comparison to other breakfast cereals.

Breakfast Food Products. *Toaster pastries* are relatively new breakfast food products. They are available in assorted fruit flavors as well as others such as chocolate fudge. Similar breakfast food products include breakfast bars, breakfast clusters, granola bars, and so on. These are for eating breakfast on the run. They are available in assorted flavors also. Ingredients include sugar, fats, and flours; oatmeal is a common constituent. An *instant breakfast milk-drink* is also available. See Table 15–4 for the comparative costs of these products. These products were developed to save meal managers time and energy and insure the eating of breakfast by family members. Time permitting, ready-to-heat-

TABLE 15–4.   *Unit Cost*[1] *of Some Ready-to-eat Breakfast Products*[2]

Items	Cost and Market Unit	Unit Cost
Breakfast Bars (6)	$1.57/8 oz.	$.26
Granola Bars (12)	1.45/10 oz.	.12
Granola Clusters (6)	1.53/7½ oz.	.26
Pop Tarts (6)	.84/11 oz.	.14
Toast'ems (6)	.64/10½ oz.	.11
Tostettes (4)	.69/6½ oz.	.17
Instant Breakfast Brand A (milk mix) (10)	2.59	.26
Instant Breakfast Brand B (milk mix) (10)	2.85	.29
Pancakes with Blueberry Sauce, frozen, single serving	.75	.75
Scrambled Eggs with Sausage and Hash Browns, single serving	.99	.99
French Toast and Sausage, single serving	.99	.99

[1] June, 1982 prices in conventional supermarket.

[2] Per-serving cost would vary with individuals because of different calorie needs.

and-eat waffles and pancakes plus a wide assortment of sweet goods can make for tasty breakfasts.

Miscellaneous Cereals

Rice, barley, buckwheat, and bulgur are cereals in this miscellaneous cereal group. Rice is more commonly used than the others. Rice is white, that is, polished or highly milled, and brown or unpolished. The latter retains some bran and the germ of the kernel; it has a higher nutritive value than polished rice (it is also more subject to spoilage). Both white and brown rice may be purchased in regular form and as instant products. Enriched rice is polished rice that has added nutrients. It should not be rinsed before or after cooking. *Parboiled* rice has been steeped in hot water, drained, steamed, and dried before milling. Parboiling or steeping effects the transfer of nutrients from the bran coat to the rice kernel; such rice has more nutrient value than polished rice. Further, because the rice grains are hardened by processing, they do not stick together during cooking. *Converted* rice is parboiled rice. Instant or *minute* rice has been precooked and dehydrated. Cooking time is reduced to as little as two to fifteen minutes. *Wild rice* is not rice, but the brown seed of a grass that grows in marshes, rivers, and shallow lakes in northern Minnesota, Michigan, Wisconsin, and Canada. It is also cultivated in paddies. It is a scarce commodity and is expensive. It can be purchased mixed with white rice.

Rice kernels are typed as long grain, medium grain, and short grain. The kernels of long-grain rice are thin; those of short-grain rice are plump; and of medium-grain, in between. Generally, two types of rice can be bought in supermarkets. The price per pound may differ. All types are packaged in different quantities; per unit of weight, the rice in the larger packages should cost less. Rice is packaged with different assortments of herbs and spices. Some of the assortments are characterized as accompaniments to certain dishes. They tend to be expensive products. As of mid-1982, one pound of long grain rice could be bought for 50 cents; the herbed and seasoned products cost approximately 85 cents for 5 to 7 ounces. The cost of rice is increased by being processed for quick cooking, perhaps as much as 100 percent. Quick-cooking rice in boil-in-bag packaging has been added to the quick-cook assortment of rice products. Ready-prepared-and-frozen rice dishes in French, Italian, and Spanish styles are available. June, 1982 they were priced $1.05 per 10-ounce carton of suggested three servings.

Barley, granular buckwheat, and *bulgur* are cereals used similarly to rice for the preparation of dishes that are to be served with meat or that include meat. Barley is a familiar ingredient in soups. It is used whole and cooked with seasonings and meats in the making of dishes sometimes called *pilaf* or *pilau*. *Roasted buckwheat* is ground to different degrees of fineness to form meal; it is sometimes called *kasha*. *Bulgur* is whole wheat that has been precooked, dried, and ground to different degrees of fineness. Both buckwheat and bulgur are also cooked with seasonings to prepare pilaf. Vegetarians and persons who espouse health foods have adopted these dishes, which are traditional in the Middle East.

LEGUMES

Dry beans and *peas*, "legumes," of assorted varieties are highly nutritious foods that are rich in protein and calories as well as being good carriers of the B-vitamins and iron. Although these foods are more expensive than they formerly were, they remain low-cost foods. They have long been known as "poor man's meat." They are used abundantly by vegetarians.

Updated methods of soaking dry beans and peas along with the use of the slow cooker and of the pressure cooker expedite the cooking process of dry beans. The updated methods are the one-hour hot soak and the overnight salt soak. For the one-hour soak, add six to eight cups of hot water per pound of beans, bring to a boil and let boil for two minutes, and set aside for an hour or more. The beans are then ready for cooking. For the overnight soak, add two teaspoons of salt and six cups of water per pound of dry beans. Let stand over night, drain, and cook. The latter method is preferred by specialists at the United States Department of Agriculture because the beans absorb the water more evenly, keep their shape better, and cook more evenly than hot-soaked beans. The use of the microwave oven in the cooking of dry beans shortens cooking time; it is possible, however, that the old fashioned baked bean flavor does not develop during the shorter cooking time.

There are numerous varieties of dry beans; some of the commonly known are the small pea or Navy bean, the baby lima, the large lima sometimes called the butter bean, light and dark red kidney beans, pinto bean, garbanzo bean or chick pea, Great Northern white bean, blackeye bean, and calico or speckled bean to name but few. Different varieties of beans are used traditionally in some dishes; there are regional differences in variety preferences for traditional dishes.

There are fewer kinds of dry peas. Dry peas are available as whole green and yellow peas and as split green and yellow peas. The green dry pea has a more distinct flavor than the yellow dry pea and is the one preferred in the United States.

Lentils are disk-shaped and of about the same size as peas. Lentils have been used in cookery for thousands of years. They have a distinct and unique flavor, and unlike most dry beans, they cook quickly. Lentils are used in soups, salads, and casserole-type dishes.

The *soybean* serves in the immature stage as a green vegetable, as does the black-eye bean. It can be used in the dry form like other dry beans and peas in a variety of dishes. The dry soy bean is treated commercially in numerous ways to produce oil; flour and grits; soy milk; soy bean sprouts; soy sauce; soy nuts; soy protein concentrate, the textured protein utilized in making simulated meats and as a meat extender; and tofu, miso, and tempeh—three Oriental foods that are relative newcomers to Americans in the United States. *Tofu* is the curd prepared from soybean milk. It has long been and remains much used in Oriental diets. Because of its bland flavor, it can be mixed with other ingredients and, hence, used in a variety of dishes including soups and salads. It is available in supermarkets where it is often displayed on the vegetable counter near the Chinese vegetables. Because of its high protein content it is abundantly used by vegetarians. *Miso* is a fermented paste of cooked soybeans and cooked rice or barley. It is not as well known nor as widely distributed as tofu. Again, vegetarians use it; it adds a distinctive flavor to dishes and soups. *Tempeh* is a fermented bean cake that can be eaten as is or cooked in various ways. Ethnic groups from Japan, Korea, and Southeast Asia have contributed to our knowledge of these foods.

Canned bean dishes, such as pork and beans, beans in tomato sauce, and chili are old-time convenience foods. Several varieties of beans canned without seasonings can also be found in the supermarket. These are ready for use in salads and casseroles because they are precooked.

NUTS AND NUT FOOD PRODUCTS

Nuts are the dry fruits or seeds of plants that consist of a kernel that is usually enclosed within a shell. Peanuts and peanut products are the nut most abundantly consumed in the United States. Nuts are rich in protein as well as fat; hence, they become rancid unless they are properly packaged and stored. Wherever nuts are abundantly produced, they are also abundantly used in regional cookery; for example, pine nuts in Mediterranean cookery and in the cookery of the American Southwest, and pecans and peanuts in the southeastern states. At one time, hickory nuts, butternuts, black walnuts, and hazelnuts were not the luxuries that they are today but were widely used in American kitchens. Today, we use these nuts stingily in cakes, pastries, and breads but eat them abundantly as snacks. Some nuts, such as macadamia and pistachio nuts, almonds, some English walnuts, filberts, and cashews, are imported. Domestic products include pecans, peanuts, and some English walnuts, almonds, and pistachios.

Nuts, except for the peanut and pistachio, are usually available in the shell only at holiday time; in general, they are purchased shelled. For culinary purposes, nuts are unseasoned, and though they can be purchased whole, they are more often broken or fragmented in different ways, even to the fineness of meal. Bits and pieces are less expensive than whole nuts.

Identity standards have been promulgated for peanut butter and mixed nuts. Fill of container has been established for shelled nuts in rigid or semirigid containers. Mixed nuts are defined as a mixture of four or more kinds of tree nuts with or without the inclusion of peanuts. Mixtures contain not less than 2 percent and not more than 80 percent of any one nut ingredient. Whenever a mixture contains more than 50 percent but less than 60 percent of a single tree nut or of peanuts, the name "mixed nuts" must be followed by the qualifying statement "contains up to 60 percent . . ." in which the single component is named. The same applies whenever a mixture contains up to 70 or 80 percent of a single nut component. Permitted nut ingredients include, in addition to the peanut, almonds, black walnuts, Brazil nuts, cashews, English walnuts, filberts, pecans, and other suitable tree nuts. Optional ingredients permitted include the use of an antioxidant to inhibit rancidity development. The fill of container is defined for shelled nuts in rigid and semirigid containers as 85 percent of the volume of the container as this is determined by defined procedures.

The identity standard requires that peanut butter contain not less than 90 percent by weight of peanuts; the other 10 percent may consist of flavoring and stabilizing ingredients. However, artificial flavorings, artificial sweeteners, chemical preservatives, added vitamins, and color additives are not considered suitable ingredients. Fat cannot exceed 50 percent. Some consumers favor a peanut butter that is 100 percent ground peanuts; without the stabilizing agent permitted in commercial peanut butters, the oil tends to separate out. In general, the larger the container purchased the cheaper will be the unit cost of peanut butter. Peanuts are subject to mold development; the Food and Drug Administration has established the limit on the quantity of aflatoxin, the toxic agent produced by molds, that may be present in peanut butter as 20 parts per billion.

SUMMARY

The meal manager has many options when purchasing grain food products. By comparison shopping the meal manager can separate the luxuries from the bargains. Policy should be, "Buy and try." There are fewer options for the buyer of dry beans, peas, and nut food products.

REFERENCES CITED

1. "Bread," *Consumer Reports* **42**:438 (1982).
2. Smallwood, David and James Blaylock, "Impact of Household Size and Income on Food Spending Patterns," Technical Bulletin #1650. Economics and Statistics Service, United States Department of Agriculture, Washington, D.C. (May, 1981).
3. "Which Cereal for Breakfast?" *Consumer Reports* **46**:68 (1981).

SUGGESTED PROBLEMS

1. Update Table 11–1. Per-Pound Cost of Selected Breads, Rolls, and Other Similar Products.
2. Update Table 11–2. Estimated Per-Serving Cost of Selected Sweet Goods.
3. Update Table 11–4. Unit Cost of Some Selected Breakfast Food Products.
4. Has there been inflation or disinflation since mid-1982? Have food prices stabilized?

SUGGESTED REFERENCES

1. Barkas, Janet, *Meatless Cooking Celebrity Style*. New York: Grove Press, Inc., 1975.
2. Bayliss, Maggie and Coralie Castle, *Real Bread*. San Francisco: 101 Publications, (1980).
3. Bread, James, *Beard on Bread*. New York: Alfread A. Knopf, Inc. (1974).
4. Cassella, Dolores, *A World of Baking*. New York: David White Company, Inc. (1968).
5. Honig, Mariana, *Breads of the World*. New York: Chelsea House Publishers (1977).
6. Landon, Mel, *Bread Winners*. Emmaus, Pa.: Rodale Press (1977).
7. Roberts, Ada Lou, *Favorite Breads From Rose Lane Farm*. New York: Hearthside Press (1960).
8. Sales, Georgia MacLeod and G. Sales, *The Clay-Pot Cookbook*. New York: Atheneum Publishers, Inc. (1974).
9. Seranne, Ann, *Good Food Without Meat*. New York: William Morrow & Co., Inc. (1973).
10. *The Breads Cookbook*. Birmingham, Ala.: Oxmoor House (1972).

Chapter 16

Shopping for Food: Miscellaneous

A family's expenditures for food products that may be classified as miscellaneous may be either large or small depending on food preferences, the culinary skill of the meal manager, and the time available for meal preparation. Miscellaneous food items that are discussed are sweeteners for food, fats and oils, beverages, jams and jellies, and miscellanea.

SWEETENERS FOR FOOD

People everywhere enjoy sweet food, but households will vary greatly in the amount of sugar used for cooking. To satisfy the desire for sweets, the average household uses sugar, syrups, and artificial sweeteners for food preparation and while dining. We also consume more sugar than we probably recognize in purchased food products.

Sugars and Syrups

Sugar is sucrose extracted from sugar cane or sugar beets. *Granulated* sugar may be more or less finely granulated; no standard terminology has been established to define it. Sugar is available in packages ranging in size from one to 100 pounds. A *superfine,* finely granulated form that can be purchased in some stores is excellent for table use, in cake making, in beverages, on fruits, and in fact, whenever rapid solution is desired. It is sold in one-pound packages and, generally, costs about twice as much as granulated sugar. *Confectioners sugar,* also described as confectioners Ten-X sugar, is finely pulverized sugar that contains a small amount of cornstarch to prevent caking. It is used in making frostings and candies, and for dusting doughnuts and other pastries. Sugar is also available in *cube* form for use in beverages. The cubes may be purchased in different sizes. Per unit of weight, the cube form is more expensive than granulated sugar. An interest in *raw sugar* surfaced with the interest in natural foods. Raw sugar, which is brownish in color, has been processed from cane and retains some of the vitamins and minerals of cane. It may contain such contaminants as molds, fiber, and waxes. Raw sugar is several times more expensive than granulated and brown sugars.

Brown sugar contains varying amounts of molasses, moisture, and other components of the product from which it is made. It varies in color from yellow to brown; the molasses flavor increases as the color darkens. Brown sugar measures out slightly more than two cups per pound (two cups per pound is the approximate measure per pound of granulated sugar). Brown sugar is also available in granulated form, which measures out about three cups per pound. Directions should be carefully followed when substituting granulated brown sugar for brown sugar or granulated sugar in recipes. The proper processing of cornstarch gives rise to products much used by the food industries: corn sugar or dextrose, maltose, and dextrins, all of which are less sweet than sucrose.

Sweeteners other than sugar that are used in or on food include corn syrups, cane syrups, molasses, maple syrup, sorghum syrup, honey, table syrups or pancake and waffle syrups, and a variety of sweet sauces for serving on ice cream. *Molasses syrups* used in cooking range from light to dark in color and mild to strong in flavor. Molasses syrup for the table is light in color and mild in flavor. Corn syrups are light to dark in color, and are used both in cookery and for the table. They are less sweet than cane syrups and also less expensive. In 1975, identity standards became effective for table syrups, maple syrup, cane syrup, and sorghum syrup. *Sorghum syrup* derived from sorghum cane has a special flavor that is highly prized in some regions within the Midwest and the South. *Maple syrup,* the most expensive of the syrups, must contain not less than 66 percent of the soluble solids of the maple sap. When maple syrup is combined with another syrup in preparing a table syrup, the quantity present must be not less than 10 percent by weight of the finished food. Whenever it is represented as the characterizing flavor in a syrup, the percentage must be declared on the label. *Table syrups,* variously called pancake and waffle syrup, must contain not less than 65 percent of soluble sweetener solids by weight. Permitted sweeteners are carbohydrate sweeteners. Some other ingredients permitted in table syrups are butter, edible fats and oils, natural and artificial flavorings either fruit or nonfruit, color additives, and chemical preservatives as well as other additives that establish certain physical properties of a syrup. Fruit syrups, which include blackberry, blueberry, raspberry, and strawberry, are often used on ice cream and puddings as well as on pancakes and waffles. They seem to taste less sweet than sugar syrups, and are also more expensive than table syrups. The available variety of table syrups priced over a wide range in cost suggests the wisdom of reading labels. Certainly any syrup with a first listing of corn syrup should cost less than one with a first listing of maple syrup.

Honey is available as comb honey, as extracted-from-the-comb honey and in a finely crystallized form called honey spread. The water content of honey is about 20 percent. Comb honey is available in only limited quantity, is expensive, and is highly prized. The color and flavor of honey depend on the flower source. Clover honey is mild in flavor, whereas buckwheat honey is strong. Interest in natural foods has led to a greater consumption of honey than in the past.

Nutritive sweeteners other than sugar include the hexitols (sugar alcohols), sorbitol and mannitol. Sorbitol has been approved for use and mannitol is in use on a provisional basis. Regulations require that beverages containing any hexitol bear a label statement as follows: "contains carbohydrates, not for use by diabetics."

No-Calorie and Low-Calorie Sweeteners

Saccharin is a popular nonnutritive sweetener. It is 300 times sweeter than sugar. In February of 1972, the Food and Drug Administration removed it from the list of substances generally considered safe. Until there was definitive proof that it was not safe, its use was permitted according to the following regulations:

1. In amounts not to exceed twelve milligrams, calculated as saccharin, per fluid ounce in beverages, fruit juice drinks, and bases or mixes for beverages when prepared in accordance with directions.

2. As a sugar substitute for cooking or table use in amounts not to exceed twenty milligrams, calculated as saccharin for each expressed teaspoonful of sugar equivalency.

3. In processed foods in amount not to exceed thirty milligrams, calculated as saccharin per serving of a designated size. Regulations required that there be label statement of the amount of the additive in milligrams per fluid ounce for beverages and for processed foods in terms of weight or size of serving.

In April of 1977, the Food and Drug Administration proposed revocation of the regulations under which saccharin and its salts were permitted in food products, because it had been definitively established that saccharin was carcinogenic in experimental animals. At the same time, the Food and Drug Administration proposed that single-ingredient tabletop sweeteners which had been regulated as foods now be considered as drugs, depending on the claims made for them. It was further proposed that the standards for artificially sweetened foods be amended to prohibit the use of saccharin as an ingredient.

Public outcry against the banning of saccharin was so great that congress passed and President Carter signed into law the Saccharin Study and Labeling Act on November 23, 1977. The act put an 18-month moratorium on regulatory action by the FDA to remove saccharin from the market but it required all foods containing saccharin to be labeled with the warning: "Use of this product may be hazardous to your health. This product contains saccharin which has been determined to cause cancer in laboratory animals." The moratorium was extended for a two-year period in 1979 and once again on June 30, 1981, another two-year extension was passed. Research continues on the safety of saccharin.

It may be easier for the public to accept a ban on saccharin, except for limited use, now that another sweetener, *aspartame* has been deemed safe for use in foods. FDA Commissioner Arthur Hayes disagreed with the recommendations of FDA's Public Board of Inquiry that further testing was necessary and declared on July 15, 1981 that aspartame could be used as a tabletop sweetener and in numerous products excluding soft drinks. The sweetener was discovered by accident; its taste could not have been predicted from its constituents. It is composed of bitter-tasting phenylalanine and flat-tasting aspartic acid; however, when the two are combined, a sucrose-type sweet product results which blends well with other foods and does not possess the bitter aftertaste of saccharin. Although aspartame contains the same number of calories on a weight basis as sugar, it is almost 200 times sweeter than sugar so smaller amounts are used.

BEVERAGES

Coffee

Coffee consumption on the green bean basis was about 8 pounds per capita in 1980; little more than one cup per person per day. The decrease in coffee consumption is the result of declining consumption by teenagers and young adults, high extraction rates in the production of instant coffees, and the high retail cost of coffee. The high cost of coffee beans at wholesale has resulted in a subtle and gradual decline in the overall quality of blends in an attempt to keep the retail cost down.

Coffee beans are derived from the fruits of an evergreen tree of the genus *Coffea* of which there are two main species: *Coffea arabica,* a native of Ethiopia and *Coffea robusta,* a native of the Congo. There are numerous varieties within each species. In general, the coffees produced in South and Central America are of the arabica varieties although both species may be grown on both continents. Trees of the *arabica* species flourish at altitudes above 2000 feet; they produce beans which when properly processed result in beverages of fine quality and flavor. The *robusta* trees grow at lower altitudes; they produce beans abundantly but the coffees they produce are not of as good flavor as those of the arabica trees. *Robusta* varieties are those used in the production of instant coffees and in low-cost brands of coffee.

Each fruit, or coffee berry, contains two seeds, or beans, covered by a parchmentlike membrane. These are embedded within the pulp of the fruit. The first step in processing the coffee berry for market is the removal of the pulp; the beans then undergo a fermentation process that is essential for flavor development. Following fermentation, the beans are cured; lastly, the covering membrane is removed. The beans are green at this stage, when they are shipped from the producing area. The green beans differ in flavor potential, and different brands of coffee differ in the basic blends of beans. The green beans must be roasted for the development of flavor and aroma. During roasting, *caffeol,* a mixture of essential oils, develops from the fat in the bean. These oils are volatile, explaining the aroma of coffee; they are also soluble in water, explaining the flavor of coffee. Further, other flavor components develop and the bean changes in color from green to different shades of brown, depending on the length of the roasting period. Roasting may be light, medium, dark, or almost black. The time required for the right amount of roasting differs with different varieties of coffee beans. For this reason, blends for the best coffees are not compounded until after roasting; however, most processors blend before roasting. After roasting, the beans are generally ground and the product is vacuum-packed in cans or in bags. Once the vacuum-packed ground coffee is opened, the coffee is perishable and should be kept in a cool place. Unground beans are available in specialty markets and some supermarkets. Some persons prefer to grind their own coffee beans for a more flavorful brew; some even choose their own blends.

Beans are ground to different degrees of fineness for the different methods of brewing coffee: a coarse, or regular, grind for percolated coffee; fine, for drip coffee; and very fine for espresso coffee. The finer the grind, the more readily are the solubles—the flavor components, the caffeine, and the tannins—removed from the coffee. Caffeine is the stimulating principle, and the tannins are bitter. The quality of a brewed coffee and of an instant coffee (which is also brewed coffee) is established not only by the blend of beans and the kind of roast but also by proper brewing. Proper brewing means the proper grind for the kind of coffee maker being used, the proper amount of ground coffee for the strength of brew desired, regulation of the length of time the water is in contact with the ground coffee, temperature control, and the use of clean equipment. The higher the temperature of brewing above 200° F and the longer the period of brewing, the less flavorful and more bitter is the brew. A coarse grind is indicated for methods of brewing when there is repeated or continuous contact of the water with the ground coffee as in percolation. A finer degree of grind is indicated for methods wherein there is only one-time contact between water and the ground coffee, as in the drip method of brewing. The strength of coffee is regulated by the amount of coffee used, not by long periods of extraction, which result in greater extraction of bitter substances. Tannins are increasingly soluble and the volatiles escape more readily as the temperature approaches the boiling point; that is, boiling during extraction results in a bitter and nonflavorful brew. Coffee oils accumulate in a rinsed-only coffee maker: they become rancid and contribute undesirable flavor components to the brew.

Instant coffee was not an instant success. Although it had been around since early in the century and had been served to the armed forces during two world wars, domestic consumption of the product did not reach 20 percent of the beverage consumed until the 1960's. In 1974, about 16 percent of the coffee beans roasted in the United States were processed to prepare instant coffee. As practiced, this processing results in about twice the volume of the beverage that is produced in the home brewing of ground beans. Instant coffees are the dehydrated beverage, and the different instants are produced by different methods of brewing, and dehydrating, especially the latter. Consumers Union (1,2) has reported the results of two coffee tastings. In each tasting, instants were compared with brewed coffee in graduated strengths from weak to strong. In the first tasting, a freeze-dried product was preferred at the medium strength; at the strong strength, freshly brewed coffee was preferred and the freeze-dried instant was second. In the second tasting, forty-five different instant coffees (thirty-three regular and twelve freeze-dried) prepared in three strengths were compared with each other and with three freshly brewed coffees, likewise prepared in three strengths. The weaker-strength brew was preferred; all coffees were about equally well liked; and differences among the brands of instant coffee were insignificant, that is, the freeze-dried products were not found to be superior to the regular instant coffees. However, there were products that rated above average.

In a third tasting, instant products were compared. The freeze-dried products were rated more flavorful than the regular products (3). One ounce of an instant product provides from 12 to 24 cups of beverage depending on the strength desired. The beverage brewed from ground beans costs more than the beverage from the regular instant product. The size of the unit and the brand purchased also affect the cost of any of these. Ground coffees marketed in paper bags are less expensive by a few cents than the same or different brands marketed in cans, the current 1982 cost of the can being 15 cents.

Decaffeinated coffees are prepared by a special treatment of the green beans. They cost about one-third more than non-decaffeinated coffees. The instant decaffeinated products contain no more than 5 milligrams of caffeine in each 5.5 ounce of beverage made with one teaspoon of the product, in contrast to a content of 41 to 68 milligrams of caffeine in the nondecaffeinated instant beverage (3).

Coffees are marketed which contain added ingredients. Chicory is a root that is dried, roasted, and ground and added at about the 10 percent level to ground coffee to produce a brew that is especially favored in Louisiana and by many persons elsewhere. It is a bitter brew. To lower the cost of coffee, cereal may be added. Mellow Roast which is available both as a ground product and an instant contains added wheat and chicory.

Tea

There are many kinds of teas, but all come from the same shrub, *Camellia sinensis*. The main domestic supply of tea is imported from Ceylon (now Sri Lanka), India, Indonesia, Taiwan, and Japan although some tea is imported from South America and Africa. The quality of the imported teas is regulated by standards established annually by tea tasters under authority granted the Food and Drug Administration by the Tea Import Act of 1897. The upward trend in tea consumption has been marked by increased use of tea bags, instant tea, and iced-tea mixes, whereas the use of loose tea has declined. An estimated 70 percent of tea consumption is as iced-tea, for which the instant product is ideal. It can be purchased with and without sweetener and with and without lemon flavor.

Although teas may be named for their place of origin, such as Ceylon or Darjeeling, most brands of tea are blends of two or more kinds or crops of tea so as to obtain desirable balances of flavor, body, and aroma. Teas are produced from the first three leaves only of a branchlet of the tea plant. The small tip leaf is called *flowery pekoe;* the next leaf is called *orange pekoe;* and the last and largest leaf is called *pekoe.* When the leaves have been processed, the best tea from a plant will be made from the flowery pekoe leaves; the next, from orange pekoe leaves; and so on. However, when different crops are compared, the largest leaves of one crop might produce a better tea than the smallest of another. Teas are typed according to the method used to treat the leaves as *black, green,* and *oolong* teas. Almost all tea consumed in the United States, 98 percent, is black tea. If leaves are fermented and then dried, the tea is *black* tea; if the leaves are dried without fermentation, the tea is a *green* tea. *Oolong* tea is processed like black tea but with a short fermentation period and is produced only from teas grown in Taiwan or China.

The steps in the production of black teas include withering, rolling, fermenting, and drying. Withered and rolled leaves may be put through a machine that crushes, cuts, and curls them prior to fermentation and drying. Teas so treated are described as "broken teas." Breaking the tea leaves intensifies the flavor of the brew and makes a stronger and darker brew than leaf grades. Broken teas are preferred in the United States. Among the most highly prized teas are the high-quality *Darjeelings,* known as the champagne of teas, *Keemuns* known as the burgundy of teas, and the *Formosa oolongs* (4).

Teas are graded according to the size and the wholeness of leaves at the end of processing and not on any inherent palatability qualities. The latter are evaluated in cup tests by tea tasters. To establish tea grades, the finished teas are passed through sieves. Leaf grades are orange pekoe, pekoe, pekoe souchong, and souchong. Broken teas are broken orange pekoe, broken pekoe, orange fannings, and pekoe fannings. Broken orange pekoe is the most expensive tea. Available loose tea is generally a mixture of pekoe and orange pekoe. To the professional tea trader, terms like orange pekoe and souchong are simply descriptions of leaf appearance and size and have no bearing on quality or taste. Teas are perishable; shelf life for loose tea and tea bags is not more than six months.

Tea leaves contain flavor oils, tannins, and caffeine. All are extracted into the beverage during brewing, that is, the infusion of the tea leaves. A cup of brewed tea contains 50 to 60 milligrams of caffeine (theine). The amount of tannins extracted into the beverage is regulated by the temperature of brewing and the length of time the leaves are in contact with the water. The addition of milk to tea reduces astringency and bitterness. The addition of lemon to tea lightens the color of the brew. The flavors and aromas of teas are delicate when compared with those of coffees. Flowers and spices are often added to impart more and different flavor and aroma. Teas do not become stale as do coffees.

Instant teas are brewed teas that are dehydrated either by spray drying at high temperatures or by vacuum drying at low temperatures. During drying, the volatile flavor and aroma compounds are lost, however, they can be recaptured and returned to the product which would then be described as aromatized. One pound of instant tea is equivalent to three pounds of loose tea.

Mixes for iced-tea contain, in addition to the instant tea, sweeteners, lemon or other flavorings, coloring, and additives to stabilize product.

Whereas one pound of coffee yields approximately 50 cups of brew, one pound of tea yields about 200 cups, that is, about 12 cups of brewed tea per ounce of tea leaves. There are 12 tea bags per ounce of tea. In general, tea brewed with loose tea costs less than tea brewed from tea bags, and instant tea costs less than tea brewed from either loose tea or tea bags. However, these cost relationships can be altered because of differing costs of different brands of teas and of packages of different size. And instant tea, depending on brand, costs slightly less than the low-calorie, flavored iced-tea mixes.

Chocolate and Cocoa

Cocoa (cacao) beans, like coffee beans and tea, are expensive. See Figure 16–1 for recent trends in price. Chocolate promises to become the luxury it was during the first century after its discovery in Mexico by the Spaniards. Because of the high cost of genuine chocolate, some products such as candies and ice creams are *chocolate-flavored,* that is the chocolate flavor is derived from a product that has the cocoa butter of chocolate replaced by another fat.

Definitions and identity standards have been established for chocolate and cocoa products. Cocoa beans are heated and shelled, the shelled units are cocoa nibs. Chocolate is prepared by grinding the cocoa nibs. Baking or bitter chocolate may have cocoa butter and/or cocoa added to the ground nibs to adjust the fat content, which is defined as not less than 50 but not more than 58 percent. Identity standards permit the addition of different sweeteners to produce sweet chocolate products,

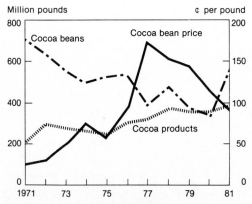

FIGURE 16–1.   U. S. cocoa imports and prices. Price is the average of nearest three active futures trading on the Coffee, Sugar, and Cocoa Exchange. (*United States Department of Agriculture, 1982.*)

and a variety of milk products to produce milk chocolate products. Further, both sweet and milk chocolate products can contain vegetable fats other than cocoa fat. White chocolate ingredients include sugar, vegetable fats including cocoa fat, whole- and skim-milk solids, lecithin, salt, artificial flavoring, and sometimes artificial color.

Cocoas differ in fat content. They are prepared by pulverizing the residue that remains after more or less cocoa fat has been removed from the ground cocoa nibs. Breakfast cocoa, medium-fat cocoa, and low-fat cocoa contain respectively not less than 22, not less than 10, and less than 10 percent of cocoa fat. Dutch process cocoa has been alkali treated, a process that alters color. Cocoa may be substituted for chocolate in recipes as follows: for each ounce of chocolate, three tablespoons of cocoa and one tablespoon of fat. Cocoa mixes are of two types: those with and those without the nonfat dry milk ingredient. Ingredients of cocoa mixes include cocoa, sugar, and various additives including flavorings. The difference in cost between the two types of cocoa mixes is not great. Similar products can differ widely in cost. Consumers who purchase these products should read labels and compare products and consider the cost of the milk that must be added to some of the mixes. All chocolate and cocoa products must bear label statements of ingredient content.

FATS AND OILS

Fats are solid at room temperatures; *oils* are liquid. Fats include butter, margarine, lard, and shortenings. Fats and oils are used in cookery. Butter and olive oil are the most expensive; corn, cottonseed, and peanut oils are comparable in cost. Recent trends have been toward an increased use of vegetable oils while the consumption of animal fats has decreased. See Figure 16–2.

Lard is 100 percent fat that is rendered from the fatty tissue of swine. It is an excellent all-purpose fat for culinary purposes and is especially good for making pastries because of its shortening power. It is good for sautéeing and for browning food. The best lard costs less than vegetable shortenings, except when the latter are specials but may cost more than shortenings compounded from vegetable and animal fats. Per capita consumption of lard has trended downward since World War II.

Shortening, as the term is generally used, refers to hydrogenated fats prepared from vegetable oils, animal fats, or combinations of the two. All fat and oil ingredients have to be identified by origin on labels, for example, beef fat or soybean oil. The oils and fats from which shortenings are made are hydrogenated to produce plastic fats of the desired degree of hardness, which are then deodorized and decolorized. Some shortenings are whipped or aerated to make them creamy and

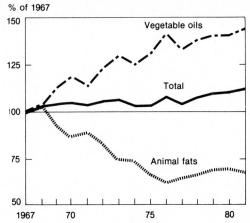

FIGURE 16–2.   Per capita consumption of fats and oils. Animal fats includes butter. (*United States Department of Agriculture, 1982.*)

to increase their plasticity and whiteness. These shortenings are the preferred choice for baked products due to their plasticity, emulsifying properties, and their ability to incorporate air. Products tend to be lighter and more uniform in texture when made from hydrogenated shortenings. Also, most cookie recipes are designed for hydrogenated shortening rather than other types of fat. Most shortenings contain added antioxidants to prolong shelf life and mono- and diglycerides are added as emulsifiers. The products are priced higher in one-pound than in larger cans, and the all-vegetable shortenings cost more than those that contain some fat from animal sources.

Oils are 100 percent fat. Food oils are pressed or extracted from corn, cottonseed, soybeans, peanuts, safflower seeds, and olives. They are then bleached and deodorized. Salad oils are further treated so that they do not crystallize during refrigeration but remain clear. Virgin olive oil is the first oil pressed from ripe black olives. A blend of olive and other soils must bear a label statement of the percentage of olive oil contained. Generally, oils smoke at higher temperatures when heated than shortenings. This makes oils more suitable than shortenings for frying.

Although there is no confirmed proof of the role of fats and cholesterol in heart disease, the medical profession recommends that some persons modify their diets by eliminating some foods and including others in order to effect changes in blood cholesterol and triglycerides. To provide truthful information and prevent misunderstandings, the Food and Drug Administration has set up guidelines for labeling the cholesterol and fat contents of some foods. Cholesterol content is stated to the nearest 5 milligram increment per serving and per hundred grams. The fat content is described in "percent of calories from fat," and by a statement of the amount of saturated and polyunsaturated fatty acids per serving. A display of the following statement on the label is mandatory: "Information on fat (and/or cholesterol, where appropriate) content is provided for individuals who, on the advice of a physician, are modifying their total dietary intake of fat (and/or cholesterol, where appropriate)."

FRUIT BUTTER, FRUIT JELLY, PRESERVES AND JAMS

Identity standards have been promulgated for fruit butters, fruit jellies, fruit preserves or jams, and artificially sweetened fruit jellies and fruit preserves and jams. Certain stipulations are true for the composition and labeling of all of these products. All may be composed from one fruit or a combination of two, three, four, or five fruits. In any combination of two or more fruit ingredients, the weight of each can be no less than one fifth of the combined weight, except that the weight of pineapple in preserves and jams may be less. A product made from a single fruit is labeled by that name. A product made from two or more fruits can be labeled "Mixed Fruit" or it can be labeled by the names of the fruits in order of predominance by weight, such as "Apple-Strawberry Jelly"; however, in the former instance, the naming of fruits in the listing of ingredients in order of predominance is mandatory so that the consumer will know from what fruits the mixed fruit jam or jelly was prepared.

Fruit butters are prepared from fruit purees prepared by the sieving of cooked fruits. The product must be composed from five parts by weight of fruit puree and two parts by weight of sugar or other sweetening agent. Concentration by heat is to no less than 43 percent soluble solids content.

Fruit jellies are made from fruit juices. The ratio of fruit juice to sugar or other sweeteners is forty-five parts to fifty-five parts by weight. Concentration with or without heat is to a soluble solids content of not less than 65 percent. *Fruit preserves* and *jams* are composed from forty-five to forty-seven parts (depending on the kind of fruits) by weight of fruit to fifty-five parts by weight of sugar or other sweetener. Whenever apple is one ingredient, the weight of the apple may not exceed 50 percent of the weight of the fruit ingredients. Concentration with or without heat is to a soluble solids content of not less than 65 percent. Jams are prepared from crushed fruits and preserves are prepared from small whole fruits or from large pieces of large fruits.

The ban by the Food and Drug Administration on the use of saccharin in food products requires that artificially sweetened jellies, jams and preserves be considered for special dietary uses; they are labeled as a dietetic product and carry a statement to the effect that use of the product may be injurious to health. Imitation jams and preserves containing about one-half of the calories of regular products are sweetened with high fructose corn syrup. They are imitation products because they contain ingredients not permitted by the standard of identity for jams and preserves. Products marketed as "Low Sugar ——————— Spreads" contain half as much sugar as standard jams or preserves, and other ingredients not permitted in the definition of identity for jams and preserves.

The costs of these products differ, jellies being more expensive than jams. Costs differ according to the fruit ingredient. Raspberry, strawberry, and blackberry products are, in general, more expensive than apple, grape, or plum products. Products made from single fruits are more expensive than those prepared from mixtures of fruits. Seedless berry jams are more expensive than those containing seeds.

MISCELLANEA

The food retailing industry classifies dressings, condiments, and spreads as one group. This classification includes such items as barbecue sauces, catsup, mustard, flavor enhancers, spices, salad dressings, and sandwich spreads. These products often offer little in terms of nutrition but they enhance palatability and many offer convenience. A good portion of the food budget is likely to be spent on these items but spending in this category should be controlled.

Dressings for Food

The Food and Drug Administration has classified mayonnaise, French dressing, and salad dressings as dressings for food and has defined these products. *Mayonnaise* as defined must contain no less than 65 percent by weight of vegetable oil. Other ingredients include one or more egg yolk-containing ingredients, one or more acidifying ingredients, and such optional ingredients as salt, sweetener, monosodium glutamate, spice or flavoring—provided it does not impart the color of egg yolk—and certain additives that assist in maintaining color, flavor, and quality. All ingredients must be declared on the label.

French dressing contains not less than thirty-five parts by weight of vegetable oil. In addition to acidifying agents, a long list of optional ingredients is permitted: salt, sweetener, monosodium glutamate, certain tomato products, sherry wine, egg or egg ingredients, spices and flavorings, color additives, plus additives that thicken, stabilize, or protect flavor and color. Label declaration of all ingredients is mandatory.

Salad dressing is composed of vegetable oil, acidifying ingredient(s), egg yolk-containing ingredient(s), a starch paste, and the same list of optional ingredients permitted in French dressings and mayonnaise. Label declaration of all ingredients is required. Of these products, mayonnaise is the most expensive. French dressing is the most easily prepared in the home kitchen, and salad dressing is the most frequently purchased product.

Dressings for salads do not conform to any of these definitions. They are marketed under such fanciful names as Spring Garden, Green Onion, Green Goddess, Caesar, and others that identify the major ingredient(s). They are tasty, convenient, and relatively expensive when their ingredient content is critically studied.

The ingredient listing of the packets of seasonings for dressings for salads should be read. One such listing reads: "Salt, monosodium glutamate, dehydrated onion and garlic, spice, dehydrated parsley, calcium stearate, and vegetable oil." This packet was to be added to one-half cup of salad oil, one-fourth cup of vinegar, and three tablespoons of water to give a measure of about one cup. The mix cost 46 cents (June, 1982). It was no bargain; a bit of salt, a small amount of sugar, and a few grains of pepper and paprika added to the oil and vinegar would suffice to produce a tasty French dressing.

In general, low-calorie dressings are composed of water, vinegar, sugar, oil, salt, various additives, and the flavor components that characterize dressings. Calorie content per serving of one tablespoon of these dressings ranges from six to twenty-five, depending on kind.

Sauces for Food

It would be quite impossible to name all of the kinds of ready-made sauces available on supermarket shelves. Some are convenience products that are used for culinary purposes such as ready-to-use hollandaise sauce, spaghetti sauce, barbecue sauce, and the like. Others, such as the steak sauces, Worcestershire sauce, Tabasco sauce, and the prepared mustards are special recipe products, rarely possible of home preparation. The sweet sauces for ice cream and desserts such as chocolate, hot fudge, butterscotch, Melba, caramel, and others are convenient and tasty. They are, in general, expensive compared to homemade counterparts.

Mixes

The use of mixes has become a way of life. Mixes for sweet goods have already been mentioned. Mixes for some items can be made at home with little effort and at reduced cost. For example, a simple ham glaze composed of brown sugar, dry mustard, and dilute vinegar can be made for less than one half the cost of a purchased ham glaze mix at $1.49/11 oz. in July, 1982. Formulas have been developed for pudding and pie filling mixes, general purpose mix for baked goods, cornmeal mix, oatmeal mix for cookies and muffins, and others.

Seasoning mixes, in addition to those already mentioned for dressings for salads, come in diverse kinds: gravy, marinade, chili, sour cream, Stroganoff, cheese, hollandaise, spaghetti, pot roast, pork chop, roast chicken, and many others. Some mixes for meats include the film bag in which the food products are cooked. Read labels and count the cost. Soup mixes have uses other than for making soup. Again, count the cost. You may be able to provide the same seasonings for a much smaller sum.

Sandwich Spreads

Meat sandwich spreads, some new and some old, are convenience foods. Depending on how generously or how stingily the product is spread, they range in cost from about seven to ten cents for one-ounce, which exceeds the cost of bologna, luncheon meats, and cold cuts when used in comparable quantities unless the latter are specialty items. Moreover, the latter meats are frequently sold as specials.

Water

Bottled drinking water has enjoyed a phenomenal sales increase in recent years. According to the industry, bottled drinking water is available in the following forms: facsimile water, artificial water, formulated water, spring-fresh water, spring-pure water, well water, natural water, artificially carbonated water, natural carbonated water, natural spring water, and mineral water. The Food and Drug Administration has established standards that limit the amount of fluoride that can be added to water, the concentration of chemicals present, bacterial count, radioactivity count, and other impurities that affect flavor and color. Water that does not conform to the standards must be so labeled. It is not required that the source of the water be revealed on the label; however, if the source is described as "well water" or "spring water," the bottler must be able to substantiate the claim. When fifty bottlers were surveyed by the Environmental Protection Agency, twenty-one gave their source as "public supply," that is, tap water. Unless the local water supply is suspect, the purchase of bottled water may not be warranted; where it is, only water bottled under federal regulations and preferably one with the source revealed should be bought.

TABLE 16–1. *The Total Cost of Selected Miscellaneous Purchases*[1]

Selected Items	Cost and Market Unit
Catsup	$1.29/24 oz.
Chicken Sandwich Spread	.37/5 oz.
Chocolate Fudge Topping	1.07/11.5 oz.
Cocoa Mix	1.89/lb.
Coffee	2.49/lb.
Cooking Wine	1.29/12.7 oz.
Dill Pickles	1.49/22 oz.
Dressing for Salad	.91/8 oz.
Ham Glaze	1.49/11 oz.
Pudding Mix	.49/31/8 oz.
Ready-to-Spread Frosting	1.39/lb.
Salad Crispins	.83/2½ oz.
Spam Sandwich Spread	.49/3 oz.
Steak Sauce	1.49/11 oz.
Total	$17.47

[1] June, 1982 prices.

SUMMARY

No discussion of food buying would be complete without a warning to the meal manager that spending for miscellaneous food products can easily get out of hand. Table 16–1 lists fifteen not unusual items with their current (June, 1982) cost. The total may not seem great, but when that total is related to a spending plan, it can become very significant. Chapter 16 explores food spending plans, that is, the food budget.

REFERENCES CITED

1. "How Good is Freeze-Dried Coffee?" *Consumer Reports* **34**:434 (1969).
2. "Instant Coffees," *Consumer Reports* **36**:32 (1971).
3. "Instant Coffees," *Consumer Reports* **44**:567 (1979).
4. Jones, Jill, "The Tale of Tea, A Fragrant Brew Steeped in History," *Smithsonian* **12**:11 (1982) pp. 99–107.

SUGGESTED PROBLEMS

1. Study the ingredient composition of one or more of the following: cocoa mixes, seasoning mixes, sauces for culinary uses, dressings for

salads, iced-tea mixes, and pudding and pie filling mixes. Which ones do you find to be "good buys?" Which are no bargain?
2. Select several brands of loose teas, tea bags, and instant teas as bought in packages of different size. Set up a table showing comparative costs for like weights.
3. Compare the cost of sandwich spreads (except peanut butter) and sandwich (luncheon) meats when used in the same quantities in sandwiches.
4. Update Table 16–1.

SUGGESTED READING

1. "Automatic Drip Coffee Makers," *Consumer Reports* **48**:115 (1983).
2. "Coffee 'Creamers'," *Consumer Reports* **48**:119 (1983).
3. "Looking for a Good Cup of Coffee?" *Consumer Reports* **48**:110 (1983).

Chapter 17
Meal Service Styles

People have always eaten in diverse ways depending on when and where they lived. Early, in all likelihood, all persons ate what they found where it was found. Later, when food was cooked, eating became an event shared by kinfolks, tribe, or clan. Still later in time, dining in contrast to just eating was born, that is, some people, because of power, wealth, social or political status deliberately had meals served in a mode and manner that set them apart from the lesser members of their respective societies. In time, the mode of dining became a means for the display of wealth and the display of culture and refinement. Rare and expensive foods and elaborately concocted dishes were offered at the table. Rooms for dining were luxuriously furnished. Appointments, beautiful beyond belief, were created for eating and serving food. Today, museums display many of them. Servants in number were essential for the preparation and serving of meals. It is possible that all persons would like to dine like kings; otherwise, having dinner in a fine restaurant would not be the great treat that it is.

The twentieth century has not been kind to the art of dining. Social and economic forces, technology, and the uncertainties of the post-industrial era seem to have been at work. Two truly significant social developments that affect mealtime are the loss of the hired girl and the entrance of the housewife into the labor market. Among economic forces are the high cost and unavailability of servants to work in the kitchen and to serve in the dining room. Today, few persons dine like kings. Though modified, some different styles for serving meals remain. They are, interestingly enough, the traditional ones with a new look.

Meal service styles differ in three ways. The first is in the manner in which the diner receives food. He may serve himself from serving dishes of food, food may be served onto his plate and presented, or he may be served from the dining table. Second, meal service styles differ in the number of courses offered; that is, the items of a meal may be offered sequentially as in formal service or in one or two courses as in family meals. Third, styles differ in that waiting on the table for the placing and removal of courses may be an essential. Some styles for serving meals are described.

AMERICAN SERVICE OR COUNTRY-STYLE SERVICE

American service, or country-style service is the oldest pattern. It is not American originally. In all ages men have helped themselves to food from a common pot. Perhaps it is named *country-style* because meals were served this way in rural regions of the United States long after the pattern was modified by Americans who left the farm and moved to the cities. This pattern remains in wide use in both rural and urban communities. It has been corrupted in the latter part of the 20th century to the extent that boxes of cereal, loaves of bread in wrappers, cartons of milk, and a host of bottles, jars, and other containers appear on the dining table. Needless to say, purists denigrate the practice.

PHOTOGRAPH 1.   Table set for self-service of food American style. (*Joe Boris.*)

For this service, individual places at the table are completely laid, including the dinner plate and salad plate. Serving dishes of food are placed on the dining table or, if the dining table does not accommodate them, on a side table placed at either the host's or the hostess's right. Each serving dish of food is passed from hand to hand usually from left to right, that is, counterclockwise, until all at the table have served themselves. Someone at the table removes the main course and serves the dessert course. The dessert may be brought in from the kitchen in individual portions, it may be served at the table, or it may be passed around the table as was the main course.

EUROPEAN SERVICE

European service is also designated as *formal service, Russian service,* and *continental service.* It is truly formal, and it is elaborate and dignified. It can be carried out only when well-trained servants and all the other essentials are available, as at the White House. European service has always been limited to an elite. The service or offering of food is from the side and not from the table. No dishes of food appear on the table other than compotes of fruits and candies, or nuts in cups at individual covers. The serving of food is accomplished by the placement at covers of plates onto which food has been served or the placement of empty plates at the covers of guests who either serve themselves from serving dishes of food proffered by a servant or the food is served onto plates by a servant. When diners are seated at the table, a service plate—a large, beautifully decorated plate—is at every cover. The plate holding a cold first course or a first course served in a stemmed glass and the hot soup plate can be sequentially placed on the service plate. The service plate is removed with the soup plate, but it is replaced simultaneously by the plate of the next course. Sequentially through the courses of the formal meal, plate replaces plate through the serving of the salad course. The salad course precedes the dessert course. The salad course is removed and for the first time during this formally served meal the cover is empty of both plate and flatware. The plate and flatware for the dessert course are placed next; then the desserts are brought; and perhaps fruits and candies follow. Finger bowls may be brought in with the service for the dessert course, or they may follow the serving of the dessert. Coffee is not offered at the table but is served in the living room. In only a few homes are meals served in this style; but this style of meal service, or a reasonable facsimile of it, is seen when dining in a very fine restaurant.

PHOTOGRAPH 2. Table set for formal service. (*Joe Boris.*)

ENGLISH SERVICE

Originally, English service was only slightly less formal than European service. It, too, was used in the homes of the privileged who had servants. The host and hostess participated in the serving of the food

PHOTOGRAPH 3.   One cover of a formally set table. (*Courtesy of Oneida Ltd. Silversmiths.*)

of the main course. The platters and serving dishes of food were placed in front of the host and hostess; he carved and served the meat onto the dinner plate, and she served the vegetables onto the dinner plate. A servant took the plate from the host to hostess to guest.

FAMILY OR COMPROMISE SERVICE

Family service or compromise service is restyled English service. Stacked dinner plates and meat and vegetables in appropriate serving dishes are placed at the cover of either the host or the hostess, generally the former. The food items of the main course are served onto the dinner plate; the served plates are passed in order from hand to hand until all at the table have been served. Salad and dessert courses may also be served from the table. Unless a meal is limited to one course, the table is cleared and the next course is brought to the table. Some person who dines at the table acts as waiter or waitress.

The use of this pattern of service implies the possession of a dining table that is sufficiently spacious to accommodate serving dishes and a dining area large enough so that the person waiting on table can, at

PHOTOGRAPH 4. Table set for the serving of food at the table.

least partly, move around it. Neither of these is an absolute requirement, however, because an accessory table may hold the serving dishes of food, and the plates to be removed may be passed from hand to hand and placed on a trolly—a table on wheels—or a tray set on a small table which can be removed to the kitchen. Compromise service is best used when the group at the table is small—not more than eight—to keep serving time to that which is compatible with the serving of hot food. A person who sits to the left of the host may assist in serving an item of the meal to expedite serving. Because a member of the group, often the hostess, performs the waiting-on-the-table duties, meals served this way are best limited to two courses at the table. Any course served before the main course is best served before diners come to the table; however, if one wishes to serve a first course at the table, the dessert might be planned so that it can be served in the living room.

BLUE-PLATE SERVICE

In blue-plate service, plates are served up in the kitchen and placed on the table just before the diners sit down. Eating begins when the hostess signals. A course that precedes the main course is best served before the diners come to the table. Removal of the main course and service of dessert are done by some member of the group at the table. This pattern of service is used when the group is small, the dining table is small, and the area for dining is small. Serving up any large number of plates is time-consuming and is likely to result in food being cold when eaten. When the number to be served exceeds six, or eight at most, another and more suitable pattern of meal service should be selected unless one has help in the kitchen. The proximity of the kitchen and the dining areas in contemporary homes makes this a much-used service pattern for family meals. In fact, family meals in the 1980's are sometimes blue-plate service and sometimes family service for quick and easy meals. Church suppers and banquets of clubs and organizations are often served in this manner. Many restaurants use this style; food is placed on the table after diners are seated.

BUFFET SERVICE

The most-used style of meal service for guest meals is buffet service; in fact, it is the only practical service for guest meals in many homes if the number of diners exceeds six. Although the buffet pattern was introduced in the United States during the last century, it was not accepted and not appreciated until the dining area and dining tables became as small as they are and homes became servantless. A *buffet* is a dining table or other suitable surface, such as a chest, a desk, a kitchen

PHOTOGRAPH 5.   Outdoor buffet—dinning from plate in hand. (*Joe Boris.*)

counter, a folding table, or a card table, that will accommodate a stack of plates and serving dishes of food. Guests are invited to serve themselves at the buffet. They dine according to the arrangements of the hostess. There are three possibilities in dining arrangements. Dining may be at a table. This may be the dining table, or card tables, or individual tables. Tables are fully set with all appointments for dining except the dinner plate, and it may even occasionally appear on the set table. Lacking room for tables, a hostess may provide each guest with a tray that holds plate and beverages and that the guest places on his or her lap. Eating from a tray on one's lap is fairly comfortable. Sometimes the tray is supported so that it becomes an individual table. Often the only arrangement made for dining is to have plenty of table space on which guests can place a beverage while they sit wherever they can and eat from the plate held in the hand. The menu for a buffet meal must be planned to be compatible with the arrangements for dining; that is, the food must be eatable under the conditions established for dining. Because the food is self-served, the buffet table must be carefully and logically set. Buffet service carried out well is excellent and practical for serving meals to large groups. Chapter 22 presents a full discussion on the management of buffet meals.

Tray Service

The popularity of the studio apartment, the ubiquitous apartment balcony, the universal acceptance of television, and the appreciation of sit-by-the-fire meals have helped make tray service a popular one, although there was a time when breakfast in bed and meals for the ill and the convalescent were the only meals served from trays. Trays are set according to the rules followed for table setting, although some modifications may be desirable for comfortable eating. Food is served onto plates, which are placed on trays. Trays are then picked up by family members and taken to guests; the meal is eaten wherever persons choose.

Meals Without Waiting on the Table

Families eat many meals at which there is no waiting on the table; it is a simple, easy way to eat a simple meal. It can be a simple, easy way to also serve a more elaborate meal. Both good and bad can be said of it. The good includes the family remaining together throughout the meal; the mother playing only the role of hostess, a role she forsakes for that of a servant when she waits on her own table; and the reduction in the total time for dining without the meal becoming hurried. The unfavorable comments include the possibility of the dining table becoming a sea of dirty dishes; poor table etiquette; and the need for special props to effect such service smoothly. In general, people do not like, although they may accept, a dining style that eliminates being waited upon. The idea of being served is old in time and old for each person, because it goes back to his infancy. Nonetheless, a meal manager may find it advantageous to acquire the few desirable props and to develop a smooth technique for managing meals served without waiting on the table. It is a style that can be used for guests as well as *en famille.*

The props desirable for such a service are few: a serving table or cart, called a *side table,* which is placed to the right or left of the hostess's chair; possibly a similar table, to be placed beside the host's chair; and an appliance for keeping coffee hot or for making coffee at the table. Given these, it is possible to serve meals of two or three courses comfortably and in good taste without any person leaving the table for the purpose of serving.

The main course could be served according to the American, compromise, or blue-plate styles—preferably the last one, to keep passing from hand to hand at a minimum. Clearing can take place by the passing of soiled plates from hand to hand to the hostess or host. The dessert and the beverage are passed from hand to hand. For further discussion see pages 429–430, Chapter 20.

SUMMARY

In summary, unquestionably, there are diverse styles for meal serving in the 1980's. Meal managers adapt the traditional to that which is practicable. They also vary meal serving styles from meal to meal and time to time. Inevitably, family meals are not what they were when there was a "hired girl"; when the housewife remained at home instead of entering the marketplace; when the lives of children were less full of planned activities; and when the life style of families was routine and family centered. It would be difficult to underestimate the importance to the family of having some meals each week when both food and conversation can be enjoyed in an environment free of tension, that is, of having times for dining and not simply eating.

Chapter 18
Setting the Table

Recent decades have witnessed few changes in the fundamentals of table setting, however much laxity there may be in following prescribed procedures. The supply of things with which to set the table has been enriched by new designs in flatware, new designs and bold color in dinnerware and linens, more synthetics and fibers for table linens, and, especially, new design and variety in throwaway appointments for the table.

Homemakers in the United States, and elsewhere, have always placed a high value on the appearance of the table they set. The ownership of both everyday and best appointments was, and remains, commonplace. The best appointments may have been used only infrequently; their possession, however, was important. Table setting was definitely the homemaker's own sphere of action. Perhaps, in prewomen's-lib days, it was one of few spheres of action in which she made the decisions and, possibly, for that reason she made much of it. Table setting provides some opportunity to be creative, to express personality, "to do one's own thing"—albeit within the framework of more or less flexible rules.

Table setting is the means to an end or ends, rather than an end in itself; but it must be recognized that not all who set a table have the same ends in mind. Of the four possible ends that are discussed, only two may be universal. First, and from the practical point of view, the purpose of table setting is to make the act of eating easy. Some rules of table setting serve this end—objects that are to be used in the right hand are placed to the right of the plate centered in a cover: knives, spoons, and beverage containers. The fork is laid to the left of the plate centered in the cover because it was, and still is in some cultures, used only in the left hand. A placement viewed (1982) in a fast-food unit

371

had all three pieces placed on the right and from right to left: knife, fork, spoon. For that institution which serves mainly sandwiches, it seems a logical placing because the knife would be used first to cut the sandwich, then possibly the fork, and perhaps the spoon. All were laid atop the napkin. Time will tell whether or not such an innovation will survive. Second, we are uncomfortable and insecure when confronted with the unfamiliar. Prescribed procedures that are accepted and used within a culture engender assurance in a recurrent and necessary act, that of eating. Persons from Western cultures are confounded when confronted with Oriental customs of dining, including the use of chopsticks; also by customs of Muslim and African cultures, which prescribe precisely the use of the hand and fingers in eating. Man derives a sense of security not only from what he eats but also from how he eats. To be asked to eat foreign food in a foreign manner is doubly disconcerting.

Third, there is overwhelming evidence that some persons seek an aesthetic experience at the table. Museums are crammed with metal, glass, and ceramic objects that have been designed for use in dining. A prodigious assortment of table linens, dinnerware, beverageware, and flatware is on the market. In many homes attention is paid to the selection and coordination of the appointments used on the table to the end that the background for dining will be pleasing to the eyes. Finally, this observation leads to another, namely that sometimes the setting of the table is for the display of objects and the sophistication and wealth that their use reflects.

When utensils were created for use in eating, customs governing their use came to be established; they in turn gave birth to the rules of table setting; that is, the rules developed through usage. Existing rules have been in use long enough to be stripped of artificiality and ostentation. They seem to have been refined according to these principles: art, common sense, concern for the comfort of those at table, and courtesy. Each rule of table setting is explainable in terms of one of these principles. Because man's ideas are subject to change, customs do change from time to time and place to place; hence, current rules may be subsequently modified.

Art principles would suggest that individual place settings and the table as a unit present a balanced appearance. *Balance* means even distribution of weight so that the parts of a composition appear in equilibrium. Balance is obtained by both symmetrical and asymmetrical arrangements. Color, texture, and shape effect balance with dissimilar objects. Small objects of dark color balance larger areas of light color; for example, the small dish of red jelly may balance the larger plate of bread. Small objects of bright luster balance larger objects of dull texture; for example, the glass at the right of the cover often balances the bread-and-butter plate at the left. There are nearly always a few items on any table that can be shifted in one direction or another to give the table better balance. A table makes a pleasing appearance when its appointments are in scale with one another and with the table. The luncheon knife and fork, the small dinner plate, and the small centerpiece are best used on a small table. Large tables can be set with appointments that are larger in scale. Further, it is desirable to keep the number of items on a table in scale with the table. Eliminating nonessentials on the small table avoids a cluttered look. The pattern obtained through the repetition of lines, shapes, and designs within the individual place settings and through the repetition of place settings around the table is pleasing. Straight lines made by flatware and linens are pleasing when they are parallel or perpendicular to the table edge. Orderly arrangement of the numerous objects on a table is pleasing; disorder is confusing.

Common sense dictates that place settings include whatever is necessary for eating a meal; it also forbids the display of nonessentials. Common sense and concern for the comfort of those at the table require that appointments be placed in convenient positions for use. Courtesy demands that all the tools essential for refined eating be provided and that they be conveniently placed.

Currently, rules allow latitude in table setting. There is no one "right" way to set the table; the pattern of table service to be used, the menu to be served, and the size of the table establish the plan for setting the table. The pattern of service establishes the position of some items, particularly dinner plates and serving dishes. The specific appointments to be placed at covers are established by the menu. The exact positions of appointments at covers may differ on small tables and on large tables.

SETTING THE TABLE

Before discussing the rules that guide the placing of appointments on the table, it is desirable to define the cover. A *cover* consists of the dinnerware, beverageware, flatware, and linens to be used by each person; it is a person's place at the table. A cover may vary in breadth from 20 to 30 inches, depending on the size of the table and the number to be seated, but dining is more comfortable if 24 inches can be allowed per cover.

The rules relating to the use of the appointments are discussed in the order in which each is usually placed on the table, beginning with the linens and proceeding to the final item, the food. It is possible to place all the flatware, then all the beverageware, and then the dinnerware, in that order—except that when butter spreaders are included in the cover, they are placed after the bread-and-butter plates have been placed.

LINENS

The kinds of linens used on the dining tables of the 1980's are diverse. *Linens* mean all of the tablecloths, place mats, and other table covers and napkins used on the dining table, regardless of fiber and including man-made materials. Easy-care, no-care, and disposable linens have, except for special occasions, replaced the linen damask and the fine linen and lace cloths of yesterday. Some tablecloths and place mats of man-made materials imitate the traditional ones in design and appearance. The dining counter and the dining table may be so constructed that the surface is imperious to water and heat; such surfaces are often set without linens, except for napkins. However, tablecloths, runners, and place mats are used some of the time by some families, and all of the time by other families. Here are some suggestions for the placing of linens.

1. Creases in fabric cloths should be ironed out whenever possible. Lay a cloth so that the overhang is the same at the two ends and the same on the two sides. An overhang of 12 to 15 inches gives a good appearance. Avoid great depth of overhang at the table where persons are seated for dining because the weight of the cloth against the legs of seated persons may become uncomfortable; also, the cloth may become entangled with legs crossed under the table.

2. Runners may be centered on a table or they may be laid along the sides as a background for the place settings.

3. On a square or rectangular table, lay rectangular place mats flush with the table edge or at a distance of one to one and one-half inches from the edge of the table. The position you choose is determined by the place mat, the table, and the line you wish the flatware to follow. Deeply hemmed and fringed place mats may look better when placed flush with the table edge. Narrowly hemmed mats may appear more pleasing if placed away from the table edge. Regardless of hemming, small place mats—those smaller than 12 by 18 inches—may look better when placed an inch away from the table edge. On a narrow table, all mats, regardless of hemming and size, may look better when placed flush with the table edge. Conversely, on a wide table, all mats look better when placed away from the edge of the table. Whenever possible, use place mats that are in scale with the table: small ones on a small table and large ones on a large table. Sometimes the fringing or hemming of a mat makes it desirable that the flatware be aligned in relation to that hemming or fringing. In such a situation, the place mat would

be placed flush with the table edge so as to have the flatware placed at a comfortable distance from the table edge.

4. In general, place oval, round, scalloped, and other mats with nonstraight edges so that some part of the edge is flush with the table edge. The large, round mat is often placed so that part of it overhangs the table. Place it so that the area on the table can accommodate the objects you wish to place on it.

5. On a round or oval table, lay rectangular mats so that the corners are flush with the edge of the table; this leaves a small arc of the table bare in front of each mat. Lay oval and small, round mats flush with the table edge.

6. The preferred shape for the folded napkin is the rectangle, but the square is also good. The triangle introduces oblique lines that make for a less harmonious whole. Fanciful folds of the napkin and the use of napkin rings are appropriate at times; however, the simpler folds produce more artful settings on the traditional dining table.

7. The napkin is usually placed to the left of the fork or forks. However, if covers are close together, the napkin can be placed in the center of a cover between the knife and the fork for the family pattern of service, on the dinner plate for the American pattern of service, or to the left of the dinner plate when the fork or forks are laid upon it. In formal service, the napkin is placed to the left of the forks or on the service plate, preferably the latter. See Figure 18–1.

8. The practice of placing the fork or forks on top of the napkin laid to the left in the cover has come into wide use. The practice necessitates sliding the napkin out from under the fork or forks, and presents an accident-prone situation to those accustomed to tradition.

FIGURE 18–1. Formal service—individual cover. The flatware from left to right are: fish fork, dinner fork, salad fork, dinner knife, fish knife, soup spoon, and cocktail fork.

FIGURE 18–2.   Alignment of napkin, flatware, and plate within a cover.

9. Place the napkin so that the edge closest to the table edge is aligned with the tips of the handles of flatware and the rim of the plate. See Figure 18–2.

10. The placing of the napkin on the place mat is determined by the size of both. It may be placed entirely on the mat, partly on the mat and partly on the table, or entirely on the table. Probably most tables look better when the napkin is entirely on the place mat. Placing the forks on the napkin is a way of keeping the napkin on the place mat. Lay a napkin so that the design and hem placement are coordinated with the place mat.

11. Napkins vary in size. The 12-inch one is usually used for breakfast and lunch. For the dinner meal the 18-inch (or larger) napkin is preferred.

Table Decorations

Table decorations always ought to be appropriate for viewing while dining, in good taste, and in scale with the table.

1. On the dining table that seats no more than twelve, keep the decorations low so that persons can see across and converse across the table. Obviously, for banquets and special dinners for crowds this is not a problem because it is not expected that persons will communicate across a table. If the dining table is placed against a wall, there is no reason why an arrangement may not be tall if it looks pleasing from the sitting position.

2. Decorations need not always be placed in the center of the table. Small arrangements can be placed at diagonally opposite corners, at all

four corners, at the two ends of the table, or at one end of the table, depending on the size and shape of the table and how people are seated at it. Asymmetrical arrangements of flowers placed away from the center of the table are handsome when balanced by candles or other objects.

3. Decorations on buffet tables and tea tables can be larger and taller than dinner table decorations because they are viewed from above.

4. With the exception of the tea table, candles are placed and lighted only after dusk. For the comfort of those at the table they should burn above eye level. Both candles and table decorations ought to be coordinated with the colors of the table appointments.

Laying Flatware

All flatware laid on a table ought to be free of spots and fingerprints. Enough flatware for comfortable and refined eating should be laid at each cover; the use of unneeded pieces is ostentatious and should be avoided. Easy-to-use and effective serving pieces should be laid for all food and dishes served at the table.

Laying Flatware at Covers.   Except for formal service, place all the flatware required for eating the full meal at the covers when setting the table; it simplifies the waiting-on-the-table duties. Lay pieces of flatware in the order of use from the outside toward the plate; this is done both for convenience during dining and because it gives the cover a balanced appearance at all times. Pieces should be laid close together, but not touching. Traditionally (see Figure 18–2), all pieces are laid so that the ends of the handles would touch an imaginary line parallel to the table edge and so that they are about an inch to an inch and a half from the table edge. See Figure 18–1. When the mat is placed flush with the table edge, the line made by the ends of the handles of flatware pieces is an inch or more from the edge of the mat; when the mat is placed away from the edge of the table, the flatware is placed so that the ends of the pieces are aligned with the edge of the mat. In some contemporary table settings forks and spoons are laid in staggered positions.

Pieces are placed in the same position at all covers for order and good appearance. Because the main plate is usually a warm one, the plates are generally among the last items to be placed; however, in laying the other items of the cover it helps one to place a plate briefly or to imagine one in the approximate center of the cover. In the directions that follow, a plate is considered to be in the center of the cover and is so indicated by a broken line.

1. Lay the dinner knife to the right of the plate with the cutting edge directed toward the plate. All knives are laid with the cutting edge directed to the left, a position that protects the fingers of the right hand as it grasps the knife.

2. Lay spoons with the bowls facing up to the right of the knife.

3. Always lay the fork or forks with the tines facing up to the left of the plate, with this exception—a fork for eating seafood is laid to the right of any spoons in the cover because this fork is used in the right hand only; however, it may be placed on the underliner of the seafood container. Lay the salad fork nearest the plate and the dinner fork to the left of it if you intend that the salad be eaten with the main course or after it. Lay the dinner fork nearest the plate and the salad fork to the left of it if you intend that the salad be eaten before the main course.

4. It is not necessary to provide a salad fork when the salad accompanies the main course.

5. When no dinner knife will be required for the eating of a simple family meal, it can be omitted from the setting. Lay the fork on the right in the place the knife would ordinarily occupy. Because the fork is used only in the right hand when no knife is needed, the position on the right is a convenient one. But if you wish to lay more than three pieces, then lay the forks on the left. See Figure 18–3. However, do not omit the dinner knife from the cover except when dining *en famille*.

6. When you provide salad forks for salads served in salad bowls, make certain that the fork will rest securely within the bowl. The preference is for broad, shallow salad bowls.

7. You may place the butter spreader on the bread-and-butter plate

(a)   (b)

FIGURE 18–3. Possible positions of the dinner fork when no dinner knife is laid.

FIGURE 18–4. Possible positions of the butter spreader on the bread-and-butter plate.

in any of three positions; choose the one that looks best on your plates and your table. See Figure 18–4.

(a) Across the upper edge of the plate in a line parallel with the table edge, the cutting edge of the knife directed toward the center of the plate.

(b) Across the right side of the plate perpendicular to the table edge, cutting edge directed to the left.

(c) Across the center of the plate with the tip of the knife a little to the left of the center of the plate and with the cutting edge directed toward the table edge. This is a good position on the coupe plate (a plate without a rim).

8. Sometimes, it is intended that the salad plate do double duty and be used also as a bread-and-butter plate. Because salads are cold and the plates for them are frequently chilled, this practice ought to be limited to use with bread that is not hot. Whenever you intend that the salad plate be also a bread-and-butter plate, arrange the salad in a lettuce cup, and leave about half of the plate free for the bread. In this case, eliminate the salad fork and the butter spreader. The salad can be eaten with the dinner fork, and the dinner knife can be used as a spreader. However, it is preferable for the dinner plate to be a repository for bread.

9. Occasionally the butter spreader is the only knife provided, particularly in covers for breakfasts and simple lunches. In this situation, lay the butter spreader on the right when no bread-and-butter plate is provided. See Figure 18–5.

10. The use of the butter spreader is optional when a dinner knife is laid; current practice is not to use it.

11. Laying the flatware for dessert is no problem unless the tool for dessert is a fork. When it is a fork, it ought to be laid so that there is no doubt about its intended use. Should a menu not include a salad, the dessert fork can be laid to the right of the dinner fork. When a salad accompanies the main course and your supply of forks does not permit the laying of three forks at each cover—one for the main course, one for salad, and one for dessert—lay one fork only on the left. Lay the fork you intend for dessert in the center of the cover above the dinner plate, handle directed to the right. See Figure 18–6. When the

FIGURE 18–5.   Position for the butter spreader when no bread-and-butter plate is placed.

FIGURE 18–6.   A possible position for the dessert fork and the beverage spoon.

fork is laid in this position, it is unlikely that anyone will use it for salad because it is not in the expected position. When a beverage is served with dessert only, lay the beverage spoon above the dessert fork with the handle likewise directed toward the right, because both are used in the right hand. Placing the beverage spoon here, along with the fork, gives the cover a balanced appearance. Further, it permits narrowing covers slightly.

Two other procedures are possible. The flatware for dessert may be laid just before dessert is served. Place both the fork for dessert and the spoon for the beverage on the right of each cover because both are used in the right hand. The hostess who is her own waitress may wish to avoid this procedure because it keeps her away from the table longer than is necessary.

PHOTOGRAPH 6.   Dessert flatware placed in the center of the cover above the dinner plate. (*Joe Boris.*)

Finally, the fork may be placed on the plate with the dessert, both when it is served from the kitchen and when it is served from the table. When you choose this procedure, covers will be better balanced if you do not place beverage spoons in the place settings. Place the beverage spoon on the saucer with the handle parallel to the cup handle when you pour.

12. When the flatware for dessert is a spoon, lay it to the right of the knife as previously directed. There is no cogent reason for laying dessert and beverage spoons in the center of the cover above the dinner plate; however, do so if you choose to. It is rather sophisticated to provide both a dessert spoon and a fork for the dessert course. If you follow this practice, the handle of the spoon is directed to the right; the handle of the fork to the left. The spoon is the tool for eating and is, therefore, used in the right hand; the fork is used as a pusher in the left hand. Because of our custom of serving coffee or other beverages with dessert, and even throughout the meal, and because we formerly used cream and sugar abundantly in beverages, beverage spoons have been traditionally laid at covers. It is quite proper to omit the beverage spoon from place settings and place it on the saucer as one serves the beverage at the table. Whether or not you use both spoon and fork for dessert service, use the dessert or place spoon as much as

you can. Make certain that the plate under the dessert bowl is large enough to accommodate it (the spoon). A plate used under a bowl, a stemmed or footed sherbet, or any dish used in this fashion is called an *underliner*.

13. Fresh fruits are often served for dessert. Some are eaten with a spoon, some may be eaten with the fingers, and a few require the use of a knife or a knife and a fork for refined eating. When both knife and fork are provided, lay the fork, handle directed to the left, below the knife, handle directed to the right, in the center of the cover above the dinner plate. Lay the beverage spoon for a beverage served only with dessert above the knife, handle directed to the right.

When a selection of fruits is offered from a tray or a large plate, it is acceptable to place the fruit knives on the tray, handles spread in a fan shape. Anyone who will use a knife for eating the selected fruit takes it from the tray. As with dessert forks, the fruit knife and fork or knife alone may be laid on the fruit plate placed by the person acting as waitress.

14. Place the tools for a dessert of cheese and crackers in the center of the cover above the dinner plate in the same way as for fruit, or lay them on the right after the main course has been eaten, using right-hand service. Either the butter spreader or the fruit knife is suitable as a cheese spreader.

Laying Serving Flatware.   The serving pieces for the self service of food at the table should lend themselves to quick and easy use. The scissors-type, two-tools-in-one combinations and tongs are excellent for chops, vegetables such as broccoli and asparagus, and salads. Serving spoons larger than tablespoons are indicated for casserole dishes and any other dish that would require several dips with the tablespoon to provide a serving.

When serving is by the host or another person at the table, two serving tools are more effective than one unless the one is a two-tools-in-one combination. Tools that can be used together—one to assist the other in serving—are two tablespoons, a tablespoon assisted by a dinner fork, a meat fork assisted by a tablespoon, a shallow flat server assisted by a dinner fork or a tablespoon, and a large serving spoon assisted by a dinner fork or a tablespoon.

1. Lay to the right of the serving dish or platter one serving tool if only one tool is essential.

2. When two serving tools are provided, lay the one that will assist to the left of the dish containing food, the one that will pick up the food to the right. See Figure 18–7. These may also be placed to the left and right of the cover of the person serving.

FIGURE 18–7.   Serving pieces laid beside serving dishes.

3. Place the carving fork to the left of the platter, the carving knife to the right with the cutting edge directed to the left or lay them to right and left in the cover of the person who will carve. Figure 18–7.

4. Lay the serving tools for small containers of food passed at the table, such as butter, jelly, and pickles, to the right of a dish that has no underliner, and on the underliner when one is used.

5. Lay spoons with the bowls facing up and forks with the tines facing up. Use a small fork such as a lemon or pickle fork for butter cut into pats.

Placing Beverageware

Some persons prefer to delay the placing of glasses of beverages until they have been filled in order to avoid a possible accident while pouring at the table. The glasses are placed on a tray, filled, carried on the tray to the table, and placed. Common sense would suggest that if you plan this way, coasters for the glasses should be placed during table setting.

1. Grasp tumblers and footed ware at the base, stemmed ware by the stem.

2. Use coasters under beverage glasses whenever humidity and temperature favor the condensation of moisture on glasses.

3. Place the water glass at the tip of the knife (or fork when placed at the right of the plate) or a little to the right or left of the knife, depending on the breadth of the covers, the width of the table, and the number of glasses to be placed. Place the water glass where it looks best and is easily grasped. See Figure 18–8.

PHOTOGRAPH 7.   Possible position of glassware when three glasses appear in the cover. Cocktail fork placed for first course. (*Joe Boris.*)

4. Ice and water may be put into the glasses about 5 minutes ahead of serving time. Water is poured to within an inch of the top of the glass.

5. Glasses of milk, when water also is served, are placed to the right and a little in front of the water glass, that is, a little closer to the table

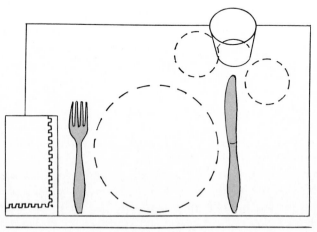

FIGURE 18–8.   Possible positions of the water glass.

edge. See Figure 18–5. This permits the easy removal of empty milk glasses before the dessert service. If no water glass is placed, as is often true in families with children, place the glass of milk or other beverage in the position for the water glass. Place a glass of juice to the right and in front of the last glass, that is, nearer the table edge.

6. Glasses placed in addition to the water glass, such as for wines, are positioned successively closer to the table edge but not so as to modify the position of flatware on the right side of the cover. Generally, no more than three glasses appear within a cover. Figure 18–6.

7. Place a saucer or small plate or coaster under a glass of iced-tea or coffee to collect condensing moisture.

Placing Dinnerware

Selecting the plates, cups and saucers, bowls, and platters that will be used in setting the table makes table setting an art. "Mix and match" sets of dinnerware have encouraged the use of plain color with patterned pieces. Although dinnerware is often purchased by the set, individual covers and the table as a whole are attractive if salad plates are different from dinner plates, dessert plates are different from cups and saucers, and serving dishes and platters are coordinated with the plates but are not all exactly alike.

1. Handle dishes and plates in such a way that you do not touch surfaces onto which food will be served. You can safely carry dishes and piles of plates if you place your thumbs on the edges and your fingers close together underneath.

2. Place the bread-and-butter plate at the left of the cover near the tip of the fork. In this position it balances the glass or glasses on the right of the cover. See Figure 18–9. In addition to serving as a receptacle for bread and butter, it is also used for celery, olives, and other relishes eaten with the fingers. At the small table, sacrifice the bread-and-butter plate to avoid a cluttered appearance. The dinner or luncheon plate, if it is not overcrowded with food, is a suitable place for bread and butter, especially when the bread is hot. The bread-and-butter plate is used when a table accommodates it, but it is not a "must" in table setting.

3. Unless served at the table, the salad is placed at each cover shortly before serving time. It may be placed in any of several positions.
   (a) If no bread-and-butter plate is at the cover, place the salad at or near the tip of the fork. This is a widely used position that allows good leverage in cutting salad vegetables. See Figure 18–10.
   (b) When a bread-and-butter plate is included in the cover, you

FIGURE 18–9.   Position of the bread-and-butter plate.

may place the salad to the left and a little below the bread-and-butter plate; however, unless covers are spacious, such a position is often not possible. See Figure 18–11. Where covers are close together you may move the bread-and-butter plate a little to the left and place the salad to the right of it; in this position, it is above the luncheon or dinner plate. See Figure 18–11. If the use of both salad and bread-and-butter plates crowds the table unduly, it may be better to omit the latter. Another, but less frequently used, position for the salad plate is to the right of the spoons and lined up with the napkin and

FIGURE 18–10.   Position of the salad plate when there is no bread-and-butter plate in the cover.

FIGURE 18–11.   Possible positions of the salad when a bread-and-butter plate appears in the cover.

the flatware. There are at least three reasons why this position is not popular. First, the salad is less comfortably eaten. Second, the long-established custom of having the salad on the left leads to mistaken eating of one's neighbor's salad, except

PHOTOGRAPH 8.   Possible position of the salad plate when a bread and butter plate appears in the cover. (*Joe Boris.*)

when covers are so spacious that there can be no doubt. Finally, wide preference for a hot beverage with the main course means that the plate at the right has been usurped. It may be well to note further that if a bread-and-butter plate is placed in a cover, and if the salad is placed at the right, then waiting on the table becomes rather complicated. These objections should not preclude the use of the position if one wishes to use it. Men like it because their cuffs are not soiled by food on the dinner plate as they may be when the salad is at the left of the cover.

4. Whenever possible, use the salad-dessert plate for a salad rather than a bread-and-butter plate, but especially for salads composed of crisp vegetables that require cutting, because the larger the plate on which the salad components are to be maneuvered, the less likely are bits to fall to the table. Whenever the salad must be served on a bread-and-butter plate, keep the salad small and compose it of fairly soft vegetables or fruits or have all pieces bite-sized. An alternative to the use of the bread-and-butter plate is the salad bowl; again, have all salad components bite-sized.

5. Some hostesses, and some hosts as well, prefer to dress, toss, and serve the salad from the table. Three positions of the salad service are possible. See Figure 18–12.

(a) The first position requires right-to-left serving of the salad onto the salad plates. Place the stacked salad plates at the position in the cover that the server's own salad plate would occupy. Place the salad bowl above the dinner plate. This arrangement leaves the last salad in the proper place within the cover.

(b) The second arrangement is similar to the first except the bowl of salad is placed to the left of the dinner plate. This position permits left-to-right serving of the salad. This arrangement also leaves the last salad served in the proper position within the cover.

(c) Place the bowl of salad above the dinner plate just left of center; place the stacked plates to the right of it. It may be necessary to move the water glass to the right. With the bowl and plates in this position left-to-right serving is easy. When the last salad has been served, it is moved to the proper position within the cover.

6. The most appropriate tool for serving salad is the two-in-one scissors-type. Otherwise, use two tools, a spoon with a fork or two spoons.

7. Set the service similarly for any vegetable or food that will be served into side dishes.

8. Place warm dinner plates last, just before dinner is announced. Put a plate in the center of each cover for the American style of meal

FIGURE 18–12. Possible positions of the salad service at the server's cover.

service. Put the stacked dinner plates at the cover of the person who will serve when the meal service style is compromise or family service. Place the served dinner plate at each cover when the service is blue-plate.

Placing a Beverage Service

In the 1980's, beverages are very much a part of meals. Soft drinks, fruit drinks, and fruit punches have been added to the milk, coffee, and tea traditionally served. In general, filled beverage glasses are placed on the table within fifteen minutes of serving time. And, in general, glasses are filled to within one inch of the top. Hot beverages are served at the table; they are also served from the kitchen at the appropriate time. For those who prefer the former practice, the service must be planned and arranged for.

1. Keeping beverage glasses filled poses some problems. Strictly *en famille,* glasses can be passed at the table and filled from a pitcher that may be on the dining table or on a small side table. Otherwise, the refilling of beverage glasses occurs between courses.

2. When a hot beverage is to be served throughout the meal and the hostess is to pour, place cups and saucers stacked by twos either to the right or to the left or above the hostess's cover. The exact position depends on the number to be served, the size and shape of the table, and the number of items already in position at her cover. Figure 18–13 shows possible positions when no more than three or four cups and saucers must be placed. Try out the several possibilities the table offers, and then adopt the one that permits the most comfortable and graceful pouring. If the dining table does not accommodate a beverage service, place it on a side table, perhaps a table-on-wheels, and set it to the right of the hostess's chair.

3. When the hot beverage is not to be served until dessert, do not place any of the appointments for it on the table; however, arrange the service as a part of the table setting. This service may be set up with or without a tray. When used, the tray should be in scale with the table. Set it with cups and saucers, creamer and sugar bowl, and perhaps spoons. For safety, the tray should be carried to the table without the pot of hot beverage on it. It may be set down to the right of, or above, the hostess's cover, depending on the size of the table and her wishes. After the tray is placed, the pot of hot beverage will be brought in and placed on it. Place the creamer, the sugar bowl, and the beverage pot on the tray in positions convenient for use. See Figure 18–14. The position above the cup and saucer into which the beverage is poured is a good one for the creamer and sugar. Leave the cover off the sugar

FIGURE 18–13.   Possible arrangements of a beverage service at the hostess's cover—beverage served during the meal and no tray used.

bowl. In the 1980s, many persons use no sugar or cream in coffee. The sugar bowl and creamer have become collectibles. It is quite possible to omit them.

4. The beverage service is more frequently placed on the table without an underlying tray because tables tend to be small, and trays that are large enough to be useful tend to be too large for the table. Again,

FIGURE 18–14. A tray arranged for beverage service.

all items for this service should be readied when one is setting the table. Have them on the serving table or on the counter in the kitchen. Chapter 20 discusses how this service is placed on the dining table.

5. Ideally, the cups, but not the saucers, are warmed for hot beverages in the same way that plates and serving dishes are warmed for hot food. This is especially important when the cup is shallow and has a large cooling surface.

6. The service for a beverage offered with or after dessert can be set up on a side table placed to the right of the hostess's chair.

Placing Accessory Items

Accessory items include bread, butter, jellies and jams, salt and pepper, food dressings, relishes, and the like.

1. Place individual salt and pepper shakers in the center of the cover above the dinner plate.

2. One pair of salt and pepper shakers is enough for two or three diners. Place them between covers in the line made by the water glasses, where they can be easily reached.

3. Place the salt to the right of the pepper shaker so that it can be taken without need for handling both objects.

4. Place dishes containing such foods as rolls, butter, and relishes to be self-served and passed from hand to hand to the right and left of the hostess's cover or on a side table placed to the right of her chair so that she can assume responsibility for passing—they move counterclockwise around the table—and so that she can be the last to serve herself. Such an arrangement permits her to control the positioning of these items on the table—she may prefer that they not remain on the dining table.

Placing the Chairs

When a table has been completely set, except for the food, the chairs, if not already at the table, may be placed. They should be set with the fronts of the seats flush with the table edge. From this position, they do not require moving when guests seat themselves.

Placing Serving Dishes of Food

Dishes and platters should be sufficiently large so that service from them is possible without spilling.

1. Warm or chill dishes as indicated.

2. When the pattern of service used is American, place serving dishes in positions where they can be conveniently reached by someone at the table. The serving tools should already have been laid.

3. When the pattern is family service, the filled serving dishes are grouped at the cover of the person who will serve, usually the host. Place the platter, chop plate, or casserole containing the main part of the meal above, but as close as possible to, the stacked plates onto which the food is to be served. Place other dishes containing food to the right and to the left of the stacked plates. If only one additional serving dish is to be placed, put it on the left for better leverage in serving. See Figure 18–15. To facilitate serving, particularly when carving is necessary, remove the server's beverage glass and salad to a small side table. On the completion of serving, the beverage glass and salad are placed on the dining table by the person who served. Emptied serving bowls can be removed to the small side table from the dining table by the person who served.

4. To hasten service to a group of eight or more, the person sitting on the host's left, because he or she can freely use the right hand, may assist by serving one or more of the dishes. The preferred position of the serving dish is above the cover of that person, especially if serving the item requires the use of two hands.

5. Although side dishes are less frequently used than formerly, some foods (such as creamed vegetables, vegetables in cream, and stewed tomatoes) are still best served in them. Place side dishes served in the kitchen at the tip of the fork or lower, depending on what other items are already placed at the cover.

6. Place the first of foods to be eaten sequentially, such as breakfast fruits and cereals, in the center of the cover; place the one to be eaten second at the left near the tip of the fork. The two dishes are ex-

FIGURE 18–15.   Dining table set for service of food at the table.

changed in position by the diner after he or she has finished the first one.

7. Place the dessert of a simple meal, to be eaten without any waiting on the table, to the left of the cover, at the tip of the fork or higher, depending on what other dishes have already been placed at the cover.

Setting the Auxiliary Serving Table

The presence of a small chest, tea cart, table, credenza, or buffet in the dining area promotes ease and speed in table service, regardless of the meal service pattern followed. Lacking one of these or room in which to set it up, set aside a part of the kitchen counter, and use it in a similar manner. This aid to service is called a *serving table* or *service table*.

1. Cover it with a runner or one or two place mats to muffle the clatter of dishes and to protect the surface if necessary.

2. Add a small tray for use while clearing and placing courses.

3. Place on the serving table the creamer, sugar bowl, and cups (if they are not being warmed) and saucers of the beverage service; the dessert plates and flatware essential for serving a dessert from the table; or the underliners for a dessert served in sherbets or bowls and brought in from the kitchen.

4. Place the water pitcher and a drip napkin here if you wish.

5. Place a small plate and a napkin for use in crumbing the table if crusty bread, such as cornbread or hard rolls, is included in the menu.

6. Do not completely cover the serving table with appointments if you plan to use it during the removal and placement of courses. See Fgure 18–16.

7. Leave on the serving table the hot pads and salt and peppers removed from the dining table when removing the main course.

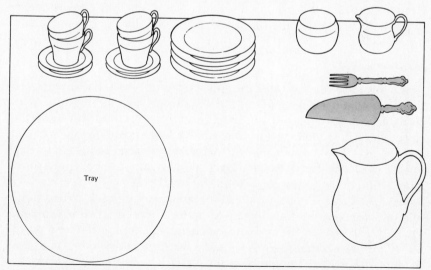

Tray

FIGURE 18–16.   A serving table arranged for convenient use.

8. The purpose of the serving table is to simplify service; use it to save steps, but do not put food for a subsequent course on it or leave it stacked with dirty dishes if it is visible from the dining table.

MISCELLANEOUS

Using a Table-on-Wheels

The small tea cart or table-on-wheels or trolley can be conveniently used in setting the table and in waiting on the table. It reduces the hand-and-foot work of mealtime. Load it with the items you must take from your kitchen to the dining table. If you wish, leave it in the dining area as a serving table if it is of a comfortable height and suitable for such use. Clear the table to it, then roll everything to the kitchen when you (or another person) wait on the table. The table-on-wheels used in this way should be of comfortable working height and should have a guard rim to prevent the sliding of dishes as it moves.

"Silent Butler" for Hosts

One last arrangement might be suggested for facilitating the smooth and unhurried service of meals even though the time devoted to dining may not be long. Place small tables, such as folding snack tables, to the right of the host's and the hostess's chair. The host's water glass and salad may be placed there while he serves second portions. The hostess may keep on her side table some of the foods that she will have passed from hand to hand at the dining table. These small side tables are especially valuable when the dining table and the dining area are small.

Serving Tools

Serving tools for food include spoons, ladles, forks, flat servers, scissors-type servers, tongs, knives, and the carving set. Serving spoons are available in assorted sizes: the large serving spoon, used for stews and casserole dishes; tablespoons; and small spoons, used for jams, sugar, and the like. Tablespoons may be pierced for serving foods from which it is desirable to drain away liquids. Ladles are also available in assorted sizes, from the large punch ladle to the small sauce ladle. Serving forks include the large serving fork and the small serving fork. When put to use, the large serving fork is pushed under a food item such as a pattie or chop; for easy service a "steadier" assists in keeping the item on the fork. The steadier is either a dinner fork or a tablespoon. The small serving fork is used for spearing small bits such as pickles, butter pats, and lemon wedges. Flat servers are of different shapes and are, generally, pierced or slotted. They lift food items from plates and platters to dinner plates; a dinner fork is a desired accompanying tool. Flat servers may serve as a cutting tool for soft foods. Except for cakes and pastries, flat servers are not used as frequently as they might be. The scissors-type tools are preferred serving tools for many food items including chops and meats in discrete units, vegetables such as broccoli, salads, and many others. The scissors-type tools are favored for the buffet. Tongs are used for sugar cubes and ice cubes, and are also a suitable tool whenever they can be efficiently used to lift or move food. Different kinds of serving knives, such as the butter knife and cheese server, have been designed. The carving knive assists the accompanying fork in picking up carved meats in much the same way that the one assists the other in carving. The serving tools that are most frequently used are the large serving spoon, tablespoon, scissors-type tool, and the carving set.

SUMMARY

Table setting is the means to an end or ends. It makes eating easy and transmutes eating to dining. It provides part of the aesthetic experience associated with dining. Table-setting rules have evolved through usage. They are functional and dynamic. The rules have flexibility that makes it possible for each meal manager to make them serve her purposes.

It has been suggested in earlier chapters that family values, and those of the homemaker especially, determine how much of the family's resources of money, time, and human energy is allocated to meals. The setting of the table makes demands on the money, time, and human energy resources and requires knowledge and skills. To maximize the uses of time and human energy, the meal manager can use the accepted rules to establish the family's own style of table setting.

Chapter 19

Table Appointments

Along with the many other changes in recent years are those that have taken place in table appointments. What we have long had—china dinnerware, glass beverageware, and sterling flatware—remains, and in addition we have much else. The traditional linens for the table have been generally forsaken because they require careful laundering and ironing. We now have little time for such tasks. No-care cloths and place mats in infinite variety have replaced linens, and some imitate the damask, lace, and embroidered linens of yesterday. In general, paper, plastics, and natural and man-made fibers are the materials from which cloths and place mats are fabricated. Not only is it possible to purchase paper table mats and cloths and napkins that are coordinated in color and design but it is also possible to purchase dinnerware and beverageware that are coordinated with them. In fact, it is possible to purchase a complete disposable dinner service that includes dinner plates, bread-and-butter plates, soup or cereal bowls, hot or cold beverage cups, napkins in two sizes, and plastic flatware. One company advertises that food can be frozen in, and heated on, its disposable line. Throwaway paper plates and beverageware and plastic flatware have been used for so long that we no longer find them strange. However, they do pose waste-removal problems.

However, all of these convenient and no-care items have not yet totally replaced ceramic dinnerware, glass beverageware, and silver and stainless steel flatware. Contemporary patterns and styles have been added to traditional patterns and styles in all of these wares, and brides continue to select patterns in china, glass, and silverware. The possession of "nice" table appointments and the ability to set a "pretty" table have long been important to families, and have provided satisfactions. But, perhaps these satisfactions, too, may fade away in the future.

The appointments for setting the table have been used by man to transmute the basic act of eating—not always a pleasant sight—into a comfortable and pleasurable act. Appointments have also been used for the purposes of the display of wealth and sophistication and as status symbols. Perhaps, this is partly true in the 1980's. But, it is also true that a person often sets a "pretty" table because it provides an opportunity to be creative and express self and from this derive some satisfactions. Further, by and through the setting of the table, a person sets the tone of meals—they become eat-and-run or sit-and-enjoy in character.

The present abundance of appointments in the marketplace makes it important to know something about them. The quality of some of them is such that they have the potential for becoming tomorrow's heirlooms, the quality of others is such that they are soon expendable. Yesterday's table appointments are today's collectibles that may have great value. The wise selection of appointments depends on knowledge of what constitutes quality so that value may be obtained for money spent, and on familiarity with art principles so that they can be coordinated. The appointments of the table are discussed in the following order: flatware, hollowware, dinnerware, beverageware, linens, and table decorations.

FLATWARE

The term *flatware* includes all the tools used for eating and serving. Flatware is obtainable in a wide variety of materials: sterling silver, plated silver, vermeil, stainless steel, and combinations of metal with bone, bamboo, ceramic, plastic, mother-of-pearl, wood, and other materials used for handles.

The first choice of many is sterling silver. It is the most expensive flatware; many brides select other flatware first and hope that someday they may own sterling. Today, many are choosing stainless steel because it requires no special care.

Sterling Silver Flatware

Sterling pieces are composed of the same material throughout, that is, they are "solid silver," in contrast to plated silverware, which is composed of a base metal covered with silver. Any silver piece marked *sterling* or *sterling silver* is made from an alloy of silver and another metal, usually copper, in the ratio of 925 parts silver to 75 parts of the other metal. The copper or other metal gives hardness and durability. Pieces made wholly of silver are soft and are easily bent and dented.

Because sterling silver pieces have the same composition throughout, they are durable and can rightfully be described as "heirlooms of to-morrow." For this reason sterling need not be put away and used only when there are guests for dinner. The family that owns sterling flatware needs no other. The small scratches that come from steady use give the silver a soft luster or patina. In order for all pieces to mellow in an equal degree, it is desirable to rotate them in use.

Durability in sterling is a matter of weight—the heavier the ware the longer it will last; however, even lightweight ware will give years of service. Sterling is made in several weights. In general, different patterns are made in different weights; however, a few patterns are made in two weights. The cost of sterling is affected by weight—heavy wares are more expensive than lighter weight wares—and by the design and workmanship of the pieces. Intricate designs are expensive to produce; hand-finished pieces are costly.

Sterling is generally sold in place settings that include some or all of the following: place knife and place fork, teaspoon, butter spreader, salad fork, and place spoon. The place spoon is a useful all-purpose spoon for eating cereal, soup, and desserts. Since there is no price advantage in buying place settings, select and buy just the pieces you think you will use. However, there may be some advantages in buying sterling ware by the set such as a service for eight. Such a purchase may buy the place settings at discount, or it may buy several serving pieces as well as the place settings. See Figure 19–1.

Identical patterns are available in both sterling and stainless steel in both traditional and contemporary designs. Purchasing the two wares

3-PIECE PLACE SETTING
Teaspoon, Place Knife and Fork

4-PIECE PLACE SETTING
Teaspoon, Place Knife and Fork,
Salad Fork

5-PIECE PLACE SETTING
Teaspoon, Place Knife and Fork,
Salad Fork, Cream Soup or Place
Spoon

6-PIECE PLACE SETTING
Teaspoon, Place Knife and Fork,
Salad Fork, Cream Soup or Place
Spoon, Spreader

FIGURE 19–1. The individual pieces included in three-piece, four-piece, five-piece, and six-piece place settings.

in the same design extends their use and definitely favors the use of limited numbers of place settings of sterling. All too frequently, the owner of a few place settings of sterling keeps them in storage until the day when there will be enough of them to set the table fully with sterling. However, design consultants consider stainless steel a modern material; they favor contemporary design that is clean-lined, simple, and without ornateness for stainless steel ware rather than traditional design that imitates sterling.

Patterns are kept open for whatever length of time they are well received; some patterns remain active longer than others. Manufacturers make it possible for consumers to purchase pieces of inactive patterns from time to time. In general, sterling patterns remain active longer than plated patterns.

Silver-Plated Flatware

Plated silver pieces do not have the same composition throughout. They are composed of a core of base metal coated with silver, the amount of the latter determining the durability or quality of the ware. The silver is added in an electroplating process, which evenly distributes the silver over the base metal. The best base metal, and the one most generally used in good quality ware because it is durable and has the color of silver, is silver nickel, an alloy of nickel, copper, and zinc. Pieces plated over this alloy are often marked EPNS; these letters inform the consumer that the ware is electroplated over nickel silver. Flatware plated over steel may rust when the silver has worn off unless the steel has been alloyed so that it is rust resistant.

The quantity of silver laid over the base metal affects the quality of plated silverware. Standard plate has two troy ounces of silver applied to a gross of teaspoons; forks and other pieces have more silver applied to them but in the same ratio. At one time, plated ware was quadruple-, triple-, or double-plated meaning that four, three, or two times more silver was applied than standard. The amount of silver on a ware will be reflected in price and in the silversmith's guarantee to replate or replace pieces that show wear within a defined period of time. Plated ware is made with as little silver as one-fourth standard; this kind would be very inexpensive. To make spoons and forks more durable, they are sometimes reinforced on bowls and handles at the points of contact with the table. Reinforcement may be by inlay or overlay; if by inlay, a part of the base metal is replaced by sterling silver at these points; if by overlay, added silver is applied at these points. Overlaid pieces may be identified by the small, slightly elevated circle of silver at these points. Inlaid pieces cannot be identified unless the manufacturer marks them, for the reinforcement is under the plating of silver.

The quality of plated flatware is determined by the kind of base metal used, the amount of silver applied, reinforcements at points of wear, the intricacy of pattern, and workmanship. Knife blades should be securely soldered to handles; tines of forks should be well-finished, completely plated, and diminish in circumference from the base of the fork to the ends of the tines. Silverplate of good quality that is given good care can be expected to last a long time. It can be replated when it shows signs of wear, but this may be expensive. Plated silverware is sold in sets of service for six, eight, or twelve; open stock; and place settings. Sets may include in addition to the requisite number of place settings such pieces as tablespoons, butter server, sugar spoon, gravy ladle, and flat server. In general, place settings do not include butter spreaders, but do include two teaspoons. One should investigate; there is sometimes a price advantage in buying by set. Patterns of plated flatware are kept active as long as they are well received.

Either kind of silverware is as suitable with china, delicate glassware, and fine linens as it is with peasant pottery, Mexican glassware, and coarse-textured linens. Design and line, rather than kind of silverware, influence the harmony of appointments.

Stainless Steel Flatware

Stainless steel flatware is made from an alloy of steel, chromium, and nickel; the quantities of the latter two materials differ in different wares. Although stainless steel is tarnish and scratch resistant, it is not totally stainless, but it requires almost no maintenance care.

The quality of the stainless steel flatware available in the marketplace varies from fair to excellent and will be reflected in the price and in the finish of the pieces. High quality steel flatware will have been carefully finished to remove sharp edges and to produce a soft luster. It will, in fact, resemble silver. One company makes sterling and stainless steel flatware in the same patterns for mix-and-use possibilities. The designs of steel flatware are both contemporary and traditional. The former may have knife blades, fork bowls, and handles of unusual shapes and the handles may be made from teak, ebony, or other different material. Traditional designs mimic silver plate and sterling silver patterns. Stainless steel flatware can be purchased in place settings and by set. The very best quality of stainless steel ware is about as expensive as silver plated ware.

Vermeil

Vermeil ware is gold-plated ware. Traditionally, it was gold plated over sterling. Contemporary vermeil is gold plated over sterling and plated silver; but much of it is electroplated over a base metal. In the electroplated ware, the layer of added gold is very thin and may quickly wear off of the bowls of forks and spoons leaving the unsightly base metal exposed. Gold is nontarnishing, and like stainless steel ware, vermeil ware requires little care. The cost of vermeil ware is greater than that of the same ware that is not gold plated; that is, gold plated sterling would cost more than sterling, and ware gold plated over a base metal would cost more than stainless steel. Much fine china is decorated in gold, and the use of vermeil ware with it makes for very beautiful table settings.

Novelty Flatware

Novelty wares have handles that make them effective in creating attractive tables. These wares may have handles of wood, earthenware or china, bone, bamboo, reed, plastic, or mother-of-pearl. The bowls and blades of the pieces are generally made of steel but may be made of plated silver. They are rarely durable wares, but since they are not continually used durability is not essential. They require the proper accompanying appointments if they are to be used effectively. Many are appropriate with pottery and earthenware and textured linens.

The Manufacture of Flatware

Regardless of composition, all flatware is made in the same manner. Forks and spoons are similarly made. The rough form, called the *blank*, is cut by steel dies from a sheet of the metal. The blanks are rolled and shaped, then clipped to the proper size, shape, and thickness. The pattern is next stamped with another set of dies or is marked by hand. Knives may be stamped all in one piece, or hollow or solid handles may be soldered to stainless steel blades. Hollow handles may be stamped in two sections, which are soldered together after the design has been stamped, or they may be drawn from single tubes of metal, in which case they are seamless. Stainless steel blades are then soldered to the handles.

After the design is applied, the individual pieces are smoothed and finished, especially the tines of forks and the edges of spoons. The workmanship employed in these operations determines both the quality and cost of a ware; good workmanship often entails many handlings of individual pieces. Silver or gold is applied to plated ware at this point. Pieces are then polished.

Buffing and polishing with different abrasives produce three different finishes: bright, a highly polished finish; butler, a satin finish; and gray, a subdued luster. Some sterling patterns combine different finishes; bowls may be bright, whereas handles may have a softer luster. In general, consumers prefer the softer lusters to the bright finish because scratches are less noticeable.

The kind and quality of workmanship that go into the production of a flatware affect its cost; the better a ware is finished and the more it is hand-finished, the more expensive is the ware.

Miscellany

Knives and Forks.   Heirloom sets of flatware often have dinner knives and forks, luncheon knives and forks, fish knives and forks, and dessert knives and forks. Most contemporary flatware has only the so-called place knife and fork scaled in size to the contemporary ten-inch dinner plate and the contemporary dining table. Knives and butter spreaders have either flat or hollow handles, which may be one-piece or of two pieces. The hollow handles are slightly more expensive, but are more easily gripped. Both are equally durable if the blade has been securely soldered into the handle. The blade is often serrated for easy cutting. Steak knives have very sharp steel blades or serrated blades. Viande knives and forks have long handles for easy cutting and comfortable handling.

Many contemporary flatware designs have pieces shaped differently from traditional pieces: the bowl of the fork is deeper and the tines are shorter; knife handles are molded and shaped to the hand, knife blades are triangular in shape; spoons are rounder and less ovoid; and the shapes of the handles of all pieces are more slender and delicate. Theoretically these alterations make tools that are more comfortable to handle and use.

Spoons and Serving Pieces.   For many years, silversmiths made an enormous number of special individual pieces and serving pieces. Many of them were limited in use. Redesigning has produced all-purpose or multiple-use pieces. The bouillon spoon, cream soup spoon, and dessert spoon have been combined in one spoon, called a *place spoon.*

Small serving spoons and forks, such as the lemon fork, the pickle fork, the butter pick, the jelly server, and the bonbon server, have been reduced to two pieces, the *small-dish serving spoon* and the *small-dish serving fork.* Large serving pieces have likewise been reduced to *large-dish serving spoon* and *large-dish serving fork;* they replace the berry spoon, round server, meat fork, and salad serving set. This trend should reduce costs at the same time that it multiplies the uses for each serving piece and reduces the amount of flatware essential for convenient service. Scissors-style serving pieces that combine in one tool a fork and spoon, or a fork or spoon wih a flattened server, or two such flattened

FIGURE 19–2.   Serving pieces. 1. Tablespoon. 2. Small serving spoon. 3. Pierced tablespoon. 4. Gravy ladle. 5. Large serving fork. 6. Small serving knife. 7. Flat server. 8. Large serving spoon. 9. Small serving fork.

parts are practical serving pieces especially for buffet service. See Figure 19–2.

Selection of Flatware

Because the purchase of flatware represents a considerable investment, buy only after you are fully informed, after you have handled and examined the individual pieces of the patterns you like, and after you have evaluated the care it requires, in relation to your way of life.

As you shop around and study the different patterns, lay each place setting on the counter, and joggle the pieces. They should lie flat and not be easily displaced. The repetition of the pattern should be pleasing because it will be repeated many times around the table. Make certain that the pattern is one you will not tire of. Look at the pieces individually; each one should be well proportioned and should be appropriate for its intended use.

Go through the motions of eating with each piece to make sure that each is comfortable to use. Handle each piece, and note the weight and thickness of the parts. The fork is thickest at the shank, the narrowest part of the handle, and from there it tapers to the ends. Pinch the tines of the fork; they should be strong, yet delicate in design. The angle of the tines should be gradual. The knife handle should be of a comfortable length and the blade should be thickened at the junction with the handle where the index finger presses.

Designs in flatware are available for every taste and every budget; some are contemporary, others are traditional. Some homemakers choose intricate patterns to use with rather plain dinnerware, glassware, and linens; others choose flatware of simple design that is suitable for use with a variety of appointments.

The Care of Flatware

Except for novelty wares, all flatware should receive much the same care. The first recommendation for the care of flatware, especially sterling, is that it be used. Rotate pieces in use so that all develop the same degree of patina.

Wash flatware as soon after use as possible; but if you must wait to wash, then remove immediately any tarnish that has developed. Wash in hot water, using a mild soap or detergent. Use a soft brush, rather than a dish mop, to remove all particles from between the tines of forks. Rinse thoroughly in hot water, and dry well. Store a flatware that tarnishes in tarnish-proof bags or chest. Silverware that tarnishes can now be polished with a polish that carries tarnish-preventative that delays tarnishing for months. Follow the directions of the manufacturer for best results.

HOLLOWWARE

Attractive table settings often include some kind of hollowware. The term *hollowware* includes pieces used as serving dishes for food and such decorative objects as trays, pitchers, beverage pots, vases, and the like, regardless of the material of which they are composed. Hollow pieces are available in sterling, plated silver, vermeil, stainless steel, pewter, copper, and brass. Those pieces that require the least care are the most usable.

Sterling pieces are made in several weights. Lightweight pieces dent easily. Some lightweight pieces may have weighted bases, which make them feel heavier and keep them steadier. Weighted articles must be stamped "Weighted" or "Reinforced."

Silver-plated hollowware is harder than sterling; and it is less easily bent and dented. Hollow pieces are usually plated over brass and steel. Plated hollowware is usually made in single or double plate; the price varies accordingly and with the kind of base metal and workmanship.

Hollowware made from stainless steel can withstand high heat. The pieces made from stainless steel are practical, both because they can withstand heat and because they do not tarnish. Pewter beverage services and pitchers, beverage pots, and candlesticks tarnish slowly; they do not require much care and many persons prefer them to have a soft patina rather than a brilliant sheen.

Many of the hollow pieces a family owns have been received as gifts, but occasionally pieces are purchased. If they are to be practical they should be easy to care for, such as pieces made of pewter, stainess steel, or brass. The use of tarnish-preventing polish on silver makes silver pieces more practical than formerly. Store pieces in plastic bags or bags made of Pacific cloth.

DINNERWARE

A set of flatware may last a lifetime or longer; rarely does a set of dishes last so long, for dinnerware is a perishable item. The degree of its perishability is determined by its kind and quality and the care it is given. Although sets of dinnerware are obtainable in glass and plastic, most dishes are either china or earthenware. Both china and earthenware are clayware, and the term *china* as generally used, may refer to either, although it properly refers to a specific kind of clayware.

Clayware

China and earthenware are similar, in that clay is the basic ingredient of both. They differ in the kind and quality of the clays used, the other ingredients used, and the firing temperature; as a result, they differ in physical properties. In general, china has a hard, dense, vitreous body that does not absorb ink applied to a fractured edge; it emits a bell-like tone if gently tapped; it is translucent when thin. In general, earthenware has a soft, porous body that absorbs ink applied to its fractured edge; it has a dull, dead sound if tapped; it is opaque. However, there are wide differences in quality within each class, and fine earthenware may excel poor china in durability.

Earthenware.   The term *earthenware* includes both pottery and a finer and more durable ware described as semivitreous ware. It is a classification so broad that it includes the crudest handcrafted pottery, as well as fine dinnerwares such as Spode and Wedgwood. The reasons for such diversity lie in the diferent clays that may be used, the vitrifying materials that may be added in production, and the different firing temperatures.

Pottery dishes are made from coarse, colored clays without added materials; firing is at low temperatures. They are thick and appear heavy. They are generally bright in color and are often decorated with gay and vivid designs. Pottery is not durable; it is easily cracked, chipped, and broken. The color of the ware under the glaze is often brown or red. Because the base is porous, once the glaze is broken, the dishes are absorbent, and therefore unsanitary, as well as unsightly. They are usually inexpensive, and they cannot be expected to give long service.

Fine earthenware is made of light clays, flint, and feldspar. The firing temperature is sufficiently high to produce semivitrification and a somewhat dense body that is fairly resistant to breaking, cracking, and chipping. Some earthenwares are of such excellent quality that they are somewhat translucent and slightly resonant.

Stoneware is an earthenware that, because of its composition, can be fired at high temperatures. It is durable and has excellent heat-retention properties.

China.   Only fine white clays are used in the manufacture of china. Although the formulas of different potters are jealously guarded secrets, we do know that the materials added to the clays in the manufacture of china include feldspar and silica. During high-temperature firing, the materials melt and fuse to produce a homogeneous, semimolten mass. This mass cools to form a hard, dense, nonporous body.

Although china objects may appear fragile, they are more durable than heavy, substantial-looking pottery objects. The hardness of china makes it the most durable of the claywares.

Bone china is made extensively only in England. Bone ash is combined with clay to produce this milky-white ware, which has a high degree of translucency. It also has a soft glaze that mars easily.

Belleek china is an Irish china named for the county in which it was originally made. It is very thin, cream-colored, and highly translucent; it has a lustrous gloss that is sometimes iridescent. The production of Lenox china was begun as an attempt to reproduce this delicate ware.

Porcelain is a mixture of clay, feldspar, and silica. It is fired first at a low temperature. After the application of the glaze, it is fired at a high temperature so that the glaze permeates the body, creating an almost opaque glass. Porcelain is brittle; hence it is not as durable as china.

Manfacture of clayware.   The materials of which a clayware is to be composed are blended with water to produce a thin paste called *slip*. The slip is refined and purified in accordance with the quality of the ware to be made from it. The slip is then filtered and aged to produce a plastic clay.

The plastic clay is next shaped into pieces called *green ware*. Shaping is by two methods—*jiggering* for plates, cups, saucers, platters, and shallow bowls, and *casting* for beverage pots, pitchers, sugar bowls, and pieces that cannot be shaped by jiggering. In jiggering, the clay is placed in a plaster-of-Paris mold on a revolving wheel. As the wheel turns the clay is shaped by the mold and a steel tool known as a *profile* that the potter operates. The profile spreads the clay evenly and smoothly to the right thickness in the mold. The face of a plate or saucer is shaped by the mold, and the reverse side is shaped by the profile. When bowls and cups are jiggered, the process is reversed—the mold forms the outside and the profile forms the inside of the vessel. After jiggering, pieces are left on molds to dry. In casting, the plastic clay is first thinned with water to form slip which is poured into molds and allowed to stand. Water passes from the slip into the mold leaving a layer of clay affixed to the mold. The remaining slip is poured out and the cast is allowed to dry. Handles, feet, spouts, and tops are molded and then affixed to shaped pieces with slip. Green ware is fragile.

The green ware is then fired. The temperature of firing affects the quality of the finished ware. China is fired at temperatures that reach approximately 2300° F; earthenware, at temperatures approximately 1800° F. The fired ware is called *biscuit ware;* it is dense and vitreous or porous, depending on its composition and the temperature of firing.

Unless the ware is to be decorated under the glaze, the next step in production is glazing. Glaze, which is similar to glass in composition, is applied to the biscuit ware by spraying, dipping, or painting. During firing, the ingredients of the glaze melt to produce a coat of fused-on glass. The brilliance and hardness of the glaze are determined by the temperature of this fire—called the *gloss fire.* The hardness of the glaze is a factor in the durability of a ware; a soft glaze is easily scratched and marred in use. To ensure perfectly glazed pieces, care must be taken in the packing of the biscuit ware in the receptacles that hold it during firing. Plates are supported on clay pins that leave unglazed pin marks. In high quality ware these marks are removed by polishing.

Different glazes and different firing temperatures produce different finishes, including a brilliant, glassy finish, a dull luster called a *matte* finish, and a semimatte finish, which is less glassy than a brilliant glaze.

If a design has been applied to the biscuit or if the glaze is the sole decoration, then the ware is complete at this point; other ware is ready for decoration.

Decorating Clayware. The kind and amount of decoration applied to clayware are large factors in determining the cost of clayware. Decoration may be applied in the glaze, as in solid-colored wares. That the color is in the glaze is evident as soon as the first piece chips and the color of the biscuit is revealed. Design may be applied in a variety of ways, either over or under the glaze. Overglaze decoration must be fused to the ware by an additional firing. It can sometimes be detected by feel.

PHOTOGAPH 9.   Well-coordinated table appointments. (*Joe Boris.*)

Handpainting is one of the oldest and most expensive methods of decorating china. This method is not in wide use today; however, filling in the printed outlines of designs by hand is not uncommon. Some decals are touched up by hand, and nearly all the bands and lines on dishes are done by hand.

Much dinnerware is decorated by decalomania. Decals make possible the use of many color shadings and of intricate design. Transfer printing with engraved copper plates permits the application of designs in one color, as in the old willow wares. Copper-plate printing is expensive, and design may be less expensively applied by stencils, hand or machine stamping, and silk screen printing.

In addition to, or instead of, applied design, some wares have design in relief. Such design is generally produced while the pieces are being shaped and is much used in English earthenware.

Each operation in the production of dishes is accompanied by losses; the further along the loss occurs, the more expensive it is. The more often a ware is handled in production, the more expensive it becomes. If a potter sells only perfect pieces, they are more expensive than the slightly flawed, but usable, ware that another potter sells.

Glass-Ceramic Dinnerware

The newest ware for dinner tables is a hard ceramic ware that was developed for use in the nose cones of guided missiles. It is manufactured from materials that are melted, formed, and cooled as glass; subsequent heat treatments produce a ceramic that is resistant to breaking, chipping, scratching, and cracking. The ware is guaranteed by the manufacturer for three years. It is available both plain and patterned. To make for variety in table settings, colored pieces that include solid brown, green, and yellow sixteen-ounce bowls and tall coffee cups and saucers and bread-and-butter plates in yellow, brown, green, and blue patterns are available. Baking dishes, saucepans, skillets, and beverage makers available in this ware are resistant to temperature changes and can go from freezer to range or vice versa.

Selection of Dinnerware

China, earthenware, and plastic ware can be purchased within a wide range of prices. The cost of any ware is affected by the kind and quality of the materials used, the kind and amount of decoration, the workmanship, and the freedom from defects of the ware.

Ceramic wares are classified according to quality as *selects, run-of-the-kiln,* and *seconds* and are priced accordingly. Selects have no defects. They are completely covered with glaze, except for the three pin marks where clay pins supported pieces in the gloss kiln. Their decorations are perfectly centered, and no parts are missing or out of position. Some manufacturers sell only ware of this quality. Run-of-the-kiln ware includes some less-than-perfect pieces, but the defects are scarcely noticeable. Much medium-to-high-priced ware is of this quality. Seconds are pieces with noticeable defects; however, these defects are not the kind that affect the durability or usefulness of the ware.

China dinnerware and earthenware can be purchased in place settings, in sets, and from open stock. Fine ware is generally sold only in place settings and from open stock. Place settings include three or more pieces. Three-piece place settings include a dinner or place plate, and a cup and saucer. In addition, a place setting may include a bread-and-butter plate and/or a salad-dessert plate. There is seldom any price advantage in buying place settings, although there is often an advantage in buying starter sets when dinnerware is sold this way. Starter sets include four place settings plus some hollow pieces. The place setting of the starter set usually includes the dinner or place plate, bread-and-butter or salad-dessert plate, and cup and saucer; it may include also the cereal or soup bowl. Hollow pieces include platter, vegetable bowl, and creamer and sugar bowl. It is desirable that additional pieces be available in open stock when starter sets are promoted.

The selection of dinnerware should not be made out of context. Any choice made should be finalized in relation to one's life-style. If all appointments used for dining are to be dishwasher-washed most of the time, then the dinnerware ought to stand up under the treatment it will receive in he dishwasher. A soft earthenware that chips easily may soon become unsightly.

Further, dinnerware ought to coordinate with other table appointments in design and in color insofar as color is relevant. Traditionally, American homemakers have rejected elaborately decorated ware. However, recent times have seen the use of more elaborate designs and color than formerly. It is in vogue to coordinate dinnerware of unmatched designs. Because some people like a little, but not too much, design on the table, sets have been made in which some pieces may be purchased plain. This mix-and-match method of selection applies to color too; many wares are available in a choice of colors.

Contemporary design has altered the shape of dishes. Some of the first free-form designs were extreme and not generally accepted; the coupe shapes are well liked, however. A coupe plate has no rim, and it curves up slightly at the edge to form a very shallow well. Other pieces of coupe shape are rounded and without rim, that is, the wide shoulder that was once so much a part of the design of dishes. Coupe shapes are pleasing and bear the repetition that is unavoidable in setting the table.

Attention should always be paid to shapes in the selection of dishes, to make certain that repetitions will be pleasing. Attention should also be directed to cups, which should be deep enough so that the beverage served in them does not cool too quickly. The most satisfactory cup for the service of hot beverages has a diameter at the cooling surface that is no greater than its depth. Furthermore, the cup should have a handle that is comfortable to grasp. Plates and saucers should support the flatware that will lie on them during dining.

There is no standard size for a plate or dish called by a specific name. Bread-and-butter plates, for example, vary from 4 to 6 or more inches in diameter; salad and dessert plates, between 6 and 8 inches; and dinner plates, from 9 to 11 inches. Bread-and-butter plates usually measure 6 inches; salad or dessert plates, 7 inches or slightly more; and dinner or place plates, 9 to 10 inches. The very large dinner plate is obtainable only in a few patterns; it is too large to be in scale with the table and dining area in many houses and apartments.

Not only are several kinds of dinnerware available but within each class there are wares at all prices—and at each price there are many different designs and colors. Yesterday, families owned one set of dishes, possibly two. Today families can own several sets of dishes without investing much money. It is very easy to acquire the dishes, but it is much more difficult to find room to store them in small apartments and homes.

The Care of Dinnerware

The rules for the care of dinnerware are much the same regardless of kind.

Store dishes carefully to prevent avoidable breakage. Hang cups from hooks for safest storage. Use pads between fine china and earthenware plates. Cover dishes that are used infrequently to prevent them from becoming dusty and greasy. Heat china and earthenware in a warm, not hot, oven at 150° F., unless the ware is ovenware. Other methods of heating dinnerware include hot water soaking for a minute or two or the use of the drying cycle of an automatic dishwasher. If overheated, the glaze may craze, and the ware may sometimes crack and break.

Rinse and scrape the dishes with a rubber scraper or soft brush immediately after use. Never leave tea and coffee cups unrinsed, because the stain is sometimes difficult to remove. Wash dishes in warm water, and use either soap or a mild detergent. Do not scour china, earthenware, or plastic dishes with scouring powder or steel wool, which can scratch them. Rinse dishes with hot water, and dry them with lintless towels, or let them drain dry, that is, if you do not have a dishwasher. When you put them away don't slide plates and saucers into place, but place them gently in position to avoid scratching the glaze.

BEVERAGEWARE

Just as technology has extended the varieties of flatware and dinnerware available to us, so has it extended the kinds of ware for beverages. In addition to glassware, which has long been the favored ware for beverages, we now have plastic ware and paper ware in variety. Paper ware remains disposable, but plastic ware is of both the disposable and continued-use kinds. In general, plastic wares resemble glassware in shapes and design. The extent to which plastic beverageware withstands heat depends on the kind of plastic utilized and the method of production. Its light weight and resistance to chipping and breakage advantage it for many users. Paper beverageware is now coordinated in color and design with paper dinnerware and paper "linens." The new paper ware is superior to the old in utility and beauty. Its wide use bespeaks ready acceptance. Although we use the paper and plastic wares from time to time, we prefer glassware for its beauty.

Glassware

Like clayware, glassware is made of earth materials and processed by fire. The main constituent of glass, regardless of kind, is silica or sand; other materials used vary with the different kinds of glass. There are three main classes of glassware, all of which may appear on the dining table: lime glass, lead glass, and borosilicate glass.

Lime Glass. Lime glass is made from sand, soda—to hasten the melting of the sand, lime—to harden the glass, and other materials that give clarity or color to both. Lime glass is hard but brittle; it does not lend itself to decoration by cutting. It does not scratch easily, it has a soft luster, and it emits a dull sound when tapped.

Lime glass can be inexpensively produced; therefore, bottles, windowpanes, and many of the tumblers, creamers, sugar bowls, plates, and other glass dishes that the homemaker uses in her kitchen and dining room are made from it.

Lead Glass. The main constituents of lead glass are sand, potash, lime, and lead oxide. Lead glass, sometimes called flint glass, is soft; it scratches easily, and it has a brilliant luster and remarkable light-reflecting properties. It emits a bell-like tone when struck. It can be cut to produce a many-faceted surface.

Lead glass objects are more expensive than similar ones made from lime glass. Glassware said to be made of "rock crystal" is made of lead glass. Fine blown glassware is made from lead glass.

Borosilicate Glass.   Perhaps the homemaker's favorite glass pieces are her heat-resistant baking dishes. Trade names for these heat-resistant glasswares include Pyrex, Glasbake, and Fire King. This glass is made from sand, soda, and boric oxide. It is durable, has little luster, and emits a dull sound when tapped. It is transparent, milk-white or colored. Color may be applied to the white ware for bowls, dinnerware, and attractive baking dishes.

Measuring equipment, casseroles, platters, baking dishes of all sizes and shapes, coffee bottles, mixing bowls, and sets of dishes are made from this glass. All are inexpensive. The availability of these heat-resistant glass pieces for use on the dining table, as well as in the kitchen, is a boon.

Manufacture of Glassware.   The materials of which glass is composed are heated to a temperature of 2500° F, to produce a molten mass called *metal.* The hot metal is worked at a temperature of 2000° F. It is shaped by blowing, molding, or a combination of both.

By means of a blowpipe, a mass of molten glass can be transformed into any desired shape. The glass blower shapes the object by blowing air into the mass and by rolling the blowpipe. Decorative elements such as handles, feet, and stems can be affixed to shaped pieces while they are still plastic. The glass object is cut from the iron blowpipe, and the edge is shaped and smoothed by reheating. Glass blowing is an art, and thus blown pieces are expensive.

Glassware is shaped in molds into which glass is either blown or pressed. In either instance, the object may take on design as well as shape in the mold. American glass makers developed the method of pressing glass into molds at the beginning of the nineteenth century. Their first pieces are collectors' items today.

After being shaped, all glass pieces must be annealed, that is, slowly cooled in special ovens. Glass is a poor conductor of heat, and when subjected to sudden changes of temperature, it breaks unless it has been annealed. Proper annealing of glass is a factor in improving the durability of glassware.

Decoration of Glassware.   Applied decoration is not essential for the making of beautiful glassware. Many glass objects are beautiful simply by virtue of the color, clarity, and luster of the glass and by virtue of their proportion and shape. The modern trend favors this kind of glassware.

Design may be applied to glass in a number of ways. Glass may be cut, engraved, carved, etched, and sandblasted to produce design by removing part of the glass. Glass may also be enameled, painted, and gilded. Bubbles of air, metals, and other kinds of glass can be imprisoned within glass as decoration. Lastly, glass may be cased or layered and patterned by cutting into one or more of the layers. Pressed glass may have the pattern introduced during molding. Many of the early American pressed glass patterns are being reproduced today.

Any decoration of glassware that requires skilled labor or hand labor is costly. Much of the cost of some glassware is the cost of decoration.

Selection of Glassware.   Factors that affect the cost of glassware include the kind and quality of the glass, the method of molding the ware, and the kind and amount of decoration on the ware.

Quality in glassware is determined by the clarity and luster of the glass; its freedom from bubbles, streaks, and other defects; and the absence of color tinges in colorless glass. High quality glass pieces are free of flaws from molding, are perfect in shape, have perfectly executed decorations, and have smooth rounded edges.

Glassware is sold in sets and from open stock. Sets include such groupings as juice sets, cocktail sets, berry sets, salad sets, dessert sets, and others. Some manufacturers of fine glassware recommend the purchase of glassware by place setting, which may include as many as five pieces; dessert or salad plate, goblet, sherbet, tumbler, and juice glass.

The most practical approach to buying glassware is to buy a ware of medium quality for day to day use, to buy it from open stock so that broken pieces can be replaced, and to buy tumblers or footed pieces because they break less readily than stemmed ware. To get the most service out of glassware, give it good care during dishwashing and store it with care.

The increasing interest in so-called "gourmet" foods and wines has led to confusion about wine glasses. Although many different shapes of wine glasses are described by different names, the names are, in general, descriptive of the place of origin rather than being specific for a kind of wine. A good wine glass is clear and free of design so that the color of the wine is not distorted. It has a stem at least two inches long so that it can be held without the temperature of the wine being altered by the hand. Finally, so that the bouquet of the wine can be concentrated, it should be tulip-shaped and hold at least 8 ounces when full. In use, a wine glass is filled one-third to one-half full. This type of glass is suitable for all still wines, champagne, and brandy.

The Care of Glassware.   Although glassware can be washed in an automatic dishwasher, many persons prefer to handwash and dry their finest glassware. Gold- and platinum-trimmed ware should definitely be hand-washed to preserve the trim. Always wash glassware in warm water with a mild detergent or soap, rinse in warm water, and dry with a linen or other lint-free cloth. When handling grasp stemware by holding the bowl in the cup of the hand with the stem between two fingers. Always place glassware on shelves with the rims upward to protect the rims from chipping. Do not stack tumblers or footed ware.

Linens

Developments of recent decades in the composition and finish of tabletops have enhanced the contemporary dining table. Tabletops impervious to heat and water have made unnecessary the table pad that limited the table cover to cloths. The table can now be used bare, but what is more important is the variety of cloths, runners, and mats that can be placed safely on it. The kinds of linens available for use have greatly increased in recent years, the term *linens* is used broadly to include table covers and napkins of all kinds regardless of the actual fiber.

Tablecloths can be purchased in a variety of fibers, colors, textures, and designs. Many tablecloths are drip-dry, no-iron, and permanent press. Their vivid or subtle colors, bold or delicate designs, and sheer or heavy textures provide whatever kind of background the meal manager desires. Plastic table covers are also available in variety. Some imitate traditional damask, embroidered, and lace cloths, whereas others are definitely modern in design and bold in color. Place mats are obtainable in many fibers, colors, designs, and textures. Plastic place mats are available in infinite variety and some imitate traditional embroidered and lace mats. Runners—long narrow strips of fabric, straw, or other fiber—are sometimes centered the length of the table or sometimes laid along the sides as a background for covers. These are often exotic in design and fiber. A table may be beautiful because of the grain of the wood, its color, or its brilliant finish. When the table makes a suitable background for the appointments to be used, it may be left bare.

Not only has custom changed with regard to table covers, but it has also changed with regard to napkins. Today, paper napkins are widely used for family and guest meals. The fact that paper napkins may be purchased in a variety of sizes, colors, and designs and in excellent soft quality has done much to make them respectable.

Linens provide the background for the composition we call the dining table, except on that rare table where the cloth, because of its beauty or design, may dominate the scene. Linens are selected to harmonize with other appointments and especially with dinnerware. In general, heavily patterned dishes look best on quite plain linens that repeat one of the colors in the pattern. Patterns of several colors provide several choices for linens, thus making possible a variety of table settings using the same dinnerware. Linens with pattern may be used effectively under dishes with pattern if the linen design is similar to that of the dishes. Plain dishes or those with bands of color or very simple design seem to offer the most opportunity for variety in linens. The kinds of design that can be used with them are not limited; nor are the choices of color as restricted as with heavily patterned dishes. The color of the linens used with quite plain dishes may match the dishes in hue but be of a lighter or darker shade or it may contrast.

In addition to being harmonious in color and design, linens should also be suitable in texture to the other appointments used. Textured fabrics and materials are suitable with heavy-looking dinnerware and glassware; fine china and delicate glassware require sheer linens or lace.

Although linens are selected to blend with other appointments, they should also be selected with care in mind. Busy homemakers are wise if they select linens that require little time for upkeep.

Care of Linens

The care of washable linens, whether made from natural, synthetic, or blended fibers, can be simplified by the following procedures.

1. For all linens of blended fibers and for all permanent press items, read directions for care, then diligently follow them. Some are subject to staining by fats and oils.

2. Remove stains while fresh, certainly before laundering. Moisten lipstick stains with glycerine, the kind purchased at the drugstore, before laundering. Coffee, fruit, and vegetable stains will be removed by soaking in cool water. If the fabric permits, pour boiling water through the spot to remove coffee and fruit stains. Check the color fastness of fabrics before using special spot removers.

3. The use of a fabric softener or a light starch, whichever is appropriate, makes ironing easier and gives a good finish to the kinds that require ironing.

4. Store infrequently used linen pieces clean, unstarched, and unironed. Press in no other creases than the center fold in a large cloth. Hand crease other folds.

5. Iron dark-colored cloths on the wrong side. Iron embroidered linens on the wrong side on a well-padded board or a thick bath towel; turn and finish on the right side. Use a thin pressing cloth when ironing lace or areas of open work.

6. Let ironed linens dry thoroughly before storing. Store in boxes

when possible. Roll runners and cloths around cardboard tubes or rolls of paper when storage facilities permit.

7. Some mats and cloths and napkins are more satisfactorily dry-cleaned than laundered.

TABLE DECORATIONS

The origins of decorating the dining table are buried in the past. The use of heavily scented flowers as table decorations probably interferes with perception of food flavors. However, flowers are preferred table decorations. Except on the buffet table, the large tea table, and the banquet table, a flower arrangement should be kept in scale with the table and this means that it will be small for most dining tables in most contemporary homes; just a few flowers, maybe only one. As mentioned previously, whatever the arrangement, it should be kept low so that persons seated at table can see over it. The flowers should be coordinated with table appointments. There is a difference in opinion about the use of artificial flowers; some persons like them, others do not. Arrangements of leaves and potted plants—in suitable containers and in proper scale—make pleasing table decorations. Arrangements of fruits and/or vegetables are effective. These, too, can be artificial—plastic, glass, or wooden. Tall candles or candles in tall candlesticks that burn above eye level, with or without other objects, are well-liked decorations. Some figurines are suitable for use on the dining table. Where the dining table is placed against the wall, a well-chosen picture placed on the wall above the table provides effective decoration.

What and how much can be used on a table as decoration is established by the size of the table and the appointments used on it. Some tables look best when nothing is added, the elegance of linens, dinnerware, flatware, beverageware, and food is enough. There is beauty in simplicity. We are prone in an affluent society to excesses in table decoration.

SUMMARY

There are so many beautiful appointments for sale that it is often difficult to decide what to buy. Beauty in table setting is not achieved through the use of expensive things per se. Beauty is achieved by the use of linens, dinnerware, flatware, and beverageware that are coordinated—these objects may cost much or little; are free of smudges and soil; and are placed in orderly fashion. Each person who sets a table expresses something of herself or himself—a feeling for color, an appreciation for design, a love of beauty, a concern for detail, or a lack of concern for such mundane matters as the mode and manner of dining.

Chapter 20

Waiting on the Table

The ritual of family meals at which all family members were present twice and even three times daily has all but vanished. In all honesty, it must be admitted that those meals were not enjoyed equally by all family members. Meals of the 1980's are different from those of the nineteenth century and pre-World War I. All too often, they are eaten alone. They are eaten hurriedly. They are not always tasty. Sometimes, they are eaten with concern for calories, cholesterol, and sodium. Infrequently, are they sit-and-enjoy meals. There is no "hired" girl to prepare and serve them. Family members assume meal preparation and waiting-on-the-table tasks for meals eaten at home. Waiting on the table is easy in the 1980's. The procedures suggested are adaptations of traditional customs; they are suited to the times; and they are, certainly, changeable if one so desires.

How to Wait on Table

The use of a serving table and/or a table-on-wheels expedites waiting on the table. A large tray can be used between the serving table and the kitchen because both hands are free to carry it; but only a small tray can be used between the serving table and the dining table because one hand must support the tray while the other hand removes something from table to tray and vice versa. Limit the use of even a small tray to the placing and removing of flatware, salt and pepper shakers, creamer and sugar bowl, dressings for food, beverageware, and other small objects.

Order for Removal and Placement of Courses

A course is removed in the following order: first, take away the serving dishes of food if there are any; second, remove the plates and the side dishes from individual covers; finally, use a small tray and take away unused flatware and other objects not to be used in the next course. The order of placing a course is the reverse: first, using a small tray, lay the required flatware and such small items as cream and sugar, a pitcher of pudding sauce, or a bowl of whipped cream; second, place any plates, bowls, and cups and saucers required; lastly, bring the food and/or beverage. For meals for which the table has been carefully set, the removal of a course may entail only the removal of individual covers, as for meals served blueplate style; and the placing of the dessert course may require only the carrying of served desserts from the kitchen to the table. The menu and the pattern of service establish how many duties must be performed in removing and serving courses.

Left-Hand and Right-Hand Serving

Some of the steps in removing and placing courses are carried out from the left side with the left hand and some from the right side with the right hand. The dinner plate is best removed from the left side with the left hand to avoid a possible collision with the beverage glass or glasses on the right. Any cover that includes a salad plate and/or a bread-and-butter plate is cleared from the left to avoid reaching in front of persons because these side dishes are placed to the left of the dinner plate. A beverage glass or an unused dinner knife would be removed with the right hand while standing on the right; and dessert flatware would be laid with the right hand while standing to the right. To serve from the left—left-hand service—stand to the left of the person being waited on so that the feet, heel to toe, are parallel to the table edge; this position brings the left hand closest to the table and puts the right hand in back of the person being served. To serve from the right— right-hand service—stand to the right of the person being served, feet parallel to the table edge; this position brings the right hand nearest to the table and puts the left hand in back of the persons being served. Except in formal table service, when standing to the left, use the left hand; when standing to the right, use the right hand. The hand nearest the table should do the work; to use the other hand would be awkward and clumsy and at the same time would introduce the possibility of bumping into the elbow of the person being waited on.

In formal service, both hands must be used because removing and placing occur simultaneously. Stand to the left, use the left hand to remove a soiled plate, use the right hand to place a clean plate onto which the next course will be served. Or, still standing on the left, use the right hand to remove the soiled plate, when the plate that will replace it has food served onto it, and place the plate with food on it with the left hand. That is, use the right hand, the one nearest the guest, to handle the plate least likely to have contents that can spill.

Order of Waiting on Persons at Table

The direction of moving around a table is from your left to your right, that is, counterclockwise. You begin at the cover of one of the following persons, depending on who is at table.

1. Begin with the hostess at a family table where parents dine alone with children; at this table the hostess is the honored person.

2. Begin with the woman seated to the host's right if she is a guest, or an elderly grandparent or aunt, or some other elderly person living with the family. A woman guest and an elderly woman are honored persons.

3. Begin with an elderly woman who may be seated to the right of the hostess because of a disability that requires assistance from the hostess. This is an uncommon situation, but one that may arise.

Removing a Course

When all have finished eating a course, if you have been delegated waiting-on-the-table duties or are the hostess and will perform these duties, casually place your napkin to the left of your cover and rise from the table, moving your chair as little as possible. Because few meals routinely consist of more than two courses served at the table, directions are for clearing the main course; but any other course would be similarly cleared. Proceed as outlined.

1. Remove the serving dishes first when these are present on a table or a side table, such as when American or compromise patterns of meal service have been used. The removal of a large platter or casserole may require the use of both hands; the removal of one or more dishes requires left-hand service; and the removal of a few dishes requires right-hand service. Stand to the left of the person in front of whom there is a large platter or casserole that will require the use of both hands; remove it from the left to avoid collision with any beverageware on the right. Take it to the kitchen immediately. Return to the table and remove to the serving table any pad or cloth that may have been placed under the platter or casserole. If one hand can support the serving dishes, stand on the left to remove those serving dishes on the left.

Take one serving dish with the left hand and transfer it to the right hand. Take a second with the left hand and then take both dishes to the kitchen. On returning to the table, remove to the serving table any protecting pads that may have been under the serving dishes. Similarly, remove the serving dishes on the server's right using right-hand service.

2. Next, remove the soiled appointments from covers. Begin with the proper person and proceed around the table in a counterclockwise direction. Exactly what you do is established by the number of plates and side dishes at the covers. Covers may include the dinner plate only or they may include, in addition, a salad plate or bowl and/or a bread-and-butter plate.

(a) When the cover includes only one plate, use left-hand service to remove the plate from the cover with which you begin. Transfer the plate to your right hand, and then remove the plate from the next cover with the freed left hand and proceed to the kitchen with these two plates, one in each hand. Avoid stacking dishes in the dining area unless you are *en famille.*

(b) When the cover includes only two items, such as the dinner plate and the salad plate or bowl or the bread-and-butter plate, remove the dinner plate with your left hand, and transfer it to your right hand. Then remove the second plate with your left hand. Proceed to the serving table; now, place the second plate quietly on top of the dinner plate. Clear the next cover in the same manner, and then pick up the plates placed on the serving table and proceed to the kitchen. Continue in the same manner until all covers have been cleared. Take your own cover in order as you proceed around the table. Strictly *en famille,* you may do this: remove one cover as suggested, proceed to the next cover, remove the salad plate or bowl or bread-and-butter plate and place atop the cover in your right hand, then with the left hand remove the dinner plate and proceed according to plan.

(c) When the cover includes three items, such as the dinner plate, the salad plate or bowl, and the bread-and-butter plate, remove the dinner plate first with the left hand. Transfer it to the right hand. Next, remove a salad plate with the left hand and place it as gently as possible on top of the dinner plate. Lastly, remove the bread-and-butter plate with the left hand. Proceed with these to the serving table, where you may place the bread-and-butter plate on top of the others. Whenever a cover includes a salad bowl, remove the bread-and-butter plate after the dinner plate, and place it on the dinner plate. Then remove the salad bowl and proceed as previously suggested. Clear the second cover in the same way, pick up the dishes on the serving table, and proceed to the kitchen. Continue in this manner until all covers have been cleared. Take your own in order as you proceed around the table.

(d) It is necessary in most kitchens to store food as it is brought from the dining area and to stack dishes on the kitchen counter or in a sink or to load them into the dishwasher as they are brought out from the dining area.

3. Finally, using a small tray (one no larger than twelve inches in diameter), remove the salt and pepper shakers, any beverage glasses not to be refilled, and unused flatware and any other remaining items not to be used in the next course. If the table has been carefully set, there will be no unused flatware to remove; should there be, remove it from the proper side—from the left if it is at the left of the cover (such as an unused salad fork), otherwise, from the right. Remove any beverage glasses that will not be refilled from the right, using the right hand. Always use the right hand for removing from the right. All such items can probably be removed in one circling of the table.

4. The course has been removed at this point; however, it may be necessary to perform two other duties: crumbing the table and refilling the water glasses. Crumbing is done only when necessary, as when hard rolls or crumbly corn bread have been served. A plate and a napkin are sufficient equipment. Do this from the left, because the crumbs, by virtue of the position of the bread-and-butter plate, will be at the left of the cover. Hold the plate below the table in your right hand and brush the crumbs onto it with the napkin held in your left hand. If there is no bread-and-butter plate in the cover, crumbs may be almost anyplace; do the best you can but avoid reaching the breadth of a cover. Leave a few crumbs if you must.

5. It is not customary to refill water glasses during a meal except when a servant waits on the table; refill empty ones at this point, using right-hand service. A napkin, called a *drip napkin*, held in the left hand, quickly catches the drip from the pitcher as you back away from the table to proceed to the next cover. Do not lift a glass from the table to refill it; if necessary, you may move the glass closer to the edge of the table by grasping it close to its base. Refill the glasses in the same order in which you removed the covers.

Serving the Dessert Course

We can serve dessert from the kitchen, from the serving table, or from the dining table. We serve a beverage with dessert much of the time, but we may offer the beverage throughout a meal, after dessert, or only after leaving the dining table. To expedite waiting on the table, especially when hostesses wait on their own tables, we are assuming that the flatware for eating the dessert was included in covers when the table was set.

Serving Dessert from the Dining Table. When a hostess pours a beverage at the table, she may delegate the serving of dessert to the host or another person at the table; on the other hand, she may choose to do all herself. In the following description of how to place the dessert course it is assumed that the hostess will serve. The procedures would be the same if another were to serve dessert such as a birthday cake, except that the appointments and the dessert would be placed at the server's cover.

1. Take the flatware essential for the serving of the dessert to the table on a small tray or plate, lay any tools that will assist the functioning tool to the left and the functioning tool—pastry server, knife, or serving spoon—to the right of the hostess's (or server's) cover or above the cover so that they will be beside the plate onto which the desset was served. At the same time place the creamer and the sugar bowl, if they are needed, in the position selected. See Fig. 20–1.

2. Place the plates onto which dessert is to be served in the center of the hostess's (or server's) cover. Whenever dessert, such as an Indian pudding or an English Trifle, is to be served into bowls, the plates they are to be placed on must also be placed. For such service, place one bowl on top of the stacked plates and set them in the center of the hostess's (or server's) cover. Place the remaining bowls, stacked one inside the other, to the left of the stacked plates. The person serving places a bowl on each plate when serving the dessert into the bowl.

3. Place the cups and saucers next. When the beverage is to be served

FIGURE 20–1. Dessert placed for serving at the table.

from a tray, carry the already arranged tray without the pot of hot beverage to the table. Place it from the right if the hostess has chosen the position on her right for it. Otherwise, place it from the left to avoid collisions with beverageware. When a beverage is served without the use of a tray, take the cups and saucers to the table either on a small tray or stacked in two's, preferably the former. Place the cups and saucers on the table with the handles of the cups directed to the hostess's right for ease in handling the cups. Set the cups and saucers down in any of three positions (see Figure 20–2). If you carry them to the table on a tray, put them down with your right hand (because you support the tray with your left hand). If you carry them by two's, a pair in each hand, put them down this way.

(a) To the left of her cover. Use left-hand service, and set those in your left hand down first; transfer those in your right hand to the left hand, and then place them.

(b) To the right of her cover. Use right-hand service. Place the cups and saucers in your right hand first; transfer those in your left hand to the right hand, and then place them.

(c) Above her cover. Use left-hand service. This position cannot be used if the hostess is serving the dessert. When an odd number of cups is to be laid, the single cup and saucer may always be placed in the position of the hostess's own cup at her cover—it is a convenient position for pouring.

4. Place the dessert in front of the hostess. Place the pot of hot beverage on the hostess's right, either directly on the table or on a tray (see Figures 20-1 and 20-2). Return to your place at the table. Your return will be a signal for the service of dessert.

Serving Dessert from the Kitchen.   Dessert is often served up onto dessert plates or into bowls or stemmed ware directly from the kitchen. A variant in the latter situation is to bring the desserts served into bowls or stemmed ware to the serving table on a tray and to serve them from it. Proceed as follows when service is strictly from the kitchen.

1. Place the beverage service on the table according to the option chosen.

2. Bring the desserts from the kitchen, one in each hand. Place from the left the one in your left hand in front of the proper person. Transfer the one in your right hand to the left hand and place it from the left in front of the person next right. Return to the kitchen for two more desserts and proceed in this way until all at the table have been served.

3. Bring the pot of hot beverage and place it at the hostess's right. Return to your place at the table.

FIGURE 20–2. Possible arrangements of the beverage service at the server's cover.

Serving Dessert from the Serving Table. This practice is a possible option when you are serving dessert from the kitchen. Proceed as follows:

1. Place the beverage service on the dining table in accordance with the selected option.
2. Bring desserts served into bowls or stemmedware (such as ice cream) on a tray from the kitchen, and place the tray on the serving table. You should have placed a stack of underliner plates for the desserts on the serving table when you arranged it. Place small paper or fabric doilies on coupe plates as you stack them. This practice prevents the sliding of the dessert dish placed on the plate as the total service is set down on the table. For easy serving of the dessert, put one served dessert on the top plate of the stack and then remove the total service with the left hand. Place a second served dessert on the next plate, remove it with the right hand. Proceed to the dining table and set them down as previously described. Continue in the same manner until all at the table have been served.
3. Bring the pot of beverage from the kitchen and place. Return to your place at the table.

Serving of Hot Beverages

Customs of beverage service differ in different socioeconomic groups, in different ethnic groups, and in different regions of the United States. Hot tea or coffee may be offered with the main course or only with the dessert course. Coffee may be served after the dessert at the table or away from the table. It may be served from the table or from the side. It is much easier to serve it from the table and pass the filled cups on saucers from hand to hand. Regardless of the arrangement of the appointments for pouring as delineated in Chapter 18, the person pouring follows the same procedure. See page 446 in the chapter on Etiquette of the Table. Once he has received his beverage, he does not pass other cups.

Whenever a hot beverage is offered throughout the meal, it is customary to refill the cups when dessert is served: the beverage pot is taken to the kitchen and refilled with the hot beverage unless the pot has been maintained at a suitable temperature. The arrangement for the beverage service should include a spill bowl into which the dregs in cups may be poured before the cup is refilled. For a spill bowl, use any bowl that is suitable in appearance and large enough to contain the cold remnants that may remain in cups. Cups and saucers are passed from hand to hand for refilling.

MEALS WITHOUT WAITING ON THE TABLE

People in the United States generally like two-course meals; they like the main course followed by something, even though that something is only a few grapes or a cookie. These two courses are occasionally served as one. The problem has been of having the dessert on the table during the main course and of eating the dessert course without removing the soiled dinnerware. Two practices have prevailed, particularly in the Midwest. Individually served desserts appear in the covers as a side dish above or to the left of the dinner plate. Dessert can be eaten without being moved, or it can be moved and placed on top of the dinner plate and eaten. Or else the dessert is taken from a common dish and served onto the dinner plate, or another plate within the cover, from which it is eaten. Neither of these practices is completely satisfactory. A more pleasing procedure suggests that the soiled dishes of the main course be passed from hand to hand to one or both ends of the table, where they are placed on a side table. The dessert is then served from the side table and passed from hand to hand until all have been served. Hot beverages are similarly served. Essential for this kind of service is a serving table that can be placed to the right of the hostess's chair, possibly a similar table that can be placed to the right of the host's chair, and an appliance for keeping a beverage hot or for brewing coffee or tea at the table.

Here are some suggestions for serving meals with finesse without waiting on the table.

1. Serve the main course in such a way that there is no need to pass plates or serving dishes. Either serve plates in the kitchen or permit guests to serve themselves at a buffet. However, if the host is unhappy when he cannot serve, by all means arrange things so that he can. Some way of limiting hand-to-hand passing will suggest itself.

2. Have no more than two plates at each cover. If a salad plate is used, omit the bread-and-butter plate; if no salad plate is used, a bread-and-butter plate may be laid.

3. When you offer a salad, avoid serving it from the table; instead, serve it up in the kitchen, and place the salad at each cover. But if you wish to offer the salad as a separate course, the bowl of salad may be passed from hand to hand and served onto the now empty dinner plate. This practice is acceptable, although some people do not favor it. You may also serve the salad course in the usual manner, but remember that this procedure means more passing from hand to hand.

4. When dessert is to be passed from hand to hand, keep to a food that can be served onto a plate. Avoid the double setup of bowl-on-

plate, which complicates passing. Should you use a double setup, place a small doily between the plate and the dish to keep the dish from slipping.

Setting the Side Table

Ideally, the side table should accommodate the dessert service, the beverage service, and the soiled plates from the first course. If it does not, a second side table placed to the right of the host's chair can be used; one table is used for the soiled plates and the other is used for the dessert and the beverage service. A three-tiered table is probably easier to work with than a two-tiered table. The dimensions of the table should be such that all soiled dishes can be placed below the top level. There are several optional procedures for arranging the table, depending on its style and size; however, certain principles are fundamental to effective use of the side table.

1. Place the dessert on the second level of a three-tiered table or on the lowest level of a two-tiered table, to keep it out of sight; place the plates and tools for serving dessert, the cups and saucers, the creamer and the sugar bowl, and the beverage pot on the top level, if possible. As soon as you are ready to clear the table and make use of the lowest level, bring the dessert up to a higher level.

2. Because you will stack plates as you receive them, place a basket large enough to accommodate the flatware on the lowest level.

3. Place accessory items such as bread and relishes on the top level or to the right or left of your cover, so that they can be passed around the table and cleared to the serving table with a minimum of passing.

4. If you intend to serve the salad as a separate course, you may prefer to put the appointments for dessert on the second level and use the top level for serving the salad.

5. To enable you to use the side table easily and without appearing awkward, use a dining chair without arms.

Using the Side Table

Experience in the use of the side table enhances its value in achieving a smooth, relaxed, and comfortable service for all. Here are some ideas for easy use.

1. Clear your own cover first or last, depending on whether you need to make room for dessert or beverage service in order to have room for stacking plates.

2. Ask each person on your left, beginning with the person on the host's right to pass his dinner plate to you. Then, beginning with the host, take dinner plates from those on your right, in turn. Stack them as you have planned but do it quietly.

3. Next, have salad or bread-and-butter plates passed to you in the same manner as the dinner plates.

4. Let saltcellars and pepper shakers, unused flatware, and other inconspicuous items remain on the dining table.

5. If you intend to serve the dessert, place the dessert plates in the center of your cover; put the dessert and the tools for serving it above the plates. Serve the dessert in the order you accepted dinner plates from those at the table.

6. Set up the beverage service according to your preference, and serve it in the order described earlier, unless you prefer to serve it in the living room.

7. Both the dessert and the beverage may be served from the side table if you so desire.

8. Should you wish to serve the salad as a course following the main course, that, too, can be managed. If one side table will not accommodate everything, place a second table beside the host. He will ask that the dinner plates be passed to him, beginning with you and then taking those on his left, then those on his right. As soon as you have given up your dinner plate, place the salad service at your cover. After all dinner plates have been removed, serve the salad.

The most serious objection to this particular style of serving meals is concerned with refilling beverage glasses. Strictly *en famille,* there is no reason why a pitcher of milk or water cannot be placed on the table: the members of the family pass their glasses rather than the pitcher. When guests are present, it is desirable to avoid this practice. A solution would be for the host to rise and refill those glasses that are empty or nearly so. Theoretically, the good guest does not drain his water glass in the first few moments of dining; instead, he sips from it, and, if the glass is moderately large, the supply of water is sufficient for the entire meal, especially when coffee accompanies dessert.

Common sense tells us that exact procedures for serving meals, when neither host nor hostess is to leave the table, will vary with menus and the number served. Until the homemaker is accomplished, one or more rehearsals of the service would be effective in producing a smooth and confident service when guests are present. Some families like this service; others do not. Some do not like to leave the table when guests are present; others do not mind. When the group is large enough, buffet service is a happy compromise.

SUMMARY

Telling takes longer and makes the task seem more difficult than actual doing. The procedures described are not the only acceptable ones, nor are they inviolate. Modify them to fit your life-style and your resources, always remembering to keep procedures comfortable for all and convenient for the person waiting on the table. The fact is that you can ignore all suggestions and "rules" that have been established and follow your own ingenious system, so long as none at the table are made uncomfortable.

Chapter 21

Etiquette of the Table

Every culture has defined who shall eat with whom, how food shall be taken or received, and how food shall be conveyed to the mouth. Customs of dining and of behavior while dining are defined for a time and a place; those of Western cultures are different from African, Muslim, and Oriental cultures. The body of definitions includes both proscriptions and prescriptions that are part of the folkways. As part of the folkways, the behavior must be taught, it must be learned, it gives order and stability in group interaction, it gives individuals a sense of security in group situations, and it is supported by the sanctions of the group.

The origins of dining customs are lost in time; ascribed origins include superstitions, religion, class delineation, and gestures of friendship. Contemporary table manners have been a long time evolving, but much of their refinement has come about during the past four centuries and parallels the widespread adoption of individual eating utensils in Western cultures. The fork was the last adopted of these tools. Although forks were known in Italy as early as the eleventh century, it was not until the sixteenth century that French society and the eighteenth century that the French middle class began to use the fork. The fork was not introduced into England until the seventeenth century and it was not until the late eighteenth century that the lower classes adopted the fork. As late as the turn of this century, the knife was used for conveying food to the mouth and a proscription in table etiquette was "don't eat with your knife."

Just as setting-the-table and waiting-on-the-table customs are modified and varied in time and place, so are customs of the table. In the United States, table customs may vary in minor detail among different ethnic groups, in different regions of the country, among different socioeconomic groups, and in metropolitan and rural areas. In the following, we offer some how-to suggestions for those in doubt. The practices delineated are those in general use. The following are described: seating arrangements at the dining table; the offering of food at the dining table; how to use the napkin and the tools for eating; directions for eating certain foods; and, lastly, how to be a hostess or a host.

SEATING ARRANGEMENTS AT THE DINING TABLE

The seating arrangements at the dining table when guests are present are simply prescribed, with few alternatives possible. The seating arrangements when the family dines alone may be varied and determined by family size, the ages of the children, the arrangements for dining, and family preference.

When the Family Dines Alone

When dining *en famille,* parents usually sit at opposite ends of the family table; children sit in between in positions determined by the amount of assistance needed. The son or eldest son may sit to his mother's right; the daughter or eldest daughter to her father's right. A grandmother or other elderly woman who is a family member sits on the host's, that is, the father's, right, unless she is so disabled as to require assistance best rendered by the hostess, that is, the mother of the family. Similarly, an elderly male relative might sit on the hostess's right. When guests join the family table, family members are disarranged to permit the seating of a woman guest to the host's right and a gentleman guest to the hostess's right.

When the Family Has Guests

When there are guests, seating arrangements at the table are established by the number to be seated, the distribution of the sexes, and the composition of the group. Insofar as possible, couples are separated and men and women are alternated around the table. The host and hostess sit opposite each other except when those at the table are couples and the number at the table is eight, twelve, or other multiples of four. The woman guest, or the most honored woman guest, sits to the right of the host; the gentleman guest, or the most honored gentleman guest, sits to the right of the hostess. When the number at the table is eight or more, it saves time and reduces confusion to have place cards at covers.

1. When the number at the table is even, but not a multiple of four, the host and hostess sit opposite each other and the sexes are alternated, when the group consists of couples, or the sexes are evenly distributed. A group in which there are more men than women or vice versa is seated so that all persons have compatible dinner companions.

2. When the number at the table is a multiple of four and the sexes are evenly divided, the host retains his position at one end of the table; but the hostess relinquishes her place to the most honored gentleman at the table. She sits at his left; he sits on her right as custom requires. Should the group at the table be unevenly divided as to sexes, the hostess may retain her position at the head of the table and seat the guests in any way she chooses, so long as the most honored guests are seated in accordance with custom.

3. When the number at the table is odd, the host and the hostess sit opposite each other; other persons are seated at the table so that they have compatible dinner companions.

4. When there is no host, a hostess sits at one end of the table. She may ask a gentleman friend to sit opposite her in those situations when a host would sit opposite her. She would seat an honored woman guest opposite her when the number at the table is a multiple of four; she would likely ask a gentleman friend to sit to this woman's left.

5. When all at the table are women, the honored woman guest sits opposite the hostess, who sits at one end of the table. In some situations, an honored woman is seated to the right of the hostess, the chairman, or the president of a group.

SERVING FOOD AT THE TABLE

Meals served at the table can be sit-and-enjoy meals. Because served plates are passed from hand to hand, it is desirable to keep passing to a minimum. For that reason, salads are frequently placed at covers rather than being served from the table. However, serving dessert, especially an unusual one, at the table provides enjoyment and it saves time in the kitchen.

The mode and manner of serving from the table should be simple and easy. The order in which served plates are accepted is established. When a meal is strictly *en famille* (father, mother, and household members), father serves and mother receives the first plate. It was passed by the server to his left and was passed from hand to hand. The next served plates are also passed to the left until all persons to the server's left have been served. The remaining served plates are passed to the server's right until all have been served. The person serving then serves himself. See Figure 21–1a. An exception to this procedure would be when an elderly, and perhaps incapacitated, family member or small

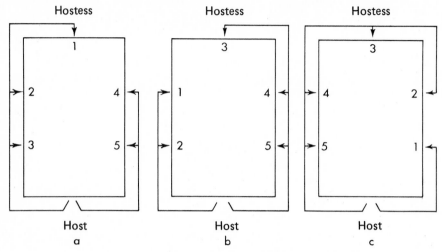

FIGURE 21–1.   Order of serving persons at the table.
a. Hostess receives first plate
b. Person to right of hostess receives first plate
c. Person to right of host receives first plate

child requiring special attention sits on the mother's right. In this instance, the first served plate is for that person so that food can be prepared for eating, such as the cutting of meat. The mother then receives the first plate passed to the right. See Figure 21–1b. When a hostess serves the salad or a dessert at the table, she follows much the same procedure in that she passes first to her left and then to her right, however, the first served plate to the left stops with the person on the host's right and the first to her right goes to him. There are many one-parent families in the 1980's. Whoever is head of the household serves as described unless the privilege of serving is granted to another member of the family.

When guests are present, procedure is as described: the first served plate to the hostess, served plates to the left, and then to right of the host with two minor exceptions. An elderly and honored woman guest sitting on the right of the host or on the right of the hostess may receive the first served plate. Figures 21–1b and 21–1c. When the person on the host's right receives the first served plate, all others are passed to the left until all are served, the hostess receives hers in turn.

When Food Is Self-served

When those at the table are to serve themselves, place the serving dishes of food on the dining table or a side table so that the host and the hostess can initiate the passing. In general, when guests are present, dishes will be offered to the woman guest on the host's right first and they will pass from person to person around the table; the host will receive them last and serve himself last. To avoid confusion, the hostess serves herself when dishes reach her; however, when she initiates the passing of dishes, she offers them to the person on her right without serving herself first. She receives them last and serves herself last. The offering of second portions is initiated in the same manner as the initial offering of food.

Offering Second Portions

Although second portions are taboo for persons who wish to control weight, it is the custom to offer second portions in some places on some occasions. It can be managed in this way. As soon as some diners may wish more food, the host moves his own plate to the right of his cover when this space is open, or to a small table placed to the right of his chair, in order to clear his cover. When guests are present, he asks the hostess if he may serve her. It is her duty to ask for something, even though she may not want it or may not eat it, to set a precedent. She passes her plate, with knife and fork laid side by side on it, to her right to the host. Her plate is returned to her by the same route. The host asks each person on his left to be served, then those on his right by simply asking, "May I serve you *this* or *that?*" Those at the table may ask for whatever they would like, even though food may remain on the plate, because this procedure expedites the serving of second portions. The order of serving second portions is the same as when the hostess receives the first plate. Strictly within the family, it is more likely that children and hearty eaters will be served twice or more without the hostess accepting a second portion; when guests are present, however, her acceptance of a second portion signals that others may feel free to do so.

TABLE MANNERS

Americans living in the United States have long been accused of having shabby table manners and recent social changes, such as eating in fast-food restaurants, in the school lunchroom, and dining alone have not led to improvement. Nonetheless, the basics of table etiquette have been little altered during this century. Later, if not sooner, the knowledge of proper table manners becomes important to many persons. Especially is this so in an upward mobile society. The following discussions will provide the kinds of information sought.

What to Do with the Napkin

1. Remove the napkin from the table with the left hand, with the right hand unfold it across your lap under the table. Open a luncheon-

size napkin fully, leave a dinner-size napkin folded in half. Except when in use, the napkin remains on your lap; do not tuck it under your chin.

2. Use the napkin as necessary. Always use it before drinking to avoid leaving greasy smears or lip-stick stains on glasses or cups.

3. When you use the napkin, blot rather than wipe with it. Women should not remove lipstick on a fabric napkin.

4. When you leave the table, place the unfolded napkin to the left of your cover.

5. Follow the same procedures for paper napkins as for fabric ones; don't shred or wad them.

How to Use the Tools for Eating

To keep the discussion of the conventions for the use of the tools for eating as simple and coherent as possible, the parts of the tools are named. Knives have blades and handles; blades have dull edges and cutting edges. Forks and spoons have bowls and handles; the parts of the bowl of a fork are the tines.

When you are a guest and if you are unfamiliar with any tools appearing in the cover, follow the lead of your hostess. Otherwise, as in restaurants, when the tools have been properly laid, use them in the order of arrangement from the outside toward the center of the cover.

The Knife and Fork.   There are two quite different customs in the use of the knife and fork. The American eats from the fork held in the right hand, tines directed upward; the European eats from the fork held in the left hand, tines directed downward. We favor the use of the fork for cutting whenever it is an effective tool for this purpose. We lay the knife across the rim of the plate when not in use; the European retains it in his hand until he has finished eating the course because he must continually put it to use. Our zigzag style of eating is more leisurely, the European's is more efficient; Americans in Europe tend to copy the Europeans, and Europeans in the United States tend to copy us. You may eat according to either style; just make certain that your technique is perfect.

1. To use the knife for cutting, grasp it in the right hand with the cutting edge of the blade directed downward, thumb extended along the handle, the cushion of the first finger pressing close to or at the union of blade and handle, and the remaining fingers curled around and under the handle, the end of which presses into the center of the palm. When the fork and knife are used together for cutting, grasp the fork with the tines directed downward in the same manner. That is, the index finger presses on the shaft of the fork, the thumb extends

along the handle, and the fingers of the hand curl under and around the handle. Do not enclose the handles of either fork or knife with a clenched fist. To hold food securely on the plate while cutting, pierce the food with the fork in the manner of a spear. Always keep the fork between you and the knife.

2. After cutting two or three bites of food, lay the knife with the cutting edge directed toward you across the upper right quadrant of the plate and transfer the fork to the right hand. Hold the fork with the tines pointing upward so that it rests on the second finger, the first finger presses on the edge of the handle, and the cushion of the thumb rests on top of the handle.

3. To use the knife as a spreader, hold it as for cutting but turn it one right angle to the left so that the first finger presses on the flat of the handle and the cutting edge of the blade is directed to your right.

4. Use the fork in the right hand to scoop food onto it except as it is turned over in the hand to pierce a bite of food. Never put more than one bite of food onto your fork; eat from the tip of the fork, tines directed upward.

5. Use the fork in the right hand for cutting food whenever it is an effective cutting tool. Grasp it in the hand the same way that you do the knife so that the edge of the bowl of the fork cuts against the plate, the handle is between thumb and second finger, the first finger presses on the edge of the handle, and the end of the handle presses into the center of the palm.

6. Use the fork for buttering vegetables including the baked potato.

7. When not in use, the knife lies across the outer rim of the plate, its cutting edge directed toward you. When not in use, the fork lies so that the bowl is centered on the plate; the handle is directed right about parallel with the table edge in front of you.

8. When you have finished eating, lift the knife and lay it beside the fork, but keep the fork between you and the knife.

Spoons. The spoon is used in the right hand only. It is a tool for cutting, as well as a tool for eating. It is held in the same way as the fork.

1. Dip the spoon away from you when eating soup, and sip from the side of the spoon.

2. In general, dip the spoon toward you when eating soft foods, and eat from the tip of the spoon.

3. Stir a beverage, or test its temperature with a spoon; always lay the spoon on the saucer after use.

4. When eating with a spoon, always lay it on the plate under the bowl into which the food was served. An exception to this rule is that

a soup spoon may remain in a soup plate. If there is no underliner plate, as when a vegetable in cream or a soft ice is served with a main course, lay the spoon on the dinner plate. Never lay a spoon that you have used on the table.

5. When iced-tea is served in a glass without an underliner and you use a spoon to stir in sugar, hold the spoon aside between your first and second fingers as you drink, or place the spoon to one side on a plate.

How to Handle Glasses, Goblets, and Cups

1. Take hold of tumblers and small glasses by encircling them at the base with the thumb and the first two fingers; the other fingers either support the glass at the base or are withdrawn into the palm of the hand, depending on the size and weight of the glass.

2. Grasp a footed or stemmed water glass at the base of the bowl between the thumb and the first two fingers; the remaining fingers encircle the stem or withdraw into the palm if the stem is short. Grasp wine glasses by the stem to avoid warming the wine.

3. Hold a cup by the handle between the index finger and the thumb so that the index finger passes through the handle and the thumb presses on the top of the handle, which rests on the second finger. Drink from the side of the cup nearest you.

4. You may drink soup from a cup if the soup is of thin consistency, but eat any ingredients that float before drinking; eat heavy ingredients that sink to the bottom of the cup after drinking the soup.

5. Drink from the handleless cup by encircling the right half of the cup with your right hand. Let the cup rest on the fingers of the open left hand, the thumb of which presses on the cup near the rim. Drink from the near side just above the right thumb.

How to Eat Different Foods

Some foods, called *finger foods,* may be taken and eaten with the fingers. Only foods that do not leave the fingers greasy, sticky, or dripping with a sauce are finger foods. Actually, what is finger food for one person may be fork food for another; individual skill and techniques in eating differ. The following sections describe how some different foods have been eaten traditionally. Confronted with the unknown, use common sense, that is, eat with the fingers only those foods that leave the fingers unsoiled except, of course, when you are dining where the hands are used for eating.

Breads and Pastries

1. Generally, breads, cookies, slices of cake, pieces of cake without soft frostings, small cakes, doughnuts, and other nonsticky pastries are finger foods. However, if they are served on a plate with a fork, eat accordingly.

2. Eat cake that has a soft frosting, is covered with whipped cream, or has a soft filling between its layers with a fork, or with a spoon if a fork has not been provided.

3. Eat cream puffs, chocolate éclairs, napoleons, and all other filled pastries with a fork, just as you would always eat pie with a fork.

4. Many sandwiches are finger foods, but use a knife and fork to eat one served with sauce and to eat some of the triple-deckers. Always break or cut a sandwich, including a hamburger on a bun, into pieces of suitable size before eating.

5. Spread a tortilla with sauce or butter; roll it; eat it from the end of the roll.

6. Eat pizza with a knife and fork unless it is a finger food for you.

7. Hot baking powder biscuits, hot rolls, cornbread, Sally Lunn, and nearly all other hot breads are buttered all at once; however, do break them into bite-size pieces for eating.

8. Do not crumble crackers into a bowl of soup except *en famille*.

Fruits. Small fresh fruits are finger foods; the mode of eating large fresh fruits is determined by kind and ripeness or juiciness. Canned and frozen fruits are eaten with a spoon.

1. Small fresh fruits, such as cherries, grapes, apricots, plums, raisins, dates, and candied fruits and fruit peels are finger foods. The pits of cherries and the seeds of grapes may be removed from the mouth between the thumb and first finger. Place them on the rim of the plate. Eat the flesh from the pits of plums and apricots; the pits end up in your hand, not in your mouth.

2. Peel oranges and tangerines, and eat the easily separated sections with the fingers. To peel, score with a fruit knife from stem end to blossom end several times around the fruit, then pull away the petal-shaped pieces of rind. Oranges can be peeled round and round, making a continuous spiral of peeling.

3. When cut in half, oranges, grapefruit, pears, and avocados are eaten with a spoon, preferably a sharp-pointed one. Eat oranges served sliced or in sections with a fork.

4. Quarter, and peel if desirable, apples, pears, and peaches. If the flesh is firm, eat with the fingers; if juicy, eat with a fork.

5. Except at picnics, watermelon is eaten with a fork; seeds are pushed to the side and remain on the plate. The flesh of segments of the other

kinds of melons may be removed from the rind with the spoon. Sometimes a knife is used to cut the flesh from the rind from end to end of the segment, the flesh is then cut into bite-size pieces which are eaten with the fork. The flesh of a small melon-half is eaten from the rind with the spoon.

6. Cut the flesh of cooked prunes, plums, and peaches from the pits with a spoon. Pits end up in the fruit dish, not in your mouth.

Meat, Fish, Poultry.   With few exceptions, be satisfied with the bites of meat and poultry that you can cut from bones and eat with a fork.

1. Never, never chew the meat from chop bones, rib bones, or steak bones except at the outdoor barbecue, picnic, or when dining *en famille*.

2. Chicken pieces (also rabbit pieces) are finger food only at picnics, barbecues or other outdoor events, and when served in a box or basket as in the fast-food shop. In general, use the knife and fork. Impale the piece of chicken—breast, thigh, or drumstick—with the fork and cut the flesh from the bone as best you can and eat with the fork. The only bones that you may nibble from are those of tiny birds and frog legs.

3. Crisp dry bacon, which shatters under the fork, is finger food. Otherwise bacon is a fork food.

4. To eat clams, oysters, and snails out of the shell, steady the shell with the left hand and remove the edible parts with the small seafood fork provided. Dip a bite at a time into butter or sauce. Use the small seafood fork for removing crab and lobster from cracked shells and claws; gently suck meat from small claws. Again dip only a bite at a time into a sauce.

5. Eat the shrimp of a shrimp cocktail with the small seafood fork; should these be giant size, impale one on the fork, bite off a suitable bite as daintily as you can, and eat in two bites.

6. Use the dinner knife and fork for eating fried shrimp, fried clams, fried scallops, soft-shelled crabs, and crab and lobster served out of the shell. However, if shrimp have tails that are intact, they may be held with the fingers; the edible part is eaten to the tail, which is returned to the plate.

7. Although people in the United States like gravy on their potatoes, gravy is properly put onto meat. To sop bread with gravy, drop a small piece of bread into the gravy and eat it with knife and fork.

8. When served an entire fish such as the Rainbow Trout, remove the head and tail to the bread-and-butter plate or put aside on your dinner plate. Using your knife and fork, slit the fish lengthwise and remove the uppermost fillet with the knife to your plate. Then remove the bone and place as the head and tail were placed. Eat the fillets with fork in either hand according to your custom. A fish knife and fork

are frequently provided—the fish knife is broad-bladed for ease in removing bones and/or skin.

9. Place accompaniments to meat, fish, and poultry to the side of the item. Place it on the item with the fork.

Vegetables.   In general, eat vegetables with a fork, but fresh crisp relishes are finger foods.

1. Place vegetable relishes on the bread-and-butter plate, salad plate, or dinner plate in that order of preference when you help yourself to them.

2. French fried potatoes and onion rings are fork foods. Potato chips and shoestring potatoes are finger foods.

3. Don't break open a baked potato and scoop the contents out onto the plate; rather add butter or sauce and eat it bite by bite from the shell. If you wish to eat a baked potato, skin and all, use a knife and fork to cut the skin into bite-sized pieces.

4. In general, pickled fruits and pickled vegetables are fork foods. Only small whole pickles and olives are finger foods. Bite the flesh of unpitted olives from the pit while holding the olive in the hand; that is, don't put the olive in the mouth, chew the flesh away, and then remove the pit from your mouth.

5. Eat vegetables served in cream and stewed tomatoes with a spoon.

6. If it is not broken into halves, break corn-on-the-cob into halves, butter it by row, and eat it by row. Hold the cob between your two hands.

7. The leaves of the artichoke are taken with the fingers, dipped into butter, and the small edible bit eaten off the leaf. Leaves are laid on the plate. The thistle part is removed with knife and fork and laid on the plate. Finally, the heart is eaten with knife and fork.

8. Use the knife with the fork in cutting wedges of lettuce or any salad ingredient that the fork alone does not cut. When salads are served as separate course, forks and knives are usually provided.

Miscellaneous Notes on Eating

The Act of Taking Food into the Mouth.   The act of eating can be quite unpleasant to observe. Eating in a more or less refined manner has to be learned and practiced. Neither the teaching nor learning is easy. Growing interest in gourmet dining in the 1980's also means new interest in the etiquette of dining.

1. Keep bites sufficiently small so that you can quickly empty your mouth should someone address you.

2. Do not drink a beverage when your mouth has food in it, unless the food is burning hot and you drink to cool the mouth.

3. Do not chew with your your mouth open.

4. To avoid appearing at your very worst, talk only when your mouth is empty.

5. Do not put your hands on your hair, ears, or face while eating.

6. Do not use your fingers to push food onto your fork. You may use your knife, held in the left hand in the same manner as held in the right hand for cutting, for this purpose. Do not use bread in your fingers to sop up gravy or sauce; you may, however, drop a piece of bread into it and, using knife and fork, eat it like any other food.

7. Do not hunch your shoulders over your plate. Move the body forward from the hips, not the waist or shoulders. Lift food to your mouth; do not lower your head to the food. Avoid placing the lower left arm on the table while you are eating with the right hand.

8. You may tip soup or dessert dishes away from you to get last spoonfuls.

9. You may drink thin soups; but spoon vegetables and other bits.

10. Never use a toothpick except in privacy in the United States, although its use is less frowned upon elsewhere in the world.

Individual Casseroles.   When food is served in individual casseroles, remove the contents to your plate, a portion at a time, if the casserole has been placed on an underliner and a spoon has been provided for this purpose. Otherwise, eat directly from the casserole. If the casserole has been brought to the table with the cover on it, put the cover on the underlying plate, not on the table.

Removing Food from the Mouth.   Remove bones and objectionable bits from the mouth between thumb and first finger with your hand cupped toward you, and place them on the dinner plate. Make an effort to conceal bits of food that have been removed from the mouth if they are unsightly. Remove the pits and seeds of fruits eaten with the fingers, such as cherries and grapes, from your mouth with the fingers to the plate. In general, eat fruits such as plums away from the pit; then place the pit on the plate. Remove a pit to a spoon if one gets into the mouth while you are eating canned fruits.

How to Help Yourself to Food

1. Do not use any of the flatware at your cover to remove food from a common container. Use the serving pieces provided for each dish.

2. Use the meat fork and the serving spoon like a scoop. Sometimes a tool for steadying a food item on the serving tool is provided; use it

in the left hand. When two serving spoons are provided, use one in each hand; if you have the skill, both may be used in the right hand.

3. In general, leave a spoon in the serving dish rather than on the underlying plate.

4. Place condiments and relishes that accompany meat, fish, and poultry beside that item on your main plate.

5. Place relishes to be eaten with the fingers on your bread-and-butter plate, salad plate, or main plate in that order, depending on what is at your cover.

6. Help yourself to finger foods so daintily that you touch only the pieces you take.

7. Place jelly or jams for breads on the bread-and-butter plate when one is provided; otherwise, place near the edge of the plate in the cover.

Finger Bowls.   Gently dip the fingers of one hand, then of the other, into the water in the finger bowl; unobtrusively dry your fingers with your napkin. You may moisten your lips causually if you think it essential; blot to dry them.

Smoking.   No longer are you free to smoke at the dining table. Smoke only when granted permission. If there are no ashtrays in sight, that signals, "no smoking" please.

When You Are the Hostess

The first duty of a hostess is to plan her menu and her work so that she can remain calm, cool, and collected at mealtime, especially if there are guests. She should be present in her living room to greet guests when they arrive, although she may soon excuse herself to complete last-minute preparations for the meal. An experienced hostess plans to serve a few minutes later than she has asked guests to arrive because she knows that someone will arrive late; she does not, however, ask guests for dinner at seven and serve at nine.

In a sense, a hostess leads the way at mealtime, and others follow; they eat when she does and they eat as she does. She is cook, butler, and waitress. Here are special notes for hostesses.

1. Enjoy a first course served in the living area with guests; do not take this time to complete tasks in the kitchen. You may do these tasks while the host and/or the children clear away the glasses and other appointments used in serving the first course.

2. Invite guests to the table. Take your position at the table quickly so that you can direct others to their places if the group is small and place cards have not been placed.

3. Make a plan for seating guests in advance, so that you can do it smoothly. You will seat guests with poise, if you simply place your hands on the top of your chair and say, "Mrs. Boss, will you sit on John's right and Mr. Boss, will you sit on my right? Mary, will you sit beside Mr. Boss, and Robert, will you sit next to Mrs. Boss?," and so forth. By grasping the back of the chair with your hands, you will avoid pointing, which makes you appear awkward. Use place cards when you have more than eight guests' for quick seating.

4. After all are seated, ask someone to say grace, if you wish, but be certain the person asked will not be embarrassed.

5. Take your napkin and unfold it across your lap. Begin eating at once if served plates are at the covers. If persons are to serve themselves, pass any serving dishes of food near you without first serving yourself. Ask others to pass nearby dishes.

6. When food is being served from the table, suggest that the first served begin eating if there are more than six at the table; otherwise, begin to eat as soon as all except the host are served.

7. When you are serving salad or a vegetable, pace your service to the host's, if he, too, is serving. In serving most dishes, use a spoon as a scoop in your right hand, and steady it with the fork held in the left hand. First, serve those on your left, beginning with the person on the host's right; serve each in order. In the interest of expediency you may next serve the host and then those on your right. Follow this serving order when you serve dessert and when you pour a beverage at the table.

8. Offer food a second time if you have planned for it. Accept a second portion so that others may comfortably do the same.

9. Continue to eat as long as any guest is eating.

10. When all have finished, signal to the person who is to clear the main course and serve desserts; a nod of the head should do. If you perform these duties, remain away from the table the shortest possible period of time.

11. Wait for the return of any person who has left the table to remove or bring in a course before beginning to eat or serve.

12. If you are to serve the beverage at the table, serve its accompaniments also; this avoids some passing at the table. Use tongs for serving lump sugar and a small fork for lemon. If you have neither, you may use a small spoon. When you do not know personal preferences for cream and sugar, ask what they are. Unless the beverage pot has a hinged cover, pouring is safer when the left hand holds the top securely in place. Pour by tipping the beverage pot, rather than by lifting it, whenever this is possible. Separate cups stacked by two's by taking the top cup in the right hand, lift with the left hand the saucer on which the remaining cup rests; place the cup in the right hand on the

remaining saucer, now transfer the cup and saucer in the left hand to the right hand, and place it in position for pouring. You will appear more graceful if you pour into a cup resting on the table. Pouring from a pot held in the right hand into a cup that rests on a saucer held in the left hand looks clumsy, but it may be the only possible procedure with some beverage pots and carafes.

13. When you are certain that all have eaten and drunk their fill, give the signal for leaving the table by suggesting that all find more comfortable chairs or that they look at John's roses, or pictures, or the like.

14. When guests offer assistance, you may accept it if you are certain it is sincerely offered. Graciously refuse if you prefer.

When You Are the Host

The host is the sole dispenser of hospitality when the hostess is absent from the room or the table. He greets guests at the door and assumes the responsibility for taking the guests' coats and hats. He may serve, or at least assist in serving, a first course in the living room. When the pattern of service permits the service of food from the table, this is the host's very special privilege. Here are special points for the host.

1. When you have guests, take the woman who will sit on your right in to dinner and seat her at the table. Pull her chair away from the table slightly and then push it under her as she sits down.

2. Be prepared to serve food from the table, if the pattern of service requires it.

3. Serving food from the table is very easy once you get the feel of it. Develop skill by requesting the privilege of serving meals when guests are not present. You will want two serving tools or two-in-one tools for serving almost all dishes. One tool does the work; the other supports the first during the transfer of food from serving dish to plate. The tool that does the work is used like a scoop in the right hand.

4. Learn proper carving procedures. Carve enough portions for all at the table before beginning to serve, unless the platter is so crowded with food that carving is difficult until at least some of the surrounding food has been served. Carving all portions before serving saves time and continual handling of the carving tools.

5. Serve meat plus any garnish present, potato, and vegetables in that order. Lift carved meat between the tines of the fork (pointed downward) and the blade of the knife. Use the flat server for serving chops, meat patties, or other meats in discrete units; assist with a fork of dinner size. Or use the scissors-type of serving tool if it is suitable.

The flat server can also serve as a cutting tool for soft foods such as meat loaves. Do not make portions too large or crowd the plates.

6. Pass filled plates in proper and logical order at the table, remembering to state for whom a plate is intended if any doubt can exist; remember, too, that once a person has accepted a plate, he should not have to pass another beyond him. The first plate may

(a) Be passed to your left to the hostess.
(b) Be passed to your left to a special woman guest seated on the hostess's right.
(c) Be passed to your right to a special woman guest seated on your right.

Decide with the hostess whom you are to serve first. If you are to serve her or a guest on her right, serve those on your left, then those on your right. If you serve a woman on your right first, pass all other plates to your left until all have been served.

7. When the person on your immediate left is assisting you in the service of food, pass all plates to her. When all those on the left side of the table, except your assistant, have been served, you and she will exchange plates until all, including you, have been served completely filled plates.

8. Serve food to the plate. Lift the plate to serve to it only to avoid spilling or dripping.

9. Watch guests, and offer second servings as soon as some guests are ready; begin by asking the hostess to be served. Ask those on your left, and then those on your right, if you may serve them. Avoid use of the words *more* and *again*. It is difficult to explain why these words should be avoided because second portions are obviously "more." However, it is considered better to say, "May I serve you this or that?" or "Would you like this or that?" Perhaps in doing so we avoid implying that guests are greedy.

10. Keep alert for lapses and awkward turns in conversation, and carry part of the conversational burden; no hostess should have to do this alone.

11. When the hostess is her own waitress, assist in the duties of removing one course and serving another. Follow her instructions. Remain at the table while she is away from it.

12. Serve the dessert from the table if such a procedure is desirable. Serve it in the same order as you served the main course.

SUGGESTED REFERENCES

1. Aresty, Esther B., *The Best Behavior*. New York: Simon and Schuster, Inc. (1970).

2. Bracken, Peg, *I Try to Behave Myself—Peg Bracken's Etiquette Book.* New York: Harcourt Brace Jovanovich, Inc. (1964).

3. Carson, G., *Polite Americans—A Wide-Angle View of Our More or Less Good Manners.* New York: William Morrow & Co., Inc. (1966).

4. Ford, Charlotte, *Charlotte Ford's Book of Modern Manners.* New York: Simon and Schuster, Inc. (1980).

5. Haupt, Enid A., *The New Seventeen Book of Etiquette and Young Living.* New York: David McKay Company, Inc. (1970).

6. Martin, Judith, *Miss Manners' Guide to Excruciatingly Correct Behavior.* New York: Atheneum (1982).

7. Miller, Llewellyn, *The Encyclopedia of Etiquette, A Guide to Good Manners in Today's World.* New York: Crown Publishers, Inc. (1967).

8. Moore, Charles, *George Washington's Rules of Civility and Decent Behavior in Company and Conversation.* New York: Houghton-Mifflin Company (1926).

9. Post, Elizabeth, *The New Emily Post's Etiquette.* New York: Funk and Wagnalls (1975).

10. Schlesinger, Arthur M., *Learning How to Behave: A Historical Study of American Etiquette Books.* New York: Cooper Square Publishers, Inc. (1968).

11. Shaw, Carolyn, *Modern Manners.* New York: Fawcett World Crest Books (1970) (Paperback).

12. Vanderbilt, Amy, *Amy Vanderbilt's Complete Book of Etiquette.* Revised and expanded by Letitia Baldridge. Garden City, N.Y.: Doubleday & Company, Inc. (1972).

Chapter 22

Meals for Guests

The decision to have guests to meals is a commitment to use the resources of money and of time and energy. The decision presupposes some knowledge of local customs, some skills and abilities in the preparation and serving of meals, and assumes the availability of the required equipment in the kitchen and of the appointments essential for dining. Put in another way, guest meals are planned on the basis of resources. These establish the size of the group invited, the menu, the pattern of meal service used, and so on. However, before the decision was made to have guests to dinner, there was a reason for having guests. This reason is important; it justifies the commitment of resources, and it affects the decisions on the menu and the style of dining. There are many reasons why we have guests to share our food: the offer of friendship; the meeting of obligations; the desire for belonging to the group; the desire for the approval of the group; the display of wealth, prestige, sophistication; the honoring of persons; the celebration of events; and others. Our reasons differ from time to time; the more compelling they are, the more likely we are to use our resources for them.

The meals to which we invite guests are dinner, brunch, and lunch, but most often dinner. Whichever meal it is, the guest meal has something about it. The food may be different, and there may be more of it than we customarily serve. The style of dining and the appointments used on the table may be different from those we use from day to day. And we ourselves are different—we are less family-centered and more other-directed.

Guest meals are easier of accomplishment in the 1980's than previously. Obvious reasons for this have to do with the ready availability of

PHOTOGRAPH 10. Table set for a small luncheon. (*Joe Boris.*)

convenience foods and catering services as well as the availability of easy-care table appointments.

Common sense suggests that the number of invited guests be limited to that number of persons who can be physically comfortable in the available space and to a number for which one can conveniently prepare and serve food. The decision on the use of money affects the meal service pattern, the use of time, and the menu. If there are no limits to the use of money, help can be hired to prepare and/or serve a meal, food can be purchased more or less ready to eat, use of time can be greatly curtailed, and the menu can be composed of just about anything desired. Although there are families who place no limits on the use of money, the great majority do.

Limits on the use of money tend to eliminate the hiring of help to serve the meal. If the number will be eight or more, it is desirable that the meal, whether dinner, lunch, or brunch, be served buffet style. Even with six at the table, the main course is often offered from a buffet. When the group is small, compromise, blue-plate, or American styles can be used. When the hostess waits on her table, she should think through the service and seek ways to keep the waiting-on-the-table time minimal.

Few decisions stand alone. A decision that puts limits on the use of money requires the use of time and human energy. Conversely, a decision to limit the use of time and human energy requires increased spending of money in the purchase of partially prepared, ready-prepared, and quick-to-prepare foods. The decision to use throwaway table appointments is a decision to use the money resource—perhaps, to save time, perhaps for other reasons. The number invited and the style of service decided upon affect the use of time. Common sense suggests that it takes longer to prepare dinner for eight than for four, and that it requires a greater investment of time and human energy to set the table for a formal dinner for eight than for a buffet supper where guests will dine from the plate held in the hand. The fact is, the decision to have guests to dinner is a decision to use time and human energy as well as money. The use of time can be controlled and with careful menu planning the use of it can be spread over several days, a real boon to the homemaker who is following a career outside the home. The truly efficient manager of time decides how much time to use and then tailors the menu and all else to it.

Although one can spend much time in menu making, it is the least time-consuming task associated with guest meals. Unless help is hired for the occasion, the meal is best limited to two courses at the table, the main course and the dessert course. Serve the first course in the living room or the family room, or the patio, or wherever guests will gather. Delay planning the first course until you have planned the main and dessert courses to avoid repetitions and to introduce foods appropriate to the rest of the menu.

PLANNING THE MAIN COURSE AND THE DESSERT

Compose the menu so that it is right for the proposed budget, so that it fits your skill in cooking, so that there is little required last minute cooking, so that it is coordinated with your planned use of time, and so that it takes into account your facilities: oven, refrigerator, freezer, pots and pans, and table appointments. And, of course, consider the rules and guidelines of menu making.

A meal consisting of excellently prepared baked beans, buttered carrots, tomato cole slaw, crisp relishes, rolls, and Indian pudding can provide wonderful eating and at the same time cost relatively little. The world is full of good things to eat. Prime rib roast of beef, thick porterhouse steak, stuffed pork chops, broiled lamb chops, roast duckling, and turkey are good. But meat loaf, spareribs with sauerkraut, lamb stew, Swedish meatballs and broiled hamburger patties are also good. Your best selections are the dishes you prepare especially well, not exotic or new and different dishes. Do not be timid: serve cheeses and crackers or fresh fruits or both for dessert; commercial sherbets, ices, and ice creams; cheesecake made from a mix; cakes made from mixes; ready-made cakes and pastries. However, if you make a wonderful cherry pie, date pudding, or caramel custard, by all means plan your menu around your specialty. But do not plan so that you have to spend two days cooking unless you want it that way. Plan so that you can prepare one or more dishes on one or more days in advance, such as gelatin salad, dessert, or even the entree that you can refrigerate or freeze until the day of your dinner. And plan a menu that frees you of kitchen duties such as broiling steak or making sauces the moment guests are expected to arrive. Last-minute preparations should only be the unavoidable ones such as taking salads to the table and putting vegetables to cook. Do not finalize the menu without first checking on the use of the oven previous to serving time; the needed roasting pans and saucepans, and the needed table appointments.

PLANNING THE FIRST COURSE

First courses are part of the image we have of special meals. Tradition has it that the purpose of the first course is to whet the appetite, a purpose that common sense discounts in the 1980's. In a weight-conscious era, many persons do not eat a first course, or a dessert either for that matter, except at special meals when they rationalize their behavior in a personally satisfying manner. It would be a pity to forego the first course in guest meals.

Favorite first courses are clear soups, fruit cups, shrimp cocktail, fresh fruits such as melon, fruit juices, tomato juice, canapés, and savory hors d'oeuvres. The predinner cocktail is almost an established custom for guest meals. With the cocktail a great variety of tidbits and savory items is suitable. What is offered differs with socioeconomic groups and from place to place. Low-calorie items such as crisp vegetable relishes served with seasoning salt or a cheese dip are in favor at one place; smoked oysters, smoked clams, shrimp with a hot sauce, sour cream and cheese dips, smoked sausage cubes, mixed salted nuts, and so on, are popular in another place. Plan a first course that follows local custom, and that looks, smells, and tastes good, but do keep it light. Avoid repetitions of those foods in the other courses, for example, do not serve tomato juice if tomato will appear in the salad, and do not serve fruit cup or a fruit juice if the dessert will be fruits. Some suggested dinner menus are presented in Appendix F.

SERVING THE FIRST COURSE

Serve the first course in the living room or the family room, or on the patio, to reduce waiting-on-the-table duties and to leave the kitchen uncluttered for serving the main course and the dessert course. You can serve almost any kind of food you might wish to offer in this infor-mal fashion. Served food and/or beverage may be taken to seated guests, or food may be arranged so that guests serve themselves. A table-on-wheels is valuable in serving this course, to transport it to and remove it from the living area and, in between, it can serve as a buffet. A desk, a lamp table, or a card table can be set up as a buffet for the food, if desirable. Here are a few specific suggestions.

1. When the first course is a fruit juice or other beverage and no food will be offered, arrange a proper number of glasses and napkins on a tray. Spread the napkins enough so that each can be easily picked up from the tray. Fill the glass to within an inch of the rim. Hold the tray low and offer it to each guest in turn (see Figure 22–1).
2. Offer soup in the same way. Arrange on your tray a suitable num-ber of cups and saucers, lay a spoon on the saucer parallel with the cup

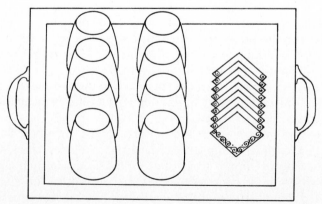

FIGURE 22–1.   Tray arranged for offering a beverage in glasses.

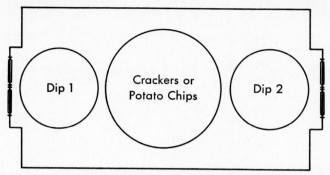

FIGURE 22–2.   Tray arranged for offering accompaniments to a beverage.

handle. Place the proper number of napkins and a small basket of salted wafers on the tray. Fill the cups no more than two thirds full. Carry the tray to the living room and set it on a table. Ask someone to assist you by offering the wafers as you offer the served soup to each guest in turn.

3. You may also serve the soup from a tureen or a deep casserole or a pitcher from a table. Arrange the cups and saucers and the container of soup on a tray. Place the napkins and spoons nearby. Serve it to the guests, who come to the table for it; each guest takes a spoon and a napkin from the arrangement.

4. Arrange the service of a hot food to be served from a chafing dish in a similar manner. Place the chafing dish, a basket of toast or pastry shells for food in a sauce, and plates on a tray. Arrange napkins and forks. Either serve this yourself or ask the guests to serve themselves.

5. Arrange an assortment of tidbits in bowls and on plates on a tray that you place on a table or directly on a draped table, desk, or card table (see Figure 22–2). Place napkins and either small plates or small cocktail trays (4 by 6 inches approximately), and picks for items that are not finger foods and that do not have picks inserted. The plate or tray should accommodate food and a beverage glass whenever the group will be milling around. Offer seafood cocktail, as a bowl of shrimp, crab, lobster, with a bowl of sauce for dipping.

6. Offer a fruit cup as a bowl or tray of fruits that have been trimmed and cut into pieces of suitable size. Have plates of suitable size and offer forks or picks.

Serving Coffee in the Living Room

A custom that adds glamour to guest meals is that of serving coffee in the living room, particularly when one has a fireplace around which all can sit.

PHOTOGRAPH 11.   After dinner coffee served in the living room. (*Joe Boris.*)

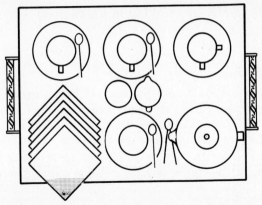

FIGURE 22–3.   Tray arranged for serving coffee in demitasse.

Coffee may be served both with dessert and in the living room if one so desires. It may be served from a tray or from a serving cart. Demitasse or coffee cups may be used, whichever are more suitable for the group present. If the small cup is used, then the correspondingly small spoon must be used. Cream and sugar are offered unless the local custom is always to drink coffee black. See either Chapter 18 or Chapter 23 for information on how to arrange a tray for serving a beverage. See also Figure 22–3.

BRUNCH

Brunch is defined in *Webster's New Collegiate Dictionary* as, "A late breakfast, an early lunch, or a combination of the two." The hours when this meal is served vary, but between 10:00 A.M. and 2:00 P.M. is usual. It may follow church on Sunday or such active sports as golf or sailing on Saturday or Sunday. The menu usually consists of some or all of the following: fruits and/or juices; such breakfast dishes as eggs with bacon, ham, or sausages; such creamed dishes as chicken, sweet breads, and chipped beef, accompanied, perhaps, by a hot vegetable; griddle cakes or waffles; hot breads and coffee cakes; assorted jams and jellies; and coffee. The meal may be a very substantial late breakfast or it may be an elaborate buffet lunch. Local custom determines whether or not cocktails or other alcoholic beverages are offered. Always offer coffee as soon as a guest arrives.

Any style of meal service may be followed; however, buffet style with table service is commonly used. For small groups, family service is good. If fruit juices are served before the guests come to the table, the meal can be composed of only one course served at the table. Suggested

menus for this combined breakfast-lunch meal appear in Appendix
F.

Late Suppers

The late supper offers breads or crackers with a variety of prepared
sandwich fillings, or a variety of meats, cheeses, and seafoods. In addition, pickles, olives, vegetable relishes, and seafood or chicken salad
may be included, as well as such hot dishes as Welsh rabbit, cheese
fondue, seafood Newburg, and chicken à la king. Local custom as much
as any other factor determines what one serves at late hours.

Buffet Meals

In a relatively short period of time the buffet pattern of meal service
has been accepted; we have adapted it to our homes; we have created
appointments especially for use on the buffet; and we have become
fairly comfortable with it. Reasons for preference for buffet meals are
several: waiting-on-the-table duties are reduced for hosts; larger numbers of guests can be accommodated than with the small dining table
in the small dining area; and the informality that people in the United
States value is fostered. Steps in the management of the buffet meal
are discussed in the following order because decisions are best made in
that order: planning the dining arrangements, planning the menu, setting the buffet table, and planning for service.

The Plan for Dining

Three patterns for dining are possible when meals are offered from
a buffet. The meal manager's decision on which pattern to use for a
particular buffet meal will depend on her facilities, her wishes, the occasion, and the number to be present. The first choice is *table service,*
that is, guests are seated at tables for dining. A second choice is *tray
service.* For this plan, guests are provided with trays on which plate,
beverages, and appointments are arranged. The tray provides a sort of
table from which to dine. Third, guests may be expected to dine from
the plate held in the hand, an arrangement we call *plate service.*

Table Service. Whenever possible, it is desirable to arrange for guests
to dine at the table. The dining table may be used for dining and the
buffet may be arranged on a chest, a serving table, or any other suitable surface in the dining area, or even in the kitchen. When the area
for dining is small, the buffet pattern of serving is ideal because it minimizes serving problems. The most frequently planned arrangement

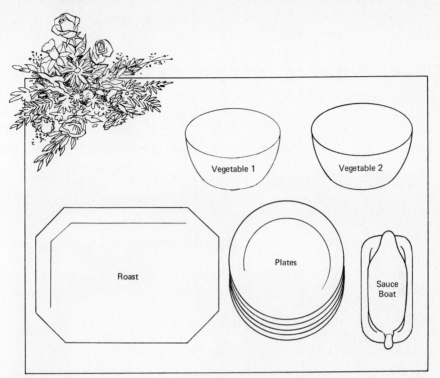

FIGURE 22–4.　Small chest set for buffet service—table service at dining table.

for dining is the use of card tables. Although they normally seat four, card tables can be enlarged to seat six by the use of round pads or plywood rounds made especially for that purpose. Individual tables for dining and small folding tables offer other possibilities. In general, the dining table serves as the buffet in the latter instances.

The tables for dining are completely set with the proper appointments: cloths or mats, flatware, beverageware, such accessories as butter, jelly, and saltcellar, cups and saucers, and accompaniments for any beverage served. When arrangements for dining are so completely made, the buffet may be quite small because only dinner plates and serving dishes of food must be placed on it. (See Figure 22–4.) However, when small tables of the collapsible variety are used, the buffet or some other table will have to present those appointments that are essential for dining. Since these collapsible tables require arrangements similar to those for trays, they are discussed in the next section.

Tray Service.　Lacking room for setting up tables, hosts may decide to provide guests with trays. Trays for this purpose usually measure about 12 by 18 inches. The tray holds plate and beverages and is placed

PHOTOGRAPH 12.   Buffet service arranged for guest to dine at table. (*Joe Boris.*)

on the lap for quite comfortable dining. Here, as in the use of table service, the buffet need present only plates and serving dishes of food; the guest ought not to acquire the tray until he has served himself. This situation is not like that in the cafeteria where food is served for the

FIGURE 22–5.   Small chest or table set with trays, appointments, and beverages.

patron. It is best to place trays, beverages, napkins, and flatware on another surface near the buffet (see Figure 22–5). After serving his plate, the guest places it on the top tray in the pile; next he places the beverage or beverages, the napkin, and the flatware on the tray; he then removes the tray and proceeds with it to the place indicated for dining.

Dining from a tray held on the lap is not as comfortable as dining at a table, and some persons like it less well than dining from the plate held in the hand. To minimize hazards, cover the trays with mats to prevent the slipping of dishes; use short tumblers for water, and mugs for a hot beverage; avoid drippy, spattery foods; and be sure that food that must be cut is fork tender. All of these precautions will reduce, if not eliminate, accidents resulting in soiled garments, carpets, and furniture. Trays and their appointments should be coordinated and should make an attractive setting for the meal.

When small folding tables, actually trays on supporting stands, are used, appointments and beverages must be provided on the buffet or on an accessory surface. Someone in the family or a guest should set up the folding tables while guests are serving themselves.

Plate Service.   Often, the only arrangement a hostess can make is to provide plenty of table space on which guests can place beverages while they dine from the plate in the hand. Table space may be provided by nested tables, stack tables, end tables, the coffee table, the corner bookcase or desk, folding snack tables, or any other available surface—ex-

PHOTOGRAPH 13.   Buffet supper—dining from plate in hand. (*Joe Boris.*)

cept the floor. When the number of guests is large relative to available space, one may have no choice but to use this plan for dining.

At wedding receptions, late suppers, and similar occasions where large numbers are present and when a beverage does not accompany the food offered, no special arrangements are made; guests are expected to stand while dining, although some chairs may be made available for elderly persons.

When plate service is used, the buffet or an accessory surface presents the following in addition to plates and serving dishes of food: forks, napkins, and beverages. Common sense dictates that guests must have both hands free for serving food and holding the plate; they cannot hold onto anything else until the serving of the plate has been accomplished. The practical and logical arrangement of the appointments on the buffet is exceedingly important, as one realizes while observing a guest making his way along or around the buffet. A guest probably serves some food onto the plate before he takes it if two tools are required for serving a food; otherwise, he takes a plate with his left hand so that he can help himself to dishes with his right hand. When he has finished serving his plate, the guest places a fork on it and takes a napkin, which he slips between the plate and his left hand; he can then take a poured beverage, or he can even pour his own, since he can still use his right hand freely.

Considerate hosts will always avoid the use of tray service or plate service at black-tie functions. If guests are to be formally dressed, it is not only highly desirable, but almost a must, that they be seated at tables for dining.

Planning the Buffet Menu

Only when the plans for seating guests have been made and arrangements for dining have been decided upon can the meal manager plan the menu for a buffet meal, because the dishes she can serve are largely determined by these arrangements. All the rules for good menu planning should be observed in planning the buffet meal; and, in addition, special considerations require that dishes be easy to self-serve and easy to eat. When guests are to be seated at tables where they can have the usual assortment of knives, forks, and spoons, there are few restrictions on the menu that a hostess may offer. However, guests should not be expected to carve for themselves; roasts and birds are carved in the kitchen or at the buffet. When guests are to dine from trays, the hostess may offer almost any meats she chooses; however, because it is awkward to use the knife at the level of a tray held on the lap, it is desirable that meats be fork tender. It is also very important that the dishes be free from sauces and juices that can drip as bites of food are lifted to the mouth. This last qualification is also important when guests are to dine from the plate held in the hand. In addition, the food must be fork cuttable, and all bread should have been buttered for this service. Pasta dishes must be made from the small varieties if served to guests who are not dining at a table. However, at potluck buffet suppers we enjoy all manner of dishes and give little or no thought to suggested rules of menu writing.

The dishes on the buffet table should lend themselves to attractive service, be easily self-served, and maintain proper temperatures during the serving period. Casserole dishes containing meat, potatoes, and vegetables are good choices for the buffet menu. If a salad is served with a casserole dish, it should be simple in composition; it ought not to be another mixture of many ingredients. It is possible to avoid the appearance of mixture by casual arrangement of a few fruits or vegetables in lettuce cups. Molded gelatin salads and salads of mixed greens are highly acceptable. Trays of relishes on which there may be a half-dozen or more choices may replace a salad or be served in addition. Relishes are not only widely acceptable, but are also easily prepared in advance of mealtime and, since they are usually finger foods, are easily eaten. Cakes, tortes, and pies are favorite desserts, especially when guests are permitted to cut pieces of the size they want. A hostess can serve any dessert she wishes; however, she will be wise to plan one that requires only one dish for adequate service lest confusion arise and a guest be embarrassed by failing to place a bowl on the proper underliner plate. Although the dessert may be brought to the guests, almost all persons enjoy returning to the buffet for dessert. This practice also frees the host and hostess from serving duties. Suggested menus for the buffet are given in Appendix F.

Except for the smorgasbord, the well-planned buffet menu will be simple; all the food of a course, including bread, will be served onto one plate. This plate will look neater and be easier to eat from if it is not completely filled. An exception is the occasion when guests serve themselves from a buffet and dine at the dining table, on which individual salads have been placed at covers.

Two courses, the main course and the dessert course, are all that should be served from the buffet table. If a first course is offered, it is best served in the living room as already suggested.

Here are some special suggestions for the planner of buffet meals.

1. For your own sake, try to have some dishes that can be prepared a day in advance. Some dishes should be prepared the day of the meal to ensure excellent quality. Some desserts, such as chiffon pies, Bavarian creams, Spanish cream, and icebox desserts, can and should be made the day before.

2. Remember the capacity of your oven; also remember that an overloaded oven lengthens cooking times.

3. Be sure that all foods to be eaten from the plate held in the hand, except finger foods, can be cut with a fork; have the bread buttered.

4. Avoid dishes with thin sauces or dressings that may spatter during serving or eating.

5. Plan so that most, if not all, hot dishes can be finally heated in casseroles or other heat-holding containers unless you have special appliances for keeping food hot.

6. More than enough of everything should be provided, so that all may feel free to help themselves to as much as they want.

Setting the Buffet Table

Decisions on what surface will be used for the buffet, where it will be placed, and how it will be set or arranged must be made. The dining table provides an excellent buffet; a chest of suitable height, a desk, a draped card table, a credenza or sideboard, the kitchen counter, or the kitchen table are all usable. Choose the buffet in accordance with your resources and the size of the group. Make certain that it will accommodate all that it must present; establish what it will accommodate by a trial setting with all the selected appointments. If one surface does not accommodate all that must be presented, use another to supplement it.

Place the buffet near the kitchen so that it can be serviced quickly and efficiently and so that there will be a minimum of movement among guests to service it. If you use a supplementary surface for trays, appointments, or beverages, place it so that guests will pass it after leaving the buffet. Place the buffet against a wall so that guests pass from one end of the buffet to the other or place the buffet away from a wall at or near the center of a room so that guests move around it (see Figure 22–6). There is less confusion when movement is from end to end of the buffet than when movement is around it (see Figure 22–7). We tend to move more gracefully from left to right and counterclockwise. At clubs, church suppers, and PTA suppers at school where crowds are large, it is expedient to have duplicate buffets. Have a full and complete buffet on the two sides of a table centered in a room; arrange two full and complete buffets on one side of a long buffet table placed against a wall; or, space permitting, arrange two or more identical buffets in different places within a room. The first and last are probably the most satisfactory arrangements.

In setting or arranging the buffet, the place to begin should be obvious; how to proceed should be equally obvious, but must also be in a direct line without the need for backtracking. Self-service of the food must be easy, and the appointments and the beverages presented on the buffet must be easy to remove and easy to handle. Whatever the arrangements for dining, all buffets present the food similarly. When dining will be from plate in hand, the buffet must present appointments and beverages, but these should follow the food so that no one is attempting to serve food onto a plate and at the same time hold the appointments for dining. It cannot be done.

If we take cues from the behavior of people at a buffet, the starting point is the pile of stacked plates. Almost without thinking guests proceed to the stacked plates on the buffet and take one from the pile. This suggests that every dish on the buffet ought to be servable with only one serving tool. Two-in-one serving tools, tongs, and large serving spoons expedite the serving food with one hand. The dishes that compose the meal can be clustered or aligned on the buffet. They ought to appear in decreasing order of importance to prevent the guests from filling their plates before the important items of the meal are taken. A buffet that presents only food can be quite small. Never place the food of the dessert course on the buffet with the main course.

The buffet that offers appointments in addition to the food must be larger, or a second surface must be used to present the napkins, the flatware, and the beverages. When dining is to be from plate in hand, the only flatware present on the buffet is the fork. A guest places the

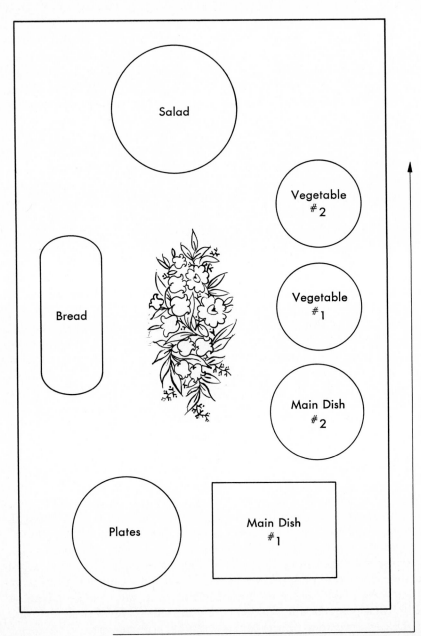

FIGURE 22-6. Buffet arranged so that guests proceed around it—table service.

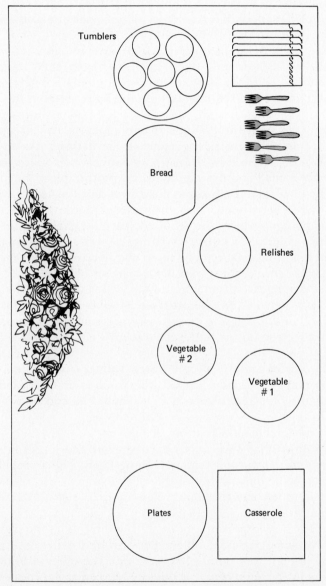

Tumblers

Bread

Relishes

Vegetable #2

Vegetable #1

Plates

Casserole

FIGURE 22–7. Buffet arranged so that guests proceed from end to end—plate service.

fork securely on the served plate, takes the napkin and slips it between hand and plate in the left hand, then takes the beverage with the free right hand. He can even serve it himself if you have carefully arranged for this, but it is desirable that there be an open area on the buffet where the guest can place the served plate while he pours his own beverage. When dining will be on trays, offer trays and appointments and beverages on a table or chest removed from the buffet. When dining is to be at individual tables that are set up as guests are serving themselves, the flatware offered may include the knife. Present the flatware and the napkins in such a way that they can be taken from the buffet gracefully. Display of the flatware on the napkin is usually space-consuming; a tight and neat arrangement of alternating forks and knives parallel with or followed by overlapping napkins uses space more efficiently at the same time that it permits the guest to place the knife and fork on the plate, take a napkin in the conventional manner, and finally take the beverage offered. The enclosure of the knife and the fork within the napkin reduces the required space for their display but is a clumsy arrangement for guests who must take a beverage. Small receptacles that hold forks stacked one upon another and similar receptacles for teaspoons are available especially for the small buffet.

The well-arranged buffet table and the well-managed buffet meal do not happen by chance. Far too often we have been guilty of just setting out the food and letting the guests carry on from there. Some specific suggestions for setting the buffet table follow.

1. The buffet table may be covered with a cloth, it may remain bare, or it may be partially covered with runners or mats to introduce color. For the best appearance, a cloth should extend halfway to the floor or farther.

2. Provide eighteen inch or larger napkins.

3. Floral or other decorations may be taller and larger in scale on the buffet than on the conventional dining table. The arrangement of the plates and the main dishes of the meal gives one part of the buffet greater weight than the remainder. Position decorations and candles to effect balance.

4. For the best appearance of the buffet table, limit the plates, cups and saucers, wine glasses, tumblers, flatware, and napkins on the table at any one time to the number in scale with the table. Additional appointments for the first course should be set on a table, chest, or other usable surface near the buffet table. It is desirable to have the appointments for the dessert course set here too; certainly, they should be collected and readily available on the kitchen counter if the serving table is not large enough to accommodate them.

5. Use the ten and one-half to eleven-inch dinner plate for the buf-

fet meal when the plate must accommodate all the food of the main course.

6. When guests dine at a dining table, these can accommodate small salad bowls. Place the salad last on the buffet, bowls beside it; include a two-in-one serving tool so that the salad can be served into a salad bowl with the right hand while the left hand holds the dinner plate. Leave an open area that will accommodate the dinner plate in case someone cannot otherwise manage.

7. When arrangements for dining permit the serving of a roast or a bird, it must be carved at the buffet or in the kitchen. The former practice is preferable.

8. To expedite service when the group is large, you may invite someone to assist in serving one or more dishes of the meal.

9. Whenever flatware and napkins are required in the buffet setting, place them beyond the food so that guests will not have to clutch them and serve themselves at the same time. If guests are to dine from the plate held in the hand, place forks only. The forks are laid close together, but it should be possible to take one without touching another. Never make them a center of interest. Do not enclose the flatware in a napkin, except for tray service.

10. Put glasses of water or other beverage on a tray. This tray should be the last item in the buffet setting, or it may be placed on another table. The beverage is the last item in a setting because once it has been taken, the guest has both hands full and cannot serve himself further. In general, use stemware for wines only, tumblers or footed ware for other beverages.

11. Coffee is often served with both courses of the buffet meal. It is easily managed when dining is at small tables where cups and saucers may be placed at table-setting time. You may fill these cups after guests are seated, or you may ask someone to do it for you. The beverage service may also be set up on the buffet table; if it is, the guest serves the beverage and takes it to the small table along with the dinner plate. When dining is from trays, the beverage service appears close to the trays; the guest pours, after placing the cup on the tray and before picking up the tray (see Figure 22–5). When dining is from the plate in the hand, cups of coffee may be taken to those who wish it, or the guests may choose between water and coffee and serve themselves.

12. Set the beverage service very carefully whenever you expect a guest to pour for himself. Leave a near area empty so that the filled plate can be set down by those who wish to do so. Do not stack cups and saucers by two's or on top of each other. To establish a pouring center, place one cup and saucer close to the edge of the table; set the pot to the right beside it. To the left, lay the spoons directly on the table, on a small plate or tray, or in a small receptacle. A spoon may be

FIGURE 22–8.   Arrangement for self-service of a hot beverage.

laid on each saucer, handle parallel with the cup handle; however, because many people do not use sugar or cream, they will not require
spoons. Set the accompaniments above the cup. This arrangement permits the guest to pour into the cup, take any accompaniments he uses,
place a spoon on the saucer if he uses one, and remove the cup and
saucer from the table with the free right hand. Group the other cups
and saucers around this center. Those who follow the first guest will
remove cup on saucer to the obvious and convenient place for pouring.
Needless to say, the beverage pot should have a hinged cover or one
that does not fall out of the pot when it is tipped in pouring (see Figure
22–8).

13. The table setting for the dessert course is determined by the service that is planned. If the group is large, it may be desirable to have
the dessert and beverage served to guests from the buffet table. Those
who serve sit at opposite ends of the table. People probably prefer to
receive the dessert before the beverage. The beverage cup may be placed
on the plate with the dessert if the dessert is not a frozen one. However, eating is both more enjoyable and more comfortable when the
cup is on a saucer, which can be set on a nearby table.

14. Set up the dessert course according to the same principles followed in setting the table for the main course. Set the dessert plates to
the right of the dessert, because service is more convenient from left to
right. Provide two serving pieces, so that the piece of cake, pie, or other
dessert item can be steadied on the pastry server while it is being moved
from one plate to another; without this steadying tool, people instinc-
tively use their fingers, thereby soiling them. Place the proper tool for
eating the dessert directly on the table beside the stacked plates. After

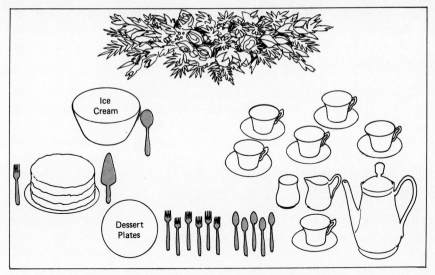

FIGURE 22–9. A dessert buffet.

taking the plate, the guest takes the tool and places it on the plate. He may then pour his own beverage with the free right hand, or he may set the plate down before pouring. If the beverage is poured for him, he can accept it with the free right hand (see Figure 22–9).

Planning for Service

One reason for using the buffet pattern of meal service is to minimize waiting-on-the-table duties. Those duties that do remain are carried out with the least confusion when they have been planned. They include the service of or waiting on the buffet during the main course, the removal of the main course, the serving of the dessert course, and the final removal of the dessert course.

Service of the Buffet Table. Replacements of food and table appointments must always be made. Additional appointments include the plates, flatware, and napkins not included in the original setting of the buffet table. Ideally, they are available from some table or chest near the buffet table; if not, they can be brought in from the kitchen, where they should have been made ready. All appointments, except plates, are best carried on a tray to the table to avoid excessive handling. The plates are supported on the open hands with the thumbs pressing on the rims of the stacked plates. Because it is customary to ask guests to serve themselves more than once at buffet meals, there should be food in plenty on the buffet at all times. Replacements are made when more than half of the food is removed from a dish. The hostess, because she is responsible for the food preparation, is the logical person to assume the duty of keeping food on the buffet if she does not have hired help in the kitchen.

Removal of the Main Course.   Whatever the mode of dining, the main course is taken from the buffet to the kitchen when it appears that all persons have finished eating it. Unless she has hired help, the main course is removed by the hostess with the assistance she requests. Since some temporary storage of food is imperative in the average kitchen, the competent hostess uses assistance here. The clearance of individual covers depends on the mode of dining.

1. When dining has been at the dining table, the table is cleared and the dessert is served in the conventional fashion.

2. When dining has been at card tables, two options are possible. Covers at card tables can be cleared in the conventional fashion; or the guest may be asked to take his plate and leave it on a designated tray or table-on-wheels as he goes to the dessert buffet.

3. When dining has been plate-in-hand style, the hostess, the host, or a helpful guest may take the plates and place them on a table-on-wheels or a tray and remove them to the kitchen. Again, the guest may simply be asked to place his plate on a designated tray or table as in (2).

4. When guests are dining from trays, it is best to clear trays as you would individual covers at the table. Use a table-on-wheels on which to collect the plates. Clear the covers of persons dining at individual tables in a similar manner.

Serving the Dessert Course.   Whenever the group is at all large, the dessert buffet is the easiest way to offer dessert. It often presents a choice of desserts, a low-calorie and a sweet-and-rich one. When guests dine at the dining table and from trays, dessert is served in the conventional manner; in all other modes of dining, guests can go to the dessert buffet to serve themselves—table by table or in small groups.

1. Place a single dessert offering on the buffet with serving tools. Place dessert plates to the right for easy left-to-right transfer of dessert to plate. Next, lay on the table the forks or other required tools for eating the dessert. Next, arrange the beverage service unless the beverage is to be or has been offered at table (see Figure 22–6).

2. Place the desserts, when more than one is offered, at intervals on the buffet. Place the proper serving tools with each dessert. Place the

PHOTOGRAPH 14.   Table arranged for a dessert buffet.

appropriate dinnerware and flatware to the right of, or in front of, each dessert, whichever effects easiest service. Arrange any required beverage service so that it follows the desserts. Dessert is always taken before beverage.

3. Serve the dessert and the beverage to persons dining from trays from a table-on-wheels.

4. Serve the beverage to guests dining at your dining table from the table.

5. Refill beverage cups by passing from table to table when the guests are dining at card tables or individual tables; pass from person to person when the guests are dining from trays or from plate in hand.

6. Set up a beverage service or services in the dining area and permit guests to wait on themselves for beverages whenever space for moving about permits.

Final Clearance. Finally, the dessert buffet and all else must be cleared.

1. When dining has been at the dining table, clear the table or leave it uncleared, depending on whether or not it is visible from the living area.

2. When dining has been at card tables, clear table by table using a

table-on-wheels. Take the tables down unless they will be used for playing bridge or other games. Use any assistance offered so that you can stack dishes in the kitchen or load the dishwasher.

3. When dining has been from individual tables, clear as in (2).

4. When guests have dined from trays, permit someone to assist you by removing the trays to the kitchen as you stack and so on.

5. When dining has been from plate in hand, use a table-on-wheels and remove plates, cups and saucers, and glasses to the kitchen.

Permit guests to help you; give them clear instructions; do not try to hurry through either the serving or the removing of courses. Above all, have some plans for doing what must be done. But do not worry if plans go awry. The buffet pattern is still new. Procedures are not as standardized as are the more conventional patterns for dining; what seems familiar to one person may seem strange to another.

MEAL PRODUCTION

After decision making comes the hand-and-foot work of meal production. Efficient use of time and human energy is contingent on thoughtful organization of tasks from shopping to clearing the table. Time spent in anticipating these tasks and in scheduling their doing saves time in the long run and reduces the stress that occasions of this kind often generate. Here are some tasks you may wish to plan in detail.

1. The shopping for food, flowers, candles, and any other items you may need to purchase.
2. The selection and preparation of the appointments you will use on the dining table: linens, dinnerware, flatware, beverageware, and perhaps serving dishes.
3. The selection of appointments and the plan for serving a first course.
4. A timetable for getting all of this accomplished.
5. A timetable for the preparation of the food of the meal.
6. A plan for waiting on the table.

ORGANIZING THE TASKS

Organizing the tasks that must be accomplished in the planning for, preparation for, preparation of, and serving of a dinner, brunch, or any other special meal, is helpful whether one, two, or twenty persons are engaged. Many decisions must be made. Following are two plans that detail decisions and schedule the doing of the various tasks, the so-called hand-and-foot work. These plans are meant to be suggestive only: they will differ as the resources of different meal managers differ. To illustrate, a menu for a buffet meal is presented. The following assumptions are made: supper will be at 8:00 P.M. on a Saturday evening; there will be eight in attendance, including the hosts; the hosts will do all the work of preparation and serving; and dining will be at card tables.

Menu for Buffet Supper
Chicken Tetrazzini
Mixed Greens with Italian Dressing
Celery   Assorted Olives   Radishes
Garlic-Buttered French or Vienna Bread
Lemon Chiffon Pie
Coffee

PART 1. *General Plan*

Tasks	When	By
Plan menu	Before Thursday	Him and her
Make shopping list	Before Thursday	Her
Check table linens	Before Monday	Her
Make plans for preparing food	Before Thursday	Him and her
Make plan for service of meal	Before Thursday	Him and her
Shop for groceries	Thursday P.M.	Him and her
Shop for flowers and last-minute items	Saturday A.M.	Him
Tidy rooms	Friday evening	Him
Get out table appointments and give needed care	Saturday A.M.	Her
Plan buffet setting	Saturday A.M.	Her
Arrange flowers	Saturday A.M.	Her
Set buffet table and card tables	Saturday 5:00 P.M.	Her
Fill water glasses	Saturday 7:30 P.M.	Her
Take food to buffet	Saturday 8:00 P.M.	Her
Take extra food to buffet	As indicated	Her
Clear main course from buffet	As indicated	Her
Take main course plates from guests	As indicated	Him
Set up dessert service	As indicated	Her
Refill coffee cups	As indicated	Him
Clear buffet table and others	As indicated	Her
Take all dishes to kitchen, load dishwasher	As indicated	Him

PART 2. *Plan for Food Production*

Items of Menu	Steps in Prepatation	When	By	Shopping List
Chicken Tetrazzini	1. Stew chicken— chill	Friday P.M.	Her	2 Chickens Mushrooms
	2. Bone and cut up	Saturday A.M.		Green and red peppers
	3. Clean mushrooms. cut peppers			Shell macaroni
	4. Sauté mushrooms and peppers			Olive oil Cream
	5. Cook spaghetti			Parmesan cheese
	6. Make sauce			
	7. Combine and put in casseroles, chill			
	8. Clean up kitchen			
	9. Put in oven	6:30 P.M.		
Mixed green	1. Wash, dry, chill	Friday P.M.	Her	Italian dressing
	2. Tear, chill	Saturday 6:00 P.M.	Him	Belgian endive
	3. Dress and toss	Saturday 8:00 P.M.	Him	Lettuce
Relishes	1. Chill olives	Saturday A.M.	Her	Bibb lettuce
	2. Wash celery and radishes	Saturday A.M.		Ripe olives Green olives
	3. Cut celery and radishes and chill	Saturday A.M.		Celery Radishes
	4. Arrange for table	Saturday 6:30 P.M.	Her	
Garlic bread	1. Prepare garlic butter	Saturday A.M.	Him	2 Vienna loaves Butter
	2. Cut and butter bread and wrap in foil	Saturday A.M.	him	Garlic powder
	3. Heat first loaf	Saturday 7:30 P.M.	Him	
	4. Heat second loaf	Saturday 8:00 P.M.	Her	
Lemon chiffon pie	1. Make crumb crust	Friday P.M.	Her	Lemons
	2. Make filling	Friday P.M.	Her	Gelatin, eggs
	3. Whip cream and spread	Saturday 7:00 P.M.	Her	Whipping cream
Coffee	1. Measure and make	Saturday 7:30 P.M.	Him	

Summary

We like to be guests and we like to have guests. These occasions are something special in our lives. They demand the commitment of resources, especially of time and human energy. They require decision making and hand-and-foot work. Experiences at home and elsewhere enrich our resources of knowledge, skills, and abilities. In time, planning menus that are compatible with resources becomes easy; the planning for serving meals poses fewer questions; and finally, the preparation of the meal becomes easier. The more decisions made and the more planning done before the hand-and-foot work begins, the less stress is generated.

Suggested References

1. Albertson, Sarah D., *The Blue Sea Cookbook.* New York: Hastings House Publishers, Inc. (1968).
2. Allen, Ida Bailey, *Best Loved Recipes of the American People.* Garden City, N. Y. Doubleday & Company (1973).
3. Arbit, Naomi and June Turner, *Ideas Quick and Easy Gourmet Treasury Cookbook.* New York: Crown Publishers, Inc. (1980).
4. Beard, James, *Beard on Food.* New York: Alfred A Knopf, Inc. (1974).
5. Beard, James, *James Beard's American Cookery.* Boston: Little Brown & Company (1972).
6. Bertholle, Louisette, *French Cuisine for All.* Garden City, N.Y.: Doubleday & Company, Inc. (1980).
7. Cheney, Winifred Green, *The Southern Hospitality Cookbook.* Birmingham, Ala.: Oxmoor House, Inc. (1976).
8. Child, Julia, *From Julia Child's Kitchen.* New York: Alfred A. Knopf, Inc. (1975).
9. Claiborne, Craig and Pierre Franey, *Craig Claiborne's New York Times Cookbook.* New York: Times Books (1980).
10. Corbitt, Helen, *Helen Corbitt Cooks for Looks.* Boston: Houghton-Mifflin Company (1967).
11. Coulson, Zoe, *The Good Housekeeping Illustrated Cookbook.* New York: Hearst Books (1980).
12. Courtney, Marion, *Brunches and Coffees.* Chicago: Reilly & Lee Company (1960).
13. Dariaux, Genevieve A., *Entertaining with Elegance.* Garden City, N.Y.: Doubleday & Company, Inc. (1965).
14. Gilbert, Edith, *All About Parties.* New York: Hearthside Press, Inc. (1968).

15. Happel, Margaret, *Quick Dinner Menus.* New York: Butterick Publishing Company (1979).
16. Harlech, Pamela, *Feast without Fuss.* New York: Atheneum (1977).
17. Hewitt, Jean, *The New York Times Heritage Cookbook.* New York: Bonanza Books (1972).
18. Hirsch, Sylvia, *The Art of Table Setting and Flower Arrangement.* New York: Thomas Y. Crowell Company, Inc. (1962).
19. *Informal Entertaining Country Style.* Garden City, N.Y.: Doubleday & Company, Inc. (1973).
20 *June Roth's Let's Have a Brunch Cookbook.* New York: Essanders Special Editions, A Division of Simon & Schuster, Inc. (1973).
21. Lee, Nata, *Complete Book of Entertaining,* Revised Edition. New York: Hawthorn Books, Inc. (1968).
22. Lowell, Florence and Norma Lee Browning, *Be a Guest at Your Own Party.* New York: M. Evans & Company, Inc. (1980).
23. Pappas, Lou Siebert, *Party Menus.* New York: Harper & Row Publishers (1974).
24. Rombauer, Irma S., and Marion Rombauer Becker, *Joy of Cooking.* Indianapolis: Bobbs-Merrill Company, Inc. (1975).
25 Roosevelt, Nicholas, *Good Cooking.* New York: Harper & Row Publishers, Inc. (1959).
26. Ross, Annette Laslett and Jean Adams Disney, *Cooking For A Crowd.* Garden City, New York: Doubleday & Company, Inc. (1968).
27. Scott, Maria Louisa and Jack Denton, *Informal Dinners for Easy Entertaining.* New York: Simon & Schuster, Inc. (1975).
28. Sorosky, Marlene and Linda Kreisbert, *Cookery for Entertaining.* Tuscon: H.P. Books (1979).
29. *The Fannie Farmer Cookbook,* 12th edition, Revised by Marion Cunningham and Jeri Laber. New York: Alfred A. Knopf (1980).
30. *The Party Snacks Cookbooks-A Southern Living Cookbook.* Birmingham: Oxmoor House, Inc. (1979).
31. Truax, Carol, *Cheese and Wine.* New York: Ballantine Books (1975) (Paperback).
32. Turgeon, Charlotte, Ed., *The Creative Cooking Course.* New York: Weathervane Books (1975).

Chapter 23

Teas, Receptions, and Other Occasions

Full meals are not the only occasions at which families and individuals serve food to guests. The times when one has guests and does not offer something to drink, with or without something to eat, are exceptions, rather than the rule. This custom stems in part from the long-held belief that to share food is a symbol of friendship.

Occasions at which we offer food are many: morning coffee, afternoon tea, afternoon coffee, receptions, the cocktail hour, "refreshments," dessert parties, and after-the-theater suppers. This is true, not only in private life but also in the social life of the community; study clubs, committees, professional groups, church groups, and even political parties lure attendance with the promise of refreshments. A common feature of all of these occasions is that the refreshments are of secondary importance; the real purpose is to provide a time and a place for people to come together, either to visit with old friends or to make new ones, to be informed, to work or play, and even to be persuaded.

These occasions with light refreshments may vary in size from "tea for two" to receptions for several hundred people. Some just happen; others are preceded by weeks or months of careful planning. A hostess can manage a tea or reception for fifty or more people, if she has good friends to help, or if she is able to hire one or two persons to work in the kitchen, and if she has enough space to accommodate this number of people. It is more than likely, however, that her experiences with large teas and receptions will, for the most part, be at church, school, and clubs. Discussions of what to serve at such functions and how to serve it follow.

WHAT TO SERVE

The light refreshments served at these various functions are similar, in the sense that they basically consist of beverage and bread, but they differ in the items served in addition to bread. The beverages served include coffee and tea, punch, carbonated beverages, cider, and the like. The bread that accompanies these beverages may be thin slices of buttered bread, sandwiches, coffee cake, sweet rolls, hot breads, cake, doughnuts, cookies, rich pastries, and crackers and similar crisp confections. In addition to bread, sweets and nuts may appear on the tea table; savory items, such as olives, seafoods, cheeses, meats, crisp vegetable relishes, dips, and pickles, may appear on the cocktail tray and the late supper table; and ices, sweets, and nuts may accompany cake at a dessert party or a reception. There are few restrictions on what may be served with a beverage except those implicit in the time of day, the occasion, and the beverage itself. Obviously, ice cream and cake or pie would be ill-chosen for the midmorning coffee.

Because only small bits of food are usually offered at teas and coffees, we try to serve food and beverages of superior quality. We also try to have beverages and the bits of food go together. For example, when we serve a sweet punch, Bohemian tea, or mulled cider, the accompanying foods are bland and not sweet, such as sandwiches made with cream cheese, fruit or nut bread sandwiches, short and crisp but not sweet cookies, pound cake, or short bread. With a fine tea of delicate aroma, plain bread and butter or pound cake would be very suitable. When the usual "garden variety" of tea is served, the tea dainties are usually more flavorful and more interesting. Since coffee is full flavored it may be accompanied by flavorful tidbits. Food served with cocktails is traditionally truly full flavored.

Food for Large Teas or Receptions

The number of items on the menu for a tea or a reception is determined by the size of the group invited. As the guest list approaches fifty, the menu may consist of a half-dozen or more items, and as it approaches one hundred, the menu may include a dozen or more items. Coffee and tea may be offered; punch can replace the coffee or tea or be offered in addition to it.

The following principles guide in the selection of the items of the tea or reception menu.

1. When two beverages are to be offered, plan so that every item on the menu will be appropriate with either beverage, because you can

never be certain that a guest will know which items are most pleasing with the beverage he or she chooses.

2. Plan so that there will be differences in the textures of the items offered, some being soft and others crisp or chewy.

3. Plan so that there will be some color in the plates and trays of dainties. It may be only a difference in intensity of color, as between plain sugar cookies and chocolate brownies, or it may be a true color difference. Sandwiches introduce true color with parsley, water cress, cucumber, green pepper, olives, pimiento, avocado, jelly, and so forth. Limit the use of artificial coloring to frostings on cakes. Color frostings delicately, and have someone with an eye for color blend the tints; colors as they come from the bottles are too harsh.

4. Plan so that more than one taste is included. The beverage may introduce bitterness, as in coffee; sweetness, as in punch; or sourness, as in tea served with lemon. The foods served introduce either saltiness or sweetness.

5. Plan to introduce a variety of flavors and ingredients. Use coconut, chocolate, citrus fruit rinds, dried fruits, nuts, candied fruits, and spices.

The following menu is suggested for a tea for one hundred guests. Ices may be offered at receptions in addition to, or in place of, some items.

Lemon Frosted Petits Fours

Frosted Brownies   Coconut Macaroons

Apricot Bread Sandwiches

Shrimp-Butter Pinwheels   Parsley Cream Cheese Pinwheels

Egg Salad Cucumber Sandwiches

Tea   Coffee

Food for the Small Tea or Coffee

Food for the small tea or coffee may be fresh bread and butter, fresh hot rolls, hot muffins, cake, doughnuts, coffee cake, cookies, or sandwiches; in fact, it may be almost anything one wants to serve and which is appropriate for the time of day. However, it should be remembered that these are occasions for light refreshments.

Food for Dessert Parties

Dessert parties are the proper occasion to serve rich and luscious desserts. When inviting guests to this kind of party, the hostess might well stress the "come for dessert." The refreshments for these occasions

PHOTOGRAPH 15.   Table arranged for afternoon tea.

may be three-layer cakes heavily iced, tortes rich in nuts and whipped cream, filled angel food cakes, meringues filled with ice cream and covered with fruit or rich sauces, ice cream and cake, cheese cake, chiffon pies, or any other kind of pie, especially when men are to be present. The possibilities are definitely unlimited and a hostess may offer two or more choices.

APPOINTMENTS FOR SERVING LIGHT REFRESHMENTS

Light refreshments are eaten in diverse ways. Guests may be seated at tables, they may dine from trays, or they may be expected to sit or stand informally and dine as best they can. The food may be finger food, it may require the use of a fork or a knife or both, or it may require a spoon. Appointments must be selected according to the kind of food and the manner in which it will be eaten; they must always provide for easy and neat eating. It is conceivable that a hostess might plan refreshments with her store of appointments in mind. Here are some general do's and don't's for selecting appointments for serving food.

1. Use plates that are large enough to accommodate the food you serve.

2. Provide all the tools that are essential for comfortable and refined eating.
3. Do not use footed cups, except when guests are seated at tables.
4. Whenever you provide a plate and a cup and saucer, be sure there is ample space for guests to put one or the other down while eating.
5. Refreshment sets that consist of cup and plate, with a well for holding the cup in position, provide a comfortable service if a cup and saucer are too small and a plate and a cup and saucer cannot be provided.
6. When you use cups on plates, place tiny soft paper doilies called "soakers" under the cups to anchor them. These doilies are now available in good design.
7. Serve cakes that guests are to cut on large cake plates so that there is ample room for cutting and serving.
8. Do not fill any dishes to the brim; it makes serving difficult and food may be spilled.
9. If you have a beautiful tray of the proper size, use it for serving sandwiches, cookies, or small cakes.
10. Do not crowd small items onto the serving plates or trays; a guest should be able to remove one item without touching another.

Following are some specific do's and don't's for selecting appointments that are appropriate to the manner in which food is to be eaten.

Finger Food

1. Do provide a saucer or a plate along with the beverage container. This underliner holds food and frees the right hand for eating and using the napkin. Most persons appear both baffled and annoyed when they attempt to manage simultaneously a cup of punch, a napkin, and even single tidbits, unless the tidbits are passed after the guests are seated with napkins on their laps, or they can gather around the table on which the tidbits are offered, as at cocktail parties.

2. Keep food tidbits in scale with the underliner of the beverage container. Have them bite-sized when it is a saucer or a bread-and-butter plate, but somewhat larger when it is a dessert plate. It is quite important not to overlook the factor of size; accidents occur if the cakes and sandwiches served are larger than the saucer or plate can accommodate; if they are too small, the food looks lost on the plate.

3. Offer spoons with a beverage to which sugar, cream, or lemon may be added and with a punch to which dips of sherbet are added.

4. You may use either tea- or cocktail-size napkins; but tea-size is preferred when a dessert plate is the underliner for a cup.

Food Requiring Flatware

Whenever the food served requires the use of a fork, such as a cake, or of a butter spreader, such as hot muffins or scones, it is desirable to provide a plate for the food and a cup and saucer for the beverage. This means that a place to set the beverage down while eating must be provided whenever guests are not seated at tables. End tables or stack tables may be used for this purpose. If they cannot be provided, the cup may be placed directly on the plate with the food as at wedding receptions and dessert parties, when cake and coffee are served on the same plate. But this plate must be large enough to accommodate both cup and food and to permit neat eating. Combine a beverage glass with a plate in this way with caution. The refreshment set is useful under these circumstances, and the well of the plate will sometimes accommodate a glass.

The fork provided may be a dinner fork or a salad fork; the knife may be a butter spreader if it will be used only for spreading, but should be a dinner knife if it will be used as a cutting instrument. Late suppers or snacks may require luncheon or dinner plates, knives and forks, and cups and saucers.

Unless guests will be seated at tables or will have trays, do not serve a dessert eaten with a spoon unless you have coupe plates with considerable depth. That is, avoid a situation where the guest must eat from a bowl, large or small, placed on a plate held in the hand. Fruit shortcakes, cobblers, and sundaes are desserts that should be served in bowls or deep coupe plates and eaten with spoons.

Use tea-size or larger napkins in all of these situations.

SERVING REFRESHMENTS

Refreshments for small groups may be served from a tray, from a table, or directly from the kitchen. Refreshments for large groups are usually served from a table. In general, the service is buffet with guests helping themselves to food, although other methods of service are also used. Guests may receive a poured beverage or they may be expected to pour their own. Much latitude in service is possible; it can be suited to the occasion, the group, the available appointments, and the refreshments, as well as to the room in which they are offered.

Serving from a Tray

When serving coffee or tea to a few persons and when serving finger foods, a hostess sets up a tray with the needed appointments. She carries it to the living room, terrace, porch, or wherever her guests have

PHOTOGRAPH 16.   A tray arranged for afternoon tea or coffee.

gathered. She then places the tray on a coffee table or other table at which she can sit and pour comfortably and gracefully. On these occasions she pours and adds the accompaniments to the beverage according to the taste of each guest; she places a spoon, if one is needed, on the plate or saucer, handle parallel to the handle of the cup; she then lifts the cup and saucer from the tray with her right hand, places a napkin between her hand and the saucer, and passes the whole to each guest in turn. Guests seated at a distance come to the table to be served, or the hostess may ask someone to take the services to guests. When the hostess has poured for all, she passes the food, unless guests have helped themselves.

Setting the Tray.   Although size and shape may necessitate variations, all trays set for beverage service are similarly set. The pattern of setting is not unlike that described previously for beverage service from the table and for the service of afterdinner coffee. Here are pointers on how to do it easily. This step-by-step procedure is for cups and saucers.

1. Place the tray lengthwise on the kitchen counter in front of you.

2. Place a cup and saucer in the center of the side closest to you.

3. Place the napkins, spread just enough so that the top one can always be grasped without fumbling, to the left of the cup and saucer.

4. Place the teaspoons, bowl inside bowl but with the handles spread in fan shape to your right for ease in removal, at the right of this cup and saucer.

5. Place the accompaniments behind the cup and saucer for ease in serving. Place cream or lemon to the right of the sugar, because they are taken more frequently.

6. Place the pot to the right of the spoons with the handle directed to the right if possible, so that you can pour by simply tipping the pot.

7. Place the remaining cups and saucers by two's, if possible; if not, stack saucers and place cups by two's. Have the handles directed to your right or directly toward you, whichever you prefer.

8. If you are left-handed and not ambidextrous, your tray arrangement will be the mirror image of the one described. This reversed arrangement is, probably, the only one in table setting that is modified for the left-handed person.

9. If space permits, cups and saucers may be set singly, with the spoons placed on the saucers parallel to the cup handles.

10. Place the plate of tea dainties on the tray. If space does not permit, remove the pot from the tray and try to fit the plate of tea dainties onto the tray—remember it is safer to carry the tray without the pot of hot beverage. If the plate of tea dainties cannot be fitted onto the tray, it may be necessary to bring it in separately. The plate of dainties and even the napkins can be removed from the tray to the table once the tray has been set down. Slight rearrangements will usually follow for easy and graceful pouring (see Figure 23–1).

Tea Dainties

FIGURE 23–1.   A tray arranged for afternoon tea or coffee.

Serving from a Table

Refreshments for tea or coffee, dessert, or supper may be offered from a table. This table may be a dining table, a draped card table, a lamp table, a tea cart, or other small table; the size of the group to be served will determine which table to use. A cloth may or may not be used depending on personal preference and the condition of the table; if one is used, it should be suitable to the occasion and in harmony with the appointments and the room. Fine lace cloths, embroidered linen cloths, sheer organdy cloth over solid colored cloths, satin cloths, and cloths of novelty weaves and fabrics are often used. The overhang of a tea cloth is greater than that of a dinner cloth and may even reach the floor. Unless a cloth is appropriate and adds something to a setting, it may be better to leave the table bare. Whatever the occasion for which the table is set, the table should be as beautiful as one can make it.

At teas, coffees, and receptions, guests help themselves to food, although the beverage is poured for them. The pourer is seated unless she is serving punch. At the dessert party or the late supper, the service may be similar, or the guests may pour for themselves. Infrequently, both the food and the beverage are served to the guests. Tables must always be set with these two goals in mind: the comfort of the person or persons pouring or serving and the comfort of guests who must serve themselves.

The Small Tea Table.   The seated hostess pours at the small tea table. Guests usually go to the small tea table to be served. Place the table on the perimeter of the room and arrange it so that you face the group.

1. Plan the setting or arrangement of the tea table well in advance of tea time. Do a trial run of the beverage service; then proceed as you plan guests to, to make certain that it works.

2. Set the beverage service on a tray or directly on the table, whichever you prefer; but if the tea cloth is a fine one, use a tray to protect it from stains. Place the cups and saucers within your easy reach. Plan to serve the accompaniments of the beverage. Plan to lay a spoon on each saucer with the spoon handle parallel with the cup handle except when the food is finger food.

3. After you have arranged the beverage service, plan for placing the food on the table; three possibilities exist, depending on the kind of food offered. To do this, move to the side of the table opposite the pouring service.

(a) When the food offered is finger food, place the teaspoons and the napkins near the pouring area, on what is now your right. Place the plate or plates of tea dainties so as to give the table a

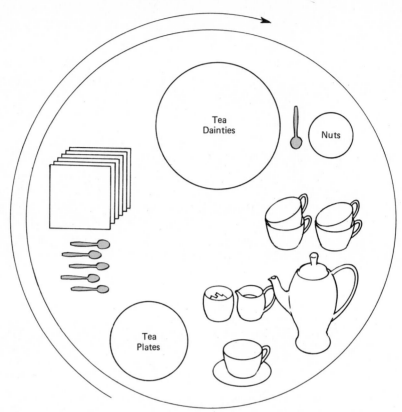

FIGURE 23–2a.   A small table arranged for tea or coffee—finger food.

balanced appearance (see Figure 23–2a). Guests approach you on your left to receive the poured beverage. They take a spoon if needed and place it beside the cup on the plate, a napkin, and then the tea dainties, so as to avoid having no place to lay a spoon as might happen were the food taken first.

(b) When the food is fork food, place the dessert on the table on your left, lay the serving pieces in position, and then place the dessert plates to the right of the dessert for easy left-to-right transfer of the food to the individual plate. Next, place the dessert forks on the table, and then the napkins. After serving herself, the guest approaches you on your left and receives the poured beverage with her free right hand (see Figure 23–2b).

(c) If the food is hot muffins, hot coffee cake, hot scones, or other food requiring the use of a butter spreader, put individual plates on your left and the plate of food to the right of them. Place the butter and the jam next; then the butter spreaders and the nap-

FIGURE 23–2b.   A small table arranged for afternoon tea or dessert—food requires the use of a fork.

kins. After serving herself, the guest approaches on your left and receives the poured beverage (see Figure 23–2c).

4. Arrange to have plenty of table space on which guests can place their plates and/or cups and saucers. Stack tables are excellent for this purpose.

5. Place an arrangement of flowers or some other decorative object on the table if space permits.

Setting the Table for a Dessert Party.   Dessert may be served for a buffet or offered to guests seated at a table, either card tables or the dining table. Setting the dessert buffet is similar to setting the dessert course of the buffet meal or setting the small tea table. The tea cart provides an excellent buffet at the same time that it permits a hostess or an assistant to pour the beverage. The dining table may be set for full self-service of dessert and beverage, or one or both may be served for guests.

1. When the food is to be self-served, set the dessert plates to the right of the dessert to provide for easy left-to-right movement in serving. Provide two serving tools. Next, lay the forks and then the napkins.

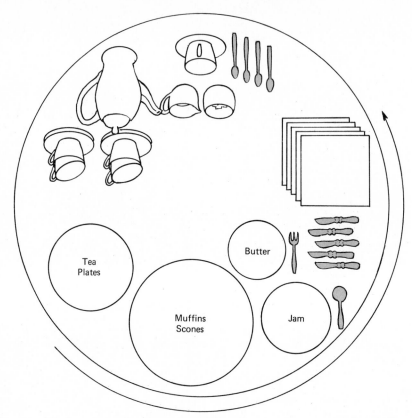

FIGURE 23–2c.   A small table arranged for afternoon tea or morning coffee—
food requires the use of a butter spreader.

2. When the beverage is to be self-served, set the service as previously described in Chapter 22. Have the beverage service follow the food service closely. Remember, cups and saucers should not be stacked by two's in this arrangement.

3. When the beverage is to be served for the guest, set the service at one end of the table as previously described. Have the person who pours serve the beverage accompaniments and place a spoon on the saucer as indicated.

4. When food is to be served for guests, set this service at one end of the table. Place the dessert plates so that they will be directly in front of the person who will serve. Place the dessert behind the plates to allow for forward movement in serving. Provide two serving tools, so that the person serving does not use the fingers to steady the dessert on the pastry server. Along the side of the table lay first the appropriate tools for eating, then the napkins. The beverage service follows.

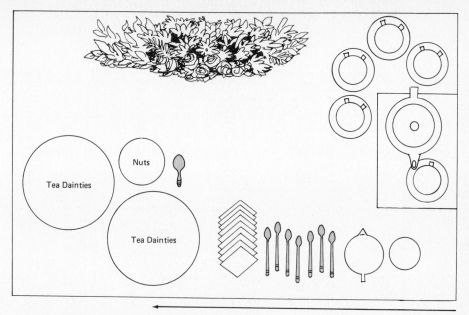

FIGURE 23-3.   Table arrangement for a large tea—a single service on one side of table and cups and saucers used.

5. The desserts may be served in the kitchen and the served desserts placed on the buffet in any number that seems suitable to balance the beverage service. The flatware, the napkins, and the beverage follow in that order.

6. Dessert may be served from the kitchen to seated guests.

Setting the Large Tea Table.   When the group invited to tea exceeds a number for whom the hostess can pour, the tea table is large. Large tea tables vary in size from the usual small dining table in the home to the enormous one put together from several tables in the schoolroom, the church parlor, or the club room. The tea table may be against a wall or away from a wall to permit traffic around it (see Figures 23-3 and 23-4). The persons responsible for serving can work most efficiently when the table is near the kitchen; at the same time the tea table ought to be in the handsomest part of the room. Compromise between these two sites is usually necessary in selecting the site of the tea table. Whatever the site and whatever the size, the table, when set, should present a well-composed picture. No other table—not even the buffet table—has so much potential for beauty, whether the appointments include exquisite linens, fine china, silver service, and orchids or peasant linens, pottery, and zinnias.

Beverages may be served from one or both ends of the table or from

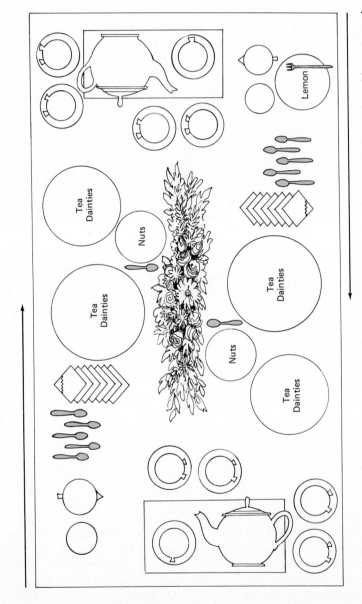

Tea
Dainties

Nuts

Tea
Dainties

Lemon

Tea
Dainties

Nuts

Tea
Dainties

FIGURE 23–4.   Table arrangement for a large tea—duplicate services on two sides of the table, cups and saucers used.

one side. The arrangement of appointments for those who pour should be carefully worked out so that they can perform with grace and poise. Arrangements for guests must be made so that they serve themselves easily and gracefully. The accompaniments for the beverage when these are self-served, the spoons, the napkins, and the food must be conveniently placed for them. Two patterns of arrangement now prevail: either guests receive the beverage first, or they take tea dainties first and receive the beverage last. Specific suggestions for setting the table for large teas and receptions follow.

1. Plan the setting in detail well in advance of the actual hour of table setting. Whenever possible, do a practice setting with the appointments to be used.

2. Decorations may be elaborate, tall, and large in scale; they should be the center of interest on the table, except when the wedding cake or other motif becomes the center of interest. The position of the flowers or other decorations may vary according to the site of the table and the number of beverage services at the table.

   (a) Center a single arrangement on a table that has two beverage services and that will have traffic around it. Place two arrangements on this table for good effect.

   (b) Decorations are not always centered on the table placed against a wall. Instead, they are placed on a lengthwise line that divides the table into thirds midway between the two ends of the table at which there are two beverage services, away from the center at the table with one beverage service.

3. Candles can be placed on the tea table. Use candles in colors that are coordinated with the decorations. Use them in different heights and place them for the best effect. Always light them.

4. Whenever possible set the beverage services so that the guest receives the beverage at the left of the pourer who is pouring from a beverage pot to avoid having the beverage pot between the pourer and the guest. A table placed against the wall and at which there are two beverage services has one service at which the beverage is received on the pourer's right, a situation the pourer can cope with. The use of a samovar or a silver urn at the left end of the table expedites the service. The samovar or urn must be coordinated with the table appointments and must be in proper scale. The urn-style coffee maker that would be appropriate in some situations would be quite unsuitable on this table. When punch is the second beverage offered, offer it at the left end of the table.

5. Any of the previously described patterns for the service of a beverage may be modified for use on the large tea table. Modifications differ, depending on whether the guest is to be served the beverage

first or last. We shall call it Plan A when the guest receives the beverage first and Plan B when the guest receives the beverage last. The beverage service may be laid with or without a tray, but the tray is preferred.

6. Here is how you go about setting the table according to Plan A—when the guest receives the beverage first. Details may differ from table to table, but in general all tables are similarly set.

(a) *Cups and saucers used.* Sit down at the table where the pourer will sit. If a tray is to be used, place it in the center of the area close to the edge of the table. Place a cup and saucer in a position comfortable for pouring. Place the beverage pot or pots to the right of it, but place behind the saucer an urn or a kettle on a swivel base that tips for pouring. Place a suitable number of cups and saucers, stacked by two's, within easy reach, either above the single cup and saucer or to the right of the beverage pot if the guest is to receive the beverage on the pourer's left. The size and shape of the table will determine the better position for the cups and saucers. Place the cups so that the handles are parallel to the table edge and directed to the pourer's right (see Figures 23–3 and 23–4).

When the beverage is to be received at the pourer's right, place the cups and saucers on her left, with the handles directed to her right for ease in separation.

When an urn is used, place the cups and saucers on either the right or the left, depending on which side the beverage will be received from.

(b) *Cups and plates used.* Place the tray, one cup with or without an underlying saucer, the other cups, and the beverage pot or urn as above, but place a pile of plates to the pourer's left. She places the filled cup on the top plate of the stacked plates and hands the plates with the cup to a guest. Use the tiny doilies that are now available to keep the cups from slipping (see Figure 23–5).

(c) Place the remaining appointments away from the beverage service in this order: the accompaniments for the beverage, the spoons, and the napkins. Finally, place the plates or trays of tea dainties. Double service from one side of a long table frequently has one plate or tray of tea dainties in common (see Figure 23–5).

7. According to Plan B, the guest receives the beverage last. Two possiblities in appointments exist: the cup may be placed on the plate; or both a cup and saucer and a plate are used. Some persons frown on the use of the cup on the plate unless the plate has a well to accommodate the cup. The disadvantage of having the cup on the plate can be partly overcome by the use of a tiny doily under the cup to keep it from slipping. Expediency sometimes leaves no choice but to use a cup and a plate.

When a plate and a cup and saucer are provided, stack tables, folding tray stands, or other table space must also be provided.

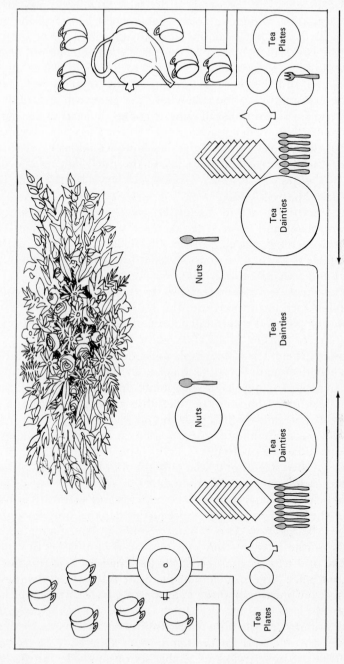

FIGURE 23–5. Table arrangement for a large tea—duplicate services on one side of table, cups and plates used.

Here is how you go about setting the table according to Plan B.

(a) *Cups and plates used.* Sit down at the table where the pourer will sit. Place a tray close to the edge of the table in the center of the area. Place a cup in the proper position for pouring. Place the accompaniments for the beverage behind this cup; place the beverage pot or pots and the kettle of hot water if one is used to the right. Place an urn behind the cup and the accompaniments to the right or left. Then, keeping the area empty on the side where the guest will approach the pourer, place a suitable number of cups—handles directed to the right—stacked by two's within easy reach on the tray or the table. According to this plan, the pourer—usually, but not always—adds the accompaniments for the beverage and then places the filled cup on the plate extended by the guest, who takes a spoon and lays it on the plate if he needs one (see Figure 23–5).

(b) Place everything else in this order, away from the pouring station: spoons, plates and trays of tea dainties, napkins, tea plates. The napkins are sometimes placed between the stacked tea plates, particularly if the table is small. The guest starts at the place where the plates are stacked and proceeds toward the pouring station.

(c) *Plates and cups and saucers provided.* In this procedure, the saucers and the spoons are introduced into the setting at the pouring station and the pourer passes the cup and saucer of beverage with the spoon laid on the saucer parallel to the cup handle to the guest.

It would be difficult to say which plan is better, as each has an advantage and a disadvantage. Service is quicker by Plan A than by Plan B; with Plan A, however, there is the possibility that an unwary guest may be jostled while he or she is at the table, thus causing an accident. Regional customs determine which plan should be used.

8. Always place a napkin of generous size at the pourer's station so that the pourer may be protected.

9. Place on the table at one time only the number of cups and saucers or plates that is in scale with the table.

10. Avoid elaborate arrangements of napkins and spoons that would make them the center of interest. Spread the napkins only enough so that each can be taken in turn without fumbling. The spoons may be laid directly on the table, or they may be placed in a basket or a bowl, or on a plate or a tray, or in a receptacle designed for that purpose.

11. Do not place large numbers of plates or trays of tea dainties on the table; instead put two or three items on one plate or tray and keep the number of plates or trays compatible with the size of the table. The total setting is improved when there are differences in the sizes or shapes of the plates or trays used for the tea dainties. One plate or tray may be common to the two services of a table set on one side for dual service.

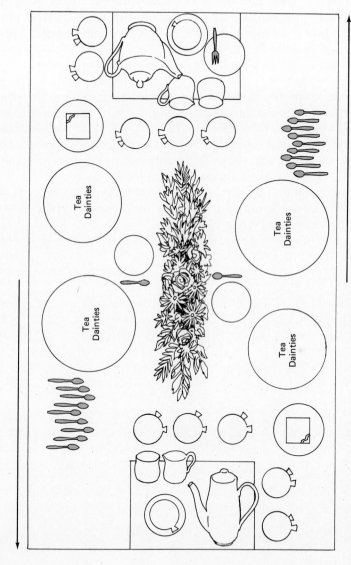

FIGURE 23–6. Table arrangement for a large tea—guest takes food, then receives beverage. Tea plates are stacked with napkins placed in between.

Setting the Service for Punch.   The setting for punch service is somewhat different from that of a hot beverage. The person who pours may
sit or stand. Punch is ladled with the right hand into a cup grasped by
the handle with the left hand. Whenever food is offered, the cup is
then placed on the plate and the whole is transferred to the guest. If
no food is offered, the pourer will transfer the cup from the left to the
right hand and offer it with its handle directed toward the guest. Here
is how you might set the service.

1. Stand in the pourer's position. Place the punch bowl on a large
plate or tray to catch any condensing moisture. Set it close to the edge
of the table, and arrange decorations around the base of the bowl. Place
a pile of small plates on both sides of the bowl. Place the cups, stacked
by two's if desirable, in symmetrical arrangement around the bowl, but
not so far to the front that they will be difficult to reach or will spoil
the effect of any decorations. Direct the handles to the left.

2. Place the napkins and the plates of food to give a balanced appearance to the table. Spoons will also have to be laid if sherbet is put
into the punch cups (see Figure 23–7).

3. If punch is being offered without food, as it frequently is at wed-

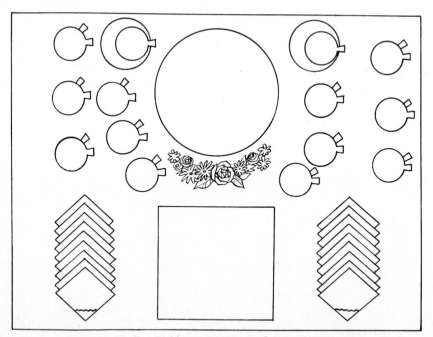

FIGURE 23–7.   Table arrangement for serving punch.

dings, the service may be set on any small table, as described, but there is no need for plates.

Serving Refreshments Directly from the Kitchen

Refreshments may be served directly from the kitchen in several ways. Some persons prefer this kind of service because it seems to be less bother, few props are required, and setting a tray or a table can be avoided. On the other hand, except when the guests are seated at tables, movement among the guests to serve them can become a nuisance unless an effort is made to control this movement. Perhaps every service has advantages and disadvantages.

1. One popular service from the kitchen is that used when guests are seated at card tables for dessert before bridge or other games. These tables are completely set with linens, flatware, beverageware, the accompaniments for the beverage, cups and saucers, and small table decorations. The dessert and the beverage may be on the tables when the guests are seated, or they may be brought later, depending on whether the group is large or small. A similar service is used when refreshments follow an afternoon or evening of cards.

2. Trays completely set with the dessert or other food and the beverage can be brought to the guests. The accompaniments for the beverage must then be passed; they are offered from a small tray or plate.

3. Often, plates of food are brought directly to the guests. They may or may not be offered from a tray. The beverage cup may be on the plate with the food, or it may be offered separately, in which case a place to set the cup and saucer while eating must be available. End tables and small stack tables can provide this space. Accompaniments for the beverage are offered from a small tray as in (2). Napkins may be offered with the plate or from the tray, depending on the manner of presenting plates.

4. When refreshments consist of a beverage and finger food, a tray that offers the poured beverage, its accompaniments, and napkins is offered to each guest. After all guests have accepted the beverage, the food is offered by the hostess or someone who assists her.

Except when guests are served at small tables, these serving patterns are very informal and casual; their use is best limited to small groups. Service from a tea tray or a table has more dignity and is more ceremonious.

MAINTAINING SERVICE

At large teas and receptions where serving continues for several hours, a crew of workers is required to maintain service at the table. In her home, the hostess may depend partly on her friends and partly on hired help; organizations appoint committees to perform the various serving duties.

Plans for Service

The following duties must be performed, and the number of workers required to carry them out is determined by the number of guests anticipated.

1. One or more persons should be available to move between the kitchen and the tea table to carry additional appointments, newly arranged plates of food, and all the other items needed on the table and to return plates that need rearranging to the kitchen. The people performing this task might be called runners.

2. One or two persons remain in the kitchen to keep a fresh supply of the beverage or beverages ready, to refill the plates of food, and to wash dishes. They might be called the kitchen helpers.

3. One or more persons should be responsible for taking cups from guests and stacking the cups in a designated place. These persons might be called cup bearers. Hostesses at large teas should not be expected to have this responsibility.

4. One or more persons should be concerned solely with greeing guests, talking with them, introducing them to other guests, and so forth. This job is for the hostesses.

At small functions, the hostess, by herself or with the help of a friend or the host, monages all of these duties.

Techniques of Service

The following suggestions lead to effective service, whether one hostess or a committee makes the plans.

1. Make definite assignments of specific responsibilities.

2. Organize the kitchen so that a place is assigned for each task.

3. Have food set up on trays, cookie sheets, or other large containers. Use one tray for each kind or for several similar kinds of food. Cover all trays of sandwiches and other foods that dry out quickly with a film wrap.

4. Have duplicate sets of all serving appointments, except punch

bowls and urns. When an object is removed from the tea table, another like it is set down in its place. Urns and punch bowls can be filled from pitchers without being removed from the tea table; they need not be duplicated. However, the pitchers should be as thoughtfully selected as all other appointments.

5. The plates and trays of food should be replaced frequently, so that the table presents a pleasing picture at all times and all plates and trays offer a generous assortment of dainties at all times.

6. Appointments such as cups and saucers, flatware, and napkins should be brought to the table on trays to avoid fingerprints and excessive handling. Stacked plates are more safely carried when they are grasped in both hands.

7. Set up a serving table near the tea table whenever possible. From it, additional cups and saucers, plates, spoons, and napkins can be taken to the tea table. Used cups and saucers can be stacked on trays on the serving table for later removal to the kitchen.

8. It is not necessary to use linen or paper doilies under the tea dainties; the gleam of silver or the color of plates may be part of the beauty of the table. Glass plates may need frequent washing to remain presentable.

9. Instruct those who work with food in the kitchen to handle it with spatulas and tongs whenever feasible.

10. Prevent foodborne illness by handling foods safely. Be sure that refrigerated storage space is adequate for the foods that need it.

Appendix A

Format for Menus

1. Capitalize all words except articles and prepositions.
2. The items that compose meals should be grouped by courses, beginning with the first. The items of courses are presented in order of greatest consequence. For example:

Broiled Sirloin Steak

Baked Potatoes   Sour Cream

Broccoli

Hot Rolls

3. When an item on the menu has a special accompaniment, you may either place the main item to the left and the accompanying item to the right, or you may center the main item and write the accompanying item underneath. For example:

Braised Pork Chops   Applesauce

or

Braised Pork Chops

Applesauce

4. When a dish is accompanied by two or more items, center the former and space the latter on the same line to the right and left, or write them on the line below. For example:

Sesame Seed Wafers   Chicken Consommé   Saltines

or Chicken Consommé

Sesame Seed Wafers   Saltines   Ry-Krisp

5. The beverage appears as the last item of the course with which it is served.

6. Such items as butter, cream, sugar, or salad dressing are not written on menus unless they are particularly interesting or different. For example:

Head Lettuce with Chutney Dressing

or

Pancakes   Maple Syrup

7. Plan the spacing and arrangement of the items on the menu so that the written menu is symmetrical. Allow extra spacing between courses; this extra space is often omitted in menus printed in books, magazines, and newspapers, in order to save space. Following is a menu for a meal of three courses.

French Onion Soup

Celery Sticks   Whole Wheat Wafers   Assorted Olives

Prime Rib Roast of Beef au Jus

Potato Soufflé

Asparagus with Hollandaise Sauce

Mixed Green Salad

Hot Rolls

Lemon Ice

Coffee

Appendix B
Purchasing Guides

Quantity food-purchasing guides become increasingly unimportant with each passing year. This is true for several reasons, some of which are proposed. Food is extensively processed and packaged in an assortment of packages of different sizes. Labeling regulations stipulate that the contents of all packages, with a few exceptions, must bear a statement of the contents in pounds and ounces for some products and in fluid measures for others. The aphorism "a pint's a pound the world around and a pound fills a pint" has only a few exceptions. One half cup of many different foods is considered a serving, that is, one pint or one pound will often be enough for four persons. See-through packaging permits rough estimates of numbers of servings, that is, of how many persons the package will feed. Trimming practices in the marketing of fresh vegetables have all but eliminated waste. Trimming practices in retailing meats have reduced both the fat and the bone contents of meats. Some food items are packaged as single servings; others, as family units. Many food purchases are made by count: pot pies, ready-to-eat dinners, apples, oranges, bananas, artichokes, fresh pears, chicken legs, eggs, and the like. Finally, the labels of many packaged food products bear a statement of a suggested number of servings.

The almost universal concern for weight control means that few persons want jumbo food servings or second servings of any food, except steak perhaps. Estimates of how much meat to buy, except when one is buying by the unit, are only guesses at best. A rule of thumb that works much of the time in buying meat is bone in, two, and bone out, three servings per pound. It must be recognized, however, that when using this rule, one can overbuy because the amount of bone and fat will vary from cut to cut and time to time. Boneless buys such as ground beef and stew can yield four servings per pound. Another rule of thumb that works most of the time in buying fresh vegetables suggests that one pound will provide four servings. Exceptions are few and are readily learned if one buys those vegetables—fresh greens, podded vegetables, and hard-shell squashes. Actually few persons desire to eat jumbo servings of vegetables: should a pound provide small servings, probably most persons would not care. For this reason, the No. 303 can and the No. 2 vacuum can of vegetables and the ten-ounce and the twelve-ounce packages of frozen vegetables will, in general, provide four suitable servings.

Although shopping for food is complicated, the quantitative aspects of the shopping are not. Only three tables are included in this appendix. Table B–1 includes some bits of information useful in meal preparation. Table B–2 gives the measure of some staples that remain in general use. Table B–3 gives the measure of some cans in which foods are commonly packed and names the foods packed in them.

TABLE B–1. *Guide to the Use of Foods in Cooking and Meal Preparation*

Item	Comment
Apples	One pound yields about 2 cups of peeled and sliced apples and will make about 2 cups of applesauce. It takes 1½ to 2 pounds to make a 9-inch pie. Allow ⅓ pound per person for baking.
Beans and peas, dry	The measure of one pound is about two cups; beans triple in volume during cooking.
Bread	Slices are not equal in weight. Two ounces will make 1 cup of soft bread crumbs; 1 cup of dry bread crumbs weighs 6 ounces.
Celery	One buys a bunch; each part is a rib.
Cereals, breakfast	Allow 1 ounce of cereal per person, regardless of kind and whether cooked or ready-prepared—except for puffed cereals and the concentrates added to cereals to enrich their nutrient content. For the latter, follow the manufacturer's directions. One half ounce of a puffed cereal fills the usual cereal bowl.
Cereals, milk for	Plan to add ½ cup of milk to each serving of ready-prepared cereal; ¼ cup to cooked cereals.
Cereal pastes, pasta	Noodles swell some during cooking; macaroni and spaghetti double in volume; a pound of any of these yields about 8 cups when cooked and serves from 8 to 16 people, depending on use. Italian spaghetti (the long kind) does not swell as much as the regular kind; 1 pound serves 4 to 8 persons, depending on the kind and quantity of sauce served. Cereals absorb between 2 and 3 times their original weight in water during cooking.
Chocolate, cocoa	Three tablespoons of cocoa plus 1 tablespoon of fat are equivalent to 1 ounce of chocolate.
Citrus fruits	One grapefruit or orange yields 8 to 10 sections. Three medium oranges yield 1 cup juice, that is, 2 4-ounce servings.
Coffee	To brew coffee for 2 persons, use 6 tablespoons of ground coffee and 3 measuring cups of water for a brew of medium strength; this volume of beverage yields 4 servings in as much as most coffee cups have a capacity of ⅔ to ¾ cup (the measuring kind). One ounce of instant coffee makes 12 to 24 cups of beverage depending on the desired strength of brew. To make coffee for 50, use 3 ounces of an instant coffee or 1 pound of ground coffee.
Flour	Two cups of flour made up into pancakes, baking-powder biscuits, muffins, or yeast breads will serve 6 people. One cup of flour made into cake or cookies will serve 6 people.

TABLE B–1. *Guide to the Use of Foods in Cooking and Meal Preparation* (*Continued*)

Item	Comment
Lettuce	Medium heads of lettuce weigh about 1 pound. Individual servings served as slices or wedges weigh about 2 to 2½ ounces. The weight of the lettuce used as underliner in a salad is approximately 1 ounce. The percentage of waste in lettuce varies from 0 to 15 percent for a quality product.
Milk	In reconstituting nonfat dry milk, 1 pound yields 5 quarts of fluid milk. Whole milk contains approximately 3.5 percent butterfat. The fat content of 1 quart of milk is 1¼ to 1½ ounces.
Potatoes	Allow ⅓ to ½ pound per person when baking; otherwise, ¼ to ⅓ pound is adequate. Follow directions of manufacturer when using instant products; however, these instructions may provide small servings.
Prunes	One-half pound of prunes cooked will yield 1 cup of pitted, chopped prunes.
Relishes	In preparing relishes, allow ½ rib celery, ½ carrot, 2 radishes, ¼ dill pickle, ½ sweet pickle, or 3 olives per person.
Rice	Rice triples in volume during cooking—cook ⅓ cup to obtain 1 cup of cooked rice.
Salad dressings	Allow 1 tablespoon French or similar dressing per serving of mixed salad. Allow ¾ tablespoon French or similar dressing per individual salad. Allow 2 tablespoons mayonnaise or "salad dressing" per serving of fish, chicken, or similar salad. Allow 1½ tablespoons mayonnaise or "salad dressing" per serving of cabbage, mixed fruit, head lettuce, or other arranged salad. Allow 1 tablespoon mayonnaise per serving in preparing sandwich fillings.
Salads, mixed green	Two ounces of mixed greens are the usual serving. There is often considerable waste to heads of endive, escarole, and romaine; only the inner portions are suitable for salads. The outer, less delicate leaves are often cooked and served as green vegetables.
Salads, mixed vegetable	The total weight of ingredients varies from 2 to 3 ounces per dinner salad. One tomato, ⅓ cucumber, and 6 to 8 ounces of lettuce will be sufficient for a tossed salad of these ingredients for 4 servings.
Shrimp	Raw, headless shrimp are about 30 percent waste. One pound serves 3 if the shrimp are mixed with other ingredients; otherwise, it serves only 2. Cooked, shucked, and deveined shrimp provide 5 to 6 servings per pound.

TABLE B–2.   *The Measure of One Pound* [1]

Items	Approximate Meausre of One Pound (Cups)
Almonds, shelled	3
Beans and peas, dry	2
Butter	2
Cheese, cheddar, grated	4
Cheese, cottage	2
Coconut, shredded	5
Coffee, ground beans	5
Coffee, instant	8
Cornmeal	3
Cornstarch	3½
Crumbs, cracker	6
Crumbs, graham cracker	4
Farina, wheat	3
Flour, bread	3½
Flour, cake	4½
Flour, general purpose	4
Flour, light rye	5
Flour, pancake	5
Flour, whole wheat	3
Lard	2
Macaroni	4
Margarine	2
Noodles	6–8
Pecans, shelled	4
Rice	2
Shortening	2½
Spaghetti	4
Sugar, brown	2¼
Sugar, confectioners	4
Sugar, granulated	2
Sugar, granulated brown	3
Tea, leaves	6
Walnuts, shelled	3½

[1] For more information see *Handbook of Food Preparation,* American Home Economics Association, Washington, D.C. (1975).

TABLE B–3. *The Measure of Cans*

Numerous sizes of cans are used for the canning of different food products; some sizes are used only for certain products. It is not possible to include all of them in this table but those most commonly purchased are mentioned herein.

Cans by Name	Approximate Weight (Ounces)	Approximate Measure (Cups)	Product Commonly Packed in Can
————	3¾	½	Salmon, tuna
6Z Tall	6	¾	Tomato and fruit juices and juice concentrates
No. ½	6½–7	1	Tuna, crab, lobster, shrimp, ham
————	7¾	1	Salmon
No. 8Z Tall	8	1	Fruits, vegetables, tomato products
————	9¾	1½	Tuna
No. 1 Picnic	10½	1¼	Condensed soups, tomato products, asparagus, gravies
2Z Tall	12	1½	Tomato and fruit juices, fruit drinks and juice concentrate
————	12½	2	Tuna
No. 300	15	1¾	Ripe olives, dry beans, tomato products, some soups
No. 303	16	2	Fruits, vegetables, pie fillings, specialties
No. 2 Vacuum	12	1½	Vegetables
No. 1 Tall	16	2	Salmon
No. 2	20	2½	Juices, pineapple, pie fillings, dry beans
No. 2½	26–29	3⅓	Dry beans, fruits, a few vegetables
No. 3 Cylinder	46	6	Juices, dry beans, fruit drinks

Appendix C
Temperature of Food and Control of Bacteria

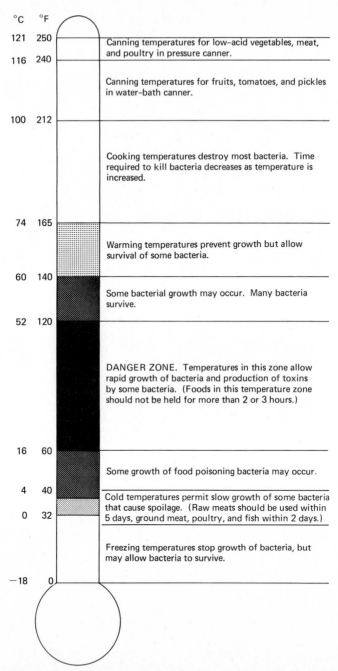

FIGURE C–1. Temperature of food for the control of bacteria. (Reprinted by permission from *Handbook of Food Preparation,* 7th ed., 1975, American Home Economics Association, Washington, D.C.)

512

Appendix D

Frozen Food Storage

TABLE D–1. *Suggested Maximum Home-Storage Periods to Maintain Good Quality in Purchased Frozen Foods Held at 0° F*

Frozen Food Products	Holding Period in Months
Baked Goods	
Angel food and chiffon cakes	2
Butter cakes	4
Sweet rolls and coffee cakes	2
Danish pastries	3
Doughnuts	3
Fruit pies, unbaked	8
Pound cake	6
White bread and rolls	3
Fish and Shellfish	
Fatty fish fillets	3
Lean fish fillets	6
Fried fish items	3
Cooked fish dishes	3
Crabmeat, clams, shucked oysters	3
Shrimp	12
Frozen Desserts	
Ice creams	1
Sherbets	1
Fruits	
Fruits	12
Fruit juice concentrates	12

Table D–1. *Suggested Maximum Home-Storage Periods to Maintain Good Quality in Purchased Frozen Foods Held at 0° F (Continued)*

Frozen Food Products	Holding Period in Months
Meats	
Beef	
Hamburger or chipped steaks	4
Roasts	12
Steaks	12
Lamb	
Ground or stew	4
Chops	4
Roasts	9
Pork, fresh	
Ground and sausage	1–2
Chops	4
Roasts	8
Pork, cured	2
Veal	
Cutlet and chops	9
Roasts	9
Cooked meat dinners and dishes	3
Poultry	
Chicken, cut up	9
Chicken, whole	12
Turkey, cut up	6
Turkey, whole	12
Duck, geese, whole	6
Cooked chicken dinners and dishes	6
Cooked turkey dinners and dishes	6
Fried chicken and fried chicken dinners	4
Vegetables, plain	12
Vegetable dishes	6

Sources: Adapted from Ruth Vettel and Carole Davis, *Home Care of Purchased Frozen Foods,* Home and Garden Bulletin No. 60, Consumer and Food Economic Institute, Agricultural Research Service, United States Department of Agriculture, Washington, D.C. (July 1973).

TABLE D–2. *Suggested Storage Periods to Maintain High Quality in Home-Frozen Food Products Held at 0° F*

Frozen Food Products	Storage Time in Months
Baked Products	
Cakes, prebaked	4–9
Breads, prebaked	3
Cake batters	3
Yeast doughs and pie shells	1–2
Butter and margarine	2
Cheddar cheese	3–6
Combination main dishes	3–6
Cooked meats and meat dishes	2–3
Cooked poultry and poultry dishes	2–3
Cured meats	1
Fresh chicken and turkey	6–12
Fresh Meats	
Beef and lamb roasts, steaks	8–12
Pork and veal roasts	4–8
Ground meats, all kinds	3
Stew meats, all kinds	3
Fried chicken	4
Fruits	8–12
Vegetables	8–12

Sources: Adapted from Marcile Allen and Mardel L. Crandall, "The Cold Facts About Freezing" in *Shopper's Guide, The 1974 Yearbook of Agriculture,* United States Department of Agriculture, Washington, D.C. (1974), p. 49.

Appendix E

Metric Conversions

TABLE E–1. *Volume Conversions*

Common Measures	Metric Equivalents
1 teaspoon	5 milliliters(ml)
1 tablespoon	15 milliliters
1 fluid ounce	30 milliliters
¼ cup	60 milliliters
½ cup	120 milliliters
1 cup[1]	0.24 liters(l)
1 pint	0.47 liters
1 quart[2]	0.95 liters
1 gallon	3.8 liters

[1] 1 cup plus 1 tablespoon equals ¼ liter.
[2] 1 quart plus ¼ cup equals 1 liter.

TABLE E–2. *Weight Conversions*

Common Weights	Metric Equivalents
1 ounce (avoirdupois)	28 grams(g)
1 pound	454 grams
1 pound	0.45 kilogram(kg)
2.2 pounds	1 kilogram

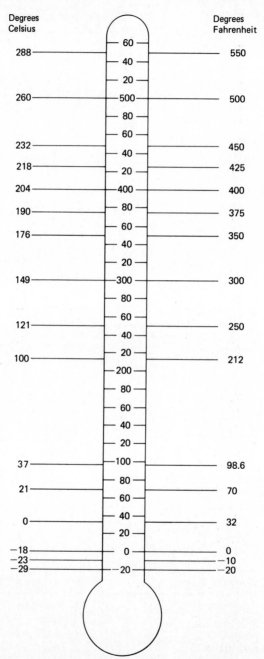

FIGURE E-1. Temperature Conversions

Appendix F
Suggested Menus

DINNER MENUS

Menu I: Patio Dinner
Broiled Sirloin Steak
Twice-Baked Potatoes
Buttered Green Beans
Mixed Green Salad
Hot Rolls
Assorted Cheeses   Crackers
Assorted Fresh Fruits
Coffee

Menu II
Braised Stuffed Pork Chops
Summer Squash   Peas
Mixed Salad of Lettuce, Celery, and Apple
Hot Rolls
Lemon Pie or Lemon Soufflé   Coffee

Menu III
Spaghetti with Meat Sauce
Assorted Crisp Relishes
Assorted Olives
French Bread
Assorted Fruits or Lemon Sherbet
Coffee

Menu IV
Prime Rib Roast of Beef
Yorkshire Pudding
Brussels Sprouts with Grapes
Salad of Bibb Lettuce and Belgian Endive
Crème de Menthe Parfait
Coffee

Menu V
Roast Leg of Lamb
Rice Pilaf
Asparagus
Mixed Green Salad
Assorted Relishes
Cherry Pie   Coffee

Menu VI
Swedish Meatballs
Mashed or Scalloped Potatoes
Broccoli
Crisp Relishes
Rye Bread
Rice and Raisin Custard   Crisp Butter Cookies
Coffee

Menu VII
Baked Fish Fillets with Egg Sauce
Baked Potatoes   Beets with Lemon Butter
Tossed Green Salad
Hot Rolls
Coconut Cake   Coffee

Menu VIII
Baked Stuffed Rock Cornish Game Hens
Creamed Onions   Lima Beans
Tomato Salad
Hot Cornbread
Caramel Custard
Coffee

Brunch Menus

Menu I

Orange Juice

Canadian Bacon   Scrambled Eggs   Sausages

Hash Brown Potatoes

Buttered Toast   Assorted Jams

Blueberry Muffins

Coffee

Menu II

Fresh Fruits in Season

Corned Beef Hash with Poached Eggs

Scalloped Chicken and Mushrooms

Toasted English Muffins

Coffee Cake

Coffee

Menu III

Fruits in Season

Blueberry Pancakes

Sausages   Ham   Bacon

Coffee Cake

Coffee

Menu IV

Assorted Fruit Juices

Creamed Ham and Eggs on Toast

Chicken Livers and Bacon

Hash Brown Potatoes

Buttered Toast   Brioche

Coffee

Buffet Menus

Menu I

(Suitable only when dining at a table)

(Roast carved at buffet)

Prime Rib Roast of Beef

Twice-Baked Potatoes

Broccoli

Assorted Relishes

Buttered Hot Rolls

Crème de Menthe Parfait

Coffee

Menu II
(Suitable only when dining at a table)
(Roast carved at buffet)

Roast Leg of Lamb
Eggplant Casserole
Mixed Green Salad
Thin Whole Wheat Bread Sandwiches
Assorted Cheeses and Crackers
Fresh Fruits
Coffee

Menu III
(Suitable when dining from table)

Baked Boned Chicken Breasts
Corn Pudding
Green Beans and Water Chestnuts
Assorted Relishes
Toasted Sesame Seed Loaf
Toffee Angel Cake
Coffee

Menu IV
(Suitable for any mode of dining)

Chicken Rice Casserole
(Chicken, rice, mushrooms, ripe olives, almonds, sauce)
Baked Tomato Halves
Assorted Relishes
Herb-Buttered Bread
Lemon Chiffon Pie
Coffee

Menu V
(Suitable for any mode of dining)

Ham Loaf
Potatoes Au Gratin
Brussel Sprouts and Tokay Grapes
Assorted Olives and Pickles
Thin Rye Bread Sandwiches
Pumpkin Pie with Whipped Cream
Coffee

Menu VI
(Suitable for any mode of dining)

Swedish Meatballs with Mushrooms
Danish Potato Soufflé
Broccoli
Jellied Fruit Mold
Rye Bread Sandwiches
Boston Cream Pie
Coffee

Index

A

Additives, *see* Food additives
Adulterated food, 34–35, 55
Afternoon tea, *see* Teas
Agriculture and food of the 1980s,
    9–11
American style of meal service, 362
Amino acid content of plant proteins,
    91
Apple varieties, 279–280
Artificial color in food, 34, 47–48
Aseptic canning, 12
Aspartame, 347

B

Bacteria, temperature control of, 512
Basic Seven food groups, 89
Beef, 174–179, 188–190
    corned, 200
    cuts, 174–179
    grades, 188–190
    ground, 204–205
    identifying cuts, 175–178
    quality in, 188–190
    tenderizing, 205
Beverage service, how to set up
    for punch, 498–499

on the buffet table, 470
on the dining table, 390–391
on the tea table, 487–499
on a tray, 390, 392, 485–486
on the serving table, 395
Beverages, 347–353
    cocoa mixes, 353
    coffee, 347–350
    fruit, 296–301
    instant coffee, 349–350
    instant tea, 351
    teas, 350–352
Beverageware, 383–385, 414–417
    glassware, 414–417
    placing on the dining table, 383–385
Blue-plate style of meal service, 367
Botulism, 71
Bread-and-butter plate
    position at cover, 385
    position of butter spreader on, 378–
        379
    use of, 379
Brownout and blackout, what to do in,
    78–79
Brunch, 457–458
    menus for, 521
Budget for food, 95–99
    factors affecting, 96–98
    guides to maximizing food dollar,
        102–103

Budget for food (*Cont.*)
  matching food choices to, 99–102
Buffet-style of meals, 367–368, 458–
    476
  dining arrangements for, 458–463
  menus for, 521–523
    planning, 463–464
  how to serve self at, 462
  how to set table for, 464–471
    main course, 464–470
    dessert course, 470–471
  table service at buffet meals, 471–
    474
Butter, 232–233
  buying guide, 242–243
  storage guide, 242
  substitute (margarine), 234–235
  whipped, 233
Buttermilk, 224
Butter spreader
  position on bread-and-butter plate,
    378–379
  when to use, 329

C

Candles, use of, 377, 419, 468, 493
Canning of food, 11–12
Cheeses, cheese food products, 245–
    275
  buying guide, 267–268
  cheese food, 262
    process of making, 247
    products, 259–264
  cold-pack, 264
  dictionary of varieties, 270–274
  processed, 259–264
  quality in, 266–267
  ripened, 249–250, 252–256
  serving, 268–269
  spread, 263
  storing, 268
  unripened, 249, 251–252
  varieties of, 249–258
Citrus fruits, 281–284
Clostridium botulinum, 71
Clostridium perfringens, 71

Cocoa mixes, 353
Codex Alimentarius, 64
Coffee, 347–350
  brewed versus instant, 349–350
  decaffeinated, 350
  demitasse, 457
  how to serve at table, 446–447
Coffee cream, 227
Coffee creamer or whitener, 233–234
Combination food store, 150
Compromise style of meal service,
    265–266
Convenience foods, 161–164
  cost or convenience of, 163
  definition of, 162
  palatability of, 163
Convenience food store, 151
Cost of food as influenced by
  brand, 149, 159
  convenience input, 161–164
  market patronized, 144–147
  size of package purchased, 160–161
  special price, 146
Coupons, 148–149
Cover
  definition of, 373
  dimensions of, 373
  items of, 373
  position of items within, *see* Table
    setting
Cream, 227
  coffee, 227
  half and half, 227
  sour, 227
Crumbs, removing from table, 424
Cyclamates, 47

D

Dairy products, 221–233
  butter, 232–233
  cheese and cheese food products,
    245–275
  cream(s), 226–227
  frozen desserts, 230–232
  milks, 222–226
  yoghurt, 225

Decision making in meal manage-
  ment, 2–3
Decorations, table, 376–377
Definitions and standards of identity,
  39–42
  authority to establish, 38–39
  examples of, 42
  labeling of defined foods, 41
Dehydration of food, 12–13
Delaney clause, 47, 49
Designed foods, 18
Dessert
  flatware for, 379–381
    how to place, 379–381
  how to place dessert course, 424–
    426
  how to serve at table, 425–426
  party, 481, 489–491, 499
Dictionary of cheeses, 270–274
Dietary standards, 82–89
  Basic Seven food groups, 87
  Minimum Daily Requirements, 82
  Recommended Dietary Allowances,
    82–84
  United States Recommended Daily
    Allowances, 84
Dinnerware, 407–414
  china, 408
  earthenware, 407–408
Direct-to-consumer marketing of food,
  152
Discount food store, 150

E

Eggs, 235–241
  buying guide for, 243
  dating, 238
  grading, 236–237
  inspection of, 29, 60
  quality in, 236–239
  sizes, 239–240
  storage of, 240–241, 243
  substitutes, 241
Energy conservation in the kitchen,
  73–79
Etiquette at the table, 433–448

drinking from cups, 440
drinking from glasses and goblets,
  440
duties of host, 447–448
duties of hostess, 445–447
finger bowls, 445
finger foods, 440
how to eat
  breads, 441
  chicken and other poultry, 442
  French fries, 443
  fruits, 441–442
  meats, 442
  pastries, 441
  salads, 443
  shellfish, 442
  vegetables, 443
  whole fish, 442–443
how to use
  forks, 438–439
  knives, 438–439
  napkins, 437–438
  serving tools, 444–445
  spoons, 439–440
order of serving persons at table,
  435–436
passing at table, 363, 435–437
removing food from the mouth, 444
seating of persons at the dining table, 434–435
of serving food, 435–436
  second servings, 437
  helping self, 436–437, 444–445
smoking at the dining table, 445

F

Family style of meal service, 265–266
Fair Packaging and Labeling Act, 49–
  55
Fats and oils, 353–355
Federal food laws, 26–56
  Delaney clause, 47, 49
  Egg Products Inspection Act, 29
  Fair Packaging and Labeling Act,
    49–55

Federal food laws (*Cont.*)
  Food Additives Amendment of 1958, 46–47
  Food and Drugs Act of 1906, 27
  Food Drug and Cosmetic Act of 1938, 28, 32–45
  McNary-Mapes Amendment, 28
  Meat Inspection Act of 1906, 25
  Pesticide Chemicals Act of 1954, 46
  Poultry Products Inspection Act, 29
  The Color Additive Amendment of 1960, 47–48
  The Wholesome Meat Act of 1967, 27–28
Federal food regulatory agencies
  Federal Trade Commission, 62–63
  Food and Drug Administration, 56–58
  U.S. Department of Agriculture, 58–62
  U.S. Department of Commerce, 62
Finger bowl, 363, 445
Finger foods, 440–443
First courses of meals, 453–454
Fish, 207–211
  grading of, 62
  inspection of, 62
Flatware, 399–406
  laying on table, 377–383
    beverage spoon, 378, 381
    butter spreader, 378–379
    carving tools, 383
    dessert fork, 379–381
    dessert spoon, 380–381
    dinner fork, 378, 380
    dinner knife, 378
    fruit knife, 392
    salad fork, 378
    serving tools, 382–383
    spoons, 378
  place settings, 400
  serving pieces, 404–405
  silver-plated, 401–402
  stainless steel, 402
  sterling, 399–401
  vermeil, 402–403
Flour, types of, 328–329
Food additives, 19–23
  amount ingested, 23
  definition, 34
Food and Drugs Act of 1906, 27, 30–31
Food buying guides
  budget and, 164–165
  butter, 242–243
  cheeses, 267–268
  eggs, 243
  fruits, 302–303
  meat, fish, poultry, 215–217
  milk, 242
  vegetables, 324–325
    quantities guide, 308–311
Food buying information
  bakery products, 329–334
  breakfast cereals, 336–337
  breakfast pastries, 338
  butter, 232–233
  cereals, 327–328, 339–340
  cheeses, 245–258, 264–268
  cheese food products, 259–264
  cocoa mixes, 352–353
  coffee, 347–350
  coffee creamer or whitener, 233–234
  coffee instant, 349
  convenience foods, 161–164
  creams, 227
  dressings for foods, 356–357
  eggs, 236, 239, 240, 242
  fats and oils, 353–355
  fruit beverages, 296–301
  fruits, 276–296
  jams and jellies, 355–356
  legumes, 340–341
  margarine, 234–235
  meat food products, 211–215
  meats, 168–183
    beef, 174–179
    cured, 198–200
    ground, 204
    lamb, 181–182
    pork, 179–180
    sausages, 200–203
    veal, 180–181
  milk, 221–226
  nondairy products, 233–235

nuts, 341–342
pasta, 334–336
poultry, 183–185, 192–194
poultry food products, 211–215
quantity guides, 305–510
salad dressings, 356–357
shellfish, 209–211
tea, 350–352
vegetables, 305–325
water, 358
Food conservation, 66–73
Food, Drug, and Cosmetic Act of 1938, 32–45
amendments to, 45–49
Food and Drug Administration, 56–58
Food flavor, 128–133
Food flavor potentiation, 133
Food packaging, 15–17
Food plans, 101, 104–107
Food preferences, 125–128
Food regulatory laws, 26–56
history of, 26–30
Food spoilage, 69–73
Food standards
fill of container, 45
identity, 39–43
quality, 60–61
reasonable quality, 43–45
Food storage guidelines, 68–69
Food waste, 67–68
Foodways, 133–134
Forks, how to place on the dining table, 378–380
Form-fill flexible package, 17
Formal meal service, 363
Freezing preservation of food, 13–14
Frozen desserts, 230–232
Fruit beverages and juices, 296–301
citrus, 297–300
Fruits, 276–302
buying guides for, 302–303
canned, 291–293
chilled, 295
citrus, 281–284
dried and dehydrated, 295–296
fresh, storage of, 303
frozen, 294–295
how to store, 303

serving size, 276–277
tropical and subtropical, 288–289
See also specific fruits

G

Glassware, 414–417
borosilicate glass, 415
lead glass, 414–415
lime glass, 414
Goals for meal managers, 5–6
Grace, saying of at meals, 446
Grade labeling, 61
Grading food for quality, 60–62
agencies responsible for, 60
defining standards, 60–61
Grapefruit, 282–283
Grapes, 284–285
Grocery stores, 142–151
competitive practices of, 144–150
nonprice practices, 147–150
pricing policies, 144–147
types of, 150–152
combination, 150
convenience, 151
cooperatives, 152
discount, 150
supermarkets, 142–150
warehouse, 151
Guest meals, 450–477
menus for, 519–523
Guides to shopping for food, *see* Food buying guides

H

Ham, 198–199
Health foods, 328
Host
duties at table, 447–448
order of serving persons at table, 435–436
Hostess
duties of at table, 445–447
begins eating, 446
ceases eating, 447

Hostess (*Cont.*)
    seats guests at table, 446
    serves beverage at table, 447
    serves salad at table, 446

I

Imitation food products, 50
Inspection of food, agents responsible
        for
    eggs and egg products, 29, 60
    fish and seafoods, 24
    meat and meat food products, 27–
        28, 58–59
    poultry and poultry food products,
        29, 60
    symbols of, 59, 60

J

Jams and jellies, 355–356
    definitions of, 355
    labeling of, 355
    low-calorie, 356

K

Knives
    butter-spreader
        when to use, 379
        where to place, 378–379, 385
    carving, where to place, 383
    dinner
        how to use, 438–439
        where to place within cover, 378
        where to place while dining, 439
Kosher food, 203

L

Label, definition of, 33
Label requirements for
    enriched foods, 52–53
    low-calorie foods, 56

net contents, 51–52
nondefined foods, 52
nutritional claims, 52–53
Labeling, definition of, 33
Lamb, 181–182, 191
    cuts, 181–182
    definitions of, 191
    grades, 191
    identifying cuts, 175
    New Zealand, 191
Liberal-cost food plan menus, 107
Linens, 374–376, 417–419
    cloths
        for buffet tables, 468
        for tea tables, 487
        how to lay, 374
    definition of, 374, 417
    napkins, 375–376
        folding of, 375
        paper, 417
        placing at cover, 376
        placing at end of dining, 438
        sizes of, 376
        unfolding at table, 437–438
Low-cost food plan menus, 105

M

Margarine, 234–235
Meal management, 1–8
    decision making and, 2
    definition, 1
    goals for, 5–6
    resources for, 4–5
    values and, 6–7
Meal manager
    definition, 1
    decisions of, 2
Meal planning, guidelines to, 134–138
Meal service, styles of, 361–370
    American, 362
    blue-plate, 367
    buffet, 367–368
    compromise or family, 365
    formal, 363
    tray, 369
Meal service, table setting, 371–397

Meal service, waiting on the table, 420–432
Meal service without waiting on the table, 429–431
Meat cuts, 172–183
Meat extenders and analogs, 206–207
Meats
  buying for the freezer, 196–197
  buying guides, 215–217
  cured, 198–200
  cuts, *see* Meat cuts
  grades, 189–191
  grading for
    wholesomeness, 185–187
    palatability, 187–191
  identity standards for meat food products, 211–215
  identity standards for poultry food products, 211–215
  inspection of, 185–187
  Kosher, 203
  serving size, 170–172
  simulated, 206
  storage of, 217–219
  tenderized, 205
  tenderness in, 188
  See also specific meats
Melon varities, 285–287
Menus
  for brunch, 521
  for buffet meals, 519–520
  for guest dinners, 521–523
  liberal-cost, 107
  low-cost, 105
  moderate-cost, 106
  planning, 134–138, 452–454
  thrifty, 104
  writing, 503–504
Milk and milk products, 221–226
  acidophilus, 225
  buttermilk, 224
  chocolate, 225
  condensed, 228
  cultured, 225
  evaporated, 228
  filled, 225–226
  Grade A, 223
  homogenized, 224
    imitation, 226
    low-fat fluid, 224
    nonfat dry, 228–229
    2 percent, 224
    UHT (ultra high temperature), 223, 224
Misbranded food, 35–36
Moderate-cost menus, 106

N

Napkins
  folding of, 375
  how to use, 437–438
  placing
    on buffet table, 462, 465, 468
    on dining table, 376
    on tea table, 487–488, 494, 496
    on tea tray, 486
    unfolding at dining table, 437–438
Natural foods, 327–328
Nectarines, 289
Nondairy products, 223–225
  coffee creamer or whitener, 233
  imitation milk, 226
  margarine, 234–235
  toppings, 234
Nutrient contribution of food groups, 90
Nutrition, 80–93
  additives to improve, 88
  and food selection, 89–90
  status of in the United States, 80–82
  value of food eaten outside the home, 87–88
Nutritional labeling, 84–87

O

Oleomargarine, 234–235
Onion, varieties, 313
Open date labeling, 153–154
Orange varieties, 281–282
Orange juice products, 297–300
Organic foods, 328

Order of
    passing at table, 435–437
    placing a course, 421
    removing a course, 422–424
    serving persons at table
        by host, 435–436
        by hostess, 436
        by person waiting on table, 422

P

Packaging food in the 1980s, 15–17
Pasta, 334–336
Pears, 287
Place cards, 446
Place mats, 374–375
    positioning on the dining table, 374
    dimensions of, 374
Planning meals
    to match budget, 99–102
    to meet nutritive needs, 89–90
    to provide satisfying eating, 137–138
Plant protein, amino acid content of,
        91
Pork
    cured, 198–200
    cuts, 179
    quality in, 190
Poultry, 183–185, 192–194
    chicken, 192–194
        classes, 192
        grading of, 192–194
        inspection of, 185–187
        quality in, 193
    ducks, 193
    turkey, 192–193
Poultry food products, 212–215
Pull date, 153–154
Punch
    arranging table for serving, 498–499
    serving, 498

Q

Quality grading of food, 60–61
    attribute of quality, 61
    grading agencies, 38, 60, 62

standards for, 61
Quantity buying guides, 505–510

R

Radiation preservation of food, 14–15
Recommended daily allowances, 84–85
Resources for meal management, 4–5
Retort pouch, 17
Rock Cornish game hen, 192

S

Saccharin, 346–347
Salad bowl
    position within cover, 385–388
    removal of, 423
    See also Salad plate
Salad greens, varieties of, 312–313
Salad plate
    position within cover, 385–388
    removal of, 423
    size of, 388
Salad service at table, 388, 446
Salmonella, 70
Salt and pepper shakers, 392
Sausages, 200–203
Seating arrangements at the dining
        table, 434–435
Second servings, offering, 437
Serving procedures
    at teas, 485, 487, 493, 496
    for host at dining table, 447–448
    for hostess at dining table of
        beverages, 446
        dessert, 425–426
        salad, 446
    when serving self, 436–437, 444–445
Serving size of
    fruits, 276–277
    meats, 170–172
    potatoes, 308
    vegetables, 308–310
Serving table
    how to arrange, 395
    how to use, 396

Serving tools, 382–383, 396–397
  how to use, 382–383
  how to place on table, 382–383
Shellfish, 209–211
Silverware, *see* Flatware
Smoking at table, 445
Spending for food, how influenced, 96–98
Spill bowl, 428
Spoons
  kinds of serving, 396, 404–405
  placing
    on dining table, 378, 380, 381
    on saucer, 381
    on tea table, 487
    on tray for beverage service, 392, 486
    using, 439–440
Standard of fill of container, 45
Standard of identity, 39–43
Standards of quality, 60–61
Standard of reasonable quality, 43–45
Staphylococcus aureus, 70
Substitute food, 50
Supermarkets, 142–151
  history of, 142–144
  promotions of, 144–150
Storage guides for
  butter, 242
  cheeses, 268
  eggs, 243
  fresh fruits, 303
  frozen foods, 72, 513–515
  meats, poultry, fish, 217–219
  milk, 242
  vegetables, fresh, 324–325
Storage materials for food, 67
Substitute foods, 17–18
Sweeteners, 344–347
Subtropical fruits, 288–289
Synthetic foods, 17–19
Syrups, 345

Table setting, 371–397
  placing on table of
    beverage service, 390–392
    beverageware, 383–385
    bread-and-butter plate, 385
    dinner plates, 377, 388, 390
    flatware, 377–382
    linens, 374–376
    salad plate, 385–388
    salad service, 388
    salt and pepper shakers, 392
    serving dishes of food, 393
    serving tools, 382–383
  principles for, 371–373
Tea
  kinds of, 350–352
  tables, how to set, 479–499
    large, 491–499
    small, 487–489
  tray, how to set, 392, 485–486
Teas and receptions, 479–499
  decorations for tables, 495
  menus for, 480–481
  service at, 500–501
  setting table for, 487–499
Temperature control of bacteria, 512
Textured vegetable protein, 204
Time management, 110–117
  alternatives to time use, 112–115
  deterrants to saving time, 115
  how to save time, 112–115
  maximizing use of time, 123
Time schedules for meal preparation, 115–122
  preparing, 117–122
Tomato products, defined, 321–322
Trading stamps, 149–150
Tray
  beverage, arrangement of, 392, 485–486
  uses in waiting on table, 395, 420
Tropical fruits, 288–289
Turkey, 192–193

T

U

Table decorations, 376–377, 419
Table linens, 374–376, 417–419

Ultra-high temperature (UHT) pasteurization, 223–224

U.S. Recommended Daily Allowances, 84–85
Universal Product Code, 154–155

V

Veal, 180–181, 190
  cuts, 180–181
  definition, 190
Vegetables, 305–325
  canned, 317–323
  cost of, per serving, 307–308
  Chinese, 311–312
  frozen, 323–324
  guides to purchase, 324–325
  guides to storage, 324–325
  grades of
    canned, 318
    fresh, 311
  frozen, 323
  onion varieties, 313
  salad greens, 312–313
  serving size, 308, 310
  sprouted seeds, 315
  squash varieties, 316–317
  tomato products, 321–322

W

Waiting on the table, 420–432
  left-hand service, 421–422
  order for
    placing courses, 421
    removing courses, 421, 422–424
    serving persons at table, 422
  right-hand service, 421–422
Warehouse grocery stores, 151
Waxes as applied to fruits and vegetables, 277